WORKERS OF ALL COUNTRIES, UNITE!

Карл МАРКС
Биография

ИЗДАТЕЛЬСТВО
ПОЛИТИЧЕСКОЙ ЛИТЕРАТУРЫ
МОСКВА

Karl MARX
A Biography

PROGRESS PUBLISHERS
MOSCOW

Translated from the Russian by YURI SDOBNIKOV

Карл Маркс

БИОГРАФИЯ

На английском языке

PUBLISHERS' NOTE

This is a translation of the second Russian edition, Moscow, 1973 (with changes), prepared by the Institute of Marxism-Leninism of the C.P.S.U. Central Committee. The group of authors consists of P. N. Fedoseyev, Irene Bakh, L. I. Golman, N. Y. Kolpinsky, B. A. Krylov, I. I. Kuzminov, A. I. Malysh, V. G. Mosolov, Yevgenia Stepanova.

English translation © Progress Publishers 1973

First printing 1973
Second revised edition 1977
Third printing 1984
Fourth (revised) edition 1989

Printed in the Union of Soviet Socialist Republics

Б $\frac{0103010000\text{-}311}{014(01)\text{-}89}$ без объявл.

ISBN 5-01-000318-X

CONTENTS

INTRODUCTION 9

Chapter One
THE ROAD TO MATERIALISM AND COMMUNISM 15

Childhood and Youth—18. Student Years in Bonn and Berlin—20. Study of Hegel's Philosophy. Among the Young Hegelians—24. Doctoral Dissertation—27. Attitude to Feuerbach—30. Start of Political Activity. Article Against Prussian Censorship—31. *Rheinische Zeitung*: Contributor and Editor—33. Revolutionary-Democratic Ideas in Marx's Journalistic Writings—34. Conflict with "The Free"—39. The *Rheinische Zeitung* Banned—40. Kreuznach. *Contribution to the Critique of Hegel's Philosophy of Law* MS. Notebooks on History—42. Preparations for Publishing the *Deutsch-Französische Jahrbücher*. Departure for Paris—47. Final Adoption of Materialism and Communism—49. Prelude to a Great Friendship—51. *Deutsch-Französische Jahrbücher*: Contemporary Assessments—54.

Chapter Two
FIRST FORMULATION OF THE PRINCIPLES
OF THE PROLETARIAN OUTLOOK 55

Break with Ruge—55. Marx in Paris in 1844—56. Scientific Pursuits—60. *Economic and Philosophic Manuscripts of 1844*—61. Work on *Vorwärts!*—67. An Historic Meeting—69. Preparation for Joint Attack on Young Hegelians—69. *The Holy Family*—71. Expulsion from Paris—77.

Chapter Three
THE MATERIALIST VIEW OF HISTORY 79

In Brussels—79. Arrival of Engels. Plan for a New Philosophical Work—81. *Theses on Feuerbach*—83. "Library of the Best Foreign Socialist Writers". Articles in the Press—85. Early Followers—86. Trip to England—88. Critical Study of Political Economy and Socialist Literature—90. Work on *The German Ideology*—93. Revolution in Views of Social Development—96. The Main Thing: Self-Clarification—103.

Chapter Four
THE START OF THE STRUGGLE FOR THE PROLETARIAN PARTY.
PROGRAMME FOR THE INTERNATIONAL
WORKING-CLASS MOVEMENT 106

The Brussels Communist Correspondence Committee—107. The Break with Weitling—110. The Struggle Against "True Socialism"—112. Disagreements with Proudhon—115. *The Poverty of Philosophy*—118. Foundation of the Communist League—124. German Workers' Society in Brussels—127. *Wage Labour and Capital*—128. Efforts to Start a Periodical—131. International Congress of Economists—134. Polemics with Karl Heinzen—136. Efforts to Unite the Revolutionary Forces—139. Second Congress of the Communist League—142. After the Congress—145. Work on the *Manifesto of the Communist Party*—147. First Marxist Programme—149.

Chapter Five
DURING THE REVOLUTIONS OF 1848-49   156

Revolutions Break Out in Europe. Marx Expelled from Brussels—156. Marx in Paris. Fight Against "Export Revolution" Plans—158. *Demands of the Communist Party in Germany*—160 Start of Activity in Revolutionary Germany—162 Opposing the Views of Gottschalk and Born—163. Proletarian Wing of the Democratic Movement—165. Editor-in-Chief of the *Neue Rheinische Zeitung*—167. Struggle to Complete the Bourgeois-Democratic Revolution—170. Support for the Oppressed Peoples' Struggle. The *Neue Rheinische Zeitung*'s Attitude Towards Foreign Policy—174. The June Uprising in Paris—176. Revolutionary Organ of the Proletariat—177. Opposing the Counter-Revolutionary Offensive. Marx in the Workers' Association and the Democratic Society in Cologne—179. Trip to Berlin and Vienna—182. September Crisis in Germany—184. The October Uprising in Vienna—188. Fighting the Counter-Revolutionary Coup in Prussia—190. First Results and Prospects of the German and European Revolutions—195. Working for the Unity of the Democratic Forces—198. Two Trials—199. Marx in February-March 1849—202. Practical Steps Towards a Mass Proletarian Party—204. The *Neue Rheinische Zeitung* and the National Liberation Struggle in Hungary and Italy—207. Defeat of the Rhine Uprisings. The *Neue Rheinische Zeitung* Closed Down—209. In South-Western Germany—212. Back in Paris. June 13—214. First Historical Test of Marxism—216.

Chapter Six
SUMMING UP THE LESSONS OF THE REVOLUTION   218

The First Months in London—218. The Founding of the *Neue Rheinishe Zeitung. Politisch-ökonomische Revue*—221. *The Class Struggles in France*—222. Efforts to Reorganise the Communist League. March *Address of the Central Authority*—226.Universal Society of Revolutionary Communists—230. Reviews from the *Neue Rheinische Zeitung. Politisch-ökonomische Revue*—232. International Reviews.Evaluating the Prospects of the Revolution—234. Fight Against the Willich-Schapper Sectarian-Adventurist Faction—236. Engels Leaves for Manchester. Correspondence Between the Two Friends—239. Plan for a Fresh Attack Against Proudhon—241. *The Eighteenth Brumaire of Louis Bonaparte*—242. Critique of Petty-Bourgeois Democracy. *The Great Men of the Exile*—247. Cologne Communist Trial—248. Communist League Dissolved. New Forms of Struggle for a Party—253.

Chapter Seven
YEARS OF REACTION   256

Oppressed by Reaction and Penury—256. Marx in the Family Circle—259. A Friendship Fortified in Tribulation—262. Economic Researches—263. Scientific Studies in Other Fields—267. Fostering Proletarian Revolutionaries. Safeguarding Revolutionary Traditions Among the German Workers—271. Marx and Chartism in the 1850s—274. Connections with the U.S. Working-Class Movement—276. Writing for the Progressive Bourgeois Press—278. Marx as a Journalist—281. Articles on Britain's Political System—283. Struggle Against Reactionary Regimes in Continental Europe—285. Exposure of the Capitalist States' Colonial Policies—288. Critique of the Ruling Classes' Foreign Policy—293. Revolutionary Tactics on the Eastern Question. Attitude to the Crimean War—296. "Revelations of the Diplomatic History of the 18th Century"—300."Revolutionary Spain"—304. Facing a New Revolutionary Upsurge—306.

Chapter Eight
THE DECISIVE STAGE IN THE FORMATION OF MARXIST POLITICAL ECONOMY — 308

Articles on the 1857 Economic Crisis—308. Work on the Economic Manuscripts of 1857-58—310. Introduction to the Economic Manuscripts of 1857-58—311. Main Manuscripts of 1857-58—316. Preparing the New Economic Work for the Press—319. First Part of *A Contribution to the Critique of Political Economy*—320. Marx and Darwin—324.

Chapter Nine
A FRESH UPSURGE IN THE DEMOCRATIC AND PROLETARIAN MOVEMENTS — 326

Das Volk—327. For a Revolutionary Unification of Italy—328. The Garibaldi Movement—330. Tactics in the Struggle for Germany's Unity—332. Differences with Lassalle—334. *Herr Vogt* Pamphlet—338. Jenny Marx's Illness—340. Trip to Holland and Germany—341. Defence of Blanqui—343. Marx and Social Change in Russia—344. Contributions to *Die Presse*—347. American Civil War. End of Contributions to the *N.-Y. Daily Tribune*—349. English Workers' Movement in Support of the North—353. Marx's Attitude Towards the Polish Insurrection of 1863-64—354. Work on a Pamphlet About Poland—357. In the German Workers' Educational Society in London—360. Loss of a Friend—361. Marx and the General Association of German Workers—362. On the Way to the International—365.

Chapter Ten
CAPITAL—MARX'S MAIN WORK — 367

Work on the Second Part of *A Contribution to the Critique of Political Economy*—367. Economic Manuscript of 1861-63—368. Economic Manuscript of 1863-65—369. Preparation for the Printers and Publication of Volume One of *Capital*—371. Russian Edition of Volume One of *Capital*—375. Second German Edition of Volume One of *Capital*—376. Authorised French Edition of Volume One of *Capital*—377. Work on Volumes Two and Three of *Capital*—379. The Production of Capital—384. The Process of Circulation of Capital—389. The Process of Capitalist Production as a Whole—393. *Theories of Surplus-Value*—398. Problems of Communism in *Capital*—402. The Method of *Capital* and Its General Importance to Science—406.

Chapter Eleven
FOUNDER AND LEADER OF THE FIRST INTERNATIONAL — 417

International Meeting at St. Martin's Hall—417. Inaugural Address and Provisional Rules—418. Head of the International Proletarian Organisation—421. The Way to the Masses—424. Corresponding Secretary for Germany—428. The Polish Question—431. Holidaying at Zalt-Bommel—432. At the London Conference of 1865—433. International's Sections Set Up in Germany. Austro-Prussian War and the German Working Class—435. International Proletariat's Economic Platform—437. Differences with English Trade Union Leaders. The Irish Question—442. Working for the International's Socialist Programme—445. Questions of War and Peace—448. The Birth of the First Mass Marxist Party—451. Start of Struggle Against Bakuninism—455. Basle Congress. International's Tactics on the Peasant Question—460. International Importance of the Irish Question—461. General Council Corresponding Secretary for Russia—463. Crisis of the Second Empire and Prospects for a European Revolution—467.

Chapter Twelve
THE PARIS COMMUNE 461

On the Threshold of a New Historical Epoch — 471. First Address on the Franco-Prussian War — 472. Helping the German Social-Democrats Formulate Revolutionary Tactics — 474. Collapse of the Second Empire. Second Address on the Franco-Prussian War — 476. Campaign for Recognition of the French Republic — 478. March 18 Revolution — 479. Contacts with the Communards — 482. Movement of Solidarity with the Commune — 484. Analysis of the Commune's Activity. Writing the General Council's Address — 487. *The Civil War in France* — 488.

Chapter Thirteen
FIGHTING FOR THE PURITY
OF THE INTERNATIONAL'S IDEOLOGICAL PRINCIPLES 494

Preparation for the London Conference — 494. Milestone in the History of the International — 496. Fight for Recognition of the London Conference Resolutions — 499. Intensified Struggle Against the Bakuninists. *Fictitious Splits in the International* — 501. Against Reformism — 503. Contacts with the Commune's Refugees — 506. Preparing for the Hague Congress — 507. The Hague Congress — 509. After the Congress. Meeting at Amsterdam — 513. The International's Last Year — 514. Dissolution of the International Working Men's Association — 518.

Chapter Fourteen
FURTHER DEVELOPMENT OF THE THEORY AND TACTICS
OF THE WORKING-CLASS MOVEMENT 521

The mid-1870s — 523. In Their Father's Footsteps — 527. Polemics Against the Anarchists on the Theory of Socialist Revolution — 529. Ideological Leadership of the International Working-Class Movement — 532. Teacher of the German Social-Democrats — 537. *Critique of the Gotha Programme* — 542. Helping to Write *Anti-Dühring* — 547.

Chapter Fifteen
THE STRUGGLE TO ESTABLISH AND STRENGTHEN PROLETARIAN PARTIES.
MARX AND REVOLUTIONARY RUSSIA 551

Theoretical Researches of the Last Few Years — 551. Studies in World History — 556. Struggle to Set Up Proletarian Parties in Various Countries — 564. Against Bismarck's Anti-Socialist Law. Critique of Opportunism — 567. Contribution to the Establishment of the French Workers' Party — 575. Towards a New Stage in the Spread of Socialism in Britain — 582. Prospects Before the Working-Class Movement in the U.S.A. — 585. Analysis of Post-1861 Development in Russia — 589. Keen Expectation of Revolution in Russia — 594. Russian Revolutionaries' Asviser and Friend — 597. Irreparable Losses. Failing Health — 605. March 14, 1883 — 608.

CONCLUSION

Name Index — 618
Index of Periodicals — 629

INTRODUCTION

Karl Marx stands out among the great men of history. Together with his close friend and associate, Frederick Engels, he worked out the most advanced, scientific world outlook, which has given mankind and the proletariat, its most revolutionary class, a great instrument for cognising and changing the world. Marx and Engels have gone down in history as the brilliant teachers of the world's working class, the great champions of its cause, the ideologists and organisers of the revolutionary working-class movement.

Marx's scientific achievements are unmatched in the long history of social thought. Even as a young man he was compared with Prometheus, who stole fire from the gods to help man escape from hunger, cold and darkness, and who is said to have given mankind the arts and sciences. Prometheus was the symbol of man's creative genius and indomitable urge for progress, freedom and happiness. Through his discovery of the laws governing social development, Marx was the first to show the working people the real ways and means of casting off social oppression and creating the necessary conditions for a dignified way of life, for human welfare and the free all-round development of each person's physical and spiritual endowments.

Before Marx came on the scene, the incipient working-class movement was groping in the dark, without a scientifically grounded goal or the right path to emancipation from the yoke of capital. Again and again, diverse social schemers and utopians befuddled the workers' minds with petty-bourgeois prejudices and confused them with fantastic projects for ridding the exploiter society of its "bad sides". Just as ignorance of natural laws induced men to seek medical cure-alls, so ignorance of social laws induced them to seek social cure-alls.

Meanwhile, the advancing emancipation movement was in great need of scientific theory, and the material and ideological prerequisites for one had already matured.

The rapid growth of productive forces in the industrial revolution created a real basis for solving the great historical task of abolishing the exploitation of man by man and emancipating labour. With the development of capitalism there arose a social force capable of tackling the task. It was the working class.

The stormy revolutions and mass workers' actions attendant on the collapse of feudalism and the establishment of capitalism had bared class contradictions and burning social problems to such an extent that they could no longer be ignored. Progressive thinkers gave them expression in one form or another, seeking answers to the questions posed by history. Thus the theoretical prerequisites for the new scientific outlook also shaped.

The teaching of Marx and Engels did not, of course, arise outside the mainstream of social thought or the development of world civilisation. It came as the legal heir to mankind's greatest discoveries in the study of nature and social life and rested on all the most brilliant advances in social thought, notably those in German philosophy, English political economy and French utopian socialism.

Marx and Engels critically assimilated all the rational elements of the leading trends in social thinking and creatively reworked them from the standpoint of the proletariat, the most advanced class of society.

The revolutionary significance of Marx's great scientific discoveries was given the most profound and clear-cut definition by Lenin, who wrote: "Marx's philosophical materialism alone has shown the proletariat the way out of the spiritual slavery in which all oppressed classes have hitherto languished. Marx's economic theory alone has explained the true position of the proletariat in the general system of capitalism." [1]

Marxism, as the scientific expression of the interests of the working class, took shape and developed in close connection with the proletariat's class struggle. The exposure of the internal contradictions of capitalism suggested the conclusion that the breakdown of bourgeois society was inevitable, while the advance of the working-class movement showed that it was the proletariat that was to be the gravedigger of the capitalist system and the creator of a new, socialist society.

Marx and Engels were the first to provide a theoretical basis for the revolutionary world outlook of the working class, thus giving the mass movement, for the first time in history, a scientific ideology in place of religious fantasies and utopian dreams.

---

[1] V. I. Lenin, *Collected Works*, Vol. 19, Progress Publishers, Moscow, p. 28.

Marx, the great scientist, was also and above all a passionate revolutionary. He most valued science as a motive revolutionary force. The main purpose, which gave supreme meaning to his life, was to help organise the working class for the revolutionary fight to overthrow capitalism and bring about the victory of socialism. He initiated, inspired and took part in the principal historical events of the working-class movement in the 19th century, and did a great deal to promote the international solidarity of the workers of all countries. In all his activities as the leader of the world proletariat, internationalism was his guiding principle.

Marx's work as the leader of the international working-class movement opened a new page in the history of the mass struggle for emancipation. Marx was an innovator in everything he did, and here too he displayed his ability to combine theory and practice in a dialectical unity. Marx was not a prophet preaching to the masses, but a man who made science serve the oppressed and turned it into a weapon which the masses themselves could wield.

The whole history of the international working-class movement, the development of the world revolutionary process as a whole, and the ups and downs of the revolutionary struggle in the various countries provided irrefutable proof that only a political party guided by the revolutionary theory and embodying in its activity the unity of science and practice, ideology and politics, can play the part of a vanguard fighter. The revolutionary essence of Marx's theory was given highly precise expression by Lenin, when he said: "The irresistible attraction of this theory, which draws to itself the socialists of all countries, lies precisely in the fact that it combines the quality of being strictly and supremely scientific (being the last word in social science) with that of being revolutionary; it does not combine them accidentally, and not only because the founder of the doctrine combined in his own person the qualities of a scientist and a revolutionary, but does so intrinsically and inseparably." [1]

Without revolutionary practice, without the translation of Marxist ideas into life, theory becomes a set of outworn dogmas and a cover for reformism and opportunism. Without science, without a strictly scientific view of social development, revolutionary action degenerates into adventurism and leads to anarchism.

* * *

Karl Marx had a hard life, but he never sought an easy one. He was above all a fighter. He devoted a lifetime to fighting for the freedom and happiness of men of labour, fighting against the exploiters and their servitors. Throughout his life he wielded the weapon of relentless criticism of erroneous ideas, spurious slogans, pseudo-scientific theories, inertness, hypocrisy, and faint-heartedness, issu-

---

[1] V. I. Lenin, *Collected Works*, Vol. 1, p. 327.

ing a challenge to the ruling classes and their ideologists and political leaders.

Born into a privileged section of society, he abandoned a brilliant academic career and the comfortable life of an affluent scientist or popular writer, and chose the hard fate of a political exile; he broke away from his environment and had to leave his native land, exposing himself, his wife, and his children to a life of wandering, privation and harassment by the police.

Marx's life was shortened by the many sicknesses caused by his titanic work and his extremely straitened, frequently dire circumstances. But he had the good fortune of seeing the first fruits of his theoretical and practical activity, winning world-wide recognition during his lifetime and commanding the ardent affections of the workers for whose sake he had performed his exploit of a lifetime.

This book tells the true story of Marx's life, the story of a personality of many facets.

Frederick Engels, Marx's great associate, wrote the first few excellent essays for a biography of the founder of scientific communism, and a number of articles shedding light on Marx's activities at various periods. In the closing years of his life, Engels wanted to write a comprehensive biography of his friend, especially to show his part in the First International, but was, unfortunately, unable to do so.

Lenin wrote a biographical sketch of Marx in 1914 for the Granat Dictionary. It was in the form of a concise article, giving a popular but profound view not only of the milestones in Marx's life, but also of the essence of his doctrine. Lenin's work is a classic model for a scientific biography of Marx, for an exposition of his life and work.

The year 1918 saw the publication of *Karl Marx. The Story of His Life* by Franz Mehring, a prominent philosopher and historian, and Left-wing German Social-Democrat. His book was the result of long research and has been appreciated for its rich content and style. However, Mehring had no knowledge of many works by Marx which had not been published at the time, such as *Economic and Philosophic Manuscript of 1844*, *The German Ideology* (written jointly with Engels) (full text), the economic manuscripts of 1857-1858, later versions of *Capital*, and other material containing important biographical facts.

Since the appearance of Mehring's book, academic Marxists have conducted fruitful research into different stages of Marx's life and activity and examined various aspects of his scientific and literary work. Efforts have been made to summarise the accumulated material in the form of biographical works. Among the books published are the first volumes of a fundamental biography of Marx and Engels by the French Marxist Auguste Cornu, a collective biographical work on Marx by the Institute of Marxism-Leninism of the Socialist

Unity Party of Germany's Central Committee, and other monographs.

Marx's life and work have been described in many books by bourgeois and reformist ideologists who make a point of falsifying the history of Marxism and the working-class movement in one way or another. The biography of the founder of scientific communism has become one of the main issues in the ideological struggle. The adversaries of Marxism have been trying to play off the young Marx against the mature Marx, Marx against Engels, and to discover contradictions in his teaching. They are especially assiduous in trying to prove that Marx's teaching is outdated, "Eurocentric", and so on. They even resort to direct and malicious slander.

A scientific biography must be based on documents and strictly verified historical facts, collating ideas and their influence, theory and practice. This is the best way to show that Marxism has been verified and confirmed by life and by the whole course of history.

The main sources used for this biography of Karl Marx are the works and letters of Marx and Engels, published in Russian in the *Collected Works* and in other editions.

Documents kept at various archives, above all at the Central Party Archives of the Institute of Marxism-Leninism in Moscow, have also provided important sources for this biography, among them Marx's manuscripts and synopses, the material of members of Marx's family, Engels' manuscripts, numerous letters addressed to the founders of scientific communism by leaders of the working-class and democratic movement, and their correspondence with each other containing valuable information about Marx. A large number of these documents have been published in the last few years by the Institute of Marxism-Leninism of the C.C. C.P.S.U. and the C.C. S.U.P.G. in *Marx/Engels Gesamtausgabe* (*MEGA*), the complete edition of the works of Marx and Engels in the original languages.

The works of V. I. Lenin, notably those dealing with Marx, Engels and Marxism, have been a most important aid and an invaluable methodological guide.

The reminiscences of contemporaries give a vivid picture of Marx as scientist and fighter, and memoirs have naturally been used in writing this biography.

A great deal of information shedding light on various aspects of Marx's guidance of the international proletarian movement can be found in the documents of various 19th-century working-class organisations. It was necessary to take account not only of the numerous available publications of these documents (Minutes of the General Council of the First International, documents of the Communist League, and other collections of documents), but also those which have yet to be published. The personal collections of the leaders of the Communist League, the First International and various national working-class organisations closely connected with Marx have been of considerable value in this study. Use was also made of material from the Prussian, Belgian and French police archives.

Periodicals published in Marx's lifetime constitute a special group of sources. A study had to be made not only of the press organs which Marx edited or to which he contributed, but also of bourgeois newspapers and journals which have brought down to us comments on his activity or reviews of his books.

The authors have relied on documents of the C.P.S.U. and fraternal Marxist-Leninist Parties containing a scientific interpretation of the theoretical problems dealt with in this book, the theory and tactics of the working-class movement and the building of socialist society.

Account has been taken of all the important studies of Marx and Marxism published in the U.S.S.R. and abroad, especially those containing valuable documentary material.

The illustrations in this book reflect Marx's life and work, and have been selected from the historical and documentary material at the Karl Marx and Frederick Engels Museum and the Central Party Archives of the Institute of Marxism-Leninism of the C.P.S.U. Central Committee.

CHAPTER ONE

THE ROAD TO MATERIALISM AND COMMUNISM

> *If we have chosen the position in life in which we can most of all work for mankind, no burdens can bow us down.*
>
> Karl Marx

Marx's childhood and youth were spent in the Rhineland, which was economically and politically the most developed part of Germany. More than any other part of Germany, it had been influenced by the French Revolution, when the Rhine valley was a scene of military operations by revolutionary armies, peasant uprisings and actions by German democrats inspired by the Jacobin ideas of liberty, equality and brotherhood. Following the French victories, the left bank of the Rhine was incorporated into the French Republic and later into Napoleon's empire. The feudal system there was abolished in the main: the big estates of the landed gentry and the church were broken up, feudal privileges were abolished, and trial by jury and the bourgeois *Code Napoléon* introduced, all of which encouraged industrial development in the area.

Under a decision of the Vienna Congress of 1815 most of the Rhineland went to Prussia, making up the Rhine Province of this biggest German state with its absolutist feudal system. The Junkers—the landed nobility—retained many of their privileges as a caste from which came the *élite* of the powerful Prussian bureaucracy and the professional officer corps with its cult of militarism. There were no representative institutions for the whole country. The Provincial Diets—Landtags—had advisory powers but no vote. The principle of representation by estates cut deeply into the rights of the bourgeoisie: in the Rhenish Provincial Diet, for instance, the two big cities of Aachen and Cologne, with populations of almost 100,000, were represented by only three deputies, while 6,520 landowners had 25 deputies.

Economically, Prussia was way behind Britain and France, and despite her industrial growth remained an agrarian country with an embryonic proletariat. The bulk of the population consisted of peasants in semi-feudal dependence on the big landowners, and an urban petty bourgeoisie (artisans and traders).

Nevertheless, there was some industrial progress going on in Germany as well. Centres of capitalist production, factories and mines were emerging in various provinces and railway construction began in 1835. The Rhine Province was ahead of the others, even the industrial areas of Prussia, and the pillars of feudalism there were so fundamentally undermined that the Prussian government failed to wipe out entirely the gains of the French Revolution, notably, to substitute Prussian Law for the *Code Napoléon*. Still, the bourgeoisie there was restricted by the absolutist police regime that had spread to the Rhine Province as well. It was discontented with the Prussian government's tax and tariff policies, which failed to provide adequate protection against foreign competition, and was largely the mouthpiece for opposition among the bourgeois circles in Prussia and the whole of Germany.

The economic and political changes in the Rhine Province in the 1820s and 1830s were a reflection of the social processes taking place in the whole of Germany and many other European countries. Everywhere there were signs of the way being paved for the bourgeois revolution, which was to remove the vestiges of feudalism in the social and political system and to clear the path for capitalism, as it had done in England and France. The country's political and economic disunity, a legacy of the Middle Ages, was the main obstacle to Germany's capitalist development. Economic development was made extremely difficult by the existence in Germany of 38 states, each with its own customs barriers, monetary units and systems of weights and measures. The establishment in 1834 of a Customs Union (*Zollverein*) of 18 states headed by Prussia, as a counterweight against Austria, her rival for hegemony in Germany, was only the first step in overcoming economic disunity. The rulers of the petty German states clung to their power and privileges and were fiercely opposed to progress in any form. One of these sovereign princelings declared: "I will not have any railway in my state, I do not want any shoemaker or tailor to travel as fast as I do."

The country's progressive forces concentrated on the question of unifying Germany. The bourgeois revolution of July 1830 in France revived the opposition among the German bourgeoisie and intelligentsia, but the bourgeoisie was hesitant and inclined to compromise with the landowners for more reasons than its relative economic weakness. A new social force was already looming up behind the bourgeoisie—the working class—which it sensed to be its future adversary. At that time the German working-class movement was only beginning.

Meanwhile, in the advanced capitalist countries—France and Britain—the proletariat was already emerging in the historical arena as the antagonist of the capitalist class and as a force objectively hostile to bourgeois society.

The advance of the industrial revolution, the switch from handicrafts and manufactures to large-scale capitalist industry based on the use of machinery, brought impoverishment to the working people, ruin to the small artisans and traders, and immense sufferings to the workers who were savagely exploited in the capitalist factories. Hundreds and thousands of workers were made redundant by the new machines. These sufferings were compounded by the crises which regularly shook the capitalist economy from 1825 onwards.

At the same time, the spread of large-scale machine production led to the concentration of masses of workers at the factories, helping them to unite and gradually ridding the one-time artisans of their petty-bourgeois mentality, and their futile dreams of once again operating their own small enterprises. As their class consciousness was awakened, the workers came to see that their enemy was not the machine, as they had once imagined, but the manufacturer himself, and the privileged propertied classes as a whole. They felt a growing urge to unite in order to resist the oppression, initially by trades and later on a larger scale, by setting up the first working-class organisations — the trade unions (in Britain, for example) and mutual-aid societies.

In 1831 and 1834 proletarian uprisings occurred in Lyons, a major industrial centre in France, when the local weavers fought on the barricades and inscribed on their banners the motto: "Live working or die fighting!" These uprisings were relatively soon put down, but they gave the bourgeoisie a great fright. When the first one took place, the government newspaper *Journal des Débats* on December 8, 1831 wrote: "The Lyons revolt revealed an important secret — the internal struggle taking place in society between the propertied class and the propertyless class." Chartism — demanding a People's Charter — arose in England in the late 1830s as the first organised mass political movement of the working class. Of its six points the main one was a demand for universal suffrage, because the Chartists believed that political struggle provided the means to improve the condition of the workers.

Spontaneous protest against exploitation by masses of people and their striving for a better life had long ago produced visions of a more equitable social system, and this was the basis of utopian socialism. In its classic form it was worked out by three brilliant thinkers of the early 19th century: Henri Saint-Simon, Charles Fourier and Robert Owen, whose works contain sharp and striking criticisms of the evils and shortcomings of the capitalist system, and remarkably accurate predictions about the future communist society. Many years later, in 1874, Frederick Engels wrote that scientific socialism "rests on the shoulders of Saint-Simon, Fourier and Owen — three men who, in spite of all their fantastic notions and all their utopianism, stand among the most eminent thinkers of all time and whose genius anticipated innumerable things the correctness of which is now being scientifically proved by us".[1]

CHILDHOOD AND YOUTH

Karl Heinrich Marx was born in the town of Trier (Trèves) on May 5, 1818, into the family of a lawyer, Heinrich Marx, who was then living in a small two-storey house at 664 Brückengasse, which is now 10 Brückenstrasse. Two years later they moved to a house in Simeonstrasse, where Marx lived until he left Trier in 1835.

Trier, which lies on the banks of the Mosel, a tributary of the Rhine, is one of the oldest towns in Germany. In the Middle Ages it was the see of a large diocese, the residence of the archbishop of Trier, but it subsequently declined in importance compared with other towns along the Rhine, such as Cologne and Düsseldorf, although it continued to be a district centre of Prussia's Rhine Province. At that time, Trier was a quiet town with a population of less than 15,000, but it did not remain isolated from the social movement that was sweeping the whole of Germany. There, too, a sharp social contrast existed between the urban poor, dragging out a miserable existence, and the prosperous minority of the townsfolk. Socialist theories were also echoed in Trier, and Ludwig Gall, one of the first German utopian socialists, issued his pamphlets there in the 1820s and 1830s.

Karl Marx's father, Heinrich Marx, was a man of no mean accomplishments. He was widely read and well acquainted with the works of the leading French thinkers of the 18th century. Prominent in his private library were the works of Rousseau and Voltaire, and Thomas Paine's *The Rights of Man*. He had a good knowledge of the works of Locke, Leibniz and Lessing. An able lawyer who acted as advocate at the High Court of Appeal, he commanded great respect among his colleagues. Marx later wrote that his father was "noted for his integrity of character no less than for legal ability." [2]

Heinrich Marx never carried his political views beyond the limits of liberalism, but even that aroused the suspicions of the Prussian authorities. The police kept their eye on him after he delivered a speech on January 18, 1834, at a festival in the Casino Hall in honour of the Rhenish Provincial Diet deputies, in which he spoke in favour of representative system.

Heinrich Marx had accepted the ideas of the Enlightenment and was something of a free-thinker on religion, although he himself came from a rabbinical family. He was quite indifferent to the concrete forms of religion and orthodox dogma. Shortly before Karl was born, he renounced Judaism and adopted the Lutheran faith,

---
[1] Marx, Engels, *Collected Works*, Vol. 23, Progress Publishers, Moscow, p. 630.
[2] Ibid., Vol. 41, p. 96.

because of the restrictions to which the Jews were then subjected in Germany. Later his wife and children were also baptised.

To Karl he was a gentle father who was constantly concerned with his son's spiritual development.

Karl responded with a warm-hearted attachment, which did not weaken even when father and son found themselves at odds over Karl's choice of way in life. Throughout his life, he retained a profound respect for his father's memory and never parted with his photograph made from an old daguerreotype. When Marx died, Engels put this photograph in his coffin.

Karl's mother, Henriette Pressburg, came from Holland. As the mother of nine children she confined herself to the business of housekeeping. Her spiritual world was narrow, and she was never a real friend to her son, as Heinrich had been. Karl had three brothers and five sisters; his brothers died young and he was survived by three sisters — the eldest Sophie, and the younger, Emilie and Louise.

Karl was the favourite of the family. His quick mind, inventiveness at play, and ability to make up and act out all sorts of fantastic stories put him at the centre of any group of children. His daughter Eleanor later recalled that her aunts had frequently said that Karl had had an immense influence on his sisters.

In 1830 Karl entered the Trier Gymnasium, where he was a good but not a top pupil, although he always shone where creative ability was required. His certificate of maturity says that his essays showed a wealth of thought and deep insight into the subject-matter, and that in Latin and Greek he was good at interpreting texts where "the difficulty consists not so much in the peculiarity of the language as in the subject-matter and train of thought".[1] Karl also had a good knowledge of mathematics. He was liked by the other boys, but they were somewhat apprehensive of his keen wit and satirical verse, in which he lampooned some of them.

Karl was fortunate in his teachers. At the time, the headmaster of the Trier Gymnasium was Johann Wyttenbach, one of the most erudite teachers of his day, who taught history and philosophy. He was a liberal, strongly influenced by the German and French Enlightenment, and believed that the young should be taught to have a "sacred belief in progress and refinement". Naturally, Wyttenbach was not trusted by the Prussian authorities and in his last few years he was even placed under police surveillance. Johann Steininger, the mathematics and physics teacher, was thought to be an adherent of materialism and there were doubts about his "patriotic frame of mind".

The solid stone walls of the Royal Frederick William Gymnasium in Trier failed to isolate its pupils from the seething life outside. In 1833 prohibited literature and satirical lampoons on the authorities

---

[1] Marx, Engels, *Collected Works*, Vol. 1, p. 643.

were discovered in the Gymnasium, and one of the pupils was arrested.

That was the period when Karl first began to feel a hatred for all things reactionary. Upon his graduation in the autumn of 1835, he refused to make a parting call on Vitus Loers, a teacher who was notorious for his reactionary views and who had been appointed assistant director with the special duty of exercising political supervision over the school.

Karl's Gymnasium examination composition "Reflections of a Young Man on the Choice of a Profession", which he wrote in August 1835, gives a good idea of his frame of mind. He said it was vital to choose the profession that would offer one the widest scope to work for mankind. He was aware that the choice was no easy one. People cannot always attain the position to which they believe they are called because "our relations in society have to some extent already begun to be established before we are in a position to determine them".[1] However, the keynote of the essay was: do not shrink into the shell of a narrow egotism, but seek ways and means to serve men. "If he works only for himself, he may perhaps become a famous man of learning, a great sage, an excellent poet, but he can never be a perfect, truly great man." Karl wrote that if a man chose the position in life in which he could most of all work for mankind, he would experience no petty, limited, selfish joy, for his happiness would belong to millions.[2]

This essay shows the influence of the 18th-century Enlightenment, its profound conviction that man's mission is to work for the common good, its idea that man depends on his environment. It is true that Karl's freedom-loving, humanistic sentiments were still rather vague, but when he came into collision with the reactionary order prevailing in Germany his keen mind helped him to take the next step.

STUDENT YEARS IN BONN AND BERLIN

Heinrich Marx had great hopes for Karl. He was grooming him for a scientific career, and once wrote: "You have still a long time to live, God willing, to the benefit of yourself and your family and, if my surmise is not mistaken, for the good of mankind."[3]

In October 1835, Karl enrolled at Bonn University and applied himself to the study of jurisprudence with the full ardour of youth, so that in his letters his father had to urge him to moderate his zeal for the sake of his health. Karl put his name down for several courses and bought a great many books on various subjects, especially history. Apart from the subjects on the law syllabus, he attend-

---

[1] Marx, Engels, *Collected Works*, Vol. 1, p. 4.
[2] Ibid., pp. 8-9.
[3] Ibid., p. 662.

ed lectures on Greek and Roman mythology, Homer and the history of modern art. His fervid imagination craved for creative effort, and he tried his hand at *belles-lettres*: he wrote verse and became a member of the university poets' circle, which was in touch with a similar circle at Göttingen University.

The students of Bonn University, as well as of other universities of Germany, set up associations (*Landsmannschaften*); Marx joined the Trier Association and was elected to its board. A lithograph is extant showing the members of this association, and among them the young Marx, with a head of thick black hair, and a serious, thoughtful face.

It was only natural that Marx as a student should question some of the traditional notions instilled in his mind at school and also at home, and this must have been reflected in his letters to his father, which are not extant. In reply to one such letter, Heinrich Marx, apparently trying to resolve his son's serious doubts about whether religion could serve as the basis for morality, wrote: "You know that I am anything but a fanatic. But ... faith is a real requirement of man sooner or later." To press home his argument he cited the example of the great scientists Newton and Leibniz, who believed in God.[1] However, Marx's critical mind was not to be swayed by an appeal to authorities.

Marx spent only two terms in Bonn, and then, on his father's advice, decided to continue his studies at Berlin University, which had among its lecturers some of the most eminent authorities on law.

Before going on to Berlin, Marx spent his summer holidays in 1836 at home. That was the occasion of his engagement to Jenny von Westphalen, a childhood friend. Born in 1814, Jenny was the daughter of Privy Councillor Ludwig von Westphalen; her grandfather, a prominent military man, had been adviser to the Duke of Brunswick and had married a lady descended from the Scottish aristocracy. However, Jenny's father was free from the aristocratic haughtiness affected by some members of his family, including his eldest son Ferdinand, Jenny's stepbrother and a future Prussian minister. Ludwig von Westphalen was on friendly terms with the "plebeian" Heinrich Marx, a baptised Jew, and was very fond of his son. It was he who first introduced Karl to the ideas of Saint-Simon. Karl responded with the most lively attachment, regarded him as one of his moral tutors, and later dedicated his doctoral dissertation to him. Jenny's mother, Caroline von Westphalen, the daughter of an official, was unaffected and warm-hearted. That the younger children of the family, Jenny and Edgar (Karl's classmate and friend), were free of the prejudices of their class was largely due to their parents.

Jenny had brains, education and looks. She had the reputation of being Trier's most beautiful woman and the belle of its balls (many

---

[1] Ibid., p. 647.

years later Marx wrote to her from Trier: "It's damned pleasant for a man, when his wife lives on like this as an 'enchanted princess' in the imagination of a whole town."[1] Nevertheless, she did not hesitate to throw her lot in with that of a young student from a family that was not well off and had no noble ancestry, and refused the many "advantageous" offers of marriage from men of her own class.

Karl and Jenny became close friends in childhood, and with time their feelings matured into a deep love. Not only feelings but a kindred spirit created a bond between the impetuous, temperamental youth and the charming girl of ready sympathy and rare feminine tact. Jenny recognised Karl's talents and outstanding personality, and strove to be a fitting companion. Karl worshipped Jenny and, as lovers are wont to do, strove to express his feelings in verse. Many were the poems he wrote to her, and he himself later spoke ironically of some of his earlier poetry which, like that of all beginners, abounded in exclamations and extravagant hyperboles. But some of it reveals a charming lyricism which gives an idea of the depth of his feelings.

> Then was I captive bound,
> Then was my vision clear,
> For I had truly found
> What my dark strivings were.
>
> . . . .
>
> And what my Soul, Fate-driven,
> Never in flight o'ertook,
> That to my heart was given,
> Was granted by your look.[2]

Their engagement was kept secret for some time for fear that Jenny's family would object, and she had to make a long and persistent stand against her aristocratic relatives in defence of her right to marry the man she loved. They were married seven years later, but by then a great deal had changed: Heinrich Marx, who approved of Karl's choice, had died in 1838, and Ludwig von Westphalen, who had treated Karl as a son, in 1842.

In October 1836, Karl Marx was enrolled as a law student at Berlin University. In the capital of the Prussian monarchy, Marx saw at first hand the acute contradictions which beset German society at that time — the sway of the Junkers, the political inequality of the bourgeoisie, and the poverty of the vast majority of the people. There were many fine scholars teaching at the university. Shortly before, Hegel had lectured there on philosophy, and Eduard Gans, a prominent progressive lawyer, was a lecturer in law. Karl attended Gans' lectures and was described by him as "exceptionally diligent". Karl may have taken part in a demonstration in honour of Gans,

---

[1] Marx, Engels, *Collected Works*, Vol. 41, p. 499.
[2] Ibid., Vol. 1, pp. 529, 530.

near his home, which the university students staged in 1838 to mark his birthday. This event attracted the attention of the police.

At first he lived in solitude and worked even harder than he had at Bonn University. He later wrote to his father: "After my arrival in Berlin, I broke off all hitherto existing connections, made visits rarely and unwillingly, and tried to immerse myself in science and art."[1] One of the results, apart from three albums of sonnets and other poems dedicated to Jenny, was a considerable number of songs, ballads, romances and epigrams.

The mood of rebellion which sprang from revolutionary romanticism runs through many of his poetical works. He also tried his hand at playwriting (*Oulanem*, a tragedy in verse) and even wrote a satirical novel (*Scorpion and Felix*), but all these were left unfinished.

Karl's poetry fell short of the high standard he set himself, and he felt that the only good thing about it was that it expressed some warmth of feeling. Of all the things he wrote in this genre only the *Wild Songs* appeared in the journal *Athenäum* in 1841; nevertheless his poetry is of great interest as a biograhical source. It reveals Karl as a young man discontented with the state of affairs, longing for vigorous activity and struggle, but as yet unaware of what to do. He seems to sense with his whole being that it is wrong to follow the well-trodden path and remain satisfied with one's lot.

> Never can I do in peace
> That with which my Soul's obsessed,
> Never take things at my ease;
> I must press on without rest.
>
> . . . .
>
> Therefore let us risk our all,
> Never resting, never tiring;
> Not in silence dismal, dull,
> Without action or desiring;
> Not in brooding introspection
> Bowed beneath a yoke of pain,
> So that yearning, dream and action
> Unfulfilled to us remain.[2]

Very frequently he expressed his discontent with abstract philosophical systems that were divorced from reality, and strove to work out an outlook which would help him to see the processes at work in life and take an active part in them. Marx's description of Hegel applies to himself to a large extent:

> Kant and Fichte soar to heavens blue
> Seeking for some distant land,
> I but seek to grasp profound and true
> That which—in the street I find.[3]

---

[1] Ibid., p. 11.
[2] Ibid., pp. 525-27.
[3] Ibid., p. 577.

However, it was not poetry but science that was Marx's main pursuit in Berlin. In the only letter to his father that has survived from that period, one dated November 10, 1837,[1] he described the books he had read, his efforts to bring order into the vast material he had studied and his own theoretical quest. The letter shows the breadth and diversity of his interests in that period, his exceptional industry, the high standard he set for himself, and his critical attitude to his own conclusions, which he relentlessly discarded whenever he found them to be untenable.

In Berlin, together with his studies of law, history, the theory of art, and foreign languages, Marx started to acquire a good grounding in philosophy. The initial impulse stemmed from an effort to write a long essay on the philosophy of law, but his interest in philosophy must also have been stimulated by his urge to comprehend the life of his day with all its contradictions.

STUDY OF HEGEL'S PHILOSOPHY.
AMONG THE YOUNG HEGELIANS

In the course of his studies, Marx realised the theoretical futility of trying to explain the world from the standpoint of subjective idealism. Marx was drawn to the philosophy of Hegel by his urge to interpret reality in terms of its intrinsic regularities, or to seek the idea in reality itself, as he expressed it in terms of the philosophical idealism he then professed. He wrote: "The object itself must be studied in its development; arbitrary divisions must not be introduced."[2]

Hegel's philosophy was a reflection of the historical changes that had taken place in Europe in the late 18th and early 19th centuries, arising as they did from the break-up of feudal social relations under the impact of the French Revolution. These social processes, together with the rapid advance of the sciences, especially the natural sciences, dealt a heavy blow at the old, metaphysical mode of thought. Later, Engels wrote: "But precisely therein lay the true significance and the revolutionary character of the Hegelian philosophy ... that it once for all dealt the death blow to the finality of all products of human thought and action."[3] Hegel's great achievement was the first systematic elaboration of the dialectical method.

Hegel's philosophy presents the world as a totality in the process of continuous development, of ascent from the lower to the higher. In Hegel's view, development proceeds through the struggle and resolution of internal contradictions, which result in the transition to a new stage, or the "elimination" (*Aufhebung*) of the old contradic-

---

[1] Marx, Engels, *Collected Works*, Vol. 1, pp. 10-21.
[2] Ibid., p. 12.
[3] Ibid., Vol. 26, p. 359.

tions and the emergence of new ones, intrinsic to the new quality. Development is seen as a unity of continuity and discontinuity, of gradual quantitative change and breaks in gradual development, of abrupt transitions to the new quality. Hegel applies this principle mainly to the history of human society. He sees world history as a law-governed development of the spirit, with the spirit's realisation of its freedom being the meaning of this development.

However, Hegel's dialectic has an idealistic basis, for he declares that the substance of all things is the Absolute Idea to whose self-development he reduces the whole process of dialectical movement. According to Hegel, wrote Engels, "the Absolute Idea ... 'alienates', that is, transforms, itself into nature and comes to itself again later in the mind, that is, in thought and in history".[1] The development of the Absolute Idea culminates in Hegel's philosophy in the form of absolute truth. This enshrinement of his own philosophical system as the ultimate goal in the development of human thought and in all development in general, is in sharp contrast with the dialectical method he himself propounded, when he insisted that all phenomena should be viewed in continuous movement and in unceasing change. The limitations of Hegel's philosophy were most glaring in his political views, for he declared the summit of society's development to be the constitutional monarchy, whose only task was to make some "improvements" in the Prussian state by adapting it to the needs of the bourgeoisie. This sacrificed the objective revolutionary content of Hegel's dialectical method to the needs of a conservative metaphysical system.

The contradiction between Hegel's dialectical method and his metaphysical system was a reflection of the inconsistent and equivocal world outlook of the German bourgeoisie, which strove to escape the fetters of feudalism but shunned revolutionary ways of doing this, preferring to compromise with the forces of reaction.

Marx knew something of Hegel's philosophy before he came to Berlin, but did not begin a serious study of it until the spring of 1837. At the time he was taking a rest in Stralow, a suburb of Berlin, after having seriously upset his health by spending nights over his books. There it was that he "got to know Hegel from beginning to end, together with most of his disciples".[2]

Meanwhile a split was developing between the pupils of the philosopher, who had died in 1831. Some of them — including Hinrichs, Gabler and Göschel — were taking a militant stand in defence of religion. These Right-wing Hegelians read Christian orthodoxy into Hegel's philosophy and vindicated the existing political order as a whole.

The Left-wing group, known as the Young Hegelians — among them David Strauss, the Bauer brothers, Bruno and Edgar, Arnold Ruge and Ludwig Feuerbach — strove to draw radical conclusions

---

[1] Ibid., p. 360.
[2] Ibid., Vol. 1, p. 19.

from Hegel's philosophy. The Young Hegelians rejected the conservative-religious interpretation of this philosophy and criticised the dogmas of Christianity and religion in general. This was first done by David Strauss in his two-volume *Life of Jesus* (published in 1835 and 1836), which treated the Gospels as a collection of spontaneous myths expressing the hopes and aspirations of the early Christian communities. By contrast, Bruno Bauer believed the Gospels to be the product of a deliberate mythogenesis, reflecting a stage in the development of man's self-consciousness, a stage that mankind was bound to overcome in the subsequent development and perfection of its consciousness. Bauer carried the critique of religion and the Gospels farther than Strauss, casting doubt not only on the divine origin but on the very existence of Christ, and connecting the origins of Christianity with the spiritual life and philosophical trends of antiquity.

This controversy between the Young Hegelians and the orthodox champions of religion was theological in form but had a definite political content: one of the main pillars of the absolutist regime was being undermined by the denial of religion as divine revelation, and the insistence that it was a product of the human spirit. By putting forward the principle of transforming reality through criticism, the Young Hegelians had moved away from the critique of religion towards a critique of the politics and ideology of reactionary romanticism and Prussian absolutism, and it is this that made their philosophy the philosophy of the German radical bourgeoisie.

Idealism was the Young Hegelians' fundamental weakness. In contrast to Hegel, they inclined to subjectivist views of history and underestimation of men's practical activity, especially mass action, by pinning their faith on the omnipotence of theoretical criticism and believing that only critical thinking by outstanding personalities could assure the progress of man's self-consciousness and, consequently, all progress in general.

Marx came to know the Young Hegelians while he was a student of Berlin University, and his sympathies were at once aroused by their bold criticism of the religious and philosophical dogmas which the philistine held to be sacrosanct, by the radicalism of the political convictions of many of them, their stand for the freedom of conscience, the press and so on. He became a close friend of the members of the Young Hegelians' circle in Berlin, known as the *Doktor Klub*, of which Bruno Bauer, a university lecturer in theology, was then the life and soul. Among the members were Karl Friedrich Köppen, a teacher of history and a great connoisseur and admirer of the Enlightenment, who soon became Marx's good friend, and Adolf Rutenberg, a teacher of geography.

Marx soon became one of the intellectual leaders of this club. His vast knowledge, powerful logic, and depth and consistency of reasoning commanded the admiration even of older men of considerable standing. Not only was Marx treated as an equal, but many were quick to concede his superiority. He had a great influence on Köppen, who in 1840 dedicated his book *Friedrich der Grosse und seine Widersacher* to Marx. In 1841, Moses Hess, a prominent Young Hegelian, wrote to his friend Berthold Auerbach: "Be ready to meet the greatest and perhaps the *only* living *real philosopher*.... Dr. Marx, as my idol is called, is still a very young man (he can be no more than 24), who will deal the final blow at medieval religion and politics; he combines the most profound philosophical earnestness with the keenest wit; imagine to yourself Rousseau, Voltaire, Holbach, Lessing, Heine and Hegel combined into one personality; and I mean *combined*, not mechanically mixed — and this will give you an idea of Dr.Marx."[1] Many shared this view.

DOCTORAL DISSERTATION

At the beginning of 1839 Marx became immersed in a study of the history of philosophy, starting with a wide-ranging survey of philosophical thinking in the Ancient world, notably Epicureanism, Stoicism and Scepticism. This choice was determined by the Young Hegelians' general interest in these philosophical systems, which they regarded as precursors of the philosophy of self-consciousness, and mainly by Marx's own interests. As his atheistic outlook developed, Marx felt a natural attraction to the philosophy of Epicurus, one of the foremost thinkers of the Ancient world, whom he called the greatest Greek enlightener. Marx had a deep interest in philosophical trends that dealt with ethical problems and man's attitude to the surrounding world. Finally, Marx's research into the history of philosophy helped to provide the answer to a burning question of how philosophy deals with the external world, whether it accepts everything that exists as being rational and necessary, or whether it contains within itself that which ought to be as opposed to that which is. We find, therefore, that in his earliest research Marx went beyond the abstract and the purely theoretical to the need to frame an outlook that would help to find an answer to this vital question: how was man to be released from bondage, how was he to be made free?

The first fruit of this study was a set of seven notebooks of preparatory material, written in 1839 and published nearly 90 years later under the title *Notebooks on Epicurean Philosophy*. In this work, Marx showed philosophy to be incompatible with religion. He was already sure that philosophy was an active force capable of exerting an influence on the world. He wrote: "As Prometheus, having stolen fire from heaven, begins to build houses and to settle upon the earth, so philosophy, expanded to be the whole world, turns against the world of appearance."[2]

---

[1] MEGA, Abt. 1, Bd. 1, Halbband 2, S. 261.
[2] Marx, Engels, *Collected Works*, Vol. 1, p. 491.

It was in the light of a philosophy actively intruding into life that Marx criticised some of Hegel's followers who held that "*mediocrity is the normal manifestation of the absolute spirit*".[1] He insisted that philosophy has the broadest cognitive possibilities and is capable of exercising a great influence on the world. He argued that man's mind is powerful, and directed his most pointed barbs at those philosophers who claimed the human spirit to be incapable of understanding the essence of things and preached a blind acceptance of a world consisting of incognisable phenomena. Among those who fell in this group were the Kantian agnostics, whom he aptly called "appointed priests of ignorance", and whose "daily business is to tell their beads over their own powerlessness and the power of things".[2]

The young Marx's radicalism and free-thinking stood out in his approach to the philosophy of Epicurus. He gave special emphasis to Epicurus' view of the problem of freedom, and praised his striving for the freedom and independence of the spirit, for release from the fetters of religion, superstition and fear of retribution in a hereafter. Marx also brought out the same congenial ideas he found in the works of the famous Roman philosopher and poet, Lucretius.

In the polemic between Epicurus and the moralist writer Plutarch, who accused the former of atheism, Marx sided with Epicurus and accepted all his atheistic conclusions; he agreed with the old atheists that religious people project their own qualities onto a supreme being whom they call God.

With his usual thoroughness, Marx worked on the history of ancient philosophy throughout 1839 and a part of 1840. At the beginning of 1841, he decided to write a doctoral thesis entitled "Difference between the Democritean and Epicurean Philosophy of Nature" many points of which he had already outlined and partially elaborated in his *Notebooks*. The formulation of his subject was in itself something of a polemic against Hegel, who took a clearly biased view of the ancient atomism and materialism of Democritus, Epicurus and Lucretius. In his foreword to the thesis, which he wrote in March 1841, Marx virtually rebuked Hegel for underestimating these philosophical systems, and pointed out that they were "the key to the true history of Greek philosophy".[3]

His thesis emphasised the importance of the views of Democritus and Epicurus, these great Greek atomists, in mankind's spiritual development, and also brought out the elements of dialectics in the philosophical system of Epicurus, notably his teaching on the spontaneous declination of atoms, which he saw as an expression of the dialectical principle of self-movement, a principle he interpreted as one of activity. He said: "Hence the good is the flight from evil, pleasure the swerving away from suffering."[4] Comparing the views

---

[1] Marx, Engels, *Collected Works*, Vol. 1, p. 491.
[2] Ibid., p. 429.
[3] Ibid., p. 30.
[4] Ibid., p. 51.

of Democritus and Epicurus on nature, he sided with the latter, whose philosophy provided the basis for his ethical views, particularly his doctrine of freedom. Marx's approach to moral problems implied philosophy's active intrusion into life, for he favoured recasting the irrational world and stressed the dialectical unity of philosophy and life. He wrote: "As the world becomes philosophical, philosophy also becomes worldly ... its realisation is also its loss." [1] What he meant was that as philosophy is translated into life it raises the latter to a new and higher stage, while itself ceasing to be pure theory and finding embodiment in practical activity. There we find in embryo his future doctrine of the interconnection and unity of theory and practice.

Marx's thesis shows an advance in his atheistic views. It was shot through with a militant atheistic spirit and hatred for superstition, and was aimed against all reactionary philosophy striving to freeze scientific quest within religious bounds and to subordinate it to the interests of religion. In his foreword Marx proclaimed atheism to be his creed. He wrote: "Philosophy ... will never grow tired of answering its adversaries with the cry of Epicurus: 'Not the man who denies the gods worshipped by the multitude, but he who affirms of the gods what the multitude believes about them, is truly impious...' The confession of Prometheus: 'In simple words, I hate the pack of gods,' is its own confession, its own aphorism against all heavenly and earthly gods." [2]

In his thesis Marx stressed that all the so-called proofs of God's existence were mere tautologies, but he realised that, while the religious outlook was irrational, religion did constitute a real force. It was the task of true science, striving to help overcome religion, not only to overthrow its dogmas but also to explain its essence, origins and wide acceptance. Marx drew the conclusion that the emergence of belief in the gods was a reflection of the first stage in the development of human consciousness, a primitive level of thinking which was still incapable of understanding and explaining the surrounding world and which ascribed to it supernatural and irrational properties. Marx pointed out that *"for whom the world appears without reason, hence who is without reason himself, for him God exists"*.[3]

Defending one's thesis at Berlin University at that time was highly complicated and involved a great deal of expense. Therefore Marx submitted his thesis to the University of Jena, where on April 15, 1841 he was awarded the degree of Doctor of Philosophy.

The doctoral thesis marked an important stage in Marx's ideological development, for while on the whole remaining a Hegelian, an idealist, he was outspokenly atheistic and insisted on philosophy taking an active stand on reality. Hegel was still a great authority for

---

[1] Ibid., p. 85.
[2] Ibid., p. 30.
[3] Ibid., p. 105.

him — a "giant thinker" — but the young man yearned to work out an approach of his own to some questions which implied conclusions differing from those of Hegel. Marx's thesis helped him to identify the problems which came to be of great importance in the shaping of his own outlook. He continued to grapple with the question of the relation between philosophy and reality and was bound sooner or later to come up against that of the relation between thinking and being. His militant atheism, fundamentally incompatible with idealism, facilitated his subsequent acceptance of materialism.

ATTITUDE TO FEUERBACH

The year Marx finished his thesis, an important event occurred in Germany's ideological life — the publication of Feuerbach's *Essence of Christianity*, which had a powerful liberating effect on the leading minds of the day. In a sense, Feuerbach was the first philosopher to overcome, within limits, the idealism of the Young Hegelians. His book was a materialist critique of religion and proclaimed that nature existed independently of the human mind, and was the basis on which men, themselves products of nature, had emerged. He declared that there was nothing outside nature and man, and that the supreme beings created by man's religious imagination were merely fantastic reflections of man's own essence. Man's concept of God embodied all the qualities which, while not characteristic of individuals, belonged to human beings as a whole, to mankind, to the human race, or to man as species-being, as Feuerbach himself put it. He wrote: "You believe in love as a divine attribute, because you yourself love, you believe that God is a wise, a benevolent being, because you regard goodness and reason as your best qualities... Hence, God is the essence of man, seen as the highest truth." [1] Consequently man had to repossess himself of his human essence, which he had himself alienated in the concept of God.

Even at that time some of Feuerbach's ideas conflicted with those the young Marx was working out for himself. He could not accept Feuerbach's contemplative approach and saw philosophy as an active factor, while Feuerbach's underestimation of dialectics clashed with his profound understanding of its revolutionary role. On the whole, however, Marx welcomed Feuerbach's book as one which helped to widen the cognitive horizons of science. Marx was also attracted to Feuerbach because of his own ideas about the earthly origins of religion. As Marx's own materialist views matured, Feuerbach, the last representative of German classical philosophy, who dealt a powerful blow at its idealistic foundations, came to exert a growing influence on him.

---

[1] L. Feuerbach, *Das Wesen des Christenthums*, Leipzig, 1904, S. 75, 77.

It is true that at the time Marx, like many other Young Hegelians, saw *The Essence of Christianity* chiefly as a manifesto of radical atheism, as a much more consistent refutation of religious superstition than was, say, Strauss' book. But being on the whole an idealist, he was still not aware of its materialist content. He realised, however, that Feuerbach's ideas were a substantial advance in understanding real human relations, and the comprehension of these ideas was one of the factors which helped to shape the materialist elements of his outlook. Feuerbach's work added to Marx's conviction that the critique of religion was a stage in the critical comprehension of the existing world order and a form of struggle for man's emancipation from his spiritual and other fetters. Subsequently, Marx wrote in this context, having Feuerbach's philosophy chiefly in mind: "The criticism of religion ends with the teaching that *man is the highest being for man*, hence with *the categorical imperative to overthrow all relations* in which man is a debased, enslaved, forsaken, despicable being." [1]

Consequently, the young Marx saw Feuerbach as an outstanding representative of advanced philosophy, whose ideas were a concentration of the "most subtle, valuable and invisible juices" of its people and of its time. [2] Open and bold defence of these ideas against the attacks of conservatives and obscurantists, and their further development became one of the main tasks which he set himself.

START OF POLITICAL ACTIVITY.
ARTICLE AGAINST PRUSSIAN CENSORSHIP

His doctoral thesis completed, Marx was full of plans for the future. He intended to join Bruno Bauer in teaching philosophy at Bonn University, to start, with Feuerbach's participation, a journal called *Archives of Atheism*, and to write a work on Christian art. In early July 1841, following a two-month stay at Trier, he went to live in Bonn, where he became a close friend of Bruno Bauer's, whom he helped to write an atheistic pamphlet, *The Trumpet Call of Hegel's Doomsday*, directed against the Right-wing Hegelians.

However, his hopes of obtaining a professorship did not materialise. King Frederick William IV, whose ascent to the throne in 1840 had given opposition circles hopes of a liberal government policy, soon made it quite clear that there were not going to be any constitutional reforms. Criticism of the Prussian monarchy, however moderate, was ruthlessly suppressed. Johann Jacoby was accused of high treason for putting out a pamphlet advocating a representative system for Prussia. Bruno Bauer was dismissed from Bonn University.

---

[1] Marx, Engels, *Collected Works*, Vol. 3, p. 182.
[2] Ibid., Vol. 1, p. 195.

The most radically-minded Young Hegelians—with Marx, Bruno Bauer and Arnold Ruge in the van—had to turn to politics because of the mounting government reprisals and the collapse of their illusions about an "enlightened monarch" introducing a constitution and a liberal order of his own accord. Once and for all, Marx opted for the lot of political fighter, and threw himself with youthful fervour into the midst of the struggle against Prussian absolutism for the democratic freedoms. He put aside the theoretical works started earlier, and between January 15 and February 10, 1842 wrote his article, "Comments on the Latest Prussian Censorship Instruction", which was the first work written by Marx as a journalist. It contained a sharp critical attack on a censorship law the government and a section of the moderate opposition press had hailed as evidence of the new king's liberal intentions.

Marx exposed the real meaning of the hypocritically worded instruction, which he said only pretended to give more freedom to the press but in fact gave a free hand to the rampant reactionary censorship. He wrote: "It is the habit of *pseudo-liberalism*, when compelled to make concessions, to sacrifice persons, the instruments, and to preserve the thing itself, the institution. In this way the attention of a superficial public is diverted." [1] Central to the instruction was a complete ban on criticism of the Christian religion, then the main outlet for opposition political views, for the government hoped that this would damp down all criticism of the existing system.

Marx condemned the Prussian government's intention to muzzle the press, for laws against frame of mind could be issued only by a government which imagined itself the sole, exclusive possessor of state reason and which opposed the people. Such a government could rely only on a bureaucratic machine and place its trust only in officials. The flaw in the Prussian state system was the power of the bureaucrats, arrogant, almighty officials, whose words and deeds were virtually sacrosanct.

Accordingly, Marx linked his criticism of the censorship with resolute and consistent condemnation of Prussian state institutions as a whole, and the fundamental defects of the absolutist feudal system itself.

There was a revolutionary ring to his conclusion: "The real, *radical cure for the censorship* would be its *abolition*; for the institution itself is a bad one." [2] This, like the whole of his reasoning, suggested to the reader that the social order in Germany did not need any partial improvements but a radical transformation. It is true that he was not yet clear about the motive forces or the class aims of such a transformation, but his debut as a revolutionary journalist was a striking expression of his revolutionary-democratic convictions.

Marx's article could not be printed in Germany under the existing censorship, and it saw the light of day only in 1843, in the first vol-

---

[1] Marx, Engels, *Collected Works*, Vol. 1, p. 110.
[2] Ibid., p. 131.

ume of a two-volume collection, *Anekdota zur neuesten deutschen Philosophie und Publicistik*, published by Ruge in Switzerland.

RHEINISCHE ZEITUNG: CONTRIBUTOR AND EDITOR

Marx's revolutionary-democratic views impelled him to seek a wide field of activity and a rostrum for his ideas. He joined the opposition *Rheinische Zeitung*, which started publication in Cologne in January 1842. It was established and financed by prominent members of the big bourgeoisie in the Rhine Province—Camphausen, Hansemann and other leaders of the liberal opposition. In an effort to recruit the best writers, they turned to the radicals, notably the Young Hegelians, and this resulted in a kind of private pact against the common enemy. On Marx's recommendation—by then he had already commanded authority in the political circles of the Rhine Province—a Berlin Young Hegelian, Adolf Rutenberg, was appointed editor. Such Young Hegelian journalists as the Bauer brothers, Hess and Köppen contributed to the paper. At first, however, its line was rather vague, with liberal overtones prevailing, and it was not widely read: in January 1842 it had only 400 subscribers.

Marx started his contributions to the *Rheinische Zeitung* in May 1842, when it carried the first of his series on the activity of the Rhine Province Assembly. The article made quite a stir throughout the country. From the summer of 1842 he became even more active on the paper, not only contributing articles but having an ever greater say in the editing. In mid-October 1842, his work on the paper induced him to move to Cologne and on October 15 he became its editor.

From then onwards the paper began to acquire distinct revolutionary-democratic features, and its criticism of Prussian absolutism and its ideological champions took on a sharper edge. This first schooling in practice brought out many aspects of Marx's talent: his organisational ability, his skill in selecting editorial personnel, his vast capacity for work and his literary endowments, both in writing and editing.

In his capacity as editor of a big daily, Marx kept coming up against socio-economic problems, which were hotly debated at weekly meetings attended by some of the editorial staff and members of the Board of Directors.

Marx recruited more contributors and made the paper much more popular. It was soon read well beyond the boundaries of the Rhine Province and even of the Kingdom of Prussia. Among its correspondents was the young Engels, who sent in his reports first from Berlin and now from England. The *Rheinische Zeitung* became the mouthpiece for the mood of democrats all over Germany. Its circulation increased from 885 in August 1842 to 1,820 in November, and to 3,400 in January 1843, a solid figure for the period. The *Mannhei-*

mer Abendzeitung commented in December 1842: "The number of the paper's subscribers in Germany and abroad has been growing from day to day, and the friends of progress and freedom ... have an organ championing their interests."

The paper's line, with Marx's articles setting the tone, gravely alarmed the Prussian government, and after the publication of Marx's first article in the series about the Rhine Province Assembly its censors became much sharper and banned the second article on the relationship between church and state. The authorities were most irate over his article on the Rhine Assembly debates on the Law on Thefts of Wood: the *Oberpräsident* of the Rhine Province, von Schaper, decided to institute proceedings against the paper, "in view of its insolent and disrespectful censure of the existing state institutions". The paper was faced with a ban. On November 30, 1842, Marx wrote to Ruge: "...We now have to put up from morning to night with the most horrible torments of the censorship, ministerial communications, complaints of the *Oberpräsident*, accusations in the Provincial Assembly, howls from shareholders, etc., etc., and I remain at my post only because I consider it my duty to prevent, to the best of my ability, those in power from carrying out their plans."[1] In these circumstances, it took exceptional self-possession and flexibility on Marx's part to continue the newspaper's fundamental line, without giving the Prussian reactionaries the pretext they were waiting for to close it down.

REVOLUTIONARY-DEMOCRATIC IDEAS IN MARX'S JOURNALISTIC WRITINGS

The sustained and acute polemics over burning political and social issues in Germany helped Marx to strengthen his revolutionary-democratic convictions and sharpen his pen as a fiery revolutionary journalist.

All his articles drove home the idea that the existing system was irrational and showed that the arguments of its apologists, advocating "the right of tyranny and violence", were false. His articles radiated a deep faith in progress and in the inevitable triumph of the new and progressive over the old and the moribund, epitomising Marx's own words about the literature of the revolutionary epoch, a literature relying in its relentless criticism on "the *new life's feeling of its own power*, which *shatters* what has been *shattered* and *rejects* what has been *rejected*".[2]

In his first article in the *Rheinische Zeitung*, "Debates on Freedom of the Press and Publication of the Proceedings of the Assembly of the Estates", Marx, as he himself said, dealt with censorship and freedom of the press from a different angle: whereas in his "Com-

[1] Marx, Engels, *Collected Works*, Vol. 1, p. 395.
[2] Ibid., p. 206.

ments on the Latest Prussian Censorship Instruction" he had dealt with the freedom of the press in general terms, he now linked the problem with the attitudes of the different social groups and estates, and extended his criticism to the social foundations of the absolutist feudal regime in Prussia—the domination of the Junkerdom and the class privileges which riddled Prussian political institutions. He launched a vigorous attack on the very principle of class representation and showed it to be directed against the people.

The Rhine Province Assembly was a typically feudal, estate-ridden institution, dominated by the nobility, which made a parody of representation. The province, whose interests the Assembly was supposed to defend, had "to fight not so much through its representatives as against them".[1]

The estate character of the Assembly also left its mark on the freedom of the press debate: the men who represented the titled aristocracy opposed freedom of the press by asserting, for instance, that it led to revolution. Marx exposed these attempts to ascribe the revolution to someone's evil machinations and showed it to be a law-governed and objective process. Revolutions were no more caused by freedom of the press than the motion of the celestial bodies by the astronomer's telescope.

One thing that stood out in Marx's journalistic writings was his criticism of the half-hearted attitude of the Assembly's bourgeois members, and Marx was perfectly aware they were impelled by narrow class interests and that theirs was the "opposition of the *bourgeois*, not of the *citoyen*".[2]

Marx backed the peasant deputy in the Assembly, whose "courageous, dignified and resolute stand" had openly contrasted with the pathetic efforts of those who opposed freedom of the press. Freedom, he argued, was to be won with spears and axes, not with futile whining and humble requests.

The article clearly revealed the essence of Marx's revolutionary-democratic views: hatred for the feudal-monarchist social-estate system, the call to win democratic freedoms for the whole people instead of privileges for some social estates, criticism of narrow-minded German bourgeois liberalism, and the opposition of resolute revolutionary action to the liberal tactics which doomed the masses to a wait-and-see attitude.

Marx the journalist declared war not only on the social and political order in Germany but also on the reactionary philosophers and historians who supported it. Among other things, he castigated reactionary romanticism, whose adherents, like the lawyer Stahl and the historian Leo in Germany, Bonald and de Maistre in France, and Haller in Switzerland, were attacking the Enlightenment, anathematising the French bourgeois revolution and singing paeans to the Middle Ages. Aristocratic feudal institutions were also being ex-

[1] Ibid., p. 147.
[2] Ibid., p. 169.

tolled by the historical school of law (Hugo, Savigny and others), which claimed that historical traditions and time-honoured institutions were not to be tampered with, because they were a product of a unique national spirit that made them exempt from rational explanation and even more exempt from change.

Marx's article, "The Philosophical Manifesto of the Historical School of Law", exposed the reactionary nature of this trend and its hostility to advanced ideas, above all to the idea of a revolutionary overthrow of the existing order. Later on, he defined it even more devastatingly as a school "which legitimates the baseness of today by the baseness of yesterday, a school that declares rebellious every cry of the serf against the knout once that knout is a time-honoured, ancestral, historical one". [1]

When he wrote the articles published by the *Rheinische Zeitung*, his view of the nature and role of the state, and the relation between material and spiritual activity was, on the whole, still idealistic, but his urge to make a critical assessment of reality, and establish the ideals of freedom in reality, not just in the sphere of pure reason, together with his desire to understand and defend the people's real interests, gave him an ever deeper and more concrete understanding of the surrounding world, social relations in particular, and this eventually brought him to materialism.

Advancing in the materialist interpretation of social phenomena, Marx expressed some penetrating ideas in the columns of the newspaper, notably, on the role of real relations in the shaping of legal rules. In one of his articles he wrote: "The *law* can only be the ideal, self-conscious image of reality, the *theoretical* expression, made independent, of the practical vital forces." [2]

Marx was quick to respond to the social issues which agitated the minds of his contemporaries. The day after Marx assumed the duties of editor of the *Rheinische Zeitung*, the paper carried his article, "Communism and the Augsburg *Allgemeine Zeitung*", rebutting the charges of communist propaganda made against his paper by the reactionary *Allgemeine Zeitung*. Marx wrote that the problem of communism was acquiring tremendous importance for the advanced European countries, above all England and France. Communism, he said, was a highly serious question of the time having "European importance". Moreover, Marx was beginning to see the close connection between communist ideas and the proletarian mass struggle unfolding in these countries. He wrote: "That the estate that today owns nothing *demands* to share in the wealth of the middle classes is a fact which ... is obvious to everyone in Manchester, Paris and Lyons." [3] There was good reason why he mentioned these three cities: Manchester was a centre of the Chartist movement, and Paris

---

[1] Marx, Engels, *Collected Works*, Vol. 3, p. 177.
[2] Ibid., Vol. 1, p. 273.
[3] Ibid., p. 216.

and Lyons were the scene of proletarian revolutionary action. Many still remembered the 1831 and the 1834 uprisings of the Lyons weavers.

Marx subsequently recalled that, realising the full importance of the problem he faced, he was aware of the inadequacy of his knowledge for passing final judgment on the essence of socialism and communism, but his reading of the works of Leroux, Considérant, and Proudhon had clearly shown him the theoretical flaws in the doctrines of these representatives of utopian socialism.

Marx criticised the widespread epigonic doctrines of utopian socialism for their clearly expressed dogmatism and efforts to reveal to the world an absolute truth. He wrote: "The *Rheinische Zeitung* ... does not admit that communist ideas in their present form possess even *theoretical reality*, and therefore can still less desire their *practical realisation*, or even consider it possible." [1]

The young Marx refrained from issuing declarations or prescribing dogmatic recipes for reality, but made a consistent and profound study of its contradictions so as to find ways of resolving them. Later, when he gained a broader and deeper view of the ideas of the outstanding utopian socialists, Marx was able to appreciate the rational elements in their theories and put them to creative use in working out his theory of scientific communism.

Marx dealt with serious social problems in his article, "Debates on the Law on Thefts of Wood", published in the *Rheinische Zeitung* from October 25 to November 3, 1842, as the third in his series entitled "Proceedings of the Sixth Rhine Province Assembly". Here he did not merely champion the interests of society as a whole against private interests, but the interests of "the poor, politically and socially propertyless many". [2] This gave his revolutionary democratism a much surer social target. He was now aiming to defend the interests of the broad masses of working people, who were oppressed under the existing system.

Marx showed that by supporting the new bill, which laid down penalties for the felling of timber and draconian punishments even for the gathering of wind-fallen twigs and branches by the poor, the Rhine Province Assembly fully sided with the private forest owners, whose interests clashed with those of the dispossessed working people. Marx had begun to realise that not only the Assembly but the state itself was safeguarding private property, although he still took the idealistic view of the institution of the state as expressive of the interests of society as a whole. He believed that the Prussian state, with its class privileges and bureaucratic-police system, nullified the very principle and character of the state as such. He wrote with indignation that in Prussia the state "stoops so low as to act in the manner of private property instead of in its own way". [3] However,

---

[1] Ibid., p. 220.
[2] Ibid., p. 230.
[3] Ibid., p. 241.

Marx had already probed his way to the main thing—the link between the interests of private property and the policy of the existing state.

In accusing the Prussian state of catering for the forest owners and becoming a slave to private interest, Marx stressed the state's hostility to the interests of the people. This concept of private interest, which he used very frequently in his writings of the period, was gradually acquiring a more concrete content. Behind the philosophical antithesis of the particular and the general were outlined the contradictions between the haves and the have-nots.

These contradictions and the anti-popular substance of the Prussian state were brought out more forcefully in Marx's article, "Justification of the Correspondent from the Mosel", which appeared in the paper on January 15-20, 1843, and which was in reply to von Schaper's attempt to declare as slanderous Peter Coblenz's reports in the *Rheinische Zeitung* about the plight of the Mosel peasant vine-growers and the government's unwillingness to help them. By polemicising against von Schaper, Marx the newspaper editor was openly crossing swords with the authorities.

His article revealed a more profound understanding of the root causes of the people's hardships under absolutism and the survivals of feudalism. He resolutely contested the views of those who blamed the weather and various mistakes by officials for the grave condition of the Mosel vine-growers. He wrote: "In investigating a situation *concerning the state* one is all too easily tempted to overlook the *objective nature of the circumstances* and to explain everything by the *will* of the persons concerned. However, there are *circumstances* which determine the actions of private persons and individual authorities, and which are as independent of them as the method of breathing."[1] Marx was suggesting that the main cause of the people's hardships lay in the nature of Prussia's social system and the Prussian monarchy. He wrote eloquently about the bureaucratic machine, which was out of touch with the people, loomed above them and ignored their interests. He said there was a constant contradiction between the people's interests and the policies of the Prussian state. One idea pervades his whole article: under the existing order, the people cannot expect anything good of the government. It is not surprising, therefore, that of the five parts of the proposed reply to the *Oberpräsident* only two saw the light of day. The rest were banned.

The article also contained indications of some change in Marx's journalistic style: there were fewer of those constructions which, while irresistible in their logic, tended to be on the abstract side, and he spoke in the loud clear tones of a champion of the people's interests. He wrote: "Anyone who often has to hear directly the *ruthless* voice of want among the surrounding population easily loses the

---

[1] Marx, Engels, *Collected Works*, Vol. 1, p. 337.

aesthetic tact by which his thoughts can be expressed in the most elegant and modest images. He may perhaps even consider it his *political* duty for a time to speak in public in the popular language of distress which in his native land he had no chance of forgetting." [1]

CONFLICT WITH "THE FREE"

The theoretical views expounded by Marx, who was increasingly moving away from the Young Hegelians, and above all his tactical line in the *Rheinische Zeitung*, led to a conflict with a group of men in Berlin who called themselves "The Free". Among them were Young Hegelians led by Edgar Bauer and Kaspar Schmidt, who later adopted the pen-name of Max Stirner. The characteristic feature of "The Free" was their indiscriminate criticism of everything, their failure to put forward any positive programme, their advocacy of utter negation, and loud ultra-radical talk about communism and atheism on the most irrelevant occasions. They rejected all compromise and convention. Their wild antics terrified the Berlin bourgeois but presented no real danger to the government and merely cast a slur on the democratic movement.

Marx repeatedly stressed that the abstract criticism by "The Free" did no good, and demanded that the correct theory should be explained and elaborated in the context and on the strength of concrete conditions. When he became editor of the *Rheinische Zeitung* he stopped publication of their articles. In November 1842, he wrote to Ruge: " 'The Free' ... had become accustomed to regard the *Rheinische Zeitung* as *their own*, docile organ, but I believed I could not any longer permit this watery torrent of words in the old manner." [2] "The Free" retaliated with demagogic charges of conservatism. In his reply to Eduard Meyen, a member of the circle, Marx demanded of them "less vague reasoning, magniloquent phrases and self-satisfied self-adoration, and more definiteness, more attention to the actual state of affairs, more expert knowledge". He said it was intolerable that communist and socialist doctrines were treated very superficially and in occasional theatrical reviews, and demanded "a quite different and more thorough discussion of communism".[3] However, "The Free" ignored this criticism, and moved deeper into subjectivism and anarchic individualism. A break with them was inevitable, and was to be the start of Marx's open break with the Young Hegelians.

---

[1] Ibid., p. 332.
[2] Ibid., p. 393.
[3] Ibid., p. 394.

THE *RHEINISCHE ZEITUNG* BANNED

Marx was finding it increasingly hard to work on the *Rheinische Zeitung*: the paper was under a double censorship—after the ordinary censor it was scrutinised by a senior official, the *Regierungspräsident*. Sometimes the mutilated issue was not fit to be published. Marx found the atmosphere of the Prussian police state stifling. In January 1843, he wrote to Ruge: "It is a bad thing to have to perform menial duties even for the sake of freedom; to fight with pinpricks, instead of with clubs. I have become tired of hypocrisy, stupidity, gross arbitrariness, and of our bowing and scraping, dodging, and hair-splitting over words." [1]

Government circles increasingly saw the *Rheinische Zeitung* as a threat to the Prussian state, and looked on the editor himself with the greatest apprehension. Saint-Paul, the government censor assigned to Cologne from Berlin in early January 1843 to keep an eye on the paper in addition to the two other censors, said Marx was the "moving spirit" behind the *Rheinische Zeitung* and the "life-giving source of its theories". The authorities were incensed at Marx's articles protesting against the government ban on democratic organs of the press like the *Leipziger Allgemeine Zeitung* and *Deutsche Jahrbücher*. His article "Justification of the Correspondent from the Mosel" was the last straw.

On January 19, 1843, the government adopted a decision to ban the paper as of April 1, 1843, and introduced an especially stringent censorship in the interim. The official notice said that the *Rheinische Zeitung* had a marked "tendency clearly aimed at spreading hostility to the existing order in the Church and the State, undermining them, inciting to discontent, maliciously disparaging the state administration ... and heaping abuse on friendly powers". [2] The latter was a reference to the paper's sharp criticism of the tsar's intervention in German affairs, which had aroused discontent among the Russian autocracy. The tsar's minister in Berlin reported to St. Petersburg with satisfaction about the banning of the paper, "whose tendency remains an openly revolutionary one". [3]

The banning of the *Rheinische Zeitung* generated a wave of protest. Throughout the Rhine Province there was a collection of signatures for petitions to the King of Prussia requesting revocation of the order. One thousand signatures were collected in Cologne in a short period. Among those who sent in petitions were the Mosel vine-growers, whose interests Marx had so fervently defended in his paper. They wrote: "We are not aware that the *Rheinische Zeitung* has spread false information, or that it has slandered the administra-

---

[1] Marx, Engels, *Collected Works*, Vol. 1, p. 397.
[2] Joseph Hansen, *Rheinische Briefe und Akten zur Geschichte der politischen Bewegung 1830-1850*, Bd. 1 (1830-45), Essen, 1919, S. 402-03.
[3] *From the History of the Working Class and Revolutionary Movement*, Moscow, 1958, p. 660 (in Russian).

tion, but we are aware that it has written nothing but the truth about our land and our condition, about our authorities, and about our destiny."[1] The opposition press saw the government's act as blatant encroachment by the reactionaries on the limited possibilities the German press still had to discuss the country's burning social issues.

However, the liberal Rhenish bourgeois who were financing the paper had no intention of doing anything radical in its defence. In fact, they were not at all pleased with the revolutionary-democratic tenor the paper had acquired under Marx's direction. When the petition to the king was being discussed, one shareholder and member of the paper's Board of Directors attacked its line in a long speech. At a general meeting of its shareholders in February 1843, one of its responsible publishers, Dagobert Oppenheim, complained that until November 1842 they had had no knowledge at all about the authorities' being dissatisfied with the articles in the paper and that "only in November did the conflict arise which has led up to this unexpected catastrophe".[2] That was outright censure of Marx's political line, for he had taken over as editor in October 1842.

In these circumstances it was impossible for Marx to continue working on the paper. On March 18, 1843, it carried an announcement of his resignation as editor. However, this did not help the shareholders to salvage the paper: its final issue appeared on March 31.

Once he had realised that public advocacy of revolutionary ideas in Prussia was impossible, Marx decided to leave. Even before his resignation, he had discussed, mainly in correspondence with Ruge, a plan to publish a revolutionary organ abroad, for he was sure that the need was not for a bulky academic collection of articles catering for a narrow circle but a periodical, preferably a monthly, for the people. At the end of May 1843, Marx went to Dresden for a few days to see Ruge and discuss the plans for such a periodical.

Marx no longer had any doubt that a revolution was approaching. "A ship of fools", as he called the Prussian state, was sailing to meet its doom, "the impending revolution".[3]

From then on, the question of the revolution, of its character, its causes and motive forces was the overriding one for Marx. In that period, his development as a theorist advanced in great strides, his practical political activity playing a crucial part in the process. His work on the *Rheinische Zeitung* marked a fundamental change in his outlook: he had begun to move from idealism to materialism, and from revolutionary democratism to communism. During this period he was not merely making ardent pronouncements in defence of the people's interests and against the feudal absolutist Prussian state oppressing them. He was gradually coming to realise that the actions of men belonging to different social sections were rooted in some kind of objective factors, and that their private interests in some way

---

[1] *Trier'sche Zeitung*, March 2, 1843.
[2] *Frankfurter Journal*, February 21, 1843.
[3] Marx, Engels, *Collected Works*, Vol. 3, p. 134.

depended on their objective status in society. Marx was gaining a clearer view of the main line of his quest, namely, uncovering the nature of the objective relations "which determine the actions of private persons and individual authorities".[1]

As an editor he had been confronted with economic problems and had come to realise not only the inadequacy of his knowledge in this field but also the primary role they had to play in life. Engels later recalled that he had "repeatedly heard Marx say that it was his study of the Law on Thefts of Wood and the condition of the Mosel peasants that had impelled him to switch from pure politics to the study of economic relations and consequently to socialism".[2]

Marx set his mind to discovering the force which was capable of changing the existing system. How true his course was can be seen from a letter to Ruge which he wrote some six weeks after the closure of the *Rheinische Zeitung*. He said: "The system of industry and trade, of ownership and exploitation of people, however, leads even far more rapidly than the increase in population to a rupture within present-day society, a rupture which the old system is not able to heal."[3]

His work on the paper also gave him much experience in another sphere relating to the state. He came to realise that the state was by no means the embodiment of universal reason, the embodiment of the universal which rose above individual private interests, as Hegel had maintained.

Consequently, Marx, who after the closure of the *Rheinische Zeitung* had temporarily retired into the study room, as he put it, pending a practical start on the publication of the new revolutionary journal, was faced with his twofold task: a critical review of Hegel's idealistic conception of society and the state, and the identification of the real motive forces behind the social process, and of ways and means to bring about the world's revolutionary transformation.

KREUZNACH.
CONTRIBUTION TO THE CRITIQUE OF HEGEL'S PHILOSOPHY OF LAW MS.
NOTEBOOKS ON HISTORY

In May 1843, Marx moved to Kreuznach, a small town on the Rhine, where his fiancée, Jenny von Westphalen, and her mother were living at the time. The marriage of "Herr Carl Marx, Doctor of Philosophy, resident in Cologne, and Fräulein Johanna Bertha Julie Jenny von Westphalen ... resident in Kreuznach" was registered on June 19, 1843.

---

[1] Marx, Engels, *Collected Works*, Vol. 1, p. 337.
[2] Marx, Engels, *Werke*, Bd. 39, S. 446.
[3] Marx, Engels, *Collected Works*, Vol. 3, p. 141.

The few months — from May to October 1843 — which Marx spent at Kreuznach were perhaps the happiest period in his long and arduous life. Not usually given to expressing his emotions, Marx wrote to Ruge shortly before his marriage: "I can assure you, without the slightest romanticism, that I am head over heels in love, and indeed in the most serious way."[1]

In Jenny Marx found a loving wife and a wholeheartedly dedicated assistant in his work. With her he shared his creative plans and his boldest ideas. Marx submitted his writings to the judgment of his well educated and intelligent wife. She was one of his first readers and frequently his first critic. She had impeccable literary taste, and he paid great attention to her critical remarks and readily followed her advice.

For Marx, the Kreuznach period was one of intense creative effort. The major problem before him was a critique of Hegel's theory of the state and law, which essentially summed up the philosopher's idealistic views of society. The outcome of this work was an unfinished manuscript which was first published in 1927 in the Soviet Union under the title *Contribution to the Critique of Hegel's Philosophy of Law*.

Marx first criticised Hegel's views of the state and law in the early months of 1842, when he condemned one of his central ideas, his eulogy of the constitutional monarchy. On March 5, 1842, Marx informed Ruge about a critical article he was planning to write on Hegel's legal and political conceptions. "The central point is the struggle against *constitutional monarchy*."[2] This article has not come down to us, and may not have been completed at all, but the direction of Marx's thinking is quite clear. He was striving to show that democratic principles were incompatible with the monarchy, but at the time he was still incapable of setting himself the task of a critical review of Hegel's doctrine of society as a whole. He did this a year later.

One work that was of great help to Marx in his critique of Hegel's idealism was Ludwig Feuerbach's *Preliminary Theses for a Reformation of Philosophy*, which was published in Switzerland in early 1843 in a collection entitled *Anekdota zur neuesten deutschen Philosophie und Publicistik*. It contained a formulation of Feuerbach's materialist views: "The real relation between thinking and being is this: *being is the Subject, thinking the Predicate*. Thinking springs from being, and not being from thinking."[3] Feuerbach showed Hegel's philosophy to be the last refuge of theology; he applied to idealistic philosophy the method he had used in his critique of religion, emphasising that "we need only substitute the *Predicate* for the *Subject*, and the *Subject* for the *Object* and the *Principle*, that is, *turn speculative phi-*

---

[1] Ibid., Vol. 1, p. 399.
[2] Ibid., p. 382.
[3] L. Feuerbach, "Vorläufige Thesen zur Reformation der Philosophie", *Sämtliche Werke*, Bd. II, Leipzig, 1846, S. 263.

losophy upside down, to obtain the plain, naked, unadulterated truth".[1]

This idea of "turning" speculative philosophy "upside down" and of establishing the real relation between thinking and being was used by Marx in the manuscript of his *Contribution to the Critique of Hegel's Philosophy of Law* as a general methodological principle for a critique of Hegel's idealism. Feuerbach's critique of Hegel's views helped Marx to advance along the path to materialism which he had discovered for himself. Marx had by then also spotted the weak points of Feuerbach's philosophy, above all his eschewal of burning political issues. In a letter to Ruge which he wrote soon after the publication of the *Preliminary Theses for a Reformation of Philosophy*, Marx observed: "Feuerbach's aphorisms seem to me incorrect only in one respect, that he refers too much to nature and too little to politics. That, however, is the only alliance by which present-day philosophy can become truth."[2] Here we find the incipient distinction between their views of man. Feuerbach saw man in the light of an abstract humanism, as a being chiefly natural and instinctive; that was the narrow anthropological principle he applied to the various philosophical questions. Even at the time Marx saw man above all as a social being, a product of historically rooted social relations.

It was natural, therefore, that the relationship between state and civil society was the central problem in Marx's manuscript, *Contribution to the Critique of Hegel's Philosophy of Law*. At the time "civil society" was the term used to designate the sphere of private, chiefly material, interests and their attendant social relations. The widely accepted idea of civil society as a sphere in which individuals confronted each other as closed, hostile entities reflected a characteristic feature of human relations under capitalism with its "homo homini lupus est" principle. A correct view of the nature of civil society and its relation to the state marked an important step towards the scientific, materialist view of the existing social order, and gave a clue to the understanding of the main causes behind the historical process as a whole.

Hegel declared that the state was at a higher stage of development than civil society and determined it. Marx took the opposite view, namely, that civil society was a prerequisite of the state. Probing for the connection between the substance of the state and the nature of concrete social relations, Marx expressed the brilliant idea that private property played the definitive role with respect to the political system. He wrote: "The political constitution at its highest point is ... the *constitution of private property*."[3] Although he still saw private property mainly in juridical terms, his line in explaining social and political institutions was already clearly materialist.

Marx concentrated his criticism on Hegel's political views, espe-

---

[1] Ibid., S. 246.
[2] Marx, Engels, *Collected Works*, Vol. 1, p. 400.
[3] Marx, Engels, *Collected Works*, Vol. 3, p. 98.

cially his apology for the Prussian bureaucracy and the monarchy with its estates. Summing up his critical analysis of Hegel's philosophy of law, with its inherent reverence for existing institutions, Marx wrote: "Hegel is not to be blamed for depicting the nature of the modern state as it is, but for presenting that which is as the *nature of the state*."[1]

As he criticised Hegel, he put forward his own idea of democracy, a social system fit for man. He saw democracy as the people's self-determination, with man's being—that is, man's interests, the people's interests—constituting its fundamental law. Using Hegel's terminology, Marx wrote that democracy was the truth of every state, that is, the ideal, ultimate goal of its development. He asserted that only in a democracy would man cease to be a plaything in the hands of the forces he had himself created—political institutions—and become their master. Only then would the state cease to stand in opposition to the people and become a "*particular form of existence* of the people".[2] Marx referred to the French, who had come to realise "recently ... that in true democracy the *political state is annihilated*".[3] He undoubtedly had in mind the great utopian socialist Saint-Simon and his idea of a future society in which the government of men would give way to government of things.

Consequently, the urge to see democracy as real, instead of nominal, rule by the people made it necessary for Marx to seek a social system under which this could be realised, thus carrying him another step towards communism, although the concept of democracy itself, as set out in the manuscript, bore signs of the influence of Feuerbach's anthropologism and abstract humanism.

The materialist elements in Marx's outlook acquired body with his deepening critique of Hegel's idealism. From the various aspects of Hegel's philosophy Marx went on to a critical review of its idealistic principles. While he did not yet claim to be a materialist, his critique of Hegel was already essentially materialist. He remarked on the fatal flaw in the idealistic method of Hegel, who "does not develop his thinking from the object, but expounds the object in accordance with a thinking that is cut and dried—already formed and fixed in the abstract sphere of logic".[4] Marx cited the evidence of Hegel to draw his conclusion that idealism inevitably led to religion and mysticism. He laid bare the connection between Hegel's idealistic philosophy and his conservative politics, and showed how in his system the Prussian monarchy, a concrete historical fact, was transformed into a stage in the development of the Absolute Idea. Hegel similarly wrapped up in mystery the other attributes of the semi-feudal state, among them the system of estates, the bureaucracy and the primogeniture.

---

[1] Ibid., p. 63.
[2] Ibid., p. 30.
[3] Ibid.
[4] Ibid., p. 14.

His work on the critique of Hegel's philosophy of law impelled Marx to look to history itself for the facts to refute Hegel's constructions. Through the entire manuscripts of his *Contribution to the Critique of Hegel's Philosophy of Law* runs the materialist tendency of starting from an analysis of concrete reality instead of abstract premises, from the "logic of the matter" and not the "matter of logic". He was aware that only a most serious study of the history of society could help to decide on the relationship between the civil society and the state. He was, therefore, not satisfied with the general presentation of the question and sought to take the historical approach. That is why, in the summer (mostly July and August) of 1843, parallel with his work on the manuscript, he made a fundamental study of history.

The five closely-written *Kreuznach Notebooks* contain many of his extracts from works on the theory and history of the state and the history of individual countries, among them England, France, Germany, the United States, Italy and Sweden, with emphasis on special histories of the French Revolution, including one by the prominent German historian Wachsmuth. He concentrated on this event because he realised its role in shaping contemporary society and also because he sought to use it for a study of the social mainsprings behind the development of society. Among the works Marx studied at that time were those of Machiavelli, the outstanding Italian thinker of the Renaissance, the French Enlighteners Montesquieu and Rousseau, and the theorists of reactionary romanticism Chateaubriand and Justus Möser.

From the topics and the nature of his extracts and the content of his indexes for them we get an idea of the range of questions claiming his attention at the time, and in some instances obtain a clear understanding of his approach to these questions. Very prominent in the extracts is the problem of feudal property and its influence on the class structure and political institutions of society. Considerable attention is devoted to an analysis of the history of the Great French Bourgeois Revolution, which helped Marx to gain a deeper view of the clash of the interests of the various classes and its impact on revolutionary developments. What is most pronounced here is his effort to trace the dependence of the bourgeoisie's policies on the economic factor, notably property relations. His grouping of the extracts is such that it tends to stress the inability of the bourgeois revolution to provide *genuine* equality, arising not from the establishment of a nominal equality of all before the law but from a radical change in property relations.

His subject indexes also show that he developed his materialist outlook not only through his criticism of idealistic social doctrines but also through his own efforts to gain a materialist understanding of historical phenomena. "Property and Its Consequences", the central head, brings together the material showing the dependence of policy on property relations.

As he studied the lessons of history he also searched for the way to advance to a social system fit to be called a truly human society. The fact that he had discovered the limited nature of past revolutions likewise carried him outside the framework of revolutionary democratism and helped to mould his communist views. His historical studies provided a scientific basis for his theoretical research and served as a reliable antidote to utopianism.

Marx's few months at Kreuznach marked an important milestone in the development of his views. Many years later Engels wrote that at the time Marx had "come to the conclusion that it was not the state, which Hegel had described as the 'top of the edifice' but 'civil society', which Hegel had regarded with disdain, that was the sphere in which a key to the understanding of the process of the historical development of mankind should be looked for".[1]

His comprehensive critique of Hegel's philosophy of law and of his idealism as a whole, together with his summing-up of the experience of past history, and his study of Feuerbach's materialist and humanistic views built up and brought out the materialist tendencies in Marx's outlook, which now became predominant. As a great dialectician who had grasped and elaborated the revolutionary substance of the dialectical method, Marx saw that existing society carried within itself the need for its own fundamental transformation. However, he charted its course only in very rough outline (in the form of an ideal state of "democracy" or "true democracy") and was still only looking for the social force capable of bringing this about.

PREPARATIONS FOR PUBLISHING THE *DEUTSCH-FRANZÖSISCHE JAHRBÜCHER*. DEPARTURE FOR PARIS

At Kreuznach, Marx continued the correspondence he had started before the closure of the *Rheinische Zeitung* concerning plans to publish a periodical to unite German and French democrats. He gave much thought to its character, aims, and prospective contributors.

In a letter to Ruge in September 1843, he outlined the programme for a journal to be published in Paris. Its main line, Marx held, should be relentless criticism of the existing world order, fearless in face of its own conclusions and unafraid of clashes with the powers that be. Marx did not regard this criticism as an aim in itself, as criticism for criticism's sake, but as a means of working out a new outlook and blazing the trail to a new world. He saw party spirit as one of the key principles of his outlook. He wrote: "...Nothing prevents us from making criticism of politics, participation in politics, and

---

[1] Marx, Engels, *Collected Works*, Vol. 21, pp. 60-61.

therefore *real* struggles, the starting point of our criticism, and from identifying our criticism with them."[1] It was here that Marx first formulated the most important idea of the unity of theory and practice.

As he criticised the existing system and set out his views of the future society, he still widely dealt with conceptions evoked by Feuerbach's humanism (such as realisation of "the true human essence"), which together with democratic, anti-absolutist feelings constituted the common basis — very short-lived, as it turned out to be — for joint action by Marx, already probing his way towards a truly scientific communist outlook, the bourgeois radical Arnold Ruge, the democrat Julius Fröbel, the revolutionary poet Georg Herwegh, the radical journalist Karl Ludwig Bernays, one of the future ideologists of "true socialism" Moses Hess, and several other men.

It was planned to invite contributions for the journal from a number of prominent French socialists, among them Lamennais, Louis Blanc, Cabet and Proudhon. Marx also tried to get Feuerbach to write an article criticising Schelling's reactionary philosophy. Lenin put a high value on his letter to Feuerbach of October 3, 1843, in which "Marx pointed out with amazing clarity the basic trends in philosophy".[2] On the whole, Feuerbach preferred to remain uncommitted, but Marx continued to have hopes of enlisting Feuerbach's active participation in revolutionary activity, as his letter from Paris of August 11, 1844 shows. This failure was to some extent offset when Heinrich Heine, the great German revolutionary poet, agreed to write for the journal.

Marx had to be in Paris to deal with all the organisational side of starting the journal. He had long since decided to leave Germany, and his departure was precipitated by the Prussian government's attempt to bribe him with the promise of a sinecure: through a friend of his late father's, Privy Councillor Esser, he was offered a position in the Prussian civil service. Marx recalled: "*After this communication*, I left Prussia for Paris."[3] Late in October 1843, Marx and his wife, Jenny, settled in Paris, at 38 Rue Vanneau.

Marx subsequently revisited the French capital on many occasions. He came to know the country well, gained a brilliant knowledge of its history, and always spoke with admiration of its working people's revolutionary fervour. His ideas were most strongly influenced by his first stay of almost 18 months in Paris, where he finally adopted the revolutionary communist frame of mind, and decided on his life purpose, which was to express the interests and to champion the cause of the most revolutionary class — the proletariat.

Within a few months, Marx came to feel the impact of the exciting social and political life in Paris, then one of the world's major seats of science and culture, and a leading centre of the revolutionary

---

[1] Marx, Engels, *Collected Works*, Vol. 3, p. 144.
[2] V. I. Lenin, *Collected Works*, Vol. 14, p. 336.
[3] Marx, Engels, *Collected Works*, Vol. 41, p. 101.

movement. Lenin described the Paris of that time as "seething with politics and the discussion of various socialist theories".[1] It offered excellent opportunities for making a study of the class contradictions and collisions rocking the bourgeois world. It was there that Marx was also to establish his first political contacts with men from the revolutionary proletariat.

FINAL ADOPTION OF MATERIALISM AND COMMUNISM

The first double issue (Nos. 1 and 2) of the *Deutsch-Französische Jahrbücher* appeared at the end of February 1844. Apart from articles by Marx, it carried two by Engels—"Outlines of a Critique of Political Economy" and "The Condition of England. *Past and Present* by Thomas Carlyle", verse by Heine and Herwegh, articles by Hess and Bernays, and a number of other items.

The section entitled "From the Correspondence of 1843" included some of Marx's letters to Ruge written during the preparations for publishing the journal, and also letters from Ruge himself, the Russian revolutionary Mikhail Bakunin, and Feuerbach. The journal's main line was determined by two of Marx's articles. One of them—"On the Jewish Question"—had apparently been written at Kreuznach, and the other—"Contribution to the Critique of Hegel's Philosophy of Law. Introduction"—in Paris in December 1843 and January 1844.

The first article attacked Bruno Bauer, who in his treatises adopted an idealistic approach to the emancipation of the Jews in Germany, who were deprived of political rights: he saw the solution in the emancipation of the Jews from religion. Marx proved this to be untenable. He showed the problem of Jewish emancipation to be part of the larger problem of mankind's emancipation from the burden of its social and political oppression, and drew a distinction between political emancipation and general human emancipation.

Marx understood political emancipation as man's release from his feudal fetters and the proclamation of bourgeois-democratic freedoms in the course of a bourgeois revolution. While attaching much importance to political emancipation, Marx saw its limits. He wrote: "*Political* emancipation is, of course, a big step forward. True, it is not the final form of human emancipation in general, but it is the final form of human emancipation *within* the hitherto existing world order."[2] Its limits sprang from the existence of private property, which the bourgeois revolution tended to safeguard as a sacrosanct social institution.

Marx made a profound materialistic analysis of the basic bour-

---

[1] V. I. Lenin, *Collected Works*, Vol. 19, p. 556.
[2] Marx, Engels, *Collected Works*, Vol. 3, p. 155.

geois freedoms, which had been achieved through political emancipation, and which the ideologists of the bourgeoisie had declared to be an expression of man's natural rights. He showed these "rights of man" to be above all the rights of members of civil society, that is, the rights of the bourgeois. Freedom in bourgeois terms was essentially freedom for the individual to dispose of his private property at his own discretion, while the individual's right to security was his right to immunity as proprietor, his right to immunity of his person and, above all, his property. Consequently, political emancipation, or political revolution — Marx used both these terms to denote the bourgeois revolution — was man's emancipation as a member of civil society, as an "egoistic man ... separated from other men and from the community".[1]

In contrast to political emancipation, Marx put forward the idea of human emancipation — man's deliverance from the vices of contemporary civil society, the elimination of real inequality, oppression and mutual alienation, and the creation of conditions in which genuine social principles would predominate over egoism and mutual hostility between individuals. Still largely employing Feuerbach's terminology, but in a new meaning, Marx wrote that "only when man has recognised and organised his *'forces propres'* [own powers] as *social* forces, and consequently no longer separates social power from himself in the shape of *political* power, only then will human emancipation have been accomplished".[2]

This reasoning is essentially the first outline of the idea of socialist revolution which works a radical change in the very foundation of civil society and establishes a true community of men. The influence of Feuerbach's anthropologism is still evident here not only in the terminology but also in the somewhat abstract approach to the question of human emancipation, whereas the criticism of political emancipation — the bourgeois revolution — is already stated in concrete terms. Nonetheless, his article, "On the Jewish Question", formulated the gist of the fundamental distinction between bourgeois and socialist revolution, and simultaneously advanced the thesis that the latter should inevitably follow on the former. His second article, "Contribution to the Critique of Hegel's Philosophy of Law. Introduction", gave the answer as to who was to carry out human emancipation, by overcoming the limits of political emancipation, and which social force was the embodiment of social progress.

His analysis of earlier revolutions led him to conclude that in revolution one social class strives to act as the emancipator of all society, while looking to its own specific condition and pursuing its own goals. However, it may undertake to do so only when objectively "its demands and rights are truly the rights and demands of society itself".[3] The class that can carry through the emancipation

---

[1] Marx, Engels, *Collected Works*, Vol. 3, p. 162.
[2] Ibid., p. 168.
[3] Ibid., p. 184.

of all men must be the one which is in contradiction with the whole of modern society, the class which consequently cannot emancipate itself without emancipating the whole of society. This class is the proletariat.

Marx's idea of the proletariat's role in world history as the destroyer of capitalist society and the creator of a new, socialist world was of tremendous significance, and marked the starting point in the transformation of utopian socialism into scientific socialism. From that point on, the moulding of Marx's outlook went hand in hand with the formulation of scientific communism, the revolutionary proletarian outlook.

Marx's second article formulated another key thesis: that an advanced theory exerts a great revolutionising effect and is a powerful factor in the struggle for a radical transformation of society. "The weapon of criticism," he wrote, "cannot, of course, replace criticism by weapons, material force must be overthrown by material force; but theory also becomes a material force as soon as it has gripped the masses." [1]

Marx saw the proletariat as the social force which was to put the conclusions of revolutionary doctrine to real use and translate them into life. "As philosophy finds its *material* weapons in the proletariat, so the proletariat finds its *spiritual* weapons in philosophy." [2]

Marx's formulation of the idea of the proletariat's epoch-making role was also an important step in his repudiation of all the theories on which classes hostile to the proletariat had left their mark. It was natural, therefore, that this article of his also contained a concise criticism of many conservative and reactionary ideological trends, going well beyond his earlier critical remarks on them. Moreover, Marx made his first public statement about the basic flaws in the Young Hegelians' theoretical views, and their urge to confine the struggle to the theoretical sphere.

PRELUDE TO A GREAT FRIENDSHIP

The two names of Karl Marx and Frederick Engels are found together in the contents of the *Deutsch-Französische Jahrbücher*, an apparent coincidence which is highly symbolic, for Engels became Marx's ally and true comrade-in-arms, with whom he spent the rest of his life, an invaluable aide in his scientific endeavours and practical struggle, the man whose name has been twinned with his own.

Engels' spiritual evolution, while having its own specific features, followed the same lines as that of Marx.

Engels also hailed from Prussia's Rhine Province. He was born at Barmen in the valley of the Wupper on November 28, 1820, into the family of a textile manufacturer, a man of rather conservative views.

---

[1] Ibid., p. 182.
[2] Ibid., p. 187.

Fervently religious, he brought up his children in accordance with strict bourgeois rules and orthodox beliefs, and this produced a sense of vigorous protest in the young Engels.

Frederick was not allowed to complete his Gymnasium schooling, and was sent to Bremen to become a businessman. Working as a clerk he devoted his leisure hours to increasing his knowledge, studying history, philosophy, literature, linguistics and foreign languages, for which he had shown exceptional aptitude from an early age. The progressive ideas of the day, above all the writings of the Young Hegelians, helped him to discard the religious views impressed upon him at home.

His revolutionary-democratic views were shaped under the influence of the progressive social trends of his day — Börne's democratism, Hegel's philosophy and Young Hegelian radical ideas — and the hard facts of life as he gained a knowledge of the working people's exploitation in his home town. His talents as a writer were soon apparent: as early as 1839 he contributed to the progressive journal *Telegraph für Deutschland*, the organ of a radical literary group calling itself Young Germany, with whose views Engels then strongly sympathised. His first journalistic work, entitled "Letters from Wuppertal", gave a picture of the harsh oppression of the working men by their masters, concealed by the guise of sanctimony. Engels' subsequent literary, critical and journalistic writings contained revolutionary-democratic ideas and vigorous criticism of the existing order in Germany.

From the latter half of September 1841 to mid-August 1842, he did military service as a volunteer in an artillery unit stationed in Berlin, then the capital of Prussia. This gave him an opportunity to attend lectures at the University of Berlin and get to know many more people. He joined the Young Hegelians, whose views he largely shared at the time, and took an active part in the ideological struggle then going on in Germany. A considerable impact on his views at the time was made by Feuerbach's works, especially his *Essence of Christianity*. Later he wrote: "One must have experienced the liberating effect of this book for oneself to get an idea of it."[1]

While in Berlin, Engels wrote a number of works (*Schelling and Revelation* and *Schelling, Philosopher in Christ*), directed against the famous philosopher, who had by then moved far to the right and was spreading mysticism and reactionary ideas. Engels' witty brilliant pamphlets exuded atheism and intolerance of obscurantism. They were very popular, and very few of his readers realised that the author was not a trained philosopher but a young army volunteer and a nonmatriculated student.

In the autumn of 1842, Engels went to Manchester to work in the office of a company in which his father was a partner, and spent almost two years there learning a great deal from his personal ac-

---

[1] Marx, Engels, *Collected Works*, Vol. 26, p. 364.

quaintance with capitalism in England, where it was then in its most advanced form with inherent acute contradictions. He also obtained much food for thought from his study of English political economy and the writings of English utopian socialists, notably Robert Owen. There, too, he found Chartism, Europe's most advanced working-class movement.

In England, Engels was active as a journalist, contributing to the Owenist and Chartist press, sending articles and reports to the *Rheinische Zeitung* and the *Schweizerischer Republikaner*; he wrote two articles for the *Deutsch-Französische Jahrbücher*.

His stay in England, his study of her economic life and political development, his close acquaintance with her working-class movement and its leaders, and direct participation in the movement, all helped him to turn decisively towards materialism and communism. Many years later he himself recalled that it was in Manchester that he had realised the crucial role in social life of economic relations constituting the basis of class contradictions and the struggle among parties.

Like Marx, Engels saw the working class as the force capable of remoulding society. These elements of the new outlook were reflected in his articles of the period, in particular those in the Owenist *New Moral World*. But the strongest evidence of his adoption of materialism and communism comes from his articles published in the *Deutsch-Französische Jahrbücher*: "Outlines of a Critique of Political Economy" and "The Condition of England. *Past and Present* by Thomas Carlyle".

At the time, the young Engels, like Marx, was still to discard the residual influence of his ideological predecessors and regarded Feuerbach's philosophy as a revolutionary one which the proletariat should adopt as a whole. Like the utopian socialists, Engels saw communism as a means of releasing not only the working people but the capitalists themselves from the narrow confines of bourgeois relations.

Engels first met Marx at the end of November 1842, when he called at the editorial offices of the *Rheinische Zeitung* on his way to England. Marx was then in sharp conflict with "The Free" of Berlin, with whom Engels was in touch during his stay in that city, and so the first meeting of the two future friends was somewhat cool. But this did not prevent Marx from valuing Engels as the *Rheinische Zeitung*'s correspondent in England, and keeping abreast of what he wrote.

Engels' articles in the *Deutsch-Französische Jahrbücher* showed Marx that their ideas were developing along the same lines; they began to write to each other, and this was the prelude to their intimate friendship. For his part, Engels too got a clearer view of the role which the editor of the journal had to play in developing socialist ideas, and of the exceptional talents of "a swarthy chap of Trier", as Marx was called in 1842 in the satirical poem *The Insolently Threat-*

ened Yet Miraculously Rescued Bible, which Engels wrote together with Edgar Bauer.

DEUTSCH-FRANZÖSISCHE JAHRBÜCHER: CONTEMPORARY ASSESSMENTS

The *Deutsch-Französische Jahrbücher* evoked a broad response and started to pick up circulation. The *Mannheimer Abendzeitung* said that almost every German who went to Paris carried away a copy of the journal with him. A number of large subscription orders came in from Leipzig, Berlin and Vienna. When the Prussian ambassador informed his government about the journal's "dangerous" line, it put a ban on its entry into the country and ordered the arrest of Marx, Ruge, Heine and several other persons if they should set foot on Prussian soil. Issues of the journal were confiscated at the border, and about two-thirds of a 3,000-copy impression is said to have fallen into the hands of the police.

Its appearance was met with vicious attacks by the Right-wing and moderate press, which clearly saw the journal's revolutionary proletarian tenor. The reactionary Leipzig newspaper, *Die Eisenbahn*, wrote on April 4, 1844 that the *Jahrbücher*'s editors and contributors aimed to "deify the proletariat of all nations, for to it alone they looked with hope and faith", which is why it was "the sacred duty of Germany's liberal press to give the most resolute expression to its indignation and vigorously to deny any kinship with them". The conservative *Allgemeine Zeitung* likewise hastened to voice its indignation. On March 10, 1844, it wrote: "The criticism of the new Paris journal is ruthless, its polemics defy all aesthetic standards, and its satirical tone, although no dagger thrust, is like the hammer blow of a great big fist."

The articles in the *Jahrbücher* summed up a whole period in Marx's life and work, in which he overcame his idealism and finally and firmly took the materialist stand, as a consistent revolutionary democrat who had become a communist and an ideologist of the working class. Lenin wrote that "Marx's articles in this journal showed that he was already a revolutionary, who advocated 'merciless criticism of everything existing', and in particular the 'criticism by weapon', and appealed to the *masses* and to the *proletariat*".[1] This marked the start of a new stage in the development of Marx's outlook, as he began elaborating dialectical materialism and the theory of scientific communism.

---

[1] V. I. Lenin, *Collected Works*, Vol. 21, p. 47.

CHAPTER TWO

FIRST FORMULATION OF THE PRINCIPLES OF THE PROLETARIAN OUTLOOK

> *With the philosophers to think, and the working men to fight for us, will any earthly power be strong enough to resist our progress?*
>
> Frederick Engels

BREAK WITH RUGE

The new views which Marx propounded in the *Deutsch-Französische Jahrbücher* were for the time being nothing but a brilliant hypothesis based on a summing up of the earlier advances of science and the historical development of society, which still required a thorough substantiation, both historical and, most importantly, philosophical and economic. From then on Marx tirelessly applied his theoretical efforts to this task.

However, his scientific and literary plans were soon to stop centring round the *Jahrbücher*, for shortly after the first issue it became clear that publication could not be continued: the ban in Germany made the obstacles to its circulation there much too formidable.

There were other, more deeply rooted reasons why the *Jahrbücher* was wound up so quickly. Even as the first issue was being prepared for press, Marx and Ruge, two of the editors, found themselves at odds over principle, and soon in open conflict. Ruge, the bourgeois radical, disapproved of Marx's communist views. As a Young Hegelian, Ruge had developed a supercilious attitude to the "uncritical" mass, the working class. He was apprehensive of the strong revolutionary ring in the writings of Marx and Engels, their implacable criticism of the existing order of things, and Marx's urge to establish close links with the workers. Readers of the first issue were quick to spot the difference between articles written by Marx and Engels, on the one hand, and those by Ruge, on the other. In a later pamphlet, *The Great Men of the Exile*, Marx and Engels stated that their articles "contained views running directly counter" to those Ruge had announced in the Preface to the first issue.[1] Once the issue was out,

---

[1] Marx, Engels, *Collected Works*, Vol. 11, p. 269.

it became obvious that the two editors were travelling along divergent roads and could no longer collaborate with each other. The erstwhile allies found themselves in different camps.

In many subsequent articles Marx was compelled to criticise Ruge as a bourgeois opponent of the proletarian movement, but when in January 1845 he learned of imminent police reprisals against his former colleague, he at once sent Ruge a letter of warning.

MARX IN PARIS IN 1844

As Marx stayed on in Paris he obtained a deeper insight into the social and political climate of the July monarchy, and the various political and socialist trends in French society at the time. He also established closer relations with various opposition circles, French socialists, revolutionary proletarians and German revolutionary emigrants.

In place of the big landed proprietors, the 1830 bourgeois revolution in France brought to power the top layers of the financial and industrial bourgeoisie — bankers, stockbrokers, railway magnates, coal and iron-ore barons, and the landowners associated with them. This financial aristocracy was deriving the maximum benefits from the rapid development of capitalism. From 1830 to 1840, the number of steam engines in France increased more than fourfold. From 1828 to 1847, iron and steel production more than doubled, and coal output trebled. Marx later aptly remarked that the July monarchy was "a joint-stock company for the exploitation of France's national wealth, the dividends of which were divided among ministers, Chambers, 240,000 voters and their adherents".[1] For the workers, the country's industrial revolution meant greater exploitation, lower real wages and longer working hours. The high property qualification withheld political rights from the working class and a sizable section of the urban and rural middle class. There was growing discontent. The working class offered the most fertile soil for revolutionary ideas, and gravitated not only to radical republican but also to socialist doctrines.

From the late 1830s, there was a spread among the workers of the ideas of utopian socialism and communism, trends which in France took a variety of forms. Utopian socialism was propounded by the epigones of Saint-Simon and Fourier in an extremely dogmatic, sectarian form, void of any objective revolutionary content. Their negative attitude to independent revolutionary action by the proletariat, their advocacy of the peaceful reformist way to socialism and class harmony, and their fear of revolutionary action made them kin to other petty-bourgeois, non-proletarian socialist trends, ranging from the "Christian" socialism of Pierre Leroux and Philippe

---

[1] Marx, Engels, *Collected Works*, Vol. 10, p. 50.

Buchez, and Louis Blanc's "state" socialism, to Proudhon's anarchist-tainted socialism. The spread of these ideas among the workers showed that the French proletariat had yet to attain ideological and political maturity.

The utopian communists' doctrines were different. While these were based on idealistic, even fantastic, notions, and while some of them, like Etienne Cabet, still believed that communism could be ushered in by peaceful propaganda and the establishment of co-operative communities, their ideals went beyond renewing existing society by modifying some of its institutions. They urged the establishment of a totally new system, and helped to generate in the minds of masses of proletarians an awareness that bourgeois society was antithetical to the future society for which they should fight. Cabet's book *Voyage to Icaria* and his newspaper *Le Populaire* had a positive part to play in this context.

The proletariat's growing discontent with the capitalist order was even more strongly reflected by the most advanced revolutionary trend in French utopian communism, that of Théodore Dézamy and Auguste Blanqui, who carried on the teaching of the remarkable 18th-century French revolutionary, Babeuf. They felt the need for a revolutionary overthrow of the existing system and the establishment of a revolutionary dictatorship. While Blanqui followed Babeuf in advocating a conspiracy by a small, well-knit minority, Dézamy rejected all conspiratorial tactics. But even they failed to see the objective conditions for a transition from capitalism to socialism and to single out the proletariat among the toiling and exploited masses as the class with the epoch-making mission of creating a socialist society.

In Paris, Marx witnessed heated debates in workers' circles over the various socialist doctrines. He knew about the ideological struggles going on in the workers' organisations, most of which operated as secret societies, and came to realise that the French working class had considerable political experience. But the French workers' minds were in a muddle which reflected the confusion of diverse socialist ideas. The ideology of the French working class was influenced by its social structure, arising from the prevalence in French industry of small and semi-handicraft enterprises. The workers had come to realise the treachery of the big bourgeoisie in 1830, but continued to put their trust in the bourgeois and petty-bourgeois republicans and followed in their political wake.

In Paris, Marx established contacts with French workers' and German emigrant organisations, met their leaders and attended their meetings. A police report sent to Germany said that Sunday meetings of German Communists were attended by 100-200 persons, and Marx was named among the speakers. In August 1844, Marx wrote to Feuerbach: "You would have to attend one of the meetings of the French workers to appreciate the pure freshness, the nobility which burst forth from these toil-worn men.... It is among these 'barbarians' of our civilised society that history is preparing the practical element for the emancipation of mankind." [1]

Marx met the leaders of the League of the Just, an organisation of German emigrant artisans, who were becoming proletarians; it had emerged in 1837 and also had communities in Germany, Switzerland, Britain and other countries. It had ties with French secret societies, notably the Blanquist Society of the Seasons. At first, it was swayed by the ideas of Babeuf and his followers, and then by those of Weitling, the first German utopian communist.

Marx also became closely acquainted with Proudhon, and in their discussions, often night-long, Marx strove to get Proudhon to accept the dialectical and materialist view of the world. Marx also was personally acquainted with Blanc and Cabet.

While being in contact with various workers' organisations, Marx did not join any of them. He did not wish to commit himself to any of the socialist sects, for he was fully aware of their weaknesses and unscientific approach. Marx believed it was his task to work out and spread a truly scientific revolutionary theory showing the proletariat the ways and means of bringing about a radical transformation of the existing system. In this way he hoped to raise the ideological level of those who were then taking part in the working-class movement, to help foster real revolutionary proletarian organisations free from sectarian exclusiveness and one-sidedness. Marx later wrote that the idea was "not a matter of putting some utopian system into effect, but of conscious participation in the historical process revolutionising society before our very eyes." [2]

Marx's numerous activities extended beyond his vast amount of theoretical work and study of the working-class movement. He had broad contacts with French radical circles, notably the petty-bourgeois democrats and socialists grouped round the newspaper, *La Réforme*, and the revolutionaries who had come to Paris from various countries. At the end of March 1844, he attended an international democratic banquet.

Among the many people who came to see Marx at his apartment in Rue Vanneau were the poets Georg Herwegh and Heinrich Heine, the leaders of the Paris communities of the League of the Just, Hermann Ewerbeck and German Mäurer, the journalist Karl Bernays and the Russian revolutionary Mikhail Bakunin. The radical-minded Dr. Roland Daniels and the journalist Heinrich Bürgers from the Rhine Province came to see him during a visit to Paris in November 1844.

Marx was on friendly terms with Herwegh, a democratic poet who wrote for the *Rheinische Zeitung* and whom Marx defended against Ruge's grossly philistine attacks, although at the time Marx and Herwegh no longer saw eye to eye, the latter taking a bourgeois-democratic stand.

[1] Marx, Engels, *Collected Works*, Vol. 3, p. 355.
[2] Ibid., Vol. 17, p. 79.

Marx and Heine were great friends, and in Paris they met often, sometimes daily. Heine recited his verse to Marx and Jenny, whose opinion he valued very highly. Marx went over some of Heine's works as their first editor. Marx's daughter, Eleanor, later recalled that the two men would work together on this or that poem, repeating it again and again, polishing every line until it was brought to perfection. Under Marx's influence the social motifs in Heine's works became more pronounced, and it is no coincidence that he wrote his *Weavers* and *Germany. A Winter's Tale*, which marked the peak of his poetic achievement, in that very period. *A Winter's Tale* was published by Marx in the newspaper *Vorwärts!* from proofs sent to him by Heine, before the poem appeared in a separate edition.

When smarting from the attacks of ill-wishers and hostile critics, the sensitive and highly strung Heine would seek solace with the Marx family. He had come to feel a great affection for the family of his younger friend, whose cast of mind he found to be so congenial to his own. One day Heine did the family a great service. Marx's six-month-old daughter, Jenny, born on May 1, 1844, suddenly had an acute fit of convulsions, and her parents and nurse were distraught. Heine, who happened to walk in, displayed great self-possession. Without waiting for the doctor, he bathed the baby and brought it back to normal again, and with her the terrified parents as well.

At that time Heine was perhaps Marx's closest friend in Paris. A brilliant poet, he was one of the most erudite men of his day, and Marx profited greatly from their association. When Marx learned of his imminent expulsion from Paris, he wrote to Heine: "Of all the people I am leaving behind here, those I leave with most regret are the Heines. I would gladly include you in my luggage." [1]

To his dying day, Heine continued to have a profound respect for Marx — man, scientist and revolutionary. Shortly before his death in 1856, he described the "leaders of the German Communists" as having "the most capable heads and the most energetic characters in Germany", as "the only men who are really alive" in that country, and who had the future with them.[2]

Among the Russian emigrants Marx met in Paris were Bakunin, V. P. Botkin, and Herzen's friend N. I. Sazonov. He met Bakunin more often than the others, and in their talks Marx propounded his materialist and communist views in an effort to influence Bakunin, whose outlook at the time was a mixture of sentimental idealism and "instinctive" socialism, as he himself called it.

In the Marx family, their friends found not only a ready sympathy but also unstinting assistance. Jenny, Marx's eldest daughter, recalled her mother telling her that soon after their wedding she had received a small legacy, and the newly-weds put the money in a casket.

---

[1] Ibid., Vol. 38, p. 21.
[2] Heinrich Heine, "Aveux de l'auteur" en Vermeil Edmond, "Henri Heine. Ses vues sur l'Allemagne et les révolutions européennes", Paris, 1939, p. 275.

Whenever needy friends came to see them, it was left open on the table for each to take according to his needs.

SCIENTIFIC PURSUITS

Once settled down in Paris, says Engels, Marx "avidly set about studying political economy, the French socialists and the history of France".[1] He often sat over his books for days on end, taking short periods off for his meals and snatches of sleep.

He sought to understand the inner workings of capitalism, its development and contradictions, and the relation between politics and economics, giving particular thought to various aspects of the class struggle in modern society. Time and again he turned to the classic examples offered by the French bourgeois revolution. He made a most thorough study of one of its key periods, 1792, and 1793, when the overthrow of the monarchy on August 10, 1792 was followed by a struggle between the Girondists, a moderate wing of the bourgeoisie, and the Jacobins, the radical bourgeois revolutionaries. Marx hoped to write a history of the Convention and collected a great deal of background material; he read the works of the Jacobin leaders Robespierre, Saint-Just and Desmoulins, and made a conspectus of the memoirs of the Jacobin Levasseur, a member of the Convention, which he entitled "The Struggle Between the Montagnards and the Girondists".

News of Marx's literary plans had apparently reached the democratic circles. In the winter of 1845, the *Trier'sche Zeitung*, commenting on Marx's expulsion from Paris, said that he was going abroad "to complete his 'History of the Convention'". He never wrote it, but in other works made extensive use of the conclusions he had drawn from his study of the history of the French Revolution. His background material was not wasted either, because his study of the class struggle in France at the time of the greatest revolutionary upheaval, his insight into the material underpinning of the struggle and the role of plebeian masses in it were a great help in his elaboration of the materialist view of history.

In his work on the origins, laws and forms of the class struggle, Marx used the writings of bourgeois historians of the Restoration, among them Thierry, Mignet, and Guizot, who, for all the limitations of their views, accepted the division of society into classes and the importance of the class struggle in history, a process which had led to the establishment of bourgeois society. They failed, however, to go to the economic origins of classes or understand the true nature of the class struggle in the capitalist epoch. By contrast, Marx's chief concern was with the economic structure of society as the basis of its class structure, and the nature of economic relations in the

---

[1] Marx, Engels, *Werke*, Bd. 22, p. 338.

modern world, which gave a clue to the class conflicts of his day. Political economy was coming to play an ever greater part in Marx's scientific research.

In the summer of 1843, in the course of his critique of Hegel's philosophy of law, he reached the conclusion that the anatomy of the "civil society", that is, the aggregation of social relations, was to be found in political economy. From then onwards for the rest of his life, economic research was his primary concern.

Among the many economic works he studied in Paris were those of Smith, Ricardo, Say, Skarbek, James Mill, Destutt de Tracy, McCulloch, and Boisguillebert. He made frequent remarks on his numerous extracts from these works, and these, especially his copious comments on James Mill's *Elements of Political Economy*, show that while the dividing line between Marx and the bourgeois economists was still a thin one and his own economic views were as yet embryonic, he was already highly critical of bourgeois economic theories. He pointed out the main flaw of bourgeois political economy: its tenet that the historically rooted and transient capitalist relations of exchange and commerce were primordial and in accordance with "man's appointed lot" itself.[1]

Marx made some highly penetrating remarks on the capitalist economy proper and the bourgeois society which rested on it. They contained — albeit in embryo — a critique of the economic foundations of the exploiting system, and pinpointed the contradictions inherent in bourgeois private ownership of the means of production.

Marx was deeply impressed by and made a précis of Engels' article "Outlines of a Critique of Political Economy", which was published in the *Deutsch-Französische Jahrbücher* and which contained the first socialist critique of bourgeois economic science and the bourgeois social system. He thought it brilliant and subsequently quoted from it in many of his works, *Capital*, in particular.

ECONOMIC AND PHILOSOPHIC MANUSCRIPTS OF 1844

Marx set out the results of his research during this period in a work which has come down to us in the form of three notebooks, known as the *Economic and Philosophic Manuscripts of 1844*, written between April and August of that year.

These *Manuscripts* contain Marx's economic and philosophic views of that period. His Preface said that he had attained his results "by means of a wholly empirical analysis based on a conscientious critical study of political economy".[2] His object had been to give a thorough critique of private property and the established political economy.

---

[1] MEGA, Abt. 1, Bd. 3, Halbband 2, S. 537.
[2] Marx, Engels, *Collected Works*, Vol. 3, p. 231.

Marx developed the idea, expressed in the *Deutsch-Französische Jahrbücher*, that man's emancipation was possible only if "civil society" were radically transformed, that is, if the exploiting capitalist system were destroyed. He is also clearly seen to address himself to the masses, the proletariat, and his political sympathies are entirely with the working people. "The brotherhood of men," he says about the proletarians of France, "is no mere phrase with them, but a fact of life, and the nobility of man shines upon us from their work-hardened bodies."[1] He exposes and brands a system under which "the inevitable result for the worker is overwork and premature death, decline to a mere machine, a bond servant of capital".[2]

Marx defines his attitude to bourgeois political economy and gives a materialist explanation of its development. He says that economic thought is developed not through the movement of some absolute spirit but through the historical metamorphoses of private property. The historical continuity of economic thought is a mirror-like reflection of the disintegration of feudalism and the step-by-step subordination of the whole socio-economic system to capital. Political economy becomes the handmaiden of almighty capital, and political economists become the scientific conscience of the "empirical operators", the capitalists. The real course of development in the sphere of production is such that the capitalist ultimately vanquishes the landowner, and highly developed private property gains the upper hand over "undeveloped", or "immature private property".[3]

Smith and Ricardo had undoubtedly made a considerable advance by recognising labour in general as the substance of all wealth — not only agricultural labour, as the Physiocrats had done. That is why Marx regarded the "enlightened political economy" of Smith and Ricardo as the highest stage in the development of the science, although he had yet to accentuate their main achievement, their labour theory of value. But his positive assessment went hand in hand with sharp criticism of the lame and downright apologetic aspects of bourgeois economic science.

Marx blamed political economy for failing to understand the "interconnection of the movement it studied", for mostly interpreting economic facts, phenomena and processes in isolation from each other, and for holding them to be the result of an act by an external force or will. This was just criticism of the metaphysical method of bourgeois economic science. By showing its metaphysical and unhistorical approach to economic phenomena and its dependence on capitalist reality itself — the source of its limitations — Marx drew a dividing line between it and the new science he was formulating. He set himself the task of comprehending the intrinsic connection between private property, avarice, competition and the value of man

---

[1] Marx, Engels, *Collected Works*, Vol. 3, p. 313.
[2] Ibid., p. 238.
[3] Ibid., p. 288.

(Marx was yet to discover the category of the value of labour-power) and his devaluation, and so on.[1]

The main part of his critique of bourgeois political economy lay in the category of alienation and alienated labour, which proceeded from the "actual economic fact" recognised by political economy itself, namely, the increasing impoverishment of the working man with the growth of the wealth he produces.

The term "alienation" had been widely used in philosophical writings even before Marx's time. Hegel, for instance, spoke of a world of the spirit alienated from itself. His absolute idea alienates itself into nature, only to return to itself in the spirit — in history and in thought — into the "ether of pure reason". For Feuerbach alienation was man's alienation from his essential "species" properties, that is, the common properties which sprang from the characteristic natural properties of all men, when man created God and made him the creator of the world. By virtue of this man on earth was forced to lead an individualistic way of life, which was alien to his real substance, while the corresponding "species" existence took place only in the religious imagination and became purely illusory. In an effort to overcome Hegel's idealistic view of alienation, Feuerbach reduced the idea to an alienation of the natural properties of abstract man, treating it in the spirit of abstract humanism, and overlooking its social content.

From the start, Marx turned to man's social life and derived alienation from its conditions, which were determined by private ownership of the means of production. He saw alienation above all as a form of social nexus, of social intercourse between men, under which their living and working conditions, the product of their activity and their relations with each other, appeared as an alien and hostile external force. He believed alienation to be the direct outcome of the private property system. Alienation in the economic sphere was the basis for other forms of alienation in the various material, and ultimately also spiritual, spheres of social relations. Taking reality as his starting point, Marx set his sights not on the "pure struggles of thought"[2] to which the classic philosophers and their epigones had called men, but on a fight against the unjust and inhuman reality which bred alienation and made it inevitable. This already implied surmounting the flaws in the philosophy of Hegel and Feuerbach in this sphere, and refuting the basic tenet of bourgeois political economy about the capitalist mode of production being rational, normal and eternal.

Alienated labour is the category Marx most fully developed. Man's vital activity and self-assertion as a conscious social being, he wrote, are expressed above all in the practical creation of the world of things, in the course of social production. The worker's making of a thing, a product, means objectification of the worker himself,

[1] Ibid., p. 271.
[2] Ibid., Vol. 4, p. 83.

while its loss due to the domination of private property is the alienation of his labour because the product stands opposed to the worker "as *something alien*, as a *power independent* of the producer".[1] The products of labour go to him who owns the capital and not to him who creates them. Marx defined capital as private property in the products of other men's labour. By his labour — his productive activity — man creates power for the non-producer over production and product. "So much does the appropriation of the object appear as estrangement that the more objects the worker produces the less he can possess and the more he falls under the sway of his product, capital."[2] The worker, who has nothing but his hands, becomes poorer with the growing power of capital. Parallel to a refinement of the requirements and the means to satisfy them, at the one pole, there arises "a complete, crude, abstract simplicity of need" at the other. Thus, the alienation of labour is expressed in a growing material inequality and a widening gap between capital and labour.

Under capitalism, working conditions and labour itself become the worker's curse, "*external* to the worker", that is, not belonging "to his intrinsic nature".[3] Under the rule of capital, the wage worker "does not affirm himself but denies himself, does not feel content but unhappy",[4] does not develop his spiritual and physical qualities, but wears out and destroys his body and soul. The producer of material values is a slave to the division of labour that has taken shape, and is tied to his occupation for life. Factory work, whatever the worker's job, is a kind of bondage, and means the worker's "loss of his self". He feels himself freely active only in his purely animal functions — eating, drinking, etc. He is himself only when he does not work, and when he works, he is not himself.

The concept of alienated labour formulated in the *Economic and Philosophic Manuscripts* is the embryo of Marx's theory of appropriation by the capitalist of the wage-labour of others, and an outline of the most important ideas which he later developed and backed up scientifically in his *Capital*.

According to Marx, man's alienation from the product of his labour, and the antagonism between men created by the very conditions in which material life is being produced, necessarily leads to a degeneration of "his species-being" and to "*the estrangement of man* from *man*".[5] Consequently, normal social connections and relations between men in harmony with human nature cannot be brought about through the substitution of some higher form of religion for conventional religion, nor through the preaching of love, as Feuerbach believed, but only through a radical transformation of society and property relations.

---

[1] Marx, Engels, *Collected Works*, Vol. 3, p. 272.
[2] Ibid.
[3] Ibid., p. 274.
[4] Ibid.
[5] Ibid., p. 277.

Private property is the basis and the cause of alienation, or the self-alienation of labour. But it is also its effect. The alienation of labour results in a reproduction of private property. Marx called private property the material, summary expression of alienated labour.[1] Hence his conclusion that society's emancipation from private property is a necessary and cardinal condition for the economic and political emancipation of the workers, which also means the really tangible supersession of alienation. Marx stressed that the workers' emancipation contained "universal human emancipation".[2]

It was chiefly the philosophical aspect of the communist transformation of society that Marx examined in his *Economic and Philosophic Manuscripts*, using the traditional, notably Feuerbachian, philosophical vocabulary, when he termed communism fully developed naturalism quite identical with humanism, or a consummate, real humanism equivalent to naturalism. But on the whole he went well beyond his predecessors to formulate fundamentally new ideas. In a variety of contexts, he set out his views of *true* communism as the highest form of abolition of private property, and consequently also of all alienation and man's self-alienation, both economic and spiritual, religious alienation, in particular.

Under private property, said Marx, the advance of the natural sciences and of applied science, as embodied in industry, produces economic wealth, on the one hand, and economic poverty, on the other. Under communism they would create conditions for the fullest expression of man's richly endowed nature and for the enrichment of his requirements. Discarding the earlier, immature ideas of communism, which distorted its meaning and discredited the very idea of it, Marx emphasised that the only social order fit to be called communism is one which eliminates the contradictions between man and nature, and between man and man, which humanises man's senses, brings them into correspondence with man's social and natural essence, and produces "the *rich* man *profoundly endowed with all the senses*— as its enduring reality".[3] Consequently, Marx saw the future society as a stage in human history which would meet the highest humanistic principles, carrying with it a flowering of man's personality, full satisfaction of his material and spiritual requirements, and a harmony of individual and social interests.

Marx sharply condemned the egalitarian approach in the various utopian communist trends, and rejected them as the ideal for the future, while recognising their importance as a historically determined form of protest against the domination of private property and material inequality. He said egalitarian communism was crude and ill-considered, for it denied man's individuality and cultivated the idea of levelling down. One of its principles was "the regression to the *unnatural* simplicity of the *poor* and crude man who

---

[1] Ibid., p. 281.
[2] Ibid., p. 280.
[3] Ibid., p. 302.

has few needs",[1] which was a parody of true communism.

Marx believed that the triumph of communism was being prepared in the inner recesses of the system resting on private property, but that it would take more than theoretical awareness to bring it about. "In order to abolish the *idea* of private property, the *idea* of communism is quite sufficient. It takes *actual* communist action to abolish actual private property."[2] This accentuated the need for mass revolutionary struggle as a means of carrying out the communist revolution.

In the philosophical plane, Marx sought to find the answer above all to this question: "How do we now stand as regards the Hegelian *dialectic?*"[3] and one of the main purposes of his work, and the subject of a special, concluding chapter, was a critical analysis of Hegel's philosophy. The *Economic and Philosophic Manuscripts* contain a thorough and fairly mature criticism of Hegel's doctrine, notably his *Phenomenology of Mind*. In the light of a consistent materialism, and using Feuerbach's positive achievements and discoveries, Marx gave a profound analysis of Hegel's philosophy, drawing a clear distinction between its revolutionary and its conservative aspects. He flatly rejected its idealism, pointing out that Hegel had detached the forms of abstraction and the forms of thinking from reality, and emphasising that "the absolute idea is nothing for itself; that only *nature* is something".[4] Taking the materialist view of the category of alienation, Marx examined and assessed the "*positive* aspects of the Hegelian dialectic",[5] and his ideas — rational, even if abstract-idealistic in form — about the process of development and the supersession of alienation.

Despite his admiration for Feuerbach, Marx laid stress on social production and social practice, his whole exposition going well beyond Feuerbach's concept of human relations consisting of no more than natural bonds, and of the human species being nothing but a natural entity of man and nature.

Marx believed that social environment had a decisive influence in shaping relations between men, and proved that it was futile to hope for any improvement of social relations so long as there was no change in the circumstances behind them, that is, the conditions in which material life was produced.

Thus, Marx's manuscripts, while terminologically still inadequate, reflected a definite stage in his formulation of various important propositions of dialectical and historical materialism, and showed the great scope of his quest, and his effort in working out the method of materialist dialectics, which was so important in criticising bourgeois social science and analysing social phenomena.

---

[1] Marxs, Engels, *Collected Works*, Vol. 3, p. 295.
[2] Ibid., p. 313.
[3] Ibid., p. 327.
[4] Ibid., p. 343.
[5] Ibid., p. 341.

WORK ON *VORWÄRTS!*

With all hope gone of continuing the publication of his own periodical Marx looked for opportunities to write for other publications, and these soon presented themselves for him and for other former contributors to the *Deutsch-Französische Jahrbücher* in the *Vorwärts!* which came out abroad twice a week.

It was published in Paris from early 1844 by an enterprising German businessman, Heinrich Börnstein. He had appointed as his editor a retired Prussian officer, Adalbert Bornstedt, who as it later turned out was a secret informer of the Prussian and the Austrian police. At first *Vorwärts!* took a fairly moderate political line and met the *Jahrbücher*'s appearance with caustic attacks, calling its contributors "communistic rabble". There was a change when the radical, Karl Bernays, became its editor in May 1844. A friend of Marx's, he was a widely-read and revolutionary-minded journalist, and succeeded, despite Börnstein's resistance, in giving the paper a democratic complexion, so that Marx could write for it. Among its other contributors were Heine, Herwegh, Ewerbeck, Bakunin, Bürgers and Ruge.

The weekly editorial meetings were so stormy that — as one of its editors recalled — it was impossible to open a window without a crowd gathering outside to find out the cause of the uproar. Marx and Ruge were the protagonists. Marx won and from the summer of 1844 began to exert an ever stronger influence on the paper's line. Under his influence, Engels wrote later, it poured "sarcastic ridicule on the pathetic German absolutism and pseudo-constitutionalism of the period".[1]

The bourgeois press took notice of the new trends in *Vorwärts!* and the Stuttgart *Schwäbischer Merkur* reported that the "ultra-radical party" had won the day on its editorial board. The German democratic journalist Alexandre Weill wrote in the July issue of the Hamburg journal *Telegraph für Deutschland*: "Marx and Ruge have now parted for good, and that is a good thing. Marx and his associates are sure to do some important things, for they are young and talented."

Marx's leading role had an effect not only on the paper's general line; some of the reports showed signs of a direct impact of his ideas, notably those he had elaborated in his *Economic and Philosophic Manuscripts*. Weitling, who was then trying to get personally acquainted with Marx, wrote to him from London in October 1844: "I believe I recognised you in some of the articles in *Vorwärts!* as I compared their spirit with what I had heard about you."[2]

The differences between Marx and Ruge soon erupted into a pub-

---

[1] Marx, Engels, *Werke*, Bd. 22, S. 338.
[2] Weitling to Marx, October 18, 1844 (Central Party Archives of the Institute of Marxism-Leninism).

lic polemic. In June 1844, the Silesian weavers staged an uprising in protest against the intolerable exploitation and extremely low wages. It was the first direct action by the German proletariat, and it aroused response throughout Germany. In June and July 1844, a wave of strikes and workers' demonstrations rolled from Bavaria to East Prussia, and there was serious unrest among the workers in Bohemia, then a part of the Hapsburg Empire. Highly alarmed, the German bourgeoisie had to recognise that the proletariat had issued clear and threatening notice of its existence and demands not only in Britain and France but also in the German states. The bourgeois press was greatly agitated. One newspaper wrote: "The weavers' uprising shows the wide gulf between the capitalists and the proletarians."[1]

Ruge's response to the uprising was typical of the bourgeois journalist. In a sharply worded article in *Vorwärts!*, which he signed "A Prussian", he attacked the proletariat for its independent action, saying that it had been a senseless and futile revolt without a "political soul".

Marx replied on August 7 and 10, 1844, with an article entitled "Critical Marginal Notes on the Article 'The King of Prussia and Social Reform. By a Prussian'" and published in the same newspaper. He stressed the great importance of the Silesian uprising, which he saw as a sign of growing class consciousness among the German workers, and a dawning realisation that they were directly opposed to the private-property society. It was, Marx said, a momentous indication of the powerful potential of the working class, the revolutionary transformer of society.

The proletarian action and Ruge's philistine response impelled Marx to formulate in more concrete terms some of his own ideas about the mission of the working class in world history, and to give even more thought to ways of renewing the world on socialist lines. In contrast to Ruge, who maintained that it was the business of the political power, the state, in that case the Prussian monarchy, and not of the proletarian masses to tackle the social question, Marx flatly rejected the idea that the men representing the existing state systems would help to bring about a radical social transformation and to remedy the working people's social plight. He reached the conclusion that poverty—a product of private property—was not to be abolished by any reform or government intervention within the framework of the existing system.

He had earlier said, in his "Contribution to the Critique of Hegel's Philosophy of Law. Introduction" and *Economic and Philosophic Manuscripts*, that it was impossible to advance to a new society without mass revolutionary action by the proletariat, without revolution, and in this article he further elaborated on the idea by

---

[1] S. B. Kan, *Two Uprisings of the Silesian Weavers*, Moscow-Leningrad, 1948, p. 363 (in Russian).

formulating the following cardinal proposition: in revolution, its political aspect — the overthrow of the existing power — and its social aspect — the destruction of the old social relations — are interdependent and inextricably bound up with each other. "Every revolution dissolves the *old society* and to that extent it is *social*. Every revolution overthrows the *old power* and to that extent it is *political*." [1] There Marx came quite close to recognising the need for the proletariat to win political power.

AN HISTORIC MEETING

At the end of August 1844, Marx had a visit in Paris from Engels, who was returning from England to Germany. During his ten-day stay in the city the two men spent almost all of their time together. Their daily forthright conversations showed their views to be completely identical on every aspect of theory and practice. Engels wrote: "When I visited Marx in Paris in the summer of 1844, our complete agreement in all theoretical fields became evident and our joint work dates from that time." [2] They liked each other, became close friends, and arranged to collaborate in every sphere of their future activity. They shared their plans and agreed to write and act together, and Engels fully endorsed Marx's intention to write a book on political economy.

Marx got his new friend to contribute to *Vorwärts!* Through Marx, Engels got to know many leaders of the French working-class movement and a number of revolutionary emigrants, among them Bakunin. Together they attended French socialist and communist meetings. By the time Engels was ready to go home, the two friends had arranged to keep each other informed of what each planned to do, and from then on they regularly wrote to each other.

Their meeting was the start of a unique partnership. Lenin wrote: "Old legends contain various moving instances of friendship. The European proletariat may say that its science was created by two scholars and fighters, whose relationship with each other surpasses the most moving stories of the ancients about human friendship." [3]

PREPARATION FOR JOINT ATTACK
ON YOUNG HEGELIANS

By the time Engels came to Paris, Marx had a plan for a work aimed against the Young Hegelians. In his article, "Contribution to the Critique of Hegel's Philosophy of Law. Introduction", Marx had openly censured the "theoretical party" which confined itself to

---

[1] Marx, Engels, *Collected Works*, Vol. 3, p. 205.
[2] Marx and Engels, *Selected Works* in three volumes, Vol. 3, p. 178.
[3] V. I. Lenin, *Collected Works*, Vol. 2, p. 26.

the sphere of philosophy in its fight against the German reactionary order, and wrote: "We reserve the right to a more detailed description of this party." [1] In the Preface to his *Economic and Philosophic Manuscripts of 1844*, Marx openly urged the need for an ideological demarcation with Young Hegelianism as "the culmination and consequence of the old *philosophical*, and especially the *Hegelian, transcendentalism*, twisted into a *theological caricature*".[2] In early August 1844, Marx informed Feuerbach of his intention to attack Bauer.

During his stay in Paris Engels found that his view of the Young Hegelians was identical with that of Marx, who invited him to join him in writing a pamphlet against the Bauer brothers. They got down to it immediately. Engels wrote his part, about 30 pages, while still in Paris, and Marx continued the work from September to November 1844, after his friend left for Germany.

There were several considerations behind the need for them to make a public critique of the Young Hegelians. They realised that they could work out a scientific proletarian outlook only by constantly defining the differences between alien ideological trends and their own. Meanwhile, the Young Hegelians, especially those in Berlin, who were grouped round the Bauer brothers, had undergone a marked change: they had renounced their democratic convictions, which had made them the ideologists of the radical bourgeoisie, and had moved to the right on many issues. They were no longer allies in the fight against religion and the Prussian state, but a group of anarchist-minded intellectuals, who scorned "the mass" as being passive and inert and an obstacle to progress. Its only impetus was "Critical Criticism" according to the Bauer brothers, of which the latter felt themselves to be the personification.

In the monthly *Allgemeine Literatur-Zeitung*, published by Bruno Bauer in Charlottenburg in 1843 and 1844, the Young Hegelians publicly repudiated their past opposition attitudes. Its eighth issue carried Bruno Bauer's article, "The Year 1842", in which he renounced the "radicalism of 1842" as "expressed in the *Rheinische Zeitung*". In a clear allusion to Marx, Engels and other German advocates of communism, Bauer spurned the views of those who "believe that they have found something new in socialism". He flaunted his contempt for politics, asserting that criticism had ceased to be political. This was an especially harmful view in Germany, which was then moving towards a bourgeois revolution, for it ignored the revolutionary action of the working class and the broad masses, the only force capable of securing victory over the semi-feudal absolutist regime.

The reactionaries were clearly benefiting from Bauer's line in the *Allgemeine Literatur-Zeitung*, as can be seen from a report by the government's censor, who wrote: "The Bauers give me real pleasure:

---

[1] Marx, Engels, *Collected Works*, Vol. 3, p. 181.
[2] Ibid., p. 233.

they have adapted themselves excellently to the censorship instructions." By contrast, the Bauer line was sharply condemned by the democratic press.

Objectively the reactionary social implications of their philosophy lay in their subjectivist view that the resolution of any contradictions in the mind was identical with their resolution in reality. Marx said they had learned "to convert *real objective* chains that exist *outside me* into *merely ideal*, merely *subjective* chains, existing merely *in me*".[1]

Marx and Engels were faced with the task of exposing the Young Hegelians' sham radicalism and countering their "Critical Criticism" with their own materialist and communist views.

As Marx worked on, the planned pamphlet against the Bauers expanded into a book of more than 20 printed sheets. In it Marx used some of the ideas and material contained in his *Economic and Philosophic Manuscripts of 1844*, his extracts from works by bourgeois economists and preparatory writings on the history of the Convention. He also made a special study of English and French materialists, among them Francis Bacon, Locke, Hobbes and Helvétius. When Engels learnt that the work was to be much larger, he wrote to Marx: "It is all to the good, for it means that much can now be disseminated which would otherwise have lain for heaven knows how long in your escritoire."[2]

Work on the manuscript was completed at the end of November 1844, but already in late September and early October reports appeared in the German press that Marx was writing a pamphlet against the Bauer brothers entitled *A Critique of Critical Criticism*, which was to "demolish"[3] Critical Criticism. Marx had an arrangement with Julius Fröbel of Zurich to publish the book, but Ruge, a companion of Fröbel's, prevented it. Marx then tried to find a publisher in Paris, but with no more success. It was issued in Frankfurt am Main at the end of February 1845 under the title, *The Holy Family, or Critique of Critical Criticism. Against Bruno Bauer and Co.*

THE HOLY FAMILY

This is primarily a philosophical work, containing a consistent materialist interpretation of some of the most important philosophical problems, and a militant attack on the philosophical opponents of the new outlook. A large part of it is a critique of the Young Hegelians' subjective idealism, which in its worse and frequently caricatured form embodied all the defects of classical German idealism, so that the critique essentially applied to idealism as a whole, to its methods and its distorted dialectics. Ridiculing the Young Hegelians'

---

[1] Marx, Engels, *Collected Works*, Vol. 4, p. 82.
[2] Ibid., Vol. 38, p. 18.
[3] *Frankfurter Oberpostamts-Zeitung*, October 14, 1844.

worship of self-conciousness, Marx and Engels wrote: "The Critical Critic ... cannot by any means entertain the thought that there is a world in which *consciousness* and *being* are distinct; a world which continues to exist when I merely abolish its existence in thought." [1]

The Holy Family gave the first materialist analysis of the history of philosophy from the 17th to the first half of the 19th century, presented as a struggle between materialism and idealism, the two main trends in philosophy, with special emphasis on the intrinsic connection between materialist ideas and those of utopian socialism and communism, and also between the history of materialism and the advance of natural science.

While recognising the great progressive importance of materialism in the history of philosophy, Marx did not identify his own views with those of the earlier materialists, for he was laying the foundations of a new materialism enriched with all the achievements of the dialectical method, dialectical materialism.

The Holy Family treated dialectics as an inherent property of the objective processes in the development of the material world, which was reflected in thinking. That is why it analysed social phenomena in their dialectical motion, where their intrinsic contradictions are the source, and their struggle the prerequisite for a revolutionary transition to a new quality.

Marx exposed the epistemological roots of idealism, notably the detachment of the individual from the general and the treatment of concrete, individual things merely as forms in which general conceptions exist. The speculative philosopher, Marx wrote ironically, "performs a *miracle* by producing the real *natural objects*, the apple, the pear, etc., out of the unreal *creation of the mind* 'the Fruit' ". [2] For the idealist philosopher, the cognition of things through an identification in them of the general becomes "an act of creation" of these things. Marx contrasted these idealistic and metaphysical conceptions with the dialectico-materialist view of the relation between the individual and the general. He said that it was quite wrong to detach the specific and the individual from the general because the only way to understand the transition from the world of concrete sensory objects to general concepts was to reveal the intrinsic objective properties in these objects.

The Holy Family also made an important contribution to an understanding of dialectics of unity and the struggle of opposites. Analysing the nature of the antagonistic contradiction between the bourgeoisie and the proletariat, Marx showed its internal structure to consist of a conservative and a revolutionary side, where "within this antithesis the private property-owner is ... the *conservative* side, the proletarian, the *destructive* side". [3] He stressed that the contending sides were irreconcilable because the private owner was the

---

[1] Marx, Engels, *Collected Works*, Vol. 4, p. 193.
[2] Ibid., p. 60.
[3] Ibid., p. 36.

source of action aimed to preserve the antagonism, and the proletariat, of action aimed to destroy it. But as opposites, the proletariat and the bourgeoisie constitute something of a relative unity, because both spring from the capitalist system. That is why the resolution of this contradiction through a proletarian revolution does away both with private property and with the proletariat as its product.

The elaboration of a number of basic propositions of the materialist view of history then being shaped was central to the content of the book. In contrast to the Young Hegelians' presentation of logical categories as something that had an existence of its own and dominated men's acts, Marx and Engels clearly said history was "human activity". They wrote: " 'History' is not, as it were, a person apart, using man as a means to achieve *its own* aims; history is *nothing but* the activity of man pursuing his aims." [1]

Marx also gained a more profound understanding of the relation between the state and civil society, and laid the groundwork for the materialist doctrine of basis and superstructure. He showed that in every historical epoch there is a definite economic structure with a corresponding political system. "Just as the ancient state had slavery as its *natural basis* the *modern state* has as its *natural basis* civil society." [2] He formulated Engels' and his own view of the bourgeois state as a "political head" of bourgeois society, thus coming very close to the view of the state as a political superstructure on the economic basis.

Marx was fully aware that there is not only some kind of correspondence but also a close dialectical bond between the state and the economic system. Any form of state is ultimately determined by the economic system of society, but the state for its part also exerts a retroactive effect on that system. Thus, the bourgeois state destroys the feudal rights and privileges hampering the bourgeoisie, and gives scope for capitalist development and promotes is.

In order to make the vague concept of "civil society" more specific he sought to define the main factor determining the development of society as a whole. He already perceived it to be the production of material goods, and saw production relations as the social relations between men which take shape in the process of production. These relations are specific, in them "the *object* as *being for man*, as the *objective being of man*, is at the same time the *existence of man for other men*, his *human relation to other men*, the *social behaviour of man to man*". [3]

Marx saw material production as the basis of mankind's history, which was a step forward from his *Economic and Philosophic Manuscripts*. No historical period can be understood "without knowing, for example, the industry of that period, the immediate mode of production of life itself". [4]

---

[1] Ibid., p. 93.
[2] Ibid., p. 113.
[3] Ibid., p. 43.
[4] Ibid., p. 150.

The Holy Family formulated the key proposition about the leading role of the masses in history—which is especially pronounced in revolutionary epochs—and its growth in the course of historical development. However, all earlier revolutions had been in the interest of a minority, which is why the masses had up till then exerted a limited influence on the course of history. But as social progress increasingly met the interests of the masses themselves, the scope of their influence on historical processes was bound to grow. Marx predicted that the socialist revolution would open an era when "together with the thoroughness of the historical action, the size of the mass whose action it is will therefore increase".[1] Lenin emphasised this idea, which he regarded as one of Marx's most profound on social development.

Marx's and Engels' formulation of the materialist view of history went hand in hand with their elaboration of the theory of scientific communism, above all the doctrine of the proletariat's role in world history as the main active and leading force of the coming socialist revolution. In *The Holy Family* Marx formulated for the first time the idea that this role of the working class is determined by socio-economic factors, and showed that capitalist society develops within the framework of a lasting antagonism between two forces—private property and the proletariat—an antagonism constantly reproduced by the development of capitalist relations, and one in whose preservation the capitalist—the private property owner—has a stake. For its part, the proletarat, whose living conditions "sum up all the conditions of life in society today in all their inhuman acuity", seeks to abolish these relations. "The proletariat executes the sentence that private property pronounces on itself by producing the proletariat."[2]

Consequently, by virtue of its objective condition, the proletariat is bound to destroy capitalist society, irrespective of what "this or that proletarian, or even the whole proletariat, at the moment *regards* as its aim. The question is... what, in accordance with its *being*, it will historically be compelled to do."[3]

As the proletariat develops an awareness of its historical mission—this awareness being advanced by the burden of capitalist exploitation—it begins to unite for the struggle against the existing system, and this transforms it into a powerful force.

Another question Marx dealt with was the emancipatory mission of the proletariat with respect to the other exploited classes. He drew on the experience of earlier revolutions to show that in each the leader had been a class impelled by its own specific interests, which, even if no more than outwardly, were expressed as the interests of all mankind. Thus, the bourgeois revolution broke up the economic

---

[1] Marx, Engels, *Collected Works*, Vol. 4, p. 82.
[2] Ibid., p. 36.
[3] Ibid., p. 37.

and political relations of the feudal system primarily in the interests of the bourgeoisie itself, although this had progressive implications for all mankind. But there the identity of bourgeoisie's interests and those of the lower classes had been temporary and extremely limited.

By contrast, the proletariat's class interests are completely identical with those of "the mass whose real conditions for emancipation were essentially different from the conditions within which the bourgeoisie could emancipate itself and society".[1] As it liberates itself from the exploiting system it also liberates the whole of society: for the first time in history, the interests of the leading class are truly in harmony with those of the broadest masses of the working people, and this makes them the interests of all mankind. This line of reasoning contained the first elements of the proposition Marx was subsequently to formulate about the proletariat's hegemony as a class which has a leading role to play in the revolutionary emancipation of the oppressed masses in modern society.

Marx and Engels saw the proletariat as the creator both of material and of spiritual values. "Critical Criticism creates nothing, the worker creates everything; and so much so that even his intellectual creations put the whole of Criticism to shame."[2] As an example they quoted Proudhon's *What Is Property?*, which they defended against Young Hegelians' criticism. They valued Proudhon's attack on big capitalist property, even though they realised his limitations, for he criticised private property from the standpoint of private ownership, and this was the core of his petty-bourgeois reformist views which later became most pronounced.

Lenin wrote that *The Holy Family* contained "Marx's view — already almost fully developed — concerning the revolutionary role of the proletariat".[3]

This new work still showed evidence, albeit to a lesser extent than *Economic and Philosophic Manuscripts*, of some of Feuerbach's influence. After rereading *The Holy Family* in 1867, Marx wrote to Engels: "I was pleasantly surprised to find that we have no need to feel ashamed of the piece, although the Feuerbach cult now makes a most comical impression upon me."[4] What Marx called "the Feuerbach cult" was an outcome of the specific formation of their views: as they worked out their outlook step by step, they only gradually came to realise that it was a fundamentally new one, and this realisation came later than the actual process of formulating their views. In other words, in *The Holy Family* they had objectively advanced well beyond Feuerbach, but subjectively still regarded themselves as his disciples. That is why even as late as August 1844 Marx believed that it was Feuerbach who had given socialism its

---

[1] Ibid., p. 81.
[2] Ibid., p. 20.
[3] V. I. Lenin, *Collected Works*, Vol. 38, p. 26.
[4] Marx, Engels, *Collected Works*, Vol. 42, p. 360.

philosophical foundation. Already materialists and Communists, Marx and Engels continued to call themselves "real humanists", a Feuerbachian term, although they endowed it with a new content, one that was unknown and alien to Feuerbach.

Apart from this dependence with regard to terminology, Marx and Engels had yet to establish their doctrine as a separate one from Feuerbach's for they were still to put the finishing touches to their materialist view of history, a task they fulfilled in their subsequent writings.

In *The Holy Family*, they still used alienation as their starting-point for analysing the regularities of social development. Marx continued to say that property, capital, industry and wage-labour were "alienated vital elements" and "concrete products of the workers' self-alienation". True, the analysis of these categories was profoundly historical, and the authors subjected to withering criticism the Young Hegelians' idolatry of alienation and their insistence that "all the attributes and manifestations of human nature can be Critically transformed into their *negation* and into *alienations* of human nature".[1] Nevertheless, they viewed social forms and institutions abstractly as various manifestations of alienated human activity. Their line of scientific inquiry led them to adopt a more concrete historical approach to social phenomena. The category of alienation, while remaining meaningful for the philosophical comprehension of important aspects of reality, was to give way in the course of the subsequent analysis of the laws of social development to more precise and concrete sociological and economic conceptions.

As a whole, *The Holy Family* was a milestone on the way to laying the theoretical foundations of the proletarian ideology and defining the differences that distinguished Marx and Engels from their predecessors and ideological adversaries. It marked an advance in the stage opened by *Economic and Philosophic Manuscripts*.

The Holy Family produced a fairly lively response in the German press. On March 21, 1845, the bourgeois *Kölnische Zeitung* had to admit that the book was an expression of socialist views since it criticised the "inadequacy of any half-measures directed at eliminating the social ailments of our times". The radical *Mannheimer Abendzeitung* printed a review on March 25, 1845, saying that *The Holy Family* was most profound and most forceful of all that Marx and Engels had recently written. By contrast, the issue for April 28, 1845 of the reactionary *Rheinischer Beobachter* which had grasped the essence of the book fairly accurately, sharply attacked its criticism of private property, its "reverence for the sensory and the material", its "ridicule of all metaphysics and philosophy", and its gibes at all things Christian and German. The *Allgemeine Zeitung*, one of the major conservative papers in Germany, was even more indignant. On April 8, 1845, it wrote: "Its every line preaches revolt ...

---

[1] Marx, Engels, *Collected Works*, Vol. 4, p. 21.

against the state, the church, the family, legality, religion and property... In short, it contains clear evidence of the most radical and the most open communism, and this is all the more dangerous as Mr. Marx cannot be denied either extremely broad knowledge or the ability to make use of the polemical arsenal of Hegel's logic, what is customarily called 'iron logic'."

Bruno Bauer reacted with an article which was both pretentious and weak, complaining that his views had been misunderstood and misrepresented. Marx and Engels countered this "anti-critique" in a short article (printed by the *Gesellschaftsspiegel* in January 1846) which ended with the following words: "By resorting to incompetent *jugglery* and the most deplorable conjuring trick, *Bruno Bauer* has in the final analysis confirmed the death sentence passed upon him by *Engels* and *Marx* in *The Holy Family*." [1]

EXPULSION FROM PARIS

The clouds over *Vorwärts!* darkened in the autumn of 1844. It had become very popular among democratic-minded readers for its revolutionary-democratic line, its discussion of burning social issues, in particular the condition of the working class, and its publication of Heine's brilliant satirical poems. It had 800 subscribers, at the time an impressive figure for an emigrant paper.

It was grossly attacked by the reactionary press. The Paris *Globe* wrote: "This paper is worse than any French handbill of the first revolution period." On September 19, 1844, the *Elberfelder Zeitung* exclaimed: "Will the governments of the German states, will the French government tolerate the existence of the handbill?", and went on to demand the most vigorous measures against this "dangerous press". However, there was little reason to fear that the French and the Prussian authorities would take a tolerant attitude to the *Vorwärts!*, because they had been extremely irritated by its accusatory tone.

As early as July 1844, the Prussian ambassador in Paris tried to persuade the French government to close down the paper on the ground that it was "preaching regicide" (a reference to the paper's comment on Burgomaster Tschech's attempted assassination of King Frederick William IV). In view of the absurdity of this charge, the French government did not risk submitting the case to a jury and imprisoned the responsible editor Bernays for his failure to comply with the deposit provisions defaulted on the payment of the statutory deposit. The editorial board decided to run the paper as a monthly, which did not require a deposit. On January 16, 1845, the French authorities issued an order for the expulsion of its contributors, among them Marx, Heine, Bürgers and Bakunin. This

---

[1] Ibid., Vol. 5, p. 18.

step, taken under Prussian pressure, aroused a wave of indignation among democratic circles in France and Germany. On February 4, 1845, the *Réforme*, a petty-bourgeois democratic and socialist newspaper, wrote about the French government's despotic act and urged other papers to protest. The March issue of the journal *Fraternité de 1845*, published by Babouvist workers, exposed the Prussian King's intrigues aimed at the expulsion from Paris of the "German writers", among them "the communist philosopher Herr Karl Marx of Trier". The radical *Trier'sche Zeitung* reported the Guizot government's expulsion order and stressed that such harsh measures had not been taken against foreigners since the Directory. Under public pressure, the French government was compelled to make some concessions, in particular, to revoke its expulsion order against Heine. However, it remained inflexible over the expulsion of Marx.

On February 3, 1845, Marx left Paris for Brussels, and was shortly followed by his wife, with their baby daughter. Jenny had had to sell their furniture for a trifling sum at short notice to obtain the price of her fare.

That was the end of Marx's Paris period. He had gone there when he was still probing for a new outlook, and in the course of his stay had embraced materialism and communism once and for all. He left with a clear goal ahead of him. It was to substantiate further and elaborate the new revolutionary doctrine, and to promote its spread and acceptance by proletarians and democrats.

CHAPTER THREE

THE MATERIALIST VIEW OF HISTORY

> *His historical materialism was a great achievement in scientific thinking. The chaos and arbitrariness that had previously reigned in views on history and politics were replaced by a strikingly integral and harmonious scientific theory, which shows how, in consequence of the growth of productive forces, out of one system of social life another and higher system develops...*
>
> V. I. Lenin

IN BRUSSELS

When he arrived in Brussels at the beginning of February 1845, Marx could not immediately find permanent lodgings within his means, and it was only in early May that he moved with his family to a house at 5 Rue Alliance in a predominantly working-class neighbourhood away from the centre. After about a year he moved to a house in Place Ste. Gudule, one of the city's oldest districts. From October 1846 to February 1848, the Marx family lived at 42 Rue d'Orléans (later renamed Rue du President). Then in February and March 1848, they again lived in Place Ste. Gudule.

Altogether Marx spent more than three years in Belgium, working very hard to elaborate further the scientific principles of the new, proletarian outlook, and making an intense practical effort to rally the advanced elements of the proletariat and form a revolutionary proletarian party. From the literary point of view, this was an exceptionally productive period. In the first eighteen months, he propounded a coherent materialist view of history in two outstanding works: *Theses on Feuerbach* and *The German Ideology*, which he wrote together with Engels.

At the time, little Belgium was one of the most economically advanced countries in Europe. The bourgeois revolution of 1830 had led to her secession from Holland and had assured her of national and considerable amount of economic independence. By the mid-1840s, Belgium had a developed mining, engineering and textile industry. The manufactory was giving way to large-scale machine production, and handicrafts and the traditional cottage industries were on the way out. This capitalist development had typical consequences for the working people: the working day was up to 14 hours long and wages were a pittance. Female and child labour was used everywhere, including the mines. Unemployment was a real scourge.

The condition of the Belgian working people provided a wealth of facts for an analysis of the social contradictions inherent in capitalism. Marx was deeply impressed by the contrast between the mass poverty and the country's outward economic "prosperity".

The undemocratic nature of the bourgeois monarchy was evident wherever you looked. Despite the country's liberal 1831 Constitution, the high property qualification meant that only one per cent of the population had the right to vote. Belgium's Minister of the Interior in the 1840s, Nothomb, declared: "The only good thing about our constitution is that the people agree not to make use of it at all!" The Catholic clergy and the clericals had considerable social influence.

However, Belgium's ruling circles were unable to stop the spread of democratic and socialist ideas. The prominent utopian communist Buonarroti settled in Brussels in 1823, and published his famous book there in 1828, *The Plot for Equality, or the So-called Conspiracy of Babeuf*. The doctrines of Saint-Simon and Fourier were also being spread. Some members of the radical-democratic opposition were under the influence of utopian socialism, and campaigned among Belgian proletarians in favour of a democratic republic. Political emigrants from Poland, Italy, Germany and France helped the progressive people in Belgian society to adopt revolutionary ideas.

The Belgian authorities were loath to grant asylum to revolutionary emigrants, and Marx's arrival in Brussels was the source of much concern to the royal government. The Minister of Justice ordered the police to keep an eye on the "dangerous democrat and Communist". On March 22, 1845, Marx was summoned to the police department and made to sign a pledge not to publish anything in Belgium on current politics. He was allowed to stay in Brussels only on that condition.

The Prussian government, which had engineered his expulsion from France, would not leave him alone either, and was now trying to get him expelled from Belgium. In December 1845, to deprive the Prussian authorities of the official pretext for meddling in his affairs, Marx abandoned Prussian citizenship.

Marx and his family soon made themselves quite at home in Belgium despite police harassment and shortage of money: their main source of income was the occasional royalties Marx received for his writings. As in Paris, the Marx household was always a happy, lively one. Marx's keen mind, brilliant wit and encyclopaedic knowledge, together with Jenny's hospitality, tact, charm and considerable erudition, all went to make their home a favourite meeting place for revolutionary emigrants and many progressive Belgian intellectuals. It became something of a political club for German socialists, French revolutionaries, and Polish, Belgian and Russian democrats. Marx and his friends spent an occasional evening at the local café in spirited conversation, discussing philosophical, political and literary topics.

His old friends in Paris wrote to him, and he met many new people who sought his acquaintance because of his reputation as an outstanding revolutionary thinker and writer. *The Holy Family* had a great part to play in this. Georg Jung, the German publicist, who was friendly with Marx, read the book and wrote to Marx on March 18, 1845: "You must now become for the whole of Germany what you already are for your friends. Your brilliant style and exceptional clarity of argument will command recognition here and will make you a star of the first magnitude."[1]

On September 26, 1845, a second daughter — Laura — was born into the Marx family, and in December 1846, a son, whom they named Edgar, after Jenny's younger brother and a close friend of Marx's, Edgar von Westphalen. During their first year in Brussels, the Marx household acquired another member — 22-year-old Helene Demuth — a maid of Jenny's mother, Caroline von Westphalen, whom she had sent over to help Jenny. Helene was deeply attached to the family and became a kind of a guardian angel. Endowed with native wit and vigour, she took over the management of the household. Every member of the family, Marx included, obeyed without a murmur the dictates of the kindly and solicitous Lenchen, for whom Karl and Jenny felt deep respect and affection.

ARRIVAL OF ENGELS.
PLAN FOR A NEW PHILOSOPHICAL WORK

In early April 1845, Engels arrived in Brussels from Barmen, and was immediately received by the Marx family as their dearest friend. When Marx moved to the Rue Alliance, Engels rented an apartment nearby at No. 7. It was on this visit that Engels made the acquaintance of Jenny, who had been away from Paris during his memorable meeting with Marx in the autumn of 1844.

Engels' book *The Condition of the Working Class in England*, published in Leipzig at the end of May 1845, was a source of great pride and sincere pleasure for Marx. He praised its depth of content, vigorous style, and realistic portrayal of the plight and struggles of the English proletariat. This work was later described by Lenin as "a terrible indictment of capitalism and the bourgeoisie".[2] It was an expression of Marx's own ideas about the great historical mission of the working class, ideas which Engels had developed independently, from his own experience and scientific knowledge. When he began

---

[1] MEGA, Abt. 1, Bd. 3, S. 458.
[2] V. I. Lenin, *Collected Works*, Vol. 2, p. 23.

elaborating his economic doctrine, Marx relied largely on the facts and conclusions contained in Engels' book.

By the spring of 1845—the time when Engels arrived in Brussels—Marx had already realised the need to develop a materialist view of history as the philosophical foundation for scientific communism. The two men had announced their intention of formulating their philosophical and social views, and criticising the latest philosophical and social doctrines, in the closing words of their foreword to *The Holy Family*, as far back as September 1844. When Engels came to Brussels, Marx was able to give him a general outline of his new, materialist conception of history. Accordingly, they decided to work together to develop this new outlook as an antithesis to German idealist philosophy.

However, both continued work on their own scientific and literary plans. Engels continued to work on the economy and history of England. Marx resumed his economic studies, hoping to set forth their results in a major economico-sociological work and in separate articles. Thus, even before Engels arrived in Belgium he worked on an article about Friedrich List's book, *The National System of Political Economy*. Both he and Engels then intended to start an open polemic with that ideologist of the German bourgeoisie and an advocate of economic protectionism. Although they did not do so at the time, an extant draft of Marx's article against List shows his profound approach to the critique of bourgeois economic thought. Marx saw List's views as a reflection of the specific features of the German bourgeoisie, which used high-flown catchwords about serving "national ideals" to cover up its greed for enrichment and its exploitative and nationalistic urges, fear of its much stronger foreign rivals and its subservience to the Junkers and the bureaucracy. That is exactly how Marx interpreted List's vague statements about "the national confederation of productive forces". In an assessment of the book Marx wrote: "The German bourgeois begins his creation of wealth with the creation of a high-flown hypocritically idealising political economy." [1]

When analysing List's work, Marx developed his own views of such categories of political economy as "labour", "exchange value", and so on. Outlining the way for a materialist interpretation of the key sociological conceptions of "productive forces", he emphatically rejected the idealist interpretation given by List, and also criticised Saint-Simon's followers for taking an abstract view of "productive forces" (the forces of nature used by man in the process of production, his own forces and the means obtained as a result of industrial activity), outside the context of the social form in which their development took place under the given social conditions. Marx pointed to the distorting influence of capitalist relations on the productive forces, emphasising that the former had become fet-

---

[1] Marx, Engels, *Collected Works*, Vol. 4, p. 267.

ters that needed to be destroyed. This carried him forward to his future discovery of the decisive role in the social process of the dialectical interaction between the productive forces and the relations of production (a proposition soon to be formulated in *The German Ideology*). Consequently, in his economic studies Marx was also constantly faced with the task of elaborating new general methodological principles for the study of social phenomena based on a scientific view of history.

By the time Marx finally, albeit still only in general terms, developed his fundamentally new view of human history he had come to realise that not only was it incompatible with Feuerbach's views of society, but diametrically opposite to them. It was also necessary to draw a line between his own communism and the pseudo-communism of Feuerbach, who spoke about his "communist convictions" and styled himself the "communist recluse of Bruckberg", and to pinpoint the fundamental difference between genuine revolutionary communist theory and these pseudo-communist views.

While being aware of the inconsistency and limitations of Feuerbach's materialism, Marx continued to value his achievements in developing the progressive philosophy. All their lives, Marx and Engels had a profound respect for Feuerbach, and when he died in September 1872, Anton Memminger, a Social-Democratic deputy of the Imperial Diet, placed a wreath on his grave on behalf of Marx and other members of the International Working Men's Association and the German Social-Democratic Workers' Party.

THESES ON FEUERBACH

These eleven theses were written by Marx in the spring—possibly April—of 1845 in a notebook he used in Paris and Brussels from 1844 to 1847. These notes hurriedly scribbled down for later elaboration ran to no more than five pages but are perhaps unequalled in concentration and depth of thought, and clarity and precision of expression. They are, Engels said, "the first document in which is deposited the brilliant germ of the new world outlook".[1]

Their central idea is the decisive role of revolutionary material practice in the life of society. Marx says that practice is the point of departure, the basis, the criterion and the purpose of any cognition, including consequently philosophical cognition.

Some philosophers before Marx had sensed and even declared that practice was the criterion and purpose of cognition, but the real role of practice in the life of society and the process of cognition and its importance as a category in philosophy could be truly understood only from the standpoint of the proletariat, the consistently revolutionary class. The introduction of the category of practice

---

[1] Marx, Engels, *Collected Works*, Vol. 26, p. 520.

into the theory of cognition marked a real revolution in epistemology, and was one of the main elements behind the revolution in the whole of philosophy.

Proceeding from the new outlook, Marx criticised the old materialism for being contemplative, and idealism for reducing practice to purely theoretical activity. That is not to say that Marx strove to rise above both materialism and idealism, but he firmly declared his outlook to be a new materialism.

In contrast to the idealist philosophers, Marx emphasised that purely theoretical criticism is not enough to change reality: it is essential to have practical-critical, revolutionary, activity; it is essential to change not only thinking but also being. Only in the process of revolutionary practice does man change both the surrounding reality and his own self.

In contrast to Feuerbach's metaphysical and unhistorical concepts of man as an abstract, isolated individual, Marx formulated another key tenet of historical materialism, namely, that the essence of man is the ensemble of all the social relations. Man exists in society, he is a product of society, and not just of society in the abstract, but in every instance of a definite form of society.

Marx saw consistent, proletarian atheism as the way to overcome religion. Pre-Marxian materialists, Feuerbach in particular, had reduced religion to its secular basis and had subjected it to profound criticism. Therein lay their historical achievement. But it was Marx who showed that religion sprang from the contradictions of this secular basis, from social antagonisms, and that in order to eliminate religion it was necessary to revolutionise existing society. He subsequently formulated the idea in its classic form in Volume One of *Capital*.

The earlier materialism had been essentially contemplative and metaphysical. Marx contrasted contemplation with revolutionary practice, and the old materialism with the new, dialectical materialism as the philosophical foundation of communism. The final thesis contained the classic formulation of the principle of the new outlook: "The philosophers have only *interpreted* the world in various ways; the point, however, is to *change* it." [1]

The new outlook, whose fundamental principles Marx had formulated with such brevity and precision in his brilliant *Theses on Feuerbach*, was elaborated by Marx and Engels in their joint work, *The German Ideology*.

---

[1] Marx, Engels, *Collected Works*, Vol. 5, p. 8.

"LIBRARY OF THE BEST FOREIGN SOCIALIST WRITERS". ARTICLES IN THE PRESS

At the same time Marx and Engels tried to carry out their plan of publishing a "Library of the Best Foreign Socialist Writers", about which Engels wrote to Marx several times from Barmen in February and March 1845. It was to acquaint German readers with the works of best French and English utopian socialists in order to stimulate an interest in socialist thought and criticism of bourgeois society by socialist writers. The first issue was to contain a general introduction giving a history of socialist ideas, and each of the works was to be supplied with a comprehensive critical commentary, concentrating primarily on its rational elements.

Some idea of the scope of the series may be gained from the cursory entries in Marx's notebook in which he later wrote his *Theses on Feuerbach*. It was to cover the works of Morelly, Mably, Saint-Simon and his school, Fourier and his disciple Considérant, Owen, Cabet, Proudhon and others, with a special study of those who favoured revolutionary methods of transforming society—Babeuf, Buonarroti and Dézamy. Marx also intended to include works by plebeian ideologists from the period of the Great French Bourgeois Revolution, among them members of the *Cercle social*, the leaders of the *Enragés* movement Roux and Leclerc, and the Left-wing Jacobin Hébert. Nor had he forgotten the Englishman Godwin, who had expounded almost socialist views.

The idea of putting out such a series shows that the new doctrine rested on the earlier development of world culture and civilisation. Their criticism of utopian socialism did not prevent Marx and Engels from seeing its valuable elements, the adoption of which facilitated rather than impeded the elaboration and spread of the new, revolutionary-proletarian outlook.

The plan fell through because of publishing difficulties and the unsound ideological attitudes of Moses Hess, a prospective co-editor. The only completed work was Engels' translation of several chapters from Fourier's *On the Three Outward Unities* which, together with an introduction and a conclusion by Engels, appeared in a periodical as "A Fragment of Fourier's on Trade".

In 1845 Marx wrote his article "Peuchet: On Suicide", which appeared in the January 1846 issue of the Elberfeld journal *Gesellschaftsspiegel*. In it Marx made a bourgeois lawyer, statistician and keeper of the police archives in Paris, Jacques Peuchet, testify against bourgeois society, by quoting from his memoirs, for which Peuchet had drawn on the archives, revealing the repugnant aspects of bourgeois morality and way of life, the social cause of suicide like penury and unemployment, and the moral and psychological stress which drove men to this act of desperation. The bourgeois world, Marx emphasised, is ruled by gross self-seeking. It inflicts constant affronts on human beings, leaving them spiritually empty and disillusioned; it is a world of bigotry, hypocrisy, debased sentiments, and degraded family relations.

EARLY FOLLOWERS

For Marx and Engels the theoretical formulation of their revolutionary principles always went hand in hand with spreading these views within the working-class emancipation movement. Recalling this period, Engels wrote: "It was our duty to provide a scientific substantiation for our view, but it was equally important for us to win over the European, and in the first place the German, proletariat to our conviction." [1] Accordingly, in their very first year in Brussels, they made a point of establishing relations with revolutionary intellectuals and progressive workers.

At first they spread their ideas not so much through the medium of the press—to which they had limited access—as through personal contacts with revolutionary emigrants in Brussels, Belgian democrats, and friends who had remained in Germany and France. The best men of the day flocked to Marx and Engels, and a nucleus of kindred spirits soon formed among those who associated with them. For many acceptance of the new outlook meant revising and shattering old ideas, and overcoming petty-bourgeois ideological influences, a process that was rarely swift or complete. Marx and Engels worked hard to promote the formation of this first band of proletarian revolutionaries.

Many of their friends, like Marx and Engels themselves, came from Prussia's Rhine Province. When Marx left Paris for Brussels he was accompanied by Heinrich Bürgers, who stayed there until the autumn of 1845 and then returned to Cologne, where he was active in spreading Marx's views. A young doctor, Roland Daniels, who had met Marx in Paris in November 1844, kept in touch with Marx when he returned home to Cologne. Daniels' meeting with Marx was a turning point in his life. It exerted a strong influence on his outlook and he soon became a devoted supporter of Marx's doctrine.

During their stay in Brussels, Marx and Engels also became friendly with a retired artillery officer, Joseph Weydemeyer, who had taken up journalism after resigning from the Prussian army in 1845 because of his oppositionist views. He began to take an interest in socialist ideas, and wrote one of the first reviews in Germany of Engels' book *The Condition of the Working Class in England*. Soon Weydemeyer became "one of the most stalwart champions of the German workers' party",[2] and was later to play an outstanding role in spreading scientific communism in the United States.

---

[1] Marx, Engels, *Collected Works*, Vol. 26, pp. 318-19.
[2] Ibid., Vol. 20, p. 24.

The talented German poet and journalist, Georg Weerth, who had made friends with Engels in England in 1843, made a short visit to Brussels in the summer of 1845 and settled there in the spring of 1846 as an agent for a German commercial firm. He had already published some essays, articles and poems about the plight of the working class and its growing revolutionary mood. In his poem *Gunsmiths* the workers say that when the hour of battle strikes, they will cast four-and-twenty-pounders for their own cause.

Weerth's close friendship with Marx and Engels after Brussels and their ideological influence helped to make his verse revolutionary and communist, so that he became the "first and *most important* poet of the German proletariat".[1] He wrote the *Songs of the Journeymen*, his best revolutionary cycle of poems, at a time when he was in close contact with Marx and Engels.

Marx also had a decisive influence on Ferdinand Freiligrath, another revolutionary poet. Until 1844 he was a romantic, enthusing over a spurious exoticism and preaching "art for art's sake", but later there were signs of his turning to reality, and revolutionary strains rang in his verse. In February 1845, Freiligrath and Marx met in Brussels, and although Freiligrath soon left for Switzerland, he carried away a strong impression of his new friend. In spite of the fact that his verse was strongly tainted with "true socialism", some of his poems indicated that he had come to accept some communist ideas as well. In *From the Depths Upwards!*, for instance, he gave this poetic expression to his sense of the mighty revolutionary potential latent in the working class, a sense he had developed under the influence of Marx and Engels:

> We are the strength! We are recasting that old,
>   rotten thing, the state,
> Downtrodden still as proletariat by God above irate.[2]

A later arrival in Brussels than the others was Wilhelm Wolff, a man destined to become one of the closest associates and friends of Marx and Engels. The son of a serf peasant, a teacher in Silesia, he had become known for his bold statements in the press, especially his descriptions of the Breslau slums, and his open stand in defence of the 1844 Silesian weavers' revolt.

Harassed by the police, Wolff emigrated to England, and in April 1846 came to live in Brussels, where he at once sought out Marx and Engels. Engels subsequently described their meeting as follows: "Marx and I were then living in a Brussels suburb; we were engaged in a joint piece of work, when we were informed that a gentleman from Germany wished to speak to us.... It was Wilhelm Wolff.... A few days were enough to put us on terms of cordial friendship with this new comrade in exile and to convince us that it was no or-

---

[1] Ibid., Vol. 26, p. 110.
[2] *Freiligraths Werke*, in einem Band, Weimar, 1962, S. 89.

dinary man we were dealing with. His cultured mind schooled in classical antiquity, his wealth of humour, his clear understanding of difficult theoretical problems, his passionate hatred of all oppressors of the masses, his energetic and yet tranquil nature soon revealed themselves; but it took long years of collaboration and friendly association in struggle, victory and defeat, in good times and bad, to prove the full extent of his unshakable strength of character, his absolute, unquestionable reliability, his steadfast sense of duty equally exacting towards friend, foe and self." [1]

Soon Marx's circle of friends and acquaintances included some emigrant workers, among them the type-setters Wallau and Born, and the German worker Junge, who had moved from Paris to Brussels.

Marx also had an influence on the more revolutionary-minded Belgian democrats, helping them to side with the proletariat. Among his Belgian friends, for instance, were Philippe Gigot, candidate of philosophy and belles-lettres, and Victor Tedesco, a Liège lawyer and revolutionary writer, who got to know Marx and Engels later, in 1847.

Marx also maintained close relations with men who were revolutionary democrats but did not accept communist views, like Joachim Lelewel, the eminent Polish historian and revolutionary, who played an active part in the Polish uprising of 1830-31 and was the leader of the revolutionary-democratic wing of the Polish emigrants. He became a friend of the Marx family, and was a frequent visitor.

TRIP TO ENGLAND

In the summer of 1845, Marx and Engels went to England, then the most developed capitalist state, to make a study of English writings, mainly economic, which were not available in Brussels, and of socio-economic conditions in that country. They stayed in London and Manchester for about six weeks, from July 12 to August 21, and this gave Marx a better view of the characteristic features of capitalist society which were not as pronounced or developed elsewhere.

Of great importance for Marx was his first-hand knowledge of the working-class movement in England and his personal contacts with its leaders. By then the English proletariat had reached a relatively high level of political awareness and organisation. For a decade the British Isles had been the arena of a powerful working-class struggle for a People's Charter, led by the National Charter Association founded in 1840, which had a network of local organisations. At the height of the Chartist movement it had a membership of almost

---

[1] Marx, Engels, *Collected Works*, Vol. 24, p. 131.

50,000. The Chartists had considerable experience in organising mass meetings and demonstrations and in publishing periodicals. When Marx arrived, the movement was just gathering momentum after a slight decline following an unsuccessful workers' strike in 1842, organised by the Chartists, and heading for its strong final upsurge in 1847 and 1848.

It was Engels who, in his book about the conditions of the working class in England, gave the first scientific definition of Chartism as a political movement of the working class with deep social roots and objectively aimed against the capitalist system. Marx and Engels were faced with the task of continuing their study of the Chartist movement in the light of their philosophical and political ideas, and of summarising its experience further to formulate their proposition about the role of the working class in world history, and to clarify the forms of its struggle and real ways of emancipation from capitalist oppression.

Equally important was the experience of the English trade unions, then a force to be reckoned with, and of the proletarian and democratic organisations established in England by revolutionary emigrants. London was one of the centres of the German League of the Just, which was developing into an international organisation. As early as 1840, its leaders had set up the German Workers' Educational Society in London.

Engels was an ideal guide. He had lived in England for almost two years, and had gained an excellent knowledge of English, which Marx was yet to learn. Engels also knew many Chartist leaders, and was correspondent for several Chartist and socialist newspapers, including *The Northern Star*, the main Chartist organ. During his stay in London in 1843, he got to know the leaders of the League of the Just, Joseph Moll, Karl Schapper and Heinrich Bauer, and he introduced Marx into their circle. Well acquainted with English scientific writings, he gave Marx many pointers in this field.

The two men spent many hours together in the reading room at a Manchester library, founded in 1653 by Humphrey Chetham, a local merchant, in what had been a medieval castle, and later a monastery. They had their favourite places, and Engels recalled this in a letter to Marx in 1870, when he wrote: "In the last few days I have often been sitting at the quadrilateral desk in the small low-window where we sat 24 years ago; I like this place very much; because of its coloured window the weather is always fine there. Old Jones the librarian is still around, but he is very old and does nothing more." [1]

In England, Marx and Engels got to know the prominent Left-wing Chartist leader, George Julian Harney, who was from the working class, a talented organiser, speaker and writer. He was a socialist follower of Babeuf's communist ideas and one of the edi-

---

[1] Marx, Engels, *Collected Works*, Vol. 43, p. 518.

tors of *The Northern Star*. Unlike many other Chartists who were somewhat wary of the revolutionary movement abroad, Harney favoured joint action by Chartists and revolutionaries on the continent. Through him, Marx and Engels later came to know Ernest Jones, another revolutionary Chartist leader, who joined the movement in January 1846.

During their stay in London, Marx and Engels did their utmost to strengthen ties between the Left-wing Chartists and members of the League of the Just. In mid-August 1845, they attended a conference of Chartists and emigrants of various nationalities at the Angel Tavern in Webber Street. Voicing his own and Marx's view of the matters discussed there, Engels warmly supported the idea suggested at the meeting of setting up an international revolutionary organisation in London. Such an organisation — the Fraternal Democrats — was indeed set up in London on September 22, 1845, after Marx and Engels had left. It was run by proletarians: Left-wing Chartists (primarily Harney and later also Jones), and leaders of the League of the Just, Schapper and Moll. Weitling was among those who attended the inaugural meeting.

The founding of the Fraternal Democrats was a clear sign that the leading proletarians were developing a sense of international solidarity. Marx and Engels maintained contacts with the society, seeking to give its activity a revolutionary proletarian orientation, and to help its leaders discard their petty-bourgeois illusions. Engels took advantage of the September 22, 1845 meeting to formulate in the press the principles of proletarian internationalism. In his article, "The Festival of Nations in London", he wrote on behalf of Marx and himself: "... Proletarians in all countries have one and the same interest, one and the same enemy, and one and the same struggle. The great mass of proletarians are, by their very nature, free from national prejudices and their whole disposition and movement is essentially humanitarian, anti-nationalist. Only the proletarians can destroy nationality, only the awakening proletariat can bring about fraternisation between the different nations."[1]

CRITICAL STUDY OF POLITICAL ECONOMY AND SOCIALIST LITERATURE

A prominent feature of Marx's scientific work in Brussels and during his visit to England was an inquiry into political economy and utopian socialist writings which were critical of the bourgeois system. Marx was collecting material for an analysis of the economic foundations of bourgeois society and a critical review of the accepted economic tenets. He made a study of the most diverse economic writings over the centuries and of his own day. In Brussels and

---

[1] Marx, Engels, *Collected Works*, Vol. 6, p. 6.

Manchester he wrote up several notebooks filled with extracts from various authors.

Marx was interested in such questions as the use of machinery in capitalist production, price formation and circulation of money, and credit and banking operations. Marx made a vast amount of excerpts on the history of economic development in Europe, America and Asia, and on population problems.

Marx's study of the social consequences of capitalist development centred on the condition of the working class—the proletariat—with special emphasis on the working and living conditions of the masses in England, the classic capitalist country. Apart from Engels' well-known book on the subject, he went through many other sources. He was also deeply concerned with the mass impoverishment in other countries.

As he read the works of contemporary bourgeois economists (among them Nassau Senior, John McCulloch, John Stuart Mill and Charles Ganilh) he perceived an increasingly apologetic trend, in general a feature of bourgeois political economy. In Smith and Ricardo's day, bourgeois economists, for all the limitations of their outlook, sought to get at the scientific truth, but those who came after them deliberately avoided the objective scientific approach by trying to obscure the contradictions of capitalism, and to put a gloss on reality so as to safeguard the exploitative system.

Marx noted signs of this deterioration when comparing John Stuart Mill's *Essays on Some Unsettled Questions of Political Economy* with the economic writings of his father, James Mill, who had drawn some radical conclusions from Ricardo's doctrine: "This *Mill Junior* provides a remarkable example of the desperate straits in which the *theorising bourgeois* finds himself." [1]

Among the bourgeois apologists Marx ranked the Free Traders, and continued to study the works of their opponents, the protectionists. In the autumn of 1845, in view of the acute polemics between the two schools, each of which was striving to present its system as a panacea for all social ills, Marx and Engels even contemplated the publication of a joint work on protectionism and Free Trade.

Marx also took a profound interest in writings criticising the capitalist system. He had read the French and German utopian socialists even before he came to Brussels, where he got down to a study of English utopian socialism. He made a thorough study of the works of Robert Owen, especially his principal work, *The Book of the New Moral World*. He also devoted much attention to the writings of John Bray, Thomas Edmonds, William Thompson and others of Owen's followers who sought to substantiate utopian socialist doctrines with the help of Ricardo's economic doctrine, and who gave his labour theory of value a socialist interpretation.

---

[1] MEGA, Abt. 1, Bd. 6, Halbband 2, S. 609.

While giving them credit for their sincere urge to do away with the exploitation and poverty of the labouring classes, Marx took a highly sceptical view of their utopian plans for arranging socialist relations in society on the basis of tenets borrowed from bourgeois political economy, such as bazaars for exchanging products at cost, and "labour money", and said that these social recipes came from an idealistic, dream world. Commenting on Thompson's fundamentally faulty methods, he said: "Thompson believes that anything can be done by talking about 'equal security', 'voluntary exchange', etc." [1]

Nor did Marx ignore the writings of those who expressed the aristocratic opposition to bourgeois society in the form of a "feudal socialism". He read the *Christian Political Economy* by the French writer Villeneuve-Bargemont, and *Chartism* by Thomas Carlyle, the English historian and idealist philosopher, who stood close to that trend. Their attacks on the existing bourgeois order went hand in hand with an idyllic view of precapitalist relations, and a reactionary call for a return to the past. This critique of capitalism from the Right betrayed a total ignorance of the laws of social development.

Marx also read *Essays on Political Economy* by Sismondi, a prominent Swiss economist, a representative of economic romanticism who criticised capitalist relations but took an unhistorical view of the past, especially petty commodity production. Marx remarked that "here and there" Sismondi "tends to idealise the ancient order of things".[2]

Marx tackled the problems of political economy and other social sciences according to a definite scheme. Ever since his *Economic and Philosophic Manuscripts of 1844,* he had been projecting in his mind's eye the outlines of a vast work analysing the whole economic structure of contemporary society and its principal political institutions in the light of revolutionary communism. Before leaving for Brussels on February 1, 1845, he had signed a contract with the Darmstadt publisher Leske for the publication of a book entitled *Critique of Politics and Political Economy.*

Informed of these plans, Marx's most intimate friends attached exceptional importance to his economic work. Roland Daniels wrote to him on March 7, 1846: "We are eagerly awaiting your Political Economy." [3] In a letter on April 30, 1846, Weydemeyer wrote: "One thing you must try to do is to have your Political Economy out as soon as possible; after all, we have essentially nothing to offer those who are eager to read something sensible about communism, because they refuse to accept general statements or believe that communism can be *introduced* through universal education." [4]

The police authorities got wind of Marx's intention to publish his

---

[1] MEGA, Abt. 1, Bd. 6, Halbband 2, S. 615.
[2] Ibid.
[3] MEGA, Abt. 3, Bd. 1, S. 514.
[4] Ibid., S. 533.

work in Darmstadt, and made their disapproval of the idea known to Leske in no uncertain terms. Marx objected strongly, when Leske tried to commit him to confine himself to purely scientific matters. On August 1, 1846, he wrote to Leske to tell him that he had no intention of adapting his work to the requirements of a reactionary censorship and of sacrificing its revolutionary content. He added that his book was a scientific one, "but not scientific as understood by the Prussian government".[1] On September 19, 1846, Leske informed Marx that he would not be able to publish his work in view of the strict censorship.

In spite of all these obstacles, Marx continued his theoretical studies. In his research on politico-economic problems, which also quite naturally helped to shape his general theoretical and general philosophical conceptions, he discovered that if he was to produce a critique of earlier economic theories and formulate a new economic doctrine the first thing he must do was reformulate the methodological principles which constituted its philosophical foundation. It was necessary to clear the ground for a new world outlook, so as to prepare men's minds to receive new politico-economic ideas. In other words, the critique of political economy had to be prefaced with a critique of the accepted philosophical and social doctrines. That is why the scheme for a book on political economy had to be shelved temporarily to give priority to the more important idea of writing a polemical philosophical work directed against the ideological opponents of proletarian socialism in Germany, a work which Marx and Engels called *The German Ideology*.

In early August 1846, Marx wrote the following about his list of priorities: "It seemed to me very important to *precede* my *positive* development with a polemical piece against German philosophy and *German socialism* up till the present. This is necessary in order to prepare the public for the viewpoint adopted in my Economy, which is diametrically opposed to German scholarship past and present."[2]

WORK ON *THE GERMAN IDEOLOGY*

By the autumn of 1845 Marx and Engels had evolved a more concrete plan for publishing a new philosophical work. This was to be a two-volume critique of German ideology—German philosophy as represented by men like Feuerbach, Bauer, Stirner, and by German "true socialism", for in an article earlier that summer, Feuerbach had publicly proclaimed himself to be a "communist", in September the "true socialists" had published several fundamental works, and, most importantly, mid-October saw the issue of Volume 3 of *Wigand's Vierteljahrsschrift*, containing articles by Bauer and Stirner.

---

[1] Marx, Engels, *Collected Works*, Vol. 38, p. 48.
[2] Ibid., p. 50.

The German Ideology was conceived as a collective work under the editorship of Marx. Some of the critical chapters were to be written by Moses Hess, but this arrangement did not materialise because Hess, a founder of "true socialism", was easily swayed by various influences (Marx ironically called him the "sponge") and so inclined to eclecticism. He had a purely superficial understanding of some features of the new materialist doctrine, and was soon back in the other camp.

Hess had written two chapters: one attacking the Young Hegelian Arnold Ruge, and the other, the "true socialist" Georg Kuhlmann, but the former was omitted from the final text, and the latter heavily edited by Marx and Engels.

In writing *The German Ideology*, Marx and Engels attained a new and higher form of co-operation, which was quite different from their work on *The Holy Family*, when their division of labour was quite simple: according to an agreed plan each wrote his own sections, and this was stated in the contents. But *The German Ideology*, especially its first volume, was literally written jointly by the two men, who believed collective research to be a basic principle of modern science, and produced a fine illustration of it. However, it was Marx who played the decisive role in working out the materialist view of history and the theory of scientific communism. Many years later, after his friend's death, Engels wrote with characteristic modesty that most of the fundamental ideas, especially their final formulation, had come from Marx. "Marx stood higher, saw further, and took a wider and quicker view than all the rest of us. Marx was a genius; we others were at best talented. Without him the theory would not be by far what it is today. It therefore rightly bears his name."[1]

Marx and Engels worked on their book day and night, totally absorbed in the task. George Harney wrote to Engels on March 30, 1846: "When I informed my wife of your very philosophical system of writing in couples till 3 or 4 o'clock in the morning, she protested that such philosophy would not suit her, and that if she was in Brussels she would get up a 'pronunciamento' amongst your wives. My wife has no objection to the manufacturing of revolutions, provided the work is done on the *short time system*."[2]

The German Ideology showed the two men to be brilliant masters of polemics, whose power was multiplied by their joint work. Sorting out Marx's manuscripts after his death, and discovering *The German Ideology* among them, Engels read one of the chapters to Marx's youngest daughter Eleanor and Helene Demuth, who were greatly entertained. Helene Demuth, Engels wrote in a letter to Marx's daughter Laura on June 2, 1883, declared: "Now at last I know why that time in Brussels you two laughed so much at night that nobody in the house could sleep." Engels added: "We were

---

[1] Marx, Engels, *Collected Works*, Vol. 26, p. 382.
[2] Central Party Archives of the Institute of Marxism-Leninism.

bold devils then, Heine's poetry is childlike innocence compared with our prose."[1]

Marx and Engels started to write *The German Ideology* in November 1845, but its final structure did not take shape immediately. They began with a general critique of Bauer's and Stirner's articles published in Volume 3 of *Wigand's Vierteljahrsschrift* and Feuerbach's works. Later they decided to present the former in two special chapters, preceded by a general introduction in the form of a chapter on Feuerbach, containing a critical analysis of his ideas and a brief exposition of their own views. Accordingly, Marx and Engels twice interrupted their critique of Stirner in order to transfer extensive theoretical digressions from this chapter to the introduction, putting mainly critical material in their place. On the other hand, the purely polemical passages directed against Bauer and Stirner were transferred from the introduction to Chapter II and Chapter III. In this way, the material of the first volume was differentiated and sorted out, and its structure crystallised.

The most important section from the theoretical point of view is the first, introductory chapter of Volume I ("I. Feuerbach. Opposition of the Materialist and Idealist Outlooks"). Here Marx and Engels expound their views directly for the most part, whereas in the other chapters this is done mostly by criticising their opponents. The preface, which remained uncompleted, gives a more or less systematic exposition of the materialist view of history and of the theory of scientific communism. The other two chapters of Volume I are mainly a critique of the Young Hegelian philosophy: one of Bruno Bauer ("II. Saint Bruno") and the other of Max Stirner ("III. Saint Max"). They satirise Bauer's and Stirner's articles in *Wigand's Vierteljahrsschrift* (which was published in Leipzig) as a "Leipzig Council", with a general introduction to these two chapters entitled "The Leipzig Council" and a special conclusion entitled "Close of the Leipzig Council".

The chapter on Stirner was the longest and structurally most complicated. Stirner's book, *The Unique and His Property,* which had appeared at the end of October 1844 in Leipzig, was in theoretical terms a characteristic product of the vulgarised and degraded classical German philosophy, with all of Hegel's accomplishments dissipated and the defects magnified out of all proportion. Hegel's objective idealism was reduced to pure subjectivism and voluntarism, his dialectics to sophistry, his criticism to phrase-mongering. Stirner preached an extreme individualism. His individualist-anarchist ideas were a reflection of the discontent among the German petty bourgeois over the development of capitalism, but were essentially hostile to communism and any encroachments on private property. It was also necessary to attack the author of *The Unique and His Property*—his article in Wigand's quarterly only served as a pretext for

---

[1] Frederick Engels, Paul and Laura Lafargue, *Correspondence*, Vol. 1, Moscow, 1959, p. 137.

criticising his main work — because in the conditions then obtaining in Germany Stirner's views were exerting some influence on the petty bourgeoisie, the intellectuals and — indirectly — the working-class movement.

Volume II of *The German Ideology* contains a critique of "true socialism" according to its "various prophets". A typical feature of this brand of petty-bourgeois socialism, which began to spread in Germany in 1844, was a conjunction of German philosophy, notably that of Hegel and Feuerbach, with utopian socialist doctrines, mainly those propounded by the French. The result was a socialist doctrine that was highly abstract and divorced from reality and practical needs. Instead of the proletariat's liberation through class struggle and social revolution, "true socialists" advocated mankind's liberation through the sentimental preaching of love. Expression of the reactionary interests of the German petty bourgeois, who was terrified by the advance of capitalism, it was an open call against revolutionary communism, said to have "grossly destructive" urges. This trend had to be combated because it stood in the way of the communist world outlook.

Chapter I of Volume II contains a critique of articles by Friedrich Semmig and Rudolph Matthäi setting out the philosophy of "true socialism"; Chapter IV contains a critique of a book by Karl Grün, the main exponent of this trend, who gave a specimen of the historiography of "true socialism"; and Chapter V a critique of a book by Georg Kuhlmann, setting out something like the "true socialist" religion. The extant manuscript of *The German Ideology* does not contain Chapters II and III. It is quite possible that Engels' article "German Socialism in Verse and Prose" published in the autumn of 1847, and criticising the verse and prose of "true socialists" was a part of Volume II.

Work on *The German Ideology* was completed for the most part in April 1846, but it went on over the following year, and culminated with Engels' article "The True Socialists" as a direct continuation of Volume II.

REVOLUTION IN VIEWS OF SOCIAL DEVELOPMENT

Up to the 1848 revolution Marx concentrated on formulating his philosophy as the foundation of all his theory. It was natural, therefore, that *The German Ideology*, the major work of that period, was principally a philosophical one. It is outstanding as the first more or less systematic exposition of the materialist view of history (historical materialism).

Marx and Engels elaborated the new world outlook in a critique of German post-Hegelian philosophy. The central issue in this polemic was: how is existing reality to be changed? The Young Hegelians criticised existing reality indirectly, by attacking religion, and so fighting not reality itself, but its shadows. In fact, they accepted existing reality, and merely sought to give it a different interpretation. Marx and Engels set themselves the task of discrediting this philosophical struggle with illusions once and for all and showed that it was not enough to criticise the world; it had to be correctly explained and — the main thing — changed.

The German Ideology presented the materialist view of history in three parts: the premises, the concept and the conclusions.

Marx and Engels started by first formulating their premises, namely, real individuals, their activity and the material conditions of their activity, which are simultaneously the premises of history itself and of the materialist view of history. In contrast to the German idealists, who followed Hegel in claiming that their philosophy made do without premises, for all premises were dogmatic, *The German Ideology* gave a consistently materialist and dialectical answer to the cardinal question of philosophy: what should be the point of departure in constructing the new world outlook? Marx and Engels admitted that they had deliberately proceeded from definite premises — in no sense dogmatic or speculative, but real — and went on to state them.

Overcoming the inconsistency of earlier materialism, which took the metaphysical view that nature was immutable, Marx and Engels showed that the natural conditions in which men live and act are also historical, and drew a distinction between the natural conditions which man finds in existence and those which are created by man's own activity. In existing society the material environment itself becomes the product of man's historical activity. Considering that Feuerbach did not understand and ignored the retroactive effect exerted by man on nature, Marx and Engels wrote: "So much is this activity, this unceasing sensuous labour and creation, this production, the foundation of the whole sensuous world as it now exists, that were it interrupted only for a year, Feuerbach would not only find an enormous change in the natural world, but would very soon find that the whole world of men and his own perceptive faculty, nay his own existence, were missing."[1] The profoundly historical approach of the new theory of social development was seen in the view that as society develops, natural conditions are increasingly transformed into the historical products of man's activity.

A definite natural environment is the objective material condition for the existence and development of human society, and men's physical, corporal make up determines their attitude to the natural environment. However, Marx and Engels did not concentrate on these two prerequisites of history but on human activity as the decisive factor behind the historical process.

There are two sides to this activity: production (men's active relation to nature, their influence on it) and intercourse (men's relations

---

[1] Marx, Engels, *Collected Works*, Vol. 5, p. 40.

to one another, principally in the process of production). While production and intercourse determine each other production is the decisive factor.

Material production marked the start of man's social history, and that is what distinguishes man from animal. "Men can be distinguished from animals by consciousness, by religion or anything else you like. They themselves begin to distinguish themselves from animals as soon as they begin to *produce* their means of subsistence."[1] Marx subsequently stated this specific distinction between man and animal in more concrete terms in Volume I of his *Capital*.

The first premise of all human history is that men must be in a position to live, which means that they need food, drink, clothes and dwellings. This is why the first historical act is the production of the means to satisfy these needs. The whole of life in a given society is determined by its mode of production, with the main aspects of social activity emerging as different lines of production.

The German Ideology was not only a comprehensive statement about the decisive role of material production in the life of society, but was also an exceptionally important step forward, for in fact it clarified for the first time the dialectical development of the productive forces and the relations of production, a most important discovery—dating back to 1845—formulated as the dialectics of the productive forces and the form of intercourse. It threw fresh light on the categories of historical materialism, which were shaping into a system, and made it possible to define the substance of the materialist view of history as a coherent conception.

This discovery boils down to the following fundamental propositions. The type of social relations, the form of intercourse, is determined by the productive forces, which at a certain stage in their development come into a contradiction with the latter which is resolved by social revolution. The old form of intercourse, which becomes a fetter, gives way to a new form corresponding to the more developed productive forces. This new form of intercourse, for its part, subsequently ceases to correspond to the developing productive forces, becomes a fetter upon them, and is replaced, through revolution, by the ensuing, more progressive form of intercourse. Thus, in the course of the entire historical development a link of continuity is established between successive stages.

Marx and Engels were clearly aware of the importance of this major discovery and said so: "Thus all collisions in history have their origin, according to our view, in the contradiction between the productive forces and the form of intercourse."[2]

This discovery was of paramount importance for an understanding of the laws of social development. Earlier on, Marx had brought out the fact that political, juridical and other relations were deter-

---

[1] Marx, Engels, *Collected Works*, Vol. 5, p. 31.
[2] Ibid., p. 74.

mined by economic relations: Marx and Engels had now established what determined economic relations themselves, thus delving more deeply into the foundation of the historical process: that all relations between men are ultimately determined by the productive forces, whose development determines the transition from one form of society to another. Marx had earlier shown material production to be the basis of all social life; now he revealed the inner working of the basis itself, thereby bringing out the connection between the main sides of social life: the productive forces and the relations of production, the whole body of production relations and the political superstructure, and also the forms of social consciousness.

Marx's discovery gave a scientific explanation of the entire historical process, and made possible a truly scientific periodisation of history. Social revolutions, which resolve the contradictions between the productive forces and the relations of production, are the milestones that mark off the principal epochs and constitute the transition from one form of society to another, or from one social formation to another, to use Marx's subsequent term.

The German Ideology brought out the main phases in the historical development of production, which rests on the development of the productive forces, whose level is indicated by the division of labour. Every stage in the division of labour determines the corresponding form of property (and, as Marx subsequently pointed out, property relations are "the legal expression" of the relations of production).

On the strength of these new ideas, Marx and Engels outlined the development of society from its inception to the forthcoming transition to communism, the truly humane society.

The first, naturally evolved, division of labour, which determined the first, tribal form of property, corresponded to the primitive historical relations. Transition from these to the following stage of social development was determined by the development of the productive forces, a transition from a natural to a social division of labour which took the form of the division of society into classes. That was a transition from classless to class society. With the social division of labour there also developed such derivative historical phenomena as private property, the state, and the estrangement of social activity. Advance in the social division of labour determines the further development and succession of the forms of property. The second form of property is ancient property, the third, feudal property, and the fourth, bourgeois property. In fact, the social formations theory started from an identification and analysis of the successive forms of property prevailing at the main stages of historical development.

Marx and Engels examined, in greater detail than other historical forms of property, the prehistory and main stages of development of the last, bourgeois form of private property: the transition from the guild system to manufacture and large-scale industry. For the first time they brought out and analysed the two main phases in the development of bourgeois society: manufacture and the large-scale industry. Earlier, in his *Economic and Philosophic Manuscripts of 1844*, Marx—in contrast to his predecessors, the utopian critics of private property—had shown the emergence of private property and its existence at a definite stage in mankind's social development, together with its inevitable abolition in the future, to be a historical necessity. *The German Ideology* demonstrated that only with the development of large-scale industry did the necessity and the material conditions for the abolition of private property arise.

The development of the productive forces in the midst of bourgeois society creates the two basic material premises of the proletarian, communist revolution. Firstly, production rises to a high level which, while being fundamentally incompatible with private property, is necessary for organising society on communist lines, and secondly, mass proletarianisation leads to the formation of a revolutionary class. This proposition has become one of the most important elements of the theory of scientific communism. Marx and Engels proved that the communist revolution abolishes private property and effects the transition to a classless society.

Marx and Engels then went on to examine the sphere of intercourse, that is, social relations, the social system, the class structure of society, and the relations between individuals, classes and society. They took the formation of bourgeois society to show the regularities behind the formation of classes, establishing for the first time the connection between the formation and development of classes and the development of material production itself, and showing, in scientific terms, how society would be rid of class distinctions.

Further, considering the political superstructure, they laid special stress on the relation of state and law to property, giving for the first time the scientific view of the essence of the state, in general, and of the bourgeois state, in particular. The state is the form in which the individuals of ruling class assert their common interests, and in which the whole civil society (that is, economic relations) of an epoch is epitomised. Marx and Engels pointed out that the bourgeois state is nothing more than a form of political organisation the bourgeois are compelled to adopt if they are to have mutual guarantee of their property and interests at home and abroad. They showed that the emergence of the state is the result of the division of society into classes, that it will therefore disappear with the abolition of classes as a result of the communist revolution.

Marx and Engels completed their exposition of the materialist conception of society and its history with an examination of the forms of social consciousness, bringing out, in particular, the relationship between the predominant consciousness and the ruling class, and showing the class character of the ideological superstructure. *The German Ideology* was the first comprehensive application of the class approach to ideological trends, and of the party principle to philosophy.

It also gave the materialist solution to the basic question of philosophy, namely, the relationship between consciousness and being: "Consciousness [*das Bewusstsein*] can never be anything else than conscious being [*das bewusste Sein*], and the being of men is their actual life-process.... It is not consciousness that determines life, but life that determines consciousness."[1] This idea of men's being was a fundamentally new one: it was not surrounding nature, as Feuerbach, for instance, believed, but chiefly social being, the real process of men's life in which their material practical activity had the decisive part to play. It was not enough to establish, as Feuerbach did, that the various products of the mind are of earthly, material origin. It was also necessary to show the growth of every form and product of social consciousness from the material, earthly basis and its contradictions. Thus Marx and Engels consistently applied materialism in examining every aspect and phenomenon of social life: production and social relations, the state, law, morality, religion and philosophy, and the general course, the concrete periods and the events of history.

The materialist view of history was summed up in these words: "This conception of history thus relies on expounding the real process of production—starting from the material production of life itself—and comprehending the form of intercourse connected with and created by this mode of production, i. e., civil society in its various stages, as the basis of all history; describing it in its action as the state, and also explaining how all the different theoretical products and forms of consciousness, religion, philosophy, morality, etc., etc., arise from it, and tracing the process of their formation from that basis; thus the whole thing can, of course, be depicted in its totality (and therefore, too, the reciprocal action of these various sides on one another). It has not, like the idealist view of history, to look for a category in every period, but remains constantly on the real *ground* of history; it does not explain practice from the idea but explains the formation of ideas from material practice, and accordingly it comes to the conclusion ... that not criticism but revolution is the driving force of history, also of religion, of philosophy and all other kinds of theory."[2]

The main conclusion from the materialist view of history is that the proletarian, communist revolution is historically necessary and inevitable. In *The German Ideology*, the theory of scientific communism appears as a corollary of historical materialism.

In contrast to the utopians, who saw communism as an abstract plan for a future social idyll, Marx and Engels saw it as a law-governed result of objective historical development: "Communism is for us not a *state of affairs* which is to be established, an *ideal* to which reality [will] have to adjust itself. We call communism the

---

[1] Marx, Engels, *Collected Works*, Vol. 5, pp. 36-37.
[2] Ibid., pp. 53-54.

real movement which abolishes the present state of things."[1]

Having established the fact that the contradiction between the productive forces and the form of intercourse is the objective basis of any social revolution, they also proved the communist revolution to be inevitable, since the productive forces created by large-scale industry come into contradiction with private property, which has become a fetter on production, and are converted into destructive forces. This objective contradiction is at the basis of the class struggle between the proletariat and the bourgeoisie, a struggle which only a proletarian, communist revolution can resolve. Having defined the material premises of this revolution, Marx and Engels set out the scientific proof that large industrial cities are the centres where communist movements originate.

The German Ideology said that to advance to a communist society the proletariat must win political power through revolution: "Every class which is aiming at domination, even when its domination, as is the case with the proletariat, leads to the abolition of the old form of society in its entirety and of domination in general, must first conquer political power."[2] That was the first general statement of the idea of the proletarian dictatorship. Many years later, after Marx's death, Engels wrote: "Marx and I, ever since 1845, have held the view that *one* of the final results of the future proletarian revolution will be the gradual dissolution and ultimate disappearance of that political organisation called *the state*.... At the same time we have always held that in order to arrive at this and the other, far more important ends of the social revolution of the future, the proletarian class will first have to possess itself of the organised political force of the state and with its aid stamp out the resistance of the capitalist class and re-organise society."[3]

Earlier in the *Theses on Feuerbach*, Marx formulated the idea that in revolutionary practice the transformation of circumstances coincides with the change in men themselves. *The German Ideology* stressed that "the revolution is necessary, therefore, not only because the *ruling* class cannot be ovethrown in any other way, but also because the class *overthrowing* it can only in a revolution succeed in ridding itself of all the muck of ages and become fitted to found society anew".[4]

Finally, *The German Ideology* gives a broad outline of the future communist society. Avoiding the dogmatic structuring of the communist system in detail, as some utopian socialists were wont to do, it sketched only those features which it was possible at the time to anticipate from an analysis of actual social tendencies.

Marx and Engels emphasised that the organisation of communism was "essentially economic".[5] It would be a society without

[1] Marx, Engels, *Collected Works*, Vol. 5, p. 49.
[2] Ibid., p. 47.
[3] Ibid., Vol. 24, pp. 477-78.
[4] Ibid., Vol. 5, p. 53.
[5] Ibid., p. 81.

private ownership of the means of production, property being under the control of associated individuals, of society as a whole. There would be no division into classes, that is, no political domination of one class over the others, or any state as an instrument of such domination. It would, in general, have no division of labour on class lines, and consequently no antithesis between town and country, or between mental and physical labour; men would no longer be tied down to a given occupation for a lifetime. Men's activity would cease to confront them as an alien force. Labour would no longer be an activity under external compulsion, and would become a truly self-activity of free men. Society would be a real association of men, a genuine and not an illusory unity. Once united, men would control the conditions of society's vital activity, consciously organising their joint efforts, regulating production, and developing the whole of society according to a general plan. Men themselves, and their consciousness, would be transformed, together with the material conditions of their activity.

Thus, on the basis of the dialectical-materialist conception, Marx and Engels elaborated the theory of the proletarian revolution and the communist society.

Engels pointed out on various subsequent occasions that two of Marx's great discoveries — the materialist view of history, and the theory of surplus value — had helped to transform socialism from a utopia into a science. The first was made in a series of works begun in the summer of 1843, when Marx commenced his criticism of Hegel's philosophy of law, was completed in general outline in the spring of 1845, and fully stated in *The German Ideology* by Marx and Engels between November 1845 and April 1846. The second was made in the late 1850s, but the first already served as the methodological prerequisite for the second.

The elaboration of the materialist view of history was a major scientific achievement, a real revolution in social science, and one of the key elements of the revolution brought about in philosophy by Marx and Engels. For the first time, materialism was extended to the cognition of social phenomena, thereby helping to overcome the inconsistency of all earlier materialism. It was the first coherent scientific view of the whole historical process, and a truly scientific method for the study of history. By elaborating the new world outlook, Marx and Engels provided the first theoretical substantiation for scientific communism. Lenin wrote: "Marx's philosophy is a consummate philosophical materialism which has provided mankind, and especially the working class, with powerful instruments of knowledge." [1]

---

[1] V. I. Lenin, *Collected Works*, Vol. 19, p. 25.

THE MAIN THING: SELF-CLARIFICATION

It was not all plain sailing for the manuscript of *The German Ideology*, as its authors had expected. At the end of April 1846, Weydemeyer, who had taken part in copying some sections of the manuscript and who was to make the arrangements for its publication, left Brussels for Germany. Preparations were also to have been made for the publication of a quarterly and for implementing an earlier plan Marx and Engels had for publishing the translations of French and English socialist writings. Weydemeyer brought with him to Westphalia the manuscript of Volume I of *The German Ideology* (without the first chapter on Feuerbach, which was incomplete). In May and June 1846 the manuscript of Volume II was sent to him. The two volumes together came to almost 50 printed sheets.

The censors were sure to produce various obstacles to their publication. True, in most German states books of more than 20 printed sheets were exempt from any preliminary censorship, but they could be confiscated as soon as they came off press. It was, therefore, very hard to find a publisher prepared to run such a risk.

In the circumstances, Marx and Engels decided to accept help from two Westphalian entrepreneurs, Julius Meyer and Rudolph Rempel, who promised to finance the publication. These two bourgeois, who styled themselves communists, turned out to be typical "true socialists". When they had read the new work, their attitude changed. By early July 1846, it became obvious that Weydemeyer's negotiations with the two men were futile. In letters written to Marx on July 9 by Meyer and July 11 by Rempel, the offer to finance the publication of *The German Ideology* was withdrawn on the plea that their money was tied up in another venture. On December 28, 1846, Marx wrote to his Russian acquaintance, Pavel Annenkov: "You would never believe what difficulties a publication of this kind runs into in Germany, on the one hand from the police, on the other from the booksellers, who are themselves the interested representatives of all those tendencies I attack."[1]

Throughout 1846 and 1847, Marx and Engels continued their attempts to find a publisher. In November 1846 they abandoned the hope of having both volumes issued by one publisher, and in April 1847 the hope of having the two volumes published in full, and sought ways of publishing separate chapters. Only in August and September 1847 did they succeed in having a chapter from Volume II on a book by the "true socialist" Grün published in the journal *Das Westphälische Dampfboot*.

The German Ideology was first published in full in the Soviet Union in 1932, years after its authors' death. Although it did not appear during their lifetime, their efforts had not been in vain. In a preface to the book *A Contribution to the Critique of Political Economy*

---

[1] Marx, Engels, *Collected Works*, Vol. 38, p. 105.

in 1859 Marx wrote: "We abandoned the manuscript to the gnawing criticism of the mice all the more willingly since we had achieved our main purpose — self-clarification."[1]

The theoretical results it embodied provided the basis for Marx's subsequent scientific and practical endeavour. He was now fully justified in saying that in its scientific form socialism addressed itself to the workers' masses not with illusory or fantastic recipes of social renovation, but with a strictly substantiated theory designed to provide a genuine theoretical platform for the proletariat's emancipation movement. Very soon Marx had the opportunity of making public the conclusions set out in *The German Ideology*, and this he did in a more polished and perfect form in *The Poverty of Philosophy* and the *Manifesto of the Communist Party*.

---

[1] Ibid., Vol. 29, p. 264.

CHAPTER FOUR

THE START OF THE STRUGGLE FOR THE PROLETARIAN PARTY. PROGRAMME FOR THE INTERNATIONAL WORKING-CLASS MOVEMENT

> *It is high time that Communists should openly, in the face of the whole world, publish their views, their aims, their tendencies, and meet this nursery tale of the Spectre of Communism with a Manifesto of the party itself.*
>
> Karl Marx and Frederick Engels

The events in Europe heralded a period of revolutionary storms. In 1847, France, Germany, Belgium, the U.S.A. and other countries were hit by an economic crisis, which was most pronounced in England. The calamities it produced were aggravated by poor grain and potato harvests in several European countries. There was a terrible famine in Ireland as a result of a potato blight in 1845-47.

Hunger riots swept across the European continent, from Eastern Prussia to Brittany and Normandy. Workers staged strikes in France. In those countries where medieval survivals and the absolutist system were still strong (Prussia, Austria and Italy), the working people's indignation was directed against the feudal nobility, the bureaucracy, and the court camarilla, and against the financial aristocracy, which had a monopoly of power in bourgeois monarchies like France and Belgium. Under the impact of the revolutionary mood of the masses, the democratic and liberal opposition took more vigorous action. A movement for the reform of the franchise started in France in early 1847. There was also a revival of the various utopian communist and socialist trends.

In Prussia an acute conflict flared up between the government and the bourgeois opposition. In April 1847, the Prussian King Frederick William IV, who found himself in financial straits, had to call a United Provincial Diet, but its bourgeois majority refused to vote a loan until a constitution was introduced. On June 26, the King dissolved the Diet, having failed to obtain any concessions. There was also growing tension in the other German states.

The national liberation struggle of the oppressed peoples rose to a high pitch. In February 1846, the Polish revolutionaries raised the banner of national independence in the free city of Cracow, which was under the joint protectorate of Austria, Prussia and tsarist Russia, but the uprising was crushed, and Cracow was forcibly annexed to Austria. In Hungary, the national opposition, led by Lajos Kossuth, issued a demand for autonomy, a demand which also gained popularity among the Czech bourgeoisie and intelligentsia. In Austria proper, there was growing hatred among the working people and the bourgeoisie for Chancellor Metternich's police regime.

Acute dissatisfaction over Austria's rule in Northern and Central Italy, together with an urge for national unity and liberation from the despotic regimes was gathering momentum in the Italian states. In January 1848, the revolutionary upsurge led to a popular uprising in Palermo against the absolutist government of the Neapolitan Bourbons.

In England, Chartism was again on an upswing, with thousands attending meetings demanding a People's Charter in all the industrial cities in England and Scotland. Radical-democratic elements gained the upper hand in the national liberation movement in Ireland.

The citadel of European reaction, tsarist Russia, was also a scene of revolutionary ferment, as could be seen from the influence exerted on Russian society by the revolutionary-democratic views of Vissarion Belinsky and Alexander Herzen (who was forced to emigrate in 1847), the response among forward-looking Russian intellectuals to the events and the development of ideas in the West, and the secret propaganda of utopian socialism in the study-circle organised by M. V. Butashevich-Petrashevsky.

THE BRUSSELS COMMUNIST CORRESPONDENCE COMMITTEE

In the prerevolutionary period, Marx and Engels concentrated their efforts on uniting the advanced elements of the proletarian movement in a practical and immediate drive to establish a proletarian party. The conclusion about the need for the working class to have a political party of its own derived from Marx's doctrine on the role of the proletariat in world history, and his understanding of the necessity for it to win political power as an indispensable condition for the revolutionary transformation of society. As he elaborated these ideas in the light of the situation that was taking shape in Europe, he came to realise the need to separate the proletariat from bourgeois democracy and to secure for it an independent position of its own in the imminent bourgeois revolution, which was to bring the working class closer to the attainment of its own, communist goals. This task could be carried out only by the establishment of a proletarian party. The experience of existing working-class organisations, including the Chartist party, which had a mixed membership and was ideologically immature, showed that a consistently revolutionary and truly independent party of the proletariat had to be set up on a correct theoretical basis.

The task of establishing a party was a truly Herculean one. In many countries, the working-class movement was in its infancy. The industrial proletariat was concentrated at the big enterprises and was still numerically small, and semi-artisans predominated among the working class, the mass of which was scattered and inclined to follow bourgeois politicians or to accept utopian socialist theories. There were very few leading workers capable of apprehending scientific communist ideas. A vast effort was required to bring them together into a solid union.

Marx and Engels saw the future proletarian party as an international organisation, assuming that the coming communist revolution would result from revolutionary action by the working class of several capitalist countries, a view borne out by the contemporary stage of capitalist development, at which the contradictions and uneven development of capitalism had not yet been aggravated to a point where the proletarian revolution could win out in one country. It was also necessary to start organising the party by bringing together the advanced workers into an international organisation so as to overcome the existing isolation of the working-class movement within the national framework, thereby laying the foundation for its international unity. Marx and Engels also believed that the party should combine the struggle for the common international goals of the working class with the efforts to achieve the proletariat's national tasks in each country.

To set up such a party, there was need to start spreading communist ideas and strengthening the ties with leading workers and revolutionary intellectuals, above all in England, France and Germany, so as to establish unity of view through an exchange of opinion, and to outline a common mode of action. This had to be done, Marx wrote, in order to shake off the "barriers of *nationality*".[1] Marx and Engels envisaged the establishment of communist correspondence committees, maintaining constant contact with each other, as organising centres for this activity.

In early 1846, they set up the Brussels Communist Correspondence Committee, whose membership was not fixed and whose leading nucleus was made up of Marx, Engels and the Belgian Communist Philippe Gigot. Among those who served on the Committee as full-fledged members were Joseph Weydemeyer, Wilhelm Wolff, Edgar Westphalen, Ferdinand Wolff, Sebastian Seiler and Louis Heilberg. Wilhelm Weitling was also a member for some time.

The Committee discussed various matters, mostly connected with communist propaganda in various countries, and its meetings were sometimes attended by men who sympathised with the emancipation movement but did not accept communist views. Thus, a meet-

---

[1] Marx, Engels, *Collected Works*, Vol. 38, p. 39.

ing on March 30, 1846 was attended by the Russian liberal writer Pavel Annenkov, who in the 1840s and the 1850s was a member of the progressive circle of "Westerners" in Russia.

On behalf of the Committee and on its instructions correspondence was carried on with workers' and socialist leaders and organisations in the various countries. Lithographed circulars were issued on important matters. Efforts were made to raise funds for revolutionary propaganda and to cover the cost of the correspondence.

Marx and Engels sought to set up similar committees elsewhere. Through Wilhelm Wolff they established connections with various towns in Silesia, while Weydemeyer made vigorous efforts to launch such committees in Westphalia and the Rhine Province. Groups were formed in some places and maintained regular contacts with the Brussels Committee.

In charting the tactical line to be followed by the Communists in Germany, Marx and Engels advised them to support the bourgeois demands for a Constitution, freedom of the press, assembly, etc., for if these demands were met, "a new era will dawn for communist propaganda".[1] Consequently, the Communists had to take an active part in mass action against absolutism and help fulfil the tasks of the bourgeois revolution so as to create more favourable conditions for the proletariat's struggle against the bourgeoisie. Otherwise, they could well degenerate into a closed sect out of touch with the general democratic movement. Those were the tactics adopted by the associates of Marx and Engels.

Through August Ewerbeck, the Brussels Communist Correspondence Committee maintained constant ties with the Paris communities of the League of the Just. Marx's proposal to set up a correspondence committee in Paris was put into effect, but only later, in August 1846, after Engels' arrival there.

Joseph Moll, Karl Schapper and Heinrich Bauer, the leaders of the League of the Just in London, approved the idea of setting up local correspondence committees, and also formed one of their own in London, but full understanding between the Brussels and the London Committee was not reached at once, because the men in London were frequently upset by the sharp criticism of the ideologists of sectarianism made by Marx and his friends. It took great patience on Marx's part to convince them that the Brussels Committee was following the correct line.

The Brussels Committee made a special point of emphasising its solidarity with the struggle of the English Chartists. On March 25, 1846, it adopted a resolution sharply censuring the petty-bourgeois radical, Thomas Cooper, who had joined the Chartists, for his slanderous attacks on the Chartist leaders. A little later, the Brussels Communists approved Cooper's expulsion from the National Charter Association, noting the great harm he had done "by propound-

---

[1] Ibid., Vol. 6, p. 56.

ing such base and infamous old women's doctrines as that of 'non-resistance' ".[1] On July 17 of that year, the Committee sent the Chartist leader, Feargus O'Connor, a special address on behalf of the German Democratic Communists, congratulating him on his victory over a rival, an advocate of Free Trade, at a meeting in Nottingham which nominated him to stand in the coming parliamentary election (the following year he was elected to the Commons for that constituency).

THE BREAK WITH WEITLING

No sooner had the Brussels Communist Correspondence Committee begun to function than Marx became aware of the obstacle to the unity of the advanced proletarian forces presented by utopian socialist doctrines, which made it hard to overcome the ideological confusion in the working-class movement and put an end to the sectarian exclusiveness and dogmatism. They also hampered the spread of the revolutionary world outlook. Among the ideological adversaries of Marxism was a movement started by Wilhelm Weitling, a Magdeburg tailor and a self-made man.

Marx readily gave Weitling credit for his part in the development of socialist ideas. In the Paris *Vorwärts!* Marx had said that Weitling's *Guarantees of Harmony and Freedom*, published in 1842, was a "*vehement* and brilliant literary debut of the German workers.... It is enough to compare these gigantic *infant shoes* of the proletariat with the dwarfish, worn-out political shoes of the German bourgeoisie, and one is bound to prophesy that the *German Cinderella* will one day have the *figure of an athlete.*" [2]

The strength and weakness of Weitling's doctrine are best seen in his main work, *Guarantees of Harmony and Freedom*, and his pamphlet, *Humanity, as It Is and as It Should Be* (1838). Although he had little understanding of the laws of social development and his ideas of the future communist revolution were quite fantastic, his proletarian class instinct suggested that communism could be attained only through a profound popular revolution. He boldly proclaimed such a revolution to be inevitable, adding that "all existing things carry within themselves the seed and the nutriment of revolution".[3] Because of this he stood head-and-shoulders above many other utopian socialists who rejected revolutionary struggle.

Weitling likewise did much to expose the capitalist system and spread communist ideas among the artisans and workers. However, he failed to single out the working class from the whole mass of the oppressed as the force that would transform society, and believed the lumpenproletariat to be the most revolutionary element. He

---

[1] Marx, Engels, *Collected Works*, Vol. 6, p. 59.
[2] Ibid., Vol. 3, pp. 201-02.
[3] W. Weitling, *Garantien der Harmonie und Freiheit*, Berlin, 1955, S. 274.

took the simplified view of the communist revolution as a spontaneous outbreak. Because he was not clear about the laws of social development, he denied the need for a bourgeois revolution in countries like Germany, and objected to any alliance between the working class and the bourgeois democrats. In general, he rejected the idea of the working class participating in the political struggle, and was in fact opposed to the establishment of a proletarian party.

Weitling's views bore the stamp of primitive egalitarianism, and as time went on the backward aspects of his outlook became ever more pronounced. He gave a religious tenor to his communist ideas in the pamphlet, *The Gospel of a Poor Sinner* (1844). Having rejected the idea of a revolutionary transformation of society, he pinned his hopes on the establishment of communist settlements.

When Weitling arrived in Brussels in early 1846, Marx and Engels did their utmost to help him understand the scientific outlook. Weitling was quick to take offence, believed himself to be infallible, and was immune to any line of reasoning. Engels subsequently wrote: "He was no longer the naive young journeyman-tailor who, astonished at his own talents, was trying to clarify in his own mind just what a communist society would look like. He was now the great man, persecuted by the envious on account of his superiority, who scented rivals, secret enemies and traps everywhere—the prophet, driven from country to country, who carried a prescription of heaven on earth ready-made in his pocket, and who imagined that everybody was out to steal it from him." [1]

Weitling also opposed the elaboration of any communist programme or its scientific and theoretical substantiation. He insisted that the Brussels Communist Correspondence Committee should spend its funds on publishing his utopian writings and took every objection as a sign of envy, and as an attempt "to keep him away from the sources of money".[2] He also resisted the intention of Marx and Engels to put out a commented collection of the great utopian socialists' works, which he took to be "unfair competition against *his own* system".[3]

When the Brussels Committee met on March 30, 1846, this disagreement flared into open conflict. Pavel Annenkov, who happened to be present, gave this description of the meeting in his memoirs. The proceedings were opened by Engels, who stood "tall and erect and as dignified and serious as an Englishman", while Marx sat at the other end of the table, "pencil in hand and his leonine head bent over a sheet of paper". Engels spoke about the need for those who had dedicated themselves to the cause of the working people's emancipation to concert their views. Weitling's attempts to back up his standpoint by means of vague statements which revealed a disregard for revolutionary theory provoked some sharp objections from

---

[1] Marx, Engels, *Collected Works*, Vol. 26, pp. 319-20.
[2] Marx, Engels, *Werke*, Bd. 37, S. 118.
[3] Ibid.

Marx, who stressed that "to call on the workers without any strictly scientific ideas or constructive doctrine ... was equivalent to vain dishonest play at preaching which assumes an inspired prophet on the one side and on the other only gaping asses". Stung by these remarks, Weitling said the advocates of revolutionary theory were armchair scholars, out of touch with life, doctrinaires indifferent to the people's sufferings. Marx could contain himself no longer, and leaping to his feet he exclaimed with indignation: "Ignorance has never yet helped anybody."[1]

In contrast to Weitling, Marx believed that the communist movement should be purged of those who propounded vulgar and obsolete doctrines. He demanded that everyone taking part in the movement should be clear on the priority of the revolutionary tasks, and the inevitability of a bourgeois revolution in Germany, and should not succumb, like Weitling, to fantastic visions about instant communism.

Very soon, Weitling began to object to the Brussels Committee's critical attacks on "true socialism". He was rebuffed once again, and left Brussels at the end of May 1846.

The leaders of the working-class movement associated with the Brussels Committee approved of Marx's attitude to Weitling, and Marx was informed of this by Ewerbeck in a letter from Paris on May 15, 1846. Marx's line was also supported by the London leaders of the League of the Just, and the Communists of Westphalia and Cologne. However, Weitling still had many supporters in Switzerland, Paris, Hamburg and elsewhere.

THE STRUGGLE AGAINST "TRUE SOCIALISM"

Marx and Engels were increasingly aware of the urgency of joining ideological battle with "true socialism", which they had criticised in Volume II of *The German Ideology*. The prospects for its publication were receding, whereas the tasks in the struggle to unite the revolutionary forces called for resolute action against "true socialism", which at the time "spread like an epidemic".[2] Its ideologists, Karl Grün, Otto Lüning, and Hermann Püttmann, among others, were putting out a steady stream of items for newspapers, journals and almanacs, and publishing pamphlets and books. The "true socialists" controlled many organs of the press. Their ideas were penetrating into the midst of the workers, who were immature and were benighted by Weitling's ideas, which were largely similar to those of the "true socialists". Both groups failed to understand that the development of capitalism was progressive, and believed that Germany could and should leap over the capitalist stage into the "communist paradise".

---

[1] *Reminiscences of Marx and Engels*, Moscow, 1957, pp. 270-72.
[2] Marx, Engels, *Collected Works*, Vol. 6, p. 512.

"True socialism" was increasingly revealing its reactionary political tendency, as its advocates mechanically applied to Germany Fourier's and Saint-Simon's criticism of bourgeois society, ignoring the existence of a great number of feudal survivals in its social and political system, compared with which the bourgeois order they criticised was a considerable advance. They opposed the demands for a constitution, bourgeois liberties, etc., put forward by the liberal opposition and the bourgeois democrats. The "true socialists'" attacks on the liberal bourgeoisie were objectively a defence of the existing absolutist feudal regime, which is why the censors hardly ever touched their publications.

Marx and Engels had more than enough grounds for launching a broad campaign against "true socialism", especially in view of the fact that the bourgeois and petty-bourgeois opponents of the Communists now and again ascribed to them the reactionary views of the "true socialists", many of whom styled themselves Communists.

That was the main reason why at the May 5, 1846 meeting of the Brussels Committee Marx raised the question of Hermann Kriege's activity in the U.S.A. This German journalist, a disciple of Feuerbach's, had met Marx in Brussels in 1845. In the autumn of that year he went to live in New York, where, with the support of emigrant German workers, he founded the weekly *Volks-Tribun* as the organ of the German branch of the American National Reform Association, which united workers and petty bourgeois and campaigned for a law against the sale of land, and for its free allotment to the working people. On the pages of his weekly, Kriege declared the Association's agrarian programme to be the basis for a transformation of society on communist lines, and propounded universal love and brotherhood in the spirit of "true socialism".

Marx and Engels were outraged by the tone and content of his propaganda, and decided at once to disavow Kriege, who claimed to be the literary representative of German communism in America. Despite Weitling's objections, the Brussels Committee adopted a "Circular Against Kriege" written by Marx and Engels.

They said that by converting the communist doctrine into "lovesickness", Kriege was "preaching *in the name of communism* the old fantasy of religion and German philosophy which is the *direct antithesis of communism*".[1] The ideals advocated by Kriege and other "true socialists", and the illusions they were spreading about the possibility of putting an end once and for all to social inequality, pauperism and exploitation by allotting plots of land to the working people, reflected the mood of bankrupt shopkeepers and mastercraftsmen or ruined peasants "striving for the bliss of becoming petty bourgeois and peasants once more in America".[2]

Marx and Engels acknowledged that objectively this movement of American petty-bourgeois reformists against large-scale landed

[1] Marx, Engels, *Collected Works*, Vol. 6, p. 45.
[2] Ibid., p. 44.

proprietorship was progressive but denied that it was a communist one, as Kriege attempted to present it. Lenin subsequently wrote: "While mercilessly ridiculing the absurd ideological trappings of the movement, Marx strives in a sober, materialist manner to determine its *real* historical content.... Marx, therefore, does not condemn, but fully approves communist support of the movement."[1]

The "Circular Against Kriege" closely argued that the communist outlook is incompatible with religion, and consequently that to clothe communism in a religious mantle, as Kriege and other "true socialists" and also Weitling did, means deliberately vulgarising and distorting it. Religion tends to paralyse men's will to struggle; it breeds humility and submissiveness, and leads ultimately to acceptance of the existing system, while producing the narrow-minded fanaticism and extreme intolerance of "heretics", that is, those who see things in a different light. By contrast, the communist outlook helps to fortify the working people's faith in their own strength, and gives them a sense of dignity, pride, independence and breadth of view, that is, the qualities required for the revolutionary transformation of the world.

Marx's and Engels' attack on the newspaper *Volks-Tribun* was also largely aimed against Weitling's egalitarian communism, for his ideas were popular among those who followed Kriege and worked on his paper.

The criticism of Kriege's views had a sobering effect on the participants in the working-class movement in Germany, France and England who had up to then taken a tolerant attitude to the propaganda of "true socialism". Kriege's authority was shaken even among his followers in New York. The second circular against Kriege, written by Marx in October 1846 for the Brussels Committee, had a similar effect. Kriege's newspaper was wound up at the end of 1846, and his advocacy of "boundless love" proved to be a complete fiasco.

In August and September 1847, the *Westphälische Dampfboot* carried Chapter IV of Volume II of *The German Ideology*, in which Marx criticised Grün's book, *The Social Movement in France and Belgium*. Through his criticism of this book Marx exposed the ideological flaws of the whole trend: its destruction of the rational elements in French utopian socialism; its extreme helplessness to explain social phenomena, its substitution of abstract talk about "true human essence" for the scientific study of social phenomena, and so on. Marx observed that the "true socialists'" highly superficial economic views made them akin to the reactionary economists who "ignored the revolutionary element in competition and large-scale industry",[2] that is, denied that capitalism was progressive as compared with the precapitalist forms of production. Marx showed that "true socialism" had an unsound ideological basis, and that its

---

[1] V. I. Lenin, *Collected Works*, Vol. 8, p. 328.
[2] Marx, Engels, *Collected Works*, Vol. 5, p. 519.

attempts to synthesise the "ideological phrases of German philosophy" (mainly Feuerbach's abstract humanism) and "the results of French social criticism", that is, the ideas of the French utopians,[1] were quite artificial. Marx also exposed the "true socialists'" national self-conceit and their laudation of "the omniscience of the Germans as compared with the ignorance of the other nations".[2]

The exposure of "true socialism" strengthened the ideological foundations of the emerging proletarian party, and helped many working-class leaders, Schapper and Weydemeyer among them, to shed the incorrect views that had been suggested by "true socialism", to gain in spiritual stature and to accept the advanced theory.

DISAGREEMENTS WITH PROUDHON

In a relatively short while, "true socialism" left the stage, having suffered its final defeat during the 1848-49 revolution. Another petty-bourgeois trend, linked with the name of Pierre Joseph Proudhon, proved to be much more tenacious. His views were an expression of the mentality and aspirations of the petty entrepreneurs and sections of the proletariat which still had some bonds with their petty-bourgeois artisan or peasant origins. They subsequently attracted quite a large following in countries where these sections constituted a sizable part of the working class—France, Belgium, Italy and Spain—and this made Proudhonism an influential trend in petty-bourgeois socialism. The Marxist struggle against Proudhonism, which began before the 1848 revolution, continued for several decades.

Marx met Proudhon in the summer of 1844 and at first their relations were friendly. Proudhon came from a poor peasant family, and had seen at first hand the plight of the working man under capitalism. Marx appreciated his innate keenness of mind and literary ability. In 1840, Proudhon published his book *What Is Property?*, in which he argued, like the 18th-century writer Brissot (a prominent Girondist during the French Revolution), that property is theft. Scientifically, the book was highly superficial, for Proudhon did not attack private property in the means of production as a principle, but only large property, because he had failed to see its historical origins, and the inevitability of property becoming concentrated as commodity production developed and capitalism grew. While condemning capitalist profit-making, usury and exploitation, Proudhon objected to the socialist demand for the socialisation of property. Still, even after the break with Proudhon and years of polemics against him, Marx admitted the merits of this book, the author's heartfelt "indignation at the infamy of the existing order", and his

---

[1] Ibid., p. 514.
[2] Ibid., p. 490.

outstanding literary qualities—his "strong muscular style".[1]

Marx hoped that Proudhon would overcome the defects of his outlook as he acquired more knowledge, especially in the sphere of philosophy, and would develop into a theorist of the French proletariat. That is exactly what Marx said about Proudhon in his article against Ruge and in *The Holy Family*. Accordingly, he sought to help Proudhon broaden his outlook and understand Hegel's dialectics.

While in Brussels, Marx continued his efforts to influence Proudhon and enlist him for co-operation with the Brussels Correspondence Committee. In a letter of May 5, 1846, he invited Proudhon to take charge of correspondence with the Committee as a representative of the French socialist movement.

However, Proudhon, in effect, refused to collaborate, having expressed a negative attitude to the communist ideas on a revolutionary transformation of society. He said the spread of these views was an invitation to "gross arbitrary acts, violence and annihilation", and countered them with the idea of gradual reform from above.

Proudhon did not see private ownership of the means of production as the root of all evil, but "non-equivalent" and "unfair" exchange of the products of labour, commercial profits and interest on loans. He expressed the mood of the master-craftsman, the peasant and the petty merchant, who were suffering from the competition of the big capitalists, usurers and bankers, and sought to establish a society of "equal" private producers, into whom both capitalists and workers would be converted. He hoped to achieve this by organising cash-free exchange on the basis of the labour value of commodities, low-cost, if not free, credit, the gradual buying up of large property from its owners, and its equal redistribution by associations of small-enterprise owners, artisans, traders and workers set up for that purpose (but not for joint production). The essential thing about Proudhon's utopia was his illusion that the capitalist system could be kept going without any dire consequences for the petty producer resulting from the big capitalists' competition and monopoly.

Marx first heard about Proudhon's social schemes from Engels who moved to Paris in August 1846 to organise, on behalf of the Brussels Committee, a similar committee on the spot, to arrange for the dissemination of communist ideas among French and German workers, and to combat the theories of Weitling and the "true socialists". Engels learned about Proudhon's reform schemes in Paris, where they were being spread among the German workers by Grün. In his letters of September 16 and 18, 1846 to the Brussels Committee and to Marx, Engels showed these ideas to be "infinitely absurd". At the end of October 1846, Engels got a meeting of the Paris communities of the League of the Just to adopt a resolution rejecting the social recipes propounded by Proudhon and Grün, and en-

---

[1] Marx, Engels, *Collected Works*, Vol. 20, p. 27.

dorsing his formulation of the purpose of the working-class movement—abolition of private property by revolutionary means.

Marx fully approved of these activities of Engels', whose letters from Paris were a source of most valuable information. From these Marx also learned, towards the end of October 1846, of the publication of Proudhon's book, *The System of Economic Contradictions, or the Philosophy of Poverty*, which he obtained in the latter half of December.

Proudhon's book claimed to be a kind of gospel that was to shake the social sciences to their very foundations and provide a key for the solution of the social question. Proudhon believed he had said the last word in philosophy and political economy, but his book showed that he had failed to understand both Hegel's philosophical method and English bourgeois political economy. What Proudhon imagined to be a great advance was in fact a step backwards from Hegel, Smith and Ricardo.

Marx saw the need to deal a crushing blow at Proudhon's reformist ideology, and to defend the idea of communism, which Proudhon had tried to denigrate. Proudhon had also grossly attacked the utopian socialists, whose views, he said, contained no rational elements at all. Accordingly, Marx at once started to write his "Anti-Proudhon", with a view to setting out—in contrast to Proudhon's dogmas—the fundamentals of the new, materialist communist outlook.

Marx gave the first concise outline of the future book on December 28, 1846, in a letter to Annenkov, who had asked for his opinion of Proudhon's work. Annenkov, neither Communist nor materialist, was highly impressed by the force of conviction and depth of the critical study of Proudhon given in Marx's letter. On January 6, 1847, he wrote: "Your opinion of Proudhon's work has really done me good by its correctness, clarity and—above all—its tendency towards the reality of things." [1]

In his letter to Annenkov, Marx proved Proudhon's methodology to be faulty and his method idealistic and metaphysical; he showed that Proudhon's sociological views were circumscribed, and that he was incapable of seeing the historical origin, nature or essence of capitalism, or any of the laws of social development in general, incapable of understanding the importance of the proletariat's class struggle. However, Marx did not treat Proudhon's views as literary oddities or the eccentricities of a muddled thinker. He regarded them as an expression of the attitudes of a definite class, and wrote: "Mr Proudhon is, from top to toe, a philosopher, an economist of the petty bourgeoisie." [2] That is why it was of fundamental importance for the proletariat that Proudhon's views should be criticised. This criticism was to establish the proletariat's theoretical and ideological

---

[1] *K. Marx and F. Engels and Revolutionary Russia*, Moscow, 1967, p. 142 (in Russian).
[2] Marx, Engels, *Collected Works*, Vol. 38, p. 105.

superiority over the petty bourgeoisie, and help the proletariat dissociate itself ideologically from the latter, and establish itself as the leading class capable of exerting an influence on the petty-bourgeois non-proletarian sections, possible allies in the forthcoming struggle.

In his letter, Marx recapitulated the basic propositions of the materialist view of history, which he had discovered and together with Engels formulated in *The German Ideology*, namely, the determining role of the productive forces in social development, the dialectical connection and interconnection between the productive forces and the relations of production, and the dependence of all other social institutions and phenomena, including ideas, on the mode of production. The historical necessity for an obsolete mode of production to give way to a new and more progressive one was determined by the discrepancy between the developing productive forces and the existing relations of production (in making his terminology more precise, Marx no longer called them "forms of intercourse", as he had done in *The German Ideology*, but "economic relations" and "social relations"). Marx gives expression to the profound idea that obsolete relations of production not only slow down social development, but may in fact retard it and deprive society of the "fruits of civilisation".[1] He exposes both the subjective idealist view of history as being the result of action by outstanding "men able to filch from God his utmost thoughts"[2] and the voluntarist notions that history can be made at will, regardless of the objective conditions. The producers of material values — the real makers of history — exert an influence on its advance mainly by their participation in developing the productive forces. But they cannot do so at will, because "man is not free to choose *his productive forces*" and every succeeding generation finds itself in possession of the "productive forces acquired by the preceding generation".[3]

Marx substantiated the historical principle in science by emphasising the need to regard the various forms of production in a given epoch as being historical and transitory. He showed this principle to be basic to any genuine scientific study of social phenomena.

THE POVERTY OF PHILOSOPHY

It took Marx a relatively short time to write his book against Proudhon. It was in French, and by early April 1847 it was completed in the main and passed on to the publishers A. Frank in Paris and C. G. Vogler in Brussels. On June 15, 1847, Marx wrote a short foreword, and in early July the book was issued as *The Poverty of Philosophy. Answer to the "Philosophy of Poverty" by M. Proudhon*.

---

[1] Marx, Engels, *Collected Works*, Vol. 38, p. 97.
[2] Ibid., p. 103.
[3] Ibid., p. 96.

While criticising Proudhon, Marx expounded in this book his own philosophical and economic views and expressed some profound ideas on the working-class movement and its tactics. For the first time in print, he set out in scientific though polemical form the fundamental principles of historical materialism, which had been formulated mainly during the writing of *The German Ideology*. These principles constituted the initial methodological basis for a critique of bourgeois political economy and the bourgeois mode of production.

Before the appearance of *The Poverty of Philosophy* Marx had already won a reputation as a serious philosopher, but was still to establish himself as an economist, so for him the book was something of a public debut in political economy. In 1880, he himself wrote: "It contains the seeds of the theory developed after twenty years' work in *Capital*."[1] Lenin considered *The Poverty of Philosophy* one of the first mature Marxist works.

Marx showed Proudhon's methodological principles to be defective, and said that Proudhon had tried to apply Hegel's dialectical method to political economy, but having failed to grasp the essence of dialectics and the fact that its scientific application to analysing economic phenomena implied the unravelling of the actual contradictions inherent in these phenomena, he went on to construct a set of artificial economic contradictions from the abstract categories of political economy. What he got instead of real dialectics was a sophistic juggling of contradictions. While borrowing the mystico-idealistic form of Hegel's doctrine of contradictions, Proudhon killed its rational elements. He completely distorted Hegel's idea of the resolution or elimination of contradictions, presenting it not as revolutionary transition to a new quality, but as elimination of the "bad side" of a given phenomenon, which clashed with the "good side". Hence Proudhon's intention not to destroy capitalism and its basis, but merely to purge commodity production of its "bad sides", of its abuses. Marx stressed that for Proudhon dialectical movement was "the dogmatic distinction between good and bad", and that he had "nothing of Hegel's dialectics but the language", while in fact remaining a metaphysician.[2]

Proudhon had borrowed from the classical bourgeois political economists their mistaken view that the economic categories of bourgeois society were everlasting, and had taken these as the basis for eliminating the "bad sides" of the existing social order and constituting a new and "equitable" one. He had repeated the mistake of the English socialists, John Francis Bray, William Thompson and other followers of Ricardo, who had tried to deduce a socialist system from the postulates of bourgeois political economy, its labour theory of value, in particular, an attempt Marx had shown to be utopian in his scientific research in 1845 and 1846. In *The Poverty of*

---

[1] Marx, Engels, *Collected Works*, Vol. 24, p. 326.
[2] Ibid., Vol. 6, p. 168.

Philosophy he showed that Proudhon's "scientific discovery" was akin to the utopian schemes of Bray and other writers of that school. However, in contrast to the English socialists, who saw these schemes only as a transitional measure to a fundamental transformation of society on socialist lines, Proudhon, like the true petty bourgeois that he was, believed them to be the cure-all for the ills of small-scale private production.

Marx attacked the metaphysical and idealistic reduction of political economy to a number of speculative abstractions and dry categories, and argued that real economic science must be based on a knowledge of the objective processes in society's material life, above all, of the conditions of material production. Abstractions and logical categories may serve as instruments of scientific cognition only when they themselves are a reflection of these processes and phenomena. But real relations, like the economic categories expressing them, are not eternal, but transitory in historical terms. From this it follows that the scientific method of cognition implies an apprehension of things, phenomena and their abstract expressions — scientific categories — in dialectical development, in movement, which is determined by the conflict of their inherent contradictions.

The German Ideology contained many examples of the application of materialist dialectics to the analysis of social phenomena, in the course of which Marx brought out the dialectical processes objectively inherent in social development (the dialectics of the productive forces and the relations of production, the unity and struggle of opposites in the form of antagonisms between classes, the transition from quantitative changes to qualitative ones and from evolution to revolution). In *The Poverty of Philosophy* he devoted special attention to the method of materialist dialectics, and generalised its essential features.

In contrast to Hegel, who turned dialectics into a property of thought alone, of Spirit, of which passive matter was allegedly the other-being, Marx saw material phenomena, life itself, of which the development of ideas and concepts was a reflection, as the primary source of dialectical movement. In contrast to Hegel's idealistic and mystical view of dialectics, Marx showed it to be profoundly materialist, and drew a distinct dividing line between Hegel's and his own scientific method.

Marx also set out in the most concise scientific form the principles of the materialist view of history, defining its essence as follows: the productive forces and the relations of production constitute a unity, so that the continuous development of the productive forces makes the change in the mode of production inevitable. He wrote: "Social relations are closely bound up with productive forces. In acquiring new productive forces men change their mode of production; and in changing their mode of production, in changing the way of earning their living, they change all their social relations. The hand-mill gives you society with the feudal lord; the steam-mill, society with the industrial capitalist." [1]

Marx defined "productive forces" as a concept which includes not only the instruments of production, but also the workers, and added: "The greatest productive power is the revolutionary class itself." [2]

In this work, Marx did not confine himself to criticising Proudhon, but pointed out the fundamental error of all bourgeois, including classical, economists — their view of value, division of labour, credit, money and so on, as hard-and-fast categories. He also sharply criticised them for their presentation of the laws of bourgeois production as natural laws that would govern social production for ever. Every phase of production had a beginning and so must have an end, and it would be wrong, for instance, to regard feudal institutions as artificial, and bourgeois institutions as natural, because the former were just as "natural" for their own period as the latter for the new one. But there will inevitably come a time when the laws of bourgeois production will become invalid and disappear off the face of the earth, together with the system of bourgeois relations itself.

Marx adopted a new methodological approach to the analysis of a number of categories of political economy, notably the fundamental category of value. Whereas Proudhon had taken value, like other categories, to be nothing but the "idea of value", that is, a purely mental concept, Marx said value had its origins in that historical stage in the development of production and exchange when the products of labour became the objects of trade. In *The Poverty of Philosophy*, Marx treats value as human labour embodied in commodities. Value is determined by the quantity of labour time socially necessary for the production of the commodity. This is what Smith and Ricardo said, but Marx also argues that the products of human labour become commodities and acquire the form of value (Marx frequently uses "exchange value" as an adequate expression) only in specific social conditions, when production is social while labour is not yet directly social. Value realises and expresses the social connection between individual commodity producers.

Proudhon saw two sides to value, as to every other category, the bad and the good. The bad (value in the proper sense of the word, exchange value) had to be eliminated, and the good (the usefulness of a thing, its use value) had to be retained and developed. He believed this contradiction, this double nature of value could be resolved through the establishment of an exchange of commodities without the use of money, the instrument of value. Marx proved that it was not money that in itself engendered the contradictions of the bourgeois system, but that the bourgeois system was at bottom contradictory, and necessarily implies the existence of value and

---

[1] Marx, Engels, *Collected Works*, Vol. 6, p. 166.
[2] Ibid., p. 211.

money. He wrote: "Money is not a thing, it is a social relation." [1] The intrinsic, organic contradictions of capitalism cannot be abolished through the elimination of money, because these contradictions spring from the form of production and are a product of capitalist private property.

Marx sets out some of the initial propositions of his theory of surplus value which he elaborated in his subsequent writings, but he still operates with concepts borrowed from the classics, like "labour as a commodity", "the value of labour" and "the price of labour". Nevertheless he fills these with a new content, which brings out the exploiting essence of relations between wage labour and capital. Ricardo saw labour as a commodity like any other. Marx regards labour as a specific commodity whose purchase and use result in the capitalist's enrichment and a worsening of the working man's condition. Marx formulates the general law of capitalist accumulation in broad terms, when he says that "in the selfsame relations in which wealth is produced, poverty is produced also". [2]

Marx's understanding of the very essence of capitalist production enabled him to adopt a new approach, as compared with Ricardo, to the origin and history of the capitalist mode of production. In *The Poverty of Philosophy* Marx elaborates on the ideas he expressed in *The German Ideology*, and gives a masterful outline of the principal stages of capitalist production: simple co-operation, the manufacture and the factory. He brings out the role of the division of labour and machine production, whose revolutionary aspect, in contrast to Proudhon, he specifically emphasises. The conditions created for the workers by the capitalist factory were certainly not humane, but it was a necessary stage in the development of industry and had powerfully promoted the growth and concentration of production. From its midst the modern working class had emerged.

Although Marx had yet to complete his critique of classical political economy, *The Poverty of Philosophy* was based on totally new methodological premises in the study of economic reality. He had begun to elaborate proletarian political economy on a totally new basis, while making use of all the rational elements in earlier writings.

In contrast to the limited, conventional notions of the bourgeois political economists and the utopian socialists, Marx indicated the real social forces that are to resolve the contradictions of bourgeois society and effect its transformation. He said that, mapping out ways of linking science and revolutionary practice, working-class theoreticians were duty-bound to give conscious expression to the advance of history, instead of seeking the scientific truth in their minds. The truly revolutionary science has the task of making the working class aware of the contradictions of capitalism and of the fact that these contradictions are also fraught with the inevitable collapse of the capitalist system.

---

[1] Marx, Engels, *Collected Works*, Vol. 6, p. 145.
[2] Ibid., p. 176.

Another fundamental issue on which Marx provided concrete proof that Proudhon was wrong was the importance of the workers' strike struggle, which Proudhon had denied, saying that the workers would not and should not associate in trade unions.

Bourgeois political economists were maintaining that it was useless for the workers to resist the existing order, while the utopian socialists offered various schemes that diverted the masses from the struggle. Marx proved that for the workers association was a school of class struggle preparing them for a revolutionary attack on the exploiting capitalist system, under which masses of working people had become impoverished, enslaved by the employers and divided by competition. But under the impact of their common interests these masses would gradually coalesce, unite, by occupation to start with, putting up ever more organised resistance to the capitalists. "In this struggle—a veritable civil war—all the elements necessary for a coming battle unite and develop." [1]

As the emancipation movement of the proletariat advances, the proletariat becomes increasingly aware of the basic contradictions between its own interests and the existing system, and of the need to organise and rally all its forces to bring about a fundamental revolutionary change in that system. The acquisition of this socialist class consciousness is of decisive importance in transforming the proletariat from a mass which "is already a class as against capital, but not yet for itself", into a "class for itself". Emphasising the importance of the workers' economic struggle, Marx observed that it was bound to grow into political revolutionary action, because any struggle of one class against another is a political struggle. This formula determined a key tactical principle of the revolutionary proletarian movement, namely, that the proletariat's economic and political struggle constitutes a unity, and that political struggle is crucial for its emancipation.

Marx said that a society based on class antagonisms is bound to experience acute social conflict. Only when a working-class victory sweeps these away will society be able to remove the obstacles to the development of the productive forces without revolutionary upheavals, while "*social evolutions* will cease to be *political revolutions*". For the time being, said Marx, quoting in conclusion the words of George Sand from the introduction to her novel *Jean Zizka:* "Combat or death, bloody struggle or extinction. Thus the question is inexorably put." [2]

Marx's friends saw the publication of *The Poverty of Philosophy* as a great theoretical success for the emergent proletarian party. With Weydemeyer's assistance, the German Communist Ferdinand Wolff published a review of the book in the journal *Das Westphälis-*

---

[1] Ibid., p. 211.
[2] Ibid., p. 212.

che Dampfboot. In his conversations with French socialists and democrats, Engels said Marx's work was "our programme".[1]

FOUNDATION OF THE COMMUNIST LEAGUE

Towards the end of 1846 there was a change in the thinking of members of the League of the Just in Paris and in London. By then, under the impact of diverse utopian socialist trends, many of them had gone through a complex ideological evolution. They inevitably became disillusioned with the various utopian systems because the latter failed to provide an answer to the practical problems of the working-class movement with which they were faced. At the same time, they felt the compelling force of the ideas of scientific communism, which was taking shape and threw light on the most complex and vital problems. The leaders of the League of the Just became convinced that Marx and Engels alone were capable of setting the working-class organisations on the right road. The artisans' traditional mistrust of the "educated" was gradually being dispelled, and there was a growing awareness of the role science had to play in the solution of social problems.

In November 1846, the seat of the central organ of the League of the Just, its People's Chamber (*Volkshalle*), was transferred from Paris to London. Its members included the shoemaker Heinrich Bauer, the watchmaker Joseph Moll, and Karl Schapper, an active participant in the revolutionary movement since his student years and now a political exile, who had of necessity been a Jack of all trades — forester, cooper, brewer and type-setter. Their address to the members of the League showed definite ideological progress under the influence of Marx and Engels. It said that there was a need to set up a "strong party" and noted the harm caused to the working-class movement by the drive to invent diverse artificial socialist systems. It put forward for discussion some really important tactical matters, such as the attitude to the various sections of the bourgeoisie, to the non-proletarian parties, and so on. The address proposed that an international communist congress be held in early May 1847.

Confronted with a number of difficulties in drawing up an agenda for the congress, the leaders of the League of the Just decided to ask Marx and Engels for their assistance, and this move was warmly supported by the most active members of the London organisation of the League. The People's Chamber sent Moll with official instructions to see Marx in Brussels and Engels in Paris and arrange the terms on which the two men would join the League and participate in drawing up the programme and other documents.

Marx and Engels had received invitations to join the League of the Just before, but had invariably rejected them, because they did not share the utopian views prevailing in it and disapproved of the

---

[1] Ibid., Vol. 38, p. 134.

sectarian-conspiratorial principles of its organisation. On the occasion in question, Marx at first had some reservations about Moll's proposal, but in the course of talks held in late January and early February 1847 it transpired that the London leaders of the League of the Just were prepared to reorganise it. This was a good opportunity for Marx and Engels to turn an existing international working-class organisation into the core of the emergent proletarian party by restructuring it fundamentally in accordance with the principles of the new doctrine. Once Marx was satisfied on this point, he agreed to join the League, and the invitation was also accepted by Engels.

The results of those talks were reflected in a second address issued by the London leadership of the League in February 1847. Without mentioning any names, it made it clear that Marx, Engels and their followers were joining the League. It added that "in France and Belgium we have temporarily organised ourselves on new lines".[1] The holding of the congress was put off from May to June, to give time for better preparation. The agenda for it was agreed with Marx, and provided for a complete reorganisation of the League, the drawing up of new rules, consideration of a programme, a printed organ, and so on. The conversations which Marx and Engels had with Moll helped the members of the London centre to clarify their attitudes to the various socialist trends.

Marx at once informed his associates in Germany and other countries about his arrangements with the People's Chamber, and invited them not only to join the League, but also to take an active part in reorganising it. In a letter to Roland Daniels on March 7, 1847, he proposed that a meeting should be held in a Belgian town to discuss party affairs. In his correspondence with Engels, he discussed various organisational matters connected with preparations for the congress and the dispatch of delegates.

The congress was held in London between June 2 and 9, 1847. Financial difficulties prevented Marx from going to London, but he gave detailed instructions to Wilhelm Wolff, the Brussels delegate, convinced that he and Engels, the Paris delegate, would be able to direct the congress along the right lines.

At the congress the League of the Just was renamed the Communist League. The congress was for all practical purposes a constituent one and inaugurated a totally new organisation, with new ideological principles and structure.

An important step was taken towards working out the programme of the League. The Congress adopted as the basis of the League's programme Engels' outline in the form of a revolutionary catechism, a form then popular among workers' societies — Draft of a Communist Confession of Faith — and decided to circulate it for discussion by its local communities. The document formulated

---

[1] *The Communist League — the Forerunner of the First International* (Collection of Documents), Moscow, 1964, p. 133 (in Russian).

the programme principles in the spirit of scientific communism.[1]

New rules were drafted with the direct participation of Engels and Wolff, and these were to be adopted at the next congress after discussion in the communities. In accordance with the arrangement between Marx and Moll, the League discarded all the practices of a conspiratorial secret society, namely, the semi-mystical ritual of swearing in new members, the oath of allegiance, the petty regulation of duties, and the excessive concentration of power in the hands of the leadership, which provided opportunities for abuses. Later, in 1877, Marx wrote about this to one of his correspondents: "Engels' and my own initial entry into the secret communist society took place solely on the condition that everything promoting superstitious veneration of authority was to be dropped from the Rules."[2] Marx and Engels believed that there was no room for a personality cult of the leaders in any proletarian organisation.

Under the new Rules, the electivity of the governing bodies went hand in hand with a sufficient degree of centralisation and the principle of the subordination of lower organs to higher ones. The highest organ of the Communist League was the congress, consisting of delegates from local organisations. Subsequently, a clause limiting the powers of the congress and giving the communities the right to accept or reject its decisions was deleted on Marx's insistence. The Central Authority was the executive organ in between congresses. The community (*Gemeinde*), with an elective chairman and a deputy-chairman, was the primary cell. In a given locality, the several communities were brought together in a circle, headed by the circle authority.

Prospective members who had acquainted themselves with the Rules were admitted to the League, with the consent of the community, by its chairman and the recommending member. Regulations were also provided for expulsion of members for various breaches of the Rules, regulations relating to the payment of membership dues and the expenditure of League funds. Members of the League were required to recognise the principles of the League, conduct a way of life worthy of Communists, observe Party secrecy, and not to belong to societies hostile to the Communist League. The latter requirement was written into the Rules some time later, once again on Marx's initiative, instead of the initial sectarian ban on League members' joining any other political or national organisation whatsoever.

The Communist League Rules for the first time introduced into the working-class movement a higher type of organisational principle than those by which earlier working-class and democratic organisations had been guided. At the same time, the Rules took account of their positive organisational experience. The congress decision expelling Weitling's followers from the ranks of the League stated that

---

[1] Marx, Engels, *Collected Works*, Vol. 6, pp. 96-103.
[2] Marx, Engels, *Werke*, Bd. 34, S. 308.

adoption of sectarian and utopian dogmas was incompatible with membership of the proletarian organisation.

The congress decided to drop the old, vague motto "All Men Are Brethren!" and to adopt instead the great rallying cry put forward by Marx and Engels—"Working Men of All Countries, Unite!" This was of epoch-making importance because it was the first call in history to embody the fundamental principle of proletarian internationalism, the idea of the international solidarity of men of labour, the idea of the unity and cohesion of the working class in the joint struggle against capitalist oppression.

The establishment of the Communist League, the first international working-class organisation which proclaimed scientific communism to be its ideological banner, was an event of great importance in the history of the proletariat's emancipation struggle. It inaugurated the fusion of Marxism and the working-class movement, and heralded the triumph of the Marxist outlook and the ideas of international proletarian solidarity.

GERMAN WORKERS' SOCIETY IN BRUSSELS

Following the first congress, the need arose to ensure the ideological and organisational consolidation of the Communist League. The communist correspondence committees and groups merged with it. On Marx's initiative, a community and a circle of the Communist League were set up in Brussels on August 5, 1847. Marx, Wilhelm Wolff, Gigot and the German worker, Junge, were on the Circle Authority. This Authority, headed by Marx, did more than direct the Belgian communities: for all practical purposes, Brussels became the governing centre of the Communist League as a whole. On all key matters, the London Central Authority consulted primarily with the Brussels Circle Authority.

Marx's closest friends and associates soon came to hold leading positions in the League, with Weydemeyer, Daniels and Bürgers acting as organisers and leaders of the League communities in Western Germany. In Paris, the communities were directed by Engels, who was on the Paris Circle Authority. At the end of July 1847, League business took him to Brussels, where he stayed until mid-October of that year.

Marx believed that the immediate aim of the Communist League should be to organise the spread of communist ideas. Considering the existing conditions in the absolutist states and the obstacles encountered by emigrants in their political activity in countries with "liberal" regimes (Belgium, France and Switzerland), the League had to remain a secret organisation, but Marx did everything to prevent it from inheriting from its predecessors—the secret workers' societies of the 1830s and early 1840s—their isolation and their lack of contact with the masses. He believed that the League's illegal and relatively narrow organisations should be surrounded with a network of open workers' societies, like the German Workers' Educational Society in London. The League was either to establish contact with existing educational societies or set up new ones.

This idea was soon put into practice. The educational societies set up by members of the Communist League organised libraries, series of lectures for workers on various subjects, choirs, and so on. There were regular political discussions. Marx later observed: "The 'League' standing behind the public educational associations, and guiding them, found them both the most convenient forum for public propaganda and also a reservoir whose most useful members could replenish and swell its own ranks." [1]

On the initiative of Marx and Engels, a German Workers' Society, consisting mainly of emigrant workers, was set up in Brussels at the end of August 1847. Its initial membership of 37 rose within a few months to almost 100, with Communist League members playing the leading part.

The Society carried on extensive propaganda and educational work, and Marx was one of its most active members. In the second half of December he read a series of lectures before the Society on political economy. There is also a record of a speech delivered by Marx at a New Year's dinner organised by the Society on December 31, 1847. He extended greetings to the leaders of the Belgian and international democratic movement present at the dinner and emphasised the importance for the workers of revolutionary struggle for democratic liberties.

WAGE LABOUR AND CAPITAL

Marx intended to prepare for publication the lectures on political economy he had given at the German Workers' Society, and a copy of them has survived written out by Weydemeyer for that purpose. They could not be published in Brussels in early 1848, however, because of the revolutionary events that broke out in Europe. Not until the first half of April 1849, eighteen months after giving these lectures, was Marx able to publish part of them in the *Neue Rheinische Zeitung*, under the general title, *Wage Labour and Capital*. The publication was incomplete, and among Marx's material there is a manuscript entitled "Wages", which is probably a rough outline of the unpublished part of his lectures.

Wage Labour and Capital is Marx's second relatively large economic work of the latter half of the 1840s after *The Poverty of Philosophy* and it reflects his profound knowledge and original views in this field. *Wage Labour and Capital* is a fine example of Marx's ability to present his scientific ideas in popular form, setting out the

---

[1] Marx, Engels, *Collected Works*, Vol. 17, pp. 78-79.

most complex economic problems in simple terms and with exceptional clarity for the workers.

He had set himself the task of explaining the essence of capitalist exploitation, and revealing the economic basis of the bourgeoisie's domination and the slavery of the wage-workers. The task was of especial importance as the numerous advocates of the bourgeois system were trying to convince the workers that they were being paid a fair wage for their labour, while the factory-owners received an equally fair reward in the form of profit, for their capital, which provided employment for the workers. Then there were also the various utopian schemes for harmonising the interests of all the participants in capitalist production.

Marx exposed all these assertions. First of all he explained to the workers what wages are and how they are determined. The worker sells his labour in a commercial transaction with the capitalist, who pays the worker for the time worked or for the definite quantity of articles produced. Wages are expressed in terms of money; they are a special name for the price of this sole commodity which the worker possesses. The worker cannot live without making this transaction, without selling his labour to the capitalist. Labour, his main form of vital activity, is his only means of securing his own existence and that of his family. That is why wage labour merely has the semblance of being free labour. Like the slave, who was sold as a thing to his owner once and for all, like the serf, who was tied to the land for which he surrendered to the landowner a part of his labour, the wage-worker too is in fact bound to the bourgeois class for life. The most he can do is to change the buyer of his labour — to switch from one capitalist to another.

The price of any commodity fluctuates with supply and demand and under the impact of competition among the sellers. But whatever these fluctuations, they invariably tend to be on a level with the production cost of the given commodity. These fluctuations are neither calm nor measured, but carry the "most frightful devastation" in their wake, and sometimes, in periods of crises, lead to real industrial anarchy.

In the category of production cost, or value, Marx then included raw materials and tools used in making the given commodities and measured by the labour-time embodied in them, and also direct living labour, which is likewise measured by time.

By analogy with other commodities, the cost of production of labour consists of the cost of training the worker and that of maintaining him as such. This is the cost of production of the worker's necessary means of subsistence, and their price constitutes wages.

Marx then went on to define profit and refuted the erroneous traditional bourgeois view of capital as a sum-total of means and resources, as accumulated labour which is used for new production. Capital has a material integument and appears as a thing, as many had pointed out, but it was Marx who proved that a thing does not always serve as capital: only under certain social relations is the product of labour, accumulated labour, converted into capital. It is the product of a definite historical stage of social development, and is itself a social relation, namely, the prevailing relation of the bourgeois mode of production, of bourgeois society. Whatever its material form, whatever the sum of its constituent commodities, it implies the existence of social conditions under which the ownership of things makes it possible gratuitously to appropriate the direct living labour of the workers, who possess nothing but their capacity for work. "It is only the domination of accumulated, past, materialised labour over direct, living labour that turns accumulated labour into capital." [1] Capital and wage labour condition and generate each other.

Marx gave the classic definition of capital and further elaborated the proposition about the exploitation of wage labour by capital. He produced vivid examples to show that the source of the capitalist's profit is that part of the value of the product produced by the worker which is in excess of the value of the means of subsistence he receives in the form of wages. Marx also drew a clear distinction between real and nominal wages, and also put forward the highly important concept of relative wages, which express the relative shares in the new product of the wage-worker and the capitalist, labour and capital. He formulated the following important regularity: even under the most favourable circumstances, the worker's share tends to shrink and that of the capitalist to grow. "*Profit and wages* remain as before in *inverse proportion.*" [2]

Marx showed that the interests of wage labour and capital are diametrically opposed, and that there is a growing gulf between the proletariat and the bourgeoisie, the two main classes of bourgeois society. With the growth of social wealth and the productivity of labour, the proletariat forges for itself only "the golden chains by which the bourgeoisie drags it in its train".[3]

However, the rapid growth of capital creates the prerequisites for a revolutionary transformation of society. In his rough outline, entitled "Wages", Marx stressed that the bourgeois system of wage labour ensures the emergence of the material means for the proletariat's social emancipation and the establishment of a new social order. Compared with the earlier forms of society, capitalism has the advantage that the domination of capital divests social relations of their "halo of sanctity" [4] and patriarchalism so that the cash relation of purchase and sale remains the only nexus. The proletariat achieves a stage of organisation and strength where it is quite capable of carrying out a fundamental social revolution.

Subsequently Marx and Engels modified, in the light of their later

---

[1] Marx, Engels, *Collected Works*, Vol. 9, p. 213.
[2] Ibid., p. 221.
[3] Ibid.
[4] Ibid., Vol. 6, p. 436.

views, some of the propositions in *Wage Labour and Capital*, where Marx had followed the classics in treating labour as a commodity. He specified that the worker does not sell the capitalist his labour but his labour-power. This was much more than a terminological refinement—it was Marx's major discovery in the sphere of political economy. He had also identified the value of the commodity with the production cost, leaving out such an essential component as the value of the surplus product, which the workers produced and the capitalists appropriated. In other words, *Wage Labour and Capital* reflected a stage in the development of Marx's economic theory before it had been finally shaped. It was the height to which he rose as an economist towards the end of the 1840s as he formulated the principles of the new, proletarian economic doctrine.

EFFORTS TO START A PERIODICAL

For the extensive dissemination of communist ideas it was essential to have a periodical. When the Brussels Communist Correspondence Committee was still active, Weydemeyer had written to Marx: "It is very regrettable that there is absolutely no organ in which small articles could be published without censorship. I am sure that you are the only person who can edit." [1]

With the foundation of the Communist League, the need for such an organ became even more acute. In August 1847, Marx worked out a plan for a critical monthly to be started in Belgium on the share-holding principle. He communicated this to his friends in Germany and France, and proposed that a subscription be started, but nothing came of the scheme.

With the support of Marx and his friends, the London leaders of the Communist League also tried to start a communist journal. They got most help from Wilhelm Wolff. A specimen issue of the *Kommunistische Zeitschrift* saw the light of day in September 1847. It bore the rallying cry "Working Men of All Countries, Unite!" (the first time it appeared in print), and its contents showed signs of the influence of Marx and Engels. Its articles criticised utopian socialist ideas and elaborated on some important tactical principles of the proletarian movement (in particular, the tactics of the working class in Germany). However, it had to suspend publication for lack of funds.

A much more important effort was made by Marx and Engels to turn the emigrant *Deutsche-Brüsseler-Zeitung* into the printed organ of the Communist League. This newspaper came out twice a week beginning on January 1, 1847. It was founded and edited by the petty-bourgeois democrat Bornstedt, who since his stay in Paris had been suspected of having connections with the police and the French Legitimists. Because he sought to have all radical-democratic and

---

[1] MEGA, Abt. 3, Bd. 2, S. 234.

socialist trends represented on its pages, the paper's ideological make-up was patchy and amorphous. Gradually, however, more and more items were contributed by followers of Marx and Engels — Georg Weerth, Ferdinand Wolff and Wilhelm Wolff, the latter doing most to turn the paper into a vehicle not only for democratic but also for revolutionary-proletarian ideas. Now and again Marx and Engels would contribute items to the newspaper.

Marx's followers were eagerly following these developments, hoping that proletarian influence would become firmly established in the newspaper. On April 19, 1847, Heinrich Bürgers wrote to Marx: "How is the *Brüsseler-Zeitung*? The whole thing will be mucked up if we take our cue from Herr von Bornstedt." [1]

By August 1847, Marx and Engels were fully determined to influence the paper's line more actively by direct participation in its publication. Marx wrote as much to Herwegh on August 8, adding that "despite its many failings", the paper "does have some merits" and that its editor "has expressed his readiness to help us in every way".[2] Bornstedt was amenable because he was in financial difficulties and undoubtedly hoped that the paper's prestige — and its shares — would soar if such well-known theoreticians and journalists as Marx and Engels took a hand in it. Nevertheless, it was not that easy to make him accept specific terms. Marx and Engels did not start their regular work on the paper until a month later, on September 12, 1847.

By the end of 1847, Marx and Engels had a commanding influence on the paper, and for all practical purposes acted as its editors until the final issue appeared on February 27, 1848. Bornstedt was only nominally its editor.

The *Deutsche-Brüsseler-Zeitung* thus became the unofficial organ of the Communist League, spreading the programme and tactical principles of scientific communism, and the idea of revolutionary struggle against the feudal absolutist and bourgeois-conservative regimes. It was in the front ranks of the general democratic movement, and at the same time took a resolute stand for the proletariat's class interests and social demands.

While working on the paper, Marx revealed himself as a brilliant revolutionary journalist. His writings combined theoretical depth and solid reasoning with keen wit and impassioned polemic. Marx the journalist freely drew on his extensive reading and his ability to make use of the apt historical analogy, literary metaphor and the imagery of the great writers.

In that period, the main purpose of the articles by Marx and Engels was to explain to the working class its role and tasks in the approaching revolution and prepare the emergent proletarian party for the coming battles ideologically and tactically. Marx sought to make the party immune to the honeyed talk of the liberal leaders

---

[1] MEGA, Abt. 3, Bd. 9, S. 336.
[2] Marx, Engels, *Collected Works*, Vol. 38, p. 120.

and to the equally dangerous blandishments of political reactionaries who wore a mask of concern for the people.

Such was the purpose of Marx's first article as a regular member of the paper's staff. It had been written in connection with a series of anonymous articles which appeared in the conservative Cologne paper, *Rheinischer Beobachter*, and which depicted the Prussian state as a champion of the working people.

In his article entitled "Communism of the *Rheinischer Beobachter*", Marx tore the "socialist" mask off the apologists of the Prussian monarchy and branded them as the worst reactionaries and demagogues. He demonstrated the complete falsehood and harm of the stories about the anti-popular Prussian state having a social mission. In his subsequent attacks on the Lassallean leaders, who flirted with Bismarck's Junker government, Marx referred to this article to show his attitude to the "royal Prussian governmental socialism".[1]

Marx also revealed the true worth of the reactionary demagogues' speculations on Christian dogmas and in general terms stated that the revolutionary-proletarian outlook was fundamentally hostile to the Christian and all other religious morality. He wrote: "The social principles of Christianity declare all the vile acts of the oppressors against the oppressed to be either a just punishment for original sin and other sins, or trials which the Lord, in his infinite wisdom, ordains for the redeemed.

"The social principles of Christianity preach cowardice, self-contempt, abasement, submissiveness and humbleness, in short, all the qualities of the rabble, and the proletariat, which will not permit itself to be treated like rabble, needs its courage, its self-confidence, its pride and its sense of independence even more than its bread."[2]

Marx's article contained a clear-cut statement of the proletariat's position in the revolutionary situation that was taking shape in Germany. He urged the masses to support the bourgeois opposition, while emphasising that the working class was dissatisfied with its insufficiently resolute behaviour in the United Provincial Diet. Marx contrasted the liberals' moderate line with the line towards a revolutionary overthrow of the absolute monarchy, abolition of the semi-medieval social institutions, and democratisation of the whole social and political system. He outlined a programme for these democratic changes, including the convocation of a truly popular representative body, abolition of the corvée system, elimination of class barriers and limitations, introduction of trial by jury, and freedom of association, assembly and the press.

The main idea that ran through the whole article was that the people is the real motive force behind the bourgeois-democratic revolution. Marx cited the English and French bourgeois revolutions of the 17th and the 18th century, respectively, to illustrate this idea. In Germany, he stressed, consistent solution of the tasks of the revolu-

---
[1] Ibid., Vol. 20, p. 80.
[2] Ibid., Vol. 6, p. 231.

tion would depend on the revolutionary activity of the masses and their readiness to "throw" the monarchy "into the gutter", and to pitchfork the lords of the manor. Marx explained that with respect to Germany "revolutionary people" meant proletarians, small peasants and the plebs, three class forces whose uniting together presented the greatest threat to the whole system of absolute monarchy.

Marx argued that the working class stood to gain from a victorious bourgeois revolution, because "the rule of the bourgeoisie does not only place quite new weapons in the hands of the proletariat for the struggle *against* the bourgeoisie, but ... also secures for it a quite different status, the status of a recognised party".[1]

In their efforts to help the working class understand its own class aims, Marx and Engels did all they could to see that the *Deutsche-Brüsseler-Zeitung* provided fuller information to its readers about the working-class movement in Belgium and other countries, and carried reports on the meetings of the German Workers' Society. The newspaper published articles and other material dealing with various aspects of the communist doctrine and the propaganda of the principles of proletarian internationalism.

INTERNATIONAL CONGRESS OF ECONOMISTS

An international congress on Free Trade met in Brussels from September 16 to 18, 1847. It was organised by bourgeois advocates of Free Trade, who wanted the lifting of all import duties, complete freedom of competition, and non-intervention by the state in business. They saw the congress as an opportunity to demonstrate the advantages of their system over protectionism. It was attended by many leading figures in bourgeois economic science and was widely advertised by the bourgeois press.

Marx, Engels and some of their associates attended the congress, having decided to use it to expose the hypocrisy of bourgeois economists. Workers were present in the public gallery, and Marx regarded the congress as a suitable arena for crossing swords with the ideologists of the bourgeoisie, and countering their views with the proletarian point of view. On its third day, when the influence of Free Trade on the condition of the working class was being debated, Weerth and Marx put their names down for the debate.

Weerth was the first to take the floor, and his speech clashed sharply with all that had been said at the congress. To cries of approval from the public gallery, he demanded an explanation of why there were no workers' delegates at a congress discussing their condition. He exploded the brazen lies of the Free Traders, who pretended that Free Trade was a blessing for the proletariat, and gave a moving picture of the plight of the proletariat.

---

[1] Marx, Engels, *Collected Works*, Vol. 6, p. 222.

Weerth's speech had the effect of an electric shock the participants in the congress, and one by one they hastened to take the floor in an effort to refute his arguments. When it was Marx's turn, the congress organisers quickly closed the debate, although the list of speakers had not run out. A resolution in favour of Free Trade was rushed through and the congress was wound up.

Marx and his associates denounced these mean actions in the democratic and working-class press. On September 29, 1847, the Belgian newspaper, *Atelier Démocratique*, published a summary of the speech Marx had prepared. Engels had articles on the congress in the *Deutsche-Brüsseler-Zeitung* and the Chartist *Northern Star*, the latter giving in detail the main points of the speech Marx was to have delivered. Thus, considerable publicity was given to the clash between the bourgeois and the proletarian trends at the congress of economists in Brussels.

In his speech, Marx gave a scientific proletarian critique of protectionism and Free Trade, exposing the false catchwords used by the advocates of both bourgeois systems and their speculation on the people's interests.

Marx took a concrete historical approach to this and other problems. He held that at the early stage of capitalism protectionism had been a factor accelerating the formation of the capitalist system and strengthening it for the struggle against feudalism. But in the 1840s, protectionism was justified, in historical terms, only in countries like Germany, where protective tariffs strengthened the economic positions of the bourgeoisie in its drive against feudal survivals. On the whole, however, at the stage capitalism had reached in its development, protectionism hampered the free movement of capital and the growth of the productive forces on an international scale. Accordingly, Marx stressed that protectionism was conservative and that Free Trade was preferable as the more progressive of the two.

Marx showed that far from being a remedy for all the social ills, as the advocates of Free Trade insisted, it tended to aggravate them and to intensify the contradictions of capitalism. However, as it deepened the antagonism between the working class and the capitalist class, Free Trade also promoted the more rapid growth of prerequisites for the overthrow of the capitalist system. "We are for Free Trade, because by Free Trade all economical laws, with their most astounding contradictions, will act upon a larger scale, upon a greater extent of territory, upon the territory of the whole earth; and because from the uniting of all these contradictions into a single group, where they stand face to face, will result the struggle which will itself eventuate in the emancipation of the proletarians." [1]

Marx pointed out that the working class did not expect salvation from any economic policy of the bourgeoisie, but that its slogan was a fundamental revolutionary transformation of the whole social sys-

---

[1] Marx, Engels, *Collected Works*, Vol. 6, p. 290.

tem. It had to pin its hopes not on the "charity" or "philanthropy" of the powers that be, but on its own revolutionary energy. "Social reforms can never be brought about by the weakness of the strong; they must and will be called to life by the strength of the weak."[1]

POLEMICS WITH KARL HEINZEN

Marx and Engels had to assert the ideological position of the Communist League in polemic not only against bourgeois doctrinaires, but also against petty-bourgeois democrats, like Karl Heinzen, who expressed the hostile attitude to communism of a group of German radical journalists and public figures (Fröbel, Struve, Ruge and others).

At one time a petty official and a contributor to the *Rheinische Zeitung*, Heinzen incurred the wrath of his superiors in 1844 by his book entitled *The Prussian Bureaucracy* and had to flee Germany to escape arrest. In 1845, in Brussels, he had long political discussions with Marx, Freiligrath and Bürgers, who tried to help him shed his liberal constitutional illusions. He soon went to live in Switzerland, where he plunged into a mood of mutinous individualism and swung to radicalism which appeared to be highly revolutionary but was in fact fairly vulgar. He urged the Germans to revolt immediately, to do away with the monarchs whom he believed to be the root of all evil, and establish a federal republic. At the same time he wrote articles for the press slandering the Communists.

In the autumn of 1847, Marx and Engels found themselves forced to start a polemic with Heinzen. In his article "The Communists and Karl Heinzen" Engels defined communism as a system of views and a social movement which had sprung from the needs of life itself. He stressed that the Communists' ultimate goal lay well beyond the establishment of bourgeois-democratic freedoms; their immediate task, however, was democracy, and in the struggle to establish it they were working together with the democrats. But the Communists could not be expected to make ideological concessions to their partners, and had the right to criticise the latter for their erroneous views. Heinzen's naive social and political views, he said, implied that social justice could be established by a single revolutionary act against the German monarchs. Heinzen had borrowed from the Communists some of their short-term social demands and set them up as the ultimate goal of any emancipation movement, turning them into philistine fantasies of a better world.

Engels' article gave Heinzen an opportunity of launching another anti-communist attack. This he did in an article entitled "A 'Representative' of the Communists" in the *Deutsche-Brüsseler-Zeitung* on October 21, 1847, which contained even more trivial moralising over

---

[1] Marx, Engels, *Collected Works*, Vol. 6, p. 281.

the Communists' "inconsistency" and "infirmity of views". This time the rebuff came from Marx in his article "Moralising Criticism and Critical Morality" which appeared in a number of issues of the *Deutsche-Brüsseler-Zeitung* in late October and November 1847.

This article, like many others written by Marx, has many facets to it: it is a brilliant satire exposing political philistinism and philistine morality, a literary-historical essay containing an incisive evaluation of various literary phenomena, a theoretical sociological treatise setting out important propositions of historical materialism, and a party document expounding the Communist League's programme and tactical principles. This wide-ranging content is clothed in an expressive literary form, with extensive use of analogies from Terence, Shakespeare, Cervantes, Goethe and the 18th-century satirist Jean Paul (Richter's pseudonym).

Heinzen had the knack of substituting abuse and "moral indignation" for relevant arguments, and Marx branded this by comparing his writings with the type of literature which in the period of the Reformation was called grobian. Heinzen, Marx observed, had the honour of reviving this literature that was "flat, bombastic, bragging, thrasonical, putting on a great show of rude vigour in attack, yet hysterically sensitive to the same quality in others".[1] Marx showed Heinzen's appeals to morality to be a philistine's response to revolutionary communist ideas, which appeared to the righteous mind of the "virtuous philistine" to be immoral and destructive. His philistine morality fitted in with his vulgar sociological views.

Criticising the latter, Marx elaborated a number of propositions of historical materialism. He refuted the superficial view of political power, widely accepted by bourgeois and petty-bourgeois democrats, as an almighty force from which all "injustice in property relations" sprang, and exploded the illusion that once the existing authority is overthrown, all the social problems can be solved at one go. By contrast, Marx expounded and formulated in concrete terms the fundamentals of his doctrine on the relationship between the economic basis and the political superstructure.

It is not property relations that are determined by political power, he wrote, but, on the contrary, it is political power that depends on the historically rooted relations of production, or property relations, and the consequent class structure of society. It is therefore impossible to abolish the political system at will, for this requires mature economic and historical prerequisites. The emergent new property relations must come into irreconcilable contradiction with the existing political superstructure. However, the latter is in no sense a passive factor in social life. Wielded by the class in the ascendant, political power helps to accelerate progressive development; wielded by the class on the decline, it is a great impediment to progress. Consequently, the new social system cannot defeat the old one without re-

---

[1] Ibid., pp. 301, 312. Thraso—a stupid, boastful soldier in Terence's comedy, *Eunuchus*.

moving the old political superstructure through revolutionary action. As Marx put it, the old political integument of society has to be exploded.

Marx cited the historical development of the absolute monarchy to illustrate the dialectics of the relationship between the economic basis and the political superstructure. At the time it was not only a task confronting historical science but also a burning political problem to reveal the essence of absolutism. The struggle against absolutist regimes was the central issue of the day in many European countries. At first, the absolute monarchy — the feudal monarchy in the period of disintegration of medieval estates and the rise of the bourgeoisie — on the whole performed a progressive centralising function, but as bourgeois relations developed the situation changed. "Formerly encouraging trade and industry and thereby at the same time the rise of the bourgeois class, as necessary conditions both for national strength and for its own glory, absolute monarchy now everywhere hampers trade and industry, which have become increasingly dangerous weapons in the hands of an already powerful bourgeoisie."[1] Abolition of the absolutist order and other medieval survivals was a vital necessity in Germany, Austria and Italy.

This could be achieved only through resolute revolutionary action by the masses, similar to that which, during the revolutionary terror at the end of the 18th century, had managed to "spirit away, as it were, the ruins of feudalism from French soil".[2] In contrast to Heinzen's brash and showy revolutionism, Marx said the Communists in Germany and other countries looked to a revolution of the 1789-94 type, in which the people would have the decisive say. The working classes would have to fulfil their revolutionary tasks in the face of the bourgeoisie's conciliatory policy, because in Germany the bourgeois generally "seek as far as possible to make the change from *absolute* to *bourgeois* monarchy without a revolution, in an amicable fashion".[3] Here we find the seed of Marx's doctrine of the hegemony of the working class in the bourgeois revolution.

Marx saw the bourgeois revolution as an intermediate stage in the revolutionary struggle, and showed that it was sheer utopia to expect its victory to solve all social problems right away. But that was precisely Heinzen's political ideal, as he projected a "federal republic with social institutions", the prototype being the United States of America, which he presented as a kind of model state.

By showing up the exploitative nature of the North American state and society, Marx dealt a blow at the myth, widespread in Europe, that the Transatlantic Republic was a land of social harmony. Marx considered the principle of federalism, as applied in the U.S.A. and also in Switzerland, to be unsuitable for feudally frag-

---
[1] Marx, Engels, *Collected Works*, Vol. 6, p. 328.
[2] Ibid., p. 319.
[3] Ibid., p. 333.

mented Germany, which at the time was in great need of centralisation. Federalism was unacceptable both from the point of view of the class tasks of the proletariat, which could be more easily united in a centralised state, and of the consistent struggle for bourgeois-democratic change. To federalise Germany in those historical circumstances would have meant preserving some of her medieval particularism. Accordingly, Marx countered the ideas of the petty-bourgeois democrats with the demand that Germany be set up as "*one* indivisible republic".[1]

The workers, wrote Marx, "can and must accept the *bourgeois revolution* as a precondition for the *workers' revolution*".[2] Once the bourgeois revolution won, their struggle against the bourgeoisie would start in earnest, confronting them with the task which had already arisen in countries where the domination of the bourgeoisie had been established earlier, namely, to "become a power, in the first place a revolutionary power".[3] In this way, Marx used his contributions to the press to elaborate one of the main propositions of his doctrine — the idea of the proletariat's revolutionary dictatorship as an instrument of the social reconstruction of society.

EFFORTS TO UNITE THE REVOLUTIONARY FORCES

As Marx and Engels criticised the dogmas and illusions of the petty-bourgeois democrats, they also worked to unite the proletarian and democratic forces against the common enemy — the antipopular regimes of Europe. Marx vigorously opposed any sectarian exclusiveness among the workers' organisations, and held that the Communist League should take an active part in the general democratic movement, while safeguarding its class independence and the purity of its ideological and political tenets. He worked to establish a union between the Communists and the democrats in the various countries and set up an international alliance of the proletarian and democratic forces.

Marx and Engels took an active part in founding the Brussels International Democratic Association, which brought together proletarian revolutionaries and forward-looking bourgeois and petty-bourgeois democrats. The idea of setting up such an association originated among Belgian and emigrant democrats towards the end of September 1847. An international banquet held in Brussels on September 27 for this purpose adopted a decision to establish an international association. At the time Marx was away in Holland, where he was visiting relatives on personal business. In his absence Engels succeeded in securing broad access to the new organisation for workers, and he himself was invited to be a vice-president. Because he was about to leave for Paris, Engels wrote to the Belgian lawyer,

---

[1] Ibid., p. 335.
[2] Ibid., p. 333.
[3] Ibid., p. 319.

Lucien Jottrand, who had presided at the banquet, and proposed Marx in his stead, as having "the best claim to represent German democracy on the committee".[1]

Marx returned from his trip to Holland at the beginning of October 1847 and threw himself wholeheartedly into preparations to establish the new organisation. On November 7, 1847, the Brussels Democratic Association was finally constituted at a meeting of 63 founding members. Its Rules provided for regular meetings, the issue of addresses and petitions, and the establishment of ties with similar societies in other towns in Belgium and abroad. The Association's Committee was confirmed as its governing body at a meeting held on November 15, with General François Mellinet, a participant in the Belgian revolution of 1830, elected as honorary president, Jottrand as president, and Marx and the French socialist Jacques Imbert, a participant in the republican movement in France, as vice-presidents. Other members were Lelewel, representing the Polish emigrants, and Weerth, the German Communists.

Until the end of his stay in Brussels (early March 1848) Marx strongly influenced the activities of the Democratic Association, seeking to turn it into a centre for rallying the revolutionary and democratic forces of Europe. Largely through his efforts, the Association established broad international ties with the Chartists, the Fraternal Democrats of London, and French, Swiss and Dutch democrats. It responded to revolutionary events abroad and gave public support to the Swiss radicals in their fight against the *Sonderbund*, the alliance of seven reactionary cantons, which started a civil war in the country in November 1847. Members of the Democratic Association discussed the convocation of an international democratic congress.

Marx worked to make the Association the leading force in the Belgian revolutionary-democratic movement as well, and it enjoyed the support of democrats not only in Brussels, but also in other towns.

There was some friction in the Association between the proletarian revolutionaries on the one hand and the petty-bourgeois democrats and bourgeois republicans (among them Jottrand) on the other. The latter sought to keep the Association's activities within the Belgian constitutional framework, viewed with suspicion the communist views of its proletarian members, and expressed dissatisfaction over Marx's criticism of the Free Trade doctrine, of which they approved. The differences between Marx and Jottrand nearly led to a breach. After an incident at an Association meeting on February 22, 1848, Marx was forced to announce his resignation as vice-president, but Jottrand adopted a conciliatory attitude and requested Marx to continue in his post, which, in view of the tense situation, Marx agreed to do.

---

[1] Marx, Engels, *Collected Works*, Vol. 38, p. 133.

Marx and Engels attached much importance to establishing contacts with the so-called socialist-democratic party in France known after its organ as the *Réforme*. It brought together petty-bourgeois democrats and socialists, and took an active part in the reform movement, demanding a democratic republic, universal suffrage, and certain social measures in the interests of the working people.

But Ledru-Rollin and Louis Blanc, the party's petty-bourgeois leaders, were carried away by revolutionary catchwords which often covered their unpreparedness for revolutionary action. Many of the *Réforme*'s active members viewed the independent revolutionary working-class movement with suspicion and adopted an arrogant, markedly nationalistic attitude to the democrats of other countries.

Marx and Engels found Louis Blanc's petty-bourgeois socialist theory unacceptable, as set out in an 1840 pamphlet, entitled *The Organisation of Labour*. It contained a keen, if superficial, critique of the evils of bourgeois society (the anarchy of production, competition, and so on), and suggested that the social question should be solved by production associations of workers by trade, set up and operated with the aid of government subsidies. He declared: "The state is the banker of the poor", thereby obscuring the class character of state power under capitalism. He spread harmful illusions about the possibility of achieving socialism through the collaboration of classes and with the help of the bourgeois state.

Marx and Engels saw clearly the shortcomings of the socialist-democratic party and its leaders, but decided in the interests of greater international solidarity of democrats to co-operate with it because, for all its weakness, the party did voice to some extent the revolutionary mood of the French masses. It was Engels who played the main role in establishing these ties. An extant letter which Blanc wrote to Marx — it is undated but unquestionably belongs to that period — shows that Marx, too, had direct contacts with the party's leaders.

However, no complete understanding was ever reached, because of differences in outlook. When Engels tried to have the *Réforme* print a summary of the speech Marx was to have delivered at the economists' congress, and a review of *The Poverty of Philosophy*, he met with an undercurrent of opposition, mainly on the part of Blanc.

In December 1847 and January 1848, Engels wrote articles for *The Northern Star* and the *Deutsche-Brüsseler-Zeitung* criticising ideas among the *Réforme* party leaders which the Communists found unacceptable, namely, that France had a special cosmopolitan role to play in world history, and that French democrats could claim a leading role in the international democratic movement.

The activities of Marx and Engels in the Democratic Association and their relations with the *Réforme* party show that their co-operation with the petty-bourgeois and bourgeois democrats was based on principle, and that they did not make any ideological concessions or refrain from criticism of their illusions and mistakes. Engels wrote: "The union of the democrats of different nations does not exclude mutual criticism. It is impossible without such criticism. Without criticism there is no understanding and consequently no union."[1] Working to bring together proletarian and democratic forces in a single camp, Marx and Engels formulated the principles of the proletarian party's policy with respect to the general democratic movement.

The revolutionary role of the Democratic Association in Belgium's political life and the international arena was determined above all by the efforts of its Left, mainly proletarian, wing, and it was the latter that the Belgian police regarded as the main danger. It always had Marx under surveillance. Ever since his arrival in Brussels, the police had kept a dossier including copies of his newspaper articles. The reactionary ruling circles of Belgium were preparing to deal summarily with Marx and his followers.

SECOND CONGRESS OF THE COMMUNIST LEAGUE

The successes achieved at the first congress of the Communist League had to be consolidated by adopting the Rules and drawing up a Programme, and this called for another congress. The situation that had developed within the League was another reason why the Central Authority in London wanted an early congress. Sectarian elements in some communities, especially in Germany and Switzerland, had intensified their fight against the leadership's line. In an address to the Brussels Circle Authority on October 18, 1847, the Central Authority said that the situation could be righted only by another congress. Schapper, Moll, and Heinrich Bauer, who signed the address, insisted that Marx should attend the congress.

Marx and Engels also attached much importance to the congress, for they realised that it would provide an opportunity for removing all the obstacles to the consolidation by the international proletarian organisation of the principles of scientific communism and its tactical platform. Both were elected delegates, Marx in the Brussels and Engels in the Paris circle of the Communist League.

During the preparations for the congress, the League communities discussed the "Draft of a Communist Confession of Faith" (a list of questions and short answers), which had been written by Engels and approved by the previous congress in the summer of 1847. In the Paris communities it was confronted by Hess' "improved" draft, which was, however, found to be unsatisfactory. At the request of the Paris members of the League, Engels edited and enlarged his draft, calling the new document *Principles of Communism*. He retained the old form but produced a fuller exposition of the

---

[1] Marx, Engels, *Collected Works*, Vol. 6, p. 409.

most important programme and tactical tenets of the proletarian party. Engels substantiated the historical prerequisites of the proletarian revolution and outlined the measures to be taken by the revolutionary proletariat after it gained power to pave the way for the transition to communism.

However, Engels himself saw this as no more than a rough outline of the programme and soon realised that it was impossible to confine to the question-and-answer form the content of a programme which called for a comprehensive historical substantiation and coherent exposition. A few days before leaving for London he wrote to Marx: "Give a little thought to the Confession of Faith. I think we would do best to abandon the catachetical form and call the thing Communist *Manifesto*. Since a certain amount of history has to be narrated in it, the form hitherto adopted is quite unsuitable."[1]

Marx fully approved the idea. Like Engels, he saw *Principles of Communism* as a preliminary variant of the Communist League Programme and felt that in its final form it should be a militant party manifesto.

On November 27, 1847, the two friends met on their way to London at Ostend, a Belgian seaside resort, where, before crossing the Channel, they put up at the Crown Hotel to thrash out the questions to be dealt with at the congress.

The congress sat from November 29 to December 8, 1847, and was, for that period, a representative forum of the international working-class movement. It was attended by delegates from Germany, France, England, Switzerland, and Belgium. Among those who took part in the work of the congress were the Chartists, Harney and Jones, both members of the Communist League, and various leaders of the Polish revolutionary emigrants. Schapper was elected Chairman, and Engels Secretary of the congress. Heated debates were held at its sessions, with Marx and Engels taking a stand for the principles of scientific communism.

The congress revealed fully the compelling logic and the conclusive reasoning which were distinctive of Marx's gift as a speaker. Everyone present was highly impressed by his personality, his powerful brain, encyclopaedic knowledge, unbending will and ebullient energy. But he showed no sign of condescension and did not strike any of the attitudes that were the stock-in-trade of the political advocates of the bourgeoisie and occasionally some socialist leaders. While his ideological adversaries and those who stubbornly insisted on confused and sectarian ideas found Marx implacable and ironic, workers and revolutionaries loyal to the working-class cause found him unaffected, friendly and attentive.

Many workers who saw Marx at the sessions of the congress, at meetings of the German Workers' Educational Society in London, or at public or private meetings, realised that here was not only a brilli-

---

[1] Marx, Engels, *Collected Works*, Vol. 38, p. 149.

ant scientist, with amazing erudition for his age, but a sage and staunch leader of the working class, who was capable of leading it through thick and thin. Friedrich Lessner, a veteran of the working-class movement and at the time a journeyman-tailor in London, found his meeting with Marx a memorable occasion. He wrote: "As soon as I saw Marx, I felt the greatness and superiority of that remarkable man. A single feeling overwhelmed me, the feeling of certainty that the working-class movement, which had such leaders to guide it, was bound to win." [1]

Lessner and others were especially impressed by the speeches Marx delivered at workers' meetings. "Marx was a born leader of the people. His speech was brief, convincing and compelling in its logic. He never said a superfluous word; every sentence was a thought and every thought was a necessary link in the chain of his demonstration." [2]

Marx was satisfied with the results of the congress. In the discussion of the Communist League's Programme, the principles of the new proletarian doctrine won a complete victory, and Marx and Engels were asked to write a programme in the form of a manifesto. On their motion, it was resolved that in its external relations the League should take an open stand as a Communist Party. The congress adopted a much improved version of the earlier written Rules. The first paragraph was couched in programmatic terms. It said: "The aim of the League is the overthrow of the bourgeoisie, the rule of the proletariat, the abolition of the old bourgeois society which rests on the antagonism of classes, and the foundation of a new society without classes and without private property." [3]

In London, Marx performed another mission which the Brussels Democratic Association had assigned to him on his own initiative. He was to establish contacts with democratic and working-class organisations in England. On November 29, 1847, he and Engels attended an international meeting to mark the Polish uprising of 1830, which had been organised in London by the Fraternal Democrats, and there was loud applause as his official credentials were read out.

In his speech at the meeting Marx formulated a number of important principles of proletarian internationalism, substantiating the idea of solidarity between the fighting proletariat and the liberation movement of the Polish and other oppressed peoples. He exposed the bourgeois cosmopolites' hypocritical talk about a brotherhood of nations under the existing capitalist system, and stressed that the working class alone was a consistent fighter against national oppression. Its victory over the bourgeoisie would be at the same time the "signal of liberation for all oppressed nations". [4]

---

[1] *Marx und Engels und die ersten proletarischen Revolutionäre*, Dietz Verlag, Berlin, 1965, S. 132.
[2] *Reminiscences of Marx and Engels*, p. 153.
[3] Marx, Engels, *Collected Works*, Vol. 6, p. 633.
[4] Ibid., p. 388.

In his speech, Engels added: "A nation cannot become free and at the same time continue to oppress other nations."[1]

Marx's trip to England helped considerably to strengthen the international ties of the Brussels Democratic Association. His talks in London on the convocation of an international democratic congress were successful and he won the support of Chartist leaders and of proletarian and democratic emigrants. There he made the acquaintance of Ernest Jones, one of the most talented revolutionary leaders of the Chartist movement.

During their stay in London, Marx and Engels participated in the work of the German Workers' Educational Society, and took the opportunity offered by its meetings to explain the principles of communist theory and tactics. On November 30, 1847, Marx presented a report to its members on various aspects of the proletarian movement and communist propaganda. He also dealt with the scientific criticism of religion, a problem to which he attached much importance in the campaign to spread the communist outlook.[2] Engels spoke twice—on November 30 and December 7—and dealt mainly with economic questions.

AFTER THE CONGRESS

Marx appears to have returned to Brussels on December 13, 1847, and Engels arrived there a few days later. Towards the end of the month, Engels went back to Paris, but his stay was short, for at the end of January 1848 he was expelled by the French authorities and returned to Brussels.

In late 1847 and early 1848, in an atmosphere of imminent revolution, Marx, the truly popular leader, worked intensely with indefatigable energy. He was engaged in a mass of activities—writing the *Manifesto of the Communist Party,* lecturing at the German Workers' Society, guiding the Communist League, speaking at public meetings, attacking the opponents of the working class in the press, writing letters and meeting friends. He also had to put a great deal of effort into the editing of the *Deutsche-Brüsseler-Zeitung,* especially when Engels was away from Brussels and Marx had to do his work as well.

Marx devoted a great deal of time and attention to the Brussels Democratic Association. On December 19, 1847, he reported to its members on the results of his visit to London. At a meeting on December 26 he seconded the motion on the admission to membership of Bakunin, who had been deported from France, and the German Communist, Dr. d'Ester. On January 9, 1848, he spoke on Free Trade at a meeting organised by the Association. Some time after January 20 he went to Ghent with a delegation from the Association

---

[1] Ibid., p. 389.
[2] Ibid., pp. 630-31.

to attend the opening of the local branch. At its meeting on February 13, he assisted in drafting a message to the Fraternal Democrats. On February 20, he chaired a meeting of the Association to hear Engels' report on the circumstances of his expulsion from France. He and Engels spoke at a meeting on February 22 honouring the fighters for Poland's independence.

Preparations were in progress for the international democratic congress and in a letter dated December 18, 1847 Harney informed Marx that the Executive Committee of the National Charter Association had agreed to take part. Agreement was reached on the date and venue of the congress; it was to be held in Brussels on August 25, 1848, to coincide with the 18th anniversary of the 1830 revolution in Belgium. This concerted and well-conceived plan was not put into effect only because Europe was plunged into a whirlpool of revolutionary events.

Marx's speech on Free Trade before the Brussels Democratic Association on January 9, 1848, was a great event in Belgium's public life. Marx spoke in French, and the enormous audience heard him with unflagging attention. When he finished, a motion was passed to have his speech published at the expense of the Association. Even before it appeared as a separate pamphlet, the *Deutsche-Brüsseler-Zeitung* published a detailed summary of it on January 16, 1848.

The "Speech on the Question of Free Trade" was based on the material Marx had prepared for the speech he was to have delivered at the congress of economists in September 1847, with the addition of a number of new theses. Lenin summed up the gist of Marx's views as follows: "The conclusion he drew from his analysis was that Free Trade signifies nothing but freedom for the development of capital." [1]

At the same time Marx again sharply criticised the bourgeois apologists of Free Trade, his criticism developing into an exposure of bourgeois liberalism as such. He showed that liberal talk of freedom was false and hypocritical, and that the bourgeoisie and its ideologists had gravely distorted the idea of freedom and equality, turning it into a cover for violence and exploitation and an instrument for deceiving the masses.

The "Speech on the Question of Free Trade" was one of the first works in which Marx dealt with colonial policy. He showed that colonial rule sprang from the predatory nature of capitalism itself, the bourgeoisie's desire to exploit which ran well beyond the national boundaries and produced both rivalry in the world market and the urge of one country to enrich itself at the expense of another. He also pointed to the grave consequences of colonial dependence for the enslaved countries, and the forcible subjugation of their economy to the interests of the bourgeoisie of the metropolis. He expressed profound indignation at the efforts to justify colonial oppres-

---

[1] V. I. Lenin, *Collected Works*, Vol. 2, p. 263.

sion with the aid of bourgeois cosmopolitan ideas, and to depict Free Trade as a means of establishing the brotherhood of nations and incorporating them in a common civilisation. Marx said: "To call cosmopolitan exploitation universal brotherhood is an idea that could only be engendered in the brain of the bourgeoisie." [1]

There was also broad agreement in proletarian and democratic circles with Marx's speech at a ceremonial meeting in Brussels on February 22, 1848, to mark the second anniversary of the Cracow insurrection. This speech, together with those of Engels and Lelewel, was also issued in a separate pamphlet. In his speech, Marx said that while supporting the national liberation movement of the oppressed peoples, the proletarian party must look to the revolutionary-democratic forces of the movement, who combined the struggle for national independence with support for peasant action against feudal oppression. In fact, the Cracow insurrection marked a great step forward, precisely because it identified the "national cause with the democratic cause and the emancipation of the oppressed classes".[2] Marx emphasised that Poland's revival should be carried out on a revolutionary-democratic basis.

WORK ON THE
MANIFESTO OF THE COMMUNIST PARTY

In this period Marx's main efforts went into the writing of the *Manifesto of the Communist Party*. He and Engels worked on it together in London for a few days after the closure of the Communist League congress, and then in Brussels until Engels' departure for Paris. Following this Marx worked on the *Manifesto* alone for a whole month, seeking to embody the fundamental ideas of the new revolutionary doctrine in a most concise literary form that combined genuine ardour and revolutionary spirit with a clear-cut, polished style. Although the *Manifesto of the Communist Party* was produced by two men — Marx and Engels — and is the fruit of their creative collaboration, and although a part of the text was based on Engels' *Principles of Communism,* it was Marx who gave these ideas literary expression. The *Manifesto* shows Marx as a genius of revolutionary thought and a brilliant master of style.

Only one page of the rough draft of the *Manifesto* has survived, but it gives a good idea of the pains Marx took in writing it. We find him working on literally every sentence, deleting and amending unsatisfactory expressions and tirelessly seeking the right word. A draft plan for Section III, which is also extant, shows that Marx continued constantly to improve the structure of the *Manifesto,* giving it greater coherence with each new version. It was completed

---

[1] Marx, Engels, *Collected Works*, Vol. 6, p. 464.
[2] Ibid., p. 549.

towards the end of January and the manuscript was sent on to London.

The *Manifesto* was printed in a small printing shop in London owned by a German emigrant called J. E. Burghard, a member of the Communist League and the German Workers' Educational Society. The first German edition coincided with the February revolution in France. In mid-March 1848, 1,000 copies were received in Paris for distribution in France and Germany. The rest of the printing went to various other countries.

In April and May 1848, the same printing shop put out another edition. From March to July 1848, the *Manifesto* was serialised in the German emigrant newspaper *Deutsche Londoner Zeitung*.

Very soon numerous efforts were made to issue the *Manifesto* in other European languages. Three or four translations of it were made in France from 1848 to 1851, and it was translated into Italian and Spanish in Paris in 1848, but these translations remained unpublished.

In April 1848, Engels, then in Barmen, was translating the *Manifesto* into English, but the first English translation made by Helen Macfarlane was not published until two years later, in November 1850, by the Chartist journal *The Red Republican* in which its editor, Julian Harney, named the authors for the first time, in his introduction. In all earlier editions and in many subsequent ones the *Manifesto* was published anonymously.

A Danish edition was put out in 1848 by the Danish members of the Fraternal Democrats Society. A Polish edition appeared in Paris at the end of 1848. A Swedish edition, which was distributed by the utopian socialist Götrek, was published in Stockholm under a different name: "The Voice of Communism. Declaration of the Communist Party." It is true that in place of the rallying cry "Working Men of All Countries, Unite!" it had "Vox populi — vox Dei!"

As the proletariat's struggle for freedom acquired ever greater proportions, new editions of the *Manifesto* appeared and the number of its readers increased. In 1890, Engels had good grounds for saying that "to a certain extent, the history of the *Manifesto* reflects the history of the modern working-class movement since 1848".[1] This great work was translated by the Spanish socialist José Mesa, the Hungarian proletarian revolutionary Leo Frankel, the pioneer of Marxism in Russia, Georgi Plekhanov, the founder of the revolutionary Bulgarian Social-Democratic Party, Dimitr Blagoev, the prominent Bolshevik journalist Vaclav Vorovsky, and the leader of the Hungarian Communists Béla Kun. It was translated into Russian by V. I. Lenin during his stay in Samara in 1893, and this translation was read there in manuscript in revolutionary circles.

Readers of the *Manifesto* at once remarked on the tremendous impact which its ideas had on them. After reading the *Manifesto*

---

[1] Marx and Engels, *Selected Works*, Vol. 1, p. 103.

Lessner recalled: "What I lost in enthusiasm and fancy I gained in consciousness of the aim and knowledge."[1]

For the ruling classes, the very act of reading the *Manifesto* was a crime. For years it was circulated in many countries only through illegal channels. The official reaction showed that Marx and Engels had dealt a telling blow at the exploiters' world.

FIRST MARXIST PROGRAMME

The *Manifesto* is the peak of the creative efforts of the founders of Marxism before the 1848 revolution, and is of immense historical importance. It was a programme which showed the working class of all countries the way to emancipation from the capitalist bondage, to a triumphant proletarian revolution. Engels was right when he said in 1888 that the *Manifesto* was "the most widespread, the most international production of all Socialist literature, the common platform acknowledged by millions of working men from Siberia to California".[2] Lenin wrote: "This little booklet is worth whole volumes: to this day its spirit inspires and guides the entire organised and fighting proletariat of the civilised world."[3]

It was the first coherent and consistent exposition of the fundamentals of Marxism. By then Marx and Engels had laid a sound philosophical foundation for their doctrine, formulating the basic principles of scientific communism and a number of key points of departure for their economic theory. The *Manifesto* shows that the component parts of Marxism constitute a single organic whole. Lenin wrote: "With the clarity and brilliance of genius, this work outlines a new world-conception, consistent materialism, which also embraces the realm of social life; dialectics, as the most comprehensive and profound doctrine of development; the theory of the class struggle and of the world-historic revolutionary role of the proletariat — the creator of a new, communist society."[4]

The *Manifesto* opens with a description of the historical situation in which it appeared, and the fear and hatred with which the powers of the bourgeois world watched the emergence of the communist movement. "A spectre is haunting Europe — the spectre of Communism. All the Powers of old Europe have entered into a holy alliance to exorcise this spectre: Pope and Czar, Metternich and Guizot, French Radicals and German police-spies."[5] Marx and Engels believed that the best way to refute the slander heaped on communism was to issue a bold and open declaration of the principles of their revolutionary doctrine.

---

[1] *Reminiscences of Marx and Engels*, p. 150.
[2] K. Marx and F. Engels, *Manifesto of the Communist Party*, Moscow, 1975, p. 19.
[3] V. I. Lenin, *Collected Works*, Vol. 2, p. 24.
[4] Ibid., Vol. 21, p. 48.
[5] Marx, Engels, *Collected Works*, Vol. 6, p. 481.

The *Manifesto* shows the origin and development of capitalism, and exposes its intrinsic contradictions and the deepening and growing class antagonism between the bourgeoisie and the proletariat. The establishment of the capitalist system, which superseded feudalism, went hand in hand with an unprecedented growth of the productive forces, economic progress and the advance of science and culture. But at a definite stage of development, the relations of production in bourgeois society—like those of earlier modes of production—ceased to correspond to the increased productive forces, and became a fetter on their further development, breeding economic crises, which rock the whole capitalist system. The *Manifesto* compares bourgeois society to the sorcerer who is no longer able to control the powers of the nether world he has called up by his spells. A progressive class during its fight with feudalism, the bourgeoisie becomes a reactionary class and an obstacle in the way of social progress.

The *Manifesto* roundly exposes the true nature of capitalist society, its brutal exploitation of the workers, inhuman morality, and unrestrained rule of money, which turns human relations into objects to be bought and sold and man's personal dignity, knowledge and skills into a mere exchange value. The capitalist system has left remaining no other nexus between man and man than naked self-interest, than callous cash payment, turning exploitation and plunder of the weak by the strong into a principle determining relations between nations. Just as the bourgeoisie makes the country dependent on the town, so it makes the countries lagging in their economic development "dependent on the civilised ones, nations of peasants on nations of bourgeois, the East on the West".[1] The rule of the bourgeoisie plunged whole nations into colonial bondage and carried with it bloody wars of destruction.

The bourgeoisie put production on a social basis, concentrating hundreds and thousands of workers at large factories, and inaugurating a higher type of social division of labour and closer connections between the various branches of the economy. However, private capitalist property and private appropriation run into irreconcilable contradiction with the social character of production. The very operation of the laws of capitalist economy is objectively paving the way for the abolition of capitalist property in the means of production, together with the whole capitalist system.

Having proved the inevitable downfall of capitalism, Marx and Engels emphasised, however, that it would not collapse of its own accord. A definite class would play the role of its grave-digger. That class has been created by capitalist society itself. "...Not only has the bourgeoisie forged the weapons that bring death to itself; it has also called into existence the men who are to wield those weapons—the modern workers—the *proletarians*." [2]

---

[1] Marx, Engels, *Collected Works*, Vol. 6, p. 488.
[2] Ibid., p. 490.

No moribund ruling class leaves the historical stage of its own accord, so the bourgeoisie can be overthrown only through bitter class struggle and proletarian revolution.

This revolutionary conclusion is based on a profound analysis of the role the class struggle has played in the history of society. Ever since the disintegration of primitive society the struggle between the oppressed and the oppressors has been the main motive force behind historical development. Bourgeois society brought to the fore the antagonism between the two main classes, the bourgeoisie and the proletariat, with the other classes and strata—the peasantry, the petty traders and artisans, the intelligentsia and the lumpenproletariat—occupying an intermediate position. As capitalism developed, the peasantry and the urban middle sections were ruined and declined. They could further progress and revolution only by joining with the working class and acting in alliance with it and under its leadership.

The *Manifesto* contains a comprehensive substantiation of the role the working class has to play in world history, as the most revolutionary class of any that have come on the historical scene. While other oppressed classes were stratified and fell apart, the proletariat was concentrated at the capitalist enterprises, grew steadily and was by its very status carried into the arena as a terrible and implacable enemy of the entire system of wage slavery. The workers' very deprivation becomes a revolutionising factor, making them consistent fighters against capitalism. "They have nothing of their own to secure and to fortify; their mission is to destroy all previous securities for, and insurances of, individual property."[1] At the same time, the working class carries on its fight against capitalism not only for its own emancipation. It fulfils its emancipatory mission in the interests of all the oppressed, of all labouring mankind, by freeing it from all oppression and exploitation for all time.

The *Manifesto* shows the various stages of the workers' struggle against the bourgeoisie, from spontaneous riots and the destruction of machinery to organised resistance by the revolutionary proletariat, which has come to realise its goals and has succeeded in rallying its forces on a national scale. This is a more or less concealed civil war, raging within bourgeois society, up to the point where it inevitably breaks out in open revolution, resulting in the overthrow of the bourgeoisie and the establishment of proletarian rule.

Elaborating the principal regularities of the proletarian revolution, Marx and Engels wrote that its first step was "to raise the proletariat to the position of ruling class, to win the battle of democracy".[2] They said that the proletariat would use its political rule to wrest, by degrees, all capital from the bourgeoisie, to centralise all instruments of production in the hands of the proletarian state, and

---

[1] Marx, Engels, *Collected Works*, Vol. 6, p. 495.
[2] Ibid., p. 504.

to increase the total of the productive forces as rapidly as possible, so as to advance to a classless, communist society.

This idea — the idea of setting up a proletarian dictatorship, a proletarian power which was democratic by its very nature and expressed the interests and relied on the support of the vast majority of the people — was the pivotal one in the *Manifesto*. It is true that the term "dictatorship of the proletariat" was not yet used in the *Manifesto*, for it took the experience of the 1848-49 revolution to help Marx and Engels chisel to perfection the formula expressing the idea of the political rule of the revolutionary proletariat. But the concept of the proletarian dictatorship itself, of the proletarian state, was not only clearly stated but also scientifically grounded.

The working class would by no means seek to perpetuate its power and would be the only class in history to take this attitude. It would establish its political rule only for the period required to do away with the exploiting classes, eliminate the conditions for the existence of classes in general, and ensure the final triumph of the social relations of the new, classless society.[1]

With brilliant insight, Marx and Engels outlined the main features of the communist system, stressing that communism would not be established all at once, but in the course of a gradual transformation of the old society into the new. They outlined the measures which the proletarian state would take to pave the way for this transformation, but were not dogmatic about them, believing that the practice of building the new society and its concrete conditions would introduce the relevant correctives. At the time, Marx and Engels were able to define the distinctive features of the future system only in the most general terms.

The communist revolution would put an end to exploitation once and for all, together with every type of social enslavement and the parasitic existence of some men at the expense of others. National oppression would be eradicated. Colonial oppression and bloody wars would disappear for ever.

Marx and Engels believed that communism would be established with the real flourishing of material production, a rapid development of the productive forces, which would be used for the fullest and most comprehensive satisfaction of the material and spiritual requirements of all members of society. "In bourgeois society, living labour is but a means to increase accumulated labour. In Communist society, accumulated labour is but a means to widen, to enrich, to promote the existence of the labourer."[2] One way to abolish the distinction between mental and physical labour would be "combination of education with industrial production".[3] The distinction between town and country would be gradually abolished. The rural

---

[1] Marx, Engels, *Collected Works*, Vol. 6, p. 506.
[2] Ibid., p. 499.
[3] Ibid., p. 505.

population would then be able to escape from the "idiocy of rural life". The inequality of women would completely disappear.

Marx and Engels stressed the high humanistic principles on which all human relations would be based under communism. True individual freedom and the harmony of individual and social interests would be established. Communist society would be an association of equal working people, in which "the free development of each is the condition for the free development of all".[1] The ideas of scientific communism set out in the *Manifesto* were an expression of genuine humanism, and charted the real way of realising the age-old aspirations of labouring mankind, its urge to be rid of oppression, and live in freedom, equality, brotherhood, peace and happiness.

A great achievement was that the *Manifesto* laid the foundations of the doctrine of the proletarian party as the organiser and leader of the working class, whose establishment was a necessary condition for the proletariat to win political power and transform society.

Marx and Engels described the Communist Party's role as the vanguard of the proletariat in these words: "The Communists, therefore, are on the one hand, practically, the most advanced and resolute section of the working-class parties of every country, that section which pushes forward all others; on the other hand, theoretically, they have over the great mass of the proletariat the advantage of clearly understanding the line of march, the conditions, and the ultimate general results of the proletarian movement."[2]

The *Manifesto* set out the fundamental tactics for the revolutionary party of the proletariat, without producing any universal recipes. It stressed the need for the Communists to act in accordance with the historical conditions, not with some stereotype. In formulating its concrete policy, the party also had to take account of general tactical principles, which were equally necessary whatever the specific local conditions. These were the ability to subordinate the immediate aims of the working class to its ultimate goals, to maintain the unity of the proletariat's international and national tasks, and to support various revolutionary and progressive trends, while maintaining a critical attitude to the illusions of its allies.

Marx and Engels substantiated the proposition that the communist movement is international and the consequent principles of proletarian internationalism. They stressed the great importance of international proletarian solidarity, that is, unity of view and concerted action by the proletariat of different countries. Their great rallying cry — "Working Men of All Countries, Unite!" — is a striking expression of the common class interests and goals of the workers of the world.

Marx and Engels castigated the bourgeois slanderers who sought to ascribe to the Communists the absurd intentions of abolishing the right of personally acquiring property as the fruit of a man's own la-

[1] Ibid., p. 506.
[2] Ibid., p. 497.

bour, doing away with personal freedom, abolishing country and nationality, the family, education and so on. The bourgeois ideologists accused the Communists of doing what bourgeois society itself had done, for it had ruined the small properties of the peasant and the artisan, and had turned the worker into a mere appendage of the machine, and was keeping him in a state of permanent ignorance, by making education the privilege of the rich. It used hypocritical cant about the sacredness of marriage to cover up official and unofficial prostitution.

Referring to the charge that the Communists intended to abolish country and nationality, Marx and Engels wrote: "The working men have no country. We cannot take from them what they have not got."[1] This statement emphasises the proletariat's hostility to the chauvinism of the bourgeoisie which seeks, under the false pretext of "defending one's country", to enslave and plunder other nations. The workers of the different countries have a common international destiny and a sense of solidarity with the working people of the oppressed nations, in contrast to their "own" bourgeoisie, which oppresses these nations.

This statement reflects only one side of the proletariat's attitude to the bourgeois country, and in other passages the *Manifesto* shows the hostile attitude Marx and Engels took to national nihilism. They said that the struggle of the working class against the bourgeoisie is at first a national struggle, and that the working class of each country must first of all put an end to its own bourgeoisie by rallying all the progressive forces of the nation. The working people will truly acquire country with the victory of the working class. The proletariat is free from all national narrow-mindedness and self-conceit, and its national interests, correctly understood, are identical with its international interests, and are completely in accord with the principles of proletarian internationalism.

The *Manifesto* made a point of characterising the diverse non-proletarian ideological trends claiming the banner of socialism as their own. It contained a profound analysis of the class essence and reactionary orientation of feudal, Christian socialism and petty-bourgeois socialism, with "true socialism", its German brand. Marx and Engels believed that the greatest harm and danger came from reformist trends, which they classed together under the heading of bourgeois, or conservative, socialism, including Proudhon's petty-bourgeois reformist doctrines.

The *Manifesto* paid tribute to the great utopian socialists—Saint-Simon, Fourier and Owen—the precursors of scientific communism, whose works greatly helped to criticise capitalism and enlighten the working class. However, as the proletariat's class struggle developed, and scientific communist ideas took shape, utopian socialism became increasingly out of touch with life and lost its

---

[1] Marx, Engels, *Collected Works*, Vol. 6, p. 502.

practical importance. Those who clung dogmatically to the defects of these doctrines degenerated into reactionary sectarians.

The *Manifesto* ends with these fiery words: "Let the ruling classes tremble at a Communistic revolution. The proletarians have nothing to lose but their chains. They have a world to win.

"WORKING MEN OF ALL COUNTRIES, UNITE!"[1]

The formulation of the first programme of the international working-class movement was a great scientific achievement. The *Manifesto* put the main finishing touches to Marxism as a coherent revolutionary outlook. It marked a decisive step in converting socialism from a utopia into a science, opening up new horizons for the development of revolutionary theory and for translating it into the practice of revolutionary struggle.

---

[1] Ibid., p. 519.

CHAPTER FIVE

DURING THE REVOLUTIONS OF 1848-49

> *In the two revolutionary years 1848-49 the League proved itself in double fashion: first, in that its members energetically took part in the movement, in all places, that in the press, on the barricades and on the battlefields they stood in the front ranks of the only decidedly revolutionary class, the proletariat. The League further proved itself in that its conception of the movement ... turned out to be the only correct one.*
>
> Karl Marx and Frederick Engels

REVOLUTIONS BREAK OUT IN EUROPE. MARX EXPELLED FROM BRUSSELS

On February 22-24, 1848, the French people overthrew Louis-Philippe, the "bankers' king", and proclaimed a republic. On March 13, an uprising was staged in Vienna, the capital of Austria, and on March 18, in Berlin, the capital of Prussia. Under pressure from the masses, Metternich's police regime collapsed and the Austrian emperor was forced to promise a constitution. A bourgeois opposition government came to power in Prussia. The people's victory in Vienna and Berlin intensified the revolutionary movement in the other German states as well.

After heroic fighting in the streets of Milan on March 18-22, the people expelled the Austrian army under Joseph Radetzky. The masses of Venice, Piedmont and Rome rose in revolt. The revolutionary tide rolled across Europe, running towards the borders of bourgeois aristocratic England in the west, and serf-holding Russia in the east.

The historical roots of the 1848-49 revolutions lay mainly in the sharpening contradictions between rising capitalism and the absolutist feudal order, which still prevailed in most European countries. In France, it had been destroyed at the end of the 18th century, and the new bourgeois-democratic revolution there was caused by the obstacles which the political rule of the top layer of the bourgeoisie, the financial élite, was creating in the way of capitalist development. In the other countries, the main tasks of the revolution were to overthrow the absolute monarchies, abolish feudal landed estates, cast off the foreign yoke, and set up united national states.

The 1848 revolutions differed from the classic type — the French Revolution — in that they brought a new class, the proletariat, into the broad political arena. Its revolutionary role was most strikingly revealed in France, where the workers fought arms in hand to set up a republic and demanded that it should be a social republic. The working class also played a decisive part during the fighting on the barricades in Vienna and Berlin, although there it was not able, as it had been in France, to put forward its own political and social demands at once.

The contradictions between the two main classes of capitalist society were most fully developed in England, the stronghold of capitalism, but they were also variously manifested in the other European countries. Thus, the very outset of the 1848 revolutions confirmed what Marx and Engels had forecast in the *Deutsche-Brüsseler-Zeitung* concerning the arrangement of forces in the revolutionary battles: "Behind them [the bourgeoisie] stands everywhere the proletariat." [1]

Marx was delighted when he heard the first reports of the February revolution in France and its reverberations in other countries, for he believed revolutionary periods to be the most important and crucial moments in world history, when masses of people make a great thrust forward, sweeping away every obstacle to mankind's progressive development.

The events in France at once had an effect on Belgium, where a movement began in favour of a republic. Marx worked to have the Communist League communities, the German Workers' Society and the Brussels Democratic Association help the people overcome their lack of organisation and leadership. At its meeting on February 27, the Association's Committee decided to launch a broad campaign and to demand that the municipal council should organise armed forces to include workers and artisans in addition to the bourgeois civil guard. The Democratic Association itself started to arm the workers. Only a fortnight or so earlier Marx had received his share of his father's estate, and contributed a large amount for the purchase of arms.

Under Marx's influence, the Democratic Association took a number of steps to establish unity of action between the democrats and proletarian revolutionaries in different countries. On February 28, its Committee sent a message of greetings to the Provisional Government of France and a letter to Julian Harney, editor of *The Northern Star* and Secretary of the Fraternal Democrats Society, expressing the hope that the Chartists would soon succeed in having the People's Charter passed as a law of the country.

Wherever Marx found himself, he never stood apart from the struggle of the masses and always devoted all his knowledge and energy to it. This won him great respect among democrats and socialists in Belgium, England and France. On March 1, he received a letter in the name of the French people from Ferdinand Flocon, a member of the Provisional Government of France, who wrote: "Tyranny exiled you, now free France opens its doors to you." [2]

---

[1] Marx, Engels, *Collected Works*, Vol. 6, p. 528.
[2] Ibid., p. 649.

Marx longed to be at the heart of the revolutionary struggle and his departure for Paris was hastened by the Belgian government, which started reprisals against democrats, foreigners, in particular. At 5.00 p. m. on March 3, he was ordered to leave Belgium within 24 hours.

Shortly before that he had been notified of the decision of the Communist League's Central Authority in London handing over all its powers to the Brussels Circle. Schapper, Heinrich Bauer, Moll and other members of the Central Authority, who were preparing to leave for the continent, believed that in the new revolutionary period Marx, the real leader of the League, should be personally in charge. However, the circumstances in Brussels had taken an unfavourable turn in view of the expulsion order issued against Marx and the arrest of Wilhelm Wolff and several other leaders of the League. Before leaving Brussels, therefore, Marx called a meeting at his home of the newly constituted Brussels Central Authority, which decided to move the Central Authority's seat to Paris, and authorised Marx to set up a new Central Authority there. The Brussels Central Authority then announced its dissolution.

Hardly had the five men who adopted this decision gone home, when the police broke into Marx's home, carried out a search and arrested him on the false pretext that he had no papers. He was maltreated during his arrest and then thrown into a prison cell.

When Jenny and the Belgian Communist Gigot went to the police department to find out what had happened to Marx, they, too, were arrested. Because they did not have their passports with them, they were charged with vagrancy, but this was so obviously absurd that the following day the examining magistrate had to release them.

The numerous protests against the arbitrary acts of the Belgian police forced them to release Marx too, but his twenty-four hours had already expired, so he and his family had to leave Brussels without any of their personal belongings.

The foul methods used against Marx and his wife by the ruling circles of the "model constitutional state" were exposed in Marx's statement to the newspaper *La Réforme* and Engels' letter to the editor of *The Northern Star*. The protests in the press and questions in Parliament forced the Belgian government to announce the dismissal of the officials who had taken the high-handed action against Marx.

MARX IN PARIS. FIGHT AGAINST "EXPORT REVOLUTION" PLANS

Immediately upon his arrival in Paris, Marx began to form a new Central Authority of the Communist League and was soon able to inform Engels, who had remained in Brussels, that the new Central Authority had been set up, with Marx as Chairman, Schapper as Secretary and Wallau, Wilhelm Wolff, Moll, Heinrich Bauer and

Engels as members. Marx urged his friend to come to Paris as soon as possible.

At the time, a very popular idea among the foreign emigrants in Paris—Germans, Poles, Belgians, Irish and Spaniards—was to form armed legions for the liberation of their countries and the establishment of republics. A German legion which was to make a raid on one of the border German states was initiated by the popular poet Herwegh and Bornstedt, one-time editor of the *Deutsche-Brüsseler-Zeitung*, who were leaders of the Democratic Society in Paris.

At first their agitation among the German emigrants, who were longing for revolutionary action, was highly successful, and was approved even by Weerth, who before Marx's arrival had been elected to the Democratic Society's Committee. At a meeting of German democrats on March 6, Karl Schapper also backed the idea of an armed legion. However, Marx soon convinced them and other emigrant workers that this was a futile and harmful undertaking, and Bornstedt was expelled from the Communist League on March 16.

Marx and Engels, who soon came to Paris, sought to explain to the workers the great harm of the reckless idea of "exporting revolution". Engels subsequently recalled: "We opposed this playing with revolution most decisively. To carry an invasion, which was to import the revolution forcibly from outside, into the midst of the ferment then going on in Germany, meant to undermine the revolution in Germany itself, to strengthen the governments and to deliver the legionaries ... defenceless into the hands of the German troops." [1]

As a counterweight to the Democratic Society, a legal German Workers' Club was set up on Marx's initiative. A joint meeting of the four Paris communities of the Communist League on March 9 approved its draft Rules, submitted by Marx. At the meetings of the Club at the Picard Café in the Rue St. Denis, Marx, Engels, and their followers urged the workers not to join the legion and to return home one by one. Marx elucidated the nature and the prospects of the revolution in France. In a long report at one meeting he explained to the workers that the February revolution was only the start of the movement, and that it was soon bound to be followed by an open struggle between the French proletariat and the bourgeoisie, a struggle on which the future of the other European revolutions would largely depend. In his efforts to foster the spirit of proletarian internationalism among the German workers, he urged those who were still in Paris to prepare themselves for the French proletariat's forthcoming struggle and told them about revolutionary events in other European countries. However, he and Engels concentrated mainly on explaining the character and specific features of the revolution which had broken out in the German states.

---

[1] Marx, Engels, *Collected Works*, Vol. 26, p. 324.

DEMANDS OF THE COMMUNIST PARTY IN GERMANY

Marx and Engels were faced with the urgent task of formulating the political platform, strategy and tactics of the Communists, the main demands that would serve as guidelines for the mass revolutionary struggle.

The general theoretical principles of communist tactics had been laid down in the *Manifesto of the Communist Party*, and the task now was to formulate them in concrete terms proceeding from the new elements that had been produced by the February revolution in France and the March events in Vienna and Berlin. It became clear just after the March revolution that the liberal bourgeoisie, which had gained power, was terrified by the revolutionary activity of the masses, the French working class in particular, and was inclined to a cowardly compromise with the forces of reaction. Only the more progressive, democratic forces of the nation could carry the bourgeois-democratic revolution to its end.

Marx and Engels believed that the unification of Germany, divided politically and economically, was the basic issue of the revolution there. Their *Demands of the Communist Party in Germany* formulated the proletariat's national programme which met the interests of the whole German people. The first, basic demand was: "The whole of Germany shall be declared a single and indivisible republic."[1] In those historical conditions only the establishment of this type of republic would make it possible to remove such obstacles to Germany's unification as the rivalry between Prussia and Austria, the numerous dynasties and the provincial narrow-mindedness, to complete the formation of the German nation and lay a broad foundation for the unity of the working class on a national scale.

Marx and Engels saw the struggle for German unification as an organic part of the struggle for democracy. They put forward a number of demands aimed at the democratic transformation of the whole political system, namely, universal suffrage for men who had reached the age of 21, salaries for members of Parliament, universal arming of the people, legal services free of charge, complete separation of Church and State, and universal and free education of the people. In contrast to the petty-bourgeois democrats, Marx and Engels saw these general democratic demands not as the ultimate aim of the revolution, but as political measures creating favourable conditions for the proletariat's subsequent struggle for socialism. They believed the struggle for democracy to be an integral part of the struggle for socialism.

A key task before the revolution was to do away not only with the political domination of the nobility, but also with its economic basis, the landed estates. Accordingly, the *Demands* formulated the Communists' agrarian programme: abolition, without compensa-

---

[1] Marx, Engels, *Collected Works*, Vol. 7, p. 3.

tion, of corvées, quitrent, tithes and other feudal obligations, and the handing over to the state of the princely and other feudal estates, all mines, and so on. Large-scale farming was to be conducted on the nationalised lands with the use of the most up-to-date scientific methods and in the interests of the whole of society. Not only were all the survivals of feudalism to be rooted out, but the very possibility of capitalist exploitation of the peasants—small holders and tenant farmers—was to be limited. The democratic state was to take over the mortgages on peasant land and receive the interest on them; all the land rent or rental dues were also to be paid to the state.

This was the most radical agrarian programme put forward by any party in the German revolution and, together with various other points of the *Demands*, it outlined measures that were to be not only the "last word" in the bourgeois-democratic revolution, but also a step forward to socialism. Apart from the nationalisation of feudal estates, mines, mortgages and rent, these transitional measures included the substitution of a state bank for all private banks, nationalisation of the railways, steamships and the posts, curtailment of the right of inheritance, introduction of steeply graduated taxes and abolition of taxes on articles of consumption, the inauguration of national workshops, state provision of work for all workers, and care for those who were incapacitated for work. All of this was to facilitate the subsequent transition to the proletarian revolution and the attainment of its main goal—the abolition of bourgeois private property. Marx and Engels believed that this goal could be achieved in the course of an uninterrupted, steadily mounting revolution.

Marx and Engels regarded the proletariat and its immediate allies—the petty bourgeoisie and the small peasants—as the social force capable of implementing the *Demands* through revolutionary struggle. The historical period this would take depended not only on the relation of class forces in Germany itself, but on the course of the revolutionary struggle in the more developed countries— France and England.

The *Demands* were the first concrete programme of the proletariat in the bourgeois-democratic revolution. They were issued as a leaflet in Paris at the end of March and appeared in a number of newspapers in Germany in early April. Together with the *Manifesto of the Communist Party*, this highly important document of the Central Authority was circulated among members of the Communist League to take with them when they left for Germany.

The Central Authority of the Communist League succeeded in sending 300-400 workers to Germany, one by one, and in early April Marx and Engels also set out for their native land to take a direct part in the revolution there.

START OF ACTIVITY IN REVOLUTIONARY GERMANY

Marx and Engels stopped for a few days in Mainz. While he was still in Paris, Marx had sent Karl Wallau, a member of the Central Authority, back to the latter's home town of Mainz, to make the first attempt to centralise the activity of the working men's societies being set up in Germany.

This was an important and highly difficult task. In England and France the industrially developed capitals were natural centres for the working-class movement, but in Germany the movement was scattered over the different states, provinces and separate industrial areas. Artisans predominated among the workers, and many of them wanted complete restoration of the guilds, which they believed would cure the ills of capitalist competition. Marx and his followers sought to help the German workers to take an intensive revolutionary course to catch up with the English and French workers, and thus be equal to the tasks with which history was presenting them.

On April 5, before the arrival of Marx and Engels, the Workers' Educational Society in Mainz issued an appeal "To All Workers of Germany", which was signed by its Chairman Wallau and Secretary Cluss.[1] It contained a call for the establishment of workers' associations across the whole of Germany to defend the proletariat's economic and political interests, and ties between these associations whose centre should be Mainz, pending the convocation of a conference, which was finally to decide on the seat of the governing body. During their stay in Mainz, Marx, Engels, Wallau and Cluss discussed a plan for further action to unite the workers' societies.

Thus, from the early days of the revolution Marx took steps to found a mass political organisation of the German proletariat on the lines of the National Charter Association, with the Communist League as its core, its ideological and political centre.

Marx regarded a revolutionary organ which he was planning to publish in Cologne as being of prime importance for the task of consolidating the German proletariat and enhancing its class consciousness.

In contrast to the bureaucratic and philistine atmosphere of the Prussian capital, Cologne was the centre of the progressive Rhine Province, with its large-scale industry, emerging proletariat, and the *Code Napoléon*, which allowed the press relatively more freedom than did the Prussian Law.

Marx arrived there on April 11 and filed an application for citizenship with the Cologne magistrates, because he had been forced to give up Prussian citizenship in 1845. Permission was granted and the Marx family came to live at 7 Cecilienstrasse.

In preparing the publication of the newspaper, Marx and Engels had to overcome considerable political and organisational difficulties. Their endeavour was facilitated by Marx's high reputation as editor of the *Rheinische Zeitung* and support from his friends and

---

[1] Marx, Engels, *Collected Works*, Vol. 7, pp. 535-36.

followers. It was called the *Neue Rheinische Zeitung*, to emphasise the continuity and to bring out the difference in its platform and conditions of publication.

The main burden of the preparation fell on Marx, whose organising talent and editorial experience helped to launch the publication of this large revolutionary daily within a very short period. There were considerable financial difficulties, because even the radical bourgeois refused to finance a paper they expected to develop into their antagonist. As a result, Marx had to begin his paper with a very small share-capital collected by subscription, of which only a small part was in cash.

Meanwhile, he faced some pressing tasks in guiding the Communist League. When he was still in Paris, Wallau, Born, Weerth and Wolff had been sent to Germany to strengthen the local League communities, the latter visiting Mainz, Coblenz, Cologne, Hanover and Berlin and temporarily stopping in his native Silesia. More emissaries were sent to the various cities after Marx and the other members of the Central Authority had arrived in Cologne. Engels visited Elberfeld and Barmen; Schapper, Mainz, Hesse-Nassau and his native Wiesbaden; Dronke, Coblenz, Frankfurt am Main, Mainz, Hanau and Kassel.

The emissaries' first-hand reports and letters showed that the workers had yet to become aware of their class interests and were still under the influence of the bourgeoisie and the petty bourgeoisie. Anti-communist propaganda had been intensified after the February and March revolutions. All of this greatly hampered the activity of the Communist League's communities, quite apart from the differences within the League which had yet to become a solid, monolithic organisation.

OPPOSING THE VIEWS OF GOTTSCHALK AND BORN

A popular physician, Andreas Gottschalk, who was a member of the Cologne community, openly came out against the line pursued by Marx and the Central Authority of the Communist League. Gottschalk, the head of the Workers' Association he had set up at Cologne, acted according to his own lights, changing his political views with quick succession. At first he advocated a "democratic monarchy", but soon appealed for a "workers' republic". In the spirit of "true socialism", he ignored the objective historical tasks of the bourgeois-democratic revolution.

He regarded the ways and means of achieving a "workers' republic" in the same spirit, trying to convince the workers that they could do so by acting within the framework of the law. Instead of clarifying the contradictions between labour and capital, he spread utopian ideas about all men being brothers and sought to provide a religious and ethical basis for communism, which he stripped of its class content.

Gottschalk's erroneous sectarian tactics sprang from his confused theories, and this was clearly seen during the elections to the all-German and the Prussian National Assembly, which he urged the workers to boycott because they were being held in two stages. His attitude tended to isolate the proletariat politically.

Gottschalk's moderate action did not match his ultra-revolutionary talk. The Workers' Association confined its activities to deluging the government and the local authorities with petitions expressing craft attitudes and artisan preconceptions.

Marx and the Communist League's Central Authority lost no time in roundly condemning Gottschalk's activities in the Cologne Workers' Association. Gottschalk bridled and handed in his resignation from Communist League. When Marx asked him, at a meeting of the Cologne community on May 11, 1848, about his attitude to the Communist League, Gottschalk said the League's Rules posed a threat to his personal freedom. The petty-bourgeois socialist found himself restricted by the constitutional framework of the proletarian organisation.

Marx held that the break with Gottschalk should not imply a break with the Cologne Workers' Association, for he realised that Gottschalk's influence was due to the existing level of the working-class movement, and so refrained from openly attacking Gottschalk for the time being because this could be misconstrued by the workers. Even when Gottschalk made slanderous charges against the *Neue Rheinische Zeitung* in the Cologne Workers' Association newspaper, which he edited, Marx displayed remarkable restraint and let the attack pass, in the hope that the patient and persistent efforts of his followers and the workers' own experience would help them to see the error of Gottschalk's tactics, Leftist in form, but opportunist in substance. Marx was proved right.

Stephan Born, another member of the Communist League, also took a special stand. In a letter he wrote to Marx from Berlin on May 11, he boastfully claimed to be the leader of the working-class movement and the chairman of a sort of workers' parliament, consisting of deputies from many trades and factories. Born wrote that the bourgeoisie had confidence in his talent as a "go-between", and that the Prussian Minister of Trade, no less, had contacted him. Born's letter revealed his high-handed attitude to the Communist League, and for a good reason. By urging the workers and artisans to concentrate mainly on the day-to-day economic needs, Born was distracting their attention from highly important political tasks. He argued that in contrast to England and France, Germany had no crystallised classes—capitalists and workers—and that the German industrialists were holding out a "friendly hand for agreement"[1] with the workers.

---

[1] *Berliner Zeitungs-Halle* No. 89, April 13, 1848, Supplement.

The documents issued by the Workers' Brotherhood, set up in Berlin in August and September 1848, also bore the mark of Born's reformism and conciliation. It is true that some of Born's articles and documents issued by this organisation showed evidence of Marx's influence. Engels said that Born "was not at all the man who could bring unity into the conflicting tendencies, light into the chaos. Consequently, in the official publications of the association the views represented in the *Communist Manifesto* were mingled hodge-podge with guild recollections and guild aspirations, fragments of Louis Blanc and Proudhon, protectionism, etc.; in short, they wanted to please everybody."[1]

Defining the differences between Marx and Born, Lenin subsequently wrote about the "*two tendencies in the working-class movement* of 1848 in Germany, the Born tendency (akin to our Economists) and the Marxist tendency".[2] Born's stand was one of the earliest manifestations of opportunism in the German working-class movement, and however much it differed outwardly from Gottschalk's "Leftist" sectarian views, they both were at root petty-bourgeois, for both hampered the political education of the proletariat and the growth of its class awareness.

But the establishment of the Workers' Brotherhood, which soon brought together over a hundred workers' societies, mainly in East Prussia, Mecklenburg and Saxony, was a positive fact in itself, and that is why Marx did not openly criticise Born either. The *Neue Rheinische Zeitung* carried without comment Born's programme for the Berlin workers' congress, which was strongly influenced by the ideas of Blanc and Proudhon. Marx soon published a statement, however, explaining that the publication of this programme did not imply acceptance of it. An editorial article in the *Neue Rheinische Zeitung*, aimed against the Turin liberal newspaper *Concordia*, contained a protest over the fact that the paper had "mistaken the programme issued by the respective commission for the Workers' Congress, and which we merely reported, for *our own*".[3]

PROLETARIAN WING
OF THE DEMOCRATIC MOVEMENT

The appeal issued by the Mainz Workers' Educational Society did not meet with a broad response. The establishment of a centralised political organisation of the proletariat was hampered by the backwardness and political immaturity of the German workers, the purely local nature of the movement, and its particularism. There was also the separatist activity of Gottschalk and Born. Other reasons for the failure were the Communist League's small membership and

---

[1] Marx, Engels, *Collected Works*, Vol. 26, p. 325.
[2] V. I. Lenin, *Collected Works*, Vol. 9, p. 139.
[3] Marx, Engels, *Collected Works*, Vol. 7, p. 272.

poor organisation and the inadequate ideological development of many of its members. Engels subsequently wrote: "As could easily be foreseen, the League proved to be much too weak a lever by comparison with the popular mass movement that had now broken out. Three-quarters of the League members who had previously lived abroad had changed their domicile by returning to their homeland; their previous communities were thus to a great extent dissolved and they lost all contact with the League.... Finally, the conditions in each separate small state, each province and each town were so different that the League would have been incapable of giving more than the most general directives; such directives were, however, much better disseminated through the press."[1]

Following an all-round assessment of the situation, Marx and the League's Central Authority which he headed found it necessary to adjust the forms and methods of the Communists' activity and their tactics. The League's continued existence as a *secret* organisation would have turned it into a sect, and this would have been tantamount to abandoning active participation in the revolution. Because the direction of the small number of communities and individual members of the League scattered across Germany had to be confined to general political directives, it was much easier to do this through the newspaper Marx was editing. Accordingly, Marx and a majority of the Central Authority members decided that there was no point in continuing with the League as a secret organisation. They did not intend to dissolve it, however, but merely to modify the organisational forms and methods of its work in view of the fundamental change which had taken place in the conditions in which it operated. Members of the Communist League, under the political guidance of the *Neue Rheinische Zeitung*'s editorial board, were now to make wide use of legal opportunities in carrying on their work among the masses. Workers' associations, to whose establishment and strengthening Marx continued to attach great significance, were an important field of their activity.

The Communists were also to become active in the democratic societies which sprang up everywhere as broad political organisations, bringing together workers and petty bourgeois. Participation in democratic societies gave the Communists opportunities to exert ideological and political influence on the workers who had not yet separated from bourgeois democracy; on the other hand, it also enabled them to influence the petty-bourgeois democrats and to draw them into the common front of struggle to complete the bourgeois-democratic revolution. Marx and his closest associates joined the Democratic Society which was set up in Cologne at the end of April 1848, and Marx advised his followers in other German towns to do likewise. The Communists joined these democratic organisations on the understanding that they would maintain their own po-

---

[1] Marx, Engels, *Collected Works*, Vol. 26, p. 324.

litical positions and openly criticise the vacillations and inconsistencies of the petty-bourgeois democrats.

The participation of Marx and his followers in the activities of the Democratic Society in Cologne roused fears among local bourgeois circles. In the middle of May, the liberal *Kölnische Zeitung* expressed dissatisfaction that the society's meetings were being influenced by the "ill-intentioned Communists".

An all-German democratic congress was held at Frankfurt am Main from June 14 to 17, with members of the Communist League taking an active part in its work. The congress elected a Central Committee and adopted a resolution to set up district committees. Steps were also taken in Cologne to establish a district centre to bring together all the democratic organisations in the Rhine Province and Westphalia, including the workers' associations. Marx became a member of the joint committee of three Cologne organisations (the Democratic Society, the Workers' Association, and the Workers' and Employers' Association), which began to play the part of a Provisional Democratic District Committee. But Marx also strove to ensure the maintenance of the organisational independence of the workers' associations.

The *Neue Rheinische Zeitung*'s political platform was determined by the entry of Marx and his followers into the democratic societies and the forms of co-operation with the petty-bourgeois democrats which they had worked out at this stage. Engels subsequently wrote: "In this way, when we founded a major newspaper in Germany, our banner was determined as a matter of course. It could only be that of democracy, but that of a democracy which everywhere emphasised in every point the specific proletarian character which it could not yet inscribe once for all on its banner."[1]

EDITOR-IN-CHIEF
OF THE *NEUE RHEINISCHE ZEITUNG*

The first issue of the *Neue Rheinische Zeitung*, with the subtitle "Organ of Democracy" and dated June 1, 1848, appeared late on May 31. On the editorial board were Karl Marx, editor-in-chief, Heinrich Bürgers, Ernst Dronke, Frederick Engels, Georg Weerth, Ferdinand Wolff and Wilhelm Wolff. This made the paper not only an organ of democracy, but also an organ of the Communist League, its directing and organising centre. The members of the board shared the same views, and worked together smoothly and efficiently, with a clear-cut division of labour, which took account of the personal qualities of each.

Work on the *Neue Rheinische Zeitung* brought out Marx's brilliant talent as editor and revolutionary journalist to the full. Engels

---

[1] Marx, Engels, *Collected Works*, Vol. 26, p. 122.

wrote: "It was above all his clear vision and firm attitude that made this publication the most famous German newspaper of the years of revolution."[1] Apart from laying down its general line, Marx wrote a great number of editorial articles, which were published unsigned, but which are easily identified by his brilliant style, his concise sentences, with their sharp antithetical constructions, and the irony with which he exposed the enemies of the revolution. His style is also imprinted on the leading articles written by his colleagues, which he edited.

Marx sought to mould the newspaper into a single whole and so made a point of reading and editing other articles and reports with his usual thoroughness. As editor-in-chief, he did a vast amount of work, for in addition to the regular daily issues, there were special issues and handbills which were circulated not only in the Rhine Province, but well beyond it. On behalf of the editorial board, Marx wrote many letters to the paper's correspondents in Germany and other countries and kept in touch with a number of progressive publications abroad.

The paper's financial affairs took up much effort, but even more strength and nervous energy went into the running battle against the authorities, the courts, and the reactionary and liberal press with their threats and slander. Occasionally the members of the editorial board had to hold the fort against Prussian militarists who raided the newspaper premises.

Engels was Marx's right-hand man, and he himself testified to how closely they worked together. "In general, it is almost impossible to distinguish Marx's articles dating to the period from my own, because we systematically shared the work."[2] Engels' broad outlook and skill and ease in writing made him an invaluable member of the editorial board, and Marx was delighted with his friend's journalistic talents. He wrote that Engels was "a veritable walking encyclopaedia", "capable, drunk or sober, of working at any hour of the day or night", and that he was "a fast writer and devilish quick in the uptake".[3] When Marx was away Engels took over as editor-in-chief.

Wilhelm Wolff was a reliable assistant of Marx and Engels on the editorial board, and his journalistic talent was best revealed in his articles on the agrarian question, for he had a good knowledge of rural life, especially in his native Silesia.

Georg Weerth's poetic talent and boundless sense of humour were put to brilliant use, and his series of pungent feuilletons "The Life and Deeds of the Renowned Cavalier Schnapphahnski", a satire on the typical reactionary Prussian Junker, was a great success.

Ernst Dronke was an experienced journalist and the author of many articles and a large book entitled *Berlin* for which he had been

---

[1] Marx, Engels, *Collected Works*, Vol. 26, p. 123.
[2] Marx, Engels, *Werke*, Bd. 36, S. 315.
[3] Marx, Engels, *Collected Works*, Vol. 39, p. 391.

imprisoned in a fortress. Although he had been "true socialist", Dronke lived up to Marx's best hopes.

Heinrich Bürgers had a place apart on the editorial board. Although a member of the Communist League, he had yet to shed all of his petty-bourgeois views. His very first article induced Marx to give up the idea of making further use of his journalistic services. While nominally remaining an editor of the newspaper, Bürgers was doing more good by representing it at popular meetings and rallies.

Ferdinand Freiligrath, a popular revolutionary poet, joined the editorial board in October 1848. His poems in the *Neue Rheinische Zeitung*, many of which had been written at Marx's request, subsequently proved to be some of his best works.

The *Neue Rheinische Zeitung* was the only periodical not only in Germany but in the whole of Europe which gave a profound scientific analysis of the major events of the German and the European revolution as a whole. It revealed a remarkable aptitude for prediction, and sought to help the people, who were making history, to find their bearings in the labyrinth of the class struggle, and to understand both the general aims of the revolution and the concrete tasks arising at its various stages. It taught the masses to be bold and to display unflinching steadfastness and readiness for resolute action.

Its persistent struggle for the German people's true national interests was combined with a spirit of proletarian internationalism: it gave resolute support to all revolutionary mass movements, wherever they developed, exposing their enemies and unmasking their false friends.

Marx kept a close watch on developments of the European revolution, attaching decisive importance to the events in France and their influence on the future of Germany and the whole of Europe. He added whole passages to the reports sent in from Paris (notably by Ferdinand Wolff and Ernst Dronke, who stayed there for some time) to show the meaning of the events and to suggest conclusions, which he subsequently elaborated in *The Class Struggles in France* and *The Eighteenth Brumaire of Louis Bonaparte*.

The *Neue Rheinische Zeitung* maintained close ties with French, English, Italian, Swiss, Belgian, Polish and other democrats, vigorously defending their cause of its pages. It had good right to call itself an organ not just of German but of European democracy.

While carrying the banner of democracy, the *Neue Rheinische Zeitung* was not an official organ of any democratic organisation in Germany. From its first issue, it criticised the weaknesses and mistakes of the German democrats and invariably advocated the proletarian standpoint in the general democratic movement.

It was not only the rostrum from which Marx and his followers addressed the masses, the proletariat above all, and formulated the "real slogans of struggle". It was also an organising centre, a kind of revolutionary headquarters, rallying the people to implement these slogans. Engels later recalled: "Those were revolutionary times, and at such times it is a pleasure to work in the daily press. One sees for oneself the effect of every word, one sees one's articles strike like hand grenades and explode like fired shell." [1]

The editorial board of the *Neue Rheinische Zeitung*, which had in fact taken the place of the old Central Authority, directed the activities of Communist League members. Through the newspaper, Marx sought to ensure the Communists' ideological and political unity and to teach them to respond, concertedly and simultaneously, to all the major events concerning Germany. A mass medium of political education and organisation of the proletariat and its vanguard, the newspaper prepared the ground for the subsequent formation of a mass German workers' party.

Lenin considered the *Neue Rheinische Zeitung* "the finest and unsurpassed organ of the revolutionary proletariat".[2]

STRUGGLE TO COMPLETE THE BOURGEOIS-DEMOCRATIC REVOLUTION

In the *Neue Rheinische Zeitung* Marx took a resolute stand against the illusions current in Germany that the March revolution had been a victory for the ideas of liberty, equality and brotherhood, and that the forces of reaction had been crushed for good. He exposed these harmful illusions, which tended to lull the people's vigilance, and argued that the March "semi-revolution" had not yet toppled a single throne, that the old army with its aristocratic officer corps was still there, that the state machine was still in the hands of the greedy, callous officials and that the landowners still held their estates and oppressed the peasants. He sought to persuade the people that the decisive battles in the German revolution still lay ahead, and wrote: *"The Bastille, however, has not yet been stormed."* [3] When, on June 14, the workers and artisans of Berlin stormed the arsenal to obtain arms the *Neue Rheinische Zeitung* said this spontaneous revolutionary outbreak was the first flash of lightning of the forthcoming second revolution.

The *Neue Rheinische Zeitung* directed its main attacks not only against the avowedly reactionary forces, but also against the German big bourgeoisie, which was disguised and was therefore the more dangerous enemy. The very first steps taken by the liberal government which came to power in Prussia after the March events showed that it was betraying the revolutionary cause. Out of fear of the revolutionary people, the government made a deal with the reactionary forces, and assumed the ignominious role of providing a "shield for the dynasty". Lenin stressed Marx's great theoretical

---

[1] Marx, Engels, *Werke*, Bd. 22, S. 76-77.
[2] V. I. Lenin, *Collected Works*, Vol. 21, p. 81.
[3] Marx, Engels, *Collected Works*, Vol. 7, p. 89.

achievement in drawing the conclusion that in contrast to the bourgeoisie of the late 18th century in France, the German bourgeoisie proved to be incapable on the whole, from the very early days of the revolution, of taking any progressive historical action and turned out to be an obstacle on the revolutionary way. On June 14, the *Neue Rheinische Zeitung* gave this clear-cut picture of the arrangement of class forces in Germany after the March events: "The big bourgeoisie, which was all along anti-revolutionary, concluded a defensive and offensive alliance with the reactionary forces, because it was afraid of the people, i. e., of the workers and the democratic bourgeoisie." [1]

The liberal government went on to draft a constitution "by agreement with the Crown", seeking to strike a balance between the people and the Crown, and to prevent either from scoring a complete victory. The *Neue Rheinische Zeitung* predicted that this "balance" would be a very short one, and that as soon as the reactionaries had secured a firm footing the bourgeoisie itself would be driven from the government with ignominy.

Marx contrasted the treacherous "theory of agreement" with the sovereignty of the revolutionary people won in the armed struggle, and explained that the revolutionary tasks facing the people—the proletariat, the peasantry, and the urban working people—could be fulfilled only by revolutionary means.

In the course of the revolution, Marx elaborated and expressed in concrete terms one of the basic propositions of historical materialism—the role of the people as the maker of history—as applied to its every task and stage. Because the fundamental issue in any revolution is that of power, Marx put forward the idea of the people's revolutionary dictatorship, and urged the masses to establish a truly revolutionary power, bold, resolute and capable of sweeping away all the medieval rubbish, putting an end to the monarchy and the landowners, and ensuring the victorious completion of the bourgeois-democratic revolution. "Every provisional political set-up following a revolution requires a dictatorship, and an energetic dictatorship at that." [2] Marx believed that one of the fundamental tasks of the people's revolutionary dictatorship was to do away with the old state apparatus, "the remnants of the old institutions", which were the mainstay of the reactionary forces.

Lenin wrote that Marx's idea of a revolutionary dictatorship implied the establishment of a revolutionary power even at the stage of the bourgeois-democratic revolution, so as to make sure that things took a democratic turn, and that its tasks were "defence against counter-revolution and the actual elimination of everything that contradicted the sovereignty of the people". [3]

In preparing the people for a fresh revolutionary attack, Marx

---

[1] Ibid., p. 74.
[2] Ibid., p. 431.
[3] V. I. Lenin, *Collected Works*, Vol. 9, p. 133.

and Engels sought to dispel their illusory hopes about the effectiveness of the representative institutions set up after the March revolution. The *Neue Rheinische Zeitung* criticised the all-German National Assembly at Frankfurt am Main, whose task was to act as the new central authority in Germany and really unite the country. The paper said: "A Constituent National Assembly must above all be an *active*, revolutionarily active assembly. The Assembly at Frankfurt is engaged in parliamentary school exercises and leaves it to the governments to act. Assuming that this learned gathering succeeds, after mature consideration, in framing the best of agendas and the best of constitutions, of what use is the best agenda and the best Constitution if the governments meanwhile have placed bayonets on the agenda?" [1]

This criticism irritated many German philistines, including some of the paper's shareholders, who immediately withdrew their financial support. However, subsequent events bore out completely what the paper had said about the "Frankfurt talking shop".

The editors of the *Neue Rheinische Zeitung* kept a closer watch on the debates in the Prussian National Assembly, which was unable to ignore the needs of real life on the pretext of discussing "all-German problems". Marx and Engels saw its main defect in its decision to frame a Prussian constitution by "agreement with the Crown". The *Neue Rheinische Zeitung* wrote: "An assembly standing 'on a revolutionary basis' does not agree, it decrees." [2] The newspaper showed the deputies the only course worthy of representatives of a revolutionary people—to turn for support to the masses, who for their part should exert pressure on the Assembly. "The right of the democratic popular masses, by their presence, to exert a moral influence on the attitude of constituent assemblies is an old revolutionary right of the people which could not be dispensed with in all stormy periods ever since the English and French revolutions. History owes to this right almost all the energetic steps taken by such assemblies." [3]

But instead of appealing to the people and relying on them the Berlin Assembly preferred to immerse itself in the backwaters of parliamentarianism. Not only the deputies of the Right and the Centre, but also those of the Left were infected with the grave disease of "parliamentary cretinism". The *Neue Rheinische Zeitung* said the deputies of the Left "dare not do anything but—*hiss*", [4] and predicted the sad consequences of their hope to secure radical decisions by purely parliamentary methods.

The cowardly and conciliatory policies of the Frankfurt and Berlin national assemblies necessarily had an effect on the resolution of the main issues in the revolution.

---

[1] Marx, Engels, *Collected Works*, Vol. 7, p. 49.
[2] Ibid., p. 76.
[3] Ibid., p. 437.
[4] Ibid., p. 100.

Although the German bourgeoisie was keenly aware of the need to end the country's fragmentation, once in power it sought to do this by making deals with reaction. It strove to unite Germany from above, round the Hapsburg Empire, or the Prussian Hohenzollern monarchy, the more popular of the two.

As for the petty-bourgeois democrats they were divided into two groups: the North Germans, who pinned their hopes on a "democratic" Prussian monarch, and the South Germans, who sought to turn Germany into a federal republic like the U.S.A. or Switzerland. In the concrete conditions of Germany at the time this meant, for all practical purposes, the formation of a very motley federation consisting of constitutional monarchies, midget principalities and tiny republics.

By contrast, the *Neue Rheinische Zeitung*, in conformity with the *Demands of the Communist Party in Germany*, campaigned for the establishment of a united German republic through the people's revolutionary struggle. In putting forward this programme, the paper took a consistent and resolute stand for the German people's real national interests and its future as a free democratic nation. This was fully in line with the proletariat's class interests. A united democratic Germany would make it much easier to put an end to the fragmentation of the working-class movement and open up broader possibilities for organising the working class, training it politically, and preparing it for the struggle for socialism.

Marx saw the task of Germany's unification as being organically connected not only with the complete democratisation of its political system, but also with deep-going social change. The *Neue Rheinische Zeitung* launched a resolute campaign to root out the survivals of feudalism in the countryside.

By the 1848 revolution only the more prosperous sections of the peasantry had come to enjoy the fruits of the agrarian reform of 1807-11, which had given the peasants the right to redeem their feudal services on extremely harsh terms. The feudal landed estates were slowly developing into bourgeois farms, a process Lenin called the "Prussian way" of capitalist development in the countryside. When the revolution broke out, the peasants spontaneously started an anti-feudal struggle, and in some places manor houses were set on fire. The peasants refused to perform any services whatsoever. The *Neue Rheinische Zeitung* wrote: "All the Government had to do was to legalise the *abolition of all feudal obligations which had in fact already been abrogated by the people's will.*"[1] Instead, the liberal bourgeoisie, out of fear for its own property, came out in defence of feudal property. The bill submitted by the Prussian Minister of Agriculture, Gierke, proposed the gratuitous abolition only of the minor services, while leaving the most burdensome ones to be redeemed

---

[1] Ibid., p. 118.

or substituted for by a plot of peasant land of corresponding value.

Marx said the Gierke Bill was the most striking proof that the "German revolution of 1848 is merely a *parody of the French revolution of 1789*.... The French bourgeoisie of 1789 never left its allies, the peasants, in the lurch. It knew that the abolition of feudalism in the countryside and the creation of a free, landowning peasant class was the basis of its rule.

"The German bourgeoisie of 1848 unhesitatingly betrays the peasants, who are its *natural allies*, flesh of its own flesh, and without whom it cannot stand up to the aristocracy.

"The perpetuation of feudal rights and their endorsement in the form of the (illusory) commutations — such is the result of the German revolution of 1848. That is much ado about nothing." [1]

Marx campaigned for a radical solution of the agrarian question — complete abolition of feudal obligations without redemption — to allow the peasant to become a free owner of his own land. A well-known series of articles by Wolff, entitled *The Silesian Milliard* (which appeared in the *Neue Rheinische Zeitung* in the spring of 1849), demanded, in opposition to the landowners and liberal bourgeoisie who insisted on the redemption of feudal obligations, that the peasants should be returned all the money these "robber knights have stolen from rural people over the last thirty years alone",[2] that is, since the start of the agrarian reforms. The paper also demanded that the larger estates be broken up to provide land for the landless and land-hungry peasants. By thus expressing the interests of the broader sections of the peasantry, the *Neue Rheinische Zeitung* was supplementing the agrarian programme set out in the *Demands of the Communist Party in Germany*.

Its articles on the agrarian questions were a strong reflection of the tactics, which Marx had worked out in the course of the bourgeois-democratic revolution, for an alliance of the proletariat with the whole peasantry, under the hegemony of the working class.

SUPPORT FOR THE OPPRESSED PEOPLES' STRUGGLE. THE *NEUE RHEINISCHE ZEITUNG*'S ATTITUDE TOWARDS FOREIGN POLICY

Marx also actively supported the revolutionary national liberation struggle of the oppressed peoples, which was spreading at the time. His support was based on a concrete historical analysis of each national movement, which helped to determine its place in the fight then taking place between the two main camps: revolution and reaction. Accordingly, the *Neue Rheinische Zeitung* board supported

---

[1] Marx, Engels, *Collected Works*, Vol. 7, pp. 294-95.
[2] Ibid., Vol. 24, p. 148.

progressive national liberation movements, which extended the front of the bourgeois-democratic revolution and swelled and fortified its ranks.

The paper's internationalist policy was formulated by Marx shortly before its publication in a letter to the editor of the Italian democratic newspaper *L'Alba*. He wrote: "We shall defend the cause of Italian independence, we shall fight to the death Austrian despotism in Italy as in Germany and Poland." [1] An editorial entitled "Germany's Foreign Policy", written by Engels in early July 1848, stressed the organic connection and interdependence between the German revolution and the liberation movement of the enslaved nations. He said: "Germany will liberate herself to the extent to which she sets free neighbouring nations." [2]

Day in day out, the *Neue Rheinische Zeitung* exposed the policy of the bourgeoisie, which on the national question followed in the steps of the old authorities. As with the peasant movement, the bourgeois government resorted to two methods: false promises and massacres. Both methods were used against the insurgent Poles in Posen, which had been annexed to Prussia following the partitions of Poland at the end of the 18th century. The paper protested angrily against these crimes and appealed to the German and the Polish peoples, the two forces which were to end Poland's oppression and secure for the Poles the chance to decide their own future.

The *Neue Rheinische Zeitung* repeatedly emphasised the tremendous importance of Poland's restoration not only for the Polish people, but also for the people of Germany, and for the course and outcome of the European revolution. The strength of reaction in Germany and Europe as a whole rested on the Russo-Prussian-Austrian alliance, cemented by the partitions of Poland. Marx and Engels saw the Polish people as a reliable ally in the struggle not only against Prussia and Austria, but also against Russian tsarism, the arch-enemy of the European revolution. Lenin wrote that "this point of view was quite correct and the only one that was consistently democratic and proletarian. So long as the masses of the people in Russia and in most of the Slav countries were still sunk in torpor, so long as *there were no* independent, mass, democratic movements in those countries, the liberation movement of the *gentry* in Poland assumed an immense and paramount importance from the point of view, not only of Russian, not only of Slav, but of European democracy as a whole." [3]

The *Neue Rheinische Zeitung* also took a whole-heartedly sym-

---

[1] Marx, Engels, *Collected Works*, Vol. 7, p. 11.
[2] Ibid., p. 166.
[3] V. I. Lenin, *Collected Works*, Vol. 20, p. 433. Lenin went on to say that in the 20th century, when an independent democratic and working-class movement started in Russia and other Slav countries, while aristocratic Poland gave way to capitalist Poland, the situation underwent a fundamental change and "under such circumstances Poland could not but lose her *exceptional* revolutionary importance" (ibid).

pathetic attitude to the awakening of another Slav people, the Czechs, who staged an uprising in Prague in mid-June 1848. It stressed that the uprising was democratic and was aimed not only against Austrian oppression, but also against the Czech feudal lords. When the Austrian militarists staged a massacre in Prague, the newspaper wrathfully branded this ignominious policy with respect to the oppressed peoples, and warned of the dangerous consequences of the Prague massacre, for it made the Czechs look to tsarist Russia.[1]

Indeed, the defeat of the Prague uprising was a heavy blow to the Czech democratic movement. The liberal-bourgeois elements, who had taken over leadership of the Czech national movement, managed to direct the full force of their struggle against the German revolution, and this objectively placed the movement in the same camp with Austrian and Prussian reaction, and Russian tsarism, which was preparing for a counter-revolutionary campaign in the West.

At the beginning of June, the *Neue Rheinische Zeitung* raised the alarm over the fact that the Russian tsar was assembling his troops along his western borders in order to go to the rescue of the "friendly" monarchies of the Hohenzollerns and Hapsburgs. In the absence of a large-scale revolutionary movement in Russia itself, this counter-revolutionary plan could be thwarted only from outside, through the joint efforts of the revolutionary peoples of Europe. Accordingly, the *Neue Rheinische Zeitung* urged European democracy to start a revolutionary war against Russian tsarism. Marx hoped that such a war would result in a fresh and powerful upsurge in Germany and the other European countries. Lenin subsequently observed that this tactic, which Marx had proclaimed on behalf of all forward-looking democrats, was in line with the objective historical conditions of the period and the character of the epoch, in which bourgeois-democratic transformations were being completed. He wrote: "*Objectively*, the feudal and dynastic wars were then opposed by revolutionary-democratic wars, by wars for national liberation. This was the content of the historical tasks of that epoch." [2]

THE JUNE UPRISING IN PARIS

While still in Paris, Marx had predicted that the internal contradictions of the recently proclaimed French Republic were bound to grow and to result in a decisive clash between labour and capital. This is precisely what happened. From June 23 to 26, 1848, Paris was the scene of a powerful uprising by the proletariat who took up arms against the counter-revolutionary bourgeoisie, which was encroaching on the gains of the February revolution and the workers'

---

[1] Marx, Engels, *Collected Works*, Vol. 7, p. 93.
[2] V. I. Lenin, *Collected Works*, Vol. 22, p. 316.

The house in Trier where Marx was born

The beginning of Marx's Gymnasium examination composition
"Reflections of a Young Man on the Choice of a Profession"

The Trier Gymnasium where Marx studied

The University of Bonn

The University of Berlin

Marx as a student

Students of the Trier *Landsmannschaft* (Association) of the University of Bonn

Georg Wilhelm
Friedrich Hegel

The house in Berlin where
Marx lived as a student

Ludwig Feuerbach

Adam Smith

David Ricardo

Marx's diploma conferring on him the degree of Doctor of Philosophy issued by Jena University

Prometheus Bound. A contemporary cartoon on the suppression of the *Rheinische Zeitung*

Cover of the *Deutsch-Französische Jahrbücher*

Page of the *Rheinische Zeitung* containing Marx's article "Communism and the Augsburg *Allgemeine Zeitung*"

Jenny von Westphalen in the 1830s

Henri Saint-Simon

Charles Fourier

Robert Owen

House in Paris, 38 Rue Vanneau,
where Marx lived (October 1843-January 1845)

Page of *Vorwärts!* with Marx's article 'Critical Marginal Notes on the Article The King of Prussia and Social Reform. By a Prussian'

Wilhelm Weitling

Heinrich Heine

Auguste Blanqui

Engels in the 1840s

Wilhelm Wolff

Ferdinand Freiligrath

Roland Daniels

Georg Weerth

Thesis XI of Marx's
Theses on Feuerbach

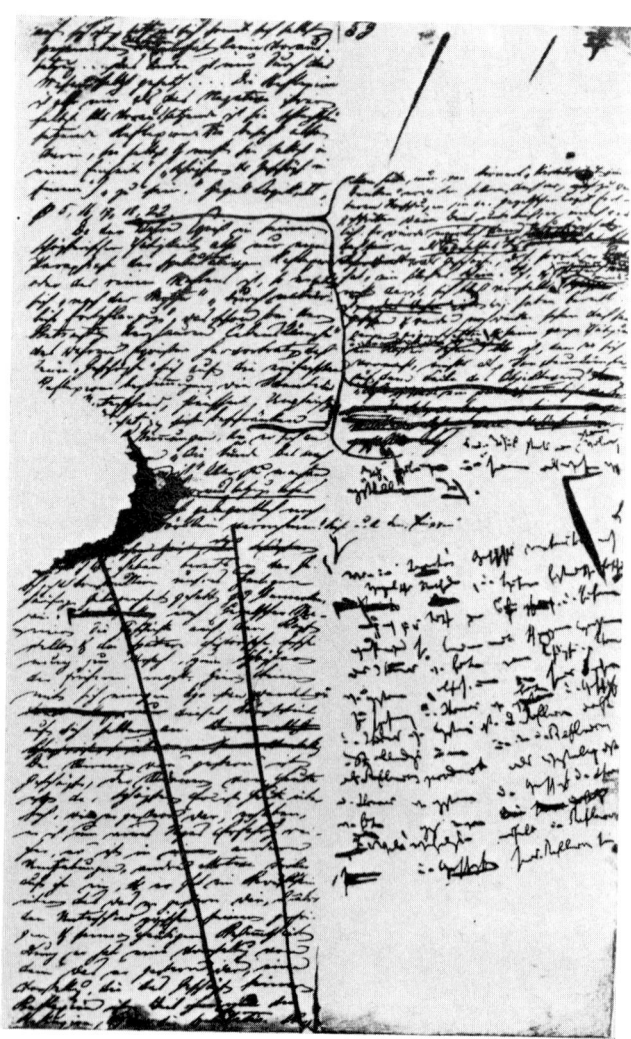

Page of the manuscript
The German Ideology

Chetham Library in Manchester, where Marx and Engels worked in 1845

George Julian Harney

Ernest Jones

Title-page of the book
The Holy Family

Cover of the book
The Poverty of Philosophy

social interests. They demanded the establishment of a democratic and social republic.

The editorial board of the *Neue Rheinische Zeitung* eagerly looked forward to every report from Paris. A series of articles written by Engels just after the events shed light on the nature of the uprising, the alignment of class forces and the course of military operations. These articles laid the foundations of the Marxist doctrine of uprising as an art.

Marx immediately appreciated the great historical importance of the June uprising as the first civil war between the bourgeoisie and the proletariat, and his remarkably powerful article on the subject entitled "The June Revolution" revealed his intense revolutionary feeling. Written on June 28, it began with these words: "The workers of Paris were *overwhelmed* by superior strength, but they were not *subdued*. They have been *defeated* but their enemies are *vanquished*."[1] A high price had to be paid for suppressing the uprising: the destruction of the illusions produced by the February revolution about liberty, equality and brotherhood, and the division of the French nation into two nations — a nation of owners and a nation of workers.

In concise, laconic terms, Marx analysed the course of the French revolution from February to June and revealed the regularities behind its development, which led to the uprising of the Paris proletariat. He showed that the uprising had been caused by the whole policy of the French bourgeoisie. And when the workers, driven to desperation, rose up in revolt, the bourgeoisie drenched the streets of Paris with their blood.

While the bourgeoisie were pouring torrents of hatred and slander on the insurgent workers of Paris, Marx raised an impassioned voice in their defence, and the closing words of his article were a paean of praise for the June fighters and their immortal cause: "It is the *right* and the *privilege of the democratic press* to place laurels on their clouded threatening brow."[2]

REVOLUTIONARY ORGAN OF THE PROLETARIAT

The *Neue Rheinische Zeitung* proved itself to be a proletarian newspaper not only by its attitude to the June uprising; while campaigning for the unity of all the democratic forces in Germany, it also took a proletarian stand of its own.

The editors laid special emphasis on those demands of the Communists' political platform — several times reprinted during the revolution — which had the most immediate bearing on the tasks of the bourgeois-democratic revolution. After a sober analysis of the situation they refrained for the time being from making demands of

---

[1] Marx, Engels, *Collected Works*, Vol. 7, p. 144.
[2] Ibid., p. 149.

a transitional nature designed for the long-term revolutionary process not only in Germany, but also in other European countries. Marx believed that the objective conditions were not yet ripe for taking these demands out of the sphere of propaganda and turning them into slogans for action.

However, even at that stage, while concentrating attention on the immediate aims of the revolution, the paper worked to muster the political army of the proletariat for the future struggle for the socialist revolution.

A class analysis of the main events of the German and European revolutions was to play an extremely important part in helping the proletariat to obtain a political education and gain an awareness of itself as a class.

Of tremendous interest in this respect were the newspaper's articles and reports about the revolution in France. In contrast to the petty-bourgeois *Réforme*, Marx argued that the post-February class battles in France were due neither to error nor accident, but were the natural result of class contradictions which were "based on economic foundations, on the existing mode of material production and the conditions of commerce resulting from it".[1] He emphasised that the differences in ideas, which the *Réforme* erroneously saw as the main source of the antithesis of the proletariat and the bourgeoisie, also sprang from the distinct status of the various classes in society, that is, from social relations. "And where do these relations derive from? From the material, economic conditions of life of the hostile classes."[2] In this way, Marx used the experience of the French revolution to help the reader to attain a materialist understanding of the class struggle and its reflection in the sphere of ideas.

England, the classic capitalist country, provided valuable and concrete historical material for the spread of his ideas, and Marx believed it to be especially important to acquaint the German workers with the revolutionary struggle of the Chartists, who constituted an organised proletarian party, and particularly to show the activity of its revolutionary wing headed by Harney and Jones. On the strength of the much richer experience of the English proletariat, Marx strove to convince the German workers of the need to set up a proletarian party of their own.

Taking the lessons of the past and the current developments in Germany and in the more advanced countries, Marx explained to the workers some of the key propositions of historical materialism, the political economy he was elaborating, and the doctrine of the class struggle and the proletariat's mission in world history. In this way, Marx helped the German workers to understand the theoretical principles of the proletarian party they were to set up.

---

[1] Marx, Engels, *Collected Works*, Vol. 7, pp. 494-95.
[2] Ibid., p. 495.

OPPOSING THE COUNTER-REVOLUTIONARY OFFENSIVE. MARX IN THE WORKERS' ASSOCIATION AND THE DEMOCRATIC SOCIETY IN COLOGNE

Following the defeat of the June uprising, which marked a turning point in the whole European revolution, the counter-revolution everywhere went over to the offensive. In Germany, the balance of class forces also tilted in its favour. The reactionary circles, forced to retreat in March, now sought to disentangle themselves from their temporary ally, the bourgeoisie, and to restore the pre-March order. The first step in that direction had already been taken by the Prussian reactionaries just before the June events in Paris. The liberal Camphausen Government was sent packing, and the political implications were described in the *Neue Rheinische Zeitung* as follows: "The Camphausen Government has covered the counter-revolution with its liberal-bourgeois cloak. The counter-revolution now feels strong enough to shake off this irksome mask." [1]

The new government was headed by the liberal aristocrat Auerswald, but Hansemann, a big Rhine capitalist and a member of the earlier ministry, was also a prominent member of it. It called itself a "Government of Action", and began by taking police action against the democratic and working-class movement on the pretext of restoring "the stability of law and order".

The "Government of Action" intended to deliver its main blow at Cologne, the centre of the Rhine Province. On July 3 it arrested Gottschalk and Anneke, the leaders of the Cologne Workers' Association. This aroused strong indignation among the workers, but the *Neue Rheinische Zeitung* realised that this was a provocative move and hastened to warn the workers against any premature and isolated action in that first-class Prussian fortress which was packed with troops. Thanks to Marx's acumen and presence of mind the government's attempt to provoke the Cologne workers into a premature uprising was frustrated.

Marx at once saw the gravity of the Cologne events in the wider context of the general scheme being hatched by the Prussian counter-revolutionaries. His article "Arrests" published on July 5 said: "Those are the actions of the *Government of Action*, the Government of the Left Centre, the Government of transition to an old aristocratic, old bureaucratic and old Prussian Government. As soon as Herr Hansemann has fulfilled his transitory function, he will be dismissed." [2]

Marx went on to predict that the same was in store for the Berlin Left, because instead of replying to the government's counter-revolutionary acts by appealing to the people, they had pinned

---
[1] Marx, Engels, *Collected Works*, Vol. 7, p. 107.
[2] Ibid., p. 179.

all their hopes on their own eloquence, and lived in anticipation of parliamentary victories to come. "Some fine day the Left may find that its parliamentary victory coincides with its real defeat." [1]

The publication of this article was used as a pretext to institute legal proceedings against the *Neue Rheinische Zeitung* for alleged contempt of the Chief Public Prosecutor Zweiffel and the police who had carried out the arrests. Consequently, it was part of the "Government of Action's" plan of reprisals to destroy the newspaper Marx was editing. On July 6 Marx, the editor-in-chief, and Korff, the responsible publisher, were summoned for questioning by the examining magistrate, after which the latter and the Public Prosecutor Hecker searched the newspaper's premises for the manuscript to find out the name of the author. This was followed by the questioning of witnesses—the owner of the printing works, Clouth, the type-setters, and the editors, Engels and Dronke. Then Engels was questioned again, this time as one of the accused. However hard the court officials tried, their investigation made little headway, and so "action" was taken against Marx himself.

Although the Cologne magistrates had granted him the right of citizenship, this was subject to approval by the local royal administration, and the latter was in no hurry to reach a decision. It was at this point, almost four months later, that Marx was informed that the local royal administration had not found it possible to grant him citizenship, and henceforth he would continue to be regarded as a foreigner. He lodged a protest over this decision with the Minister of the Interior, Kühlwetter, stressing the underlying political motives. He wrote: "Such tendentious reasons could only be employed in the old police state, not however by revolutionary Prussia and her responsible Government." [2]

The refusal of the Cologne authorities to grant Marx the right of citizenship drew protests from workers and democrats in the city. The Democratic Society sent a deputation to the local authorities demanding an end to the police action against Marx. Nevertheless, on September 12, the Minister of the Interior confirmed the decision of the local administration, and although the protest campaign prevented the reactionaries from doing their worst right away, the threat of expulsion from Prussia hung over Marx like the sword of Damocles.

In these extremely trying conditions, Marx sought to retain control of such a powerful instrument of influence on the people as a large daily. While devoting most of his time and energy to the newspaper, he took part, together with his friends and followers, in the activity of the working men's and democratic organisations in Cologne, striving to spread the experience of the Cologne Workers'

---

[1] Marx, Engels, *Collected Works*, Vol. 7, p. 179.
[2] Ibid., p. 409.

Association and the Democratic Society among the members of the Communist League and the working men's and democratic organisations in other parts of Germany.

This activity won ever greater respect and confidence for Marx and his followers among the masses. After the arrest of Gottschalk and Anneke, Marx's friend, Joseph Moll, was elected chairman of the Committee of the Workers' Association at its meeting on July 6. Together with Schapper, who had recently arrived from London, he represented the Workers' Association on the Committee which, as has been said, brought together three Cologne democratic organisations, and which functioned as the Provisional Democratic District Committee.

The new leadership of the Workers' Association, which had constant assistance from Marx, now concentrated on the ideological and political education of workers, with discussions playing an important part. At one of these, Moll and Schapper explained to the workers that the evil did not lie in the machines, as many workers and artisans believed, but in the existing social relations. Marx's followers gave a vivid *exposé* to the workers of the main ideas contained in the *Manifesto of the Communist Party*. During a discussion on labour organisation in contemporary society, they in fact substantiated and advocated a number of points contained in the *Demands of the Communist Party in Germany*. The discussion ended with a report on the social question delivered by Engels at a meeting of the Committee on September 11.

The ideological and political restructuring of the Cologne Workers' Association went hand in hand with some changes in its organisational structure, including the abandonment of the old narrow-craft principle, and the introduction of fixed membership dues. Marx and his followers found the Association to be an ever more reliable support.

They also took an active part in the work of the Democratic Society. As a member of the Provisional District Committee, Marx was directly concerned with its leadership and spoke at its meetings at the Stollwerk Hall. In the summer of 1848, the Society held a discussion between Marx and Weitling, who had returned from America and was paying a visit to Cologne. In his speech at a meeting of the Society on July 21, Weitling claimed to be a "democrat, socialist and communist", and urged the establishment of a dictatorial provisional government consisting of a handful of persons, having himself in mind above all. On August 4, Marx delivered a speech criticising Weitling. Judging by the fragmentary record of this speech, he argued that Weitling was wrong to separate political and social interests, because they were "interwoven with each other". He showed Weitling's sectarian view of dictatorship to be "impracticable" and his idea of a one-man dictatorial power altogether absurd. Whereas Weitling had denied that the revolution was bourgeois and democratic, Marx set the task of constituting a revolutionary government from among the representatives of all the trends in the democratic movement.[1]

Marx and his followers initiated the Democratic Society's adoption of a number of resolutions and addresses on important political questions. These addresses, signed by thousands, were sent to the National Assemblies in Berlin and Frankfurt.

The First Democratic District Congress of the Rhine Province and Westphalia, held in Cologne on August 13 and 14, showed the authority and influence Marx enjoyed in revolutionary-democratic circles. When, in connection with a report by the Trier delegate, Schily, about the republican feelings among the local civil guard, the chairman announced that Marx was also a native of Trier, the audience stood and gave three cheers. The Bonn delegate, a student by the name of Karl Schurz, recalled that at the congress he "met face to face some of the most outstanding men of his day, among them Karl Marx, the socialist leader. Marx was thirty years old at the time and already the acknowledged leader of a socialist school of thought. The thick-set man with his broad forehead and dark flashing eyes, his jet-black hair and full beard immediately attracted general attention. He had the reputation of being a remarkable scholar in his own field and, in fact, what he said was weighty, logical and clear.... I still remember the sharply sarcastic tone he used to pronounce the word 'bourgeois'." [2]

The congress adopted a resolution transforming the Cologne Provisional District Committee into the permanent Rhenish District Committee of Democrats. It was headed by the lawyer, Karl Schneider II, and apart from Marx included Moll and Schapper.

The practical revolutionary activity of Marx and his followers led to the establishment in Cologne of a stronger and politically more mature organisation of democrats than in any other German town.

TRIP TO BERLIN AND VIENNA

On August 23, soon after the Democratic District Congress, Marx set off for Berlin and Vienna to strengthen ties with the democratic and workers' organisations in the capitals of the two largest states of the German Confederation, and also to collect funds for the *Neue Rheinische Zeitung*, which had been abandoned by its remaining shareholders after the articles on the June uprising.

In Berlin, Marx had talks with some Left-wing deputies of the Prussian National Assembly, notably d'Ester, a member of the Communist League. He also met other leaders of the democratic movement, including Bakunin, with whom he resumed the friendly relations they had established in Paris.

---

[1] *Der Wächter am Rhein*, 2. Dutzend, No. 1, 23. VIII, 1848.
[2] *Reminiscences of Marx and Engels*, Moscow, 1956, p. 285 (in Russian).

From there Marx went on to Vienna, where political tension had increased. The Austrian counter-revolutionaries, heartened by the defeat of the Prague and the Paris uprisings, and the invasion of Milan by Radetzky's troops on August 6, had gone over to the offensive. By reducing wages and abolishing unemployment relief, they had provoked disturbances among the workers, leading on August 23 to a bloody clash between the bourgeois national guard and a workers' demonstration.

Upon his arrival in Vienna, Marx contacted the leaders of the workers' and democratic movement, who knew him well as editor-in-chief of the *Neue Rheinische Zeitung*, which was valued for its penetrating analysis of the political situation.

On August 28, Marx spoke at the Democratic Association in a discussion of the latest events in Vienna, which brought out serious differences between him and Julius Fröbel, a visiting member of the Berlin Democrats' Central Committee. Fröbel supported the proposal to send a deputation to the Emperor requesting the dismissal of the Minister of Labour Schwarzer, the main culprit in the August 23 events.

Marx objected and spoke angrily about the "Berlin theorists" who called themselves democrats, but in fact sought "agreement" with sovereigns. *Der Radikale*, a democratic Vienna newspaper, reported that his speech was "very witty, sharp and instructive". Marx had emphasised that in Vienna, as in Paris, "it was now a question of the struggle between the bourgeoisie and the proletariat".[1]

On August 30, Marx delivered a report before the first Vienna Workers' Educational Society. In extending his greetings to the members of the Society, he said that it was an honour for him to address representatives of the workers of Vienna, as he had earlier addressed workers' societies in Paris, Brussels and London. His report dealt with social relations in Europe and the proletariat's role in the revolutionary struggle. He remarked on the participation in the June uprising in Paris of German emigrant workers, who had shared the terrible but glorious fate of their French brothers. The German workers could be proud of their fellow countrymen. He reported on the latest Chartist action in England, and the struggle for the emancipation of the proletariat in Europe. He also dealt with the situation in Belgium. On September 2, he spoke before a workers' audience in Vienna on wage labour and capital.

He also showed much interest in the relations between the nationalities in Austria, that "prison-house of the peoples", and in Vienna met Alois Borrosch, the leader of the German-Bohemian group in the Austrian National Assembly. Borrosch complained about fanatical hostility between the Czechs and the Bohemian Germans, but when Marx asked him whether this also applied to the workers, Borrosch said: "As soon as the workers enter the movement, that stops;

---

[1] Marx, Engels, *Collected Works*, Vol. 7, p. 570.

there is no more talk about Czechs or Germans, and they all stick together."[1]

As the political situation grew more tense in Berlin and Frankfurt, Marx hastened to return to Cologne. On the way he stopped in Dresden and Berlin, where he attended a sitting of the National Assembly, and had more talks with the local Leftists. He met Wladyslaw Kościelski, a Polish leader, who on behalf of the Polish democrats gave him 2,000 talers for the *Neue Rheinische Zeitung*. Marx was back in Cologne about mid-September.

SEPTEMBER CRISIS IN GERMANY

By then an acute political conflict had flared up in Berlin over the National Assembly's second vote on a motion by a Left-wing deputy called Stein, suggesting that the reactionary Prussian officers should be dismissed from the army. It had been adopted on August 9, but the War Minister had refused to recognise it. Stein renewed his motion on September 7, and it was adopted by a majority vote. As a result, the Auerswald-Hansemann Government announced its intention to resign. Marx wrote in the *Neue Rheinische Zeitung* that there were only two possible outcomes for this acute political conflict: either the Assembly would win, the king's power would be broken, and a government of the Left would be set up; or the Crown would win, in which case the Assembly would be dissolved, the right of association would be abolished, and an electoral law based on property qualifications introduced, that is, a coup d'état would be carried out at bayonet point.[2]

The *Neue Rheinische Zeitung* explained that the fate of the Assembly depended on whether it called on the masses to stand up in its defence, or vacillated and ultimately submitted to the Crown, something that would lead to its removal from Berlin as a prelude to its dissolution. "The French Constituent Assembly transferred its sessions from Versailles to Paris. It would be quite in character with the German revolution if the Assembly of Agreement were to move from Berlin to Charlottenburg."[3]

History has made only a small, and purely geographical, correction to this forecast: in November, Brandenburg, another small provincial town, was designated as the Assembly's new official seat before its final dissolution.

Frankfurt am Main was the other centre of the September political crisis. There, the all-German National Assembly was about to discuss the ignominious armistice Prussia had concluded with Denmark on August 26. In contrast to the counter-revolutionary wars of the Austrian militarists in Italy and the Prussian militarists

---

[1] Marx, Engels, *Werke*, Bd. 22, S. 403.
[2] Marx, Engels, *Collected Works*, Vol. 7, p. 429.
[3] Ibid., p. 438.

in Posen, the war against Denmark over the mainly German-populated Schleswig-Holstein was a popular one, and the armistice with Denmark was rightly seen as a betrayal of Schleswig-Holstein's revolutionary government and Constituent Assembly. The Prussian government hastened to conclude it not only because of pressure from England and Russia, but also because it sought to call back General Wrangel's troops from the front to use them in the fight against the people.

The *Neue Rheinische Zeitung* said that the people alone could frustrate this counter-revolutionary scheme, and its editorial board acted as organiser and leader of the masses. Together with the Cologne Workers' Association and the Democratic Society it organised large indoor and open-air mass meetings, which developed into impressive political manifestations.

On September 13, the *Neue Rheinische Zeitung* editorial board, the Cologne Workers' Association and the Democratic Society called a public meeting in the Frankenplatz which was attended by some 5,000-6,000 people. On a motion by Wilhelm Wolff, seconded by Engels, Hermann Becker and Dronke, a Committee of Public Safety consisting of thirty members was elected, whose members included Marx, Engels, Wolff, Bürgers, Dronke, Schapper and Moll. This was followed by the unanimous adoption, on a motion by Engels, of a draft address to the Berlin Assembly, demanding that if an attempt were made to dissolve it the deputies would remain at their posts, even against the force of bayonets.

The formation of the Committee of Public Safety meant the establishment of an organ elected directly by the people which was to become an organising centre for the revolutionary struggle and the embryo of a new and truly revolutionary power. This terrified the Cologne bourgeoisie, and the same day it issued a protest on behalf of many members of the Board of the Cologne Citizens' Association, a constitutional monarchist body. As a result, some members of the Committee, including Schneider II, Chairman of the Democratic Society, announced their withdrawal from the Committee. This showed the sharpening contradictions between the petty-bourgeois and the proletarian wing of the Democratic Society.

A public meeting held at Worringen, in the suburbs of Cologne, on September 17, played an important part in enhancing the authority of the Committee of Public Safety. Besides people from Cologne, it was attended by peasants from neighbouring villages, and delegations from Neuss, Düsseldorf, Krefeld and other towns. On the rostrum, the red flag flew alongside the black-red-and-gold flag, which symbolised German unity. As at the September 13 meeting, the *Demands of the Communist Party in Germany* were extensively circulated among the audience. The meeting declared in favour of a democratic social red republic and approved with great enthusiasm the establishment of the Committee of Public Safety. It unanimously adopted, on a motion by Engels, an address to the Frankfurt

Assembly over the Prusso-Danish armistice, saying that in the event of a conflict between the Prussian government and the all-German Parliament, those present would "be ready to sacrifice their lives and property on the side of Germany".[1]

As the *Neue Rheinische Zeitung* had anticipated, on September 16 the Frankfurt Assembly ratified the Prusso-Danish armistice. The workers of Frankfurt, Offenbach and Hanau and the peasants of the neighbouring villages rose up in defence of Germany's revolutionary honour.

In view of these developments, the Committee of Public Safety, the Democratic Society and the Cologne Workers' Association called a public meeting in the Eiser Hall on September 20, which was attended by Marx and the other members of the *Neue Rheinische Zeitung* editorial board. In a brilliant speech Engels branded the traitorous decision of the all-German National Assembly, and reported on the course of the uprising in Frankfurt. A proclamation was adopted declaring the ratification of the armistice to be a betrayal of the German people, and branding as traitors the deputies of the Assembly, with the exception of those who had announced their readiness to resign.

When the *Neue Rheinische Zeitung* published the proclamation, it gave the authorities a pretext for commencing fresh proceedings against the newspaper and its editor-in-chief, this time on charges of libelling the deputies of the Frankfurt Parliament.

Following the suppression of the Frankfurt uprising, the Cologne Public Prosecutor's office preferred charges against Engels, Wilhelm Wolff and Bürgers on conspiring against the existing system, on the strength of their speeches at the public meetings. The Minister of Justice of the Imperial Government at Frankfurt issued orders that legal proceedings should be started against the Committee of Public Safety, the leaders of the Democratic Society and the Workers' Association, and also against the *Neue Rheinische Zeitung's* circulation department for collecting funds for the support of the Frankfurt insurgents and their families.

The tension in Cologne was growing. On the morning of September 25, Marx went to attend a meeting of the second democratic district congress, but it did not take place because of the arrests which had started in Cologne. Schapper and Hermann Becker were arrested early that morning, but the police failed to find Wolff. An attempt was made to arrest Moll, one of the most popular leaders of the Workers' Association, but he was released by the people who had flocked to his house.

By midday, a meeting of the Workers' Association had been convened at the Im Kranz Hotel in the Old Market. Marx urged the workers not to allow themselves to be provoked, and warned them against any premature or isolated uprising. At 3 o'clock, he issued

---

[1] Marx, Engels, *Collected Works*, Vol. 7, p. 587.

a similar call at a meeting in the Eiser Hall, which was also attended by members of the Democratic Society.

That night, a great crowd of people gathered in the Old Market, and there were rumours of approaching Prussian troops. The workers hastened to erect barricades, but the authorities did not risk moving in the troops because a section of the civil guard was "unreliable". However, these events provided them with a pretext for declaring a state of siege. All meetings and democratic and workers' organisations were banned; the publication of the *Neue Rheinische Zeitung* and other democratic newspapers was suspended, the civil guard was disarmed and disbanded.

A tide of indignation swept across Germany over the declaration of the state of siege at Cologne. Resolute protests were voiced in the Prussian National Assembly by the Left-wing deputies d'Ester, Borchardt and Kyll. The government was forced to make concessions. On October 2, the Cologne Public Prosecutor's office ordered the state of siege to be lifted. On October 3, subscriptions to the *Neue Rheinische Zeitung* were resumed.

However, it took Marx some time to recommence its publication. The paper had lost several of its editors. Engels and Dronke had gone to Brussels to escape imprisonment just when things were coming to a head. They were arrested by the local police and sent to France. Dronke stayed in Paris, while Engels walked his way to Switzerland. He settled down in Berne and took an active part in the Swiss working-class movement, helping Marx as best he could by sending in reports. Wilhelm Wolff escaped arrest by going to Pfalz, but aware of the difficulties facing Marx he returned secretly to Cologne and settled near the newspaper's premises at 17 Unter Hutmacher Str. Every day he walked across the yard to the editorial office, without having to go into the street. In addition to Weerth and Wolff, Marx now also had Freiligrath as an assistant.

The financial difficulties, caused by the purchase, before the state of siege, of an expensive, high-speed printing machine, were exacerbated by the paper's suspension. In order to save it, Marx put in all the money left of the sum he had inherited from his father — over 7,000 talers. In contrast to various other newspapers, the *Neue Rheinische Zeitung* never sought "to make a milch cow of the revolution", as Marx wrote later; "rather that paper was kept on its feet only at considerable financial sacrifice and at great personal risk to myself."[1]

The sale of the paper in the streets of Cologne was resumed on October 12. Marx issued something of a challenge to the authorities, who had ordered the arrest of almost all the editors, by announcing that *"the editorial board remains the same. Ferdinand Freiligrath has newly joined it."*[2]

At this time, the leaders of the Cologne Workers' Association

---

[1] Marx, Engels, *Collected Works*, Vol. 41, p. 100.
[2] Ibid., Vol. 7, p. 456.

found themselves in a very tight spot. Schapper was in prison and Moll had been forced to emigrate to London. Gottschalk's followers jumped at the chance to win back the positions they had lost. The Association's Committee then decided to send a deputation to Marx requesting him to accept the post of chairman. Despite the long hours he put in at the newspaper, the uncertainty of his position in Cologne because of the authorities' refusal to restore his rights of citizenship, and the judicial harassment, Marx agreed to accept this office temporarily. At a meeting of the Committee on October 16, he said: "The Government and the bourgeoisie ought to realise that, despite their acts of persecution, there were always persons to be found who would be ready to put themselves at the disposal of the workers."[1] Marx's election as chairman was approved by a general meeting of the Association on October 22. He performed these duties up to February 1849.

At a meeting of the Cologne Workers' Association, Marx remarked on the workers' outstanding role in the armed uprising that had started in Vienna. On his motion, a decision was unanimously adopted to send a message of greetings to the Vienna Workers' Association.

THE OCTOBER UPRISING IN VIENNA

The very first issue of the *Neue Rheinische Zeitung* after the lifting of the state of siege carried an article by Marx on the Vienna uprising, which had been sparked off by an imperial decree dissolving the Hungarian Diet and appointing as Governor of Hungary the reactionary Josip Jelačič, the ban of Croatia, who had just been heavily defeated by the fighters for Hungarian independence. On October 5, the troops stationed in Vienna were ordered to join Jelačič's routed army for a fresh campaign against the Hungarian revolution. The next day there was an uprising by the people, the students' Academic Legion and the National Guard of Vienna, who resisted the dispatch of the troops. By nightfall the people had won.

From then onwards the course of the struggle depended largely on how united and well organised the people of Vienna were. In his very first article, Marx sounded a warning about a possible betrayal by the Vienna bourgeoisie, and this was borne out. The Austrian reactionaries also managed to make use of national contradictions: in addition to the Southern Slavs, deceived by their landed *élite*, the Czech bourgeois national-liberal party also sided with the Hapsburgs. Under pressure from the liberals and a section of the officer corps, the leaders of revolutionary Hungary displayed a timid circumspection: the Hungarian troops were in no hurry to go to the aid of the Vienna insurgents.

---

[1] Marx, Engels, *Collected Works*, Vol. 7, p. 595.

Accordingly, special importance was attached to support for insurgent Vienna by all the democratic forces of Germany. In view of the forthcoming Second German Democratic Congress, Left-wing deputies of the Frankfurt, Berlin and several other German parliaments held a meeting in Berlin at the end of October. When the Frankfurt deputies, Simons, Zitz and Schlöffel stopped in Cologne on their way to Berlin, Marx made a point of seeing them in the hope of swaying the other Left-wing deputies. However, the Berlin meeting turned out to be small and far from united, and a majority, refusing to act otherwise than "within the law", rejected an appeal to the German people, written by d'Ester, Jacobi and Simons.

The Second German Democratic Congress, which met from October 26 to 30, was just as ineffective. The indignant *Neue Rheinische Zeitung* wrote that just when the fate of Vienna—and apparently of the whole of Germany—was at stake, the congress wasted time in endless debates on minor organisational matters. Only on the third day did it get round to discussing the Vienna events. The Leftists proposed that a mass meeting should be held at the Tiergarten to call for action by the people. A large section of the delegates walked out in protest, while the rest issued an appeal to the people to demand their governments to go to Vienna's aid.

This appeal was harshly criticised by Marx, who wrote: "Did the 'Democratic' Congress have the right to assume for one moment this childish and conservative attitude to the German governments?" He expressed the hope that the people would "aid the Viennese in the only way it is still able to do at this moment, by defeating the counter-revolution at home".[1]

The remaining participants in the congress took a more radical stand when they discussed the social question on October 30. The report was delivered by the delegate of the Cologne Workers' Association, Beust, who proposed a draft programme which envisaged, following the establishment of a democratic republic, practical measures based on a number of points in the *Demands of the Communist Party in Germany*. Most of these were reproduced verbatim, but some were amended in the petty-bourgeois democratic spirit. The report was circulated among the democratic societies for discussion.

The closure of the Second Democratic Congress almost coincided with the fall of Vienna. On November 6, Marx spoke on the question at a meeting of the Committee of the Cologne Workers' Association, and within a few days, at a meeting of the Democratic Society. Lessner, who was present, later recalled: "Marx broke the news that Robert Blum had been shot by sentence of a field court-martial in Vienna.... Silence immediately fell over the hall. Marx went up to the rostrum and read out the dispatch from Vienna on Blum's death. We were horrified. Then a storm seemed to blow through the hall."[2]

---

[1] Marx, Engels, *Collected Works*, Vol. 7, pp. 491-92.
[2] *Reminiscences of Marx and Engels*, Moscow, 1957, p. 157.

In his article, "The Victory of the Counter-Revolution in Vienna", Marx wrathfully branded the bourgeoisie's betrayal of the Vienna insurgents and wrote: "History presents no more *shameful and pitiful spectacle* than that of the *German bourgeoisie*." Assessing the impact of the Vienna events on the German and the European revolution as a whole, Marx wrote: "The second act of the drama has just been performed in *Vienna*, its first act having been staged in Paris under the title of *The June Days*.... We shall soon see the third act performed in *Berlin*." [1] He anticipated a decisive offensive by the counter-revolution in Prussia and took a realistic view of the balance of forces there. Accordingly, he pinned his main hopes on an initiative by revolutionary France, emphasising the lessons the peoples had to learn from the experience of the battles fought: "The purposeless massacres perpetrated since the June and October events, the tedious offering of sacrifices since February and March, the very cannibalism of the counter-revolution will convince the nations that there is only *one means* by which the murderous death agonies of the old society and the bloody birth throes of the new society can be *shortened*, simplified and concentrated — and that is by *revolutionary terror*." [2]

Marx used this bitter experience of defeat to again substantiate the need to establish a true revolutionary power capable of preventing any further counter-revolutionary atrocities, and so facilitating and bringing on the victory of the masses.

FIGHTING THE COUNTER-REVOLUTIONARY COUP IN PRUSSIA

As Marx had anticipated, the defeat of the October uprising in Vienna spurred the Prussian reactionaries to resolute action. On November 2, King Frederick William IV asked the diehard reactionary, General Brandenburg, to form a new government. The royal decree transferring the National Assembly from Berlin to the provincial town of Brandenburg was issued on November 9, and marked the start of the coup in Prussia, which Marx summed up in the following words: "*Brandenburg in the Assembly and the Assembly in Brandenburg! ... The guardroom in the Assembly, the Assembly in the guardroom!*" [3] Marx demanded that the Assembly should take revolutionary action, believing that it "should have had the Ministers *arrested as traitors, traitors to the sovereignty of the people*. It should have *proscribed* and *outlawed* all officials who obey orders others than those of the Assembly." [4] For the Assembly this was much too vigorous and revolutionary. It did decide to continue its

---

[1] Marx, Engels, *Collected Works*, Vol. 7, pp. 504-05.
[2] Ibid., pp. 505-06.
[3] Ibid., Vol. 8, p. 14.
[4] Ibid., p. 15.

sittings in Berlin, but announced that it intended to confine itself to passive resistance.

Marx condemned the tactics of the "whining, hair-splitting and irresolute National Assembly" and urged it to appeal to the masses and to the soldiers of the Prussian army and to use French-type, Jacobin, plebeian methods. He asked the people: "And what should we do at the present time?" And answered: *"We should refuse to pay taxes."* [1]

Thus, on November 11, with the political fight at its crucial stage, Marx issued a basic slogan of struggle the realisation of which would, on the one hand, have weakened the counter-revolution and undermined its financial basis, and on the other, helped to draw into the struggle the broad masses of the people and pitted them directly against the government. This would have increased the political army of the revolution.

Seeking to win time, the counter-revolution hastily implemented its own plans. On November 11, its soldiers prevented the deputies from entering the theatre where the National Assembly was meeting, and they had to assemble at a shooting gallery. A decree was issued disarming and disbanding the Berlin civil guard and declaring a state of siege in the city. Marx said this was another piece of high treason and urged the deputies to resort to extra-parliamentary forms of struggle: *"The National Assembly has its seat in the people and not in the confines of this or that heap of stones."* [2]

While assigning the most active role to the proletariat and its vanguard — the Communists — Marx strove to unite the country's progressive forces, so as to frustrate the plans of the counter-revolution and deal it a crushing blow. Marx himself became the heart and soul of a broad revolutionary movement in the Rhine Province. On his initiative, the Democratic Society and the Workers' Association held a number of mass meetings in Cologne and its environs. A meeting held in the Eiser Hall on November 11 adopted an address to the Berlin National Assembly, urging it to persist in its refusal to submit to the royal decree. By noon on November 12, the address had 7,000 signatures. The meeting declared itself to be a standing body and on November 13 elected a People's Committee with twenty-five members, on which all the democratic trends and the Communists were represented. The People's Committee was set up on a broader basis than the Committee of Public Safety which had operated in Cologne in September. Apart from representatives of the workers and the petty bourgeoisie, it included some progressive bourgeois. The Committee's task was to rally all the forces to resist reaction that was encroaching on the gains of the revolution.

Arming the people became the vital question. Already on November 11, the Eiser Hall meeting had called on the Cologne municipal council to return the arms confiscated in September to their owners

[1] Ibid., p. 18.
[2] Ibid., p. 25.

without delay, a demand to which the "city fathers" turned a deaf ear. The Democratic Society took steps to re-establish the disbanded civil guard. The Cologne Workers' Association started to form its "flying squad". An appeal was issued for the collection of funds for the purchase of arms. The *Neue Rheinische Zeitung*'s circulation department announced that it was prepared to receive donations for that purpose.

Meanwhile, much was being done in the army. On November 12, the Democratic Society adopted an address to the soldiers of the Cologne garrison, urging them to stop being a tool in the hands of the despots. A special supplement to the *Neue Rheinische Zeitung* No. 143 issued on November 15 bore the headline "The Fatherland Is in Danger" followed by an announcement that a meeting would he held in the Eiser Hall that day by members of the Cologne *Landwehr* and reservists. This meeting demanded that the Berlin National Assembly should "call on the *Landwehr* to rise up as it did in 1813 and destroy the internal enemy as it then destroyed the external enemy".[1] Despite strict orders to the contrary, many *Landwehr* meetings were attended by soldiers of the Cologne garrison, indicating that the army was also in a state of revolutionary ferment.

In order to draw the peasantry into the struggle, the Democratic Society, the Workers' Association and the People's Committee sent their emissaries to the surrounding villages.

Marx also worked to co-ordinate action with the democrats in various towns of the Rhine Province. In a letter dated November 13 to Ferdinand Lassalle, who played a prominent role in Düsseldorf, Marx, writing on behalf of the Democratic District Committee, recommended that the people of Düsseldorf should adopt the following decisions: 1) to refuse totally to pay taxes, with special emphasis on carrying the idea to the countryside; 2) to dispatch a volunteer detachment to Berlin, and 3) to dispatch money to the Democratic Central Committee in Berlin.

An important step in translating the demand to refuse to pay taxes into a mass action slogan was the signing by Marx and Schneider II of an appeal from the Democratic District Committee on November 14 urging all democratic organisations in the Rhine Province to hold public meetings at once and induce the whole population of the Province to refrain from paying taxes. But until the slogan was adopted by the Berlin National Assembly and actively supported in the other provinces, Marx believed the people should not, for the time being, use force to resist the collection of taxes.

The District Committee's appeal at once met with a sympathetic response among the people in a number of towns and rural localities in the Rhine Province. There were also reports of revolutionary ferment in Saxony, Silesia and Westphalia. But again the movement was unco-ordinated and mainly spontaneous. In order to bring to-

---

[1] *Neue Rheinische Zeitung* No. 145, November 17, 1848.

gether the local centres of resistance in a nation-wide revolutionary struggle, the grassroots revolutionary action had to be reinforced by action from above, by the Berlin National Assembly, the only body capable of centralising the movement.

In putting forward slogans for struggle, Marx also suggested the tactic to be used by the Prussian National Assembly, notably its Left wing. At the same time, he was preparing effective support for it. In an editorial article carried in the *Neue Rheinische Zeitung* on November 14, he called on the people of the Rhine Province "*to hasten to the assistance of the Berlin National Assembly with men and weapons*". [1] In those critical days, Marx established regular ties with the Berlin Left-wing deputies, making use for the purpose of a special messenger service manned mainly by members of the Cologne Workers' Association.

On November 15, under the influence of innumerable appeals which were coming in from the Rhine and other provinces, the National Assembly adopted a decision on the refusal to pay taxes, to become effective on November 17. At long last, Marx's slogan acquired nation-wide importance and binding legal force. Henceforth, he wrote, "*it is high treason to pay taxes. Refusal to pay taxes is the primary duty of the citizen!*" [2]

Marx displayed his genius as revolutionary strategist and tactician by his ability to keep abreast of the rapidly changing political situation and to modify the forms and methods of struggle accordingly. The National Assembly's decision now warranted the slogan of armed resistance to the forcible collection of taxes. At this responsible moment, when the weapon of criticism was to be superseded by criticism through the use of weapons, Marx again took the initiative by outlining, in a fresh appeal by the District Committee on November 18, a programme of action for the whole of revolutionary democracy. The appeal was signed by Marx, Schneider II and Schapper, and contained three new slogans: 1) resistance to the forcible collection of taxes all over the country, by every possible means; 2) organisation of people's volunteer detachments to beat back the enemy; and 3) establishment of committees of public safety to confront authorities refusing to abide by the National Assembly's decision.

The counter-revolutionaries tried to cut short Marx's revolutionary activity. The day after his appeal in the *Neue Rheinische Zeitung* to refuse paying taxes, he was summoned by the examining magistrate. On November 14, the city learned that Marx was faced with arrest, and an impressive crowd gathered outside the court-house. The Cologne Chief Public Prosecutor, Zweiffel, informed the Ministry of Justice that the crowd was prepared to use force to release Marx if he were arrested. When Marx emerged from the court-house, he was

---

[1] Marx, Engels, *Collected Works*, Vol. 8, p. 19.
[2] Ibid., p. 36.

greeted with enthusiastic cries and escorted to the Eiser Hall, where he thanked everyone for their support.

The authorities were again thrown into confusion by the District Committee's appeal of November 18. The Cologne *Regierungspräsident* [1] wrote to the Minister of the Interior, Manteuffel, that the arrest of the authors of the appeal—Marx, Schapper and Schneider II—would "remove the main elements stirring up trouble here". [2] When on November 20 the judicial authorities issued a fresh summons, carrying a charge of incitement to open revolt, Marx, Schapper and Schneider II warned the democrats of the Rhine Province that another provocation was being plotted in Cologne and that the state of siege could be reimposed. They wrote: "Frustrate this hope. Whatever may befall us, conduct yourselves calmly." Meanwhile they were preparing the people for the battles ahead, declaring that the Rhine Province would not "submit to the rule of the sword". [3]

The People's Committee sent a deputation to Chief Public Prosecutor Zweiffel to demand an explanation about the rumours of impending arrests. On that occasion, in view of the highly tense political atmosphere, the authorities confined themselves to instituting judicial proceedings, but this did not rule out more arbitrary acts by the police, and Marx expected to be arrested at any time.

In these very trying circumstances, Marx firmly and vigorously implemented the tactics he had outlined. From November 19 to December 17 the *Neue Rheinische Zeitung* carried the front page headline *Keine Steuern mehr!!!* (No More Taxes!!!)—and the idea was driven home in special placards and handbills.

The Second Democratic District Congress met in Cologne to discuss further revolutionary steps with Marx taking an active part in it. The *Neue Rheinische Zeitung* carried only this laconic report: "The Rhine Democratic Congress held on November 23 approved the decisions taken by the Rhine District Committee.—The delegates are to inform their associations of the detailed instructions." [4] Thus, the congress approved Marx's action slogans, and the delegates were given instructions on how to translate them into practice.

Marx and his followers in the Rhine Province had done everything to prepare the people for the decisive battle against the counter-revolution, but the success of the struggle throughout the country largely depended on the Prussian National Assembly, which limited itself to tactics of passive resistance within the law, cowardly tactics which demobilised the masses and which Marx ironically compared with the resistance put up by a calf as the butcher drags it to the slaughter.

---

[1] Regional representative of the central government in Prussia.
[2] G. Becker, *Karl Marx und Friedrich Engels in Köln, 1848-1849*, Berlin, 1963, S. 159.
[3] Marx, Engels, *Collected Works*, Vol. 8, p. 46.
[4] *Neue Rheinische Zeitung* No. 153, November 26, 1848.

The counter-revolutionary royal clique was quick to take advantage of this, and on December 5 issued two decrees: one dissolving the National Assembly and convening new Chambers in February 1849, and the other announcing the royal grant of a Prussian Constitution, without its consideration by any assembly whatsoever. That put the finishing touches to the coup d'état in Prussia.

Marx commented: "The National Assembly now reaps the fruits of its chronic weakness and cowardice. For months it allowed the conspiracy against the people to carry on its work unmolested, to grow strong and powerful, and hence has now become its first victim."[1]

FIRST RESULTS AND PROSPECTS OF THE GERMAN AND EUROPEAN REVOLUTIONS

In a series of articles entitled *The Bourgeoisie and the Counter-Revolution*, Marx gave an unsurpassed analysis of the specific features and main stages of the German revolution from March to December 1848.

His analysis of the basic distinction between the German revolution, on the one hand, and the English revolution of 1648 and the French revolution of 1789, on the other, enabled Marx to draw a highly important theoretical conclusion about the different types of bourgeois revolution. In the English and French revolutions, "the bourgeoisie was the class that *really* headed the movement. The *proletariat* and the *non-bourgeois strata of the middle class* had either not yet any interests separate from those of the bourgeoisie or they did not yet constitute independent classes or class sub-divisions."[2]

Nothing of the sort happened in the March revolution in Prussia. "The German bourgeoisie developed so sluggishly, timidly and slowly that at the moment when it menacingly confronted feudalism and absolutism, it saw menacingly confronting it the proletariat and all sections of the middle class whose interest and ideas were related to those of the proletariat.... Without initiative, without faith in itself, without faith in the people, without a world-historic mission, an abominable dotard finding himself condemned to lead and to mislead the first youthful impulses of a virile people so as to make them serve his own senile interests — sans eyes, sans ears, sans teeth, sans everything, such was the *Prussian bourgeoisie* which found itself at the helm of the Prussian state after the March revolution."[3]

Summing up developments in Prussia up to December 1848, Marx answered a question that was of great concern to the people, namely, what were the prospects for the German revolution. He

---

[1] Marx, Engels, *Collected Works*, Vol. 8, p. 135.
[2] Ibid., p. 161.
[3] Ibid., pp. 162-63.

wrote: "The history of the Prussian bourgeois class, like that of the German bourgeois class in general between March and December, shows that a purely *bourgeois revolution* and the establishment of *bourgeois rule* in the form of a *constitutional monarchy* is impossible in Germany, and that only a feudal absolutist counter-revolution or a *social republican revolution* is possible." [1]

Thus, Marx clearly formulated two possibilities: either a final victory for the feudal absolutist counter-revolution and the total abolition of representative institutions, freedom of assembly, association and the press — all of which had been won in March — or another revolution in which the proletariat, the peasantry and the urban petty bourgeoisie would set up a truly democratic republic capable of becoming an instrument of social change and implementing the programme outlined in the *Demands of the Communist Party in Germany*.

Marx continued to see an organic connection between the prospects for the revolutionary movement in Germany and the advance of the European revolution, whose results in 1848 and further prospects Marx outlined mainly in two articles: "The Revolutionary Movement in Italy", which he wrote on November 29, and "The Revolutionary Movement", on which he worked at the very end of 1848.

In the first article, Marx described the following main stages in the counter-revolutionary offensive which had followed upon the triumphant advance of the European revolution in February and March: the prevention of the Chartist demonstration in London on April 10, which had blocked the way of the revolution in England; the defeat of the Paris workers on June 25, which had dealt a heavy blow at the European revolution; the recapture of Milan by Austrian troops on August 6; and the final defeat of the October uprising in Vienna on November 1. Soon after the article was written came the coup in Berlin.

In the face of this discouraging outcome, Marx was not inclined to despair, because he realised that the peoples learned both from their victories and from their defeats. At the start of the revolution, people everywhere had been carried away by illusions and vague enthusing about universal brotherhood. But the counter-revolutionary atrocities had taught the revolutionary fighters a great deal. "The chief result of the revolutionary movement of 1848 is not what the peoples won, but what they lost — the *loss of their illusions*." [2]

Analysing the prospects for the European revolution in 1849, Marx said he still expected the revolutionary initiative to come from France, with the European peoples once again being roused by the crowing of the Gallic cock. He saw an even closer connection between the overthrow of the absolutist regimes and the winning of in-

---

[1] Marx, Engels, *Collected Works*, Vol. 8, p. 178.
[2] Ibid., p. 197.

dependence by the oppressed nations, on the one hand, and a victorious uprising by the French workers, on the other.

Marx saw capitalist England with its industrial and commercial hegemony as the main enemy of the proletarian revolution in France. "*England* seems to be the rock against which the revolutionary waves break.... A revolution of the economic relations in any country of the European continent, in the whole European continent without England, is a storm in a teacup." [1] If a social revolution in France was not to be suppressed by the English bourgeoisie, old bourgeois-aristocratic England had to be crushed. Marx believed, therefore, that in those conditions the first outcome of a victorious working-class revolution in France would be a European war, and since England would be involved it would become a world war, in the course of which conditions could also be provided for a successful Chartist uprising. "England will head the counter-revolutionary armies, just as it did during the Napoleonic period, but through the war itself it will be thrown to the head of the revolutionary movement and it will repay the debt it owes in regard to the revolution of the eighteenth century." [2]

It was the historical situation that made Marx believe that a French proletarian uprising would lead to a great clash between the revolutionary and the counter-revolutionary forces in the international arena. It was impossible at that time for the European revolution to rise to a new and higher stage without fresh victorious action by the French working class. Marx also believed that this revolutionary process would succeed with a victory of the proletarian revolution in England, economically the most developed country. He saw the prerequisites for a proletarian revolution in the aftermath of the economic crisis of 1847, the incredibly savage forms and methods of exploitation of the workers typical of the early stages of industrial capitalism, the mass impoverishment of the artisans, and the dire plight of the peasantry.

At that time Marx and Engels regarded all this as signs of an imminent socialist revolution. They tended to exaggerate the "senility" of contemporary capitalism and erred on the side of optimism in their hopes for an early victory of the proletarian revolution. Lenin wrote: "But *such* errors — the errors of the giants of revolutionary thought, who sought to raise, and did raise, the proletariat of the whole world above the level of petty, commonplace and trivial tasks — are a thousand times more noble and magnificent and *historically more valuable and true* than the trite wisdom of official liberalism, which lauds, shouts, appeals and holds forth about the vanity of revolutionary vanities, the futility of the revolutionary struggle and the charms of counter-revolutionary 'constitutional' fantasies." [3]

---

[1] Ibid., p. 214.
[2] Ibid., p. 215.
[3] V. I. Lenin, *Collected Works*, Vol. 12, p. 378.

WORKING FOR THE UNITY OF THE DEMOCRATIC FORCES

After the coup in Prussia there was a temporary lull. The forces of revolution and counter-revolution appeared to be preparing for the final showdown.

In January and early February 1849, Marx concentrated on the elections to the Second Chamber of the Prussian Provincial Diet, which were, in the main, to be held on the basis of the universal and equal but not direct suffrage introduced in April 1848. If the results were favourable to democracy, an opposition could emerge in the Second Chamber to resist any future schemes of the counter-revolution. That is why Marx and Engels, who had returned to Cologne in mid-January, attached much political importance to the elections and once again worked to unite all the democratic forces.

It was most important for a victory of democracy that the liberal bourgeoisie, which had accepted the imposed constitution and was beguiling itself and the people with hopes of securing its partial revision, should be fully exposed and isolated. In a series of articles entitled *Montesquieu LVI* Marx ironically explained that the bourgeoisie would be given an opportunity of revising the constitution only "insofar as it suits the King and the Second Chamber consisting of country squires, financial magnates, high-ranking officials and clerics".[1] He condemned the *Kölnische Zeitung*, the mouthpiece of the liberals, which had tried to deceive the people by saying that the imposed constitution could help to solve both political and social questions, without in any way modifying the existing social relations.

While working to unite all the democratic forces, Marx made no effort to gloss over the differences in the democratic camp. Thus he levelled frank and stern criticism at the *National-Zeitung*, the organ of the Berlin former Left, which while declaring its adherence to a "*genuinely* democratic-constitutional order" opposed any continuation of the revolution, and stood for "law, tranquillity and order". Marx wrote: "These gentlemen 'want' the very things they will never obtain except by a new revolution. But they do not want a new revolution."[2] Marx criticised the petty-bourgeois democrats and demanded that they should be consistent, firm and energetic in working for general democratic tasks.

A meeting of the Committee of the Cologne Workers' Association on January 15 discussed its tactics in connection with the elections to the Second Chamber. Some of Gottschalk's adherents still remaining in the Association opposed an electoral bloc with the democrats. In a big speech, Marx attacked the sectarians and once again

---

[1] Marx, Engels, *Collected Works*, Vol. 8, p. 257.
[2] Ibid., p. 279.

argued the need for unity with the democrats in the elections, and this move was a success: of the electors returned in Cologne on January 22, two-thirds were democrats, who also won in many other towns and rural localities in the Rhine Province. These primary elections showed that "the petty bourgeoisie, peasants and proletarians emancipated themselves from the big bourgeoisie, the upper nobility and the higher bureaucracy".[1]

The elections to the Second Chamber, held on February 5, once again vindicated Marx's tactics. The candidates Kyll and Schneider II, nominated by the general democratic front, were returned. The election of Schneider II was of especially great political importance, because in three days' time he was due to appear in a Cologne court before a jury together with Marx and Schapper. Thus, even before the trial opened, a voters' majority had passed a verdict acquitting them.

TWO TRIALS

By the end of 1848, Marx had lost count of the trials started by the authorities against the *Neue Rheinische Zeitung* and some of its editors.

The first case, over the publication on July 5, 1848 of the above-mentioned article entitled "Arrests", had been postponed by the authorities on several occasions in expectation of a more favourable political situation and was heard on February 7, 1849. In the dock were Marx, Engels and Korff, the responsible publisher. Schneider II, a trained lawyer, acted as defence counsel for Marx and Engels, but the highlight of the trial were the bold speeches of the accused in defence of the *Neue Rheinische Zeitung* and freedom of the press in general in the Rhine Province and the whole of Germany.

Lessner, who had been at the trial, subsequently recalled: "It was a delight to see and hear with what great superiority the black-and-white [2] reaction was opposed. Even these two men's opponents could not help admiring them."[3]

Marx had set himself the task of beating his opponents on their own ground with their own weapons and was eminently successful. He gave a detailed legal analysis of the indictment and proved beyond all doubt that the articles of the Criminal Code, under which the charges of insult of the Cologne Chief Public Prosecutor Zweiffel and libel of the police were being preferred, were absolutely irrelevant. Proceeding from this Marx showed the overall political significance of the trial. By sanctioning the application of the laws in this manner, he told the jury, "you abolish freedom of the press ... whereas you have recognised this freedom by a Constitution and won it

---

[1] Marx, Engels, *Collected Works*, Vol. 8, p. 288.
[2] Black and white were the Prussian colours.
[3] *Reminiscences of Marx and Engels*, p. 176.

by a revolution. You sanction every arbitrary action of the officials, you permit every official villainous action, you punish only the denunciation of villainy." [1]

Marx further declared that he personally would have preferred to deal with epoch-making events, instead of grappling with the local police and the officials at the Public Prosecutor's office. "I consider we are making a real sacrifice when we decide to break a lance with *these* opponents. But firstly, it is the duty of the press to come forward on behalf of the oppressed in its immediate neighbourhood.... The press must decide to enter the lists against a *specific* police officer, a *specific* Public Prosecutor, a *specific* Landrat." To cries of approval from the public gallery, he added: "What caused the defeat of the *March revolution*? It reformed only the highest political summit, it left all the groundwork of this summit intact — the old bureaucracy, the old army, the old boards of prosecuting magistrates, the old judiciary which had been created, had developed and grown grey in the service of absolutism. The first duty of the press now is *to undermine all the foundations of the existing political state of affairs.*" [2]

Thus, in the dock, Marx stood up for the freedom of the press and spread the idea of a people's revolution which was to crush the old officialdom, the army and the courts.

Engels, who spoke after Marx, said that the facts given in "Arrests" had been confirmed to the letter, as had also been its general political conclusion about the "Government of Action" being transitional to the old aristocratic and old bureaucratic government. Addressing the court and the jury, Engels said that his and Marx's crime apparently consisted in having "correctly reported correct facts and drawn the correct conclusions from them ".[3]

Marx's and Engels' case was so strongly reasoned that the jury had to bring in a verdict of not guilty, which was met with cries of jubilation from the large audience.

The following day, Marx, together with Schapper and Schneider II, was arraigned in court on a charge of "incitement to revolt" in connection with the second appeal of the Rhine District Committee of Democrats of November 18, 1848. The *Deutsche Londoner Zeitung* reported that, as on the previous day, "the crowd of people was extraordinary".[4]

In a long speech Marx gave a profound theoretical analysis of the causes behind the coup in Prussia and showed its true nature, arguing in favour of the tactics followed by the Rhine District Committee of Democrats.

Marx criticised the idea that a revolution had to confine itself to the "framework of legality", and drew a highly important theoreti-

---

[1] Marx, Engels, *Collected Works*, Vol. 8, p. 313.
[2] Ibid., pp. 316-17.
[3] Ibid., p. 322.
[4] Ibid., p. 521.

cal conclusion on the attitude of the revolution towards the obsolete legal superstructure. In contrast to the idealistic views then held by jurists that society was based on the law, Marx argued that "the law must be founded upon society, it must express the common interests and needs of society ... which arise from the material mode of production prevailing at the given time".[1] Marx stressed that the old laws could not serve as a basis for new social development, and so the revolution had the vital task of destroying the old legal superstructure.

Marx also criticised, in the light of materialism, the treacherous "theory of agreement". He showed that the conflict between the Crown and the National Assembly had been inevitable, and explained its social essence. It was "a *conflict between two societies,* a social conflict, which had assumed a political form: *it was the struggle of the old feudal bureaucratic society with modern bourgeois society*, a struggle between the society of *free competition* and the *society of the guild system*, between the society of landownership and the industrial society, between the society of faith and the society of knowledge".[2]

Referring to the Rhine District Committee's appeal of November 18, Marx cited examples from history to show that refusal to pay taxes was a legitimate means of popular self-defence against a government that was violating the people's interests. On that occasion, it was the royal power that had strayed from legality by resorting to force. Marx's main idea was that the people had the inalienable right and duty to resist such arbitrary acts, by countering the violence of despots with revolutionary violence even to the extent of overthrowing the existing political system. Rebutting the Prosecutor's charge that in their appeal the accused had gone farther than the Prussian National Assembly itself, Marx said that the Assembly had been inconsistent and its majority cowardly. "The conduct of the National Assembly was by no means a criterion for the people.... If the Crown makes a counter-revolution, the people has the right to reply with a revolution." In conclusion, Marx stressed that the struggle was far from over, and that this was merely the end of the first act of the drama. Ahead lay either "*complete victory of the counter-revolution* or a *new victorious revolution*".[3]

Engels subsequently wrote that Marx confronted the bourgeois jury as a Communist who had to explain that the bourgeois themselves should have done the things he was being tried for. Marx's speech left such a strong impression on the jury that the foreman thanked him for his instructive explanations. Once again the accused were acquitted.

The authorities were at a loss as to how to deal with Marx. The commandant of the Cologne fortress suggested that he should be de-

---

[1] Ibid., p. 327.
[2] Ibid., p. 335.
[3] Ibid., p. 339.

ported, as the chief source of "the disturbances in the Rhine Province".[1] Consequently the police authorities, though fearful of popular protest, applied for permission, and this was granted by the Minister of the Interior, Manteuffel, who left it to the Cologne authorities to decide the time and pretext. The latter merely bided their time, hoping to get rid of the dangerous revolutionary by this means.

MARX IN FEBRUARY-MARCH 1849

The only purpose for which the Second Chamber was convened, on February 26, was to put the stamp of legality on the coup. The people were to be kept quiet by three reactionary bills—on clubs and assemblies, on placards, and on the press—and by analogy with the anti-popular Act of 1819 in England, Marx called them the "gagging laws".

In those conditions Marx believed that it was especially important for the people to keep the deputies under vigorous pressure. The people of Cologne set the example. A big meeting of electors on March 11 voted into being a committee of nine, which included Communists, among them Marx and Wolff. The election of Marx, formally not a voter because he did not have Prussian citizenship, was in itself a political demonstration. The committee had the task of calling meetings of electors and conveying their addresses, protests, etc., to the deputies in the Second Chamber. The same meeting called on the deputies to demand an end to the state of siege in Berlin. A meeting on March 16 discussed the "gagging laws", and thousands of people signed the address, which was written in the style of the *Neue Rheinische Zeitung*. A special letter addressed to the Cologne deputies, Kyll and Schneider II, contained the demand, formulated by Marx, that the Rhine Province deputies should withdraw from the Second Chamber if the bills were approved. The commandant of the Cologne fortress at once sent in a report about these meetings to the Ministry of War stressing the leading part played by the editors of the *Neue Rheinische Zeitung* in arranging them.

However, despite pressure from the people, the deputies, even the Leftists, behaved in a cowardly manner. That is why in nearly every article written by Marx and Engels about the Second Chamber there was a sharp criticism of the Leftists.

Democratic banquets arranged to mark the anniversaries of the February and March revolutions were another form of political work among the masses, the first being organised at Mülheim am Rhein on February 11 by the local Workers' Association. In a speech before a large audience, Marx described the German workers' participation in the revolutionary movement in other countries, including France, England, Belgium and Switzerland. One of the

---

[1] G. Becker, *Karl Marx und Friedrich Engels in Köln*, 1848-1849, S. 206.

toasts was in honour of the guests, who "like the redacteur en chef of the *Neue Rheinische Zeitung Karl Marx*, who was present, had in words and deeds upheld the rights of the working class long before the February revolution".[1]

Another democratic banquet was held in Cologne on February 24 by the Workers' Association and the Democratic Society. The great Eiser Hall was filled to capacity, and the keynote of the banquet was the international solidarity of the democrats of all countries. All present stood in memory of those who had died in the February and June uprisings in Paris.

The editors of the *Neue Rheinische Zeitung* received many invitations to banquets in honour of the anniversary of the March revolution in Prussia, but did not feel inclined to celebrate the occasion. "We confess to our readers that we do not know how to write any leading article for today. The March revolution in Berlin, that feeble echo of the revolution in Vienna, never aroused our enthusiasm," [2] they wrote.

However, Marx and the other editors of the *Neue Rheinische Zeitung* did attend a banquet held on March 19 by the Workers' Association and the Democratic Society to mark the fighting on the barricades in Berlin. In the presence of almost 6,000 persons, Engels proposed a toast to the June insurgents in Paris, Schapper to the English Chartists, and Dronke to the proletarian revolution. Freiligrath wrote the *Reveille*, an inspiring revolutionary anthem to the strains of the *Marseillaise*. It drew a comparison between June and March and called for a new revolution under the red banner. The banquet ended with a general toast to the Red Republic. The *Neue Kölnische Zeitung* called the banquet a "proletarian festival".

A large part of the credit for spreading the communist influence in Cologne belonged to Marx's followers in the Workers' Association. In February it adopted a new set of Rules based on the territorial principle. The Association had nine branches empowered to enroll new members who paid monthly membership dues. Political discussion was now centred in the branches and as a rule dealt with the most pressing political issues analysed in the *Neue Rheinische Zeitung*'s leaders.

The Association gave much attention to the defence of the economic interests of the workers and artisans, whose condition, undermined by the 1847 crisis and unemployment, continued to be grave. Fearful of a spontaneous explosion, the Cologne authorities employed some of the jobless on public works, all of whom had to sign a "Worker's Card" and to abide by stringiest disciplinary regulations. In "A Bourgeois Document", an article written in early January 1849, Marx branded this savage and cynical system and showed that the Prussian bourgeoisie had wedded charity to revenge like the

---

[1] Marx, Engels, *Collected Works*, Vol. 8, p. 522.
[2] Ibid., Vol. 9, p. 108.

English bourgeoisie which had set up workhouses for the poor with a prison-like routine.

PRACTICAL STEPS TOWARDS A MASS PROLETARIAN PARTY

In their effort to turn the proletariat into an independent political force, Marx and his followers worked steadily to prepare the workers for an ideological, political and organisational separation from petty-bourgeois democracy and for the establishment of a party of their own. But while members of the Communist League in Cologne were in direct contact with Marx and the other members of the Central Authority, elsewhere they were not. The organisational ties between the League's communities in other cities in Germany, and also in London, Paris, Switzerland, and Belgium, on the one hand, and the Central Authority in Cologne, on the other, gradually weakened and eventually faded away.

Soon after his arrival in London, Joseph Moll, who had apparently never quite accepted the idea of winding up the Communist League's secret activity, joined Heinrich Bauer and Johann Georg Eccarius in setting up a new central authority. In the winter of 1848-49, the London Central Authority sent Moll to Germany to reorganise the Communist League, with or without the consent of Marx and the Cologne Central Authority, to reconvert it into a secret society under a new set of Rules framed in London.

A member of the Communist League, Peter Gerhard Röser, later reported that in the spring of 1849 a meeting with Moll was held on the *Neue Rheinische Zeitung* premises and was attended by members of the Cologne Central Authority—Marx, Engels, Wolff and Schapper—and members of a secret League community set up in Cologne by Schapper—Röser, Nothjung, Reiff, Haude, Esser and Müller. Schapper and Moll insisted on resuming the secret League, while Marx, Engels and Wolff objected, because conditions for legal communist activity still existed in Germany. They came out strongly against the London Central Authority's Rules, designated as the "Rules of the Revolutionary Party", apparently for fear that the "spectre of communism" would frighten away the workers. Instead of giving a clear-cut formulation of the League's communist aims, as Paragraph One of the old Rules had, the new one said: "The aim of the League is to establish a united and indivisible social republic." Paragraph Two, formulating the conditions of membership, said nothing about accepting communism, and Marx declared that the new Rules were essentially not communist. He also criticised them for reducing revolutionary struggle to conspiratorial activity. Far from promoting the establishment of a mass proletarian party, such Rules actually hampered it.

The differences between London and Cologne were being aggravated by the intrigues started earlier by Ewerbeck, chairman of the

Communist League's Paris Circle Authority and a correspondent of the *Neue Rheinische Zeitung*, together with Hess and Gottschalk. While attending the Second Democratic Congress in Berlin as a delegate of the German democrats of Paris, Ewerbeck began to put through his and Hess' plan to set up a new governing centre for the League in the capital of Prussia as a counterweight to the Cologne Central Authority. An attempt was also made to drive a wedge between Marx and Engels. Marx's response to the attempt was described by Ewerbeck in a letter to Hess which he sent from Cologne on November 14. He said that Marx was "very enthusiastic about Engels, whom he regarded as outstanding 'intellectually, morally and as regards his character'".[1]

Despite the increasingly complicated situation in the Communist League, Marx and his friends steadfastly continued to pursue the firm line they had adopted at the beginning of the revolution to set up a mass legal political organisation of the German proletariat, with the Communists as its core. As Marx had expected, the practical revolutionary struggle, especially the events of November and December 1848, gave the workers an excellent political schooling. Life itself was breaking up the shell of the narrow-craft unions and forcing them to turn to politics. Meanwhile, the workers who had found themselves following in the wake of the petty-bourgeois democrats were coming to realise the latter's indecision and seeking to take a political stand of their own.

The experience of the revolution necessarily had an effect on the Workers' Brotherhood and Stephan Born, its leader, whom the November events and the threatened dissolution of the National Assembly had forced to change his tone. Obviously under the influence of the November 18 appeal of the Rhine District Committee, the Brotherhood's Central Committee urged all its local and district committees to do their utmost to arm the workers. Born wrote that the Germans were faced with a choice between the knout and the "sword of freedom".

The deep changes, of which there was evidence in the working-class movement in Germany, were mirrored by a number of congresses in the winter and spring of 1849. At the end of January 1849, the Heidelberg Congress adopted a decision to unite the governing bodies of the Workers' Brotherhood, whose influence had spread mainly to North Germany, and the General German Workers' Congress, which brought together many workers' associations in the South of Germany. The United Central Committee, which was to have its seat at Leipzig, was to call a national workers' congress to establish a general German workers' union, with political and social purposes. Similar decisions were adopted by workers' congresses in Hamburg, Thuringia (Altenburg), Württemberg (Göppingen) and Bavaria (Nuremberg).

---

[1] *The Communist League — the Forerunner of the First International*, p. 218 (in Russian).

Marx and Engels took account of these new tendencies in the working-class movement: the urge for unity, the striving to do away with the narrow-craft spirit and "economism", disenchantment with petty-bourgeois democracy, and the groping towards an independent political stand. They sensed the need to join the emergent nation-wide organisation of German workers and to turn it into a mass political party of the proletariat.

This required more vigorous propaganda of the proletarian outlook, a change in the form of co-operation with the democrats, and various measures to ensure the influence of the Communists in an all-German organisation of the proletariat.

Marx believed that his *Wage Labour and Capital* (lectures he gave in December 1847 to German workers in Brussels) had an important part to play in the ideological preparation of the progressive German workers for the establishment of their own party, and it was serialised in the *Neue Rheinische Zeitung* from April 5, 1849, a fact, said Engels, which indicated the social purpose of the paper's policy.

In a small preface, Marx wrote: "Now, after our readers have seen the class struggle develop in colossal political forms in 1848, the time has come to deal more closely with the economic relations themselves on which the existence of the bourgeoisie and its class rule, as well as the slavery of the workers, are founded." [1]

The Cologne Workers' Association acted as the ideological centre of the whole German working-class movement when, at a meeting of its Committee on April 11, it decided to urge all its branches — and all other workers' associations in Germany — to discuss the social question on the basis of the articles on wage labour and capital.

To help the workers establish complete organisational as well as ideological and political independence, Marx and his followers adopted a highly important decision on April 14 calling for a withdrawal from the democratic associations, so as to achieve an organisational separation from the petty-bourgeois democrats. At a meeting of the Rhine District Committee of Democrats, whose membership following the resignation of Schneider II, who had been elected to the Second Chamber, consisted of Hermann Becker, Marx, Schapper, Anneke and Wilhelm Wolff, the last four issued the following statement:

"We consider that the present organisation of the democratic associations includes too many heterogeneous elements for any possibility of successful activity in furtherance of the cause.

"We are of the opinion, on the other hand, that a closer union of the workers' associations is to be preferred since they consist of homogeneous elements, and therefore we hereby from today withdraw from the Rhenish District Committee of Democratic Associations." [2]

---

[1] Marx, Engels, *Collected Works*, Vol. 9, p. 198.
[2] Ibid., p. 282.

The withdrawal of Marx and his followers from the Rhenish District Committee of Democratic Associations did not in any sense signify an abandonment of the alliance with the democrats, but merely indicated that in the new political circumstances it had assumed a new form, that of joint action by two independent organisations in the fight against a common enemy, against the forces of counter-revolution preparing for a fresh drive.

The Cologne Workers' Association likewise decided to draw a dividing line between itself and the democrats. On April 16, its general meeting unanimously resolved to withdraw from the association of democratic societies in Germany and to join the union of German workers' associations (with its Central Committee at Leipzig). It also decided to send delegates to a general workers' congress in Leipzig and before it was called to hold in Cologne a congress of all the workers' associations in the Rhine Province and Westphalia. Marx was on the commission appointed to prepare it, but was unable to take a direct part in its work because he had to leave Cologne in mid-April for some time. In connection with this the publication of *Wage Labour and Capital* was interrupted, never to be resumed. The reasons for Marx's journey, during which he called at Bremen, Hamburg, Bielefeld and Hamm, were the fresh financial difficulties besetting the newspaper and his desire to establish closer ties with Communists and workers' associations, an urgent need in view of the preparations under way to set up a mass proletarian party in Germany.

THE *NEUE RHEINISCHE ZEITUNG* AND THE NATIONAL LIBERATION STRUGGLE IN HUNGARY AND ITALY

The revolutionary war in Hungary, in the course of which Hungarian revolutionary forces inflicted a number of heavy defeats on Austrian troops, was an important element in Marx's political strategy in the spring of 1849. He was hoping that the bright flame of revolutionary struggle in Hungary would set alight the inflammable material that was once again accumulating in Germany, France and Italy.

At his request, Engels followed up his first article about the struggle in Hungary which he had sent in from Switzerland in January 1849, with a series of articles giving a political analysis of the Hungarian war of national liberation and a review of the military operations. Engels expressed his admiration for the courage of the Hungarians, their swift organisation of arms manufacture, and their energy and uncompromising attitude to those who stood in the way of the revolutionary struggle.

While analysing the alignment of forces during the revolutionary war in Hungary and examining every national movement in the light of the revolutionary interest, Engels assessed the role of the various peoples in these events. In a society based on exploitation, class antagonism is compounded by national contradictions which the exploiter classes use for their own selfish ends. Depending on the situation, they use fraud or violence to involve the peoples in wars of aggrandisement and wars against other peoples fighting for national liberation and social emancipation. In 1848 and 1849, when the fight against absolutism and the survivals of feudalism was aggravated by acute national collisions, the ruling classes sought to make some nations play a reactionary role by setting them against others fighting for the victory of the bourgeois-democratic revolution. In this context, Engels classified nations either as revolutionary or reactionary, depending on their role in the revolution.

Lenin regarded this in the concrete historical conditions of 1848 and 1849 as a correct assessment, which in no way clashed with proletarian internationalism. He wrote: "Marx and Engels at that time drew a clear and definite *distinction* between 'whole reactionary nations' serving as 'Russian outposts' in Europe, and 'revolutionary nations', namely, the Germans, Poles and Magyars. This is a fact. And it was indicated *at the time* with *incontrovertible* truth: in 1848 revolutionary nations fought for liberty whose principal enemy was tsarism, whereas the Czechs, etc., were in fact reactionary nations, and outposts of tsarism." [1]

As well as correct assessments of the objective role of Slav national movements in Austria during the 1848-49 revolution, articles in the *Neue Rheinische Zeitung* contained certain imprecise and even erroneous views. Thus, Engels elaborated on the idea that the small Slav peoples on the territory of the Austrian Empire, with the exception of the Poles, were no longer capable of maintaining an independent national existence and would inevitably be absorbed by their stronger neighbour. He noted the capitalist tendency towards centralisation and the establishment of large states, but not the other tendency, namely that of the small peoples to fight against national oppression, and for their independence, and their desire to set up states of their own. It must be stressed that Engels immediately made the important reservation: "If at any epoch while they were oppressed the Slavs had begun a *new revolutionary history*, that by itself would have proved their viability. From that moment the revolution would have had an interest in their liberation, and the special interest of the Germans and Magyars would have given way to the greater interest of the European revolution." [2]

This possibility allowed by the *Neue Rheinische Zeitung* subsequently became historical reality. As the small Slav nations of the Austrian Empire developed economically, as ever greater masses of

---

[1] V. I. Lenin, *Collected Works*, Vol. 22, pp. 340-41.
[2] Marx, Engels, *Collected Works*, Vol. 8, p. 371.

them were drawn into the national liberation struggle, and as their consciousness and organisation grew, their national movements became more democratic and helped to extend the front of the revolutionary struggle. Once oppressed and enslaved in the Austrian Empire, the small Slav nations not only displayed a capacity for independent national development and the establishment of their own states, but took the socialist way and made a worthy contribution to the establishment of the most advanced social system.

Marx and Engels kept a close watch on the Hungarians' hard and heroic struggle and were aware that its outcome depended not only on the alignment of forces in the Austrian Empire. The Russian tsar had long since arrayed his troops along his western borders, and was merely waiting for an opportune moment to intervene. The Hungarians' only hope was a fresh upsurge in the German and the European revolutions.

The resumption on March 20 of military operations in Italy between the Piedmont army and General Radetzky's troops was an important and encouraging event. However, the Piedmont army was routed on March 23, mainly because it did not use revolutionary methods of warfare. Engels wrote in the *Neue Rheinische Zeitung*: "A nation that wants to conquer its independence cannot restrict itself to the *ordinary* methods of warfare. Mass uprising, revolutionary war, guerrilla detachments everywhere — that is the only means by which a small nation can overcome a large one, by which a less stronger army can be put in a position to resist a stronger and better organised one."[1]

DEFEAT OF THE RHINE UPRISINGS.
THE *NEUE RHEINISCHE ZEITUNG* CLOSED DOWN

From early May 1849, Saxony, Rhenish Prussia and South-Western Germany became an arena of struggle between the forces of revolution and counter-revolution. It was sparked off by a campaign for recognition of the Imperial Constitution, which had been slowly and painfully drawn up by the Frankfurt Assembly. It was rejected by most German governments. On April 15, Austria recalled her deputies from Frankfurt. On April 27, the Second Chamber of the Prussian Provincial Diet, which had dared to insist on recognition of the Imperial Constitution, was dissolved.

Frederick William IV sent a note to the Frankfurt Assembly and all the German governments, which the *Neue Rheinische Zeitung* saw as a threat to disband the Assembly. And Prussia was indeed concentrating her troops along the Saxon border and on the Rhine. These counter-revolutionary acts aroused profound indignation among the people.

---

[1] Ibid., Vol. 9, p. 171.

On May 3, an uprising broke out in Dresden, with Born and Bakunin playing a prominent part. Despite the courage displayed by the insurgents, mainly workers and artisans, they were defeated by Saxon and Prussian troops after a six-day fight.

On May 5, the day before the various political organisations were to hold district congresses in Cologne, there were rumours that the authorities intended to reimpose the state of siege, and the *Neue Rheinische Zeitung* warned the workers not to let themselves be provoked just when "all Germany is on the threshold of *civil war*, and when perhaps they will soon have the opportunity to *come forward with their own demands*". [1]

On May 6, the democratic societies and workers' associations held their congresses in Cologne. A joint meeting of delegates decided to support the Imperial Constitution, provided that the Frankfurt Assembly acted as a sovereign revolutionary constituent body. When the Prussian government announced a partial call-up of the *Landwehr*, which it intended to use against the people, the disturbances in the Rhine Province increased. On May 9, an uprising broke out in Elberfeld. When Engels heard of this he at once set out for his home town, where the local Safety Committee put him in charge of building the barricades. Engels urged a spread of the uprising over the whole Berg and Mark district, but under pressure from Elberfeld's terrified bourgeois the Safety Committee soon decided to expel him from the town. The workers took a firm stand in his defence, but Engels did not wish to split the ranks of the insurgents and left.

"Let the workers of the Berg Country and the Mark," wrote the *Neue Rheinische Zeitung*, "who have shown such astonishing affection for and devotion to a member of our editorial board, bear in mind that the present movement is only the prologue to another movement a thousand times more serious, in which the issue will concern their own, the workers', most vital interests. This new revolutionary movement will be the result of the present movement and as soon as it occurs Engels—on this the workers can confidently rely—like all the other editors of the *Neue Rheinische Zeitung*, will be at his post, and no power on earth will induce him to forsake it." [2]

Then followed the defeats of the isolated uprisings in other towns in the Rhine Province, including Düsseldorf, Solingen, Iserlohn. Only in the South German states of Baden and Pfalz did the insurgents meet with some success, and set up provisional governments supported by the insurgent army.

In the critical days of the May uprisings the *Neue Rheinische Zeitung* spoke out with even greater wrath and passion. Engels later recalled: "'Out there, in the Reich', wonder was expressed that we car-

---

[1] Marx, Engels, *Collected Works*, Vol. 9, p. 403.
[2] Ibid., p. 449.

ried on our activities so unconcernedly within a Prussian fortress of the first rank, in the face of a garrison of 8,000 troops and confronting the guardhouse; but, on account of the eight rifles with bayonets and 250 live cartridges in the editorial room, and the red Jacobin caps of the compositors, our house was reckoned by the officers likewise as a fortress which was not to be taken by a mere *coup de main*." [1]

The government was increasingly alarmed over the newspaper's bold, challenging articles. In April and early May, the Minister of the Interior, Manteuffel, made several requests to the Cologne authorities for legal proceedings against the editors. By then 23 cases had been commenced against them, but the Public Prosecutor's office, which had twice failed to get a jury to convict them, was unwilling to risk another legal contest with the *Neue Rheinische Zeitung*. Only after the uprisings in the Rhine Province had been put down, did the authorities muster the courage to do what they had prepared well in advance. When Marx returned from a journey on May 16, he was handed a government order to leave Prussia within 24 hours as a foreigner who was being deprived of the hospitality "he has so outrageously abused".

Then followed repressions against the other editors. Dronke and Weerth, both non-Prussian subjects, were also ordered to leave Prussia. Criminal proceedings were started against Engels for his part in the Elberfeld uprising. The other editors were also faced with legal proceedings.

This meant the end of the *Neue Rheinische Zeitung*, and its last issue, in red print, appeared on May 19.

In a leading article Marx exposed the hypocritical political motives behind his expulsion order. It had been alleged that in the "last few pieces" the paper had been stirring up contempt for the government and calling for a violent revolution and the establishment of a social republic. Marx wrathfully responded: "Did we therefore have to advance our social republican tendency only in the 'last pieces' of the *Neue Rheinische Zeitung*? Did you not read our articles about the *June revolution,* and *was not the essence of the June revolution the essence of our paper*?

"Why then your hypocritical phrases, your attempt to find an impossible pretext?

"*We have no compassion and we ask no compassion from you. When our turn comes, we shall not make excuses for the terror*. But the *royal terrorists*, the terrorists by the grace of God and the law, are in practice brutal, disdainful and mean, in theory cowardly, secretive and deceitful, and in both respects *disreputable*." [2]

The revolutionary organ of the proletariat, Marx wrote with pride, had also been a courageous and consistent champion of the German

---

[1] Marx, Engels, *Collected Works,* Vol. 26, p. 127.
[2] Ibid., Vol. 9, p. 453.

people's true national interests: "We have saved the revolutionary honour of our country." ¹

The paper's address to the Cologne workers said: "In bidding you farewell the editors of the *Neue Rheinische Zeitung* thank you for the sympathy you have shown them. Their last word everywhere and always will be: *emancipation of the working class!*" ²

At Marx's request Freiligrath wrote these parting lines:

> Farewell now, farewell, O you World ever warring.
> Farewell now, you struggling hordes,
> You battlefield, black with the powder-smoke pouring,
> You lances, you guns, and you swords!

> Farewell, brothers; but it shall not be forever,
> Our spirit they could not dismay.
> With a clashing of arms up as mighty as ever,
> I shall be returning one day!

> With the word, with the sword, by the Danube and Rhine,
> A true ally in all times of trouble
> I shall be to those Throne-smashing people of mine—
> A warrior, an outlaw, a rebel! ³

Engels subsequently recalled: "We had to surrender our fortress, but we withdrew with our arms and baggage, with band playing and flag flying, the flag of the last issue, a red issue." ⁴

IN SOUTH-WESTERN GERMANY

Marx left Cologne immediately after the publication of the "red issue", but even then the Prussian authorities did not cease their harassment and instituted fresh legal proceedings against him, Weerth and Dronke. It is remarkable that even when the counter-revolution in Prussia was already celebrating its triumph, on May 29 the police reform court in Cologne which was hearing the case in the absence of the accused returned a verdict of not guilty.

From Prussia Marx went to Frankfurt am Main, and together with Engels, who had also arrived there, tried to influence the Left-wing deputies in the all-German National Assembly, who were in a majority following a walk-out by the reactionaries and the liberals. At this time the position of the Frankfurt Assembly was by no means a hopeless one. The people of South-Western Germany had taken up arms, and the troops everywhere were wavering. Austria had her hands full with the war against the Hungarians, and there was instability in Prussia. A great deal depended on how resolute and bold a stand the Assembly would take.

During their meetings with Left-wing deputies in the Assembly,

---

[1] Marx, Engels, *Collected Works*, Vol. 9, p. 454.
[2] Ibid., p. 467.
[3] *Freiligraths Werke*, in einem Band, Weimar, 1962, S. 140-41.
[4] Marx, Engels, *Collected Works*, Vol. 26, p. 128.

Marx and Engels advised them to side openly with the uprisings that had already broken out, to call on the people to take up arms everywhere, to summon the insurgent armed forces to Frankfurt to provide protection for the Assembly, to outlaw all the monarchs, ministers and other counter-revolutionaries, to set up a solid and vigorous revolutionary executive, and to win over the peasants by abolishing the feudal obligations. All this would have converted the uprising into an all-German one, and would have helped it to abandon its defensive tactics and mount a resolute offensive. However, the deputies preferred to let events take their own course, and did not support this bold political and military plan. Once Marx and Engels saw the futility of any further efforts, they left for insurgent Baden.

There they also met with indecision and hesitation among the petty-bourgeois democrats. The government set up at Karlsruhe was taking no action at all, although it had an army, weapons and money at its disposal. At a meeting with members of the government, Marx and Engels declared that the first thing that should have been done was to advance on Frankfurt, but now that the opportunity had been missed, there was no hope of victory without resolute action in Hungary or another revolution in Paris. Most of those present resented this view, but events proved Marx and Engels to be right.

From Baden, Marx and Engels travelled to Pfalz, another insurgent centre. At Kaiserslautern they found the same state of extreme unconcern, and the provisional government, with the exception of d'Ester, who was one of its members, was doing nothing even to defend itself. Marx and Engels left Kaiserslautern within a few days, but on their way to Bingen they were arrested, together with a few friends, by Hessen soldiers and conveyed to Darmstadt and from there to Frankfurt, where they were finally released.

Upon their arrival in Bingen, Marx and Engels issued a final statement on behalf of the *Neue Rheinische Zeitung* editorial board, which they sent to the *Frankfurter Journal* on May 31. It informed the paper's former correspondents and readers that there was no connection between the *Neue Rheinische Zeitung* and the *Westdeutsche Zeitung*, which had started publication in Cologne on May 25, with Hermann Becker as editor, and which claimed to be the successor of the *Neue Rheinische Zeitung*. The statement made it clear that Marx intended to resume publication of the paper at the earliest opportunity.

The two friends parted at Bingen, Marx travelling to Paris with a mandate from the Democratic Central Committee, issued to him by d'Ester, and Engels to the Palatinate, where he intended, "should a suitable opportunity offer itself, [to] take up at the outbreak of fighting the only position that the *Neue Rheinische Zeitung* could take up in this movement: that of soldier".[1]

---

[1] Ibid., Vol. 10, pp. 186-87.

Soon Engels became aide-de-camp to Willich, commander of a volunteer detachment which included many workers, who proved themselves to be fine, disciplined fighters. Engels fought in four battles including the one at the fortress of Rastatt. On July 12, 1849, Willich's detachment, providing cover for the defeated, retreating Baden-Pfalz army, was the last to leave German territory and cross the border into Switzerland.

BACK IN PARIS. JUNE 13

Marx went to France in the hope that the mounting revolutionary crisis there would end in a victory for the proletariat, giving powerful support to the revolutionary struggle in South-Western Germany, Hungary and Italy, and a fresh impetus to the European revolution.

He arrived in Paris in early June and at once established contacts with leaders of the democratic and socialist movements, and of secret workers' societies. On June 7, he wrote to Engels in Kaiserslautern: "I consort with the whole of the revolutionary party." [1] Decisive events were in the offing. The President, Louis Bonaparte, had resumed military operations against the Roman Republic, thereby flagrantly violating the Constitution, which said that the French Republic would never encroach upon another country's freedom. The Left-wing press urged the parliamentary opposition—the petty-bourgeois Mountain—to take vigorous action. On June 11, Ledru-Rollin, leader of the Mountain, declared in the Legislative Assembly that the Republicans would compel respect for the Constitution with all the means at their disposal, including armed force.

The subsequent events were described by Marx in an article entitled "June 13", published in the democratic newspaper *Volksfreund*. It showed him to be not only a witness of the events, but also a participant who was clearly seeking to influence their course. He reported that a secret socialist committee had been set up in Paris which called for an uprising to catch the government unawares. If it won, the committee was to proclaim itself a Commune, a proletarian power operating alongside the new official government. However, the Mountain flatly turned down the proposal for an immediate uprising. Although it had threatened in the Assembly to use force, it now decided to stage an unarmed demonstration on June 13.

Weerth, who had arrived from Belgium early that morning, gave a detailed description of the demonstration in a letter to his brother on June 16. Together with a few friends, who "belong to our party", he had gone to 45 Rue de Lille where Marx lived. From there he evidently went off with Marx, Ferdinand Wolff and Dronke.

When they reached the boulevards, they joined the head column of

---
[1] Marx, Engels, *Collected Works*, Vol. 38, p. 199.

demonstrators moving towards the Legislative Assembly. When the column reached the Rue de la Paix it was attacked by mounted troops. A call to arms was heard, and Weerth and his comrades hastened to the Palais National, where they expected to obtain arms, but it turned out that government troops had already taken over the arms caches that had been laid up for a possible uprising. Here and there attempts were made to put up barricades, but these did little to slow the charge of the cavalrymen, who cut down unarmed men with their swords.[1]

The Mountain's "parliamentary uprising" came to an inglorious end. The workers had all along regarded its plans with suspicion, and did not support its call to the people to take up arms after the demonstration had already been dispersed. "Taken as a whole," wrote Marx, "June 13, 1849 is only the retaliation for June 1848. On that occasion the proletariat was deserted by the 'Mountain', this time the 'Mountain' was deserted by the proletariat." [2]

June 13 was not only a day of defeat for French petty-bourgeois democracy. Marx said it was a day of ordeal "for our party throughout Europe".[3]

A state of siege was declared and mass reprisals started in Paris. From day to day, Marx expected to be arrested or deported. His position was complicated by the fact that his wife Jenny and their three children had arrived in Paris in early July. In order to reach Paris, she had been obliged to pawn the family silver in Frankfurt am Main with Weydemeyer's help. It had only recently been redeemed from a Brussels pawn shop. Marx was in great financial straits. When the newspaper was being wound up, all the money received from subscribers and from the sale of the high-speed printing press had been used to pay off the printers, compositors, newsprint suppliers and correspondents, and to enable the editors to escape. In fact, a debt of 300 talers had been incurred. Marx found himself literally penniless in Paris and had to turn to Lassalle for a loan. Although Marx had asked him to avoid publicity, Lassalle started a public collection, which drew vehement protests from Marx, who was most scrupulous on this point. He wrote to Freiligrath: "The direst straits are better than public begging." [4]

On July 19, Marx was informed by the French authorities that he was being ordered to leave for the Morbihan Department in Brittany. He lodged a protest with the Minister of the Interior, and the expulsion order was suspended.

At the end of July, Marx finally got news from Engels, about whom he had been highly worried. In a letter from Vevey addressed to Jenny, Engels recounted what had happened to him since their parting in Bingen. Engels asked Jenny whether there was any truth

---

[1] See G. Weerth, *Sämtliche Werke*, in fünf Bänden, Bd. 5, Berlin, 1957, S. 309-18.
[2] Marx, Engels, *Collected Works*, Vol. 9, pp. 478-79.
[3] Ibid.
[4] Ibid., Vol. 38, p. 204.

in the rumours he had heard in Baden about Marx having been arrested in Paris. "You can imagine the state of anxiety I am in as a result, and I beg you most urgently to set my mind at rest and to put an end to my doubts about Marx's fate."[1]

Marx at once replied: "I have suffered a great deal of anxiety on your account and was truly delighted when yesterday I received a letter in your own hand."[2] He advised Engels to write a history of the Baden-Pfalz revolution or a pamphlet about it, expressing the *Neue Rheinische Zeitung*'s standpoint. He also informed Engels of the whereabouts of the other editors.

Marx's own future depended on the French authorities. On August 23, a police sergeant called at his home with the following order: "Karl Marx and his wife are to leave Paris within 24 hours." This draconian measure had dogged his footsteps since 1845, when he was expelled from Paris, then in 1848 from Brussels, in 1849 from Cologne, and finally once again from Paris.

Marx informed Engels about his expulsion to a marshy, unhealthy part of Brittany: "I need hardly say that I shall not consent to this veiled attempt on my life. So I am leaving France." He could not obtain a passport to enter Switzerland, and so decided to go to London, where he also had hopes of starting a journal. Marx urged Engels to join him: "In London we shall get down to business."[3]

Being short of money, Marx had to leave Jenny, who was pregnant, and the children in Paris for the time being. She had a hard time obtaining police permission to stay on until September 15.

On August 26, Marx arrived in London, a new — and as it turned out to be, lifelong — place of exile.

FIRST HISTORICAL TEST OF MARXISM

The years of revolution, which greatly taxed all of Marx's capacities, fully revealed his genius, inexhaustible energy, unbending will, dedication and revolutionary drive. Lenin regarded Marx's direct participation in the mass revolutionary struggle of 1848-49 as "the central point" of his activity.[4]

The various historical periods each brought out different aspects of the rich and varied ideological content of the great theory of Marxism. Up to 1848 the formation of Marxist philosophy was of primary importance. In 1848 and 1849 its political ideas, strategy and tactics were brought to the fore.

The brilliant tactical solutions proposed by Marx in 1848 and 1849 show him to be the first revolutionary leader in history to base

---

[1] Marx, Engels, *Collected Works*, Vol. 38, p. 203.
[2] Ibid., p. 207.
[3] Ibid., pp. 212, 213.
[4] V. I. Lenin, *Collected Works*, Vol. 13, p. 37.

his policies on a scientific foundation, and are an invaluable contribution to the international proletariat's treasure-house of revolutionary experience.

The policy hammered out by Marx did not bring about a victory for the revolution because of the specific features of "that epoch in world history when the revolutionary character of the bourgeois democrats was *already* passing away (in Europe), while the revolutionary character of the socialist proletariat had *not yet* matured".[1]

Despite the defeat of the revolution, the stormy years of 1848 and 1849 not only demonstrated in practice the vital force of Marxism and its superiority over all the other socialist theories, but also provided a powerful source for the development and enrichment of that great doctrine. The experience of the revolutionary struggle of that period served as a basis for the subsequent great advances in Marx's theoretical thinking, which were given a classical formulation in his works summing up the lessons of the revolution.

---

[1] Ibid., Vol. 18, p. 26.

CHAPTER SIX

SUMMING UP THE LESSONS OF THE REVOLUTION

> *A time of apparent stagnation, like the present one, must be used to explain the preceding period of revolution, the character of the contending parties, and the social relations which determine the existence and the struggle of these parties.*
>
> Karl Marx and Frederick Engels

THE FIRST MONTHS IN LONDON

By the time Marx arrived in London, rampant reaction either had been or was on the way to set in in all the European countries which had only recently been swept by the tide of revolution. After the events of June 13, 1849, in France, the counter-revolutionary policy of the ruling "Party of Order", consisting of two monarchist factions — the Legitimists and the Orleanists — was paving the way for the establishment of a Bonapartist dictatorship. In the summer of 1849, after the last revolutionary centres had been stamped out in Germany, the Austrian imperial army crushed the revolution in Hungary with the help of tsarist troops. The Italian revolutionary movement was also stifled by the joint forces of the European counter-revolution.

The defeat of the 1848-49 revolutions did not quench Marx's energy or shake his confidence in the inevitability of change in Europe. In fact, his faith in the ability of the working class to play a key role in bringing about such change was increased by the behaviour of the various classes in the course of the revolution itself.

For all the bitterness of these reverses and losses, Marx was clearly aware that the battles of 1848 and 1849 had not been fought in vain, for they had shaken the feudal-monarchist foundation in a number of countries, advanced the establishment and development of capitalism, and prepared the ground for the further growth of the proletariat's consciousness and organisation. They had initiated the release of the masses from their illusions, and had dealt a blow at every brand of petty-bourgeois socialism, demonstrating the incontestable superiority of the policy based on the theory of scientific communism.

Marx saw the situation as a forced break in the open revolutionary struggle which was sure to be followed by act two of the revolutionary drama. There were various indications that the break would not be a long one, and it was some time before Marx realised that there was little hope of an early revolutionary upsurge. But even while hoping that the break would be short, Marx was quite free from the delusions of the bourgeois and petty-bourgeois emigrants, who were sure that almost any day now they would be summoned to rule the destinies of the peoples. He realised that, regardless of the turn of events, regardless of whether the period of reaction was long or short, a great deal had to be done to unite the scattered revolutionary forces, to resume and extend the broken ties, to brace up the apathetic and despondent, and to organise and train the proletarian cadres for the forthcoming revolutionary battles. Those were the pressing practical tasks which faced Marx in the first few months of his exile in London.

A revived Communist League, which Marx continued to regard as the core of a future and larger proletarian party, was to be the organisational form for uniting the proletarian revolutionaries. In the new situation, practical revolutionary work was once again to be centred in the secret League's illegal activity. Engels wrote: "The situation again forbade, as in 1848, any open organisation of the proletariat; hence, one had to organise again in secret."[1] The League itself needed to be reorganised and consolidated. The Central Authority, as such, had virtually ceased to function, and most of the communities and districts had fallen apart. Many League activists had been killed in the fighting or arrested, others had withdrawn from the movement, and most of the addresses and connections had been lost.

As soon as he arrived in London, Marx re-established the guiding body of the Communist League. By then, most members of earlier central authorities had come to London, with the exception of Engels, Schapper and Moll, the latter having been killed in the campaign for an Imperial Constitution. At Marx's insistence, Engels left Switzerland for London, where he arrived on about November 10, after travelling via Genoa, and then sailing for five weeks round the Iberian Peninsula and across the Bay of Biscay. He was at once included in the Central Authority. Schapper, who was serving a prison term in Wiesbaden, did not come to London until early July 1850, and also became a member of the Central Authority. Among the new members was August Willich, who had shown himself to be a capable commander during the campaign in Baden and the Palatinate and, on Marx's motion, was elected to the Central Authority in October 1849. He had arrived from Switzerland with a recommendation from Engels. Another new member was Konrad Schramm, an active participant in the German revolution of 1848-49, who had staged a bold escape from a Prussian fortress in

---

[1] Marx and Engels, *Selected Works*, Vol. 3, p. 186.

September 1849. Prominent League members, Georg Eccarius and Karl Pfänder, were also included in the Authority.

In early September 1849, Marx joined the German Workers' Educational Society in London, which was closely allied with the Communist League. He attached much importance to the theoretical training of the workers, and from November 1849 to the autumn of 1850 lectured in the Society on political economy and the *Manifesto of the Communist Party*.

Assistance to the revolutionary emigrants was one of the pressing needs in the effort to bring together the scattered revolutionary forces. Every day, hundreds of political refugees arrived in London. To escape persecution at home they came to England, a country where there was relative political freedom. However, they were faced with bitter privation, and most were homeless and lacked the bare necessities.

Marx himself faced poverty. On September 5, 1849, he wrote to Freiligrath: "I am now in a really difficult situation. My wife is in an advanced state of pregnancy, she is obliged to leave Paris on the 15th and I don't know how I am to raise the money for her journey and for settling her in here." [1] The money was obtained with great difficulty, and in mid-September Jenny and the three children arrived in London. But despite his own hardships, Marx did everything to rescue revolutionary fighters from poverty and sometimes even from death.

On September 18, 1849, he arranged a meeting of the German Workers' Educational Society and the newly arrived political refugees, which elected a Committee of Support for German Political Refugees, with Marx as one of its members. Among these were petty-bourgeois democrats as well as members of the Communist League.

The Committee announced that it would help all political refugees whatever their convictions or party affiliations, but the struggle which broke out between the various groupings of the emigration soon spread to the aid effort. Refusing to allow the intrigues of the various groupings to intrude into the sphere of aid to the needy, Marx and his followers decided to part company with the leaders of the petty-bourgeois democrats. At a general meeting of the German Workers' Educational Society in November 1849, the Committee was reconstituted as the Social-Democratic Refugee Committee, consisting only of Communists: Marx, who was elected chairman, Engels, Heinrich Bauer, Pfänder and Willich. The Committee announced that its aid would go primarily to the proletarian and socialist sections of the emigration.

---

[1] Marx, Engels, *Collected Works*, Vol. 38, p. 216.

THE FOUNDING OF THE *NEUE RHEINISCHE ZEITUNG. POLITISCH-ÖKONOMISCHE REVUE*

Marx was sure that the practical tasks before the working-class movement had to be tackled simultaneously with extensive theoretical work in helping the proletarian masses to learn the lessons of the revolutionary battles of 1848 so as to be better prepared for the next revolutionary upsurge. There was a need to bring together into a system the ideas which had emerged in the years of the revolution, to take a fresh look at the ebb and flow of the class struggle in the various countries, to draw the necessary theoretical conclusions, and so to advance the revolutionary doctrine of the proletariat.

Referring to Marx's theoretical generalisation of the lessons of the 1848 revolution, Lenin wrote: "Here, as everywhere else, his theory is a *summing-up of experience*, illuminated by a profound philosophical conception of the world and a rich knowledge of history."[1]

Marx believed that if the results of the revolution were to be generalised in scientific terms, and revolutionary theory developed and spread further, it was highly important to resume publication of a proletarian periodical, if only in the form of a journal for the time being. He had been thinking about this ever since the closure of the *Neue Rheinische Zeitung*. In the new conditions the journal was to continue the newspaper's militant revolutionary line and serve as an instrument for the ideological education and theoretical training of Communist League members and proletarians allied with them. It was to become an organ of the League and a mouthpiece for its ideas. Accordingly, it was decided to call the journal the *Neue Rheinische Zeitung. Politisch-ökonomische Revue,* a name which also showed that the editors had not reconciled themselves to the police closure of the proletarian revolutionary paper, and were prepared to resume its publication at the earliest opportunity.

Marx spent the autumn and winter of 1849 making intensive preparations for the publication of the journal. He turned to his many friends and acquaintances for money and help in finding a publisher and contributors, and in selling the shares.

At the end of 1849, an agreement on the publication and circulation of the journal was concluded with Köhler, the owner of a printing works in Hamburg, and Schubert & Co. booksellers.

On December 15, 1849, Marx and Engels issued their "Announcement of the *Neue Rheinische Zeitung. Politisch-ökonomische Revue*", which said that it would be published under the editorship of Karl Marx from January 1850 onwards and would permit "a comprehensive and scientific investigation of the *economic* conditions which form the foundation of the whole political movement".[2]

---

[1] V. I. Lenin, *Collected Works*, Vol. 25, p. 412.
[2] Marx, Engels, *Collected Works*, Vol. 10, p. 5.

However, despite their vigorous efforts, Marx's friends were unable to obtain the necessary money by January, and it was not collected until March. The first issue of the journal appeared in Hamburg on March 6, 1850. On its cover, it carried the names of London, where Marx and Engels were resident, Hamburg, where the journal was printed, and also New York, where Marx and Engels expected to find a readership among the many participants in the 1848-49 revolutions who had emigrated to the United States.

Six issues appeared in 1850, Marx and Engels being unable to have it published at shorter intervals. The final, double, issue — Nos. 5 and 6 — appeared at the end of November 1850. Police harassment in Germany and lack of money made it impossible to continue its publication.

The bulk of the material for the *Revue* was written by Marx and Engels, including Marx's *The Class Struggles in France* and *Louis Napoleon and Fould*; Engels' *The Campaign for the German Imperial Constitution*, *The Peasant War in Germany* and *The English Ten Hours' Bill*, and a number of joint reviews and international surveys.

Among those whom Marx and Engels had enlisted for work on the *Revue* were Wilhelm Wolff and Georg Eccarius. Marx did much to help the latter write a long article entitled "Tailoring in London or the Struggle Between Big and Small Capital". Marx encouraged contributions to the press by leading workers, who showed themselves to be highly observant and adept at analysing the facts on the basis of the materialist views they had assimilated. Editorial comment by Marx and Engels on Eccarius' article said: "Before the proletariat fights out its victories on the barricades and in the battle lines it gives notice of its impending rule with a series of intellectual victories."[1]

Although the journal was short-lived, it fulfilled the task set by Marx and Engels. Its six relatively small issues contained an exceptional wealth of ideas and dealt with a great diversity of theoretical and historical problems.

THE CLASS STRUGGLES IN FRANCE

This is one of the most important works written by Marx to sum up the results of the revolution. Most of it was written from January to March 1850 and published in the first three issues of the *Revue* under the laconic title: "1848-1849". Reissuing this work many years later — in 1895 — Engels introduced as a final, fourth chapter, the sections on France from the third international review (October 1850), which Marx and he had written together, and titled the whole publication *The Class Struggles in France, 1848 to 1850*.

He had good reason for turning to France. Since the French Rev-

---

[1] Marx, Engels, *Collected Works*, Vol. 10, p. 485.

olution, France had been playing the leading role in European history, with its class struggle assuming the most pronounced and acute forms. Nowhere else had the working class displayed such vigour and courage during the 1848-1849 revolution as it had in France.

In *The Class Struggles in France* Marx applied the method of materialist dialectics for the first time to the study of an entire historical period and gave an unsurpassed analysis of the causes, character and course of the French bourgeois-democratic revolution of 1848. He formulated in more concrete terms and elaborated further the most important propositions of historical materialism: the interconnection between the basis and the superstructure, and the definitive role of the economic basis in social life; the importance of the struggle of classes and parties; the role of revolutions in history and the decisive role of the masses; the role of the state and social ideas in the historical process. Marx did not use his materialist view of history as a universal stereotype, but as a guide for concrete analysis. While recognising the crucial importance of the economy, he did not in any sense ignore the role of the political and ideological superstructure — the state, political parties, ideological trends — and outstanding individuals. In fact, it helped him to clarify the concrete forms in which the superstructure — politics and ideology — exerts an active influence on the historical process. At the same time, in contrast to bourgeois idealist historians, Marx clearly saw the limits of this influence, and the dependence of the attitudes taken by the various parties, ideologists and political leaders on the various material and class interests, reflecting the tendencies in the development of social production, which ultimately determines the course of history.

Marx gives a comprehensive elaboration of the idea that revolutionary periods are law-governed and are of tremendous importance in the life of society, and that revolutions are powerful motivators of social progress. He calls them "the locomotives of history", for they give history an exceptional impetus and boost the inexhaustible creative energy of the masses, which then become politically active, break up the old social relations and create new and historically progressive forms of social life. "In this vortex of movement, in this torment of historical unrest, in this dramatic ebb and flow of revolutionary passion, hopes and disappointments, the different classes of French society had to count their epochs of development in weeks where they had previously counted them in half centuries." [1]

The French experience provided the clearest confirmation of Marx's conclusion reached during the revolution about the European bourgeoisie's increasing dissipation of its revolutionary traditions, which dated back to the period of its struggle against the feudal system. With exceptional skill and historical insight, he gave

---

[1] Ibid., p. 97.

a picture of the French bourgeoisie's political degeneration, as it sank into reaction. Its counter-revolutionary character had been most pronounced in its attitude to the proletarian movement. As soon as the revolution broke out, the bourgeoisie acted not only as the sworn enemy of the proletariat, provoking it into an uprising in June 1848 and then putting it down in a blood bath, but also as a reactionary force blocking the country's advance along revolutionary and democratic lines.

In these conditions, the working class became the main force of the revolutionary movement and of historical progress. It faced the task of carrying the bourgeois-democratic revolution to its end, and then of tackling the socialist tasks.

Owing to its immaturity which stemmed from the insufficient development of capitalist relations in France, the French proletariat was unaware of its class tasks at the first stage of the revolution, labouring under bourgeois illusions and believing that the February victory had established a social republic standing guard over the interests both of the bourgeoisie and of the proletarian masses. Marx showed that the proletariat could become aware of its own class interests only in a life-and-death struggle against the bourgeois counter-revolution. The June 1848 uprising in Paris was the turning point of the formation of the class consciousness of the French and largely of the international proletariat as well: "The first great battle was fought between the two classes that split modern society." [1]

Despite the defeat of the insurgents and the savage massacre that followed, Marx believed the most important positive outcome of the uprising to be the French proletariat's awakening from its illusions. The defeat opened the eyes of the working class to the truth that it was utopian to hope to escape from exploitation within the framework of a bourgeois republic. Only after the June defeat, wrote Marx, "there appeared the bold slogan of revolutionary struggle: *Overthrow of the bourgeoisie! Dictatorship of the working class!*" [2]

The Class Struggles in France gave an historically substantiated answer to the question of the proletariat's allies in the revolution. Just before and during the 1848-49 revolution, Marx had expressed in various forms the idea that the working class needed to enlist the support of the non-proletarian sections of the working people. The lessons of the revolutionary years helped him to turn this idea into a clearly and comprehensively formulated proposition, which has become part of the Marxist doctrine of the proletarian revolution, and of the strategy and tactics of the proletariat's revolutionary struggle.The immaturity of the proletariat apart, Marx believed that the main cause of the defeat of the June uprising lay in the fact that the peasantry and the urban petty bourgeoisie had failed to support the workers. He was sure, however, that that was a transient attitude and that it clashed with their own true interests. As the class

---

[1] Marx, Engels, *Collected Works*, Vol. 10, p. 67.
[2] Ibid., p. 69.

struggle advanced, "peasants, petty bourgeois, the middle classes in general, stepping alongside the proletariat, [were] driven into open antagonism to the official republic and treated by it as antagonists". [1]

The peasants were induced to side with the working class because they were exploited by a common exploiter—capital—even if in different ways. "Only the fall of capital can raise the peasant; only an anticapitalist, a proletarian government can break his economic misery, his social degradation." [2] Thus, the French revolution suggested to Marx the key theoretical and political conclusion, namely, that the proletariat cannot unhinge the bourgeois system unless it has on its side the mass of peasants and petty bourgeois, who accept it as their leader in the fight against capital.

Marx also showed the urban petty bourgeoisie to be an ally of the proletariat, but sharply criticised their political spokesmen and ideologists. He cited the action by the petty-bourgeois *Montagne* on June 13, 1849 to show its total inability to give a lead in the revolutionary struggle.

The 1848-49 revolution exposed both petty-bourgeois democracy and petty-bourgeois utopian socialism. In *The Class Struggles in France* Marx gave a more profound critique of non-proletarian socialist trends, showing them to be untenable in both theory and practice. He gave a full-scale analysis of Louis Blanc's petty-bourgeois socialism. Blanc's behaviour during the revolution and his participation in the bourgeois Provisional Government sprang from his false tenet that socialism could be achieved through collaboration between classes and the bourgeois government's assistance to workers' associations. While claiming the status of leader of socialist democracy, Blanc in fact acted as a hanger-on of the bourgeoisie, and was a "plaything in their hands". [3] As chairman of the commission on the workers' question (the Luxembourg Commission) he spread harmful illusions among proletarians about the bourgeois bosses of the Second Republic being seriously prepared to tackle the social question by "organising labour". Marx said that the Luxembourg Commission was a "socialist synagogue" and "a ministry of impotence, a ministry of pious wishes", [4] and that its failure epitomised the collapse of Blanc's utopian doctrine and conciliatory tactics.

To the various doctrinaire socialist systems, which ignored the class struggle, Marx counterposed revolutionary socialism, driving home the main idea that in the course of the class struggle the working class wins political power and sets up a dictatorship of the proletariat as an instrument of the real transformation of society. Marx wrote: "This Socialism is the *declaration of the permanence of the rev-*

---

[1] Ibid., p. 125.
[2] Ibid., p. 122.
[3] V. I. Lenin, *Collected Works*, Vol. 25, p. 61.
[4] Marx, Engels, *Collected Works*, Vol. 10, pp. 55, 56.

olution, the *class dictatorship* of the proletariat as the necessary transit point to the *abolition of class distinctions generally*, to the abolition of all the relations of production on which they rest, to the abolition of all the social relations that correspond to these relations of production, to the revolutionising of all the ideas that result from these social relations." [1]

It was here that Marx first used in print the term "dictatorship of the proletariat", which was not a mere terminological refinement, but a more profound definition of the idea of proletarian power. Marx emphasised that it was to be the product of a deep-going revolutionary process, an instrument and a form of its further development. In 1848, he drew the conclusion that a revolutionary dictatorship of the people — a vigorous power capable of putting down the scheming counter-revolutionaries — was required to carry the bourgeois-democratic revolution to its end. A dictatorship of the working class, faced with even more complex and majestic tasks, was to have this capacity to an even greater extent. This was Marx's line of reasoning as he formulated the very essence of his doctrine of the communist revolution.

The Class Struggles in France contained a strictly scientific formulation of the basic tasks of the proletarian dictatorship in the economic transformation of society: "The appropriation of the means of production, their subjection to the associated working class and, therefore, the abolition of wage labour, of capital and of their mutual relations." [2]

EFFORTS TO REORGANISE THE COMMUNIST LEAGUE. MARCH *ADDRESS OF THE CENTRAL AUTHORITY*

The reconstituted Central Authority of the Communist League soon started to reorganise the League's local branches. In early 1850, Marx sent a letter to Peter Röser, a member of the League in Cologne, requesting him to re-establish the community there, and to do his utmost to set up communities in other towns of the Rhine Province.

Of great importance in reorganising the League were the Central Authority's addresses to it written by Marx and Engels, which outlined a programme of action for its members, in Germany above all, informed them about the state of the branches in the various countries and gave the relevant slogans and demands.

The first of these — *Address of the Central Authority to the Communist League* written in March 1850 — was the ideological basis for the efforts to restore the League, but its importance goes well beyond the League's activities during that period, for it was one

---

[1] Marx, Engels, *Collected Works*, Vol. 10, p. 127.
[2] Ibid., p. 78.

of those works in which Marx and Engels summed up the experience of the 1848-49 revolution and outlined the proletariat's tactics in the coming battles. It reflected the development of those programme and tactical aspects of the Marxist doctrine whose great importance was fully revealed only during later stages of the proletariat's liberation struggle. Lenin said it was "extremely interesting and informative",[1] and used it as a basis for formulating the revolutionary tactical line for the proletarian party in the bourgeois-democratic revolution, and for substantiating the theory of its growing over into a socialist revolution.

The Address declared the need for the proletariat to consolidate its independent political stand by drawing an ideological and an organisational line of demarcation with the petty-bourgeois democrats, and this was the more important since the forthcoming revolution in Germany would, because of the liberal bourgeoisie's bankruptcy, most probably bring the petty-bourgeois democrats to power. The political doctrines and behaviour of the petty-bourgeois — democratic constitutionalists and republicans — in 1848-49 made it clear that they would prevent the revolution from developing in depth and would betray the people as the liberal bourgeois had done in 1848. That is why the proletariat had the duty there and then of resolutely resisting any attempts to involve it in petty-bourgeois organisations and turn it into a throng wildly applauding the bourgeois democrats. The main task before the German workers and particularly the Communist League was to set up an independent working-class party in Germany with a secret and an official organisation, and to turn each League community into a centre and core of the legal workers' associations.

However, Marx and Engels never displayed any sectarianism and did not in any sense deny the importance of joint action by workers and petty-bourgeois democrats at a definite stage of the struggle. The Address explained that in order to fight the counter-revolutionary forces the proletarian party could enter into temporary alliances and blocs with the petty-bourgeois democrats, but that it should always remain independent and pursue a revolutionary policy distinct from that of the latter. In the same light, Marx and Engels considered and stressed the importance of the workers' participation in elections to central and local representative institutions, observing that as a counterweight to the petty-bourgeois democrats the workers should everywhere nominate their own candidates, as far as possible from among the members of the Communist League. Marx and Engels explained that while the petty-bourgeois democrats wanted to finish the revolution as soon as possible and confine themselves to a few reforms, it was in the proletariat's interests to make the revolution permanent and develop it in depth.

---

[1] V. I. Lenin, *Collected Works*, Vol. 8, p. 467.

In his earlier works, Marx had outlined his doctrine of the permanent revolution, but it was fully formulated in the March Address. In essence, Marx's doctrine of the permanent revolution meant that the revolutionary process was to pass through a number of phases, without there necessarily being a long period of quiet, non-revolutionary development between the bourgeois-democratic and the proletarian stages of the revolution. On the contrary, Marx and Engels allowed for the possibility of a relatively swift transition from the former to the latter, a transition taking place as the revolutionary energy of the masses steadily increased, and as the bourgeois and petty-bourgeois elements were ousted from power and the dictatorship of the proletariat established. They believed this turn of events to be the most favourable for the working people and historical progress as a whole. "It is our interest and our task to make the revolution permanent, until all more or less possessing classes have been forced out of their position of dominance, [until] the proletariat has conquered state power.... For us the issue cannot be the alteration of private property but only its annihilation, not the smoothing over class antagonisms but the abolition of classes, not the improvement of the existing society but the foundation of a new one." [1]

Accordingly, they outlined a programme of action by the proletariat to ensure the conditions for transition to the proletarian revolution. Alongside the new official petty-bourgeois government, to be set up if the revolution won, the workers were to constitute their own revolutionary governments in the form of organs of local self-government or workers' clubs and committees, so as to exercise control over the activity of the bourgeois-democratic government. They were also to arm themselves everywhere and to form their own military organisations, including contingents of the proletarian guard. Marx and Engels believed the "workers' governments" and proletarian military organisations to be a force capable of developing a revolutionary political crisis in breadth and in depth. They saw these "governments" as the seeds of the proletariat's future revolutionary power.

The Address also dealt with the proletariat's tactics on the agrarian question. Elaborating the propositions they had formulated in the *Demands of the Communist Party in Germany*, Marx and Engels said that once the bourgeois-democratic revolution was victorious the workers were to see that the confiscated feudal estates were turned into state property, instead of being distributed among the peasants, as the petty-bourgeois democrats planned to do. These lands should be used to set up large-scale farms run by associated rural proletariat. Marx and Engels believed that this would strengthen the bonds between the workers and the poor and most exploited sections in the countryside, something that was of excep-

---

[1] Marx, Engels, *Collected Works*, Vol. 10, p. 281.

tional importance for the transition to a socialist revolution. The other sections of the peasantry would be given a clear example of the advantages of the large-scale farming on collective principles.

Marx and Engels did not set themselves the task of providing a full-scale programme on the peasant question in their Address and merely accentuated the tasks which were bound to arise at the second, proletarian, phase of the revolution. Nevertheless, it did reflect some aspects of the great idea of the alliance between the working class and the peasantry, showing that Marx and Engels regarded this as an important element of their permanent revolution doctrine. In contrast to the democrats' urge to establish a solid petty-bourgeois peasant class, they made it clear that only a permanent revolution could release the German peasants from the effects of bourgeois relations in agriculture—impoverishment and growing indebtedness. That is why the German peasants had an objective interest in the victory of the proletariat, if they were to escape the lot of their fellow-peasants in France. Also, the working class required strong-points in the countryside, including large-scale collective farms established on lands once owned by the gentry.

The Address is dominated by this idea: the revolution must be carried forward as far as possible, until the establishment of proletarian rule. The workers' militant slogan should be "Permanent Revolution!"

The Address was handed to Heinrich Bauer, whom the Central Authority sent to Germany at the end of March 1850 to speed up the reorganisation of the League. With the assistance of members of the Cologne and other communities, he succeeded in duplicating and widely circulating the document.

Bauer's mission was a success. Apart from Cologne, League communities were either reorganised or established in Frankfurt am Main, Hanau, Mainz, Wiesbaden, Hamburg, Schwerin, Berlin, Breslau, Göttingen, Liegnitz, Glogau, Leipzig, Nuremberg, Munich, Bamberg, Würzburg, Bielefeld, Stuttgart and a number of other localities. The League's communities spread their influence to many legal workers' organisations. Marx and Engels insisted that the Communist League could become strong and effective only if it succeeded in establishing close ties with the masses and turning the legal workers' organisations into its mainstay.

Marx also took steps to revive the Communist League in other countries, notably, Switzerland, where Ernst Dronke went as an emissary, but mainly because of strong petty-bourgeois influence among the emigrants, his mission was less than successful.

In early June 1850, Marx and Engels wrote the second *Address of the Central Authority to the Communist League*, giving detailed information about the state of the League's organisations in Germany, Belgium, Switzerland, France and England, and giving advice to local leaders on tactical and organisational matters. It was taken for distribution in Germany by the League's emissary, a grinder called Wilhelm Klein.

The activity of the Social-Democratic Refugee Committee in London was of great importance in consolidating the revolutionary forces, for it did more than give assistance to the victims of the counter-revolution. It became increasingly political and helped to restore the Communist League and get the best political emigrants to work with it.

Apart from the English papers, all the addresses, reports and statements by the Committee were published in the German democratic press, reminding the advocates of the liberation struggle in Germany that the revolutionary forces abroad were not idle, but were preparing for fresh battles. Another highly important point was that all the Committee's documents were signed by Marx, who was well known in revolutionary circles.

The efforts of Marx and his followers to reorganise the Communist League were fruitful, especially in Germany. Despite a few reverses, by mid-1850 the League was functioning as a well-constituted and smoothly working organisation with reliable local branches.

UNIVERSAL SOCIETY OF REVOLUTIONARY COMMUNISTS

Marx expected another European revolution to take place shortly, and believed that an international association of revolutionary representatives of the working class from various countries would help to bring about its victory. In the spring of 1850, he enlisted the help of Left-wing Chartists and Blanquist emigrants in setting up a broader international proletarian organisation of which the Communist League would be the nucleus. This was to have enhanced the League's international importance and helped to spread the ideas of scientific communism in the English and the French working-class movement.

Marx was drawn to establish a closer alliance with the Chartists and the Blanquists by his knowledge of the part they had played in the working-class liberation struggle, although he was quite aware of their weaknesses. Harney, Jones and other Left-wing Chartists had displayed a bent for scientific communism even before the 1848 revolution, and even while the proletarian struggle in England was generally on the decline they had continued to voice the revolutionary tendency in the English working-class movement. Of all the French socialist groups and trends, the Blanquists were closest to scientific communism. Although the views of Blanqui himself and his closest associates were on the whole confined to Babouvist utopian communism and although they continued to favour the conspiratorial tactics of the secret revolutionary societies of the 1830s, Marx regarded Blanqui as an outstanding political fighter and put a great value on his practical experience and revolutionary instinct. During the revolution, Blanqui was on the Left of the democratic and proletarian movement, and his implacable stand earned him the hatred of all bourgeois circles. In April 1848 he was sentenced to ten years in prison, and Marx and Engels called him "the noble martyr of revolutionary communism".[1] *The Class Struggles in France* had paid tribute to this courageous revolutionary, and Marx now sought ways of working together with his followers.

In mid-April 1850, an agreement was concluded in London setting up a Universal Society of Revolutionary Communists. It was signed by Marx, Engels and Willich on behalf of the Communist League, by Harney on behalf of the Left-wing Chartists, and by Vidil and Adam on behalf of the Blanquist emigrants. Article 1 of it containing the programme principles of the Society said: "The aim of the association is the downfall of all privileged classes, the submission of those classes to the dictatorship of the proletarians by keeping the revolution in continual progress until the achievement of communism, which shall be the final form of the constitution of the human family."[2]

Consequently, the Society's programme contained some of the basic ideas of scientific communism — permanent revolution and the dictatorship of the proletariat.

However, the ties with the Blanquists proved to be tenuous. They soon began to break the terms of the agreement, in an effort to establish contacts with the petty-bourgeois Democratic Alliance, which took a fiercely hostile attitude to the communist purposes set out in Article 1 of the agreement establishing the Universal Society. Subsequently, the Blanquist emigrant leaders became openly antagonistic to Marx and his followers, and this led Marx and Engels to abrogate the agreement with the Blanquists in the autumn of 1850.

Their relations with the Left-wing Chartists took a different turn. Even before the signing of the agreement Marx and Engels had done much to help Harney in his fight against the reformists' conciliatory factions grouped round the movement's former leader, O'Connor. They had helped Harney to start publication of the *Democratic Review* and spread revolutionary ideas through it. With the establishment of the Universal Society, the ties between Marx and Engels and the Left-wing Chartists were further strengthened. They made regular contributions to the renascent revolutionary Chartist press. The *Democratic Review* carried extracts from Marx's *The Class Struggles in France* and articles by Engels. Another journal edited by Harney, *Red Republican*, carried in its November 1850 issue the first English translation of the *Manifesto of the Communist Party*.

In the spring of 1851, however, Harney became more closely asso-

---

[1] Marx, Engels, *Collected Works*, Vol. 10, p. 537.
[2] Ibid., p. 614.

ciated with the petty-bourgeois democrats and broke with the revolutionary wing of the Chartists. Marx and Engels condemned this sharply. However, they continued to give full support to Jones, who remained loyal to revolutionary Chartist traditions. He had accepted some elements of Marx's doctrine and was working to revive the Chartist movement on a socialist basis. The programme which the Chartist Convention adopted in 1851 through Jones' efforts officially proclaimed socialist goals for the first time in the history of Chartism.

Marx and Engels were active contributors to *Notes to the People*, a weekly published by Jones in 1851 and 1852, which in the summer of 1851 carried Marx's article "The Constitution of the French Republic Adopted November 4, 1848". On many points it supplemented his critical analysis of the Constitution in *The Class Struggles in France*. Marx also helped Jones to write a series of articles on the co-operatives, which exploded the utopian idea that the proletariat's social ills could be cured under capitalism through a development of producers' and consumers' co-operatives, and explained that these could become an instrument of social change only when political power was in the hands of the working class. Recalling these articles, Marx said in 1864 that he and Jones had essentially anticipated the polemics against the co-operativist ideas propounded by bourgeois theorists of the "workers' question" like Schulze-Delitzsch, for whose exposure Lassalle claimed all the credit.

Marx and Engels helped Jones to maintain the principle of the Chartist movement's independence and to resist attempts by reformists to deprive it of its proletarian character and to subject it to bourgeois radical influence.

REVIEWS FROM THE *NEUE RHEINISCHE ZEITUNG. POLITISCH-ÖKONOMISCHE REVUE*

Marx believed that explaining the impact of revolutionary events on ideology was an important part of learning the lessons of the revolution. Together with Engels, he wrote several reviews of books by bourgeois and petty-bourgeois writers published in 1849 and 1850. These appeared in the second and fourth issues of the *Revue* and criticised the interpretation of the revolutionary events of 1848-49 and the role of revolutions in history given by the proletariat's ideological adversaries. They analysed the latest bourgeois historical conceptions and pseudo-socialist theories, bringing out their class and political significance and assessing them from the standpoint of the revolutionary proletarian movement.

With keen insight, Marx and Engels realised that the 1848 and 1849 revolutions marked the turning point in the development of bourgeois ideology and showed that, confronted with proletarian action, even once progressive bourgeois historians lost their capacity for scientific, objective reasoning and in fact repudiated their own rational ideas.

Marx and Engels illustrated this by their critical analysis of a pamphlet by François Guizot, *Why Has the English Revolution Been Successful?* Guizot, a conservative bourgeois politician and one of a brilliant group of historians of the Restoration who accepted the role of the class struggle in the formation of contemporary bourgeois society, had moved further to the Right as a result of the 1848 revolution. His latest pamphlet on the English revolution, published in 1850, showed that "even the most capable people of the *ancien régime*, people whose own kind of talent in the realm of history can by no means be disputed, have been brought to such a state of perplexity by the fatal events of February that they have lost all understanding of history, that they now even fail to comprehend their own former actions".[1]

Guizot had earlier recognised revolutions to be natural, but now sought to minimise their historical importance and to prove that in his day revolutionary acts were accidental. Among the revolutionary events of the past, Guizot emphasised and presented as ideal those which had entailed the least disruption of traditional institutions and had ended in a compromise. But even these he interpreted idealistically, without trying to identify their material and class causes.

Marx and Engels showed that it was absurd for Guizot to say that the 17th-century revolution in England had "been successful", that is, had ensured the country's further constitutional development without revolutionary upheavals, because, in contrast to the destructive French Revolution, it had been religious and moderate. They proved that the French Revolution was superior to the English one, which had only gone halfway, well short of completion, leaving England's constitutional monarchy intact, because of the durable alliance between the English bourgeoisie and the bulk of the big landowners, who had remodelled their estates on bourgeois lines. By contrast, the French Revolution had destroyed the large-scale, fundamentally feudal, landed estates through vigorous revolutionary measures and parcellation.

The review of Guizot's pamphlet ended with these words: "*Les capacités de la bourgeoisie s'en vont.*"[2] This conclusion was also largely borne out by the evolution to the Right in the views of Thomas Carlyle, the prominent English historian and publicist, whose book *Latter-Day Pamphlets* was also reviewed by Marx and Engels. They deflated his subjective, idealistic conception of history based on reactionary "hero-worship" and the juxtaposition of "wise and noble" leaders and the crowd. Behind the screen of hero-worship, Carlyle in fact "justifies and exaggerates the infamies of the bourgeoisie".[3]

---

[1] Marx, Engels, *Collected Works*, Vol. 10, p. 251.
[2] The talent of the bourgeoisie passes away.
[3] Marx, Engels, *Collected Works*, Vol. 10, p. 310.

The petty-bourgeois democrats also inflated and enhanced the role of various individuals, notably, members of the bourgeois and petty-bourgeois opposition, and Marx and Engels exposed this in a review of two books about the revolutionary movement in France written by Adolphe Chenu and Lucien de la Hodde, both police agents. Marx and Engels wrote: "Nothing is more to be desired than that the people who were at the head of the active party, whether before the revolution in the secret societies or the press, or afterwards in official positions, should at long last be portrayed in the stark colours of a Rembrandt, in the full flush of life. Hitherto these personalities have never been depicted as they really were, but only in their official guise, with buskins on their feet and halos around their heads. All verisimilitude is lost in these idealised, Raphaelesque pictures."[1]

This review was a strong expression of the proletarian revolutionaries' negative attitude to adventurism, sectarianism and conspiratorial tactics in the revolutionary movement. The conspirators, those "alchemists of the revolution", were not intent on organising real revolutionary struggle, but on spurring the revolution by violent means, "bringing it artificially to crisis-point, launching a revolution on the spur of the moment, without the conditions for a revolution".[2]

In their review of a book by the German theologist Daumer, *The Religion of the New Age*, Marx and Engels showed the bankruptcy of the ideology of the German philistine, who was terrified by the revolution. In the light of materialism, they showed religion to be a form of social consciousness, which determined its role in history, and made its disappearance inevitable as men acquired knowledge about the real laws of social development. They added that one of the prerequisites for overcoming religious superstitions was the triumph of the materialist outlook both in the natural and in the social sciences.

Marx and Engels were sure that consistent exposure of unscientific sociological views was a way of bringing ideological education to those who took part in the proletarian struggle.

INTERNATIONAL REVIEWS.
EVALUATING THE PROSPECTS OF THE REVOLUTION

In the course of 1850, Marx and Engels wrote three international reviews, which appeared in the second, fourth and final issues of the *Neue Rheinische Zeitung. Politisch-ökonomische Revue*. They contained a profound analysis of current political and economic events in Europe, North America and Asia, and forecasts which were subsequently borne out by historical developments. The experiences of

---
[1] Marx, Engels, *Collected Works*, Vol. 10, p. 311.
[2] Ibid., p. 318.

1848-49 induced Marx and Engels to devote the most serious attention to economics. As Marx probed for the root-causes of these events he came increasingly to realise the need for a thorough study of economic processes.

In their international reviews, Marx and Engels expressed the idea that economic crises give an impetus to revolutionary crises, and that, on the contrary, economic prosperity tends to slow down revolution and create the ground for a consolidation of reaction. This idea was subsequently spelled out in detail in their letters, and Lenin observed: "Crisis paves the way for *proletarian* action (as the cavalry for attack)."[1] Concerning Engels' remark that a long period of prosperity had had a demoralising effect, Lenin emphasised: "*The demoralisation of the workers by a time of peace.*"[2]

Until the middle of 1850, Marx and Engels were sure revolution would come soon, believing that another economic crisis would break out shortly in Europe and that this would spark off a new revolution. This view is reflected in the first and second international reviews. However, as they developed their study of the shaping economic outlook, they came to see that this forecast was unjustified and drew different conclusions concerning the immediate prospects for Europe's social development.

Marx and Engels made their premature forecast of revolution partially because at the time they had a general tendency to overestimate the maturity of capitalism and the proletariat's revolutionary capacity, and therefore expected the forthcoming revolution soon to become a socialist one. In his introduction to Marx's *The Class Struggles in France*, Engels wrote in 1895: "History has proved us, and all who thought like us, wrong. It has made it clear that the state of economic development on the Continent at that time was not, by a long way, ripe for the elimination of capitalist production."[3]

In the summer of 1850, having made a study of economic development in the preceding decade, Marx drew the conclusion that the effects of the 1847 economic crisis, which had played a great part in paving the way for the revolutionary events of 1848, had completely died away and that a new industrial boom had started while the revolution was still on. In 1849 and 1850 it had risen to a very high level, thereby helping European reaction to entrench itself. This conclusion was substantiated in the third international review, written by Marx and Engels in the autumn of 1850, which marshalled a vast body of facts to show the economic upswing in England, France, Germany and the U.S.A., and stated that a temporary non-revolutionary period had opened in the development of capitalist society. "With this general prosperity, in which the productive forces of bourgeois society develop as luxuriantly as is at all possible

---
[1] V. I. Lenin. *Synopsis of the "Correspondence of K. Marx and F. Engels, 1844-1883"*, Moscow, 1968, p. 30 (in Russian).
[2] Ibid., p. 34.
[3] Marx and Engels, *Selected Works*, Vol. 1, p. 200.

within bourgeois relationships, there can be no talk of a real revolution. Such a revolution is only possible in the periods when *both these factors*, the *modern* productive *forces* and the *bourgeois forms of production*, come *in collision* with each other.... A new revolution is possible only in consequence of a new crisis. It is, however, just as certain as this crisis." [1]

This reconsideration of the prospects for revolution led Marx and Engels to review the tactics of the Communist League, which could no longer be directed towards an outbreak of revolution in the immediate future. Assuming a relatively long period of reaction new tactical forms of party activity had to be sought. The important thing was to get the other members of the League, its leading core, to accept this, and there again Marx and Engels faced great difficulties.

FIGHT AGAINST THE WILLICH-SCHAPPER SECTARIAN-ADVENTURIST FACTION

In the summer of 1850, a "Left" faction developed within the Communist League. It was headed by August Willich, who was a Communist only by instinct, and Karl Schapper, who had failed entirely to break with the sectarian-conspiratorial traditions of the early period of the working-class movement. Willich, Schapper and their followers were unable to understand the specific features of the new historical situation and to take account of them in formulating the tactical tasks of the working-class movement. They advocated essentially adventurist tactics, which was especially dangerous when the revolutionary movement was at an ebb.

Marx and Willich had already clashed in the winter of 1849-50, when Marx was lecturing on the *Manifesto of the Communist Party* at the German Workers' Educational Society in London. In these lectures he said that communism could not be achieved overnight but had to be arrived at through a number of phases in revolutionary development, and that the tasks of the bourgeois-democratic revolution had to be tackled before proceeding to communist transformations. Willich had no idea of the laws governing the development of society and the revolutionary process, and denied the need for any material prerequisites for the establishment of communism, hoping to set it up at one go, through an effort of will by a handful of men.

These differences remained in the background as long as Marx was hoping for an early revolutionary explosion, but the situation changed after he and Engels had reached their conclusion in the summer of 1850 about the start of non-revolutionary period in Europe and had made the relevant changes in the League's tactics. While main-

---

[1] Marx, Engels, *Collected Works*, Vol. 10, p. 510.

taining their strategic line towards an inevitable revolution, they believed that in the given situation the main task was to preserve and bring together the proletarian cadres and to give them a theoretical grounding in preparation for the battles ahead.

Willich, Schapper and their followers objected strongly to the new tactics and tried to push the League into reckless action aimed at instant revolution in Germany. This was a harmful and adventurist "playing at revolution", instead of serious preparation for the coming revolutionary battles.

By mid-September 1850, the Willich-Schapper faction had disrupted the League's work in London. In breach of the Rules, they started to oppose the Central Authority's decisions in the German Workers' Educational Society, at general meetings of the League's London District, and in the Social-Democratic Refugee Committee. In a minority on the Central Authority, they began to spread ideas among the workers that clashed with the *Manifesto of the Communist Party* and the Central Authority's addresses.

The split occurred at an extraordinary meeting of the Central Authority on September 15, 1850. The representatives of the majority — Marx, Engels, Schramm, Pfänder, Heinrich Bauer and Eccarius — were all present. The minority group was represented by Willich, Schapper and Lehmann. Fränkel was unable to attend.

Marx pointed to the real cause of the differences between the majority and the minority, arguing that, contrary to what Willich asserted later on, these were not personal but absolutely fundamental, because the urge of the Willich-Schapper faction to substitute imaginary for actual conditions and to invest a subjective factor like volition with the principal role in revolution was ideologically and tactically untenable. Marx said: "A German national standpoint was substituted for the universal outlook of the *Manifesto*, and the national feelings of the German artisans were pandered to. The materialist standpoint of the *Manifesto* has given way to idealism. The revolution is seen not as the product of realities of the situation but as the result of an effort of *will*. Whereas we say to the workers: You have 15, 20, 50 years of civil war to go through in order to alter the situation and to train yourselves for the exercise of power, it is said: We must take power *at once*, or else we may as well take to our beds." [1]

Marx proved that voluntarism and subjectivism were the ideological basis of their adventurist policy and sectarian tactics, which ignored life. With the approval of the majority he resolutely rejected the idea, which was being advocated by the Willich-Schapper group, that the League should look to an instant take-over of power by the working class in Germany.

Marx assumed quite rightly that the Central Authority majority was empowered by the Rules to expel the representatives of the mi-

---

[1] Ibid., p. 626.

nority from the League, because their views clashed with the League's principles, but he was loath to do this, for he hoped that events would make them realise their mistakes. At the same time, he believed it necessary to make an ideological break with the faction, and therefore proposed a demarcation formula that would prevent both a split in the League and a take-over by sectarian elements. His proposal was that the Central Authority should transfer its powers to the Cologne District Committee, and set up two separate districts in London, one consisting of the supporters of Marx and Engels, and the other of those of Willich and Schapper. Both districts would be members of the same League and would work under the leadership of the same Central Authority, with whom each would maintain contacts independently and abide by its decisions. Marx emphasised that he was proposing this solution for the sake of keeping the League united.

Speaking for the factionalists, Schapper rejected Marx's plan. When the debate was over Willich and Lehmann walked out. Schapper, who stayed on, made a point of abstaining from voting. The others all voted for Marx's proposal.

Willich, Schapper and the other factionalists refused to abide by the Central Authority's decision and got a general meeting of the League's London District to adopt a decision setting up its own Central Authority and expelling Marx, Engels and their supporters from the League. They achieved this by resorting to slander and playing on the craft-union prejudice of many of the League's members, who naively expected an early revolution. Marx and Engels gave the new sectarian organisation the ironic name of *Sonderbund* (Separatist Union), by analogy with the separatist union of reactionary Catholic cantons in Switzerland in the 1840s.

Having failed to keep the League united, because of the factionalists' splitting tactics, Marx and Engels felt that it was useless to maintain all other forms of co-operation with the Willich-Schapper group, and so, on September 17, 1850, they and their supporters announced their withdrawal from the German Workers' Educational Society in London, in view of the fact that most of its members had sided with the splitters, and also from the Social-Democratic Refugee Committee. In early October 1850, Marx and Engels officially broke with the emigrant Blanquists, who backed the factionalists.

The *Sonderbund* managed to prevail in the French and Swiss communities, which were small and poorly organised, but almost all the communities in Germany remained loyal to Marx and Engels.

The Cologne District Committee, supported by all the local Communists, approved the Londoners' decision of September 15, 1850, and set itself up as the Central Authority. At its meeting on September 29, the new Central Authority annulled the *Sonderbund*'s decision expelling Marx, Engels and their supporters from the League, announced the dissolution of the London organisation, and authorised Eccarius and Schapper to establish two independent districts in London.

The Willich-Schapper group refused to abide by the decisions of the Cologne Central Authority, following which the London District, newly established by Eccarius from among the supporters of Marx and Engels, submitted a proposal to the Cologne Central Authority on November 11, 1850, to expel all the members of the *Sonderbund* from the Communist League. The Cologne Central Authority agreed, and passed a decision on their expulsion.

Following the split in the Communist League, the Willich-Schapper group developed into a narrow sect isolated from the proletarian movement and was increasingly drawn into adventurist schemes by petty-bourgeois emigrant circles, while the *Sonderbund* (which continued to exist until early 1853) became a mere appendage of the petty-bourgeois emigration.

ENGELS LEAVES FOR MANCHESTER. CORRESPONDENCE BETWEEN THE TWO FRIENDS

In November 1850, Engels had to move to Manchester, to start work in the office of Ermen & Engels. He was forced to resume his "damned business" activity largely because of his desire to give the Marx family regular financial support and to help Marx to get on with his theoretical work. Resident in two different cities, the two men continued to maintain close spiritual contact with each other. Now and again Marx would go to see Engels in Manchester to work on some piece of writing together or take a rest. Engels also took every opportunity to spend a few days with Marx and his family in London. However, for many years letters were the main form of contact between the two friends. They got into such a habit of writing regularly to each other that any slight delay in the post at once became a source of acute anxiety.

Their correspondence is something of a chronicle of their life and struggle. Its most valuable aspect is that it is a very full reflection of the vast theoretical and practical work of these two great thinkers and their creative co-operation in various fields of science and revolutionary practice. Marx valued Engels' opinion extremely highly and invited his opinion on all his scientific discoveries, observations and conclusions. For his part, Engels shared with Marx his experience and the results of his research.

The two men discussed a vast range of questions—philosophy and natural science, political economy and socialism, history and linguistics, military science and technical developments, literature and the arts. Their letters give a picture of the development of the three component parts of their doctrine, and also of their creative contribution to a number of special branches of knowledge. Now and again they reflect literary plans which for various reasons were not realised. Thus, alongside the outlines of important propositions subsequently amplified in their printed works, the letters contain many valuable ideas which were not subsequently taken up.

They constantly discussed and criticised in their letters the views of bourgeois scientists. Frequently their comments took the form of general statements, showing the essential features of bourgeois historical, philosophical and economic science. Many pages of their letters are filled with assessments of books they had read and remarks on various outstanding events in science and the publication of important works.

Marx and Engels constantly kept living reality within their field of vision—the economic and social processes taking place in the world around them and the political developments in the various countries. Sometimes these served as subjects for their articles and reports. Their assessments of political leaders in their letters are, as a rule, much sharper than in their articles and reports.

The strategy and tactics of the proletariat's class struggle is another important subject dealt with in their letters, which show very well the tremendous attention Marx and Engels paid to the condition of the working class in various countries, the various forms of proletarian resistance to the capitalists, the liberation movement of its allies—the peasantry and the peoples of the oppressed countries—and the formulation of the proletarian tactical line on a number of issues. Analysing this aspect of their correspondence, Lenin observed: "There unfolds before the reader a strikingly vivid picture of the history of the working-class movement all over the world—at its most important junctures and in its most essential points. Even more valuable is the history of the *politics* of the working class. On the most diverse occasions, in various countries of the Old World and the New, and at different historical moments, Marx and Engels discuss the most important principles of the *presentation* of the *political* tasks of the working class."[1]

Lenin repeatedly pointed to the vast wealth of ideas in the letters of Marx and Engels, and always regarded them as being a most important part of the treasure-house of Marxist thinking. He wrote: "If one were to attempt to define in a single word the focus, so to speak, of the whole correspondence, the central point at which the whole body of ideas expressed and discussed converges—that word would be *dialectics*. The application of materialist dialectics to the reshaping of all political economy from its foundations up, its application to history, natural science, philosophy and to the policy and tactics of the working class—that was what interested Marx and Engels most of all, that was where they contributed what was most essential and new, and that was what constituted the masterly advance they made in the history of revolutionary thought."[2]

---

[1] V. I. Lenin, *Collected Works*, Vol. 19, p. 553.
[2] Ibid., p. 554.

PLAN FOR A FRESH ATTACK AGAINST PROUDHON

In July 1851, Marx read Proudhon's book *The General Notion of Revolution in the Nineteenth Century*, which had just been published in Paris and which showed very clearly the characteristic features of Proudhon's outlook as an ideologist of petty-bourgeois socialism, together with his reformist and anti-revolutionary tendencies. Proudhon's was a utopian programme for social revolution by peaceful, purely "economic" means, mutual assistance and credit, an exchange bank, lower interest on loans, and similar reforms. He was sure these would result in the establishment of a "society without power". This book gave a fuller exposition of his anarchist views than any of his earlier works. He rejected any idea of using political power for revolutionary and socialist purposes, declaring any state to be reactionary and all democracy to be useless.

Marx decided to publish a critique of Proudhon's book, which was the more necessary since Proudhonism was already crystallising as a definite petty-bourgeois reformist trend, presenting an especial danger for the working class in the conditions of reaction. Its least steadfast section had grown apathetic and despondent over the defeat of the revolution, doubted the need for political struggle, and responded to Proudhon's advocacy of political indifference and his calls for a class peace and the solution of the social issues through reform. This was greatly hampering the revolutionary education of the proletariat.

In his letters to Engels of August 8 and 14, 1851, Marx outlined the basic idea expounded in Proudhon's book and summed it up as "a polemic against communism".[1] He told Engels that he planned to write a polemical work against Proudhon and asked for his comments.

By the end of October Engels had sent in his critical analysis of Proudhon's book, and Marx found it highly satisfying. On November 24, 1851, he wrote to Engels: "I have been through your critique again here. It's a pity that there's no means of getting it printed. If my own twaddle were added to it, we could bring it out under both our names."[2] For a long time, Marx entertained the idea of using Engels' analysis in publishing a polemical work against Proudhon and sought an opportunity to realise his plan. At one point it appeared to be close to fruition. In the autumn of 1851, Joseph Weydemeyer emigrated to the U.S.A. and informed Marx in mid-December that he was proposing to start publication in New York of a communist weekly, *Die Revolution*, beginning in January 1852. Weydemeyer invited Marx and Engels to send in their contributions, and Marx in turn asked Weydemeyer to insert an announcement about the forthcoming publication of an anti-Proudhon pamphlet.

---

[1] Marx, Engels, *Collected Works*, Vol. 38, p. 423.
[2] Ibid., p. 492.

On December 19, 1851, he wrote: "For the following numbers you can announce a serialised work of mine, to appear article by article, namely, *Neuste Offenbarungen des Sozialismus, oder 'Idée générale de la Révolution au XIXe siècle' par J. P. Proudhon.— Kritik von K. M.*" [1] This advertisement appeared in the first issue of the weekly in January 1852.

However, until April 1852 Marx was engrossed in work dealing with the recent Bonapartist coup in France, which he considered to be the more pressing task of the two. By the time he was free *Die Revolution* was no longer being published as a periodical because the editor was short of money, so there was no chance of publishing a pamphlet against Proudhon.

THE EIGHTEENTH BRUMAIRE OF LOUIS BONAPARTE

On December 2, 1851, the supporters of President Louis Bonaparte staged a coup d'état and dispersed the Legislative Assembly. Bonaparte's dictatorship was set up, and a year later Bonaparte proclaimed himself Emperor Napoleon III.

In a letter of December 16, 1851, Engels suggested that Marx should write an article about the events in France for Weydemeyer's weekly. Marx got down to it at once. However, he soon found himself writing much more than an article, and within a short period produced one of the most remarkable of his works, *The Eighteenth Brumaire of Louis Bonaparte*. He sent Chapter Seven, the final one, to New York on March 25, 1852.

As he wrote *The Eighteenth Brumaire*, Marx exchanged ideas with Engels and took his advice into account. For his source he had, apart from the press and the official material, the letters of Richard Reinhardt, Heine's secretary, who was resident in Paris. He also obtained some important information from his talks with French revolutionary emigrants.

He had to write his work in very difficult circumstances. He was seriously ill throughout almost the whole of January, and the family was so short of money that in February he had to pawn his clothes and was unable to go to the library. Still he worked with abandon and produced a work written in an extremely precise and expressive style. Wilhelm Liebknecht said: "The words of *Brumaire* are arrows, javelins—it is a style that brands and kills. If ever hate, scorn and ardent love of liberty were expressed in burning, devastating, lofty words, it is in *The Eighteenth Brumaire*, which combines the indignant severity of a Tacitus with the deadly satire of a Juvenal and the holy wrath of a Dante." [2]

There were great difficulties over the publication of the new work,

---

[1] Marx, Engels, *Collected Works*, Vol. 38, p. 519.
[2] *Reminiscences of Marx and Engels*, p. 103.

for Weydemeyer's weekly had proved to be short-lived. Not until May 1852 did Weydemeyer succeed in issuing it as a separate edition in the form of the first "non-periodical issue" of the journal *Die Revolution*. Marx was unable to reprint his work either in Germany or in Britain.

Like *The Class Struggles in France*, *The Eighteenth Brumaire* turned to the French revolution of 1848 and 1849 and examined the vicissitudes of the French political life in the light of their ultimate outcome — the Bonapartist coup of December 2.

Marx's bourgeois and petty-bourgeois contemporaries were unable to show the social roots and significance of the events in France. In his pamphlet *Napoléon le petit* issued almost simultaneously with Marx's work, Victor Hugo achieved the opposite effect, when he tried to deflate the hero of the coup. In fact, he built him up to tremendous proportions by depicting the coup as the result of the French president's sinister will and ascribing to a fairly mediocre personality "a personal power of initiative such as would be without parallel in world history".[1] Proudhon's book *The Social Revolution in the Light of the December 2 Coup*, published at the time, contained an attempt to explain the coup which was basically a false vindication of its protagonist and an apologia of Bonapartism. Marx alone succeeded in unravelling the skein of social and political phenomena which had led up to the coup in France and showing its real character. Engels wrote: "This eminent understanding of the living history of the day, this clear-sighted appreciation of events at the moment of happening, is indeed without parallel."[2]

Marx's key to the events in France was his materialist view of history and his theory of the class struggle. He saw the Bonapartist coup as the inevitable result of the development of the class struggle in France, whose course created "circumstances and relations that made it possible for a grotesque mediocrity to play a hero's part".[3] Class antagonisms in bourgeois society in France had reached a stage when any further advance of the revolution in depth would have entailed the implementation of socialist measures. That is why the bourgeoisie abandoned such clear-cut and direct forms of domination as the bourgeois republic and in order to preserve the exploitative system handed over power to a reactionary clique of wild adventurers. Hence, Marx saw the Bonapartist coup as a natural consequence of the bourgeoisie's growing counter-revolutionary character. The Bonapartist regime sprang from a balance of class forces under which the bourgeoisie was no longer able to rule by using conventional parliamentary methods, while the proletariat was still too weak to frustrate the former's counter-revolutionary schemes.

Marx showed Bonapartism to be the dictatorship of the most coun-

---

[1] Marx, Engels, *Collected Works*, Vol. 21, p. 57.
[2] Marx and Engels, *Selected Works*, Vol. 1, p. 411.
[3] Marx, Engels, *Collected Works*, Vol. 21, p. 57.

ter-revolutionary elements of the bourgeoisie and revealed its distinctive features: a policy of manoeuvring between the classes, which invests the state power with some independence, gross demagogy designed to cover up the defence of the interests of the exploiting *élite* and combined with political terrorism, the total sway of the military, corruption, the use of the criminal world, blackmail, bribery and other base means. The experience of the first few months of the Bonapartist regime enabled Marx to lay bare its internal contradictions. He predicted its downfall while the Bonapartist clique was still celebrating its victory.

Marx took a close look at the stand of the various parties in France, brought out the characteristic features of the history of bourgeois society, and showed how social processes and the clash of classes were reflected in the political and ideological sphere. He urged the need to draw a distinction between the objective side of social and political phenomena and their reflection in the minds of those taking part in the events. That was an important contribution to the development of historical materialism. He wrote: "...in historical struggles one must still more distinguish the language and the imaginary aspirations of parties from their real organism and their real interests, their conception of themselves from their reality." [1]

Marx had some very important things to say about the relationship between the ideologists and the political and literary spokesmen of a class and the class itself, and warned against the vulgar view that ideologists must necessarily have the same social status and way of life as the whole mass of the class they represent, that, for instance, the ideologists of the petty bourgeoisie must necessarily be shopkeepers and owners of small workshops. A politician or a writer becomes an ideologist of the given class because in theoretical terms he arrives at the same conclusions and sees the same tasks to which the rank-and-file members of that class are led up by their immediate material interests and their own experience.

Marx devoted much attention to the condition of the peasantry, the most numerous class of French society, and its attitude to the revolution and the Bonapartist coup. The peasants had voted for Louis Bonaparte because they were politically backward and ignorant and out of touch with cultural and political developments in the cities. Because of the tax levies of the bourgeois governments under the Second Republic the peasants became disillusioned with the revolution and supported Bonaparte. They also did so because, as small-holders, they were attached to their plots of land and believed the representative of the Napoleonic dynasty to be their traditional patron. Marx wrote: "Historical tradition gave rise to the belief of the French peasants in the miracle that a man named Napoleon would bring all the glory back to them." [2]

---

[1] Marx, Engels, *Collected Works*, Vol. 11, p. 128.
[2] Ibid., p. 188.

Marx showed the twofold social character of the peasants, emphasising that there were two sides to their outlook—the conservative and the revolutionary—the urge to maintain and consolidate their plot of land and the traditional way of life it bred, on the one hand, and the urge to escape from these conditions, on the other. It was the peasants' conservative aspirations that had provided Bonaparte with a temporary foothold. The Bonaparte dynasty "represents not the enlightenment, but the superstition of the peasant; not his judgment, but his prejudice; not his future, but his past".[1] The inevitable ruin of the small-holding peasant and his enslavement by the money-lenders was bound to help the peasant escape from the pernicious influence of the *"idées napoléoniennes"*. While the peasant's prejudices had impelled him to side with the Bonaparte dynasty, his judgment, his awareness of his own interests must impel him to joint action with the worker. "Hence the peasants find their natural ally and leader in the *urban proletariat*, whose task is the overthrow of the bourgeois order."[2] Marx stressed that with the peasants *"the proletarian revolution will obtain that chorus without which its solo becomes a swan song in all peasant countries"*.[3]

We find, therefore, that in this book Marx set out an even more comprehensive argument for the proposition concerning the alliance between the working class and the peasantry, with the proletariat playing the leading role. Four years later, he was to elaborate this idea as applied to the conditions in Germany, in connection with the prospects for revolutionary struggle in that country. In a letter to Engels of April 16, 1856, he said: "The whole thing in Germany will depend on whether it is possible to back the proletarian revolution by some second edition of the Peasants' War. In which case the affair should go swimmingly."[4]

The Eighteenth Brumaire contains a further elaboration of the theory of revolution. Marx re-emphasises that revolution is a powerful accelerator of social processes and makes them develop "by an abbreviated ... method". He draws an even deeper distinction between the bourgeois and the proletarian revolutions. Whereas the former are "short-lived and soon attain their zenith", the proletarian revolutions are not short outbursts, but long periods of fundamental social change. They "criticise themselves constantly", in other words, they "interrupt themselves continually in their own course, come back to the apparently accomplished in order to begin it afresh, deride with unmerciful thoroughness the inadequacies ... of their first attempts",[5] and are marked by an indomitable striving to advance.

The attitude of the proletarian revolution to the bourgeois state,

---

[1] Ibid., p. 188.
[2] Ibid., p. 191.
[3] Ibid., p. 193.
[4] Ibid., Vol. 40, p. 41.
[5] Ibid., Vol. 11, pp. 106-07.

which Marx formulates in *The Eighteenth Brumaire*, is of enormous theoretical importance. In this work, on the strength of the experience of the 1848-49 revolutions, Marx first draws the conclusion about the need for the victorious proletariat to break up the old state machine. By way of example, he traces the growth of the military-bureaucratic state apparatus in France, and says that "all revolutions perfected this machine instead of breaking it".[1] The proletarian revolution needs a totally different type of power and so cannot merely take over the existing state machine of the bourgeoisie and set it in motion, leaving intact this fundamentally exploitative instrument which was used to oppress the labouring masses. The task of the proletarian revolution is therefore "to concentrate all its forces of destruction against it".[2]

Analysing these conclusions, Lenin wrote: "In this remarkable argument Marxism takes a tremendous step forward compared with the *Communist Manifesto*. In the latter the question of the state is still treated in an extremely abstract manner, in the most general terms and expressions. In the above-quoted passage, the question is treated in a concrete manner, and the conclusion is extremely precise, definite, practical and palpable: all previous revolutions perfected the state machine, whereas it must be broken, smashed.

"This conclusion is the chief and fundamental point in the Marxist theory of the state."[3]

While working on *The Eighteenth Brumaire*, Marx gained a fuller understanding of the main distinction between his doctrine of classes and the class struggle, on the one hand, and the views of those bourgeois economists and historians who recognised the existence of class contradictions. He also found a highly lucid formulation for it. He summed up his conclusions in a letter to Weydemeyer of March 5, 1852: "Now as for myself, I do not claim to have discovered either the existence of classes in modern society or the struggle between them. Long before me bourgeois historians had described the historical development of this struggle between the classes, as had bourgeois economists their economic anatomy. My own contribution was 1. to show that the *existence of classes* is merely bound up with *certain historical phases in the development of production;* 2. that the class struggle necessarily leads to the *dictatorship of the proletariat*; 3. that this dictatorship itself constitutes no more than a transition to the *abolition of all classes* and to a *classless society*."[4]

---

[1] Marx, Engels, *Collected Works*, Vol. 11, p. 186.
[2] Ibid., p. 185.
[3] V. I. Lenin, *Collected Works*, Vol. 25, p. 411.
[4] Marx, Engels, *Collected Works*, Vol. 39, pp. 62, 65.

CRITIQUE OF PETTY-BOURGEOIS DEMOCRACY.
THE GREAT MEN OF THE EXILE

Marx worked hard to keep pure the proletarian revolutionaries' ideological and tactical principles, and took steps to protect the proletarian movement from bourgeois and petty-bourgeois influence. The loud and noisy activity of various democratic groups of the emigration was doing much harm to the democratic and working-class movement. The petty-bourgeois emigrants in London, Switzerland and the U.S.A. were issuing bombastic proclamations and manifestoes heralding an early revolutionary explosion, and were forming committees and provisional governments in an effort to build up artificially the prestige of their leaders who had failed badly during the revolution.

Marx and Engels believed that there was a need for a public exposure of the adventurist activity of the petty-bourgeois emigrants, to show the true face of many of their "leading lights". They were also impelled to do this by the malicious attacks, slander, and insinuations directed against the Communists by the leaders of the emigration and the leaders of the *Sonderbund* allied with them.

In the spring of 1851, Marx and Engels wrote an article for the press to expose the sponsors of the so-called Banquet of Equals, a meeting called in London to mark the third anniversary of the February Revolution in France. Blanc, Willich and other organisers of the meeting had concealed from the audience the text of a speech which Blanqui had written for the banquet and had smuggled out of the Belle Isle prison, and which exposed the traitorous behaviour of members of the French Provisional Government, including Blanc and Ledru-Rollin. Marx and Engels translated it into German and English and wrote a short preface, mentioning its indecent suppression at the "Banquet of Equals".

In a number of letters Marx also sharply criticised the petty-bourgeois leaders of the emigration for their careerism and popularity hunting. Well in advance, they had shared out among themselves all the senior posts in the future republican governments, and Marx ridiculed their adventurist idea of floating a German-American revolutionary loan designed to promote instant revolution.

In April 1852, Marx decided to write, together with Engels, a special pamphlet against these leaders, and in May and June they worked on a long polemical work, most of which was written together during Marx's stay in Manchester. They called it *The Great Men of the Exile*. In early July, the manuscript was delivered for publication in Germany by a Hungarian emigrant, Janos Bangya, who had close connections with prominent Hungarian revolutionaries and had offered his services. However, it soon transpired that Bangya was a police agent (Marx subsequently exposed him in the press on many occasions). Bangya sold the manuscript to the Prussian police, but Marx had kept the original, and made several fresh attempts to publish it in Germany and elsewhere, notably, the U.S.A. However, he was unsuccessful, and it was first published in the Soviet Union in 1930.

The pamphlet is a brilliant political satire on the German petty-bourgeois emigrant circles of the early 1850s, who were in the habit of engaging in empty and pseudo-revolutionary chit-chat. It is a determined criticism of all vulgarisation of the great revolutionary cause. It presents a gallery of brilliant portraits of the "great men" of the emigration, revealing the seamy side of their ways, the poverty and vulgarity of their spiritual world, and their extreme political unreliability. It gives a glimpse of the everyday life of the German petty-bourgeois leaders of the emigration and shows that behind the façade of their debates about principle lay nothing but a "war between the frogs and the mice", petty squabbles between various groupings. It was a condemnation of every brand of empty talk, the striking of attitudes, and demagogic speculation with revolutionary catchwords.

What made the adventurist behaviour of the leaders — Kinkel, Struve, Ruge and Heinzen, among others — especially dangerous was that it provided "the governments with the pretext they needed to arrest many people in Germany, to obstruct the movement throughout the country and to use these wretched strawmen in London as scarecrows with which to frighten the German middle classes".[1]

In their pamphlet, Marx and Engels also found a way of exposing the sectarian Willich-Schapper group, although for reasons of secrecy they were unable to discuss openly the split in the Communist League and their differences with the factionalists. That is why they gave a portrait of Willich in the emigrant leaders' gallery. It was fully justified because his petty-bourgeois views differed little, if at all, from those of the other "great men". Marx and Engels showed that Willich was incapable of comprehending the great strategic and tactical tasks facing the revolutionary movement, and he is presented as a fanatically stubborn, narrow-minded man, with a set of rigid ideas, working hard to subordinate the general interests of the whole movement to those of a small sectarian group.

COLOGNE COMMUNIST TRIAL

In May and June 1851, a wave of arrests swept across Germany. Among the victims were many Communist League activists, including Nothjung, Bürgers, Daniels, Hermann Becker, Röser and Lessner. In an attempt to stamp out the revolutionary movement, the

---

[1] Marx, Engels, *Collected Works*, Vol. 11, p. 311.

forces of reaction aimed their blows above all at the followers of Marx and Engels, for the most farsighted members of the police were well aware that the real threat to the existing system did not lie in the loud ultra-revolutionary talk by members of the diverse emigrant organisations, but in the highly secret and dedicated efforts of the proletarian revolutionaries grouped round Marx. Berlin's chief of police, Hinckeldey, wrote in a secret report in April 1852: "It can now rightly be said of the Marx-Engels Party that it stands far above all the emigrants, agitators and central committees, because it is unquestionably the strongest in knowledge and ability. Marx himself is well known personally, and everyone realises that he has more intellectual power in the tip of his finger than the rest of the crowd have in their heads." [1]

The Prussian government decided to stage a trial at Cologne of the arrested members of the Communist League on a charge of participation in a "conspiracy having the character of high treason". The trial was deliberately organised on a large scale, for the Prussian authorities intended to use it as a pretext for stamping out the workers' organisations and the democratic and even the liberal opposition.

Its main organiser was Stieber, a police official, but some very high-ranking persons, including the King of Prussia himself, had a hand in staging it. Stieber and his men were given the task of producing forged evidence of the guilt of the accused, and Stieber worked in close contact with the chiefs of police in France and other countries. In London, his secret assignments were carried out by a group of spies: among them Greiff, an attaché at the Prussian Embassy, Fleury, a merchant, and Hirsch, a commercial-house clerk. Prominent Communists resident in London were kept under strict watch. In December 1851, Hirsch managed to find his way into the London District of the Communist League, but was soon suspected of having connections with the police and expelled with ignominy. Marx and his friends tightened up their security, and altered the time and place of the League's weekly meetings.

The police provocateurs' job was made easier by the reckless behaviour of the Willich-Schapper group and the carelessness they displayed in looking after Party documents and keeping Party secrets. In the summer of 1851, a Prussian police agent managed to get away with the *Sonderbund*'s archives in London. In the autumn of that year, the Prussian and the French police jointly fabricated in Paris a case about the "German-French conspiracy" involving persons belonging to the *Sonderbund*. On the strength of these facts and the stolen documents, the police and the organs of inquiry issued the charge that the followers of Marx and those of Willich were at odds over personal matters only, and that they had a common tactical

---

[1] K. Obermann, *Zur Geschichte des Bundes der Kommunisten 1849 bis 1852*, Berlin, 1955, S. 92.

platform, so that the Cologne defendants would be held responsible for all the statements and documents of the Willich-Schapper group.

Moreover, the Prussian police ordered Hirsch, together with Fleury and Greiff, to forge a Minute Book of meetings of the Central Authority of the Communist League which they alleged had been set up by Marx in London following the arrest of the Cologne Central Authority members. On the strength of the inventions contained in this "original Minute Book", the Prussian police and judiciary were hoping to prove that the threads of imaginary anti-government plots in Germany could be traced to Marx in London.

The trial of eleven Communists at Cologne did not begin until October 4, 1852, after all the forged evidence had been collected.

After learning of the arrest of the Communists, Marx kept a close watch on the proceedings against his comrades, maintaining constant contact with Germany and receiving regular information about their condition from Adolph Bermbach, a Cologne lawyer, who was to be a witness for the defence. For months, Marx, Engels and their associates worked hard to help the accused and to expose the foul methods and arbitrary acts of the Prussian government and police. On December 1, 1851, Marx sent a number of statements to the press in Paris, but these were not published because of the Bonapartist coup the following day. At the end of January 1852, Marx and Engels sent a letter to the bourgeois newspapers, *The Times* and *The Daily News*, giving the facts about the harsh treatment of the accused and the unlawful acts of the Prussian judicial authorities, who had ordered a new inquiry even after a judicial ruling that the evidence did not warrant a bill of indictment. However, this letter was not published either.

Marx acted most vigorously in support of his Party comrades when they were brought before a jury in the court at Cologne. Marx and Engels finally succeeded in exposing the Prussian authorities publicly: on October 28-30, five English newspapers carried their statement, also signed by Wilhelm Wolff and Freiligrath, which branded the trial as a series of "police tricks, perjury, forgery of documents, falsification of dates, thefts, etc., unprecedented even in the records of Prussian political justice".[1]

During the trial, the defence of the accused was, for all practical purposes, concentrated in the hands of Marx, who wrote almost daily to Engels about the most effective ways of helping the Cologne Communists. Marx displayed great inventiveness and outstanding ability as a revolutionary conspirator in organising the dispatch to Cologne of evidence refuting the charges against the accused, despite the numerous obstacles and secret surveillance by the Prussian police. Aware that all his correspondence was being scrutinised, and some confiscated, Marx sent his letters with the necessary material and documents via Frankfurt, Düsseldorf, Paris and other cities,

---

[1] Marx, Engels, *Collected Works*, Vol. 11, p. 378.

frequently dispatching several copies to make sure that the letter got through. In order to confuse the police sleuths, he sent many letters as commercial correspondence to addresses provided by Engels, frequently not from London but from Manchester and other cities. In this way, Marx kept his friends in Cologne who were at liberty supplied with documents, which provided the defence with the means of exposing the whole system of foul methods used to fabricate the charges. In this way he in fact determined the conduct of the defence at the trial.

The atmosphere of high tension in which Marx spent the five weeks of the trial was described by Jenny in a letter of October 28, 1852 to Adolf Cluss, a member of the Communist League who had emigrated to the U.S.A. She wrote: "As you can imagine, the 'Marx party' is busy day and night and is having to throw itself into the work body and soul... A complete office has now been set up in our house. Two or three people writing, others running errands, others scraping pennies together so that writers may continue to exist and provide proof of the most outrageous scandals ever perpetrated by the old world of officialdom. Add to this the singing and whistling of my three rollicking children, who now and again get a scolding from their strict old dad."[1]

Marx saw through to the inner workings and secret mainsprings of the trial, although the Prussian government kept most of the charges in strict secrecy until they were presented in court. He at once put his finger on the most vulnerable spots of the indictment at which he aimed his devastating counter-blow. As soon as he received the German papers reporting fresh facts about the trial, Marx wrote to the lawyers to give them his ideas and the necessary information.

To help the defence rebut the charges that the accused were involved in a conspiracy, Marx told the lawyer, Schneider II, how he could distinguish the Communist League's documents from those of the *Sonderbund*, and show their fundamental difference. He sent evidence to Cologne proving that the accused and the Communist League as a whole had absolutely nothing to do with the so-called German-French conspiracy. He believed the most important thing was to expose the forgery of the "original Minute Book", which Stieber presented in court on October 23 as the main evidence for the prosecution. Marx helped the lawyers to prove that it was a base forgery by putting at their disposal a number of documents, including facsimiles of the handwriting of Hirsch, the man who had actually forged the records, and the facsimiles of the handwriting of the League members, Liebknecht and Rings, who were alleged by Stieber to have taken down the minutes in question. Thanks to Marx, Stieber and the other organisers of the trial were virtually driven into a corner by the defence lawyers, and the Public Prosecu-

---

[1] Marx and Engels, *Selected Correspondence*, p. 247.

tor, Saedt, was forced to admit openly that the Minute Book was "unauthentic".

Marx and Engels helped the defence to rebut completely the absurd charges made against the arrested Communists, charges which it had taken the Prussian police and judicial authorities 18 months to concoct. Marx said the accusatory material sent from London to Cologne had helped to lay a countermine which was to explode the whole government fraud.

Nevertheless, despite the absence of incriminating evidence, most of the accused were found guilty on November 12, 1852. As Marx wrote, they had in fact been convicted in advance because they represented "the revolutionary proletariat" who "stood defenceless before the ruling classes who were represented by the jury".[1] To make sure that the Communists were not acquitted, the government installed a handpicked jury consisting of six reactionary Junkers, four members of the financial aristocracy, and two senior civil servants—a panel unprecedented in the history of the Rhine Province. Seven of the accused were sentenced to various terms of imprisonment in a fortress: Bürgers, Nothjung and Röser to six years, Reiff, Otto and Becker to five years, and Lessner to three. Four—Daniels, Klein, Jacobi and Erhardt—were acquitted.

After the trial a committee was set up in London on Marx's initiative to provide material assistance to the prisoners and their families. It included many of Marx's associates. On behalf of the committee, Marx wrote an appeal to the workers of the United States on December 7, 1852, saying that it was the duty of every class-conscious worker to help ease the lot of the proletariat's front-ranking fighters.

Marx also felt it to be his party duty to write a special pamphlet exposing the methods used by the Prussian state in fighting the communist movement. The idea had first occurred to him during the trial. He began writing it at the end of October and completed it in early December 1852. He called his sharply satirical pamphlet *Revelations Concerning the Communist Trial in Cologne*, and had to write it in especially trying circumstances because he and his family were suffering from exceptional privation at the time. In a covering letter of December 7, 1852 to Adolf Cluss, who was to publish the pamphlet in the United States, Marx wrote: "You will appreciate the humour of the brochure better when you realise that its author is as good as interned because he lacks pants and shoes and that, moreover, *his family* risked and still risks being plunged into *really distressing poverty*. The trial dragged me even deeper into penury, for I had to spend five weeks working for the party against the government's machinations, instead of earning some money. In addition, it has totally estranged the German booksellers with whom I had hoped to sign a contract for my *Political Economy*."[2]

[1] Marx, Engels, *Collected Works*, Vol. 11, p. 457.
[2] K. Marx, F. Engels, *Letters to Americans*, p. 51.

The pamphlet was published in Basle in January 1853, but in March almost the whole printing (2,000 copies) was confiscated by the police at the Baden border village of Weill, as it was being transported to Germany. In the United States it was first serialised in the democratic Boston newspaper *Neu-England-Zeitung*, and was issued by the paper's publishers as a separate pamphlet at the end of April 1853. However, the Boston edition, which was fairly well known among the German emigrant workers in the U.S.A., could not be widely circulated in Germany at the time, and became available to a mass readership there only after it was reprinted in 1875.

Marx wrote his pamphlet not only as an impassioned fighter taking a courageous stand in defence of the proletarian party's honour, but also as a stern prosecutor of those who had staged the fraudulent trial and had subjected the leading men of the working class to police harassment. He exposed the criminal acts of those who had actually organised the prosecution of the Communists, and pilloried the Prussian state with its police and bureaucratic regime. He proved that Prussian justice was biased, and that the bourgeois jury was "a court-martial of the privileged classes; it was created to bridge the gaps in the law with the broad bourgeois conscience"[1].

Prior to the Cologne Communist Trial, Marx had been unable for reasons of secrecy to make any public statements about the differences with the Willich-Schapper group. Now that the fact of the split had come out in the reports of the trial, he was no longer so constrained and in his pamphlet showed that the group expressed the petty-bourgeois frame of mind and voluntarist and dogmatic views, and that its adventurist and conspiratorial tactics were harming the working-class movement, alienating it from the masses and creating favourable conditions for all manner of police provocations.

COMMUNIST LEAGUE DISSOLVED.
NEW FORMS OF STRUGGLE FOR A PARTY

The arrests of the Communist League members and the Cologne Trial virtually marked an end to the League as an organisation in Germany and other countries on the continent.

As reaction gained ground, Marx and Engels realised that the Communist League had worked itself out and that there was no point in trying to continue it in its old form. A meeting of the League's London District on November 17, 1852 adopted, on Marx's initiative, a decision to dissolve the local organisation, and announced that it considered the further continuation of the League on the continent to be equally purposeless. This marked the winding up of the League's activity as an organisation, although some of its communities and groups continued to exist for some time in some parts of Europe and the U.S.A.

---

[1] Marx, Engels, *Collected Works*, Vol. 11, p. 457.

However, Marx believed that the dissolution of the Communist League did not mean an end to the effort to bring together forward-looking proletarians in a revolutionary party, and that in the new situation party activity should run along the lines of preserving and fostering the cadres of the proletariat's revolutionary fighters, strengthening their ties with the working-class organisations where they still functioned, and taking every opportunity to spread scientific communism. Those were the tasks to which Marx and Engels now dedicated themselves.

For all the merits of the Communist League, Marx certainly did not insist that it was a model proletarian party organisation for all time. Its general programme, its tactical and many of its organisational principles were of lasting importance, but on the whole it reflected the effort to set up a proletarian party at the early stage of the proletarian emancipation movement, when the movement was still immature ideologically and weak organisationally, and when it was not the worker of the big industrial enterprise but the artisan-journeyman in the process of becoming a worker that was still its leading member. All of this largely explains why it had a small membership (not more than 400). Marx and Engels had repeatedly failed in their attempts to turn it into the nucleus of a broader, and more solid and influential proletarian organisation. But it marked the first and perhaps the most difficult step in the establishment of the proletarian party as the true vanguard of the working class giving a lead to the broad proletarian masses, a goal that was itself still to be achieved. Ahead lay long and persistent struggle to attain it in the forms and with the means that corresponded to the new historical conditions.

Marx, Engels and their followers continued this effort, with the Communist League's ideological legacy as a basis, tirelessly emphasising the League's outstanding role in the history of the proletariat's emancipation struggle, and the bonds of continuity between its activity and the subsequent advance of the working-class movement. It was the proletariat's first political organisation, which at the dawn of the working-class movement proclaimed the principles of scientific communism as its ideological banner, and began to spread it among the proletarians. For its programme, it had the immortal *Manifesto of the Communist Party*, and the spread of its ideas helped the League to pave the way for the subsequent advances in the proletarian struggle.

The Communist League, the first historical form of proletarian party, which emerged on the basis of scientific communism and marked the start of its integration with the working-class movement, was the forerunner of the large-scale revolutionary workers' and communist organisations which were set up later. The League not only brought together German workers, but sparked off the unity of the advanced proletarian forces on an international scale, with the most progressive revolutionary doctrine as its platform. It was the first international communist organisation of the proletariat, the forerunner of the First International.

The Communist League played a great part in fostering the first nucleus of proletarian revolutionaries. Engels wrote that the League had been an excellent schooling in political activity for those taking part in the revolutionary struggle. From its ranks came a number of men who later led the International.

Marx and Engels themselves benefited greatly from their activity in the Communist League, for it gave them an opportunity to display their great gifts as strategists and tacticians in the proletarian struggle, and helped them to gain in stature as organisers and propagandists. Marx's leadership of the first communist organisation of the working class, like his participation in the revolutionary events in 1848 and 1849, added immensely to his experience in life and politics and helped him very soon to put himself at the head of a mass international proletarian movement.

CHAPTER SEVEN

YEARS OF REACTION

> *In times that were most peaceful, seemingly "idyllic", as Marx expressed it,... Marx was able to sense the approach of revolution and to* rouse *the proletariat to a consciousness of its advanced revolutionary tasks.*
>
> V. I. Lenin

OPPRESSED BY REACTION AND PENURY

Rampant reaction reigned in Europe during the 1850s. Absolutist regimes had been re-established in many states, supplemented here and there, as in Prussia, with deformed relics of representative institutions. The democratic and working-class press had been stamped out and workers' associations destroyed. The proletariat had been deprived of any legal possibility of uniting its forces. It was "publicly debarred, *igni et aqua*, from writing, speaking and meeting".[1]

The triumph of reaction on the continent also left its mark on domestic life in bourgeois-aristocratic England, where two ruling parties—the Whigs and the Tories—fiercely resisted any progressive change. They did not dare to attack the right of asylum for political emigrants openly, but kept them in fear of being handed over to their despotic governments. Many of these emigrants were under police surveillance, and the reactionary press depicted them as dangerous malefactors.

Marx himself felt the tight grip of reaction. He was unable to address the proletarian masses on the continent through the revolutionary press, which had been muzzled almost everywhere, with the exception of England. He had no money to put out a periodical of his own, and contacts with revolutionary workers and fellow-thinkers in other countries were made extremely difficult. The publication of major works, always very difficult because of police harassment, now became altogether impossible. After Becker's unsuccessful attempt to publish a collection of Marx's works in 1850—Becker had managed to publish only a volume containing Marx's two articles for 1842—there followed a long period in which the publishers refused to touch anything written by Marx.

For a long time Marx had no regular income at all, and this was an exceptionally hard period for the Marx family. Engels shared

---

[1] Marx, Engels, *Collected Works*, Vol. 11, p. 446.

what he had, but that was precious little, for he was then only a clerk at the Manchester office of Ermen & Engels. Not until the summer of 1851 did Marx become a correspondent for the *New-York Daily Tribune*, but his earnings were small and irregular and he was unable to pay off his debts or provide adequately for his family.

For years Marx lived in utter destitution. There was sometimes not a spare penny in the house, so the family had to go without newspapers, writing paper, stamps, medicine and doctors. Sometimes Marx was unable to go out because his coat and trousers were in pawn. The family was short of almost everything and used to live for weeks on bread and potatoes. His creditors made his life a misery, threatening to send in the bailiffs to distrain his personal belongings.

Marx suffered greatly making futile efforts to improve his family's lot and obtain the bare necessities, wasting a great deal of time to settle his monetary affairs, obtaining loans in expectation of forthcoming royalties, and deferring payments. At one such very trying moment, he wrote: "I would not wish my worst enemy to have to wade through the quagmire in which I've been trapped for the past two months, fuming the while over the innumerable vexations that are ruining my intellect and destroying my capacity for work." [1]

The family lived in very poor conditions because for a long time Marx could not afford to lease any tolerable premises. From the autumn of 1849 to April 1850, they were crowded in a small flat at 4 Anderson Street in Chelsea in south-west London. Marx's fourth child, his son Heinrich Guido, was born there on November 5, 1849. The landlady arbitrarily cancelled the lease when her demand for the immediate payment of the rent arrears was not met, and the family had to move out in truly tragic circumstances. In a letter to Weydemeyer of May 20, 1850, Jenny wrote: "Since this [2] was not ready to hand, ... two bailiffs entered the house and placed under distraint what little I possessed — beds, linen, clothes, everything, even my poor infant's cradle, and the best of the toys belonging to the girls, who burst into tears. They threatened to take everything away within 2 hours — leaving me lying on the bare boards with my shivering children and my sore breast." [3]

Marx managed to obtain some money from his friends to settle with his landlady, thereby securing the release of his possessions, but these were immediately sold to pay off his various small debts to the chemist, the baker, the butcher and other creditors.

The Marx family found a temporary refuge at a German hotel in Leicester Street. In early June 1850 they moved to 64 Dean Street and then, in December 1850, to a small two-room flat at number 28. This was in the densely populated quarter of Soho, which was not

---

[1] Ibid., Vol. 40, p. 331.
[2] The money to be paid to the landlady.
[3] Marx, Engels, *Collected Works*, Vol. 38, p. 557.

famous for its amenities, and was one of the main breeding grounds of cholera during the 1854 epidemic. Many French and Italian emigrants lived in the area and there, in damp and crowded premises, Marx and his family spent almost six years. The front room served as study, living room and dining room, and the back room as bedroom for the whole family. Only in the autumn of 1856, when Jenny received a small legacy from her late mother, were they able to rent a small cottage in a north-west suburb of London. There, at 9 (subsequently 46) Grafton Terrace, Maitland Park, Haverstock Hill, a somewhat better part of London, the family lived until March 1864. The area was just being built up, however. It was littered with rubbish, there was no lighting, and on rainy days the dirty roads became impassable.

Marx's titanic effort and his constant fight against privation undermined his health, and disease wedded to poverty, bad food and constant worry was a frequent visitor to the family. Marx himself began to suffer from inflammation of the eyes and rheumatism, and in March 1853 developed a liver complaint. His wife and children were very often ill.

Soon there were losses in the family. Only three of the seven children survived. The one-year-old Heinrich Guido died of pneumonia on November 19, 1850, and Franziska, born on March 28, 1851, died less than eighteen months later, on April 14, 1852, just when the family was plunged in extreme distress. A warm-hearted French emigrant helped to pay for the coffin and the funeral expenses. Jenny gave birth to another child in early July 1857, but it died at birth.

The most painful blow for Marx was the death on April 6, 1855 of eight-year-old Edgar. He had been a gifted and friendly boy, with an inquiring mind, the favourite of the family, known as "Little Sparrow"—Musch—and Marx and Engels frequently called him Colonel Musch. In the spring of 1855, Edgar developed a grave gastric complaint, and from then on Marx and Jenny lived in a virtual nightmare, alternating between hope and despair, depending on the child's state. When Edgar died the whole family was in a state of shock. Marx wrote to Engels: "I've already had my share of bad luck but only now do I know what real unhappiness is." [1]

The sufferings of Marx and his family were due mainly to the cruelty of the bourgeois world, which had doomed a great revolutionary thinker to a life of destitution. Mehring wrote: "For such a genius bourgeois society has nothing but sufferings and tortures still more cruel than the punishments of antiquity or the stake of the Middle Ages though outwardly they may appear less brutal." [2]

Marx bore all these trials with a truly heroic stoicism and nothing could make him swerve from his path. He remained true to his lifetime goal. In August 1866, he wrote to Paul Lafargue, who was later

---

[1] Marx, Engels, *Collected Works*, Vol. 39, p. 533.
[2] Franz Mehring, *Karl Marx, Geschichte seines Lebens*, Berlin, 1964, S. 229.

to marry one of his daughters: "You know that I have sacrificed my whole fortune to the revolutionary struggle. I do not regret it. Quite the contrary. If I had to begin my life over again, I would do the same." But he added: "I would not marry, however." [1]

There is a genuine humanism, spiritual grandeur and nobility in these words: "I laugh at the so-called 'practical' men and their wisdom. If one wanted to be an ox, one could, of course, turn one's back on the sufferings of humanity and look after one's hide." [2] Marx was sustained in all his personal trials and misfortunes by the lofty idea of service to toiling mankind.

MARX IN THE FAMILY CIRCLE

Although the sufferings of his nearest and dearest caused Marx much anguish, he never regarded his family as a burden, but as his mainstay in the struggle, a source not only of care, but also of much joy. Marx was a profoundly happy family man. Whatever the circumstances, a spirit of optimism, an atmosphere of complete mutual trust, warm-heartedness and cordiality to their friends always prevailed in the family, mainly because of the example set by the parents.

Jenny's fine character was most fully revealed in the difficult circumstances of life in emigration. She was not only a considerate friend to her husband and a loving mother and tutor to their children, who skilfully guided their development and the moulding of their character and taste, but also a loyal fellow-fighter sharing Marx's convictions and displaying a better understanding than most of his friends of the greatness of his ideas and creative schemes. In her reminiscences, Jenny wrote of the tremendous satisfaction she derived from reading and copying her husband's manuscripts. In addition, she also handled his correspondence.

Marx remained very much in love with his "charming, dear and only" Jenny like a young man. When she went from Manchester to Trier to see her mother, who was on her deathbed, she received a letter which her husband wrote to her on June 21, 1856. It said: "There are, indeed, many women in the world, and a few of them are beautiful. But where else shall I find a face of which every lineament, every line even, reawakens the greatest and sweetest memories of my life? In your sweet countenance I can read even my infinite sorrows, my irreplaceable losses, and when I kiss your sweet face I kiss away my sorrow." [3]

The misfortunes and calamities of Marx's life, and his truly heroic endeavour did cause white strands to appear in his jet black hair, but this did nothing to change his generous and buoyant nature. His

---

[1] Marx, Engels, *Collected Works*, Vol. 42, p. 308.
[2] Ibid., p. 366.
[3] Ibid., Vol. 40, p. 56.

daughter Eleanor had good reason to say that nothing was more ridiculous than the story depicting as stern and haughty Jupiter Fulgur, "the cheeriest, gayest soul that ever breathed, ... a man brimming over with humour and good-humour, whose hearty laugh was infectious and irresistible, ... the kindliest, gentlest, most sympathetic of companions".[1]

Children brought out all his warmth and kindness, and Wilhelm Liebknecht recalled that "Marx could not do without the society of chidren, which was his rest and refreshment".[2] His readiest sympathies were with the children of the poor, and on his innumerable visits to working-class neighbourhoods he was always upset by the sight of the underprivileged and ragged children. He sought to put heart into them by showing them some little kindness and making them happy, if only for a little while.

His own children Marx loved with heart and soul, and he was never irked by their presence, whether he was at his writing desk or resting after a hard day. He was not irritated by their scuffles, laughter or noisy games, in which he himself often joined, falling in with the general mood of merriment like a child himself. One of their most popular games was "cavalry", when the girls sat astride their father's back, or "omnibus", when they "harnessed" him to the chairs. "Sea battles" between squadrons of paper ships were fought out in a basinful of water. But the most memorable events, for the children and the grownups, were the Sunday outings to Hampstead Heath, a rugged sandy heathland spreading over the hills and valleys of a verdant range, to which the whole family repaired in the company of a few close friends. These were occasions for boisterous contests — races, wrestling, throwing stones to knock down the ripest chestnuts from the trees, and so on. On one occasion, Marx joined in the stone throwing with such gusto that he was afterwards unable to use his right arm for a whole week. As the girls grew up, the games became more sophisticated: chess and comic questionnaires, with the answers requiring considerable intellectual powers.

Marx loved reading aloud to his children and telling them fairy-tales and funny stories, frequently of his own invention. His fairy-tales sometimes developed into whole cycles. The hero of one of them was Hans Röckle, a sorcerer, who owned a toy-shop and who, for all his magic art, was unable to settle his debts and had to give his toys away to his creditors. However, after numerous remarkable adventures, his toys eventually returned to his shop. Marx's small audience was enchanted by the humour and poetic quality of these fairy-tales, which conveyed in symbolic form the vagaries of the story-teller's own life and expressed a winning faith in the triumph of good over evil.

---

[1] *Reminiscences of Marx and Engels*, p. 250.
[2] Ibid., p. 116.

The children grew up to be avid readers, for Karl and Jenny had introduced them to the great classics, by opening up before them the magic world of the fairy-tales of the Grimm brothers, Hoffmann, and *The Thousand and One Nights*, Homer's poems, and the medieval legends recounted in the *Song of the Nibelungs* and *Gudrun*. Among the family's favourite writers and poets were Aeschylus and Sophocles, Dante, Cervantes and Goethe, Fielding and Robert Burns, Balzac, Heine and Freiligrath, Rückert and Chamisso. Shakespeare was revered above all the others, and the girls knew by heart whole scenes from his plays. Like Marx himself, the rest of the family loved adventure stories and historical novels, particularly those by Walter Scott, Captain Marryat and Alexander Dumas.

As a father, Marx was gentle and indulgent. He commanded a rare obedience in his children without resorting to his parental authority. He never allowed himself to neglect his children or to ignore their childish worries. For them he was a friend and an older comrade who could always be relied upon for sound advice. Like everyone else in the family, he had a nickname, being known as the Moor because of his swarthy complexion.

The children were brought up to tell the truth and hate falsehood and hypocrisy. The whole family sympathised with the fighters for freedom and yearned to take part in their struggle.

Everyone was delighted with the accomplishments of Jenny and Laura, the two elder daughters. They both won prizes at school, wrote fine essays in English, which had become their mother tongue, spoke French very well, and read Dante in the original. But for all their parents' efforts they had a hard time with their German. Jenny was good at drawing, and many of her pictures were pinned up on the walls, while Laura had a great inclination for music and singing.

Eleanor (Tussy), the youngest daughter, born on January 16, 1855 shortly before Edgar's death, was the family favourite. The affection the elder sisters had had for their dead brother now went to Tussy, a vivacious, playful girl, who was very fond of games and who amazed everyone by her precocious flights of fancy.

Helene Demuth continued to be a full-fledged member of the family, and life in exile fully brought out her affection and loyalty to the family and her miraculous skill in cooking, sewing, mending, darning, keeping the house in order and even creating some comforts with the family's highly limited resources. Marx believed that Helene was endowed with genuine organisational and administrative talent. He used to say "that under reasonable conditions of society she would have been as invaluable to society as she was in a small way to us".[1] A great lover of chess, he would often play with Helene, and now and again be beaten.

---

[1] Letter of Eleanor Marx to Wilhelm Liebknecht, March 12, 1896 (Central Party Archives of the Institute of Marxism-Leninism).

A FRIENDSHIP FORTIFIED IN TRIBULATION

Marx was despondent at being unable to see Engels every day, and wrote: "The only thing that vexes me is our not being able to be together now, to work and have fun together." [1] But their joint creative endeavours were never interrupted, and spiritually their life was one. The creative efforts of the one constantly supplemented, and frequently made up for, the scientific quest of the other. They shared the results of their research in their letters and, of course, at their infrequent meetings.

They continued to collaborate both in science and party affairs, informing each other of their contacts with working-class leaders. They also continued to write together, but not as they once used to, sitting at the same table and working on the same piece of writing. Now they had to formulate a common standpoint, topic and plan for their work, and each as a rule dealt with the subject he knew best. Now and again Marx would incorporate what Engels had written into some report of his, or one of the friends would edit and put the finishing touches to what the other had written.

This was a period which fully proved Engels' devotion as a friend, his selflessness and ready sympathy. His remittances arrived from Manchester whenever the family found itself in a tight spot. Engels wanted Marx to go on with his economic research, and took over a large part of his journalistic duties. His concern for the Marx family was evident in all things, great and small: he took care of their debts, and sent Christmas presents to the children, and fruit and wine to anyone who fell ill. His visits to London caused great jubilation in the family. Engels always looked forward to Marx's visits to Manchester, and it was there that Karl and Jenny found refuge after the death of their son in the spring of 1855.

Marx valued their friendship very highly. He treated Engels' worries as his own, and was most upset when his friend was ill. Thus, he wrote on September 21, 1857: "Nothing could please me more than to hear that your health is progressing." [2] Marx resented the fact that in order to help his family, and for other mundane reasons, Engels had to waste so much time at the office and do his research at odd moments. Marx was always delighted to help his friend in any small way, such as obtaining a book he needed, making an extract from some rare source, or collecting some information in London.

The two men preferred deeds to verbal expressions of friendly feeling, and this added weight to the heartfelt words of gratitude they pronounced in time of strong emotion. The day Marx's son died in his arms, he wrote to Engels: "I shall never forget how much your friendship has helped to make this ghastly time easier to us." [3] After his son's funeral, he added in a letter dated April 12: "Amid all

---

[1] Marx, Engels, *Collected Works*, Vol. 39, p. 403.
[2] Ibid., Vol. 40, p. 173.
[3] Ibid., Vol. 39, p. 530.

the fearful torments I have recently had to endure, the thought of you and your friendship has always sustained me, as has the hope that there is still something sensible for us to do together in the world."[1]

The relations between the two men were based on high principles and complete sincerity. They always told each other the truth in all things, large and small. Neither was obstinate when proved wrong. Marx found his friendship with Engels invaluable in his scientific endeavour, and in the whole of his life and struggle.

ECONOMIC RESEARCHES

Once settled as an exile in London, Marx resumed his economic studies, which had been interrupted by the 1848-49 revolution. From the spring of 1850, he once again immersed himself, with exceptional persistence and purposefulness, in the study of political economy.

He set himself the task of exploring the mechanism behind the movement of capitalist society and giving the proletariat a clear understanding of the laws which lay at the basis of this movement and which worked for the destruction of the capitalist system. Once again he considered writing a large work on political economy.

He now took a more mature view of the subject than he had before the revolution. He was also aware of the importance of studying the new economic facts which had come to light during the revolution and especially in the first few years after it. His work was greatly facilitated by the fact that he had settled in London, which was then the centre of the capitalist world and presented a "convenient vantage point for the observation of bourgeois society".[2] The most diverse information about the state of industry and agriculture in England and many other countries, the condition of the domestic and foreign markets, banking and the stock exchange flowed to London as the capital of the most developed capitalist state and the largest colonial empire. Marx was able to work regularly at the British Museum, one of the world's major libraries, founded in 1753 and containing a rich collection of literature, rare books and publications not available elsewhere.

Marx worked intensely and with great vigour. Almost every day he was to be seen in the reading room of the British Museum from 9.00 a.m. to 7.00 p.m., going through stacks of books and other material. For years he would work there in the daytime, continuing his studies at home in the evenings, and frequently at night.

The material on which Marx had to work was "so damnably involved".[3] From the summer of 1850 to August 1853, he filled 24

---

[1] Ibid., p. 533.
[2] Ibid., Vol. 29, p. 264.
[3] Ibid., Vol. 38, p. 377.

notebooks of extracts from the bourgeois economists, official documents and periodicals. These show that he made a profound and comprehensive study of the theoretical problems of political economy, the history of the national economy, and the economics of the contemporary capitalist world.

Marx also found it necessary to cover some fields of natural science and engineering. Thus, while studying land rent, he dealt with agronomical sciences, particularly agro-chemistry. That is when he made a summary of the book *Chemistry in Application to Agriculture and Physiology* by the outstanding German scientist Justus von Liebig, and other works in this field. Marx also sought to acquaint himself with the technological side of capitalist production, and kept abreast of technical inventions and scientific discoveries. He went to the World Industrial Exhibition held in London in 1851, displaying especial interest in technical advances, notably, the new raw materials (guttapercha), machinery and technological processes. His profound understanding of the importance of technical progress in the evolution of capitalist production induced him to make a deep study of the history of the applied sciences. He made use of various aids, among them the works of the German technologist and economist Johann Beckmann and the historian of science and engineering Johann Poppe, and Ure's *Dictionary of Arts, Manufactures and Mines*. In his 1851-53 extracts, Marx reproduced a picture of the application of physics, mathematics and other sciences to the various types of production over a period of several centuries.

Marx frequently reread books he had first read in the 1840s. He wrote a new summary of Ricardo's *On the Principles of Political Economy and Taxation*, making some very profound conclusions and critical remarks. He also gained a more profound understanding of the role of the classic economists in developing economic theory, both in their achievements and their historically rooted limitations.

Marx explicitly stressed Ricardo's scientific superiority over Smith, an economist of the manufactory period, whose relative inadequacy of scientific concepts and inconsistency in applying the principle of labour-value stemmed from the low development of social relations at that time. Ricardo, however, wrote at a time when capitalist relations were more mature, so his views were more mature and consistent than those of Smith. In his new summary Marx wrote: "The important thing about Ricardo is that, whereas even Adam Smith and Say still take a *definite product* of labour to be the regulator, he everywhere takes labour, activity, industry itself, not the product but production, the act of creation. Hence the whole epoch of bourgeois industry." [1]

The aggravation of capitalist contradictions and the sharpening of the class struggle induced the ideologists of the bourgeoisie to re-

---

[1] K. Marx, *Grundrisse der Kritik der politischen Ökonomie (Rohentwurf) 1857-1858*, Berlin, 1953, S. 808.

ject Smith's and Ricardo's conclusions and traditions in the field of political economy. The labour theory of value propounded by Smith and Ricardo was in particular the target of general attack. This amounted to vulgarising economic science, and in a letter to Engels of April 2, 1851, Marx said: "*Au fond*,[1] this science has made no progress since A. Smith and D. Ricardo, however much has been done in the way of individual research, often extremely discerning."[2]

Already pronounced though not yet clearly formulated in Marx's statements at this time was the distinction he drew between the classic school of bourgeois political economy and its vulgar trend, bearing the mark of degeneration and downright subservience to capital.

A large part of Marx's extracts dealt with the theory of money and the circulation of money. In 1851, after consolidating and systematically arranging his notes on this problem, Marx produced a short rough manuscript (about 3.5 printed sheets) which he entitled "The Complete Monetary System".[3] Money epitomises the contradictory nature of the capitalist world, being connected with such categories as commodity, value, price, cost of production, and so on, an understanding of which must be attained for any correct scientific examination and analysis of capitalism as a whole.

In effect, Marx refuted Ricardo's quantitative theory of money. Going beyond his own view of a few years earlier, Marx no longer regarded the value of money as being a magnitude derivative from the quantity of money in circulation. On the contrary, he believed that the quantity of money itself depended on the sum-total of the prices of commodities being exchanged through the medium of money. In a letter to Engels of February 3, 1851, he argued that the quantity of money in circulation was not regulated by the ebb and flow of precious metals, as Ricardo, Lloyd and many other theorists and practitioners of finance and banking had believed, but by the state of industry and trade. Marx said: "The *circulation* would *only* rise if business increased to the extent that additional currency was required to conduct it.... Its increase is ultimately the *consequence* of a greater amount of capital put to use, not vice versa."[4] Engels agreed with this view and felt that this approach would help to "go a long way towards reducing the crazy theory of circulation to simple and lucid fundamental facts".[5]

In his economic summaries of 1851-53, Marx gained a deeper understanding of the substance of capital. He made the following observation concerning Ricardo's view of capital as that part of the country's wealth which is applied for the purpose of future production and can be increased in the same way as wealth itself: "Here Ri-

---

[1] Basically.
[2] Marx, Engels, *Collected Works*, Vol. 38, p. 325.
[3] Central Party Archives of the Institute of Marxism-Leninism.
[4] Marx, Engels, *Collected Works*, Vol. 38, p. 275.
[5] Ibid., p. 299.

cardo confuses capital with the *material* of capital. Wealth is only the material of capital. Capital is always the *sum-total of values* which is again designated for production, a sum not only of products nor even for the production of products, but a sum for the production of values."[1]

These and other statements show clearly the fundamentally different views of capital taken by Ricardo and by Marx. According to Ricardo, capital is a simple sum of things, and according to Marx, capital is a definite social relation, one which is characteristic of a definite historical stage of commodity production.

For the time being, in his polemics with Ricardo, Marx merely outlined the way towards the scientific discovery of the secret of capitalist enrichment, in other words, the approaches to formulating the theory of surplus-value. He wrote: "Bourgeois wealth and the purpose of all bourgeois production is *exchange-value* and not consumption. In order to increase this exchange-value, there is no other means — reciprocal swindling apart — but to multiply the products, to produce more.... However, the purpose of bourgeois production has *never* been the increased production of commodities, but the increased production of *values*."[2]

Marx refuted the vulgar bourgeois theories that profit results solely from the skilful distribution and redistribution of an "aggregate surplus" within the class of capitalist proprietors. Before any sharing out can be done, it is essential to have something that can be distributed and redistributed. The surplus itself is not to be derived from trade, although "now and again super-profits" do indeed accrue in this sphere. "The surplus does not arise in this exchange, although it is realised in it. It arises because out of this product, which costs 20 working days, the worker receives the product of only 10, etc., working days. The value of wages decreases to the same extent that the productive force of labour increases."[3] The term "surplus-value" is not yet used here, but its source, the sphere where the roots of capitalist exploitation and profits are to be found, is indicated.

Among Marx's cardinal scientific achievements of the early 1850s is his theory of rent, which he set out briefly in a letter to Engels of January 7, 1851. As he was analysing it, he came to realise that Ricardo's theory of rent was wrong and proceeded to make a fundamental review of its basic points.

Ricardo was inclined to assume that the inclusion of the worst lands in cultivation made it possible for the sum-total of rent to rise merely through an increase in the price of grain. This doctrine failed to take account of the economic consequences of scientific and technical progress, and meant acceptance of the notorious law of di-

---

[1] K. Marx, *Grundrisse der Kritik der politischen Ökonomie (Rohentwurf) 1857-1858*, S. 805.
[2] Ibid., S. 804.
[3] Ibid., S. 829.

minishing returns, which the Malthusians were spreading in an effort to blame the poverty of the mass of people on "insuperable" natural phenomena. Marx proved Ricardo's views to be wrong and, at the same time, the law of diminishing returns to be completely untenable. He showed the connection between the formation of differential rent and the development of the productive forces in agriculture, stressing that rent does not necessarily have to drop as the prices of farm products fall. In practice, rent tends to increase as prices fall with the growing productivity of agriculture.

Engels at once accepted Marx's theory and became its ardent advocate. He wrote: "You have now cleared up the matter, which is yet another reason why you must make haste to finish the Economy and get it published." [1]

From 1854 to 1856, Marx did not work as intensively on political economy, because he was very busy writing for the press and studying other scientific problems not directly connected with political economy, and also because for the time being there were still no prospects of getting his book published. In this period, among other things, he reread his summaries, "the intention being, not so much to elaborate the thing, as at any rate to master the material and get it ready to work on"; [2] he once again went over his old notebooks, adding brief comments and heading his manuscript *Money, Credit, Crises*.

By 1857, when Marx was once again intensively engaged in economic research, he had at his disposal a vast amount of background material, and had advanced so far theoretically that he was soon able to produce a real revolution in political economy.

SCIENTIFIC STUDIES IN OTHER FIELDS

Concentrating on the formulation of his new economic doctrine, Marx went to great pains to see that it took into account all the advances in human knowledge in every sphere of the social and natural sciences.

He also attached much importance to a study of the natural sciences in further substantiating the materialist world outlook and improving the dialectical-materialist method. The natural sciences, he subsequently wrote in a rough outline for his *Capital*, "constitute the basis of all knowledge". Marx was happy to see Engels devote much attention to this problem and fully approved of the latter's idea, which began to materialise in the late 1850s, of summing up in philosophic terms the advances in the natural sciences—physics, physiology, and so on.

Although all Marx's research in that period was based on the use of dialectical-materialist methods, which were thereby greatly en-

---

[1] Marx, Engels, *Collected Works*, Vol. 38, p. 271.
[2] Ibid., Vol. 39, p. 522.

riched, he lacked the time to produce special philosophical works, but he did continue to believe the further elaboration both of general and particular philosophical problems to be highly important.

In the spring of 1857, Marx devoted some time to aesthetics, intending to write an article on it. In this connection, he made a study of the fundamental work by the Hegelian Friedrich Fischer, *Aesthetics, or the Science of the Beautiful*, Eduard Müller's *A History of the Theory of Art Among the Ancients*, and other writings.

While Marx and Engels each worked in his own field, their scientific interests were largely identical and overlapping. Thus, Marx frequently dealt with the problems of military history, either for his own purposes or by way of collecting the facts for Engels, who was a great specialist in military theory and history. However, Marx made no systematic study of military history, relying fully on Engels, whom he called the "Ministry of War in Manchester".[1] Philology was another field in which Engels specialised, and there, too, Marx recognised his friend as an authority. But he himself also expressed many fundamental ideas on problems of language, and was constantly improving his own knowledge in this field. His followers later recalled one of his favourite sayings: "A foreign language is a weapon in the struggle of life."[2]

During his exile in London, Marx was in the habit of speaking, thinking and writing in three European languages: German, English and French. His excellent knowledge of Greek and Latin was a great help in his scientific research and in reading the classics. By the time he arrived in London he was also able to read Italian well, and read in the original not only Dante's *Divine Comedy*, his favourite, but also the poems of Ariosto and Bojardo, the verse of the satirist Pietro Aretino, the comedies and historical writings of Machiavelli, and the works of the 19th-century Italian writers and publicists Guerrazzi, Massimo d'Azeglio, and others. He read the works of Giordano Bruno, the great Italian thinker and martyr of science, in Italian and Latin.

In the spring of 1854, Marx began studying Spanish on his own, seeking to master it from the best Spanish classics: Calderon's *El Mágico prodigioso* and Cervantes' *Don Quixote*. Within five or six months he was able to read Spanish sources for his study of a history of Spain.

Philological research also had a bearing on Marx's economic and historical studies. Thus, he went through various philological reference works, including Du Cange's *Glossary of Medieval Latin*, in order to establish the origin and medieval use of terms like "capital", "interest", "profit", and "product".

One of his main subjects in that period was world history, to which he was impelled to refer by his approach to economic problems. His method required that logical analysis with the aid of sci-

---

[1] Marx, Engels, *Collected Works*, Vol. 39, p. 376.
[2] *Reminiscences of Marx and Engels*, p. 75.

entific abstractions should go hand in hand with analysis of the concrete historical development of the phenomenon he was studying and should rest on it. At the same time, Marx was aware of the importance of improving historical materialism by considering the development of historical science and summing up its advances. A further incentive in his historical studies was his journalistic work, and his urge to gain a deeper insight into contemporary events and to bring out their historical roots.

Now and again, depending on the lines of his work on economic theory or the needs of his writing for the press, he had to change the subjects of his historical researches but on the whole they were geared to the task of verifying the general regularities underlying the historical process, and their concrete manifestation. His attention was focussed on bourgeois society, its historical origins, its triumph over feudalism, the development of the class struggle in it, and the reflection of bourgeois ideology in historical science.

Marx vividly expressed his attitude to bourgeois historiography in a letter to Engels of July 27, 1854, when writing about a book by Augustin Thierry, one of the leading historians of the Restoration period. The book was *A History of the Formation and Progress of the Third Estate*, which held that French history was pivoted on the struggle by the third estate against the feudal aristocracy, and made a detailed examination of the rise of the free cities (communes), the cradle of the French bourgeoisie. Marx called Thierry "*le père* [the father] of the 'class struggle' in French historiography".[1]

Marx gave Thierry his due, but used his book to show the defects of bourgeois historical writing even in its heyday. Thierry and other historians of his school had failed to reach down to the material basis of class contradictions, and had believed that foreign conquest was the main cause of society's division into classes. Marx stressed that Thierry had been wrong to identify the third estate with the bourgeoisie, and to regard it as a single class, failing to notice the origination of antagonistic contradictions within it. Thierry had revealed the narrowness and inconsistency of his views by his attempts to confine the sphere in which the law of the class struggle operated to feudal society, and by his unwillingness even to consider the nature and character of the class struggle under capitalism. Marx's critique of Thierry's views showed the profound antithesis between the revolutionary-proletarian and the liberal-bourgeois views of the class struggle.

Positivist sociology and historiography, which succeeded the Thierry school, marked a considerable step back in understanding the substance of historical processes, a fact that Marx was quick to notice. In the spring of 1853, he read some works by the English philosopher and sociologist, Herbert Spencer, a founder of positivism, notably his book *Social Statics* which already revealed the vulgar

---

[1] Marx, Engels, *Collected Works*, Vol. 39, p. 473.

tendency inherent in positivism to make a mechanical application of biological laws to social life.

Marx devoted much time to the study of precapitalist epochs, and his extracts from various books in the 1850s show that he took an interest in ancient history and the fortunes of the Celtic, Germanic and Slavonic peoples in the early Middle Ages, and in feudalism at the height of its development.

Aware of the importance of colonial policy in the past, and especially in the mid-19th century, Marx made the history of colonial conquests one of his most important subjects. In the autumn of 1851, he studied a number of books on the history of colonisation in Asia and Africa, and the Spanish conquest of Mexico and Peru. In April 1853, when he decided to expose the colonial system in the press, he began an especially intensive study of the history of the East. He read the parliamentary Blue Books and the reports of parliamentary commissions dealing with British policy in India, geographical and statistical manuals and other writings about India, China and Indonesia. He acquainted himself with the ancient and medieval history of the East from the writing of orientalists, and also read the notes of European travellers, among them François Bernier and A. D. Saltykov.

On the strength of all this Marx drew some important conclusions, notably about the material prerequisites for the emergence and essence of Islam, and in general about the class roots of religious movements in the East.

Following the examination of the social system of India, Iran and Arabia, Marx wrote to Engels on June 2, 1853 that "all the manifestations of the East" have "a common basis, namely the *absence of private property*. This is the real *clef* [key] even to the eastern heaven." [1] Marx held that the prevalence of state ownership of land was largely due to the need for artificial irrigation by the central authority. He saw the concentration of public works in the hands of a despotic state, the viability of the rural communities, their isolation and seclusion as factors which had determined the slowed-down, "static character" of development in the Asian countries. At the time when the West was moving from feudalism to capitalism, the ripening of a more advanced social order in the East slowed down, a fact which had fatal consequences. It weakened the Asian peoples' resistance to the European colonialists and led to the colonial subjugation of many Asian countries.

Marx was faced with diverse problems in formulating his revolutionary tactics in foreign policy. To sort out the historical roots of the so-called Eastern question, Marx collected extensive material on the history of the Balkan peoples in his 1853-54 notebooks, and also studied a number of published diplomatic documents, including those in the *Portfolio* almanac.

---

[1] Marx, Engels, *Collected Works*, Vol. 39, pp. 333-34.

For several months of 1856 and the first half of 1857, Marx made an especially intensive study of 18th-century Russo-English relations, collecting material from pamphlets, memoirs, foreign-policy documents and historical works on the period (such as Schlosser's *History of the 18th Century*) and works on the history of England, Sweden and Russia.

These extracts show that Marx, a resolute opponent of tsarism, was already displaying an interest in the conditions, customs, everyday life and history of the peoples of Russia. He also took an interest in the Russian people's historical and literary monuments. When he came across a French translation of the ancient Russian poem *The Lay of Igor's Campaign* in Eichhoff's *History of the Language and the Literature of the Slavs*, he remarked on the heroic, epic character of this outstanding work. He wrote to Engels on March 5, 1856: "In essence, the poem is a call for unity on the part of the Russian princes just before the invasion by the Mongol hordes proper."[1]

In this period, Marx also made a study of the history of Poland, and in early 1857 read a work on the subject by Lelewel, the democratic historian, Mieroslawski's *On the Polish Nationality within the European Equilibrium*, and other works.

As a proletarian scientist, Marx devoted special attention to the history of popular movements and revolutionary events, especially where they were interwoven with the national liberation struggle. In May and June 1854, he made a special effort to collect the facts about the Italian revolution of 1848-49 and the activity of Mazzini's followers in that period. On September 2, 1854, at the height of the revolutionary struggle which had started in Spain, he informed Engels: "My principal study is now Spain."[2] His five copious notebooks of extracts from various sources show that he studied the epoch of bourgeois revolutions in Spain in the context of the country's whole history and the international situation.

FOSTERING PROLETARIAN REVOLUTIONARIES. SAFEGUARDING REVOLUTIONARY TRADITIONS AMONG THE GERMAN WORKERS

So long as there were no practical conditions for setting up a proletarian party, Marx and Engels worked gradually to prepare the ground for it. Marx took every opportunity of keeping in touch with participants in the working-class movement and collecting information about the condition and mood of the workers and the existence of underground groups. In England and the United States, where

---

[1] Ibid., Vol. 40, p. 19.
[2] Ibid., Vol. 39, p. 480.

the working-class movement was not banned, Marx sought through his friends and associates to influence its development. He helped to start workers' periodicals and carry on the propaganda of scientific communism in these countries. In spite of all the difficulties, he worked to establish international ties between the proletarian leaders of various countries.

The first thing Marx strove to do was to exert an ideological influence on the revolutionaries fostered within the Communist League, and to induce his comrades-in-arms to use every opportunity to increase their knowledge. He worked hard to encourage his followers and associates — Liebknecht, Wolff, Eccarius, Schramm, Pfänder, Lochner, Imandt and Pieper, among others — to enlarge their mental horizons, to become steadfast revolutionaries, skilled in overcoming all the hardships, firm in spirit and confident in the triumph of the revolutionary cause. In his reminiscences of Marx Liebknecht wrote: "Study! Study! That was the categoric injunction that we heard often enough from him and that he gave us by his example and the continual work of his mighty brain." [1]

Himself in constant privation, Marx displayed tireless concern for his party friends and shared his last few pennies with them on many occasions. His home was a very modest one indeed, but frequently became a sanctuary for revolutionary emigrants. When Dr. Abraham Jacobi, one of the accused at the Cologne Communist Trial, arrived in London in June 1853, he was warmly received in the Marx home. Despite his acquittal Jacobi had been forced to go abroad for fear of a fresh arrest. Wilhelm Pieper frequently lived in Marx's house for long periods. Other emigrants kept coming and going.

Marx devoted a great deal of effort to help his comrades arrange their financial affairs and earn a living. In 1853 he tried to find a salaried correspondent's job in the United States for Eccarius, whose tailoring was proving to be a poor source of livelihood. When Eccarius had an attack of tuberculosis in February 1859 Marx pawned his wife's dresses to help him and his family. Together with Engels, Marx took care of Konrad Schramm, when he returned to England in the summer of 1857 after a futile attempt to find work in the United States and had to settle on the Island of Jersey because of the state of his health.

Marx was greatly saddened by every loss suffered by the band of early proletarian revolutionaries in the years of reaction. He grieved at the death from tuberculosis on August 29, 1855 of Roland Daniels, who had been incarcerated in a Prussian prison for 18 months during the preparations for the Cologne Trial. Marx wrote wrathfully to Engels: "He is no more nor less than a victim of the infamies of the Prussian Police." [2] Georg Weerth died of a tropical fever in Cuba on July 30, 1856, and Konrad Schramm, whom Marx had vis-

---

[1] *Reminiscences of Marx and Engels*, p. 102.
[2] Marx, Engels, *Collected Works*, Vol. 39, p. 547.

ited a short time before in Jersey, succumbed to tuberculosis in mid-January 1858.

Marx was deeply pained by evidence that some former members of the Communist League were vacillating and lapsing into philistine habits, unable to withstand the temptations of the bourgeois world. Among those who withdrew from active participation in the working-class movement was Dronke.

Intolerant of political desertions, Marx did not hesitate to break with those who had betrayed the working class. Thus, in the late 1850s and the early 1860s, once he was convinced that former members of the Communist League, Hermann Becker, Heinrich Bürgers and Johannes Miquel, had gone over to the bourgeois camp, he refused to consider them either as friends or acquaintances. However, he was tolerant and lenient with those who admitted their mistakes. In the spring of 1856, Marx was reconciled with Schapper, who had led a sectarian faction in the Communist League.

Despite all the difficulties, Marx managed to keep in touch with proletarian and democratic circles in various countries and valued especially highly his contacts with the leaders of the working-class movement in Germany, where former League members had gone underground to carry on revolutionary work.

At the end of December 1853, Marx had a visit from Gustav Levy, a German socialist from Düsseldorf, who came as a representative of the League's former communities in Western Germany. He told Marx about the revolutionary mood of the workers in the Rhine Province and tried to obtain his moral sanction for an armed uprising. Marx had a hard time explaining that in view of existing conditions this idea was reckless and untimely.

A couple of years later, in February 1856, Levy again came to see Marx on behalf of the Düsseldorf workers. What he told Marx made it clear that revolutionary propaganda was still being carried on among the workers of the Rhine Province, and that they still regarded Marx and Engels as their leaders. Their request was that in the event of a proletarian uprising in the Rhine Province Marx and Engels should come and take over political and military leadership. Marx displayed great patience and tact in explaining to Levy the principles of revolutionary tactics, and asked him to tell the workers that any uprising in the Rhine Province was doomed to failure unless there was a general revolutionary upsurge in Germany and a revolutionary situation in Europe. Marx stressed that once the Paris proletariat gave the signal for revolution, revolutionary action should be taken with the utmost vigour and resolution. For the time being there was need for restraint and patience.

Marx regarded his contacts with the German workers and the maintenance and strengthening of Communist League traditions among them as a most important means of educating the German proletarians in the revolutionary spirit and as true internationalists.

MARX AND CHARTISM IN THE 1850s

Marx continued to help the leaders of the Left revolutionary wing of the Chartists, who made truly heroic efforts in the 1850s to resume Chartist agitation on a new, socialist basis. Marx and Engels believed that although its membership had declined, the National Charter Association could, given the right conditions, become the nucleus of a mass proletarian party in England, virtually the only country where there was at the time some chance of setting up such a party. That was why Marx and Engels devoted so much attention to the English working-class movement.

Marx gave great support to the Chartist leader Ernest Jones in starting *The People's Paper*, a Chartist weekly whose first issue appeared on May 8, 1852. Marx wrote unpaid articles for the paper himself and also got Eccarius, Pieper and Cluss to contribute. In the first 18 months the paper carried, apart from various statements, 17 articles by Marx, including his famous series entitled *Lord Palmerston*. He explained to the paper's readers the principles of revolutionary proletarian tactics as applied to conditions in England in the 1850s.

Marx always came to Jones' aid at critical moments, when the paper was either short of editorial matter or money. He wrote to Engels on September 2, 1852: "In spite of my own money bothers I have spent days with him traipsing all over the place in connection with his paper's financial affairs."[1] Now and again Marx took a hand at editing the paper. With his assistance, *The People's Paper* became a militant and truly revolutionary proletarian periodical.

In 1853 the Chartists tried to make use of the wave of strikes which swept over England to involve the workers in the fight for the People's Charter. In his articles, Marx emphasised the importance of the strike movement and wrote that if the workers had failed to resist the employers' offensive against their economic interests, "the working classes of Great Britain, and of all Europe, would be a heart-broken, a weak-minded, a worn-out, unresisting mass, whose self-emancipation would prove as impossible as that of the slaves of Ancient Greece and Rome".[2] At the same time, Marx approved highly of Jones' speeches at meetings and in the press in which he argued the inadequacy of fighting for economic demands only, and the need to combine it with political struggle.

In late 1853 and early 1854, the Chartists took steps to set up a broad working-class organisation called the Mass Movement, which was to include the trade unions, non-unionised workers and Chartist groups, with a Labour Parliament meeting at regular intervals to act as the governing body.

---

[1] Marx, Engels, *Collected Works*, Vol. 39, p. 175.
[2] Ibid., Vol. 12, p. 169.

The first Labour Parliament in England, convened on Jones' initiative, met in Manchester from March 6 to 18, 1854. Marx was invited to attend as an honorary delegate, but because he was unable to go to Manchester, he sent a letter to the Labour Parliament, dated March 9, 1854, and this was published in *The People's Paper*. In his letter Marx called on the English proletariat to undertake the militant task of organising "the labouring classes on a national scale".[1]

The hopes Marx had pinned on the Labour Parliament did not materialise, however, for it became dominated by typical trade unionists, who ignored the important practical matters before the working-class movement and concentrated on plans for solving the social question on petty-bourgeois socialist lines. When the programme was being drawn up, Jones and his comrades made important ideological concessions to the trade unionists and the bourgeois co-operativists and abandoned the idea of writing Chartist political demands into it. This produced a programme which could not serve as a basis for the efforts to set up a proletarian party, and the Mass Movement was soon wound up.

In the summer of 1855, the Chartists organised two huge public demonstrations in London in protest against the Sunday Trading Bill, passed by Parliament, which hit the workers, who normally received their week's wages on Saturday night. On Sunday, June 24, 1855, and the following Sunday, July 1, thousands gathered in Hyde Park. Marx and Liebknecht took part in these events, and narrowly escaped arrest during the second demonstration when it was attacked by squads of police.

Despite such flare-ups, the working-class movement under the banner of Chartism tended on the whole to decline, and there were signs of apathy and disillusion with the political activity. But even in face of these difficulties, Marx never tired of giving support to the Chartists, trying hard to put heart and backbone into the movement. At a banquet marking the fourth anniversary of *The People's Paper* on April 14, 1856, Marx delivered one of his most inspired speeches full of unflagging faith in the inevitable socialist revolution and the creative revolutionary forces of the proletariat.

He gradually became concerned and pained over the behaviour of Jones himself. Instead of working hard among the masses, he got involved in various short-lived and futile political campaigns to set up, together with bourgeois radicals and petty-bourgeois emigrants, diverse international committees, associations, and so on. Marx kept warning Jones that close association with the radicals could result in the proletarian movement losing its independence, and advised him to concentrate on work in the factory districts and not to waste energy on supporting the bourgeois and petty-bourgeois elements.

However, Jones did not heed this advice. His compromise with

---

[1] Ibid., Vol. 13, p. 58.

the radicals made it impossible for Marx to go on working on *The People's Paper*. By early 1858, the National Charter Association had collapsed for all practical purposes. In June of that year, *The People's Paper* fell into the hands of bourgeois businessmen. Although Marx found it difficult to break with one of his old comrades-in-arms, he stood firm on this kind of vacillation. On February 1, 1859, he wrote to Weydemeyer: "I have broken with Ernest Jones."[1] In the early 1860s, the old Chartist leader readopted his revolutionary attitude, and Marx resumed friendly relations with him.

Marx and Engels saw Jones' ideological vacillations as stemming from the intensified reformist trends in the English working-class movement as a result of England's world industrial and colonial monopoly, the excessive wealth accumulated by the English bourgeoisie through colonial plunder, and its flexibility and readiness to keep the working-class *élite* happy with handouts from its coffers. The English proletariat was split and paralysed when the bourgeoisie won over the labour aristocracy, whose influence was expressed in the domination of liberal trade unionist elements and the abandonment of revolutionary Chartist traditions.

CONNECTIONS WITH THE U.S. WORKING-CLASS MOVEMENT

The republican system and some democratic freedoms made it possible to organise the working class in the north of the United States, although the slave plantations in the South fettered the country's economic and political development. Workers kept moving into the wild areas of the West. There was strife between native-born American workers and immigrant workers from Germany, Italy and Ireland. Ideologically, the mass of proletarians was highly immature.

Marx kept in touch with the leading U.S. workers through Joseph Weydemeyer and Adolf Cluss, both members of the Communist League. Marx corresponded regularly with Cluss from 1851 to the second half of 1854, when Cluss abandoned the effort to disseminate communist ideas. Marx remained a close friend of Weydemeyer's until the latter's death in 1866. Cluss and Weydemeyer pioneered the spread of Marxism in the U.S.A., published several of Marx's works in the United States, and spread the ideas of scientific communism through the press. They were given some help by Abraham Jacobi, who had emigrated to the United States in 1853.

Marx supported Weydemeyer's efforts to set up a proletarian organisation in the U.S.A. on the same lines as the Communist League, and particularly approved of Weydemeyer's participation

---

[1] Marx, Engels, *Collected Works*, Vol. 40, p. 375.

in founding the broad American Labour Union in March 1853. Most of its members were emigrant workers, and Weydemeyer sought to turn it into the backbone of a political party of the American workers.

Marx's friends strove to spread scientific communism in the U.S.A. through the New York German-language newspaper, *Die Reform*, which had been started on March 5, 1853 and soon became the organ of the Labour Union. It was closed down at the end of April 1854. Marx warmly approved of Weydemeyer's and Cluss' efforts to establish their influence on its editorial board and turn it into a proletarian organ. He did his best to supply them with material from Europe and to get Jones, Eccarius and Pieper to write for the paper. He allowed Cluss to publish in *Die Reform*, without payment of fees, German translations of the articles he and Engels wrote for the U.S. press as regular correspondents. He suggested subjects which were important for U.S. readers and helped in the fight against bourgeois ideology, notably the theory of the vulgar U.S. economist Henry Carey, which was just coming into vogue.

Thanks to Marx's help, *Die Reform* became one of the best workers' newspapers in the U.S.A. When the paper was wound up because of financial difficulties and internal dissension caused by the attitudes of the petty-bourgeois members of the editorial board, he wrote to Engels on May 22, 1854: "Collapse of the *Reform* deplorable." [1]

In October 1857, a group of German emigrants connected with Weydemeyer, among them Friedrich Kamm and Albrecht Komp, founded the Communist Club in New York. One of its active leaders was Friedrich Adolf Sorge who had taken part in the Baden uprising. The members of the Club studied the writings of Marx and Engels and used them for their propaganda among the workers. Its leaders sought to establish direct contact with Marx. Kamm wrote to him in December 1857: "There is no doubt that, since you are carrying on the scientific and critical struggle for the idea of communism and will always continue to carry it on, you are also the teacher and the Party leader of the Communists of the Old World, and in virtue of this the threads of the organisation run to you as its central point...." [2]

When members of the Communist Club suggested that Marx should revive the Communist League in Europe, he said that it was out of the question to return to such a relatively narrow framework for rallying the forces of the working class in the new circumstances in which the working-class movement was developing in the European countries. That is why he regarded paving the way for a massive organisation, and above all elaborating revolutionary theory, as the main task.

---

[1] Ibid., Vol. 39, p. 453.
[2] Central Party Archives of the Institute of Marxism-Leninism.

WRITING FOR THE PROGRESSIVE BOURGEOIS PRESS

Marx believed that even when conditions were favourable for the proletarian press, it was advisable for proletarian revolutionaries to write for the bourgeois-democratic and generally progressive periodicals. It was even more important to use this channel to influence public opinion at a time of reaction. Accordingly, Marx accepted the offer in early August 1851 to act as London correspondent of the U.S. bourgeois newspaper, the *New-York Daily Tribune*. At the time he was badly in need of this job because he had no other source of livelihood.

The *New-York Daily Tribune* was one of the most widely read periodicals in the United States. It was founded in April 1841 by Horace Greeley, who had himself risen from humble origins to become a leading publisher. The *Tribune* became a vehicle for the economic and political ideals of progressive bourgeois circles. It campaigned for restrictions on the spread of slavery, and on the whole supported the movement for Negro liberation, without backing its most resolute spokesmen. In view of the imminent conflict between the bourgeois North and the slave-holding South, the line taken by the *Tribune* was in accord with the mood of even broader social sections and commanded a mass readership. It was also popular because it was cheap.

More radical views were expressed by Charles Dana, another influential member of the editorial board, who at one time had been in close touch with the followers of Fourier in the United States and had shown a sustained interest in socialist theories. In the autumn of 1848, he met Marx in Cologne and was highly impressed by the latter's knowledge and power of thought. It was he who suggested that Marx should be invited to act as correspondent for the *Tribune*.

Engels approved of Marx's decision to accept Dana's proposal. To enable Marx, then engaged in his economic research, to back up his acceptance with something tangible, Engels undertook to write at Marx's request a series of articles entitled *Revolution and Counter-Revolution in Germany*. In August 1852, Marx himself joined in the writing. At first he wrote in German, and his manuscripts were mailed to New York after Engels had translated them into English in Manchester. However, in January 1853, Marx "ventured for the first time to write an article *in English* for Dana".[1] After Engels had read one of Marx's first articles in English, he wrote: "*Je t'en fais mon compliment.*[2] The English isn't merely good; it's brilliant."[3]

Subsequently, the two friends arranged for some division of subjects, Marx dealing mostly with the economic situation, the domestic and foreign policy of the European states and the development of

---

[1] Marx, Engels, *Collected Works*, Vol. 39, p. 275.
[2] I congratulate you.
[3] Marx, Engels, *Collected Works*, Vol. 39, p. 329.

the working-class and democratic movement, and Engels almost entirely handling the analysis of military events, but also writing many articles on other subjects. Some of their reports were written by the two men together.

Marx took great pains in writing his reports. Very often he put in a great deal of research to produce one item or a short series of articles. Engels subsequently wrote that "these were not conventional reports but circumstantial reviews of the political and economic situation in the individual European countries based on a thorough study and frequently consisting of a whole series of articles".[1] Compared with the other items in the *Tribune* they were distinguished for their depth and precise analysis of situations, events and public figures and contained important theoretical generalisations.

Marx's work as a correspondent was closely bound up with his theoretical research, especially in the field of political economy. In his articles he used many of the facts he had unearthed and the scientific conclusions he had drawn. On the other hand, the constant need to keep abreast of current events and facts and to look at concrete economic developments helped to enlarge the basis for his analysis of economic theory. Marx subsequently used in his major economic works some of the ideas he had expressed in the *Tribune*. In the Preface to *A Contribution to the Critique of Political Economy* he observed that regular journalistic work had helped him to gain a knowledge of many practical details which "lie outside the sphere of political economy".[2]

Very soon readers began to pay special attention to Marx's articles in the *Tribune*, and this helped to enhance the paper's prestige. The members of the editorial board also had to recognise that the theoretical standard of these articles was unusually high. Thus, in a leading article on April 7, 1853, the editors paid tribute to their correspondent's remarkable capabilities. They wrote: "Mr Marx has very decided opinions of his own, with some of which we are far from agreeing, but those who do not read his letters neglect one of the most instructive sources of information on the great questions of current European politics."[3] In a letter to Jenny Marx of July 1, 1853, Dana assured her that her husband's articles were highly valued by the proprietors of the *Tribune* and the public.[4] Some of Marx's articles were reprinted or quoted by other American newspapers, among them *The New York Times*. They were also read in Europe.

But while the editors of the *Tribune* may have been progressive, they took the purely employer approach to their correspondents and sought to get as much value out of them as they could for their money. Initially, there was no agreement at all on what Marx was to be paid, and the little that was paid arrived after long delays.

---

[1] Marx, Engels, *Werke*, Bd. 22, S. 340.
[2] Marx, Engels, *Collected Works*, Vol. 29, p. 265.
[3] Ibid., Vol. 39, p. 315.
[4] Central Party Archives of the Institute of Marxism-Leninism.

The editors did not publish many of the articles by Marx and Engels because they felt the bourgeois readership wanted something different or because they did not like what the two men were saying. In the summer of 1856, Dana returned to Marx a series of articles by Engels on pan-Slavism, and the same thing happened to Marx's own articles against the policies of tsarist Russia and Bonapartist France in the Danubian principalities. Nor were the editors too careful about how they edited the articles, frequently abridging the text or making insertions whose meaning clashed with the content. A considerable number of the contributions sent in by Marx and Engels were published as unsigned leading articles. Marx strongly resented this "annexationist policy",[1] but his protests were to no avail.

Now and again, the editors' rule that no definite party standpoint should be taken was an insuperable obstacle to writing on this or that subject. Thus, in December 1853, Dana asked Marx to write a series of articles on German philosophy, but stressed that they "must not contain anything to shock the religious sensibilities"[2] of Americans, in other words, that Marx should not in any way advocate atheism. Marx naturally found these terms unacceptable. Dana stipulated the same terms when he invited Marx, in April 1857, to write for *The New American Cyclopaedia*. This, of course, made it impossible for Marx to write articles on the history of philosophy, Chartism, socialism and communism, and so he had to confine himself mainly to military subjects, "the good old military stuff", as Engels jocularly put it in a letter,[3] and also the biographies of outstanding men. Most of these articles were written by Engels, while Marx wrote several biographical sketches about Napoleon's marshals and diplomatists—Brune, Berthier, Bessières, Bernadotte and Bourrienne, about Simon Bolivar who led the Latin American national liberation movement, and Robert Blum, a participant in the 1848 revolution in Germany.

Now and again, Marx was on the verge of breaking with the *Tribune*, but did not do so because he was aware of the importance of keeping in touch with a mass readership even through a channel like that newspaper. He managed to expound revolutionary proletarian ideas in his articles through a flexibility of form and the use of innuendo. In fact, despite the intentions of its editors, Marx and Engels used the bourgeois paper to expose the bourgeois system. Even when writing for *The New American Cyclopaedia*, Marx managed to get round the editors' instructions that the articles should be couched in dry academic terms, and his articles were a reflection of revolutionary-materialist convictions and the party attitude to the events he dealt with.

In the autumn of 1854, Marx received another invitation, through

---

[1] Marx, Engels, *Collected Works*, Vol. 39, p. 395.
[2] Dana to Mrs. Marx, December 16, 1853 (Central Party Archives of the Institute of Marxism-Leninism).
[3] Marx, Engels, *Collected Works*, Vol. 40, p. 124.

Lassalle, to write for the *Neue Oder-Zeitung*, a German bourgeois-democratic newspaper. It was founded in Breslau (Wroclaw) in March 1849, during the revolution, and was one of the few opposition newspapers which had managed to survive in the early years of reaction. For all its defects, it was then the only legal democratic periodical in Germany. In a letter to its editor, Karl Elsner, Marx wrote: "The *N. O.-Z.* expresses the most extreme views possible in the present condition of the Press."[1] Writing for the paper gave Marx the opportunity of establishing direct contacts with German readers. Being aware of the censorship and other difficulties faced by the publishers of a progressive periodical in reactionary Germany, he considered it his duty to give them the utmost support in their "underhand struggle against the established powers".[2]

Marx's first article was published in the *Neue Oder-Zeitung* on January 2, 1855, and for the next few months he regularly contributed two or more reports every week. When he learned that the paper was short of funds he expressed readiness to write without being paid. He wrote some of his items for the *New-York Daily Tribune* and the *Neue Oder-Zeitung* simultaneously and also translated for the latter the reviews of military operations in the Crimean War which Engels wrote in English for the American press.

In the autumn of 1855, the newspaper faced even greater difficulties and was threatened with closure. With much effort its publication was dragged out to the end of the year.

Marx and Engels used their articles in the *Neue Oder-Zeitung* to suggest the leading democratic circles in Germany and the whole of Europe revolutionary tactics which corresponded to the intricate international situation caused by the Crimean War. A number of their articles were aimed against the continued flirtation by the Prussian ruling clique with Russian tsarism. In allegorical language they also criticised the attitudes of the German, above all Prussian, bourgeoisie. In many of his articles, Marx exposed the anti-popular features of the English constitutional order and exploded the political ideals of the liberals, who regarded it as a model order for a future German state, thereby also dealing a blow at the constitutional illusions of the bourgeois democrats themselves. By describing some of the actions taken by the English proletariat, Marx tried to drive home to German readers that there were signs of a fresh upsurge of revolutionary energy in the masses, and that the militant spirit of the working class had not been stamped out even in the period of reaction.

MARX AS A JOURNALIST

Marx's articles and reports in the *New-York Daily Tribune* and in the *Neue Oder-Zeitung* are a vivid reflection of his qualities as a pro-

---

[1] Ibid., Vol. 39, p. 554.
[2] Ibid., p. 507.

letarian publicist who was able in the incredibly difficult conditions of reaction to awaken revolutionary feelings in the masses by his impassioned *exposés* of capitalism, the reactionary political system of the European states, and the anti-popular policies of the ruling classes. He relentlessly criticised the hypocritical optimism exuded by the reactionaries and well-intentioned bourgeois, who argued that the period of reaction was the dawn of an era of stability, ruling out any revolutionary upheavals in the life of society. He had nothing but scorn for the "official economic fortune-tellers", who presented the short-lived revival of industry and trade as the start of lasting affluence. Marx wrote: "There never was a single period of prosperity, but they profited by the occasion to prove that *this time* the medal was without a reverse, that the inexorable *fate* was *this time* subdued." [1] In contrast to bourgeois economists, he predicted at the very height of the economic boom that the next crisis would be much deeper and more extensive than that of 1847.

The ideologists of the bourgeoisie, Marx argued, were falsely asserting that the economic prosperity had brought lasting welfare to the working people. He cited hundreds of facts to show that the economic upswing had not at all eased the working people's sufferings, or eliminated the growing impoverishment of the lower orders, the social deprivation and the spiritual and physical mutilation of those who worked at the factories. Nor had it done away with unemployment, that terrible scourge of the working class.

Marx said that two social phenomena—starvation and forced emigration—brought out most forcibly the true price that working people had to pay for capitalist prosperity, as men in the prime of life died of malnutrition in Great Britain, abounding in goods and accumulating the wealth of the whole world, and as thousands fled across the ocean, driven from their native soil by privation and lack of land. In capitalist society, Marx never tired of emphasising, public wealth grew at the price of ruin and incredible suffering for the vast majority, while a handful of exploiters enjoyed the fruits of it. In such a society, progress resembled the "hideous, pagan idol, who would not drink the nectar but from the skulls of the slain".[2]

While presenting a true picture of capitalist reality, Marx never lapsed into the sentimental tone of petty-bourgeois writers who did not go beyond complaints and lamentations. A true revolutionary, he regarded the successes of the capitalist economy and the attendant deepening of the contradictions of capitalism as a source of the prerequisites for a future social revolution which was to lay the foundations of a new social system. He wrote: "Bourgeois industry and commerce create these material conditions of a new world in the same way as geological revolutions have created the surface of the earth." [3]

---

[1] Marx, Engels, *Collected Works*, Vol. 11, p. 363.
[2] Ibid., Vol. 12, p. 222.
[3] Ibid.

With sustained revolutionary feeling Marx expressed his conviction that the proletariat was bound to gain in strength, and that history's each stride forward brought nearer the time when it would commence its great mission of transforming the world. Marx keenly discerned and noted in his articles every sign of consolidation of the working class on which he pinned his main hopes in the struggle against the reactionary regimes. Whatever the external situation, be it flaming revolution or darkest reaction, Marx remained true to his purpose: to help the proletariat realise its historical tasks and call it tirelessly to struggle.

ARTICLES ON BRITAIN'S POLITICAL SYSTEM

Marx devoted much attention to Great Britain, then the most developed capitalist country, and studied the processes going on in the capitalist world mainly on the basis of economic development in this "metropolis of capital". He also made a comprehensive analysis of the British state system, the policy of her ruling classes, and the attitudes of her various political parties and groupings, in such articles as "The Elections in England—Tories and Whigs" and "The Chartists", a series of reports analysing the Aberdeen coalition ministry of 1852-55, the pamphlet *Lord John Russell*, the articles "The British Constitution", "Palmerston and the English Oligarchy", "The English Election", and many others.

One of the tasks Marx set himself was to explode the liberal legend that capitalist Great Britain was a bulwark of freedom and political equality. He destroyed this imaginary aura of a country where, of all other countries, "the despotism of Capital and the slavery of Labour" had been developed on the greatest scale.[1] Marx showed that despite some of the democratic freedoms the British people had won, the country's political system as a whole rested on conservative principles. Nothing had shaken the political privileges of the landed aristocracy and the bourgeois *élite* (mainly financial and commercial), which had a monopoly in the government, civil service and Parliament. Political power shuttled between one ruling party and the other: now to the Tories who voiced the interests of the landed aristocracy and were "enthusiasts for nothing but the rent of land", now to the Whigs, "the *aristocratic representatives* of the Bourgeoisie, of the industrial and commercial middle class".[2] This two-party system had enabled the ruling bourgeois-aristocratic oligarchy to manoeuvre in building up its domination, and to deceive the masses by what looked like a free contest of political forces.

Marx observed a process that was then taking place, namely the coalescence of the landed and the financial aristocracy with the industrial bourgeoisie, the increasing adaptation of the oligarchic re-

---
[1] Ibid., Vol. 13, p. 57.
[2] Ibid., Vol. 11, pp. 328 and 330.

gime to the interests of the bourgeoisie, and the incipient restructuring of the old parties, which were gradually acquiring a patently bourgeois character. The Tories were being transformed into the party of the big bourgeoisie, the Conservatives, and the Whigs, into the Liberal Party involving ever wider sections of the middle and petty bourgeoisie.

Marx stressed that the bourgeois-oligarchic regime was fettering the country's development and preventing any kind of democratic change. Parliament's legislative activity was reduced to a set of palliatives, and this was especially evident in the budgets and the financial reforms. In framing their budgets, the representatives of the oligarchy took care not to overstep the margin "beyond which the working man would gain — the aristocrat and middle classes lose".[1]

Marx frequently exposed the British oligarchy through his political sketches of its most prominent members. His gallery of British 19th-century statesmen — Palmerston, Russell, Aberdeen, Clarendon, Gladstone, Derby and Disraeli, among others — is colourful, satirically sharp, and remarkably precise in conveying the characteristic features of these bourgeois-aristocratic politicians. Marx also took a highly critical view of Bright and Cobden, the bourgeois opponents of the oligarchy and the leaders of the Free Trade industrial bourgeoisie. The Free Traders' policy was half-hearted and full of fear of mass action and hostility to any independent working-class movement. They preferred "to compromise with the vanishing opponent rather than to strengthen the arising enemy, to whom the future belongs, by concessions of a more than apparent importance".[2]

While condemning the anti-popular political order in England, Marx, the objective proletarian politician, took the concrete historical approach to it. The regime in England may have been conservative, but it was more favourable for the workers than those which had been established on the continent. However curtailed, England did have freedom of assembly, association and the press. The British proletariat was able to exert some influence on Parliament and government through "pressure from without". In contrast to other European countries, the British working class constituted a sizable majority of the population. Nor did England at the time have a sprawling, continental-type military and bureaucratic state machine. Taking all this into consideration Marx concluded that in contrast to the continental countries England could have a peaceful transfer of power to the working class. To bring about a political take-over by the British proletariat — by peaceful or non-peaceful means, depending on the situation — Marx believed that the existing parliamentary system had to be radically overhauled and the whole political order democratised. That is why he attached so much importance to the Chartist programme and gave such active support to the efforts to revive Chartist agitation.

---

[1] Marx. Engels, *Collected Works*, Vol. 12, p. 66.
[2] Ibid., Vol. 11, p. 335.

In England, said Marx, the Chartist demand for universal suffrage had a different meaning than it had on the continent, where it did not go beyond the framework of a bourgeois-democratic programme and was now and again even put to demagogic use, as in Bonapartist France, by the counter-revolutionary forces. In England, combined with other radical demands, it was a proletarian slogan. The introduction of universal suffrage in England and the implementation of other points of the Charter would have led to the working class winning political power, of which the most important prerequisite was the growing political awareness and organisation of the British proletariat and the establishment of a revolutionary proletarian party of the British workers.

STRUGGLE AGAINST REACTIONARY REGIMES IN CONTINENTAL EUROPE

Marx and Engels regarded Bonapartism as one of the chief opponents of the working class and democracy in France and the whole of Europe, and the struggle against it became a primary task before the international working-class movement.

In his articles written for the press, Marx enlarged the profound analysis of the Bonapartist regime which he had made in *The Eighteenth Brumaire of Louis Bonaparte*. Each of his articles on the subject was a pamphlet wrathfully branding the arbitrary acts of the Bonapartist clique in France, another page added to the scientific study of the counter-revolutionary evolution of the ruling *élite* in bourgeois society and its state, a study of the character of the Bonapartist monarchy as one of its forms.

In his articles "The France of Bonaparte the Little", "The Beginning of Louis Napoleon's End", "The Rule of the Pretorians", among others, Marx stressed that the Bonapartist state reflected the growing counter-revolutionary tendencies of the bourgeoisie and its switch to openly dictatorial rule with the aid of the "naked sword", unmitigated violence and police despotism. The Bonapartist regime also bore the mark of the corruption that was spreading in the top strata of bourgeois society. Bribery and embezzlement spread to all spheres of the parasitic state machine including the war ministry. In the spring of 1856, Marx wrote: "The cancer that eats up the French army is the organic principle of the Lower Empire—theft and embezzlement."[1]

In his article "The Project of Regulation of Prices on Grain in France" and other writings Marx observed Napoleon III's typical Bonapartist tight-rope walking between the various classes, in an effort to act simultaneously as the patron of rural France, "a sort of socialist providence to the proletarians of the towns" and the "saviour of property" in the eyes of the French bourgeoisie.[2] Marx point-

---
[1] Ibid., Vol. 14, p. 618.
[2] Ibid., Vol. 16, p. 114.

ed out that this policy of "appeasing all classes" was fundamentally false, but he by no means regarded the attempts by the Bonapartist authorities "to purchase the conscience of the French working classes" as a harmless farce.[1] He felt it to be his duty to warn of the danger of Bonapartist social demagogy and its corrupting influence on vacillating workers.

Marx also saw the Bonapartist clique's efforts to use national movements in its own interests as a great threat, and warned Kossuth and Mazzini against having anything to do with it, as this could turn them into unwitting tools of Bonapartist intrigues and harm the cause of national liberation in Hungary and Italy. In an article "Mazzini and Napoleon" written in March 1858, he noted with satisfaction that the outstanding Italian democrat had become aware of the substance of Bonapartist policies on the national question.

Marx's articles helped to expose the class basis of the Second Empire regime, which had opened the floodgates of plunderous profits for the big financial barons and industrialists. Unrestrained agiotage, he wrote, had turned France into a "gambling house", while speculation on the stock exchange had become a "vital principle of the present Empire", which was grossly neglectful of economic laws.[2] In one series of articles, Marx dealt with *Crédit Mobilier*, a bank which enjoyed the special patronage of Napoleon III. Analysing its operations, which included investments in industrial enterprises, canals and railways, Marx noticed the changes in the economic role of the banks, the beginnings of a process which was to develop fully later, at the last stage of capitalism. He wrote prophetically that "the application of joint-stock companies to industry marks a new epoch in the economical life of modern nations".[3]

Marx saw quite clearly that the attempts by the Bonapartist press to exaggerate France's economic "successes", the showy sumptuousness of the court and the reconstruction of the capital — whose secret purpose was "to protect it from its own ebullitions"[4] — served only as a means to camouflage the Second Empire's intrinsic instability and imminent bankruptcy, which the ruling clique sought to escape by engaging in gambles abroad. Dissatisfaction with the regime was spreading among the broadest sections, and in 1857 "we find the surface of society already heaving and rocking with the movement of the subterranean fires".[5]

Marx sought to show that it was not the bourgeois opposition but the mass of the people, the staunch French proletariat above all, that would play the decisive role in the inevitable overthrow of the Second Empire. On March 25, 1853, after a demonstration against the Bonapartist regime had been staged by workers taking part in

---

[1] Marx, Engels, *Collected Works*, Vol. 15, p. 478.
[2] Ibid., Vol. 14, p. 657; Vol. 15, p. 276.
[3] Ibid., Vol. 15, p. 21.
[4] Ibid., p. 503.
[5] Ibid., p. 302.

the funeral procession of the wife of a prominent revolutionary, Raspail, Marx wrote to Cluss that "the proletarian lion isn't dead".[1] Marx pinned great hopes on the indomitable revolutionary energy of Auguste Blanqui, the leader of the French workers, who was then languishing in a prison cell.

The reaction in Europe, as Marx repeatedly said, was sustained by the joint efforts of the counter-revolutionary governments, with Hohenzollern Prussia taking an active part in this peculiar community of gendarmes and police.

Many of Marx's reports dealt with the situation in Prussia, and they all exuded a spirit of relentless struggle against the domination of the hidebound and reactionary Junkerdom and the bureaucratic-police order under the Prussian monarchy, the citadel of counter-revolution in the German Confederation.

Marx's articles "The King of Prussia's Insanity" and "Affairs in Prussia", among others, showed that the Prussian reactionaries were intent on eradicating every trace of political reform which had been carried out during the 1848 revolution and obliterating the very memory of that terrible year. That was the meaning behind the numerous revisions of the 1848 Constitution, "all this tedious process being gone through in order to wipe out the last features recording the revolutionary offspring of the patchwork".[2] Marx said that the Prussian Provincial Diet was a "mere sham" and a "mock institution".[3]

His article "The Divine Right of the Hohenzollerns" showed that the very rise of that dynasty revealed the specifically reactionary features of Prussian politics which had been carried on into the 19th century. Petty theft, perfidy and traitorous deals with the strong powers behind their neighbours' backs, with the aim of benefitting at their expense, were among the means traditionally used to attain their plunderous aims by the Brandenburg Electors, who subsequently became the Kings of Prussia.

Marx said that the actual restoration of absolutism in Prussia had been the result of the indecision and cowardice of the German bourgeoisie, and finally reached the conclusion that the bourgeoisie in Prussia, and Germany as a whole, had lost its ability to take resolute anti-government action and was living in mortal fear of popular movements. All its thoughts and aspirations were concentrated on boosting its profits. It had ceased to take an interest in progressive philosophy that reflected opposition to the existing order; "speculation in ideas has given way to speculation in stocks".[4]

However, the arrogance of the Junkers and bureaucrats and the bourgeoisie's slavish submissiveness did not prove that the reactionary order in Germany was solidly based. The country had a bur-

---

[1] Ibid., Vol. 39, p. 300.
[2] Ibid., Vol. 16, p. 76.
[3] Ibid., Vol. 12, pp. 509, 510.
[4] Ibid., Vol. 14, p. 657.

geoning industry and trade. Berlin, once an aristocratic showplace, was a growing centre of engineering. The number of new banks was well in excess of the number of princes in the German Parliament. The upshot of the industrial revolution—the formation of a proletariat and the ruin of the petty bourgeoisie and the peasantry—together with the unsolved historical task of unifying the country, all injected tension into the social situation in Germany, and led Marx to expect social and political change in that part of Europe shortly.

The Austrian Empire was one of the pillars of reaction in Europe. A patchwork, multi-national absolutist state, it was maintained by strife among the nations under Hapsburg rule. Nevertheless, Marx emphasised in his article "Austrian Bankruptcy" and other writings, the tide of history was washing away the foundations of the reactionary monarchy which had stood for centuries. Bureaucratic and police methods could not stem the growth of centrifugal forces, the national liberation struggle, the deepening of the internal crisis and the aggravation of financial and other difficulties.

Surrounded by their guards, their gibbets and their gaols, the reactionary rulers "feel the thrones of Europe vibrate to their foundations at the first forebodings of the revolutionary earthquake".[1] Marx's readers were left in no doubt as to what would happen to these corrupt regimes once the revolutionary storm again swept across the continent.

EXPOSURE OF THE CAPITALIST STATES' COLONIAL POLICIES

From the 1850s there are signs of Marx's taking a growing interest in the history of the colonial and dependent peoples. By then the colonial enslavement of the backward countries by the capitalist states had been considerably advanced. With her annexation of the Punjab in 1849, Britain completed the conquest of India; in 1852, she seized the Burmese province of Pegu, and was engaged in colonial wars against China (1840-42, 1856-58 and 1860), Afghanistan (1838-42) and Iran (1856-57), and was extending her possessions in South Africa. The French colonialists were engaged in the conquest of the Far East and were mounting punitive expeditions against the Arab and Kabyle tribes in Algeria. The U.S. bourgeoisie was beginning to take an active part in colonial expansion. But there was also growing resistance to the colonialists from masses of people in Asian and African countries.

Marx and Engels kept a close watch on events in the East and regularly commented on them in the press. They showed the essential features of colonial policies and formulated the working-class attitude to the liberation struggle of the oppressed peoples, thereby ela-

---

[1] Marx, Engels, *Collected Works*, Vol. 11, p. 516.

borating the principles of the revolutionary-proletarian doctrine on the national and colonial question and providing a profound theoretical backing for the principles of proletarian internationalism. Marx's study of colonial problems also gave him additional background material for examining important aspects of the capitalist mode of production, and this was later reflected in his *Capital*.

However, Marx went beyond the purely theoretical analysis to expose the colonial policies and their architects. In the mid-19th century, when even prominent European democrats had a supercilious attitude to the peoples of the East, it took great courage to express the consistent proletarian revolutionary stand and issue an impassioned plea in defence of these peoples' rights to independent development. This was flying in the face of established tradition and prejudice.

Marx gave especially much attention to India, Britain's largest colony, whose situation he examined in such articles as "The British Rule in India", "The East India Company—Its History and Results" and "The Future Results of the British Rule in India". He also kept a close watch on the events in China. His articles "Revolution in China and in Europe", "The British Quarrel with China" and "History of the Opium Trade" branded the policy of aggrandisement pursued in the Far East by the British, French and other colonialists to which China had fallen a victim. He also showed what the European invaders were doing against Iran, Turkey, Afghanistan and Burma. His articles "Question of the Ionian Islands", "The Indian Question—Irish Tenant Right" and "The Excitement in Ireland" analysed the status of the Greek population of Corfu and other islands of that group (a British protectorate from 1815 to 1864), and the situation in Ireland, which had become an English colony in the Middle Ages.

Colonial policy was a reflection of the most disgusting and bloodthirsty aspects of the capitalist system. About British rule in India, Marx wrote: "The profound hypocrisy and inherent barbarism of bourgeois civilisation lies unveiled before our eyes, turning from its home, where it assumes respectable forms, to the colonies, where it goes naked."[1] He was profoundly indignant at the hypocritical efforts of bourgeois ideologists to invest the colonialists with a civilising mission and to present them as being solicitous of the welfare of the peoples they conquered. Colonial wars, he insisted, were the most blatant piracy, and acts of gross lawlessness and arbitrariness.

The British conquest of India, which went hand in hand with a fierce struggle between Britain and her colonial rivals—Portugal, Holland and France—constituted a series of piratical acts carried out with brazen cynicism, gross perfidy and unprecedented savagery. An important role in this bloody conquest of a vast country with an ancient civilisation was played by the East India Company,

---

[1] Ibid., Vol. 12, p. 221.

a "Company of English merchant adventurers, who conquered India to make money out of it".[1]

Marx exposed the base methods used by the colonialists to achieve their aims: divide-and-rule, feudal fragmentation, rivalries between local rulers, caste and religious divisions, bribery of members of the local nobility who were quick to betray their own, and so on.

Marx commented indignantly on the military gambles launched by the British and other colonialists to enslave China, and said the so-called Opium Wars waged by the capitalist powers against the Chinese Empire represented the implementation of a piratical policy with respect to the Chinese people. He branded the atrocities committed by the European conquerors, who trampled on every rule of international law. "The violations of women, the spittings of children, the roastings of whole villages, were then mere wanton sports, not recorded by mandarins, but by British officers themselves."[2]

Marx showed that the development of the colonial system of capitalism rested on the most abominable forms of the exploitation of man by man, which revived obsolete and barbarous institutions long since condemned by mankind, like slave labour on plantations and trade "in human flesh and blood".[3] In her colonial possessions capitalist Britain was widely resorting to feudal methods of extra-economic coercion. The land, salt and other taxes collected like Danegeld were the main instrument for extracting the surplus and a part of the necessary product. The land tax system introduced by the British in India virtually put the seal on feudal relations in the Indian countryside, adapting them to the colonial needs of British capitalism. In the Bengal Presidency, they saddled the peasants with an army of local exploiters, the zamindars, feudatories, who acted as intermediaries between the cultivators and the East India Company. In the Madras and the Bombay Presidencies, the peasants were converted into tenant bondmen of the Company itself.

In Ireland, their colony in Europe, the British invaders also used precapitalist forms of exploitation, and established and maintained relations between the foreign landlords and the local tenant farmers which reminded Marx of relations "between the robber who presents his pistol, and the traveller who presents his purse".[4] As in India, so largely in Ireland and other colonies, all the senior posts in the colonial administration, the judiciary and the army — a vast parasitic tumour — were filled by the British, and this emphasised the deprived state of the conquered people.

Marx showed that the forms and methods of exploitation in the colonies had evolved with the development of capitalism. At its ear-

---

[1] Marx, Engels, *Collected Works*, Vol. 12, p. 179.
[2] Ibid., Vol. 15, p. 354.
[3] Ibid., p. 573.
[4] Ibid., Vol. 12, p. 160.

ly stage, which Marx subsequently called the epoch of the so-called primitive accumulation, the local population was openly and rapaciously plundered. Since the industrial revolution in Europe, fresh forces of the rising bourgeoisie — industrialists and manufacturers — had been seeking to secure a share of the colonial spoils, which is why transformation of the colonies into profitable markets for industrial goods and sources of cheap raw materials became the main form of colonial exploitation. The colonies were being turned into agrarian and raw-material appendages of the capitalist countries. Their economy was entirely subordinated to the interests of the metropolitan country, its development was one-sided and distorted, and their natural resources were being plundered. Trade with the colonies was inequitable, frequently assuming the form of openly piratical operations, like the smuggling of opium into China.

Even Marx, with his vast knowledge of history, could not readily find a yardstick to show the tragic consequences of colonial rule for the peoples plunged into bondage. The damage inflicted on Hindustan by British rule was far worse than everything that had been inflicted on the area earlier by all the enemy invasions, destructive wars and conquests. Under British rule in the East, the irrigation system, which had always been maintained even by local despots, fell into a state of neglect, resulting in a decline of agriculture, frequent crop failures and recurrent famines, which took the life of millions. Colonial rule doomed the population of India, Ireland and the other colonies to utter poverty, to the status of rightless pariahs labouring under a double yoke imposed by the local exploiters and the foreign oppressors.

While exposing the system of colonial rule, Marx also pointed out its inherent contradictions and vulnerable spots. With keen insight, he discerned the future trend in the economic and social development of India and the other conquered countries and pointed out that by destroying the patriarchal communal order and allowing — for the purpose of colonial gain — the beginnings of the capitalist economy to develop, even if in a colonially distorted form, the British were quite unwittingly helping to establish the prerequisites for a growth of anti-colonial forces: the national bourgeoisie and the local proletariat. In so doing, they were also undermining the basis of their own domination.

Even at the dawn of the anti-colonial movements, Marx was considering ways of liberation for the colonies. He wrote: "The Indians will not reap the fruits of the new elements of society scattered among them by the British bourgeoisie, till in Great Britain itself the now ruling classes shall have been supplanted by the industrial proletariat, or till the Hindoos themselves shall have grown strong enough to throw off the English yoke altogether."[1] This contains the most fruitful idea of the liberation of the colonies either through

---

[1] Ibid., p. 221.

proletarian revolution in the metropolitan country or through a victorious national liberation struggle by the peoples in the colonial countries themselves. Marx did not believe these two ways to be mutually exclusive. On the contrary, even then he saw them as being two sides of one and the same revolutionary process of liberation.

Marx saw the great national liberation uprising in India from 1857 to 1859 as one of the most vivid manifestations of the growing resistance of the oppressed peoples to the colonialists. The causes, nature, and motive forces of this uprising were analysed in a series of articles ("Investigation of Tortures in India", "The Approaching Indian Loan", "British Incomes in India", "The Annexation of Oudh", "Taxes in India" and others). He brushed aside the biased attempts by the British bourgeois press to present it as a military mutiny and insisted that it was "in truth a national revolt".[1] Although it was defeated, it dealt a mighty blow at British colonial rule, forcing a change in method, notably the winding up of the East India Company in 1858.

Marx also gave close attention to another major event in the East, the Taiping rebellion in China (1850-64), a powerful peasant war aimed against the feudal and national oppression of the Manchu dynasty, and also indirectly against the foreign colonialists who were encroaching on China's independence. In 1853, Marx wrote in the *New-York Daily Tribune* about the Taiping movement as a revolution which was to shake the foundations of that ancient empire. Nine years before the open intervention by the capitalist powers against the Taiping state, Marx predicted their action in support of the Manchu reactionaries under the hypocritical pretext of "restoring order" in China. In 1862, following changes in the Taiping state and the emergence of its own aristocracy and bureaucracy, Marx wrote in his article "Chinese Affairs" about the conservative features which had come to light at that stage of the Taiping movement. However, he continued to regard it as being revolutionary. Without idealising the peasant movements in the East, and clearly realising their shortcomings, notably the negative role of their monarchist-religious ideology, which marked the Taiping uprising and the Indian uprising of 1857-59, Marx invariably stressed their progressive historical role.

Marx regarded the liberation wars of the Latin American peoples against Spanish domination from 1810 to 1826 as exemplifying the victorious struggle by the colonies for their independence. In an article written for *The New American Cyclopaedia* and entitled "Bolivar y Ponte", he showed the people's role in the struggle. It is true that Marx made a one-sided study of Bolivar because he was not in possession of the objective sources, having been forced to draw on tendentious writings by various European adventurers who had exaggerated Bolivar's drive for dictatorial power. However, Marx as-

---

[1] Marx, Engels, *Collected Works*, Vol. 15, p. 316.

sessed the Latin American movement itself as liberatory and revolutionary.

The keynote of many of his articles on the colonial question was the idea of a deep-going internal connection between the national liberation movement in the East and the maturing of socio-economic prerequisites for the proletarian revolution in the West. Marx emphasised that the drawing of colonial and dependent countries into the orbit of world capitalist development, and their internal upheavals, particularly the start of a powerful popular struggle against the colonialists, were all bound to affect the capitalist system as a whole, to accelerate the growth of its contradictions, and to make its economic and political crises more acute. Marx was sure that the national liberation movement in the colonial and dependent countries helped to weaken the general positions of capitalism, thereby making it easier for the working class to win out. During the Indian uprising, Marx wrote to Engels in mid-January 1858: "In view of the drain of men and bullion which she will cost the English, India is now our best ally." [1]

At the same time, Marx issued ever more insistent appeals to the proletarian revolutionaries to give consistent support to the colonial peoples' struggle for their liberation. Largely under his influence, an internationalist stand with respect to the colonial and dependent peoples was taken by the Chartist leader, Ernest Jones, whose wrathful articles in *The People's Paper* in 1853 exposed the policy of the British colonialists in India and China. Jones took a courageous stand in defence of the Indian insurgents.

Marx's conclusion that the oppressed peoples' liberation movement and the proletariat's struggle against capitalism were interconnected and interdependent was of primary importance for the development of revolutionary theory on the national-colonial question, which Lenin used to formulate his doctrine of the national liberation revolution in the colonies as an important component part of the revolutionary anti-imperialist process.

CRITIQUE OF THE RULING CLASSES' FOREIGN POLICY

International relations and foreign-policy issues constituted an important element of Marx's publicistic writings. During the 1848-49 revolution, he became aware of the importance for the working class and revolutionary circles to unravel the secrets of diplomacy and formulate, in contrast to that of the ruling classes, their own revolutionary attitude on all foreign-policy issues. By the 1850s, Marx and Engels had become firmly convinced that the

---
[1] Ibid., Vol. 40, p. 249.

working class was the only force in bourgeois society capable of rallying all the progressive elements and impeding policies of aggrandisement, and that even before its take-over it should seek actively to influence the respective governments' foreign policy and make them abandon their counter-revolutionary and aggressive plans. Marx's articles in the press helped to awaken among the workers an interest in foreign-policy issues. He regarded the effort to expose the anti-popular substance of the ruling classes' foreign policy as a way to muster the proletarian and democratic forces and prepare them for the coming revolutionary battles.

Marx dealt with the underlying causes and various aspects of contemporary international conflicts: the struggle between Austria and Prussia for supremacy in Germany; the complications caused by Napoleon III's striving for hegemony in Europe; the clash of the great powers' interests in the Balkans and the Middle East; the Franco-Prussian quarrel over the Prussian king's dynastic claims to the Swiss cantons of Neuchâtel and Valangin; the intervention by Russia, England, Prussia and other states, which engendered international friction, in the struggle carried on by the German population of Schleswig and Holstein against the centralising policy of Denmark's ruling monarchy (a struggle which continued even after the 1848-49 revolution) for the purpose of fortifying their positions in the basin of the Baltic and the North Sea and suppressing seats of the national liberation movement in the region, etc. Delving down to the historical roots of these contradictions, Marx pinpointed the traditional features of international policy, which went back to the epoch of absolutism, to the period of the struggle waged by the feudal monarchies against the French bourgeois revolution, and to the activities of the Holy Alliance of 1815. In his articles and letters Marx repeatedly recorded the counter-revolutionary moves, the cynical breaches of international law in dealings with weaker opponents or partners, the fanning and taking advantage of national strife, perfidy, and deals with the enemy behind the back of one's ally. Marx and Engels condemned as gross arbitrariness the diplomatic preparations made by Prussia, Austria and tsarist Russia for the partition of Poland and its three partitions in the late 18th century. Marx exposed the counter-revolutionary role of the members of the Holy Alliance in stamping out the revolutionary movements of the 1820s, and castigated the very idea of interference in the domestic affairs of another people and of armed intervention for the purpose of fortifying the tottering thrones of "legitimate" monarchs.

Analysing the diplomacy of the new period, Marx showed that bourgeois statesmen had borrowed their base diplomatic methods from the absolutist feudal governments, and had even improved on the latter's diplomatic machinations. Once in power, the bourgeoisie also inherited the practice of using foreign policy for counter-revolutionary purposes. Thus, the decisions of the Vienna Congress of 1814-15 were an expression not only of the desire for restoration among the landed aristocrats of Austria, Prussia and Russia, but also of the counter-revolutionary aspirations of the West-European bourgeoisie, which wanted a solid "order" in the wake of the revolutionary storms. There was good reason why the French diplomatist Talleyrand-Périgord, the idol of the big bourgeoisie, was one of the leading figures at the congress.

Marx regarded the international system based on the Treaties of Vienna as a reactionary anachronism, whose main aim was to perpetuate the counter-revolutionary regimes, to keep Germany and Italy fragmented, and to block the restoration of the national independence of the Polish, Hungarian, Italian and other oppressed peoples. The counter-revolutionary governments, including the bourgeois ones, saw the maintenance of what was left of the 1815 status quo mainly as a means of resisting the primed revolutionary-democratic change.

Marx's pamphlet *Lord Palmerston*, written from October to December 1853 and widely circulated, was a vivid *exposé* of bourgeois diplomacy. It was published in England and the U.S.A., and in an abridged form in Germany. A publicistic masterpiece, it combined a critique of the whole British system of government with a portrait of Lord Palmerston, the leading statesman of bourgeois-aristocratic England and the architect of her foreign policy over many years. It laid bare the true class nature of the policies pursued by Palmerston and other English statesmen and revealed the connection between their foreign and domestic policies. Their main concern was to prevent any clouds from darkening "the bright sky of the landlords and moneylords".[1] Palmerston was adept at covering up his defence of the self-seeking interests of the landowners and the financial barons with a pretended concern for England's national prestige, while striking the attitude of a "truly English minister".

Palmerston had an especially unseemly role to play in respect of the Italian, Hungarian and Polish national liberation movements. This "truly English minister", claiming to be a champion of constitutionalism, feigned a sympathy for the peoples fighting for their independence which he dangled as a bait to lure them into a trap. A past master of provocation and diplomatic chicanery, Palmerston delivered these peoples into the hands of the despotic powers, a fact which best showed England's counter-revolutionary role in international affairs.

---

[1] Marx, Engels, *Collected Works*, Vol. 12, p. 351.

REVOLUTIONARY TACTICS ON THE EASTERN QUESTION. ATTITUDE TO THE CRIMEAN WAR

In view of the heightening of tension between tsarist Russia and the Western powers in the Middle East and the Balkans, which was soon to lead to another European war, Marx and Engels took a growing interest in the so-called Eastern question. It was extremely important to bring out its substance and formulate a correct tactical line for the revolutionary forces.

They sought to find the solution to the Eastern question whch would best accord with the interests of the oppressed peoples, the European proletariat and democracy, and approached the issue from the standpoint of the "sixth power", as they called the European revolution. At Marx's request, Engels had written in the press on the subject in the spring of 1853. Marx himself soon began to deal in his reports with the development of the Eastern conflict, and then with the political aspect of the Crimean War, while Engels concentrated on analysing the military operations.

They saw as the essence of the problem the skein of contradictions between the European powers fighting for key positions in the Middle East and the Balkans, for the straits and for a division of Turkey's possessions, and the collisions caused by the Balkan national liberation movements against the Ottoman Empire. By then, Greece, Serbia and, to a certain extent, Moldavia and Walachia had won actual independence and were seeking to shed the final vestiges of their dependence on Turkey. Bulgaria, Macedonia, Bosnia, Herzegovina and Albania remained under the Turkish yoke. The situation was further complicated by the striving of the major European powers — England, France, Austria and Russia — to subordinate these countries and Turkey herself to their own influence.

Both belligerent sides were striving for territorial aggrandisement in this conflict, but Marx and Engels regarded tsarist Russia as being the most dangerous aggressive force, for ever since the late 18th century it had been the citadel of international reaction, stamping out the freedom of its own and other peoples, and serving as the mainstay of the counter-revolutionary forces of Europe.

"Half a century ago," Lenin wrote in 1909, "Russia's reputation as an international gendarme was firmly established. In the course of the last century our autocracy rendered no small support to various reactionary causes in Europe even to the point of crushing by downright military force the revolutionary movements in neighbouring countries." [1] Marx's publicistic writings wrathfully branded tsarist Russia's despotic regime, exposing tsarism as the sponsor of the aggressive foreign policy, and revealing the machinations of tsarist diplomats. He explained that the tsarist government sought to

---

[1] V. I. Lenin, *Collected Works*, Vol. 15, p. 461.

use for its aggressive and counter-revolutionary purposes the sympathies which the peoples of the Balkan Peninsula, the Southern Slavs especially, had always felt for the Russian people. Whereas the victories scored by Russian armies in the wars against Turkey objectively helped these peoples to escape from the Turkish yoke, tsarism, donning the mask of "protector of its Slav coreligionists" and spreading pan-Slavist ideas, was in fact seeking to establish its domination in the Balkans.

In their Middle-East policy, tsarist Russia's rivals — England and France — were guided by equally self-seeking motives. Their cover was a feigned concern for the integrity of the Turkish Empire, but they were as avid as tsarist Russia herself in trying to lay their hands on Turkish possessions. Under the pretext of helping their Turkish "ally" they meddled in her internal affairs, used her armed forces, and tightened the financial grip they had long had on her government. In April 1854, Marx wrote: "The Turks ... begin to look on France and England as more dangerous enemies than the Czar himself." [1] In his pamphlet *The Fall of Kars* Marx exposed the perfidious attitude of British diplomacy towards its ally.

The main protagonists in the anti-Russia coalition — France and England — also had widely divergent aims. Whereas the British bourgeois oligarchy was trying to destroy the Russian navy, seize the Crimea and the Caucasus and establish its supremacy in these areas, Bonapartist France strove not only to preponderate in the Middle East, but also to establish her hegemony over the whole of Europe, and to extend her borders at the expense of her neighbours. Marx was sure that after the Crimean War the French rulers would start fresh wars. He saw the inevitable collapse of the Anglo-French alliance, which is exactly what happened at the Paris Peace Congress in 1856.

But on one point the British and French ruling circles saw eye to eye. While seeking to weaken Russia as their rival in the East and in many parts of Europe, they had no intention at all of destroying the tsarist autocracy. Marx and Engels observed that conservative Europe — the "Europe of the monarchs, the feudals and the capitalists" — needed tsarism as a defender of anti-popular regimes and exploitative social systems. What the West-European politicians feared most were the revolutionary consequences of a collapse of tsarism. They hoped to maintain a "conservative millennium", as Marx wrote in his article "Eccentricities of Politics". [2] These counter-revolutionary aspirations were matched by the Western powers' strategy. In order to avoid revolutionary complications, they made a point of carrying the military operations to Russia's outlying areas, so as to keep the theatres of war as far away as possible from any potential centres of revolutionary uprisings and national liberation movements. Their policy of a "local war for local purposes"

---
[1] Marx, Engels, *Collected Works*, Vol. 13, p. 160.
[2] Ibid., Vol. 14, p. 284.

was not at all designed to save lives or reduce the devastations of war, but to prevent the Crimean War from being converted into a popular war against tsarism, for that would also jeopardise the existence of the anti-democratic regimes in France and England.

Marx also dealt with the stand taken by Austria and Prussia on the Crimean War. He said the policy pursued by the ruling classes of the Hapsburg Empire was a twofold one. On the one hand, they feared a strengthening of the national movements of the oppressed peoples (Hungarians, Czechs, Poles and Southern Slavs), which could be put down only with tsarist help, and on the other, they had their own aggressive schemes in the Balkans, which impelled them to regard Russia as a rival and seek to weaken her. Marx believed that fear of revolutionary developments in the heart of Europe, if military operations were carried into that area, was the factor which ultimately kept the Prussian ruling clique neutral in that war.

Marx and Engels were sure that the European proletariat and democracy wanted military operations to take a totally different turn. Marx never shared the vulgar view that war invariably led to revolution, but once a war had started contrary to the will of the people, the working class and the democratic forces were duty-bound to turn the military crisis to their own account. That was one of the central premises of the revolutionary tactics worked out by Marx and Engels in the Crimean War period.

They expected the Anglo-French bloc's "local" war against Russia to develop into a revolutionary war of the European peoples against the tsarist autocracy and the counter-revolutionary forces supporting it. If that happened, there was bound to be a fresh upsurge in the revolutionary and national liberation struggle, and it would then be possible to find revolutionary-democratic ways of fulfilling the historical tasks remaining from the 1848-49 period, and the anti-popular regimes in Europe — including those in France and England — would be swept away. In that event, the European proletarians, Marx wrote in an article entitled "Prospect in France and England", would "resume that position which they lost, in France, by the battle of June 1848". [1]

Marx and Engels believed that only a popular revolution could open the real way to freedom for the oppressed nationalities of the Turkish Empire. Marx countered the idea of maintaining this most reactionary oppressor state, a bulwark of feudal barbarism, by emphasising the need to destroy it in the revolutionary way and establish independent national states on its ruins. Marx explained that the Western powers' defence of the "integrity" of the Ottoman Empire was a threat to the national liberation movement of the Balkan peoples, and pushed them into the arms of tsarism. A revolutionary-democratic solution of the Eastern question implied above all total liberation of the Southern Slavs and all the other peoples of the Bal-

---

[1] Marx, Engels, *Collected Works*, Vol. 14, p. 145.

kan Peninsula from Turkish oppression. Marx was aware that it was impossible to anticipate the forms of statehood which the peoples rising to independence would establish, but he did not rule out the possibility of a "Federal Republic of Slavonic States" being set up in the Balkans.[1]

Marx and Engels held that conversion of the war into a revolutionary one was bound to bring to life forces resisting tsarism in Russia herself, and anticipated the possibility that the European revolution would extend the sphere of its operations to Russia as well. Expressing also Marx's view, Engels wrote: "The revolutionary landmarks have been steadily advancing ever since 1789. The last revolutionary outposts were Warsaw, Debreczin, Bucharest; the advanced posts of the next revolution must be Petersburg and Constantinople. They are the two vulnerable points where the Russian anti-revolutionary colossus must be attacked."[2]

In that period, Marx and Engels already began to take a profound interest in the prospects for the revolutionary movement in Russia. Marx kept in touch with Russian revolutionary writings published abroad, and continued to maintain ties with Russian emigrants, notably, N. I. Sazonov, who lived in Paris.

Nor did Marx fail to take note of the establishment in London in 1853 of the "Free Russian Press" by Alexander Herzen. Marx had read several works by this outstanding revolutionary writer, including *On the Development of Revolutionary Ideas in Russia*, but because of Herzen's close association with petty-bourgeois circles of the emigration, and some of his utopian views (the idea of "renovating" Europe by means of the Russian peasant commune, etc.), Marx took a highly circumspect attitude towards him. There was also Herzen's participation in 1853 in a campaign started against Marx in the liberal *Morning Advertiser* by the Russian liberal landowner I. G. Golovin and the German vulgar democrat Ruge. They accused Marx of slandering Bakunin on the strength of an item against the latter signed "F. M.", which had in fact been written by the British conservative publicist, Francis Marx. Karl Marx had to write to the press on several occasions to refute this charge.

The Crimean War did not develop in the way Marx and Engels had hoped and did not result in direct revolutionary changes in Western Europe. The problem of national independence of the peoples still under Turkey's yoke remained unsolved. For Russia, however, the consequences of the war were much more considerable. Fifteen years after the war, Marx wrote in his outlines of *The Civil War in France* that "however Russia might have saved her honour by the defence of Sevastopol and dazzled the foreigner by her diplomatic triumphs at Paris", the Crimean defeat "laid open at home the rottenness of her social and administrative system".[3] The revolu-

---

[1] Ibid., Vol. 12, p. 212.
[2] Ibid., p. 34.
[3] Ibid., Vol. 22, p. 459.

tionary situation that was coming to a head in Russia not only heralded major social change in that country, but also markedly tilted the balance between the revolutionary and the counter-revolutionary forces in Europe, a fact which Marx and Engels subsequently took into account.

"REVELATIONS OF THE DIPLOMATIC HISTORY OF THE 18th CENTURY"

With the impressions of the Crimean War and West-European diplomatic efforts to prevent the fight against Russia as a rival from doing damage to the reactionary tsarist regime still fresh in his mind, Marx conceived a plan for a fresh *exposé* of the back-stage policies of the Western powers, in particular bourgeois-aristocratic England. In December 1855 he published an article entitled "Traditional English Policy", arguing that indulgence of tsarism had been a typical feature of British diplomacy in the 18th as well as the 19th century. In his new work he intended to support this idea with solid historical facts dating from the Northern War of 1700-21.

The idea first occurred to Marx in the spring of 1856, when during his studies in the British Museum he came across some ancient editions of diplomatic documents and political pamphlets. In March of that year, Marx negotiated with Trübner, a German publisher in London, about writing a book of 20 or so printed sheets on the strength of this and other material. No agreement was reached, and Marx decided to publish his future work in periodicals issued by the English publicist and politician David Urquhart and his followers.

Urquhart had around him a small group of journalists and politicians who were dissatisfied with the ruling oligarchy, the Whigs especially. These men were mostly of a conservative cast of mind, although some of them were radical-minded, like Charles Dobson Collet, editor of the group's London periodical *The Free Press*. While Urquhart sought to enlist the support of the workers, he continued to be a fierce opponent of any independent working-class movement. But whatever the conservative motives behind their criticism of the government's foreign policy, its colonial gambles in the East, and the methods it used to suppress the uprising in India, the Urquhart group made the workers give thought to political questions.

It was the group who invited Marx to write for their periodicals. Following the publication of his articles from the *Lord Palmerston* series, Urquhart wrote to Marx on December 9, 1853, conveying a proposal from the publisher, Tucker, who was close to the Urquhart group, for a separate reprint of one of the articles. Urquhart soon began to seek a personal interview with Marx, and the two men met in early February 1854. In the course of their talk it transpired that they had "only one thing in common", viz. Marx's "views on Palmerston", and took a diametrically opposite view on all other matters. [1] As before, so after this meeting, Marx argued in the press that Urquhart, "an innate conservative", was expressing untenable idealistic and subjectivist views, especially the idea that diplomacy had the decisive role to play in social development, and exposed his absurd attempts to present the tsar as a secret participant in the European revolution, and his idealisation of the Turkish and the Austrian Empires. [2] But Marx considered it possible to make use of the Urquhartist press because its attacks on Palmerston's foreign policy contained rational elements of use to the working class. Marx drew a distinction between the subjective motives behind these attacks and their objective significance. In 1860 he wrote about Urquhart: "He is, I grant you, subjectively reactionary (romantic); ... this in no way precludes the movement in foreign policy, of which he is the head, from being *objectively revolutionary*." [3]

Marx's relations with the Urquhart group show that the revolutionary proletarian tactics allow temporary agreements even with the opponents of the proletarian movement in order to fight a more dangerous enemy. On another occasion, Marx wrote: "In politics a man may ally himself, for a given object, with the devil himself— only he must be sure that he is cheating the devil, instead of the devil cheating him." [4] Marx stressed that his collaboration with the Urquhart group did not imply any ideological concessions or abstention from criticism of views which were hostile to the proletarian outlook.

Apart from *Lord Palmerston*, the Urquhartists also published some of his other articles from 1856 to 1859, the most important of these being his work on the diplomatic history of England and Russia in the 18th century, written in June 1856-March 1857. It was first serialised in the provincial *Sheffield Free Press* in the summer of 1856, as the author submitted each part. However, it was published carelessly, with deliberate omissions, and this made Marx stop sending material to Sheffield. When Urquhart learned of the friction between Marx and the editors, he suggested that the publication should be transferred to the London *Free Press*, where the whole of Marx's text was printed from August 1, 1856 to April 1, 1857. It was printed under the title "Revelations of the Diplomatic History of the 18th Century". After Marx's death, a separate edition was prepared by his daughter, Eleanor, and this appeared in 1899 under the title *Secret Diplomatic History of the Eighteenth Century*.

Seeking to bring out the historical roots of the foreign policy pursued by contemporary counter-revolutionary rulers, Marx did not hesitate to expose the defects of their historical predecessors— English diplomatists and politicians of the 18th century. He said

---

[1] Marx, Engels, *Collected Works*, Vol. 39, p. 455.
[2] Marx, Engels, *Werke*, Bd. 28, S. 735.
[3] Marx, Engels, *Collected Works*, Vol. 41, pp. 152-53.
[4] Ibid., Vol., 11, p. 382.

that his purpose was to acquaint the reader with the "infamies of English diplomacy"[1], and its cringing to tsarism. Engels subsequently wrote that the work was an *exposé* of "the continued self-interested dependence of English Whig ministers upon Russia"[2]. Lenin made a similar comment.

Marx keenly observed the community of counter-revolutionary aspirations between Russian tsarism and the English bourgeois-aristocratic oligarchy, which after the revolution had "usurped wealth and power at the cost of the mass of the British people"[3], but he could not avoid a somewhat one-sided view in analysing Anglo-Russian relations, partly because of the pamphleteering nature of his work. The character of these relations was determined not only by the desire of the English ruling classes to use tsarism in the fight against revolution, but also by their own aggressive aspirations, which frequently impelled them to regard Russia as a rival. Both during the Northern War and when Palmerston was in office, the architects of British foreign policy repeatedly hatched plans to strengthen England at tsarist Russia's expense, and gave support to her adversaries. In his articles on the Eastern question, Marx himself drew attention to Anglo-Russian contradictions as an important factor causing international complications. In his "Revelations of the Diplomatic History of the 18th Century" and partly in *Lord Palmerston*, he had left these facts in the background, and British connivance at tsarism's aggressive schemes was seen as an isolated phenomenon, not in a wider context. Nevertheless, the general idea of the work, that it was fatal to encourage the aggressive forces and make cowardly and self-seeking concessions to them, was of fundamental importance in appraising West-European diplomacy and in formulating an independent working-class stand on foreign-policy issues.

The "Revelations" contain a few pages dealing with the history of Russia. Marx had no intention of producing any sort of detailed essay on the subject, being mainly interested in the historical prerequisites of the aggressive foreign policy pursued by the tsarist autocracy. Another thing to bear in mind is that Marx obtained his facts about Russian history solely from the works of West-European historians (for instance, Ségur's *History of Russia and of Peter the Great*), and these were frequently full of ill will towards Russia and contained a number of tendentious propositions, subsequently rebutted by historians, like the Norman theory of the origin of the Kiev State, which said that it had been set up by the Vikings. Marx was unable to take a critical view of these ideas because he lacked the relevant facts. In the course of his subsequent historical studies he largely corrected his views. Thus, in the early 1880s, he noted in his *Chronological Notes* the role of the Russian people's heroic

---

[1] Central Party Archives of the Institute of Marxism-Leninism.
[2] Marx, Engels, *Werke*, Bd. 22, S. 345.
[3] *The Free Press*, November 8, 1856.

struggle in liberating the country from the Mongols. In the "Revelations" it appeared to be rather the result of diplomatic efforts by the Moscow Grand Princes.

Nevertheless, Marx's 1856-57 observations on various aspects of Russia's historical development reveal keen insight. The history of Kiev Rus suggested the conclusion, important in clarifying the whole period of early feudalism, that the formation of feudal states in the early Middle Ages was based on a "vassalship without fiefs, or fiefs consisting only in tributes". He gave a vivid analysis of the instability of "incongruous, unwieldy and precocious" empires of that period, such as those of Charlemagne, the Rurik dynasty, etc., which were inevitably doomed to disintegrate and fragment into appanages as feudalism developed.[1] He gave a classic description of the Mongol conquest, started by Genghis Khan. Marx stressed its terrible consequences: mass bloodshed, material destruction, and a life of slavery under the conquerors' yoke. This was "a yoke not only crushing, but dishonouring and withering the very soul of the people that fell its prey".[2] The "bloody mire of Mongolian slavery" had a corrupting influence on the feudal *élite* in the conquered countries, who borrowed the cunning, cruel method of administration used by the Mongolian conquerors.

As he examined the formation of the absolute monarchy in Russia in the 15th century (on subsequent occasions Marx and Engels repeatedly remarked that this process had been on the whole historically progressive), Marx revealed the ugly aspects of the absolutist system, already in evidence at that early stage. Even in pursuing centralisation and other progressive tasks (such as the subordination of the appanage princes, etc.) the autocratic rulers constantly resorted to the despotic and perfidious methods of Machiavellian politics. Of great interest were Marx's observations about the causes for the downfall of the feudal republics of medieval Rus in the struggle against the Moscow princes. He said that in the Novgorod Republic an important factor was the internal class struggle, which Ivan III made use of, and also "the dissensions between the patricians and plebeians raging as well in Novgorod as at Florence".[3]

In Peter the Great's policy, Marx discerned not only an autocratic despotism and a craving for conquest, but also breadth of vision and boldness of his undertakings as a statesman. He remarked on the resolution with which Peter the Great "transferred the capital of the empire from the inland centre to the maritime extremity", his role of reformer, his fight against inertia and routine, his urge to civilise Russia, to do away with stagnation and the Asiatic barbarism, and to prepare her for acceptance of "the technical appliances of the Western peoples"[4] without infecting them with the latter's ideas.

---

[1] Ibid., February 4, 1857.
[2] Ibid.
[3] Ibid., February 25, 1857.
[4] Ibid., April 1, 1857.

The "Revelations" contain Marx's first excursus into Russia's historical past, and while it may have been undertaken for a very limited purpose—exposure of tsarist diplomacy and its origins—it did acquaint Marx—even though through a prism of other people's subjective and, as a rule, one-sided assessments and judgements—with some pages of Russia's history and paved the way for him for a subsequent circumstantial and comprehensive study of Russia.

"REVOLUTIONARY SPAIN"

The events which broke out in the Peninsula in late June 1854 stood in sharp contrast to the overall reactionary situation in Europe. An armed rebellion, started by generals dissatisfied with the reactionary royal camarilla, grew into a bourgeois revolution, the fourth in 19th-century Spain. Power passed into the hands of the liberal party of Progressists.

Marx saw the revolution in Spain as heralding a fresh upsurge of popular movements. While explaining its progress in his reports, he noted both the general historical and the specific national features of Spanish revolutions, "some incidents in the Spanish revolutions peculiarly belonging to them".[1] Since the Middle Ages, popular movements in Spain had been isolated in the various provinces, and the army long remained the only force capable of taking a stand against the royal court on a national scale. However, the class prerequisites common to all bourgeois revolutions also constituted the basis there: as elsewhere, the mass of people played the part of the main motive force and repeatedly created situations in which "a mere military rebellion" developed into a "general movement" in the Peninsula.[2]

While putting a high value on the revolutionary energy of the Spanish masses, Marx was very suspicious of their political leaders, the bourgeois liberals. He had no doubt that the Spanish liberals would go the way of the cowardly, conciliatory liberal bourgeoisie in other European countries.

His fears proved to be well founded. The liberal government's policy led to the reactionaries being put back in power in the summer of 1856, and they proceeded to wipe out almost completely the gains of the fourth bourgeois revolution in Spain.

To gain a deeper understanding of the revolutionary processes in Spain, Marx turned to her history. In August 1854, he began publishing in the *New-York Daily Tribune* a series of articles entitled "Revolutionary Spain", with the intention of showing the connection between contemporary events and the Spanish people's revolutionary past, its traditions of fighting against absolutism and against Napoleonic domination, and the earlier Spanish revolutions of

---

[1] Marx, Engels, *Collected Works*, Vol. 13, p. 374.
[2] Ibid., p. 286.

1808-14, 1820-23 and 1834-43. The series was not completed, only eight articles having been published (the last one on December 2, 1854), which brought the story up to the start of the second bourgeois revolution (1820-23). The three subsequent articles Marx sent to the *Tribune* were not published, and we now have a rough manuscript of only one of them, analysing the causes of the defeat of the 1820-23 revolution.

In this series Marx took a fresh look at the historical role of the absolute monarchy, and on the strength of his Spanish studies made some essential corrections in his earlier conclusions, emphasising the need for a concrete historical approach to this question as well. He showed that at its origin absolutism did not always or everywhere operate as an instrument of progressive centralisation. In Spain, for instance, Marx saw it as a despotic oriental, specifically Turkish, form of rule, combining unlimited power of the monarch and local particularism, thereby largely responsible for the country's economic and social decline.

However, the absolutist regime was unable to stifle the Spanish people's energy for ever, a people who had shown their strength particularly in the fight against the foreign invader, Napoleon. Marx saw the war of liberation against Napoleonic rule as a heroic epic, showing that "Spanish society was full of life, and every part of it overflowing with powers of resistance".[1] It is true that he also observed contradictory tendencies in the resistance movement: the people's striving for liberation clashed with the urge of the feudal *élite* to preserve its social and political privileges. Accordingly, Marx said, the national liberation movement acquired genuine stability only "when social changes were to be blended with measures of national defence".[2]

Stressing the incapacity of the movement's bourgeois-landowner leaders to blend these two tasks, Marx pinpointed the most vulnerable spot of Spanish bourgeois revolutions in the first half of the 19th century, namely, the fact that the "revolutionary party did not know how to link the interests of the peasantry to the town movement". That is why the peasantry "remained passive observers of the party strife",[3] and was sometimes used by counter-revolutionary circles.

The lessons of the last Spanish revolution, Marx stressed in his summing-up articles on Spain which he wrote in July and August 1856, were highly symptomatic and showed that the changes taking place in Europe had also had an effect on backward, semi-feudal Spain: the bourgeoisie was degenerating into a counter-revolutionary force, while the proletariat had emerged in the historical arena as the force which was to carry the bourgeois revolution to the end in alliance with the peasant masses. The emergent Spanish

---

[1] Ibid., pp. 396.
[2] Ibid., p. 437.
[3] Ibid., p. 657.

working class first took part in the 1854-56 events, although it had yet to achieve self-determination and still followed in the wake of the bourgeois republicans. On that occasion, the peasants also gave wholehearted support to the revolution. The 1854-56 revolutionary movement gradually discarded traditional military and dynastic features, and all this, despite the temporary victory of the counter-revolution, gave Marx grounds to express the hope that "the next European revolution will find Spain matured for co-operation with it".[1]

FACING A NEW REVOLUTIONARY UPSURGE

Marx's creative energy was not weakened either by the oppressive atmosphere of reaction or the burden of personal adversity. In this difficult time, his fruitful and multifarious scientific and publicistic activity was of exceptional importance for the development of revolutionary theory and tactics. In his economic research of that period, Marx stood on the threshold of great discoveries. He had further deepened and concretised his materialist understanding of history, which he applied both to his analysis of general historical processes and to his studies of the concrete history of a number of countries, including those which he had not studied in detail before (Russia, Spain, the Balkans and the Eastern countries). A major accomplishment was his transition beyond the fairly narrow geographic horizons of bourgeois historical science, which as a rule confined its research to the history of Europe, and now and again combined this "Europacentrism" with a racist sense of superiority with respect to non-European peoples. By analysing the history of the peoples of Asia, and to some extent those of Africa and Latin America, showing its organic connection with the development of the European countries, and stressing the closely interwoven processes taking place in the metropolitan countries and in the colonial areas of the capitalist world, Marx laid the foundations for a scientific view of history as the historical development of the whole of mankind, as universal history in the true sense of the word.

As he shed light in the press on contemporary phenomena from day to day, he gave models of profound analysis of the most diverse aspects of life in bourgeois society, and the most diverse spheres in which capitalist relations were manifested—the economy, the political system of individual states and its evolution, domestic and foreign policy, and ideology. As in his capital works, his publicistic writings showed him to be an outstanding economist, sociologist, historian and politician.

In that period, Marx did a great deal to develop the revolutionary strategy and tactics of the working class, formulating the principles

---

[1] Ibid., Vol. 15, p. 108.

which determined the proletarian attitude to the liberation movement of the colonial peoples, the principles of an independent working-class line in international conflicts and wars, and fruitful ideas about temporary blocs and agreements between proletarian revolutionaries and other opposition forces, and about the terms on which these could be arranged. Marx and Engels believed that in the coming revolution the main centres would lie in the countries which since 1848 had given evidence of the most acute need for bourgeois-democratic change, and continued to expect the French proletariat to display revolutionary initiative, but saw that the revolution could run on different lines, and in particular could advance farther to the East, to Russia. They arrived at this conclusion by taking account of the social changes which had been taking place in various countries since the 1848-49 revolution.

Despite the difficulties of exerting an influence on the masses in the years of reaction, Marx's voice and the revolutionary ideas of his articles and reports did reach the leading workers. His publicistic writings promoted the growth of revolutionary feelings, of hatred for the existing counter-revolutionary regimes, and this was strongly brought out when the fresh revolutionary upswing came. Marx remained in touch with working-class leaders in various countries and used every means to establish closer ties with the proletarian movement. He was going forward to fresh revolutionary events, rallying round him a group of comrades-in-arms, fully armed with theoretical knowledge and a clear understanding of the pressing tactical tasks, and with the readiness of the experienced fighter to join open battle against the enemy.

CHAPTER EIGHT

THE DECISIVE STAGE IN THE FORMATION OF MARXIST POLITICAL ECONOMY

> *Ever since political economy had put forward the proposition that labour is the source of all wealth and of all value, the question became inevitable: How is this then to be reconciled with the fact that the wage-worker does not receive the whole sum of value created by his labour but has to surrender a part of it to the capitalist? Both the bourgeois economists and the socialists exerted themselves to give a scientifically valid answer to this question, but in vain, until at last Marx came forward with the solution.*
>
> Frederick Engels

ARTICLES ON THE 1857 ECONOMIC CRISIS

Throughout the period of reaction, Marx had displayed a keen interest in everything that determined the economic and political development of the capitalist world. In a short period, its productive forces had noticeably increased. The factory system had been most successful. Hundreds of factories bringing together unprecedented numbers of workers under one roof had been started. At the large enterprises, steam and mechanical machines were rapidly displacing manual forms of industrial labour. There was a simultaneous revolution in transport and communications. The length of railways throughout the world increased from 25,000 kilometres in 1847 to 83,000 in 1857.

Between 1850 and 1860, the volume of transactions in the world market almost doubled. Credit and banking assumed exceptional proportions. There was a rapid growth in the number of diverse banks, which began to operate on an unprecedented scale. The stock market hummed. This was used by the bourgeois economists and the press to extol the capitalist system.

However, Marx's precise scientific analysis of the economic development of the capitalist system enabled him to predict the onset of a new cyclical crisis of over-production, which was to succeed the boom phase in industry and trade. This prediction was fully borne out. The crisis broke out in 1857, taking the form of sharp cut-backs in the volume of production, massive close-downs of factories, numerous cases of bankruptcy, clogged-up markets, plummeting commodity prices, mounting unemployment, and so on. This was capitalism's first economic crisis which assumed truly world-wide proportions.

Marx set out his analysis of the economic situation in Europe regularly in his articles for the *New-York Daily Tribune*, and many of these revealed the prerequisites, causes, symptoms and specific features of the 1857 crisis.

Marx gave the 1857 crisis special attention, firstly, because the facts and processes relating to it helped to provide a more profound formulation of the theoretical problems of political economy; and, secondly, because it looked like directly aggravating the political situation in the most developed capitalist countries.

Marx's articles, written just after the events on the basis of his personal observations and reports in newspapers and special journals in England, France and Germany, contain not only vivid publicistic sketches of the ups and downs of the pre-crisis period and the crisis itself, but also generalisations which are of lasting value and which are a part of the Marxist theory of economic cycles and crises.

Marx argued that the 1857 crisis, whatever its specific symptoms and manifestations, was in no sense an accidental slowdown or setback in the commercial and financial sphere, but a typical cyclical crisis of over-production, which was an organic and inevitable part of capitalism, and which no government was able to avert. It had been prepared by the whole contradictory course of development in industry and trade.

One highly popular view prevailing among economists at the time was that banks of issue could exert an influence on the level of prices by regulating the amount of money in circulation, thereby striking the necessary balance between supply and demand for industrial goods, and stimulating or, on the contrary, slowing down current production. Many believed that over-production was caused by the issue of money over and above the necessary quantity, and the consequent sharp rise in prices. Marx used information issued by the Bank of England to prove the absurdity of these ideas. There was as little ground to blame the crisis on the stock-market speculations which had accompanied the industrial boom. Marx ridiculed the "crystal-gazing" theorists who said that "trade was sound, but that, alas! its customers ... were unsound".[1]

When the crisis broke out it exploded all the superficial declarations by bourgeois journalists, who had for years insisted that "the era of commercial convulsions was finally closed with the introduction of Free Trade".[2]

The reverse side of the prosperity in industry and commerce, which had culminated in the crisis, was savage exploitation of the working class. English employers prolonged the working day in defiance of the Factory Acts, which had been passed by Parliament as a result of stubborn class struggle. They reduced wages and preferred to employ children instead of adult workers. In one of his articles, Marx said that the capitalists of England were "vampires, fattening on the life-blood of the young working generation".[3] The

---

[1] Marx, Engels, *Collected Works*, Vol. 15, p. 383.
[2] Ibid., p. 400.
[3] Ibid., p. 253.

plight of the working people was further worsened by the crisis. The effect of "the palsy of industrial activity" was a rapid spread of indigence among the working class throughout Europe. Marx exposed the practices of the bourgeois governments who sought in every possible way to compensate the factory owners and big traders for their losses at the expense of the "fortune of the whole community",[1] in particular, by increasing the burden of taxes on the bulk of the people, and handing out to the barons of industry and commerce generous government subsidies and guarantees. This was the cynical practice of shifting the consequences of the crisis onto the shoulders of the poor sections of the population.

Marx objected to the tendency to exaggerate the specific features of the 1857 crisis and regard it as some sort of isolated phenomenon. He declared that "the distinctive features ... peculiar to every new commercial crisis, must not be allowed to overshadow the aspects common to all of them".[2] Marx believed that economic crises were organically built into the capitalist system of production, and that "so long as the system lasts, they must be borne with, like the natural changes of the seasons".[3]

WORK ON THE ECONOMIC MANUSCRIPTS OF 1857-58

Convinced that the triumph of reaction would be short-lived, Marx and Engels expected the economic upheavals in the capitalist world, arising out of the 1857 crisis, to have political consequences and to bring on the "deluge" — another revolution. In these conditions, Marx felt it to be a primary task to write a work on political economy to give the working class a knowledge of the economic laws of social development. He believed that a work of this kind would help the proletarian fighters to become aware of their revolutionary tasks, and would promote the growth of the proletariat's class consciousness and cohesion. At the height of the crisis Marx began to sum up all the economic research he had carried out. But before addressing himself to the public, he decided to produce a preliminary rough manuscript to clarify the problems for himself.

This was the origin of a series of economic works written from January 1857 to May 1858. The chief of these is an extensive manuscript running to 50 printed sheets, written from October 1857 to May 1858.

The economic manuscripts of 1857-58 are a true masterpiece of Marx's scientific genius.

It is also highly remarkable that this great work was produced in

---

[1] Marx, Engels, *Collected Works*, Vol. 15, p. 405.
[2] Ibid., Vol. 16, p. 34.
[3] Ibid.

a very short time and when "poverty weighed heavily on Marx and his family".[1] The extant letters of Marx and members of his family show the terrible poverty into which the great man and his family were then plunged. On January 20, 1857, he wrote to Engels: "So here I am, without any prospects and with growing domestic liabilities, completely stranded in a house into which I have put what little cash I possessed ... I am utterly at a loss what to do, being, indeed, in a more desperate situation than 5 years ago. I thought I had tasted the bitterest dregs of life. *Mais non!* And the worst of it is that this is no mere passing crisis. I cannot see how I am to extricate myself."[2] Subsequently, his condition became even more oppressive. When the 1857 crisis broke out, the *Tribune* editors dismissed all their European correspondents, the only exception being Marx, who the editors feared would be asked to write for other U.S. papers. But he was now guaranteed publication of only four articles a month, instead of the usual eight, and this meant a halving of his fees.

In this trying period, Engels helped his friend in every way he could. Lenin emphasised that "had it not been for Engels' constant and selfless financial aid, Marx would not only have been unable to complete *Capital* but would have inevitably been crushed by want".[3]

Despite the hardships, Marx worked with the greatest inspiration. On December 8, 1857, he wrote to Engels: "I am working like mad all night and every night collating my economic studies so that I at least get the outlines clear before the *déluge*."[4] He was fired with boundless loyalty to the cause of the revolution and his high sense of duty to the working class.

Marx worked on his 1857-58 economic manuscripts in an effort to realise a plan for six books on the following subjects: capital, landed property, wage labour, the state, foreign trade, and the world market.

INTRODUCTION TO THE ECONOMIC MANUSCRIPTS OF 1857-58

The general Introduction to the planned work, written by Marx in August 1857, is also one of the new series of manuscripts, which is theoretically one of the best specimens of mature Marxism. It is of immense scientific importance because it gives the fullest formulation of Marx's view of the subject and method of political economy as a special science.

Political economy deals with the social relations which arise between men in the process of the production of material values, and

---

[1] V. I. Lenin, *Collected Works*, Vol. 21, p. 48.
[2] Marx, Engels, *Collected Works*, Vol. 40, p. 94.
[3] V. I. Lenin, *Collected Works*, Vol. 21, p. 48.
[4] Marx, Engels, *Collected Works*, Vol. 40, p. 217.

with the objective economic laws governing its movement. One of the main tasks of political economy is the study of the specific features and distinctions of individual historical forms of social production, but it also examines the general laws of all modes of production.

The Introduction elaborates the key questions relating to the role of and dialectical interaction between the individual elements of social production. When men produce they adapt the products of nature to their needs; distribution establishes the proportion in which the produced goods are used; exchange supplies the individual with the products which he himself does not possess but wants to possess; in consumption the products become the objects of individual acquisition. In this series, production is the beginning and consumption the end, with distribution and exchange in the middle as the mediating element between production and consumption. Marx specifically stresses and argues the primacy of production with respect to distribution, implying that in every instance the mode of distribution is determined by the mode of production. While operating as the prerequisite of new production, distribution itself is always the product of production, in general, and of its specific historical form, in particular.

The section dealing with the method of political economy sheds much light on the part scientific abstraction has to play in political economy, and sets out the basic principles for correct scientific analysis and exposition.

Abstraction means separating from the real world of the relations being studied a definite element in them, a definite relation, the starting point for an analysis of an aggregate of such relations, which have their own historical features and their own laws. That is why abstraction, a logical category, a specific instrument of research, gives simultaneous expression to the properties of reality and to the movement of cognition, and is consequently similarly applicable in defining real phenomena and scientific concepts.

Marx held that the fruitful way of research should start from the surface, from what is given in the notion, and run into the depths of phenomena, until one finally arrives at the simplest definition. From there the researcher can start on "a return journey", from the analysis to the synthesis, from particular abstractions and definitions to "a rich totality of many determinations and relations".[1] Thus, for instance, while the category of population in general is in itself an abstraction of little content, in the aggregation of its particular definitions (classes, economic basis of their existence, etc.), which have been studied and subjected to scientific analysis beforehand, it becomes tangibly clear and concrete, and no longer appears as some chaotic whole.

The ascent from the simplest elements (such as labour, division of

---

[1] Marx, Engels, *Collected Works*, Vol. 28, p. 37.

labour, demand, exchange-value, etc.) to more complex elements (such as the state, international exchange, the world market, etc.) is the "correct scientific method".[1] But this method of proceeding from the abstract to the concrete, which implies "a synthesis of many definitions", "a unity of diverse aspects", is only a means by which the mind perceives the concrete and reproduces it in the process of cognition. It is in no sense a process in which the concrete itself emerges. Categories reflect reality, but do not create it.

Of special methodological interest is the treatment in the Introduction of the relationship between the historical and the logical in the process of cognition. Marx comes out in favour of the logical method, stressing that it makes possible the examination of economic categories not in the sequence in which they have come to play a decisive role historically, but with an eye to their relationships in contemporary bourgeois society. A correct understanding of existing and extinct forms requires the determination in every instance of decisive forms in series of logical categories. But it does not follow that Marx rejected the historical method which reproduces phenomena in accordance with their actual historical sequence. Political economy is essentially an historical science, because it studies the economic laws of social development and the conditions in which forms of production function and succeed each other. A cognition of the historically less developed forms implies an analysis of the more developed ones. "The anatomy of man is a key to the anatomy of the ape."[2]

Setting forth the methodological principles of his approach to the analysis of the categories of political economy, Marx formulated the principle of the unity of the historical and the logical in research. He showed that this unity was dialectical, being based not on an identity of the two methods, but on their interaction, interpenetration and mutual enrichment. Logical analysis cannot be an arbitrary mental operation: it is determined by the character of the economic phenomena being studied and the objective ties existing between them. Both bear the marks of their historical origins, and their essence cannot be fully understood unless these are clarified. That is why the use of the logical method in the study of economic phenomena should be organically combined with a clarification of their evolution in time, with detailed and scrupulous historical analysis. Such a combination is a necessary condition for all-round and deep-going analysis of the subject-matter and a means of obtaining correct and scientifically authentic results.

The Introduction shows clearly that Marx formulated the problems of political economy and the method of analysing economic phenomena in close connection with the general philosophic questions of the revolutionary-proletarian outlook. While assuming production relations to be the economic basis of social development, he

[1] Ibid., p. 38.
[2] Ibid., p. 42.

constantly dealt with the processes relating to the sphere of political and ideological superstructure, and traced their dependence on the basis and their retroactive effect on it.

Marx also made a profound study of the arts as a form of social consciousness. On the strength of his vast erudition and knowledge of the finest products of human culture, he formulated, as early as the 1840s, a number of conclusions constituting the basis of the new, materialist aesthetics.

Marx was the first to bring out the materialist prerequisites for the arts. In his *Economic and Philosophic Manuscripts of 1844* he had pointed to the role of labour in the development of man's capacities to perceive and reproduce the beautiful and to shape "objects in accordance with the laws of beauty".[1] At the same time, he stressed that the capacity to create works of art does not stem so much from man's anthropological, natural qualities, as from the social and historical conditions of his existence. Any change in these conditions tends to bring about a change in aesthetic ideals, requirements and standards.

Marx believed that art has a great part to play in social life, and saw creative art both as a form of reflection of the world and as a mode of its mastering. He was sure that progressive art exerts a progressive influence on the social process and on the education and spiritual development of the members of society.

Marx revealed that by its very nature art is social and develops historically, and showed the influence exerted on it—in an antagonistic class society—by class contradictions and the policies and ideology of definite class forces. The content of artistic works and the prevalence of this or that genre in literature and the arts are determined by the level of society's development and its social structure, and Marx saw this as one of the basic reasons why the art of different epochs is unique, and why it is impossible in contemporary conditions to recreate, say, the myths and epic poems of the ancient Greeks. "Is the conception of nature and of social relations which underlies Greek imagination and therefore Greek [art] possible in the age of selfactors, railways, locomotives and electric telegraphs?"[2]

In a warning, as it were, against the vulgar-sociological approach, Marx said that there was nothing straightforward or mechanical about the reflection of social life and the ideology of definite classes in the sphere of art. Creative art, while being subordinate to the general laws of social development, has, as a special form of consciousness, its own specific features and regularities. One of these is that periods of flourishing art may not coincide with periods of social upswings in other spheres, including the sphere of material production. It is also necessary to take into account the relatively independent development of ideology, art especially. Although works of

---

[1] Marx, Engels, *Collected Works*, Vol. 3, p. 277.
[2] Ibid., Vol. 28, p. 47.

art are historically connected with definite social forms, it does not follow that the importance of the former declines with the disappearance of the latter. By way of example Marx referred to the art and epic poems of the ancient Greeks, which "give us aesthetic pleasure and are in certain respects regarded as a standard and unattainable model".[1] Marx went on to give a profound explanation of this phenomenon. The reason lies in the fact that Greek art reflected a naive yet healthy, normal perception of reality, a striving for "natural veracity", full of a unique attractiveness and fresh human charm, a view of the world that mankind held at its earliest stages of development, in the period of its infancy.[2]

This example expresses an important aesthetic principle of Marxism: in examining works of art ultimately as a reflection of definite social conditions and social relations, it is necessary to bring out in them that which is of lasting value, the truly human element, which meets the aesthetic needs of subsequent generations as well. The nihilistic attitude to the artistic legacy of the past is deeply alien to Marxism. Marx himself provided a fine example of how people should cherish the world art treasures and study and use all mankind's great achievements in the sphere of spiritual culture in the interests of progress.

Analysing the status of art in the contemporary capitalist world in his *Economic and Philosophic Manuscripts of 1844*, Marx expressed the idea that capitalist reality is hostile to genuinely creative art, an idea that does not, however, deny the development of literature and art under capitalism. It means that by its very nature the capitalist exploitative system is profoundly antagonistic to the humanistic principles which inspire great writers and artists. The more profound their awareness of the contradiction between their ideals and the real capitalist world, the more vibrantly in their works, frequently contrary to their class origins, rings the protest against the inhumanity of capitalist relations. Even in bourgeois literature, the hostility of bourgeois society to creative art leads to criticism of capitalism in various forms, and the portrayal of capitalist reality as one which is full of dramatic and tragic collisions. That is the dialectical aspect in the development of creative art under capitalism, which is why bourgeois society produced Shakespeare, Balzac and other writers of genius, who, as artists, rose above their epoch and their class milieu and castigated, with tremendous artistic power, the vices of the exploitative system: the callous attitude to the dispossessed, the power of money, the offences of human dignity, etc. Marx's generalisations in his Introduction and other writings and letters form a solid part of the treasure-house of Marxist aesthetic ideas, and constitute the fundamentals of the scientific theory and history of art and literature.

---

[1] Ibid.
[2] Ibid., p. 48.

MAIN MANUSCRIPTS OF 1857-58

The Introduction was never completed, but the wealth of its content reflects the multitude of ideas set out in the main sections of the economic manuscripts of 1857-58.

The "Chapter on Money" gives a fairly detailed exposition of the main questions of the general theory of value and money. Marx reconsiders his earlier view of money, when, notably in *The Poverty of Philosophy*, he followed Ricardo in placing gold and silver in an exclusive category of commodities whose value is allegedly not determined by the costs of production.

Marx criticises the false theory of supply and demand as a factor behind the value of money, and shows that it is not the quantity of precious metals in circulation, but the cost of their production that determines the commodity prices as measured in the value of the metal. "If the costs of production of the precious metals rise, the prices of all commodities fall; if the costs of production of the precious metals fall, the prices of all commodities rise. This is the general principle." [1]

Step by step, Marx retraces the long path travelled by money. Like the state, money is not the result of contract. It is the product of exchange, which for its part is the product of division of labour. "Commodity circulation is the basic premiss of money circulation." [2] Initially, the role of money was performed by a commodity which was most frequently accepted in exchange, being the object of consumption by the whole of society or by a certain part of it. At the early stages of exchange, salt, hides, cattle and slaves functioned as money. Only very much later, the needs of exchange as such began to be serviced by a commodity which was least of all used for the purposes of individual or productive consumption. "In the first ... case a commodity becomes money because of its special use value; in the second case, it acquires its particular use value by serving as money." [3]

The functions of money likewise developed gradually. At the lowest stages of exchange and barter, money for the most part functioned as a measure of value, and not at all, or only in exceptional instances, as an instrument or medium of exchange. Marx observes that for Homer, oxen primarily served as a measure, whenever they were treated as money.

The bulk of the main economic manuscripts of 1857-58 consists of the "Chapter on Capital", which takes up almost six out of the seven notebooks.

It contains the initial exposition of the theory of surplus-value, the cornerstone of Marx's economic doctrine. It shows the historical

---

[1] Marx, Engels, *Collected Works*, Vol. 28, p. 128.
[2] Ibid., p. 122.
[3] Ibid., p. 103.

development of commodity production from its lowest form to its full-scale form, when labour-power becomes a commodity, and when the process of purchase and sale becomes all-embracing, subordinating to its laws society's whole way of life and activity.

Marx regards money as the primary form of capital, and analyses in detail the metamorphoses of industrial capital. The manuscript shows how capital alternates between being commodity and money. Capital itself signifies a replacement of both these definitions, a replacement whose ultimate result and purpose is a certain increment in the money compared with the amount originally invested by the owner of the means of production in the industrial and commercial turnover. This emphasises the essential distinction between money as such, as a commodity, even if a privileged one, and money which has acquired the capacity for "self-increase".

However, at a definite stage of social production money is converted into capital not of its own accord, not because of something intrinsic in its nature, but solely because the worker's capacity for labour, or labour-power, becomes an object of purchase and sale, that is, a commodity alongside numerous other commodities. The capitalist purchasing labour-power pays for its value, which is on average equal to the value of the worker's means of subsistence and the cost of his training as a worker. But what the capitalist obtains for his own use is the use-value of the labour-power, and this he uses in such a way as to obtain the gratuitous part of the finished product, once he has recouped the cost of labour-power, capital's costs incurred in the maintenance of this labour-power, as expressed in wages. Like the whole product, this part is made by the wage-worker. It embodies the surplus-value, which is the source of every form of unearned income derived by the exploiting classes of bourgeois society.

Consequently, the exchange between capital and labour merely has the semblance of an exchange of equivalents, and it is this semblance that bourgeois economists present as a real fact in order to justify capitalist relations.

The 1857-58 economic manuscripts first formulated the concepts of constant capital (the value of the means of production) and variable capital (the value of labour-power). This discovery was of crucial importance, for it made it quite clear that profit is generated in the process of production not by capital in general, not by aggregate capital, but only by that part of it which is expended on wages. As for that part of capital which goes into the basic assets, the cost of raw and other materials, its value does not increase in the process of production but is merely transferred to the finished product.

Bourgeois classical economists had never analysed the unpaid part of the product, which the worker is forced to give up to his employer, "in its integrity as a whole", [1] although they were aware that profit and rent were merely parts of this unpaid portion. But

---

[1] Karl Marx, *Capital*, Vol. I, Moscow, 1986, p. 14.

Marx in his "Chapter on Capital" notes that *"au fond* [at bottom], surplus-value — to the extent to which it constitutes the basis of profit, but is also distinct from what is commonly called profit — has never been analysed". [1]

Marx's great scientific accomplishment is his analysis of surplus-value independently of its specific forms: profit, interest and rent. In fact, this is one of the main dividing lines between Marxist economic doctrine and classical bourgeois political economy which constantly confuses the specific and general forms of profit.

Marx also examines the historical tendencies of capital, anticipating the general development of the productive forces for decades ahead. He speaks about "exploring the whole of nature so as to discover new useful properties in things", [2] and about the universal exchange of products between all climatic zones and all countries, the development of new methods of manufacturing "natural objects" and producing objects used in personal and productive consumption, the all-round exploration of the earth to discover new objects fit for consumption and new useful properties of old objects. A high level of natural science is a necessary prerequisite for this development.

Capital promotes the development of the productive forces, and therein lies its "great civilising influence". [3] But sooner or later it reaches the internal limits of its development: "Its production moves in contradictions, which are constantly surmounted, but just as constantly generated." [4] At a certain stage, the tendency of capitalism towards a boundless and wholesale development of productive forces begins to come up increasingly against the fundamental nature of the social system itself.

Marx's profound and truly prophetic words about the future application of science are of special interest. In large-scale capitalist production, there is already a tendency for "production to assume a scientific character", with the "technological application of science" as its most important factor. [5] The technical level, attained by industry in the first place, and "the development of constant capital is an indication of the extent to which general social knowledge is transformed into an *immediate productive force"*. [6] Marx said that this process would be even more intensive in a society in which the development of production and of the productive forces was released from the fetters of social antagonisms.

Marx expressed another highly important idea about some other aspects of the communist formation, under which collectiveness becomes the basis of production and the individual's labour operates

---

[1] K. Marx, *Grundrisse*..., S. 288.
[2] Ibid., S. 312.
[3] Ibid., S. 313.
[4] Ibid.
[5] Ibid., S. 587.
[6] Ibid., S. 594.

as collective labour from the very outset. It is not exchange that will make labour universal, but the collective character of production that will make the product a collective, universal asset from the very start.

Marx said that under collective production, economies of time, like the balanced distribution of labour-time among the various branches of production, become the primary economic law, a law "to a much greater extent". Every real economy is expressed as a saving of labour-time and a reduction of production costs to a minimum. This is the same as developing the productive power of labour. Economies in labour-time are equivalent to an increase in leisure-time, that is, the time to be used for the working people's full and all-round development, which should have a retroactive effect on the productive power of labour. Free time—both leisure and time for loftier pursuits—would enable every member of society to develop his spiritual and physical forces to the full.

Bearing in mind the range of questions discussed and the level of scientific analysis, the 1857-58 economic manuscripts can well be regarded as the first version of *Capital*, the first draft of the fundamental work which it took Marx over 20 years of intense endeavour to produce.

PREPARING THE NEW ECONOMIC WORK FOR THE PRESS

Even before the manuscript was completed, Marx began to prepare it for the press. First he compiled a detailed subject index making it easier to use the various hand-written notebooks. Between early August and mid-November 1858, Marx used the manuscript as a basis for writing the original version of *A Contribution to the Critique of Political Economy*. He also looked around for a publisher. Help came from Lassalle, who arranged with the Berlin publisher, Duncker, to have the work printed in consecutive parts, each between 4 and 6 printed sheets, a procedure suggested by Marx himself, because he was then unable to publish the whole work at one go. Marx intended to send the first book to the printers at the end of May 1858, hoping to produce a relatively self-contained work which would provide the theoretical basis of the subsequent exposition.

The preparation of the manuscript for the press was greatly hindered by Marx's illness and financial difficulties. He was often in such pain that he was quite unable to work, or even "to ply his pen", and after he did manage to work a little in spite of his pain, he was "to lie quite fallow for a couple of days".[1] This delayed the completion of his work and also affected its style. Marx himself was dissatisfied with what he was writing, particularly because it was the re-

---

[1] Marx, Engels, *Collected Works*, Vol. 40, pp. 303-04, 310.

sult of fifteen years of intense research, and he had hoped to do much better. "In it [this work] an important view of social relations is scientifically expounded for the first time. Hence I owe it to the Party that the thing shouldn't be disfigured."[1] Marx always set himself very high standards in his research and political activity. For him it was part of his code of behaviour, a firm ethical principle.

While working on his manuscript, Marx learned from *The Economist* about the publication of a work by the bourgeois economist James Maclaren, *A Sketch of the History of the Currency*, which he very much wanted to read. "My theoretical scruples won't permit me to proceed without having looked at it."[2] As a rule, there was considerable delay in new books arriving at the British Museum Library, and Marx could not afford to buy it although it cost only 9s.6d. His family continued to live in the grip of penury. Marx did not even have "a farthing" to pay for the posting of his manuscript to Berlin.[3] His finished work lay on the shelf until a money order arrived from Engels.

Finally, on January 26, 1859, the manuscript was sent to the publisher Duncker. It was twice as long as had been agreed. About a month later, on February 23, Marx also sent his preface.

The first part took quite a long time to be printed. Marx voiced his dissatisfaction over the fact that Duncker was "procrastinating".[4] An edition of 1,000 copies was issued on June 11, 1859.

FIRST PART OF *A CONTRIBUTION TO THE CRITIQUE OF POLITICAL ECONOMY*

One of Marx's most brilliant works, *A Contribution to the Critique of Political Economy*, opens with his preface, giving a concise outline of the history of his economic research and a classic definition of the materialist view of history, which suggests highly revolutionary conclusions equally important for theory and practice. Marx says: "In the social production of their existence, men inevitably enter into definite relations, which are independent of their will, namely relations of production appropriate to a given stage in the development of their material forces of production. The totality of these relations of production constitutes the economic structure of society, the real foundation, on which arises a legal and political superstructure and to which correspond definite forms of social consciousness. The mode of production of material life conditions the general process of social, political and intellectual life. It is not the consciousness of men that determines their existence, but their social existence that determines their consciousness. At a certain stage of development,

---

[1] Marx, Engels, *Collected Works*, Vol. 40, p. 354.
[2] Ibid., p. 318.
[3] Ibid., p. 369.
[4] Ibid., p. 408.

the material productive forces of society come into conflict with the existing relations of production, or — this merely expresses the same thing in legal terms — with the property relations within the framework of which they have operated hitherto. From forms of development of the productive forces these relations turn into their fetters. Then begins an era of social revolution."[1]

This classic definition of the basic conclusions and propositions of materialism as applied to social relations makes the preface a document with a scientific value of its own.

The preface ends with the words of the great Dante, which Marx quotes as his own motto in research and in the revolutionary struggle:

> Qui si convien ogni sospetto
> Ogni viltà convien che qui sia morta.[2]

Apart from the preface, the first part of *A Contribution to the Critique of Political Economy* consisted of two chapters: "The Commodity" and "Money or Simple Circulation".

The chapter "The Commodity" is the most difficult in terms of exposition and comprehension. Marx brings out in the most simple form of commodity the contradictory character of capitalist production, thereby establishing the initial theoretical principles for a further analysis and criticism of the economic categories of bourgeois society. An important feature of Marx's method is that he starts with the more elementary forms and then proceeds to the more complex ones. His analysis of commodities and value is not an end in itself. It paves the way for a logical transition to an analysis of money and capital.

At first sight, bourgeois wealth appears to be a vast accumulation of commodities, with the individual commodity as the elementary existence of this wealth. The commodity — the object of purchase and sale — is defined by Marx as a contradictory unity of use-value and exchange-value.

Use-value signifies the capacity of a thing to be necessary, useful, to be the object of human requirement. Use-value constitutes, in any society, under all social forms of production, the material content of wealth, and is produced by concrete labour, the labour of the cobbler, the tailor, the carpenter, the ploughman, and so on.

By contrast, exchange-value represents an economic relation. The labour which produces it and is embodied in the commodity is indifferent to the specific substance of use-values and to the specific form of labour itself. It is labour deprived of distinction and lacking quality, "labour in which the individual characteristics of the workers are obliterated".[3] This labour, which constitutes the substance of

---

[1] Ibid., Vol. 29, p. 263.
[2] Here must all distrust be left; All cowardice must here be dead. (The English translation is taken from Dante, *The Divine Comedy*, Illustrated Modern Library, Inc., 1944, p. 22.)
[3] Marx, Engels, *Collected Works*, Vol. 29, p. 271.

value, is called abstract-universal labour by Marx. In the 1857-58 economic manuscripts, he suggested that labour has a twofold character, and that abstract labour is a source of exchange-value. He elaborated this idea in detail in the first part of *A Contribution to the Critique of Political Economy*. Abstracting universal human labour means reducing various types of labour to simple average labour, that is, to the labour which the average individual of a given society is capable of performing. The labour represented in value is performed as the labour of a separate individual, but through the medium of exchange and market relations it assumes the form of its opposite and becomes abstract-universal labour. Thus this labour is the specific social form of labour.

By declaring labour to be the only source of value, Marx accepts the fundamental concept of the origin and substance of value advocated by classical bourgeois economists, but takes a substantial, qualitatively new step forward, notably as compared with Ricardo, the most consistent advocate of the labour theory of value.

Although his predecessors, including Ricardo, drew a distinction between use-value and value, they were unable to define their real relationship. Having discovered labour as the source of value, they were unable to establish the specific feature of labour which creates value. Concerned solely with the magnitude of value, and defining it as labour-time embodied in the commodity, they were unable to see the qualitative side and show the specific nature of the forms of labour represented in use-value and value.

Marx was the first to do this. His great scientific accomplishment is his detailed exposition, in the chapter "The Commodity", of his doctrine on the twofold nature of the commodity as a unity of use-value and exchange-value, and the twofold character of labour as concrete labour and abstract-universal labour.

He dispelled the mistaken notion that the sphere of commodities consists of relations between things, and set out the scientific prerequisites for a profound and general critique of all the distorted forms in which the economic laws of capitalism appear.

The second chapter, "Money or Simple Circulation", turned out to be more extensive and basically more elaborate than the chapter "The Commodity". The first chapter contains some points which are barely outlined and were subsequently developed in his *Capital*, but the second chapter, by contrast, contains some "circumstantially elaborated" propositions which he set out only in concise form when summing up the whole part in Volume One of *Capital*. Whereas the first chapter was roughly doubled in size and extensively rewritten for Volume One of *Capital*, the second chapter was reduced to about half its original size and was not substantially revised.

On the whole, this chapter is a fully mature and most circumstantial exposition of Marx's theory of money and money circulation, and the fact that it is much more detailed than the corresponding chapter in Volume One of *Capital* and contains an important historical sketch, which *Capital* does not, determines, together with other factors, the scientific importance of *A Contribution to the Critique of Political Economy* as an outstanding work of Marxist thought.

Marx produced a truly scientific theory of money and money circulation, and showed that money is not introduced into the circulation for the sake of convenience, but is produced by circulation itself. A specific commodity begins to function as money, because its natural properties—ease of transportation, divisibility, and so on—enable it, and no other, to serve as an adequate expression of value, and to appear in the process of exchange between private commodity producers as the embodiment of social labour. Money has value not because it performs a definite social function, but because it is a product of labour, and consequently possesses a real value, like all other commodities, not an imaginary or conventional one. Money is the supreme expression of value, which has evolved from the development of the contradiction between concrete labour and abstract labour, between use-value and the value inherent in commodities. It is the form in which individual labour appears as social labour.

Having analysed all the functions of money—money as the measure of value, as a means of circulation, as a means of hoarding, as a means of payment, and as world money—Marx formulated the law governing the quantity of money required for circulation, and other laws of the circulation.

A Contribution to the Critique of Political Economy was a real revolution in political economy. In a letter to Weydemeyer of February 1, 1859, Marx wrote: "I hope to win a scientific victory for our party,"[1] an aim which was achieved with the publication of the work.

Marx demonstrated the superiority of his economic views over the theories and dogmas of the bourgeois economists. The advantages of his method and his uniquely correct approach to the subject of political economy enabled Marx to draw conclusions in his study of the fundamental categories of bourgeois economics which exploded notions that had seemed established and well-nigh unshakable. He also gave further evidence of the theoretical flimsiness of Proudhon's critique of bourgeois property and all his plans to eliminate its "evil sides" through the reforms, which Proudhonism, a false brother of scientific communism, was advocating. Consequently, the publication of *A Contribution to the Critique of Political Economy* was a twofold theoretical victory for the revolutionary party of the working class, a victory over bourgeois political economy and a victory over the petty-bourgeois brand of political economy, as represented by Proudhon and his followers.

The first part of *A Contribution to the Critique of Political Econ-*

---

[1] Marx, Engels, *Collected Works*, Vol. 40, p. 377.

omy remains the world's finest work on money and money circulation, but it is of particular importance because it was the first to set out the Marxist theory of value, which is the foundation of Marx's economic doctrine.

Engels' review of the book was all the more instrumental in propagating its ideas. He declared that Marx's work was an outstanding scientific achievement and marked a new stage in the development of political economy. The edition was rapidly sold out. The book was read not only in Europe, but also in the United States. Marx was encouraged by its success and at once set about preparing the second part. At the same time he wanted to prepare an English edition of the first part, but had to abandon the plan for various personal reasons.

MARX AND DARWIN

The year that Marx published *A Contribution to the Critique of Political Economy* also saw the appearance of Charles Darwin's *On the Origin of Species by Means of Natural Selection*, which marked the emergence and establishment of Darwinism as one of the most important accomplishments of human reason in unravelling the innermost secrets of nature.

Marx was one of the first to appreciate Darwin's work. On December 19, 1860, he wrote to Engels, just after reading *The Origin of Species*: "Although developed in the crude English fashion, this is the book which, in the field of natural history, provides the basis for our views." [1] By asserting the idea of development in nature, Darwinism dealt a heavy blow at the metaphysical idea that the world was immutable, and cleared the ground for a spread of scientific views on social development. Marx regarded Darwin's theory as one of the great achievements in natural science which, together with a scientific analysis of social phenomena, should constitute the basis for the revolutionary-materialist outlook. Darwin's book struck at the very roots of the idealistic concept of design in nature, and gave a scientific explanation of its rational meaning.[2]

Marx also remarked on some of the weaknesses in Darwin's outlook, notably his tendency to oversimplify the analogy between the laws operating in the plant and animal world and the competitive struggle, a "war of all against all", which he witnessed in contemporary capitalist society. But that was not the main flaw. What was much more dangerous, Marx believed, was the efforts by the so-called social Darwinists to apply the biological laws discovered by Darwin to human society in order to explain the social contradictions of capitalism by the operation of the "eternal" laws of nature. In a letter to Paul and Laura Lafargue dated February 15, 1869, Marx said that while the universal fierce competition in English so-

---

[1] Marx, Engels, *Collected Works*, Vol. 41, p. 232.
[2] Ibid., pp. 246-47.

ciety had suggested to Darwin the idea of the struggle for existence and natural selection among animals and plants, the social Darwinists vulgarised and distorted the theory of the great naturalist by considering this competition "a conclusive reason for human society never to emancipate itself from its bestiality".[1]

Relations between Marx and Darwin were based on mutual respect and recognition of each other's scientific achievements, although differences in outlook prevented them from becoming close friends. Upon receiving a copy of *Capital*, Darwin wrote to Marx on October 1, 1873:

"Dear Sir,

"I thank you for the honour which you have done me by sending me your great work on Capital; and I heartily wish that I was more worthy to receive it, by understanding more of the deep and important subject of political economy.

"Though our studies have been so different, I believe that we both earnestly desire the extension of knowledge and that this in the long run is sure to add to the happiness of Mankind.

"I remain, Dear Sir,
          Yours faithfully
                    Charles Darwin."[2]

The theories formulated by Marx and Darwin developed in close interaction, interweaving and reinforcing each other. Darwinism presented a vast array of facts which confirmed, substantiated and developed Marxist philosophy. The spread of Darwinist evolutionary ideas in society as a whole helped to create more favourable ground for the assimilation of the Marxist doctrine by the working people. For its part, Marxism played an outstanding role in providing a dialectical-materialist interpretation of Darwin's theory and in developing its methodological principles. Marx, Engels and Lenin highly appreciated Darwin's ideas and showed their great scientific importance, thus promoting their extensive dissemination.

Comparing Marx's scientific achievement and Darwin's discovery, Lenin wrote: "Just as Darwin put an end to the view of animal and plant species being unconnected, fortuitous, 'created by God' and immutable, and was the first to put biology on an absolutely scientific basis by establishing the mutability and the succession of species, so Marx put an end to the view of society being a mechanical aggregation of individuals which allows of all sorts of modification at the will of the authorities (or, if you like, at the will of society and the government) and which emerges and changes casually, and was the first to put sociology on a scientific basis by establishing the concept of the economic formation of society as the sum-total of given production relations, by establishing the fact that the development of such formations is a process of natural history."[3]

---

[1] Ibid., Vol. 43, p. 217.
[2] Central Party Archives of the Institute of Marxism-Leninism.
[3] V. I. Lenin, *Collected Works*, Vol. 1, p. 142.

CHAPTER NINE

A FRESH UPSURGE IN THE DEMOCRATIC AND PROLETARIAN MOVEMENTS

> ...Marx was, as in 1848, most of all concerned with extending the scope of the bourgeois-democratic movement and bringing it to a head through the participation of broader and more "plebeian" masses, the petty bourgeoisie in general, the peasantry in particular, and finally of the poor classes as a whole.
>
> V. I. Lenin

Although the world economic crisis did not immediately result in revolution, it did provide an impetus for a fresh revolutionary upsurge in Europe and America in the late 1850s and early 1860s. The movement for national unification once again flared up in Germany and Italy, where the basic tasks of the bourgeois-democratic revolution had yet to be fulfilled. A revolutionary situation was developing in Russia and the United States. The struggle against national oppression in Poland and Ireland entered a new phase. There was revolutionary ferment among the masses in Bonapartist France and the Austrian Empire.

The political activity of the working class was growing in Germany, England, France, the U.S.A. and other countries. The proletarian movement was steadily parting ways with the bourgeois-democratic movement and pursuing its own path of development.

The vital needs of the working-class movement made Marx pay increasing attention to the practical side of the struggle for a proletarian party. It was necessary to rebuff the hostile circles and to help the working class in every way to escape from the political influence of the bourgeois parties and play an independent part in completing bourgeois-democratic change. The desire to prepare the working class theoretically for this role impelled Marx to try and finish his economic research as quickly as possible. Following the publication of the first part of *A Contribution to the Critique of Political Economy*, he worked with tireless energy on his old economic manuscripts and on new ones. At the cost of incredible effort, he succeeded in carrying on extensive research while performing the duties of proletarian organiser and publicist which had increased in the new circumstances.

He had to spend a particularly large amount of time on formulating the tactical line of the proletarian revolutionaries in the new international conflicts and wars, and also in connection with the revolutionary events in a number of countries.

In early 1859, Marx took steps to extend and strengthen international proletarian ties. In February 1859, he resumed a vigorous correspondence with Weydemeyer, whom he had helped to arrange the publication of a newspaper for the Chicago workers. The establishment in 1860 of contacts between Marx and Johann Philipp Becker, veteran of the German and Swiss revolutionary movement, helped the latter to adopt the communist stand. The circle of Marx's correspondents in Germany was enlarged. At the end of 1862, he began a regular correspondence with the Hanover physician Ludwig Kugelmann, a participant in the 1848-49 revolution, who had long followed Marx's activity with sympathy.

Marx established closer relations with former Communist League members—Lessner, Pfänder, Lochner and Imandt among others—who were resident in London and other towns in England. He wanted to see each of his comrades-in-arms engaged in the tasks confronting proletarian revolutionaries in the new upsurge of the revolutionary movement.

In the new situation it was particularly important to establish a proletarian periodical, which would act as an open party rostrum for the spread of revolutionary ideas and the organising centre for the proletarian fighters. On May 18, 1859, Marx wrote to Engels: *"It will be of crucial importance that, not just our enemies, but we ourselves should be able to publish our views in a London paper."* [1]

DAS VOLK

In early May 1859, Marx and his comrades-in-arms discussed the dissemination of proletarian ideas in the press. Within a few days, Marx was invited to contribute to a new weekly, *Das Volk*, which first appeared on May 7, 1859, as the organ of the German Workers' Educational Society and other German workers' societies in London. The invitation came from its editor, the petty-bourgeois democrat Elard Biscamp. Marx's reply was evasive, because he wanted to find out whether it was possible to exert an ideological influence on the newspaper. He refused to contribute officially but promised Biscamp his constant support, and did help to edit articles, raise funds for the paper, and select material for it. Thus, its second issue contained an item about Engels' pamphlet, *Po and Rhine*, which had just appeared. Issue No. 4 of May 28 carried an article by Engels written at Marx's request and entitled "The Campaign in Italy". Under Marx's influence, the tenor of the leading articles gradually began to change, with domestic and foreign-policy events being ana-

---

[1] Marx, Engels, *Collected Works*, Vol. 40, p. 439.

lysed from the proletarian class standpoint. Initially an emigrant sheet reflecting the narrow interests of predominantly German petty-bourgeois circles, the newspaper was being converted into a militant revolutionary organ, voicing the views of the proletariat. This enabled Marx and his comrades-in-arms to establish closer relations with the newspaper in June 1859. Its issue No. 6 for June 11 contained an official announcement by the editors that Marx, Engels, Freiligrath and Wilhelm Wolff were working for the paper.

In early July, Marx became the virtual editor and manager of the newspaper, which was by then an organ of the proletarian revolutionaries.

In the columns of *Das Volk*, Marx and Engels explained various aspects of the revolutionary theory and tactics of the proletariat. The paper carried Marx's Preface to his book *A Contribution to the Critique of Political Economy*, and also Engels' review of it, which showed the great importance for science and practice, for the revolutionary movement, of the materialist view of history discovered by Marx. Engels explained the basic features of the method of materialist dialectics worked out by Marx.

Das Volk defended the interests of the proletarian masses and reported on the proletariat's class battles. Thus, it informed its readers about a strike of London building workers at the end of July 1859, which played a major part in rousing the English working class to action.

Marx believed that one of the paper's main tasks was to combat petty-bourgeois ideology. A number of issues included press reviews, written by Marx with Biscamp's participation, containing devastating criticism of the lack of political principle of petty-bourgeois ideologists, and their views which bore the stamp of philistinism and nationalism.

The paper devoted particular attention to the Italian War (as the Austro-Italo-French war of 1859 was called at the time), to the proletariat's tactics in the war, and to an exposure of Bonapartism and of the foreign policy of England, Prussia and Russia.

Das Volk did not last long: in August 1859, the financial difficulties which faced it from the outset became insuperable. Marx made great efforts to obtain money to continue its publication, but failed. The last (sixteenth) issue of the newspaper appeared on August 20, 1859. But in spite of its short life, *Das Volk* made a substantial contribution to the spread of the ideas of scientific communism and the proletarian party's tactical principles.

FOR A REVOLUTIONARY UNIFICATION OF ITALY

In early 1859, Italy was on the verge of a revolutionary outbreak. The need to unify the country and liberate its northern part (Lombardy and Venice) from Austrian oppression became ever more acute. The Italian big bourgeoisie and the liberal gentry were hoping to unify the country from "above", dynastically, without popular participation. The moving spirit behind this policy was Count Cavour, a rich landowner and Prime Minister of the Sardinian Kingdom of Piedmont. He believed his plans could be realised through a joint war by Piedmont and France against Austria. At the same time, Napoleon III was hoping that a successful "local" military campaign, under the pretext of Italian "liberation", would help to prop up his tottering regime in France and to acquire more territory at Italy's expense.

However, contrary to the expectations of Napoleon III and Cavour, the war of France and Piedmont against Austria, which started at the end of April 1859, resulted in a powerful revolutionary upsurge in Italy, with popular uprisings sweeping Tuscany, Parma and Modena. The absolutist regimes in these states were overthrown. Uprisings also occurred in Romagna and other Papal provinces. Revolutionary excitement was growing throughout the country.

Marx and Engels rightly regarded the Italian question as one affecting the whole of Europe, believing that the struggle in Italy would influence the development of the revolutionary movement in other countries as well. In January 1859, before the war broke out, Marx wrote that "a successful revolution in Italy will be the signal for a general struggle on the part of all the oppressed nationalities to rid themselves of their oppressors".[1]

Marx and Engels took a resolute stand in favour of a revolutionary solution of the Italian question. In an article, "On Italian Unity", written in early January 1859, Marx expressed his conviction that "the burning hate of the Italians towards their oppressors, combined with their ever-increasing suffering, will find vent in a general revolution".[2] Marx supported the truly patriotic forces, which he called the "Italian National party", and exposed the anti-popular and counter-revolutionary plans to unite Italy under Piedmont's Savoy dynasty. He was hoping that the Italian democrats would succeed in rallying the middle and petty bourgeoisie, the peasantry, the progressively minded intellectuals and the still small working class, and "initiate the great national insurrection".[3] He believed that that was the only way to achieve national liberation, unite Italy on truly democratic principles, and solve the pressing social and political questions—elimination of the survivals of feudalism, abolition of the monarchist regimes, and so on—in the interests of the broad masses.

In his articles dealing with the events in Italy, Marx wrote with great warmth about the Italian people, expressing faith in its capac-

---

[1] Marx, Engels, *Collected Works*, Vol. 16, p. 153.
[2] Ibid., p. 148.
[3] Ibid., p. 153.

ity to paralyse the counter-revolutionary pro-Bonapartist activities of the bloc of the nobility and the big bourgeoisie. He praised the exposure by Mazzini, the leader of the Italian democrats, of Napoleon III's counter-revolutionary plans with respect to Italy, observing that Mazzini had "performed an admirable act of moral courage and patriotic devotion".[1]

For his part, Marx did his utmost to show up the true nature of Napoleon III's policy in Italy. In a number of articles written during the period when the war was being prepared diplomatically and militarily—"The War Prospect in Europe", "Louis Napoleon's Position", "The War Prospect in France", and others—Marx showed that Napoleon's intervention in Italian affairs was dictated by his urge to prevent a revolutionary explosion in that country, to keep it fragmented under counter-revolutionary regimes, and also to consolidate his own position in France. "The mock glories of the Second Empire are vanishing fast away, and blood is wanted to cement that monster imposture anew,"[2] he wrote. This was fully borne out at the very start of the Italian War.

Marx was hoping that the revolutionary-democratic forces would make use of the situation to rouse the people to activity, thereby helping to transform the dynastic war into a revolutionary one.

The results of the war, which ended with the signing of the provisional treaty of Villafranca on July 11, 1859, were analysed in Marx's articles "What Has Italy Gained?", "The Peace" and "The Treaty of Villafranca". Marx said that Napoleon III had hastened to conclude peace because in spite of its initiators the Italian War was "tending to become a revolutionary war".[3] But the Treaty of Villafranca made it especially clear that Louis Napoleon's aims, hypocritically presented as action in defence of the oppressed nationalities, had little to do with liberating and uniting Italy. Marx stressed how humiliating the treaty was for the Italians: Lombardy was first handed over to France, and then "as a French gift to the Savoy dynasty",[4] with Napoleon claiming compensation for this in the form of Savoy and Nice. Venice remained under Austria's rule (up to 1866). Marx said: "It will be long before Louis Napoleon can again delude even the sentimentalists and enthusiasts into regarding him as a champion of Freedom."[5]

THE GARIBALDI MOVEMENT

In July 1859, Marx wrote under the immediate impact of the Treaty of Villafranca: "Very possibly, however, an Italian Revolu-

---

[1] Marx, Engels, *Collected Works*, Vol. 16, p. 354.
[2] Ibid., p. 157.
[3] Ibid., p. 413.
[4] Ibid., p. 418.
[5] Ibid., p. 413.

tion may intervene to change the aspect of the whole peninsula, and to bring Mazzini and the Republicans once more upon the scene."[1] He was proved right within less than 10 months. A popular uprising broke out in Sicily in April 1860 against the social and political oppression of the Bourbons. Giuseppe Garibaldi, the outstanding Italian revolutionary, hastened to join the insurgents, and in May 1860 led a contingent of volunteers—the famous "thousand"—which landed in Sicily. From there, Garibaldi's victorious army advanced on Naples and entered it in early September, thereby completing the liberation of the whole of Southern Italy from the Neapolitan Bourbons. Garibaldi then began to prepare to march on Rome.

Marx and Engels followed the developments in Italy closely, expressed their warmest support for the heroic struggle being waged by Garibaldi and his volunteers, and praised the revolutionary tactics adopted by this truly popular leader.

Marx greatly approved of Garibaldi's resolution in fighting against Napoleon III's intrigues in Italy. Analysing Garibaldi's negative attitude to the French Emperor, he wrote to Lassalle on September 15, 1860: "Garibaldi shared my opinion of *Bonaparte's mission*, just as Mazzini did."[2] He believed that Garibaldi's success not only opened up prospects for Italy's revolutionary unification but also shook the foundations of the European policy of Napoleon III and of the whole Bonapartist regime.

Marx exposed the counter-revolutionary policy of Piedmont's ruling circles, who were resisting Garibaldi's revolutionary activities. He learned with alarm that the government of the Sardinian Kingdom had made arrangements with Louis Napoleon for an invasion of the Papal region by Piedmontese troops to frustrate Garibaldi's march on Rome. Marx wrote: "Cavour is actually Bonaparte's tool."[3]

For all his great successes, Garibaldi failed to carry the revolutionary struggle through to the end. Despite the insistence of Mazzini and other democrats, he did not dare to proclaim a democratic republic in Naples and continue, under its banner, the fight to unify the whole of Italy. In October 1860, he abandoned his march on Rome, allowed Piedmontese troops to enter Naples, and relinquished his powers, thereby displaying the political shortsightedness and inconsistency so typical of him. His greatest concern was the unity of the whole of Italy, but he did not attach sufficient importance to the question of the form of unity, so that while being a republican and a democrat, he did not object to the country's unification under a constitutional monarchy. Thus, Garibaldi the politician turned out to be—contrary to the hopes of Marx and Engels—of a much lower stature than Garibaldi the revolutionary general.

---

[1] Ibid., p. 420.
[2] Ibid., Vol. 41, p. 193.
[3] Ibid., p. 203.

At the end of October 1860, a plebiscite in Southern Italy supported her integration with the Kingdom of Piedmont, which handed the fruits of the victory, won by the Italian people under Garibaldi's leadership, to the Savoy dynasty, and the bloc of liberal nobility and big bourgeoisie supporting it.

TACTICS IN THE STRUGGLE
FOR GERMANY'S UNITY

The Italian War brought about a national upsurge in Prussia and the other states in the German Confederation. Public circles in Germany rightly regarded Napoleon III's attack on Austria as a prelude to his open territorial claims on the left bank of the Rhine. Demands were voiced in the press, at meetings and in clubs for nation-wide resistance to these aggressive plans. The national upsurge in Germany in 1859 once again raised the question of the unification of the numerous German states in a single state.

Marx and Engels formulated the proletarian tactics on this question, linking it closely with the tactical stand taken by the proletarian revolutionaries on the Italian conflict. Their point of departure was that Bonapartism, which had stifled the various revolutionary and national liberation movements in Europe, was the greatest obstacle in the way of Germany's unification. Marx and Engels believed that the defeat of Bonapartist France was the most important prerequisite for a European revolution, and urged the need for Prussia and the other German states to enter the Italian War on Austria's side. Their tactics did not, of course, in any sense signify an appeal to support the reactionary regime of the Austrian Empire or its rule in Italy, and they continued to condemn Austria for oppressing the Italian and other peoples. In his article "The War Prospect in Prussia" Marx wrote: "While decidedly taking part for Italy against Austria, they cannot (the German people—*Ed.*) but take part for Austria against Bonaparte." [1] Such was the dialectical approach to the solution of one of the most intricate problems of contemporary world politics in the interests of the proletarian and democratic movement.

Marx was sure that the entry of the German governments into the Italian War on Austria's side, quite irrespective of their intentions, would create the most favourable conditions for converting the dynastic war into a revolutionary one, and consequently for Italy's real liberation from Austrian rule. In the event of joint action by Austria and the German states, France's defeat could result in a revolutionary outbreak in Europe, leading to the overthrow not only of the Bonapartist system in France, but of the reactionary regimes in Austria herself, Prussia and the other states in the German Confedera-

---

[1] Marx, Engels, *Collected Works*, Vol. 16, p. 269.

tion, and to the unification of Germany and of Italy on revolutionary-democratic lines. Elaborating this idea, Marx observed in his article "Spree and Mincio" that in the situation that had arisen, an alliance between Prussia and Austria *"means revolution"*.[1] If events were to develop along these lines, tsarist Russia's entry on the side of France against Germany would be inevitable, and this would accelerate and intensify the revolutionary crisis, making the European revolution even more probable.

In his articles "A Prussian View of the War", "Quid pro Quo", "Spree and Mincio" and others, Marx condemned the cowardly neutralist policy pursued by the Prussian government as being outright support of Bonapartism. He showed that its refusal to come out against Napoleon III sprang from its fear of a revolutionary outbreak and its desire to take advantage of Austria's weakness to carry out its dynastic plan for unifying Germany under Prussia, and "by trickery eventually to gain hegemony in Germany at a discount".[2] His brilliant and profound article "Erfurtery in the Year 1859" directly stated the alternative which history was presenting to Germany: either the urgent tasks — national unification and the necessary changes — would be carried out in the revolutionary way, or they would be performed from above by the ruling clique, with ways and means that corresponded to its own interests. Marx warned that "in the hands of reaction ... this revolutionary programme turns into a satire on the relevant revolutionary forces".[3]

In his press articles, Marx emphasised that the end of the war in Italy did not mean that the question of revolution in Europe should be shelved. Indeed, the national upsurge in Germany continued even after the conclusion of the Treaty of Villafranca.

The constitutional conflict in Prussia in 1860 over the refusal of the Lower House of the Provincial Diet to pass a government bill for reorganising the army and increasing military spending gave a fresh impetus to the movement for Germany's unification. A revolutionary situation began to develop in Germany. In his article "Public Feeling in Berlin", written in April 1860, Marx noted the marked growth of revolutionary ferment.

The letters exchanged by Marx and Engels during the culminating phase of the conflict in 1862 show that they believed the situation in Prussia had been further aggravated and that a revolutionary outcome of the crisis was possible. But they very much feared that, as in 1848, the liberal opposition would display cowardice and capitulate treacherously to the Junker government. Indeed, the Prussian liberals did not go further than empty statements of opposition and allowed the counter-revolutionary forces to consolidate their positions. In September 1862, William I, who had become King of Prussia in 1861, appointed as his Prime Minister Prince Otto von Bismarck,

---

[1] Ibid., p. 381.
[2] Ibid., p. 452.
[3] Ibid., p. 404.

a Pomeranian Junker, who began to carry out a military reform without the consent of the Provincial Diet. Its liberal majority, the progressists, confined themselves to issuing verbal protests, and in fact allowed Bismarck to commence the unification of Germany from above, with "blood and iron", as he himself put it in one of his speeches.

DIFFERENCES WITH LASSALLE

During the upsurge in the proletarian and democratic movements, the differences between Marx and Lassalle became most pronounced. For a number of years, Marx had sought to persuade Lassalle to accept the revolutionary theory and work for the proletariat.In his letters to Engels and Lassalle himself, Marx had repeatedly criticised the latter's theoretical views, and observed that Lassalle was taking an idealist Hegelian stand. He stressed that Lassalle's philosophic writings were superficial and eclectic, and the author himself pretentious.

In a letter to Engels on February 1, 1858, Marx gave a sharp criticism of Lassalle's book *The Philosophy of Heraclitus the Dark of Ephesus*. He wrote: "*Heraclitus, the Dark Philosopher* by Lassalle the Luminous One is, *au fond*,[1] a very silly concoction. Every time Heraclitus uses an image to demonstrate the unity of affirmation and negation — and this is often — in steps Lassalle and makes the most of the occasion by treating us to some passage from Hegel's *Logic* which is hardly improved in the process; always at great length too, like a schoolboy who must show in his essay that he has thoroughly understood his 'essence' and 'appearance' as well as the 'dialectical process'." [2]

Marx kept in touch with Lassalle in the hope that the latter would accept his criticism and renounce his erroneous views. In fact, however, Lassalle remained a petty-bourgeois democrat even though he assured Marx that he supported the latter's views. The socialist views to which Lassalle slightly inclined at that time were a very far cry from scientific communism and sprang from various utopian socialist doctrines, mainly those of petty-bourgeois socialists. At the end of the 1850s, the profound differences in outlook and approach to current political issues resulted in a fundamental divergence of opinion between Marx and Engels, on the one hand, and Lassalle, on the other, over theoretical questions and the tactics of the revolutionary movement.

In 1859 Marx and Engels wrote a friendly but fairly critical review of Lassalle's historical drama, *Franz von Sickingen*, about an uprising of knights in 1522-23, on the eve of the Peasant War in Germany. In their letters to Lassalle (Marx's dated April 19 and Engels'

---

[1] At bottom.
[2] Marx, Engels, *Collected Works*, Vol. 40, p. 259.

dated May 18, 1859) they formulated the key principles of Marxist aesthetics. Their analysis of the literary aspect of Lassalle's drama revolved round the problem of realism, and their statements on this point constituted, as it were, a foundation for their views on the theory and history of literature.

Marx and Engels believed that realism, as a trend in literature and as an artistic method, was the highest achievement in the development of the arts. They held that the realistic method made it possible to give the most adequate, comprehensive and profound reflection of reality in artistic form. Realistic portrayal was in no sense a copying of reality, but a method of penetrating into the essence of phenomena, generalising them in artistic terms, and bringing out the typical features of a given epoch. That is precisely what Marx and Engels valued in the writings of the great realists such as Shakespeare, Cervantes, Goethe, Balzac and Pushkin. In particular, Marx valued Balzac so highly as an unsurpassed artist in depicting the life and customs of French bourgeois society in the first half of the 19th century, whose works were marked by "profound understanding of real relations", that he intended to write a special work on his *Comédie humaine* after he had finished his own *Capital*. In an article written in 1854 Marx said that the English realists of the 19th century — Dickens, Thackeray, Charlotte Brontë and Elizabeth Gaskell — were a "splendid brotherhood of fiction-writers ... whose graphic and eloquent pages have issued to the world more political and social truths than have been uttered by all the professional politicians, publicists and moralists put together".[1]

Marx's criteria in assessing Lassalle's drama reflected a profound understanding of the substance of realism. He noted its merits, namely, its excellent composition and liveliness of the action. At the same time, he showed how it departed from realistic principles, by its rhetoric and excessively abstract description of characters. By turning the characters into "mere mouthpieces for the spirit of the times",[2] Lassalle deprived them of their authenticity and individuality. Another departure from realism was that the drama lacked a real social background, the people. Lassalle had also failed to convey the historical atmosphere.

These critical remarks expressed important principles of realistic art. Marx and Engels insisted on authentic portrayal and a concrete historical approach to the phenomena depicted. The characters must be endowed with convincing individual features that reflect the typical aspects of the nature and mentality of the class milieu to which they belong. The author of a truly realistic work does not convey his ideas to the reader in the form of didactic exhortations but through the medium of full-blooded, lifelike characters, acting on the reader's mind and heart by the various means of artistic expression. Marx and Engels believed that Lassalle had intensified

[1] Ibid., Vol. 13, p. 664.
[2] Ibid., Vol. 40, p. 420.

some of the weaker aspects in the writing of the great German poet and playwright, Schiller, namely, his tendency towards high-sounding rhetoric which turned his characters into abstract, one-dimensional mouthpieces for various ideas. In this respect, they preferred Shakespeare to Schiller, and told Lassalle that by imitating Schiller's manner he was ignoring the need for the realist writer to combine ideological depth and lofty ideals with Shakespearean ability to portray genuine passions and diverse characters.

Marx also set a high standard for writers with respect to artistic form. He said to Lassalle: "Since you have chosen to write in verse, you could have put a touch more artistry into the iambics." [1]

In their letters to Lassalle, Marx and Engels also dealt with the connection between literature and life, the contemporary scene. Marx did not in any sense censure Lassalle for his idea of drawing an analogy between the 16th-century events depicted in the drama and the situation in the middle of the 19th century, and pinpointing the truly "tragic conflict upon which the revolutionary party of 1848-49 justly foundered".[2] What he considered to be a mistake was the idealistic and incorrect interpretation of the conflict itself and the reduction of its causes to an allegedly eternal and abstract "tragedy of revolution", deprived of any concrete historical, class content. Marx did not criticise Lassalle because there was a political tendency in his drama but because it was basically incorrect from the point of view of the materialist interpretation of history and the proletarian revolutionary outlook. On the whole, Marx and Engels believed that a political tendency, the reflection of any political opinion, of this or that outlook, was an integral part of any literary work. They took a highly critical view of the attempts to place literature above politics, and of the various theories of "art for art's sake". In the same period, Marx censured Freiligrath's neglect of party interests and remarked regretfully that the latter's departure from a revolutionary position had had a negative effect on his writings.

Marx and Engels were deeply convinced that the best books must give authentic expression, in vivid artistic form, to the contemporary processes in life, that they must herald progressive ideas and champion the interests of society's progressive forces. It was in this noble sense that they understood the concept of party spirit in literature. They believed that an organic blend of ideological content, aesthetic form and literary craftsmanship, which was precisely what Lassalle's drama lacked, was a necessary quality of truly realistic art.

Their critical analysis of Lassalle's drama was not confined to pointing out its literary merits and defects, but also involved fundamental political principles. Marx resolutely censured Lassalle for having portrayed the opposition nobility, led by the knight Sickingen, as the vehicle of revolutionary ideas. He wrote to Lassalle:

[1] Marx, Engels, *Collected Works*, Vol. 40, p. 419.
[2] Ibid.

"Have not you yourself—like your Franz von Sickingen— succumbed, to some extent, to the diplomatic error of regarding the Lutheran-knightly opposition as superior to the plebeian-Münzerian?"[1]

There was, in fact, good reason for Lassalle's error. His views of the Peasant War in Germany sprang from his general underestimation of the people's revolutionary potential, notably, that of the peasantry, which he regarded as an altogether reactionary class. During the struggle for the various ways of bringing about Germany's national unification and solving the country's important sociopolitical problems, Lassalle was inclined to side with the bourgeois-Junker bloc. In analysing the political tendencies of Lassalle's drama, Marx was, in fact, having a discussion with him about the motive forces not only of past revolutionary events, but of Germany's future development.

Marx and Engels did not succeed in their efforts to win Lassalle round to their view. In response to their critical remarks he wrote to them, among other things, that peasant wars were "*not* revolutionary", but were "*ultimately—reactionary*".[2]

The question of ways to unify Germany led to especially serious differences between Marx and Lassalle over the Italian War of 1859. Lassalle was well aware of the view taken by Marx and Engels from the pamphlet, *Po and Rhine*, but far from supporting them, he adopted a hostile attitude. In May 1859 he issued an anonymous pamphlet in Berlin, entitled *The Italian War and Prussia's Tasks*, voicing solidarity with the Prussophile bourgeoisie and the Prussian Junkers, and supporting a plan for a dynastic unification of Germany with Prussia at the head. In contrast to the appeal for the country's unification as a democratic republic, which Marx issued in 1848, Lassalle favoured the absorption of the other states by the Prussian monarchy. His pamphlet was addressed not to the German people but to the Prussian government.

Lassalle vindicated the Prussian government's neutralist policy and advised it to take advantage of Austria's difficulties and implement its unification programme. Instead of exposing the Bonapartist demagogy on the Italian question, Lassalle insisted that in Italy Napoleon III was working for "a cause that is great and just, civilising and supremely democratic, and therefore a cause cherished by *all* peoples".[3]

Marx and Engels expressed their displeasure with Lassalle's pamphlet, justly regarding it as an open attack on their views on German unification. Marx wrote to Engels on May 18, 1859: "Lassalle's pamphlet is an enormous blunder."[4] He told Lassalle that his stand

---

[1] Ibid., p. 420.
[2] F. Lassalle, *Nachgelassene Briefe und Schriften. Herausgegeben von Gustav Mayer*, Bd. 3, Stuttgart-Berlin, 1922, S. 205.
[3] F. Lassalle, *Gesammelte Reden und Schriften*, Bd. 1, Berlin, 1919, S. 43.
[4] Marx, Engels, *Collected Works*, Vol. 40, p. 435.

had nothing in common with that of the proletarian revolutionaries. However, Marx continued to keep in touch with Lassalle in the hope of persuading him to change his views.

Lenin explained the fundamental differences between Marx and Lassalle in 1859 as follows: "Lassalle was adapting himself to the victory of Prussia and Bismarck, to the lack of sufficient strength in the democratic national movements of Italy and Germany. Thus Lassalle deviated towards a national-liberal labour policy, whereas Marx encouraged and developed an independent, consistently democratic policy hostile to national-liberal cowardice (Prussia's intervention in 1859 against Napoleon would have stimulated the popular movement in Germany)." [1]

HERR VOGT PAMPHLET

Marx and Engels believed that one of the important tasks in setting up a proletarian party was to protect the proletarian cadres, which were still in their infancy and had yet to gain in strength, from slander and harassment by the ideologists and agents of the bourgeoisie, such as the vulgar democrat Karl Vogt, who in December 1859 put out a pamphlet called *My Lawsuit against the "Allgemeine Zeitung"* which was full of malicious slander against the proletarian revolutionaries. Vogt was particularly anxious to denigrate the activity of Marx and his associates in the Communist League, and he depicted them as conspirators who were secretly in touch with the police and printing counterfeit money to incite revolution. He sought to cast a slur on *Das Volk* by alleging that it was a branch of the reactionary Bavarian *Allgemeine Zeitung* and received money from dubious sources.

Marx saw Vogt's attack as an attempt by the bourgeoisie to discredit the incipient proletarian party in the eyes of the public. He did not usually respond to personal attacks but this was a slur on the party's honour, and he could not ignore it. He wrote: "In the previous ten years a vast number of verifications of myself had appeared in the German and German-American press, but they only rarely drew any literary response from me, and then only if a real party interest seemed to be at stake, as with the Cologne communist trial." [2]

Marx's response to Vogt's pamphlet was *Herr Vogt*, a pamphlet published in London in December 1860, with a twofold task. The first was to expose Vogt himself not as a casual figure but as "an individual who stands for a whole trend",[3] and as a typical lackey of the bourgeoisie. In addition, while donning the mask of a democrat and enjoying the reputation of a naturalist, Vogt was in fact, as

---

[1] V. I. Lenin, *Collected Works*, Vol. 21, p. 141.
[2] Marx, Engels, *Collected Works*, Vol. 17, p. 259.
[3] Ibid., p. 26.

Marx established later, acting as a secret Bonapartist agent in the political sphere.

Marx's second task was to strengthen the authority of the proletarian revolutionaries among the masses by showing their past and present activity and their views and aims in a true, undistorted light. He wrote to Freiligrath on February 23, 1860, saying that the fight against Vogt was "crucial to the *historical vindication* of the party and its subsequent position in Germany".[1]

Marx began to collect material for his pamphlet at the end of January 1860, and worked on it tirelessly for almost a year, temporarily interrupting even his economic studies. In order to obtain information to rebut Vogt's inventions and to expose Vogt himself, he sent over 50 letters to friends, acquaintances and even strangers in many towns in Europe, and studied a large number of documents and various publications. In addition, he went to see Engels in Manchester and stayed there from mid-February 1860 to March 25, to discuss the plan for the polemical work against Vogt, and to look through material which Engels possessed on the history of the Communist League. Many of Marx's friends failed to understand why he was putting so much effort into this, and believed he was wasting his time. But Marx was quite clear on the main point: he had to convey to the masses the ideas of the proletarian party in all their greatness and purity, and to deny the enemies of the working class any opportunity to denigrate and defame the party.

In the pamphlet, Vogt was presented mainly as a political figure, but the philosophical views expressed in his scientific writings were also analysed. With sharp irony Marx ridiculed Vogt's primitive ideas, for the latter belonged with Ludwig Büchner and Jakob Moleschott to the German vulgar materialist trend of the mid-19th century.

Step by step, Marx exposed Vogt's slander of the proletarian party, showing him up as a flagrant liar. Vogt's malicious story was such a tissue of lies and contradictory statements that the "fat scoundrel" himself had been unable to tie up all the loose ends. While hurling the foul charge of working with the police at the proletarian revolutionaries, Vogt carefully glossed over the facts of his own base collaboration with the police authorities.

In contrast to Vogt's inventions, Marx gave a true picture of the development of the international communist movement. On the basis of numerous documents, he portrayed the heroic struggle of the proletarian revolutionaries to establish a revolutionary proletarian organisation. In bold, concise terms, Marx told the story of the Communist League, describing the historical background to its activity, its character and aims, and the importance of its struggle against sectarian elements and vulgar petty-bourgeois democrats.

The central point of Marx's pamphlet was his exposure of Vogt as

---

[1] Ibid., Vol. 41, p. 54.

a paid Bonapartist agent. After reading Vogt's book *Studies of the Present Situation in Europe* which was published in March 1859, Marx was convinced that it had been written on direct orders from France and was being used by Napoleon III to exert an ideological influence on European public opinion. He wrote: "*Vogt* was merely one of the countless mouthpieces through whom the grotesque ventriloquist in the Tuileries spoke in foreign tongues."[1] But Vogt had also rendered other services to Napoleon III. Marx revealed that he had been connected with the ramified network of Bonapartist agents in many countries and had in fact been one of its recruiters.

Documents made public later, which Marx had not been aware of at the time, fully confirmed his view that the "democrat" Vogt had been actually in the service of the Bonapartist government. The accounts for the expenditure of secret funds by Napoleon III, made public after the fall of the Second Empire, showed that in August 1859 Vogt received 40,000 francs from the French Emperor.

Marx exposed the counter-revolutionary nature of Napoleon III's policy, including his role in starting the Italian War. He also denounced the Bonapartist demagogy on the national question and the notorious "nationalities principle", which the French Emperor had used to disguise his efforts to use the national movement of the small peoples for his counter-revolutionary ends. Of equal importance was Marx's warning of the danger for the working-class movement presented by the flirtation of the Bonapartist ruling circles with vacillating elements of the proletariat.

Marx showed that in respect of Germany the pro-Bonapartist stand of Vogt and others of his kind was expressed in their Prussophile attitudes and their efforts to spread Prussia's "unifying mission". The critique of those who advocated German unification under the aegis of Prussia was, undoubtedly, also aimed against Lassalle, although Marx did not name him. Marx wrote to Engels on November 26, 1859, saying that Lassalle "in point of fact was piping the same tune as Vogt".[2]

The pamphlet *Herr Vogt* is profound in content and brilliant in form. From a literary point of view it ranks among the world's best satirical writings. In a letter to Marx dated December 19, 1860, Engels wrote: "This is, of course, the best polemical work you have ever written."[3]

JENNY MARX'S ILLNESS

Vogt's slander had a bad effect on Marx's wife. Throughout the months when Marx was working on his pamphlet against Vogt she suffered from nervous tension and frequent attacks of insomnia. She also worked hard to produce a fair copy of the pamphlet, and on

---

[1] Marx, Engels, *Collected Works*, Vol. 17, p. 159.
[2] Ibid., Vol. 40, p. 542.
[3] Ibid., Vol. 41, p. 231.

November 19, 1860, when it was finished, she took to her bed. The doctor diagnosed smallpox. She had been run down and her resistance was so lowered that she had contracted the disease despite having been inoculated against it twice.

This was an especially trying time for Marx. The children had to be put into the care of the Liebknechts, who lived nearby. Karl and Hélène Demuth took turns sitting at Jenny's bedside. Jenny later described the first few days of her illness to Luise Weydemeyer as follows: "I was in great suffering. I had severe burning pains in my face and was completely unable to sleep. I was mortally anxious about Karl, who took the most tender care of me. In the end I lost all use of my outward senses although I was fully conscious all the time. I lay constantly by the open window so that the cold November air would blow over me, while there was a raging fire in the stove and ice on my burning lips, and I was given drops of claret from time to time. I could hardly swallow, my hearing was getting weaker, and finally my eyes closed so that I did not know whether I would remain enveloped in eternal night." [1]

For a whole week they feared for her life. Then came the turning point and her condition improved. Marx wrote to Engels on November 26, 1860: "My wife's condition has improved, in so far as this is possible under the circumstances. It is going to be a lengthy business. What might be called the paroxysm of the disease is now over." [2]

Jenny's illness upset Karl's routine, and in the early stages he was unable to work at all. He wrote to Engels: "Writing articles is almost out of the question for me. The only occupation that helps me maintain the necessary quietness of mind is mathematics." [3]

By the end of December, Jenny was feeling so much better that the doctor allowed the children to be sent home. This was a great occasion for their parents, who were deeply grieved even by the shortest separation from their daughters. But the physical and emotional strain during Jenny's illness had its effect, and hardly had Jenny started to improve when Karl himself fell ill in early January with an especially acute attack of his chronic liver complaint that kept him in bed for almost the whole month.

TRIP TO HOLLAND AND GERMANY

Marx's illness coincided with another bad patch in the family's financial affairs. In early 1861, there was a sharp drop in fees from the U.S.A. Because of the impending civil war, *The New American Cyclopaedia* suspended publication and the editors of the *New-York Daily Tribune* once again, as they had during the 1857 crisis, dis-

---

[1] *Reminiscences of Marx and Engels*, p. 247.
[2] Marx, Engels, *Collected Works*, Vol. 41, p. 218.
[3] Ibid., p. 216.

missed all their European correspondents with the exception of Marx, whom they asked to refrain from sending in reports for a certain time, and after that to send in only one article a week instead of two.

At the end of February, to help put his financial affairs in order, Marx went to see his uncle, Lion Philips, a fairly rich merchant, who lived in the Dutch city of Zalt-Bommel. He hoped that Philips, who was administering his mother's estate, could help him to obtain some money on account of his share of the inheritance. His hopes were realised and on May 7, 1861, upon his return to London, he informed Engels: "For a start, I squeezed £160 out of my uncle so that we were able to pay off the greater part of our debts." [1]

From Holland, Marx went on to Berlin, the Prussian capital, where he stayed from March 17 to April 12, hoping to discuss with Lassalle a plan for the joint publication of a newspaper, and also to get himself reinstated as a Prussian subject on the strength of an amnesty issued by the Prussian government, following the accession to the throne of King William I. In Berlin, Marx was the guest of Lassalle, whom he was meeting for the first time after the 1848-49 revolution. Lassalle and his friend, Countess Sophie Hatzfeldt, gave Marx a warm welcome but made a point of advertising their close acquaintance with the famous revolutionary thinker to their aristocratic friends. They sought to introduce him to their "select society", held a dinner party attended by persons of high rank, and took him to the theatre. Marx had to spend a tedious evening in a box next to the royal box, watching a pompous ballet. He enjoyed even less Freytag's comedy, *The Journalists*, which was "full of Prussian self-glorification".

Marx witnessed a session of the Chamber of Deputies from the press gallery. Comparing it with the Prussian National Assembly, which he had seen in September 1848, he found that the changes in Prussia's representative institutions had, by no means, been for the better. "A cramped assembly room. Nothing much in the way of visitors' galleries. The fellows sit on benches (as compared with the arm-chairs of the 'Gentlemen'), an odd combination of government office and school-room. A Belgian Chamber is imposing by comparison. Simson or Samson, or whatever the president's name is, avenges himself—with all the grotesque and brutal magisteriality of a ministerial *huissier*—for the kicks dealt him by Manteuffel when dispensing discipline with his ass's jawbones among the philistines cowering below.' [2]

Nor were his impressions of his other meetings in Berlin any more favourable. He wrote to his cousin Antoinette (Nannette) Philips, with whom he had made friends during his stay in Zalt-Bommel, that "a world of Philisteans hemmed me in". [3] However, he derived

---

[1] Marx, Engels, *Collected Works*, Vol. 41, p. 279.
[2] Ibid., p. 288.
[3] Ibid., p. 274.

great pleasure from a visit to his friend of student days, the well-known historian, Karl Köppen.

However unpleasant Marx found his particular situation in the Prussian capital, he observed with satisfaction the signs of growing opposition and general ferment. He wrote to Engels: "Berlin is in a cheeky, frivolous mood. The Chambers are despised.... Among a broad section of the public there is much dissatisfaction with the existing press.... Under the circumstances it might, in fact, not be inopportune if we could bring out a paper in Berlin next year."[1]

However, Marx's talks with Lassalle about jointly publishing a newspaper were unsuccessful. Lassalle's terms were designed to give him full control of the paper. Upon his return to England, Marx consulted with Engels, and sent Lassalle a refusal. Nor was Marx tempted to collaborate with Lassalle by the latter's excessive vanity, haughty manner, and his longing to move in high society, all of which Marx had observed at first hand.

With Lassalle's aid, Marx took steps in Berlin to get himself reinstated as a Prussian subject, so as to be able to live in or at least make fairly long visits to Germany now and again and to take a hand in guiding the German working-class movement. On March 25, 1861, he sent in his application to the Berlin chief of police, von Zedlitz.

His request was turned down even before he left the Prussian capital, on the pretext that he had renounced Prussian citizenship of his own accord in 1845. The authorities regarded Marx as being too dangerous a revolutionary to be allowed to live in Prussia. He left Lassalle power of attorney to pursue the matter, but the applications filed by Lassalle on Marx's behalf were also rejected in June 1861 by the Berlin chief of police, and in the following November by the Minister of the Interior. In this connection Marx wrote that the so-called amnesty was a "mere delusion, sham and snare".[2]

From Berlin Marx paid a short visit to Elberfeld, Barmen and Cologne. In Cologne, he met the lawyer Schneider, who had acted as defence counsel at the Communist Trial in 1852, and also a former member of the Communist League, Karl Klein, one of the accused in the trial. On April 19, he went to Trier to pay a two-day visit to his mother. That was their last meeting, for Henriette Marx died two and a half years later, on November 30, 1863.

From Trier, Marx went, via Aachen, for another visit to Holland, where he stayed in Rotterdam and Amsterdam, as well as Zalt-Bommel. He returned to London on April 29.

DEFENCE OF BLANQUI

During his stay in Berlin Marx learned that Blanqui, who had returned to France following the 1859 amnesty, had been arrested in

---
[1] Ibid., pp. 280-81.
[2] Ibid., p. 312.

Paris in March 1861 on a charge of organising a secret society. Sophie Hatzfeldt informed Marx that democratic-minded circles in Berlin were highly indignant over the actions of the Bonapartist police and expressed sympathy for Blanqui. During the trial, Blanqui was detained at Mazas prison, where he was brutally treated by the prison warders. In the summer of 1861, despite lack of evidence, he was sentenced to four years in prison.

Upon his return to London, Marx launched an active campaign to help Blanqui. He arranged with Simon Bernard, a French emigrant who had taken part in the 1848 revolution, and Ernest Jones, the former Chartist leader, to hold a meeting in protest against Blanqui's arrest and brutal treatment in prison. At the same time, Marx started corresponding with Louis Watteau, a French revolutionary and a close friend of Blanqui's, who had emigrated to Brussels and wrote in the press under the name of Denonville. Through Watteau, Marx succeeded in establishing contact with Blanqui. Informing Engels of this, Marx wrote on June 19, 1861: "Blanqui himself has, through Denonville, expressed his heartfelt gratitude to me and to the *parti prolétaire allemand* [German proletarian party] ... for the sympathy we have shown him. I consider it a very good thing that we should again have direct links with the decidedly revolutionary party in France." [1]

Marx took vigorous steps through the press to organise a movement in defence of Blanqui. In May, he wrote to Countess Hatzfeldt requesting her assistance in publicising the harsh treatment of Blanqui in prison and circulating a demand for his release. Thanks to Marx's efforts, reports about the fresh reprisals against Blanqui appeared not only in German, but also in Italian and American progressive newspapers.

Marx gave full backing to Watteau's intention to issue a pamphlet exposing the Bonapartists who were victimising the fiery French revolutionary and keeping him in jail. Through Countess Hatzfeldt, he appealed to democratic circles in Germany to raise funds to cover the cost of issuing the pamphlet. He also took steps to raise funds among the emigrants with the aid of the German Workers' Educational Society in London. On November 10, 1861, Marx sent Watteau the money collected by the Society, together with a letter containing high praise of Blanqui. He wrote: "Rest assured that there is no one more interested than myself in the lot of a man whom I have always regarded as the brains and inspiration of the proletarian party in France." [2]

MARX AND SOCIAL CHANGE IN RUSSIA

From the end of the 1850s, Marx kept a close watch on internal developments in Russia, gradually reaching the conclusion that tsar-

---
[1] Marx, Engels, *Collected Works*, Vol. 41, p. 298.
[2] Ibid., p. 326.

ism had been weakened by its defeat in the Crimean War. The war had not merely exposed tsarist Russia's economic and political backwardness, but had also caused widespread disturbances among the serfs, which were eroding the foundations of the feudal serf system. On October 8, 1858, Marx wrote to Engels about his view of the growing revolutionary mood in the Russian Empire: "The Russian war of 1854-55 ... nevertheless clearly precipitated the present turn of events in Russia." [1] That same year, Marx observed that the crisis of the serf-holding system was rapidly coming to a head, and that there were signs of a developing revolutionary situation in Russia, which in turn was weakening tsarism as a bastion of European reaction. That is what he pointed out in his letters to Engels, emphasising that the "movement for the emancipation of the serfs in Russia" marked the beginning of an internal development that might "run counter to the country's traditional foreign policy." [2]

Marx also saw clearly the socio-economic causes of the imminent changes in Russia. The obsolete feudal relations were a great impediment to the development of capitalism. In this situation, the formation of the capitalist system entailed especially acute suffering and hardship for the exploited masses, which were labouring under a twofold oppression: that of the feudal landowners and of the capitalists. All of this intensified the revolutionary ferment even more.

Realising that the collapse of serfdom was inevitable, Marx saw that Russia was faced with a choice of ways in which to abolish it, and that this was the point at issue between the contending class forces in the country. The ruling circles, aware that it was impossible to govern in the old way, were seeking a way out of the crisis through reform, while the millions of peasants were striving to solve the problem in the radical, revolutionary way. Marx wrote: "The Russian serfs happen to interpret the emancipation differently from the government." [3] Marx was fully aware of the disagreement within the ruling class over the reform, and the disputes between the liberal landowners and the serf-owners, but he believed that the motive forces behind the reform lay elsewhere. In contrast to the West-European press, he regarded it primarily as the result of the irreconcilable class struggle between the peasantry and the landowners.

Even before the peasant reform was introduced Marx commented on some of its important features, using information which had leaked into the press, in his articles which appeared in the *New-York Daily Tribune* from 1858 to 1860. Two of these—"The Question of the Abolition of Serfdom in Russia" and "The Emancipation Question"—dealt wholly with the mooted reform. He emphasised that absolutist governments agreed to the emancipation of the pea-

---

[1] Ibid., Vol. 40, p. 346.
[2] Ibid., p. 310.
[3] Ibid., Vol. 17, p. 141.

sants only "with the support of revolution or war". [1] He was sure that like all such measures taken from above, the proposed reform would be inconclusive, merely marking a step towards necessary bourgeois changes in Russia, and would not be able to resolve all the pressing issues, which was something that could be done only through revolution.

Analysing the proposed reform, Marx showed, even before Alexander II's Manifesto of February 19, 1861, that it was aimed against the people, and was designed to give utmost protection to the interests of the landowners and to preserve various aspects of the serf system. He believed also that these measures could not for long check the degradation and decline of a dying class like the landed nobility. For the peasants, the reform was only illusory emancipation, a change in the type of bondage, a means of robbing them through redemption payments, etc. It would not help to abolish their dependence on the landowners. It would substitute a "civilised form" of servitude for a "patriarchal" one. [2]

Marx hoped that the tsarist government would not be able to stem the peasant revolutionary movement by this reform, and that this movement would grow as the peasants became aware of its real significance. He spoke of a possible bourgeois-democratic revolution in Russia, pointing out that the government's attempt to put through its type of reform might be "the signal for a tremendous conflagration among the rural population of Russia". [3] That would mean that "the Russian 1793 will be at hand", with a reign of terror, and that this would mark a "turning point in Russian history" and would bring it "real and general civilisation". [4] While looking to a revolutionary outbreak in Russia, Marx believed that because of the inadequate development of capitalist relations it would assume the form of an agrarian revolution, and said so, in particular, in a letter to Lassalle on February 4, 1859.

On the eve of and during the Crimean War, Marx had believed the revolutionary prospects in Russia to be still relatively remote, and therefore regarded the country primarily as the mainstay of reaction in Europe. Now his views began to change: while remaining a firm opponent of autocracy, he increasingly concentrated on unofficial Russia, the Russia of the people, who were ranged against tsarism within the country itself. He was pleased to see evidence that these forces were growing rapidly, and that a popular revolution was maturing in Russia. From that point on, Marx regarded the Russian revolutionary movement — revolutionary Russia — as a counterweight to tsarist Russia, and as a constant factor to be reckoned with in overall revolutionary strategic plans and in mapping out the possible course of any future revolution in Europe. He wrote

---

[1] Marx, Engels, *Collected Works*, Vol. 16, p. 52.
[2] Ibid., Vol. 17, p. 486.
[3] Ibid., Vol. 16, p. 147.
[4] Ibid.

in June 1858: "There is another great power which, ten years ago, most powerfully checked the revolutionary current. We mean Russia. This time, combustible matter has accumulated under her own feet, which a strong blast from the West may suddenly set on fire." [1] In the summer of 1858, Marx still believed that revolutionary action in Western Europe would trigger off a revolutionary explosion in Russia, but the growing peasant disturbances soon suggested that the revolution might flare up in Russia before it did in the West, and might in fact spread to the West from Russia. In December 1859, he wrote to Engels: "In Russia the movement is progressing better than anywhere else in Europe." [2]

Marx saw the Russian revolutionary movement as an ally of the proletariat and democracy in the West. Comparing events in Russia with the struggle against Negro slavery in the U.S.A., Marx wrote to Engels on January 11, 1860: "In my view, the most momentous thing happening in the world today is the slave movement — on the one hand, in America ... and in Russia, on the other." [3]

Even after the promulgation of the peasant reform in March 1861, Marx continued to look to a revolutionary outbreak in Russia, and his view was borne out by reports of continuing and even increasing unrest among the peasants. Marx had good historical grounds for regarding the situation in Russia on the eve of and during the reform as pre-revolutionary. Lenin subsequently wrote: "Even the most cautious and sober politician could not but acknowledge the possibility of a revolutionary outbreak and the serious danger of a peasant revolt." [4] That the revolutionary situation of 1859-61 did not in fact develop into a revolution does not detract from the value of Marx's conclusion that a popular revolution was maturing in Russia, and that a truly inexhaustible store of revolutionary energy was latent in her people.

CONTRIBUTIONS TO *DIE PRESSE*

Max Friedländer, the editor of the liberal Viennese *Die Presse*, tried to get Marx to write for his paper in 1859, and renewed his invitation in early June 1861.

Die Presse had 30,000 subscribers, and was read in Germany as well as Austria. Its considerable popularity at the time was due to its anti-Bonapartist stand on foreign-policy issues. However, Marx did not send his first articles to *Die Presse* until October 1861, when he became sure that the paper had also taken a progressive stand on domestic issues, and had ceased to support Chancellor Anton von Schmerling's reactionary domestic policy. On September 28, 1861,

---

[1] Ibid., Vol. 15, p. 568.
[2] Ibid., Vol. 40, p. 552.
[3] Ibid., Vol. 41, p. 4.
[4] V. I. Lenin, *Collected Works*, Vol. 5, p. 39.

he wrote to Engels: "The *Vienna 'Presse'* ... has finally revised its attitude towards Schmerling and hence it may now be possible to establish a connection with the paper." [1] It was extremely important for Marx to be able to spread his views directly among the Germans.

In October 1861, Marx sent two trial articles on the American Civil War to Vienna, at the request of the editors. Both were approved and prominently featured. Marx was informed that as of November 1861 he was being enrolled on the staff of *Die Presse*, with a fee of £1 per article and 10s. per report.

Many of the articles Marx wrote for *Die Presse* dealt with the American Civil War and its influence on the international situation. Marx had good reason to believe that the war would help to intensify the revolutionary movement in Europe, and so attached much importance to providing European readers with accurate reports on developments in the United States. On April 28, 1862, he wrote to Engels about the need "to disseminate correct views on this important matter in the land of the Teutons". [2]

A number of articles which Marx wrote for *Die Presse* dealt with the economic situation in England and the standard of living of the working people. He gave a vivid picture of the disastrous state of England's textile industry due to the suspension of cotton exports from the U.S.A. because of the Civil War. His articles "The Crisis in England" and "Workers' Distress in England" revealed the terrible poverty of the unemployed weavers. Marx also observed the rising political activity of the English working class, which since the decline of the Chartist movement had been under the strong influence of trade unionism.

Marx's articles in *Die Presse* continued to expose the corrupt regime of the Second Empire with its vast expenditure on arms and the extravagance of the court. Following the armed intervention by France, England and Spain in Mexico, which began in 1861, Marx wrote a number of articles to expose Napoleon III's foreign-policy ventures. He showed that the real purpose of the intervention, launched on the pretext of combating anarchy, was to overthrow the progressive government of Juárez, and to turn the Mexican Republic into a colony of the European Powers. Marx's articles on the intervention in Mexico were a fresh contribution to the fight against colonialism.

The bourgeois editors of *Die Presse* regarded many of Marx's articles as being too revolutionary. By the end of 1861, Marx realised that some of his articles were not being printed. He wrote to Engels on December 27, 1861: "The rotten *Presse* is printing barely half my articles." [3] Among the unprinted articles were some dealing with the Mexican expedition and condemning the European Powers' policy of colonial aggrandisement.

---

[1] Marx, Engels, *Collected Works*, Vol. 41, p. 321.
[2] Ibid., p. 353.
[3] Ibid., p. 338.

In 1862 the editors reduced their publication of Marx's articles even further. Just before the second World Industrial Exhibition opened in London in 1862, Friedländer tried to confine Marx's writing entirely to reports on the exposition, with no more than one article a week on other matters. The upshot was that in December 1862 Marx stopped writing for the paper.

AMERICAN CIVIL WAR. END OF CONTRIBUTIONS TO THE *N.-Y. DAILY TRIBUNE*

From the spring of 1861, Marx and Engels concentrated their attention on developments in the United States. The election as President, in 1860, of the Republican Party candidate, Abraham Lincoln, an opponent of Negro slavery, who believed that the first step towards its abolition should be to limit the territory on which it was being practised, induced the Southern slave-owners to rise in open revolt. One by one, the Southern States declared their secession from the Union. On February 4, 1861, the representatives of the secessionist states set up a separate Southern Confederation. On April 12, 1861, the rebel troops launched military operations against the armed forces of the Union. This was the start of a civil war on an unprecedented scale.

Marx saw the American Civil War, which continued until April 1865, as an event of great historical importance, and wrote over 40 articles on it, mostly for *Die Presse*. The military aspect was still commented upon by Engels. After December 1862, however, Marx was no longer able to report on the course of the war in the periodical press. He was forced to break with *Die Presse* and the dispatch of his articles to the *New-York Daily Tribune* stopped even earlier. His contributions to the latter, following a decade of continuous collaboration, began to taper off in early 1861, when the editors suggested that he should temporarily suspend submitting reports. The publication of his articles was not resumed until October. However, in March 1862, Marx broke his relations with the *Tribune*.

Marx's break with the *Tribune* and then with *Die Presse* once again played havoc with his earnings. Instead of calmly continuing the writing of his economic work, which he had resumed in 1861, he was forced into frantically searching for a means of subsistence. In early 1863, Marx even considered working as a railway clerk, but was rejected because of his poor handwriting. The situation improved somewhat towards the end of 1863, when he inherited a small estate from his mother.

Thus, for reasons beyond his control, Marx dealt in his journalistic writings only with the early stages of the American Civil War, but these were well supplemented by his letters to Engels and other persons ranging over the whole period of the war and containing incisive political comments on the events and personalities.

Marx considered the events in the United States as a keen-sighted sociologist, a passionate fighter against reaction and a champion of the common interests of the American and European working people. His articles and letters revealed the economic and social roots of the American Civil War and analysed its character and motive forces. The war was caused by the struggle between two social systems: the capitalist "system of free labour" predominant in the Northern States, that is, the wage labour of industrial workers, and the labour of artisans and also of farmers; and the system of slavery, the precapitalist form of exploitation of the direct producers, prevailing in the South. "The struggle has broken out because the two systems can no longer live peacefully side by side on the North American continent." [1] The continuation of slavery was becoming increasingly incompatible with the capitalist development of the United States.

Marx emphasised that the Civil War centred round the issue of slavery. In October 1861, he wrote: "The whole movement was and is based, as one sees, on the *slave question*. Not in the sense of whether the slaves within the existing slave states should be emancipated outright or not, but whether the 20 million free men of the North should submit any longer to an oligarchy of 300,000 slaveholders; whether the vast Territories of the republic should be nurseries for free states or for slavery; finally, whether the national policy of the Union should take armed spreading of slavery in Mexico, Central and South America as its device." [2]

Referring to the historical origin of the Civil War in America, Marx said that the fight between the antagonistic forces — the industrial North and the slave-holding South — had been the "moving power of its history for half a century". [3] In this struggle, he stressed in an article entitled "The North American Civil War", the South had constantly acted as a militant, aggressive force, scoring one victory after another over the North on the issue of slavery. The success of the slave-owning oligarchy was due to the fact that it had always met with support from the big bourgeoisie in the Northern States, who were linked with the slave-owning planters and who made their money by trading in cotton and other products of slave labour. "All the attempts, periodically repeated since 1817, to resist the ever increasing encroachments of the slaveholders" had foundered on this counter-revolutionary alliance. [4] Meanwhile, the progressive circles of the bourgeoisie, mainly the industrial bourgeoisie, had also intensified their struggle against slavery, and together with the mass popular movement against slavery this resulted in Lincoln's victory in the presidential elections.

Marx exposed the lies in the British bourgeois press concerning

---

[1] Marx, Engels, *Collected Works*, Vol. 19, p. 50.
[2] Ibid., p. 42.
[3] Ibid., p. 11.
[4] Ibid., p. 38.

the allegedly peaceable nature of the secession, and firmly rebutted the attempts of the European press to obscure the true aims of the slave-owners of the South and present them as champions of State rights in the face of the Federal Government's encroachments, as champions of local autonomy who were merely acting in self-defence. Marx stressed that in the South a small exploiting clique was engaged in a usurpatory act which ran counter to the interests of the vast majority of the population even in the Southern States. Quite apart from the Negroes, the slave-owning oligarchy in the South "is confronted with many millions of so-called poor whites, ... whose condition is only to be compared with that of the Roman plebeians in the period of Rome's extreme decline". [1] The secession was in fact a counter-revolutionary rebellion, a slave-owners' riot, and not in any sense a "war of defence, but a war of conquest, a war of conquest for the spread and perpetuation of slavery." [2]

While stressing that the North was fighting a progressive war, Marx sharply condemned the indecision and hesitation displayed by bourgeois circles in the Northern States, and criticised the bourgeois republican government for its unwillingness from the outset to turn the war into a nation-wide revolutionary one. Marx saw this as an expression of the limited nature of U.S. bourgeois democracy. It was this policy during the initial stages of the war that was the main cause of the Northerners' military defeats, despite their superiority in terms of economic potential and manpower.

Marx wrote with indignation that the Northern Army was infested with reactionary officers, who sympathised with the Southerners. He criticised the Northern leaders most strongly for their policy on the Negro issue. Fearful of revolutionary upheavals, they were at first unwilling to allow Negroes to enlist. Marx believed that enlisting Negroes in the Northern Army would have had a tremendous impact on the course of the war, greatly increasing the North's chances and undermining the position of the Southern slave-owners. On August 7, 1862, he wrote to Engels: "One single nigger regiment would have a remarkable effect on Southern nerves." [3]

Marx never tired of stressing that the fight against slavery was in the interests of the U.S. working people, the proletariat above all, because slavery was an obstacle to the unity of the working class, divided the whites and the blacks in their struggle against their exploiters, and weakened the working-class movement. "In the United States of North America, every independent movement of the workers was paralysed so long as slavery disfigured a part of the Republic." [4]

Marx believed that the decisive role in the fight against slavery would be played by the people. He expected the freedom-loving American farmers and workers to exert a powerful influence on the

---

[1] Ibid., pp. 40-41.
[2] Ibid., p. 44.
[3] Ibid., Vol. 41, p. 400.
[4] Karl Marx, *Capital*, Vol. I, p. 284.

government of the North and make it change its mode of warfare. The mounting activity of the masses in the course of the Civil War would transform it into a real revolution in whose flames both the rule of the planters' oligarchy and the treacherous schemes of their accomplices in the North would collapse. Marx felt sure that "the North will, at last, wage the war in earnest, have recourse to revolutionary methods and overthrow the supremacy of the border slave statesmen".[1] In August 1862, he wrote: "So far, we have only witnessed the first act of the Civil War—the *constitutional* waging of war. The second act, the *revolutionary* waging of war, is at hand."[2]

Marx's forecasts were fully borne out. In the second half of 1862, mass popular pressure forced the Lincoln government to implement a number of revolutionary-democratic measures which ultimately brought victory to the North. Marx welcomed Lincoln's acts—the permission to form Negro regiments, the law on the confiscation of rebel property, etc. He was especially pleased with Lincoln's Emancipation Proclamation issued on September 22, 1862, freeing all Negro slaves owned by rebel planters. Marx saw clearly the shortcomings of a proclamation that freed the slaves without giving them land, but he emphasised its tremendous revolutionary importance. It his article "Comments on the North American Events", he said Lincoln's proclamation was the "most important document in American history since the establishment of the Union".[3] It marked the transition to a new stage of the war—a war fought the revolutionary way.

Marx gave a vivid description of President Lincoln as an outstanding statesman who heeded the voice of the people. Marx liked Lincoln as a man of the people and a plebeian in sentiment and way of life. Marx stressed his simple manners, his efficiency, his refusal to posture and to engage in high-flown rhetoric. While criticising Lincoln for his bourgeois limitations and a certain inconsistency, Marx praised his actions highly: "Lincoln's place in the history of the United States and of mankind will ... be next to that of Washington!"[4]

Marx also assessed the Civil War in the light of the overall prospects of the revolutionary movement. He believed that the struggle to destroy Negro slavery was a prime factor in rallying both the American working class and the whole international proletariat. He observed that the slave-holders' rebellion had sounded the "tocsin for a general holy crusade of property against labour",[5] and that the future of the working people of the whole world hinged on the victory or defeat of the North. He believed that however hard the American bourgeoisie tried to appropriate the fruits of the people's vic-

---

[1] Marx, Engels, *Collected Works*, Vol. 41, p. 400.
[2] Ibid., Vol. 19, p. 228.
[3] Ibid., p. 250.
[4] Ibid.
[5] Ibid., Vol. 20, p. 20.

tory, or preserve Negro inequality, the abolition of slavery in the U.S.A. by revolutionary means would give a powerful impetus to the liberation struggle on either side of the Atlantic. That is why he attached such importance to solidarity between the European working class and the American Abolitionists, and the oppressed Negroes themselves. All his articles about the American Civil War drove home the idea that, regardless of nationality and colour, the working people of all countries have a common interest, and this was a further elaboration of the principle of proletarian internationalism.

ENGLISH WORKERS' MOVEMENT IN SUPPORT OF THE NORTH

Marx believed that protests by the English working class against the intention of English ruling circles to intervene openly in support of the South had played a major part in educating the proletariat in a spirit of international solidarity. From the very beginning of the war, the English government supported the Southern planters, supplying them with arms and other materials and allowing their ships to be built in English shipyards. The English bourgeoisie and aristocracy were plotting to intervene against the North and establish a coalition of reactionary European states to give armed assistance to the South. However, these schemes were vigorously resisted by the English people, particularly the working class.

In his articles "English Public Opinion" and "A London Workers' Meeting", among others, Marx considered active influence on foreign policy as a key task before the revolutionary proletariat and showed that the English working class had remained true to its internationalist duty. At the numerous meetings beginning in the winter of 1861 the English workers voiced their determination to prevent the disgraceful aggression in defence of slavery. Marx said that the English working class remained steadfast even in the face of severe privation caused by the crisis in the textile industry due to the American Civil War. The government did not succeed in taking advantage of the workers' indigence and generating hatred among them for the Northern States.

Despite the efforts of the ruling *élite*, there was growing sympathy in England for the North. Mass workers' meetings were held in London, Manchester and Sheffield in 1862 and 1863 to voice solidarity with the fighters against Negro slavery. On March 26, 1863, Marx attended a most impressive workers' meeting held at St. James's Hall by the London Trades Council. Unlike English bourgeois-aristocratic circles, speakers at the meeting voiced resolute support for the Northern government. Describing his impressions of the meeting to Engels, Marx wrote on April 9, 1863: "The working men themselves spoke *very well indeed*, without a trace of bourgeois rhetoric or the faintest attempt to conceal their opposition to the capitalists."[1]

Marx valued this internationalist stand by the English proletariat most highly. In October 1863 he observed: "The English working class has won immortal historical honour for itself by thwarting the repeated attempts of the ruling classes to intervene on behalf of the American slaveholders by its enthusiastic mass meetings, even though the prolongation of the American Civil War subjects a million English workers to the most fearful sufferings and privations."[2]

Marx's articles on the anti-interventionist campaign of the English workers taught the proletariat how to work out and assert its own revolutionary line in international conflicts.

MARX'S ATTITUDE TOWARDS THE POLISH INSURRECTION OF 1863-64

Another centre of revolutionary struggle erupted in early 1863. On January 22 and 23, guerrilla warfare started and a national liberation insurrection broke out in the Polish lands belonging to tsarist Russia.

Marx thought it most significant that, in contrast to earlier Polish uprisings, this one began against the background of revolutionary upsurge not only in Western but also in Eastern Europe, in Russia, where revolutionary ferment continued among the masses because of discontent with the 1861 Reform. This opened up new prospects for the insurrection in the Polish lands. Marx and Engels believed that, given a favourable turn of events, it could become the starting-point for an all-European revolution. They expected the Polish insurrection to help spark off a Russian revolution, and then together with it to carry the revolutionary flames into neighbouring Germany, particularly Prussia, then going through an acute political crisis, and also into the other West-European countries. On February 13, 1863, Marx wrote to Engels: "What do you think of the Polish business? This much is certain, the era of revolution has now fairly opened in Europe once more.... This time, let us hope, the lava will flow from East to West and not in the opposite direction."[3]

Throughout the insurrection, Marx and Engels wrote to each other analysing the insurgents' chances of victory and the impact of the Polish events on the revolutionary movements in other countries, keeping a close watch on the struggle between the parties within the insurgent camp, and assessing the foreign political forces influencing the course of the insurrection.

---

[1] Marx, Engels, *Collected Works*, Vol. 41, p. 468.
[2] Ibid., Vol. 19, p. 297.
[3] Ibid., Vol. 41, p. 453.

Marx and Engels believed that the success of the insurrection depended primarily on two factors: the participation of the broad mass of Polish peasants in the struggle and an agrarian revolution in Russia, which would help integrate the Polish people's liberation struggle with the Russian revolutionary movement. Their views coincided with those of the Russian revolutionary democrats and the members of the "Red" revolutionary party in Poland, which had been set up in 1861. The most far-sighted Russian and Polish revolutionaries worked hard to unite the revolutionary forces of Russia and Poland. In 1862 they concluded an agreement that the Russian revolutionaries would support a Polish insurrection planned for the spring of 1863. Although Marx and Engels were not aware of this arrangement they, too, hoped that given the right conditions the Polish insurrection would provide an impetus to revolutionary action by masses of peasants in Russia and would obtain powerful support from the Russian revolution.

However, by the summer of 1863, Marx and Engels reached the conclusion that the Polish insurrection's chances of success were dwindling, and observed with regret that the movement in Poland had failed to develop into an agrarian revolution, while in Russia the peasant unrest began to subside. Marx saw the main cause of the unsuccessful development of the Polish insurrection in the fact that the overall leadership of the insurgent forces had been seized by the "White" party, which did not look to mass revolutionary struggle but to assistance from France and England. The "White" party, representing the interests of the big landowners and the bourgeois *élite*, was doing its utmost to prevent the Polish insurrection from developing into a peasant revolution. The "Whites" laid claims to Ukrainian and Byelorussian lands. They established contacts with Polish aristocrats abroad. Through Prince Czartoryski, who lived in Paris, they maintained relations with the governments of Napoleon III and Palmerston. The pro-Western policy of the "Whites", like their conservative stand on the peasant question, had a fatal effect on the insurgent movement. On August 15, 1863, Marx wrote to Engels: "The Polish affair has gone completely off the rails because of this same Boustrapa,[1] and the influence his intrigues have given the Czartoryski party."[2]

In a number of his letters to Engels, Marx denounced the provocative policy pursued by France and England with respect to the Polish insurgents, showing that the ruling circles of these states were in fact acting as accomplices in suppressing the insurrection, in covertly helping tsarism to carry out its punitive operations. The governments of France and England made hypocritical professions of sympathy for the insurgents, but at the crucial moment abandoned them to the mercy of fate. They went through diplomatic motions, but gave the Poles no real assistance. Marx stressed that France and

---
[1] A nickname for Napoleon III.
[2] Marx, Engels, *Collected Works*, Vol. 41, p. 489.

England had intervened in Polish affairs because they had an axe to grind. Napoleon III was hoping to aggravate the international situation and create a favourable opportunity for seizing the left bank of the Rhine and for other ventures. Marx saw through the French Emperor's schemes soon after the insurrection began. On February 21, 1863, he wrote to Engels: "My chief anxiety about the Polish affair is that beastly Bonaparte will find a pretext of moving up to the Rhine and extricate himself from a nasty situation again." [1]

Marx also realised the true motives behind Palmerston's declaration of sympathy for the Polish insurrection: the English Prime Minister was hoping to complicate Russia's diplomatic position, provoke France into action and frustrate the incipient Franco-Russian rapprochement after the Crimean War.

From the very outset Marx had no doubt that the Prussian government headed by Bismarck would give tsarism the most active assistance in putting down the insurrection, and he was proved right. On February 8, 1863, the tsarist and Prussian governments signed a convention of joint suppression of the insurgents, a counter-revolutionary act which the Prussian liberal bourgeoisie actually supported, having confined itself to some timid criticism of it in the Provincial Diet. Marx angrily denounced the cowardice of the Prussian liberals, who were grovelling to Bismarck.

For his part, Marx did his utmost to help the Polish insurgents. He believed that the sympathy for the oppressed Polish people among workers and democratic circles in Western Europe should be used both to organise the most effective assistance to the Poles and to consolidate the international brotherhood of the workers of all countries. Marx encouraged the German Workers' Educational Society in London to support the Poles, and organised the raising of funds in aid of the Polish insurgents among German workers in England, Switzerland, the United States and Germany herself.

In September 1863, Marx warmly responded to a request from the Polish Colonel Lapiński to help form a German legion to support the insurgents. On September 12, 1863, he informed Engels: "The cause as such would appear to be excellent," [2] requesting him to arrange the collection of the necessary money in Manchester. Whereas in early 1848 Marx was quite right in regarding Herwegh and Bornstedt's idea of artificially causing a revolution in Germany by sending in an émigré legion as a dangerous gamble, the dispatch of a German volunteer detachment to Poland in 1863 was a totally different matter. Marx believed that this would be an effective form of international support for an insurgent movement that had already started in the country itself, a revolutionary act similar to the participation of foreign volunteers in Garibaldi's campaigns in Sicily and Southern Italy. However, the Lapiński expedition did not take place, not only because of lack of funds, but also, apparently, be-

---

[1] Marx, Engels, *Collected Works*, Vol. 41, p. 460.
[2] Ibid., p. 493.

cause of the negative attitude on the part of the "Whites" to the idea of sending foreign revolutionary legions to help the insurgents.

From the experience of the Polish insurrection and the solidarity campaign Marx and Engels drew the conclusion that the Polish people's national liberation struggle could succeed only in close alliance with the revolutionary movement in Russia and with the European working class. They believed that an important condition for victory was for the oppressed nation to combine its struggle for national independence with internal revolutionary change, above all, with a democratic solution of the agrarian question in the interests of the broad peasant masses.

WORK ON A PAMPHLET ABOUT POLAND

Marx also hoped to help the insurgents through the periodical press. As soon as he learned about the convention which Prussia and Russia had concluded on joint suppression of the insurrection, he decided, together with Engels, to write a special pamphlet about Poland to help expose the police collaboration between Berlin and St. Petersburg and to induce Germany's democratic circles to take resolute action in defence of Poland and against domestic reaction. Marx was to write the historico-diplomatic and Engels the military part of the projected pamphlet. In a letter to Marx written on about February 21, 1863, Engels sketched out a rough plan and proposed the following title: *Germany and Poland. Politico-Military Considerations on the Occasion of the Polish Uprising of 1863.*

The pamphlet was not completed mainly because of Marx's ill health. In March he had an acute attack of his liver complaint, and this continued until the end of May. Nevertheless, in these three and a half months, he did a vast amount of preparatory work. He took notes from almost 50 books, filling up two large notebooks and a smaller one. Examining the Polish question in connection with the policies pursued by the leading European Powers, Marx made a study of the documents, memoirs, correspondence, and historical writings bearing on the diplomatic and domestic history not only of Poland, but also of Russia, Prussia and France. The smaller notebook also contained numerous extracts from the press about the progress of the 1863 insurrection.

Marx subsequently collated all this material in a systematic way, classifying it by subject, and arranging each subject in chronological order. This gave him two rough manuscripts. One of them entitled "The Prussian Scoundrels" dealt with Prusso-Polish relations from 1640 to 1863, and the other, without a title, was a chronological record of the history of Polish-French relations. When he set out to write the pamphlet itself, he used the preparatory material to produce two versions of the first chapter. He began with the Middle Ages, going up to 1792 in the first draft, and up to 1770 in the second, a more polished one, entitled "Poland, Prussia and Russia".

That was the state of his work at the end of May 1863. On May 29, he informed Engels: "Despite various repeated attempts, I have *not managed* the stuff on Poland."[1] Marx and Engels appear to have stopped writing the pamphlet because they decided that it would take too much time to complete, and that it could not be published early enough to be of any practical use to the insurrection.

However, the extant manuscripts not only reveal Marx's overall scheme, but also help to determine the content of a sizable part of the work he was going to write. The rough manuscript of "The Prussian Scoundrels" and in part the initial versions of the first chapter trace the territorial ambitions of Prussia and tsarist Russia with respect to Poland over a period of two centuries. Marx concentrated on exposing Prussia and attacking the "dismal House of Hohenzollern".[2] The pamphlet was a continuation and elaboration of Marx's articles in which he had castigated the Prussian reactionaries beginning with the period preceding the 1848 revolution.

Marx described in detail the rise of the Brandenburg line of the Hohenzollern dynasty, showing the petty intrigues, deceit and treachery by which they had managed to wrest control of the Duchy of Prussia from Poland, thereby increasing their territory and acquiring the royal title. As the Polish aristocratic republic declined, the former vassal acted true to form, revenging himself with the baseness of a lackey on his former suzerain, and like a jackal seizing upon every opportunity to snatch at his prey. Marx's manuscripts show Prussia's treacherous role in the three partitions of Poland effected in the late 18th century in close alliance with tsarist Russia and Austria. Marx believed that participation in the partition of Poland was the decisive factor behind Prussia's rise. Since then, Prussia had played the part of gendarme in every uprising of the Polish people. Marx gave a vivid picture of the ignominious and brutal methods Prussia used to carry out her conquests. He described the acts of the Prussian militarists in Poland on the eve of the first partition as follows: "In early 1771, whole regions of Prussian Poland were overrun by Prussian mercenaries, who perpetrated unheard-of plunders, atrocities, infamies and all manner of brutalities."[3]

In his manuscripts, Marx elaborated the idea, using the policy pursued by Hohenzollern Prussia and tsarist Russia towards Poland as an example, that joint enslavement of other nations shackles the oppressors to each other and intensifies their mutual dependence, with the stronger becoming to a large extent the ruler of the destinies of the weaker. He saw the fact that the Prussian kings had relied on tsarist Russia in seizing Polish territory as one of the main reasons for the Hohenzollerns' servile devotion to the tsar of Russia. Prussia and tsarist Russia were also held together by their common hatred

---

[1] Marx, Engels, *Collected Works*, Vol. 41, p. 474.
[2] Ibid., p. 460.
[3] Karl Marx, *On the History of the Polish Question. Manuscripts of 1863-64, Marx-Engels Archives*, Vol. XIV, Moscow, 1973, p. 213 (in Russian).

for the European revolutionary movement, the bourgeois revolution of the late 18th century and the liberatory influence it had exerted on Europe. The Hohenzollerns and the Romanovs always regarded the Polish people's urge to restore Poland's independence as an expression of a revolutionary tendency. "Since the Jacobin war ... Prussia has seen Poland as the Eastern analogy of France and a revolutionary crater." [1]

One idea that runs right through Marx's manuscripts is that ever since the establishment of Prussia the Hohenzollerns had pursued a policy towards Poland which, far from having anything in common with Germany's true interests, in fact clashed with these interests and inflicted harm both on the neighbouring Slav peoples and on the Germans themselves. As in 1848-49, Marx developed the idea that the Prussian monarchy was the main obstacle to German unification by revolutionary-democratic means, and that its overthrow should be the first step in Germany's revolutionary development. At the height of his work on the pamphlet, he wrote to Engels: "Since ... the existence of Poland is necessary to Germany and completely incompatible with the State of Prussia, the State of Prussia must be erased from the map." [2]

Another task Marx set himself in the planned pamphlet was to expose the treacherous policy of the Western powers, especially of the Bonapartist Second Empire, towards beleaguered Poland. Taking the history of Franco-Polish relations as his example, Marx showed that both during the period of absolutism and of bourgeois domination, the rulers of France invariably used Poland as a pawn in their diplomatic calculations and moves, making the Poles shed blood for alien interests. While tantalising them with hopes of independence, they did everything to prevent its restoration. The English bourgeoisie conducted a similar policy on the Polish question.

Marx traced the diplomatic struggle between the powers over Poland in close connection with his analysis of the internal socio-economic and political development both in these countries and in Poland herself. In his manuscripts, he studied the social structure of Polish society and the class composition of the national liberation movement. He observed that the anti-Polish policy pursued by Prussia, Austria and Russia enjoyed the support of the corrupt Polish aristocracy, which was even prepared to give up its national independence so long as it retained its feudal privileges. Because the national bourgeoisie was weak, the progressive sections of the Polish gentry had long carried the banner of struggle against the aristocratic oligarchy and in support of national independence. The Polish aristocracy, said Marx, "should be distinguished from the *Polish gentry*, which in Poland had the same status as the bourgeoisie in the European states". [3]

---

[1] Central Party Archives of the Institute of Marxism-Leninism.
[2] Marx, Engels, *Collected Works*, Vol. 41, p. 462.
[3] Central Party Archives of the Institute of Marxism-Leninism.

Marx showed the leading circles of the Polish gentry as progressive and receptive to the liberatory ideas of the day and the ideals of the French bourgeois revolution by citing their resistance to the partition of Poland, and their attempts to clear the way inside the country for political and social progress. From this standpoint, he praised the Constitution of May 3, 1791, which had resulted from the struggle by the Polish patriotic forces against the aristocratic clique. Despite their limitations for class reasons, these revolutionaries continued to play a prominent part in the struggle for Poland's liberation, and in Polish uprisings against alien oppression, beginning with the 1794 uprising by Tadeusz Kościuszko.

Marx's manuscripts on Poland constitute an important part of his theoretical legacy on the national question. They also enable us to take a closer look at his creative methods, and show that whatever the sphere he dealt with he was always highly conscientious as a scientist in working for the interests of the oppressed.

IN THE GERMAN WORKERS' EDUCATIONAL SOCIETY IN LONDON

In the 1860s, Marx was highly active in the German Workers' Educational Society in London. He and Engels had withdrawn from the organisation in September 1850, when it was under the influence of sectarian elements. Towards the end of the 1850s, the situation had changed, and a prominent part began to be played in the Society by Johann Eccarius, Friedrich Lessner and other proletarian revolutionaries who sought to overcome the sectarian mistakes of the old leadership and to establish closer contacts between the Society, English working-class organisations and proletarian elements of other nationalities. Accordingly, Marx was able to resume his work in the Society.

He sought to educate the workers in a spirit of international solidarity, and it was on his initiative that in 1861 the Society held a meeting of French and German workers which unanimously adopted a protest against Blanqui's arrest.

During the Polish insurrection, Marx worked hard to turn the Society into a centre for organising concerted action by the West-European workers in support of the Polish national liberation movement. Together with other proletarian and democratic emigrant circles, the Society took part in action by English and French workers in defence of Poland, and its representatives attended the meetings and rallies staged for that purpose in London, notably the one held at St. James's Hall on July 22, 1863.

In October 1863, Marx wrote on behalf of the Educational Society a "Proclamation on Poland" for collecting funds in aid of the Polish insurrectionists. It summed up his views on the importance of the Polish question for Germany, views which he had expressed in his unfinished manuscripts on Poland. His main thesis was: "Without an independent Poland there can be no independent and united Germany." He accused the German bourgeoisie of looking on, "silent, passive and indifferent, at the slaughter of the heroic nation", and stressed that the struggle for Poland's independence was a vital cause of the proletariat, especially of the German proletariat. "It must inscribe the *Restoration of Poland* in letters of flame on its banner." [1]

The proclamation was issued as a leaflet and was circulated among German emigrants in England in the latter half of November. On Marx's instructions 50 copies were sent to Germany for distribution among workers.

Marx's activities in the Educational Society helped to strengthen his ties with the leading representatives of the working-class movement. He became more widely known not only among German emigrant workers, but also in those circles of the English and the French working-class movement with which the Society maintained constant contact.

LOSS OF A FRIEND

Wilhelm Wolff, who came to live in Manchester in the autumn of 1853, was active in helping Marx and Engels to organise the working class. He warmly supported Marx's "Proclamation on Poland". On December 2, 1863, Wolff wrote to Jenny Marx: "As soon as I read the first few lines, I realised that this short vigorous proclamation could have come from no one but the Moor". [2] Wolff did his utmost to circulate the proclamation among German emigrants in Manchester, believing that it would help to overcome the nationalistic attitudes still taken by some of them.

Marx regarded Wolff as his next best friend after Engels, and constantly consulted with him on the most important political problems. For his part, Wolff sought to help Marx in his party-political activity.

In the 1860s, Wolff was frequently seriously ill, his health having been undermined by his terms in Prussian prisons and the privations of life in emigration. Feeling that the end was approaching, Wolff made a will at the end of December 1863 leaving Marx and his family most of his small savings. This money largely helped Marx to complete his work on Volume One of *Capital*.

On May 3, 1864, Marx went to Manchester to visit his dying friend. Wolff, who had been in a coma, regained consciousness briefly, showed signs of having recognised Marx and Engels, and

---

[1] Marx, Engels, *Collected Works*, Vol. 19, pp. 296-97.
[2] *Marx und Engels und die ersten proletarischen Revolutionäre*, Dietz Verlag, Berlin, 1965, S. 206.

then relapsed again. He died on May 9. Marx wrote to his wife: "In him we have lost one of our few friends and fellow fighters. He was a man in the best sense of the word." [1]

At Wolff's funeral on May 13, Marx delivered a short oration, and was so grief-stricken that he had to pause several times.

MARX AND THE GENERAL ASSOCIATION OF GERMAN WORKERS

The revival of working-class activity in Germany, the German workers' desire to unite their forces and take an independent stand on the issues of concern to the people induced Lassalle to start agitating for a political workers' organisation. He claimed to be the theorist and leader of the German working-class movement, and strove to formulate its programme and tactics.

Marx learned of the main points of Lassalle's platform during the latter's stay in London in July and August 1862, before the start of his mass agitation in Germany. Lassalle held that the workers must try to win social emancipation through universal suffrage and producers' associations established with the help of the state, that is, even of the Prussian Junker state. This programme did not hold out any revolutionary prospects for the working class and spread illusions about the possibility of achieving socialism without a class struggle. During their talks in London, Marx told Lassalle that this clashed with the principles stated in the *Manifesto of the Communist Party*.

There was nothing original about Lassalle's views, for the idea of associations with state aid had been propounded in the 1840s by Philippe Buchez, an ideologist of French Catholic socialism, by the petty-bourgeois socialist Louis Blanc, and others. Lassalle had borrowed his demand for universal suffrage from the Chartists, without however taking account of the different conditions in England and Germany. Marx said that in a country like Germany, with a predominantly peasant population, and a working class whose political consciousness was still low, this demand could be used by the counter-revolutionary forces as well, in much the same way as the Bonapartists had used it in France during the coup d'état in 1851. Of course, it was not universal suffrage as such that Marx opposed, but merely Lassalle's insistence on it as the one and only sure means of emancipating the working class.

Marx also criticised Lassalle for ignoring all continuity between the past struggle of the working class in Germany, the revolutionary traditions of 1848 and of the Communist League, and the present. He disliked Lassalle's excessive ambition and his constant efforts to present himself in the best possible light. "Since I last saw him a year ago, he's gone quite mad," Marx wrote to Engels about his talks with Lassalle. "He is now indisputably, not only the greatest scholar,

---

[1] Marx, Engels, *Collected Works*, Vol. 41, p. 523.

the profoundest thinker, the most brilliant man of science, and so forth, but also and in addition, Don Juan *cum* revolutionary Cardinal Richelieu." [1] Lassalle made a highly unfavourable impression on Jenny, who wrote ironically about his megalomania and his tendency to surround himself with flatterers and hangers-on: "He was almost crushed under the weight of the fame he had achieved as a scholar, thinker, poet and politician." [2]

Soon after this meeting, Marx finally broke with Lassalle. In a letter to Kugelmann on February 23, 1865, he gave the following reasons: "Whilst he was pursuing his agitation, our relations were suspended, 1. on account of his bombastic self-adulation, which he managed to combine with the most shameless plagiarism of writings by myself and others; 2. because I *condemned* his *political* tactics; 3. because, even *before* he began his agitation, I had fully explained and 'proved' to him here in London that direct *socialist* intervention by a '*Prussian state*' was an absurdity. In his letters to me (from 1848 to 1863), as well as when we met personally, he had always declared himself a supporter of the party I represent. As soon as he had become convinced in London (at the end of 1862) that he could not play his game *with* me, he resolved to set himself up as 'workers' dictator' *against* me and the old party." [3]

However, even after his break with Lassalle, Marx kept a close watch on his activity. When in May 1863 the General Association of German Workers was founded, headed by Lassalle, Marx saw it as a revival of an independent working-class movement in Germany, and an important step in releasing the workers from the tutelage of the liberals who, like Schulze-Delitzsch and others, sought to restrict the proletariat's tasks to the establishment of co-operative societies, loan and savings banks, etc. Marx said: "After fifteen years of slumber, Lassalle—and this remains his immortal service— re-awakened the workers' movement in Germany." [4] Considering the positive role which the struggle for the political unification of the German proletariat was playing objectively, Marx and Engels abstained for the time being from publicly attacking Lassalle's erroneous dogmas and tactics.

However, they were quite clear that under Lassalle's leadership the General Association of German Workers was operating as a sectarian and reformist organisation. Lassalle's dogmas about producers' associations with state aid and about universal suffrage as the political cure-all were adopted by the Association as its basic principles. Lassalle held the vulgar view that workers' wages could not rise above a given minimum (because of the operation of the "iron law of wages"), and denied the importance of the struggle to improve the economic conditions of the working class. Because of this, the

---

[1] Marx, Engels, *Collected Works*, Vol. 41, p. 389.
[2] *Reminiscences of Marx and Engels*, p. 234.
[3] Marx, Engels, *Collected Works*, Vol. 42, pp. 101-02.
[4] Ibid., Vol. 43, p. 132.

Association initially refused to take part in establishing trade unions and organising strikes. Under the influence of Lassalle, who saw the peasantry as a reactionary class, the Association totally ignored the task of involving the mass of peasants in the emancipation struggle, and did not demand the elimination of feudal survivals. The Association's leadership displayed nationalistic tendencies by refusing to develop international contacts with proletarian organisations abroad. The Association's organisational structure corresponded to Lassalle's dictatorial methods and clashed with the democratic principles of the working-class movement. The President—Lassalle himself—had such extensive powers that he could deal with the affairs of the Association alone and almost without control. For all practical purposes, Lassalle was implanting within the Association a personality cult of the President.

Marx and Engels believed that the greatest flaw in Lassalle's tactics was his attempt to make the workers' organisation take the dangerous path of flirting with the ruling Junker circles. Lassalle's attacks on the exploiting classes were one-sided: he attacked the bourgeois liberals (Party-of-Progress men)—a fact of great importance in itself—but did not fight against Bismarck's government and the Junkers. On the contrary, he oriented the working class towards an alliance with these forces against the bourgeoisie.

At the time, Marx and Engels were not aware that Lassalle was in secret correspondence with Bismarck, that he had met him on several occasions, and that the two men had made a secret arrangement. Lassalle had promised Bismarck the assistance of the workers' organisation in the fight against the Party-of-Progress men, and its support for Bismarck's unification plans, in exchange for an undertaking to introduce universal suffrage and to help set up producers' associations. However, from what Lassalle was saying Marx guessed that he had been in touch with representatives of the Prussian royal power. In January 1865, after Lassalle's death—he was killed in a duel on August 31, 1864—Marx and Engels learned that his flirtations with Bismarck had gone much farther than they had suspected, and that Lassalle had promised the head of the Prussian government the Association's assistance in annexing Schleswig-Holstein. That is why they branded his behaviour as an act of treachery to the working-class movement, despite the fact that all the details of Lassalle's relations with Bismarck were not fully revealed until decades later.

In criticising Lassalle, Marx and Engels did not identify him with the General Association of German Workers, let alone the German working-class movement as a whole. They hoped that, through the sound elements within the Association, the workers who remained loyal to revolutionary traditions, they would succeed in changing its programme, tactics and organisational principles, and in transforming it into a militant organisation of the working class. Reports from Germany showed the existence of such revolutionary forces within and without the Association, especially among the proletariat of the Rhine Province. Lassalle and his followers had failed to eradicate among the leading workers memories of the Communist League and its leaders, Marx and Engels. In the spring of 1864, during the anniversary celebrations of the Association in the Rhine city of Ronsdorf, the audience loudly applauded the mention of their names. In the summer of 1864, two Solingen workers who came to London to escape persecution by the Prussian authorities told Marx about the Rhine Province workers' loyalty to his and Engels' ideas.

Marx and Engels pinned great hopes on the activity within the Association of their comrades-in-arms, particularly Wilhelm Liebknecht, who had returned home in 1862 and regularly informed them about the state of the working-class movement in Germany. Marx and Engels gave Liebknecht advice and instructions about disseminating the ideas of scientific communism, for they saw the spread of these ideas as the best means of overcoming the influence of Lassalle's petty-bourgeois socialism, exposing his sectarian and reformist tactics, and forming—in contrast to Lassalleanism—a revolutionary wing of the German proletarian movement.

ON THE WAY TO THE INTERNATIONAL

The fresh revolutionary upsurge in the late 1850s and the early 1860s was marked by considerable success in the international working-class movement. Workers' strikes assumed extensive proportions. Workers' organisations, ranging from mutual assistance societies and trade unions to political associations, like the General Association of German Workers, were set up in many countries. The working class reacted vigorously to political events at home and abroad, revealing an urge to take an independent stand. The activity of the proletarian masses was determined by important changes within the composition of the working class itself. Not only had it grown numerically, but its structure had changed. With the advance of the industrial revolution, workers in large-scale industry constituted a growing section as compared with the semi-artisan proletariat which had prevailed at the time of the Communist League. The role of the working class was also increasing in some countries where it had just made its appearance at that time.

The development of the working-class movement made it an urgent task to unite the forces of the international proletariat. There was an instinctive urge among the workers to establish international ties. Ideas for the establishment of a mass international working-class organisation were advanced. An impetus to practical steps in this direction was given by the above-mentioned meeting of solidarity with the Polish insurgents held in London on July 22, 1863, following which the English and French workers set up an organising committee to prepare such an association.

However, the establishment of a mass revolutionary international proletarian organisation required more than the instinctive desire of the workers for unity. There was also a need for an ideological basis for the cohesion of their forces, and this could be provided only by a revolutionary theory giving scientific expression to the basic interests of the working class of all countries. This theory was the doctrine of Marx and Engels. Despite the fact that by the 1860s most workers were under the influence of bourgeois ideology and pre-Marxian utopian socialism, the working-class movement was already sufficiently mature for gradually adopting Marxist ideas. Marx's theory provided the means for overcoming bourgeois and petty-bourgeois influence among the workers, their ideological confusion, sectarian isolation and national exclusiveness.

On the eve of the 1848-49 revolution, Marx and Engels had given a scientific basis for proletarian internationalism, and had created, by setting up the Communist League, the prototype of a future broad international proletarian organisation. They fostered the revolutionary cadres which could constitute its leading core. In the period of reaction, and especially in the period of the upsurge of the proletarian and democratic movements, Marx carried on an intense struggle to unite the proletarian forces round the banner of scientific communism. His publicistic writings in those years helped to mould revolutionary views among the leading participants in the working-class movement, to educate them in a spirit of internationalism, and to intensify their urge for unity.

Marx's practical activity also promoted the international cohesion of the proletariat of all countries: his participation in the early 1860s in the German Workers' Educational Society in London, his statements in defence of Blanqui, his support of the meetings organised by English workers as a mark of solidarity with the Polish national liberation movement and with the fighters against Negro slavery in the U.S.A., and his contacts with the leading revolutionary elements in the General Association of German Workers. Marx's contacts with representatives of the working-class movement in various countries helped to draw the workers into the common international struggle.

The theoretical and practical activity of Marx and his associates, and their efforts to spread the ideas of scientific communism and proletarian internationalism and to establish a proletarian party played the decisive role in laying the ideological foundation for the International Working Men's Association (International).

While seeking to give the working class a theoretical weapon in its fight against the capitalist system, Marx had all this time been putting an intense effort into the writing of *Capital*, his main work.

CHAPTER TEN

CAPITAL — MARX'S MAIN WORK

> *"Capital" is our sword, our shield, our weapon of attack and defence.*
>
> Johann Philipp Becker

WORK ON THE SECOND PART OF *A CONTRIBUTION TO THE CRITIQUE OF POLITICAL ECONOMY*

After dispatching to the publisher the first part of *A Contribution to the Critique of Political Economy* in January 1859, Marx at once set about preparing the second part, a chapter which was to complete the first section — "On Capital" — of his planned work on political economy. With the economic manuscript of 1857-58 as a basis, Marx first of all sketched out a detailed plan of this chapter.

Its first part was to show the process of the production of capital, and the second the circulation of capital. The third part was entitled "Capital and Profit". The final part of the plan, entitled "Varia", was to deal with agriculture, landed property and capital. There he must have planned to give an exposition of his theory of rent of land.

Marx had expected to take only a short time in preparing the second part of his *Contribution* and to publish it immediately after the issue of the first part, but, says Engels, no sooner had the first part been published than Marx began to feel that he was not yet quite clear on all the details in elaborating the principal ideas in the second and subsequent parts. There arose the need for an additional study of a whole range of questions, before expounding the subject for the press. Accordingly, Marx launched a fresh assault on the book repositories of the British Museum. Once again he went over much new material. Among other works, he reread Engels' *The Condition of the Working-Class in England* and made a thorough study of the Factory Reports between 1855 and 1859.

This intensive and fruitful research was interrupted from early 1860 to mid-1861 mainly because of Marx's work on a pamphlet against Vogt.

ECONOMIC MANUSCRIPT OF 1861-63

Not until the summer of 1861 was Marx able once again to devote himself almost entirely to political economy. He himself said that he worked like "a Trojan".[1] He had to interrupt his studies, sometimes for weeks on end, mainly because of the never-ending "domestic disturbances",[2] illness among the members of the family, and various other concomitants of extreme penury and privation.

From August 1861 to July 1863, he produced a great manuscript, *A Contribution to the Critique of Political Economy*, consisting of 23 notebooks running to almost 200 printed sheets. That is what the continuation of the first part proved to be in practice. In effect, this is the second version, after the economic manuscript of 1857-58, of the whole of *Capital*.

On June 18, 1862, Marx informed Engels: "I am expanding this volume, since those German scoundrels estimate the value of a book in terms of its cubic capacity".[3] However, it would be wrong to see this as the only reason for the vast dimensions of the 1861-63 manuscript. This was due more to Marx's grand scheme and the truly vast amount of material that he had mustered initially to write a single but very important chapter.

The manuscript sets out in detail the most important aspects of the general problem of the production of capital: the conversion of money into capital, absolute surplus-value, relative surplus-value, formal and real subordination of labour to capital, co-operation, division of labour, machines and the consequences of their capitalist use, the reconversion of surplus-value into capital (the accumulation of capital), and the primitive accumulation of capital. We find, therefore, that the manuscript reflects the problems which will be dealt with in the future Volume One of *Capital*, constituting "the first extant draft thereof",[4] as Engels put it.

Some notebooks of the manuscript deal with subjects relating to Volumes Two and Three of *Capital*, like the movement of money in the process of capitalist production, reproduction (mainly simple reproduction), surplus-value and profit, the conversion of profit into average profit, loan and commercial capital, commercial profit, and the tendency of the rate of profit to fall with the advance of capitalist production.

As Marx worked on the manuscript, he reorganised the whole project and by the end of 1862 had conceived his outline scheme to publish the second part of the work not as a direct continuation of his *A Contribution to the Critique of Political Economy* (published in

---

[1] Marx, Engels, *Collected Works*, Vol. 41, p. 384.
[2] Ibid., p. 352.
[3] Ibid., p. 380.
[4] Karl Marx, *Capital*, Vol. II, Moscow, 1986, p. 2.

1859), but as an independent work entitled *Capital* with the subtitle *A Contribution to the Critique of Political Economy*. His letter to Kugelmann of December 28, 1862 shows that at the time he already considered the manuscript of his book to be essentially complete. It set out the "principles of political economy" and, according to Marx himself, was to constitute, together with the first part, the theoretical quintessence which would make it relatively easy to elaborate the subsequent sections of political economy, which were to deal with more concrete relations. In the same letter, Marx also expresses his intention of having a fair copy of the manuscript made and putting the finishing touches to it for publication.

Actually, the manuscript was not only copied and polished, but also expanded with the addition of new material. In the first half of 1863, Marx expended a great deal of effort on giving greater depth to his study of the history of technical development and the technology of production, the character and specific features of the industrial revolution, and its influence on the condition and struggle of the working class. Once again he spent long hours at the British Museum, studying various writings on the history of political economy.

Marx was unable to complete his work earlier because he was unwell. In a letter to a friend, Bertha Markheim, dated July 6, 1863, Jenny wrote: "My dear Karl had a great deal of trouble with his liver this spring. However, despite all the setbacks, his book is now making gigantic strides towards completion. It would have been finished sooner, had he kept to his original plan of limiting it to 20 or 30 sheets. But since the Germans really believe only in 'fat' books, and the far more subtle concentration and elimination of all that is superfluous counts for nothing in the eyes of those worthies, Karl has added a lot more historical material, and it is as a volume of 50 sheets that it will fall, like a bomb, on German soil."[1]

An historico-critical analysis of bourgeois economic views constitutes a sizable section of the 1861-63 manuscript, which Marx himself called "my handiwork" in which he had to "demolish everything and even build up the *historical* section out of what was in part quite unknown material".[2]

As his manuscript increased in volume, Marx began to feel that this work, which appeared to be finished, should be divided into three books.

ECONOMIC MANUSCRIPT OF 1863-65

From August 1863, Marx turned mainly to elaborating the sections of his economic research which had not been formulated in sufficient depth in twenty-three notebooks of his economic manuscript of 1861-63, namely, questions bearing on the circulation of capi-

---

[1] Marx, Engels, *Collected Works*, Vol. 41, p. 582.
[2] Ibid., p. 488.

tal and the converted forms of surplus-value. In other words, he concentrated on the problems of the future Volumes Two and Three of *Capital*. As far as circumstances permitted, he continued to combine writing the new manuscripts with an intensive study of new sources and writings. His attention was drawn to French sources, new data on Japan, and the works of the German agrochemists, Liebig and Schönbein.

However, in this period also there were interruptions in his work. Once again he was seriously ill. It took him almost the whole of December 1863 and January and February 1864 to settle his personal affairs in Germany and Holland. In September 1864 the International Working Men's Association was set up, and practical activity took up a great deal of his time because he had to "run the whole Association himself".[1] His work in the International naturally distracted him from his study of political economy and inevitably delayed the completion of his writings.

For Marx, the interests of revolutionary science and of the working-class movement were paramount, and he devoted every moment he could spare from other urgent business to *Capital*. When his health somewhat improved, he worked day and night to complete his work as soon as possible. He said jokingly that in his research he had applied a "system of shifts", similar to the one of the English factory-owners ("factory dogs") had imposed on the workers from 1848 to 1850. "I have been going to the Museum in the day-time and writing at night."[2]

On July 31, 1865, Marx informed Engels that he had only three more chapters to write to complete the theoretical part of *Capital* (the first three books). The first book could have been sent to the printers', but Marx did not do this, because he preferred to have the whole work in front of him.

Moreover, according to the arrangement with the publisher, Otto Meissner of Hamburg, who had agreed to publish *Capital*, it was not to exceed 60 sheets. Accordingly Marx felt that it was absolutely necessary to complete the whole of the manuscript, so as "to know how much to be condensed and crossed out"[3] for a balanced and proportional exposition of the separate parts within the space permitted.

Thanks to his heroic efforts and extreme determination, the new version of the manuscript of the whole of *Capital* was ready by the end of December 1865. It was so large that the chapter on land rent alone could have been a separate book.

---

[1] Marx, Engels, *Collected Works*, Vol. 42, p. 328.
[2] Ibid., p. 227.
[3] Ibid., p. 175.

PREPARATION FOR THE PRINTERS AND PUBLICATION OF VOLUME ONE OF *CAPITAL*

On January 1, 1866, on Engels' advice, Marx began to prepare for the printers not the whole work, but only the first book dealing with the production of capital. This he did with great satisfaction and genuine inspiration. He "enjoyed licking the infant clean after long birth-pangs".[1] In actual fact, of course, he was producing yet another version of the work. At this point, his health deteriorated again. In a letter in April 1866 to Ernestine, Wilhelm Liebknecht's wife, Jenny wrote: "Karl, who was more or less all right until then, started to copy out his new book at the New Year. He was getting on famously, and I cannot tell you with what quiet satisfaction I watched the manuscript grow proudly to such large proportions after so much long, anxious, almost hopeless waiting; then suddenly, at the end of January, signs of Karl's old wretched illness reappeared once again."[2]

For over two months he was bedridden, but continued "to work assiduously although only for short intervals in the day-time".[3] In this way he enlarged the historical part of the chapter on "The Working-Day".

Marx felt bound to take into account every published work which might be of any interest and to go over all the available documentary sources, from which the necessary information could be gleaned. At the very end of 1866, he asked Engels to obtain for him as quickly as possible a book by James Edwin Th. Rogers, entitled *A History of Agriculture and Prices in England*. "I must have a look at the book and have left a gap in one chapter for the purpose. Although it has already been out for a long time, it is not yet in the library."[4] In February 1866, Marx asked Engels to help him obtain a book by John Watts, entitled *Trade Societies and Strikes. Machinery. Co-operative Societies*, which had been mentioned in one of the factory reports. In the course of 1866, Marx again and again returned to the parliamentary Blue Books, the official reports on the use of child and female labour in English industry, and the living conditions of the English proletariat. He worked very hard, without sparing himself, until April 2, 1867, when he informed Engels that the book was ready and that he would deliver it in person to the publisher in Hamburg. He left London on April 10 and arrived at Hamburg at noon on April 12. It was a rough crossing, but after his voluntary seclusion in his study and the reading-room, Marx paid no heed to the weather and, in fact, enjoyed himself "tremendously".When he met Meissner, it turned out that the latter did not have enough printers and trained proof-readers at his disposal,

---

[1] Ibid., p. 228.
[2] Central Party Archives of the Institute of Marxism-Leninism.
[3] *Lettres sur "Le Capital"*, Editions Sociales, Paris, 1964, p. 150.
[4] Marx, Engels, *Collected Works*, Vol. 42, p. 339.

and it was decided to have the book printed by Otto Wigand in Leipzig. The printers began work on it on April 29, 1867.

From Hamburg Marx went on to Hanover to see his friend Ludwig Kugelmann, with whom he had corresponded since 1862, but had never had an opportunity of meeting personally. He was given the warmest possible welcome, and hosts and guest easily found common ground and felt a great liking for each other. Gertrud, Kugelmann's wife, had imagined Marx to be a "morose revolutionary", and was highly surprised to find him a "smart, good-humoured gentleman whose warm Rhenish accent at once reminded her of home. Young dark eyes smiled at her from under a mane of grey hair.... Marx was unpretentious and amiable.... He took an interest in everything and when he was particularly attracted by anybody or a witty remark was made he would adjust his monocle and survey the person in question with a friendly interest." [1]

Marx spent almost a month at the Kugelmanns' home and read the first page-proofs there.

Engels took a keen interest in the page-proofs, and Marx sent them on to him for perusal. After reading some 36 printed sheets Engels congratulated his friend wholeheartedly on the ease with which he had set out in simple and clear terms the most abstruse economic problems. [2] He advised Marx to describe the historical development of the form of value in somewhat greater detail, backing up with historical examples what had already been demonstrated dialectically. Engels wrote: "It was a serious mistake not to have made the development of these rather abstract arguments clearer by means of a larger number of short sections with their own headings." [3] Kugelmann advised to do the same.

Marx did so at once. On June 22 he wrote to Engels: "With regard to the development of the *form of value*, I have both followed and *not* followed your advice, thus striking a dialectical attitude in this matter, too. That is to say, 1. I have written an *appendix* in which I set out *the same subject* again as simply and as much in the manner of a school text-book as possible, and 2. I have divided each successive proposition into paras. etc., *each with its own heading*, as you advised." [4]

The letter which Marx wrote to Engels at 2.00 a.m. on August 16, 1867, is a most stirring and historic document. It said:

"Dear Fred,

"Have just finished correcting the *last sheet* (49th) of the book. The appendix—*Form of Value*—*in small print*, takes up 1¼ sheets.

"*Preface* ditto returned corrected yesterday. So, *this volume is finished*. I owe it to *you* alone that it was possible! Without your self-

---

[1] *Reminiscences of Marx and Engels*, p. 274.
[2] *Lettres sur "Le Capital"*, p. 172.
[3] Marx, Engels, *Collected Works*, Vol. 42, p. 382.
[4] Ibid., p. 384.

sacrifice for me I could not possibly have managed the immense labour demanded by the 3 volumes. I embrace you, full of thanks!" [1]

Twenty-five years of dedicated labour and persistent quest lay behind him. It was quite natural for Marx to express in the most touching words his heartfelt affection and gratitude to Engels, who had always given him support and assistance with the selflessness of a true friend.

Capital is the book for which, as Marx put it, he had sacrificed his "health, happiness, and family" [2]. Jenny had good reason to say: "There can be few books that have been written in more difficult circumstances, and I am sure I could write a secret history of it which would tell of many, extremely many unspoken troubles and anxieties and torments. If the workers had an inkling of the sacrifices that were necessary for this work, which was written only for them and for their sakes, to be completed they would perhaps show a little more interest." [3] From the hands of the genius, the working class received a great ideological weapon. *Capital*, as Marx himself said, was the most terrible missile ever aimed at the heads of the bourgeois and the landowners.

The volume was published on September 14, 1867, in an edition of 1,000 copies. Marx expected the royalties to help him right his financial affairs, pay off his old debts, and buy something for the home, but they proved to be so small that, as Marx himself wittily remarked, they did not even cover the cost of the tobacco he had smoked when writing the book.

He dedicated his work to Wilhelm Wolff, a remarkable man with whom he and Engels had been close friends and fighters in the revolutionary struggle for many years. The title-page of the book said: "Dedicated to *my unforgettable friend, Wilhelm Wolff,* intrepid, faithful, noble protagonist of the proletariat. Born in Tarnau on June 21, 1809. Died in exile in Manchester on May 9, 1864."

As with the publication of the first part of *A Contribution to the Critique of Political Economy*, the German bourgeoisie tried to surround Volume One of *Capital* with a "conspiracy of silence", a fact which disturbed Marx and his friends. Just before the book was due to appear, Engels suggested to Marx that the book should be attacked "from the bourgeois point of view" to attract the attention of the public at large.[4] Marx definitely liked Engels' idea and he wrote on September 12, 1867: "Your plan to attack the book *from the bourgeois point of view* is *the best tactic.*" [5] Accordingly, when the volume appeared, Engels published a number of reviews in the bourgeois press.

These reviews, which appeared to have been written by an objec-

---

[1] Ibid., pp. 402-05.
[2] Ibid., p. 366.
[3] Ibid., pp. 578-79.
[4] Ibid., p. 426.
[5] Ibid., p. 427.

tive bourgeois scholar, started out by saying that the Germans had done very little in the sphere of political economy. Official, professional German economists had tended to avoid the contradictions and difficulties of economic development, imitating the unscientific views of Bastiat, and rejecting the classics, including Ricardo and Sismondi. "For the sake of momentary popularity", they had disavowed the classical legacy. Against this background, Engels stressed, Marx stood out as a man whose earlier writings, especially his 1859 treatise on money, were "distinguished by a strictly scientific spirit as much as by ruthless criticism". Considering that Germany's official economists had been unable to counter Marx's conclusions earlier, it would be even more difficult for them to contest the conclusions set out in his latest work, Volume One of *Capital*, which has the merits of the "greatest scientific subtlety" and the "masterly, dialectical arrangement of the whole",[1] and gives a convincing and penetrating picture of the various historical states of society. Engels went on to list Marx's most important discoveries at deliberate length.

His articles unquestionably did much to popularise Volume One of *Capital*. Another factor of positive importance was the publication of extracts, arranged by Marx's friends, from the author's Preface to the volume in German, English and French newspapers.

Very soon, German bourgeois science was forced to abandon its "conspiracy of silence", for it would have been the height of absurdity to continue pretending that Marx's book did not exist. Its importance began to be publicly acknowledged. The review in a German journal by Eugen Dühring, a vulgar philosopher and economist and an assistant professor at Berlin University, which revealed "embarrassment and funk"[2] was typical.

There was an interesting comment from Ludwig Feuerbach, the great German materialist philosopher, who wrote in his work *Concerning Ethics: Eudaemonism* about *Capital*'s accusatory power and wealth of facts. He said: "Where men are packed together as, for instance, in the English factories and workers' dwellings, if pigsties can be called dwellings, where they do not even have a sufficient amount of oxygen in the air—in this connection see K. Marx's *Capital*, a work which is at least rich in incontrovertible facts of the most interesting if terrible kind—morality is deprived of any scope, and virtue is, at best, only a monopoly of messieurs the industrialists, the capitalists."[3]

Marx's book was given an enthusiastic reception in the leading circles of the scientific intelligentsia in Russia.

The best reward for Marx was the understanding his work met with among the workers. It was welcomed in the working-class press as soon as it appeared. The official organ of the German sections of

---

[1] Marx, Engels, *Collected Works*, Vol. 20, pp. 208-09.
[2] Ibid., Vol. 42, p. 511.
[3] Ludwig Feuerbach, *Sämtliche Werke*, Zehnter Band, Stuttgart, 1911, S. 266-67.

the First International in Switzerland, the jounal *Vorbote*, said in its September issue for 1867 that for the working class Marx's work meant "a battle won". In September 1868, on the motion of the German delegates to the Brussels Congress of the International, it passed a resolution recommending that workers of all countries should study *Capital* and that efforts should be made to have it translated into the various languages. It also emphasised the invaluable service rendered by the author, who had been the first to give a scientific analysis of the capitalist system.

RUSSIAN EDITION OF VOLUME ONE OF *CAPITAL*

In September 1868, Nikolai Danielson, a young clerk at the St. Petersburg Mutual Credit Society, a revolutionary Narodnik who subsequently became a prominent leader of the liberal Narodniks, wrote to Marx concerning the publication of *Capital* in Russian. He said: "The importance of your latest work—*Capital. A Critique of Political Economy*—has induced a local publisher (N. P. Poliakoff) to undertake the translation of this work into Russian."[1]

The idea of translating *Capital* into Russian was first mooted by Hermann Lopatin, a young graduate of St. Petersburg University, and an ardent follower of Nikolai Chernyshevsky, who had rallied round him revolutionary-minded young people of St. Petersburg and several other towns.

In 1870 Lopatin made a special trip to London to see Marx and was warmly met there by the latter in early July. The two soon became fast friends. The 25-year-old Lopatin, who had a critical mind, a noble, steadfast character, and was well read, became a favourite with Marx, who said: "There are few people in the world of whom I am so fond and whom I esteem so much."[2] Lopatin worshipped Marx and called him "one of the most remarkable writers on political economy and one of the most widely educated men in the whole of Europe".[3] In London, the two men frequently discussed the publication of a Russian edition of Volume One of *Capital*, for which Lopatin suggested the corresponding terminology in Russian. For this edition, at his request, Marx promised to rewrite, in a more popular form, his first chapter on "Commodities and Money".

On Marx's advice, Lopatin began his translation of the book with its second chapter ("The Transformation of Money into Capital"), and by the end of November 1870 he had also translated Chapter Three ("The Production of Absolute Surplus-Value") and part of Chapter Four ("Production of Relative Surplus-Value"), that is, roughly one-third of the book. He then returned to Russia to organ-

---

[1] Central Party Archives of the Institute of Marxism-Leninism.
[2] Marx, Engels, *Werke*, Bd. 33, S. 478.
[3] *Reminiscences of Marx and Engels*, p. 201.

ise the escape of Chernyshevsky from exile in Siberia, but was arrested in Siberia and did not manage to get free until the summer of 1873.

The translation of *Capital* was completed by Lopatin's friend, Nikolai Danielson, with the participation of Nikolai Lyubavin, subsequently a professor of chemistry at Moscow University. Chapter One was translated in its original form, because Marx had been unable to rewrite it in view of the great pressure of other urgent business. He did, however, make a few minor changes and additions to this and other chapters.

The Russian translation came out on March 27, 1872, in an edition of 3,000 copies, a fairly large one for those days, but the demand was also considerable. By May 15, 900 copies had been sold and by the end of the year almost the whole edition.

This was the first translation of *Capital* into any foreign language, and Marx praised its high standard. The translators had made a fine job of a task of exceptional complexity, with the personal assistance of the author himself. Many of the terms they introduced were accepted by Russian readers and subsequently incorporated into scientific usage.

The appearance of Volume One of *Capital* in a Russian translation was a great event. Friedrich Lessner, a German worker who knew Marx well, recalled: "He attached great importance to the movement in Russia at the time and spoke with great respect of those who made such great sacrifices for the study and spreading of theoretical works and of their understanding of modern ideas. When he at last received a copy of *Capital* in Russian from Petersburg he considered the event an important sign of the times and an occasion for him, his family and his friends to celebrate." [1]

The prominent tsarist censor who authorised the printing of *Capital*, predicted that "*few people in Russia would read, let alone understand it*".[2] However, in 1880 Marx observed with satisfaction that *Capital* was being read and praised more highly in Russia than anywhere else. It was helping Russian revolutionaries to spread Marxism in Russia and to set up the first Marxist circles and groups. The first few editions of *Capital* played a great part in paving the way for the establishment of the future Marxist Party of the Russian proletariat.

SECOND GERMAN EDITION OF VOLUME ONE OF *CAPITAL*

By the autumn of 1871, the first German edition of Volume One had been sold out. The growing demand for the book induced the publisher Meissner to ask Marx to prepare a second edition quickly.

This required a great deal of work, and Marx's changes affected

---

[1] *Reminiscences of Marx and Engels,* p. 170.
[2] *Krasny Arkhiv,* Vol. 1 (56), Moscow, 1933, p. 7.

above all the structure of the book. Instead of the six chapters of the first edition, it was now divided into 7 parts and 25 chapters. Almost all the chapters were subdivided into smaller paragraphs or sections. By improving the structure of the book, Marx was taking account of the suggestion Engels had made in 1867.

Many new footnotes were written for the second edition, some of them at Lopatin's suggestion. A great number of changes and additions were made in the text. Jenny, Marx's eldest daughter, recalled that he was satisfied with the improvements he had made, and for him this "did not happen often".[1]

While hard at work on the second edition of *Capital*, Marx had to devote much time to the International and help participants in the Paris Commune who had fled to London to settle down. In a letter to Kugelmann, dated December 21-22, 1871, Jenny said that her father not only had to fight the governments of the ruling classes, but to skirmish constantly with "fat, fair and 40-year-old" landladies who attacked him wildly for this or that Communard failing to pay the rent.[2] Night seemed to be the only time when Marx could get down to work on his *Capital*.

The second edition was published in 1872 and 1873, initially in nine separate parts, the first appearing in mid-July 1872. In January 1873, Marx wrote an afterword to the whole edition. In early June 1873, the volume was put out as a book in an edition three times larger than the first one.

AUTHORISED FRENCH EDITION
OF VOLUME ONE OF *CAPITAL*

A French edition of Volume One was produced between 1872 and 1875 in separate parts. This was the second foreign edition, the Russian being the first. Marx himself helped to prepare it, because he wished to improve the work and make it more comprehensible to the French reader.

The French edition was prepared in the period which followed upon the defeat of the Paris Commune, the first attempt to establish proletarian power.

Even the members of the Commune were mostly socialists by instinct only and had no clear understanding of the key principles of scientific communism. In a letter to Kugelmann of May 18, 1874, Marx observed that "in France the absence of a theoretical foundation and of practical common sense is very evident".[3] Proudhonism continued to be a source of dangerous influence on the workers. In a letter to Ludwig Büchner of May 1, 1867, Marx explained the reasons why he wanted to have a French edition published in Paris, af-

---
[1] Marx, Engels, *Werke*, Bd. 33, S. 695-96.
[2] Ibid., S. 687.
[3] Ibid., S. 628.

ter the publication of *Capital* in Germany. "I consider it to be of the greatest importance to emancipate the French from the erroneous views under which Proudhon with his idealised petty bourgeoisie has buried them." [1] *Capital*'s scientific logic exploded Proudhon's principal illusions and cleared the way for a truly proletarian movement.

In addition, French was a language more widely known than German in Belgium, Spain and Italy, where the anarchists were seeking to secure control of the working-class movement, particularly in Spain and Italy. The spread of the ideas of *Capital* in these countries helped to undermine the positions of the anarchist leaders.

Marx accepted a proposal from the publisher La Châtre to have *Capital* serialised. He wrote: "In this form, the book will be more accessible to the working class, a consideration which to me outweighs everything else." [2]

Volume One of *Capital* was translated into French by Joseph Roy, who had also translated the works of Feuerbach. Although, according to Marx, Roy had a fine knowledge of both languages, his translation turned out to be too literal and did not satisfy the author. Marx had to work extremely hard on this particular translation. On May 12, 1874, he wrote to La Châtre: "Roy's manuscript ... had to be re-worked from start to finish." [3] Marx did not confine himself to editing the translation, but expressed many of his ideas in a new form.

The French edition differs substantially from the first two German editions, and there are also some differences between it and the fourth German edition, published under the editorship of Engels in 1890, which is regarded as the final one, although Engels took into account most of what Marx had done for the second German and the French editions.

The second and subsequent German editions contain 7 parts consisting of 25 chapters. The French edition has 8 parts and 33 chapters. Chapter 24, "The So-Called Primitive Accumulation", is presented in the French edition as a separate Part Eight, which is entitled simply "Primitive Accumulation".

The title-page of the French edition of Volume One of *Capital* says, and with good grounds: "Completely revised by the author." In correspondence with his friends, Marx frequently quoted ideas from *Capital* as set forth in this particular edition adding that they were not as cursorily presented there as in the other editions. He strongly advised translators of Volume One to use the French edition. With reference to the second Russian edition he wrote to Danielson on November 15, 1878: "1) I wish that the *division into chapters*—and the same holds good for the *subdivisions*—be made according to the French edition.

---

[1] Marx, Engels, *Collected Works*, Vol. 42, p. 368.
[2] Karl Marx, *Capital*, Vol. I, Moscow, 1986, p. 30.
[3] Central Party Archives of the Institute of Marxism-Leninism.

"2) That the translator compare always carefully the second German edition with the French one, since the latter contains many important changes and additions...." [1] Marx believed that the more popular character of the French edition of Volume One would make it easier to translate it from the French into English and the Romance languages.

In an afterword to the French edition, dated April 28, 1875, Marx addressed the reader as follows: "...Whatever the literary defects of this French edition may be, it possesses a scientific value independent of the original and should be consulted even by readers familiar with German." [2]

WORK ON VOLUMES TWO AND THREE OF *CAPITAL*

Earlier on, in 1867, Marx began to put the finishing touches to the rest of the manuscripts which he had written by the end of 1865, and which were to make up the other volumes of *Capital*. He continued this work, with some interruptions, up to his death.

First and foremost, he made a much deeper study of agrarian relations in the various countries, and of new phenomena in capitalist economy. In a letter dated July 4, 1868 to Sigfrid Meyer, a leader of the German and American working-class movement, Marx asked him to send him American newspapers from time to time: "In particular, it would be of great value to me if you could dig up some antibourgeois material about landownership and agrarian relations in the United States." [3] Marx needed this material for his polemics against the bourgeois economist Henry Carey on the question of land rent. On October 7, 1868, he wrote to Danielson saying that he was unable to prepare Volume Two for the press "until certain official enquiries, instituted during last year (and 1866) in France, the United States and England, have been completed or published". [4] In addition, Marx also began to see the special importance of Russian material. As a result he decided, in 1871, that the whole manuscript of Volume Two needed to be radically revised.

In the late 1860s and the early 1870s, Marx did his utmost to complete *Capital* as soon as possible, but he had other important duties to perform. In a letter to Danielson on November 9, 1871, he complained that he had been so busy over the last few months that he could not resume his theoretical studies. On May 28, 1872, Marx wrote to him: "I am so overworked, and in fact so much interfered with in my theoretical studies, that, after September, I shall *withdraw* from the *commercial concern* which, at this moment, weighs principally upon my own shoulders, and which, as you know, has its

---
[1] Ibid.
[2] Karl Marx, *Capital*, Vol. I, p. 31.
[3] Marx, Engels, *Collected Works*, Vol. 43, p. 61.
[4] Ibid., p. 123.

ramifications all over the world."[1] For reasons of secrecy, he referred to the General Council of the First International as a "commercial concern". Marx had earlier repeatedly expressed his intention to withdraw from day-to-day practical work in the International. On November 24, 1871, he wrote to César De Paepe, a leader of the Belgian working-class movement: "As I told you in London, I have often asked myself if the time has not come to resign from the General Council. The more society develops, the more time is taken up and I must, after all, finally have done with *Das Kapital*."[2] His work on *Capital* and his leadership of the International were two totally different fields of activity, and it is amazing how much strength and energy Marx devoted to both. One wonders how both activities could be carried on simultaneously by a man who was ill, no longer young and tormented by bitter privation and endless everyday worries. A great goal generates great energy capable of performing miracles.

At the end of 1869, Marx began to learn Russian, his profound interest in the language and Russian social thinking being stimulated by N. Flerovsky's *The Condition of the Working Class in Russia*, which he had received from St. Petersburg and which made a great impression on his very first reading of it. Marx believed it to be absolutely necessary to make a study of Russian economic writings and original sources, especially on relations involving landed property.

Having made a rapid study of the grammar, he started to read Russian works with a dictionary, his first being a copy of Herzen's "Prisons and Exiles" (a part of *My Past and My Thoughts*), which Engels had studied before him. The translations and Russian roots which he had jotted down in the margin were a great help to Marx and he was soon able to start Flerovsky's book. On February 10, 1870, he informed Engels with satisfaction that he had already read 150 pages.

Marx made a note of unknown words in the margin, and these became fewer and fewer as he neared the end of the book, for by then he was reading fairly fluently. He also jotted down remarks on the substance of the book, some of them critical ones. Although Marx highly valued the content of the work and the material it contained, showing the existence of a capitalist sector in Russia, the disintegration of the village commune and the development of commodity production, he did not ignore the flaws in the author's outlook, his idealisation of the communal way of life, and his illusions about the "class harmony", which were akin to some of Proudhon's views. Thus, where Flerovsky expressed the wish that the capitalist and the worker should not feel themselves to be "employer and hired hand", but "comrade" and "brother", Marx wrote: "*An old illusion!*"[3]

---

[1] Central Party Archives of the Institute of Marxism-Leninism.
[2] Marx, Engels, *Werke*, Bd. 33, S. 338.
[3] *Marx-Engels Archives*, Book IV, Moscow-Leningrad, 1929, p. 376.

On the whole, Flerovsky's book, presenting as it did a wide array of facts, gave Marx what he would otherwise have obtained only in part from other sources distorted by official optimism or subjectivist notions. He wrote to the Lafargues: "After the study of his work, one feels deeply convinced that a most terrible social revolution — in such inferior forms of course as suit the present Muscovite state of development — is irrepressible in Russia and near at hand. These is good news. Russia and England are the two great pillars of the present European system." [1]

After this, in the first half of 1870, Marx appears to have read Volume Three of the Geneva edition of Chernyshevsky's works, which included his "Additions and Notes to John Stuart Mill's First Book on Political Economy". In the summer of that year, he ordered Volume Four from Geneva, for he had an extremely high opinion of the works of the great Russian socialist and democrat.

A year later, Marx was able to sum up the initial results of his efforts to study Russian. He wrote to Sigfrid Meyer: "The result was worth the effort that a man of my age must make to master a language differing so greatly from the classical, Germanic, and Romance languages. The intellectual movement now taking place in Russia testifies to the fact that fermentation is going on deep below the surface. Minds are always connected by invisible threads with the body of the people." [2]

Having mastered Russian, Marx set about making a systematic study of official publications and monographs on agrarian relations and socio-political development in Russia. According to Engels, Marx was "engaged in entirely new special studies". [3] For over a decade, large crates of Russian books kept travelling between St. Petersburg and London, in both directions, as Marx's friends (Danielson among them) sent him various books that he frequently returned after reading them.

Marx's extensive and numerous extracts, with his comments, from the *Transactions of the Tax Commission, Reports of the Commission on the State of Agriculture, A Summary of Reports by Gubernia Offices on Peasant Affairs, Statistical Data on Landed Property and Populated Localities in European Russia*, and the works of various Russian authors are themselves a reflection of Marx's wide range of interests and knowledge, and show how much energy and effort was going into his *Capital* even after the first volume had become a standard work among leading proletarians in various countries, and after the preliminary manuscript of the subsequent volumes had been written.

He always sought to supplement data referring to one geographical area or country with data on other areas or countries.

---

[1] Marx, Engels, *Collected Works*, Vol. 43, p. 450.
[2] Marx and Engels, *Selected Correspondence*, p. 241.
[3] Karl Marx, *Capital*, Vol. III, Moscow, 1986, p. 7.

On January 24, 1870, he wrote to César De Paepe: "As I treat of landed property in Volume Two of *Capital*, I believe it useful to go into some detail there on the structure of landed property in Belgium and of Belgian agriculture. Will you have the goodness to send me the *titles of the principal books* which I must consult?" [1] De Paepe did so very quickly.

In April 1876, Marx asked Sorge whether it was possible to obtain catalogues of American books from New York, and at what price, to find out whether anything "that might, perhaps, be of use" had been published in the U.S.A., since 1873, as regards American agriculture and landed property, credit, and financial and monetary relations. [2] He added that the English papers did not give him any idea about the current scandals in the U.S.A. (apparently meaning speculation in land and commercial machinations in connection with the extensive railway construction, etc.), and wondered whether Sorge still had any of his old American papers.

To be fully armed with the facts, Marx continued to study agronomy, agrochemistry and the physiology of plants. The latest achievements in these sciences were to enable him to give a deeper and more convincing critique of the unscientific "law of diminishing returns".

From May to August 1875, he made extensive calculations to illustrate the difference between the rate of surplus-value and the rate of profit, calculations which constituted the basis of Chapter III of the future third volume of *Capital*—"The Relation of the Rate of Profit to the Rate of Surplus-Value". In mid-February 1876, he wrote a short but theoretically important study entitled "Differential Rent and Rent as Mere Interest on Capital Incorporated in the Soil", which Engels subsequently included in Chapter XLIV of the published text of Volume Three of *Capital*.

From November 1870 to July 1878, Marx was engaged in preparing for press his manuscript entitled "The Circuit of Money-Capital", which is now Chapter I of Volume Two of *Capital*. In 1880, he worked on problems dealt with in the section "The Law of the Tendency of the Rate of Profit to Fall", Book III and on other parts and chapters of Volumes Two and Three.

However, in the late 1870s and early 1880s, Marx deliberately slowed down the preparation of his final text, and explained the reasons for this "moratorium" in some of his letters. On April 10, 1879, he wrote to Danielson: "*Firstly*: I should under no circumstances have published the second volume before the present English industrial crisis had reached its climax. The phenomena are this time singular, in many respects different from what they were in the past....

"It is therefore necessary to watch the present course of things until their maturity before you can 'consume' them 'productively', I mean '*theoretically*'....

---

[1] Marx, Engels, *Collected Works*, Vol. 43, p. 412.
[2] Marx, Engels, *Werke*, Bd. 34, S. 179.

"*Secondly*: The bulk of materials I have not only from *Russia*, but from the *United States*, etc., make it pleasant for me to have a 'pretext' of continuing my studies instead of winding them up finally for the public.

"*Thirdly*: My medical adviser has warned me to shorten considerably my 'working day' if I were not desirous to relapse into the state of 1874 and the following years where I got giddy and unable to proceed after a few hours of serious application." [1]

Shortly before his death, Marx asked his daughter Eleanor to pass the *Capital* manuscripts to Engels, who was to "make something" out of them. [2]

As Marx's best friend and literary executor, Engels saw it as his right and duty to prepare the remaining manuscripts of *Capital* for publication immediately, even though this involved putting off his own scientific studies. He divided the author's manuscript of Volume Two into two separate volumes, Two and Three. With his usual modesty and affection, which verged on veneration for his late friend, he strove to do this "exclusively in the spirit of the author", confining his work wherever possible to the "mere selection of a text from the available variants". [3] Actually, what Engels did, especially in Volume III, was so considerable that Volumes Two and Three of *Capital*, published under his editorship, should be regarded, as Lenin pointed out, as the work of both men.

Engels spent almost ten years giving Volume Three its final form. He supplied some of its chapters with footnotes, inserted numerous passages to connect fragmentary texts, wrote a new text for Chapter IV on the basis of the author's notes, revised the whole of Part V three times, and wrote a preface and supplement to the volume ("Law of Value and Rate of Profit" and "The Stock Exchange").

His work on Volume II did not require as much effort but was also demanding and complex. Even the sections of the manuscript which had been prepared for the printers could not be published right away, because they required amending in accordance with Marx's later formulations and studies. The bulk of the material had not been style-edited. The four manuscripts written from 1865 to 1870 and the four written in 1877 and later had to be brought together into a single coherent whole, and it took Engels over two years to do this.

Volume Two was published in 1885 and Volume Three in 1894. In a preface to Volume Two, Engels indicated that Marx had wanted Books II and III to be dedicated to his wife, Jenny.

Engels also intended to publish the historico-critical section of the work—"Theories of Surplus-Value"—in the form of the fourth and final volume of *Capital*, but was unable to do so.

---

[1] Marx and Engels, *Selected Correspondence*, pp. 296, 298.
[2] Karl Marx, *Capital*, Vol. II, p. 5.
[3] Ibid.

THE PRODUCTION OF CAPITAL

Marx's *Capital* is the work of a lifetime and the principal work of scientific communism. Its first volume deals with the process of the production of capital. As Marx himself said, at the beginning of this volume (Chapter I of the first German edition and the corresponding Part I of subsequent editions) he "summarised" the substance of the first and only part of *A Contribution to the Critique of Political Economy*.

Once again Marx begins with an analysis of the commodity, the elementary cell of bourgeois wealth. This was a vital prerequisite for his analysis of the higher and more complex forms of capitalist production. For over 2,000 years mankind had sought to comprehend the commodity, the form of value, which at first sight appears to be a simple thing. This proved to be an exceptionally difficult task which it fell to the lot of Marx to fulfil: the profound analysis of the form of value up to and including money, a peculiar commodity of commodities, is one of Marx's greatest scientific achievements. His analysis of the form of value paved the way for his success in analysing capital.

The main content of Volume One of *Capital* is an analysis of the exploitation of wage labour by capital, the dominant relation of production under capitalism.

As commodity production develops, money is transformed into capital, and the simple commodity economy into a capitalist one based on the exploitation of wage labour.

Marx discovered the secret of capitalist exploitation and gave a truly scientific theory of surplus-value which, Engels said, came like a bolt from the blue. Classical bourgeois economists had been unable to explain the origin of surplus-value or its true nature.

Just as the commodity itself is a unity of use-value (the property of satisfying some human want) and value (the socially necessary labour-time embodied in a product), so the process of commodity production must simultaneously express the process of labour and the process of the creation of value. Because this happens to be capitalist production, the creation of value also implies the production of a definite excess of value for the sake of which the capitalist organises production. "His aim is to produce not only a use-value, but a commodity also; not only use-value, but value; not only value, but at the same time surplus-value."[1]

Marx discovered the fact that it is not labour itself, as bourgeois economists had imagined, but labour-power, or the capacity for labour, that is the commodity which the worker sells and the capitalist purchases. This discovery provides the key to understanding the mechanism of capitalist exploitation and helps to solve one of the problems which the Ricardian school had been unable to solve: to

---

[1] Karl Marx, *Capital*, Vol. I, p. 181.

establish the connection between the exchange between capital and labour and the determination of the value of commodities by labour. Labour-power, like any other commodity, has use-value and value. The use-value of labour-power is its capacity to create value, moreover, a greater value than that which labour-power itself has. Its value is the value of the means of subsistence necessary for the maintenance of the worker and his family. The value of labour-power is determined by the labour-time necessary for the production, and consequently also for the reproduction, of this particular commodity. The value of labour-power in terms of money is expressed in wages, which, depending on the concrete economic situation, the traditional way of life in a given country, the organisation and strength of the working class and many other factors, may fluctuate around the value of labour-power and assume various forms. Wages merely appear to be the price of labour. As a converted form of value and the price of labour-power they appear as the price of labour, thereby obscuring the process of exploitation. It looks as though the worker sells his labour and the whole of his labour is paid for, but in fact wages are always lower than the total value of the product created by wage-labour. The worker produces the value of the means necessary for the reproduction of labour-power within a given part of the working-day (necessary working-time). He spends the rest of the working-day (surplus working-time) creating an additional value over and above the value of his labour-power, or surplus-value.

Bourgeois political economy declared capital to be all accumulated labour, any means of production, and regarded it as a lasting condition for the existence of human society. Marx disproved this and showed that the means of production become capital only under given conditions, namely, when they are the property of capitalists and are used to exploit wage-labour. Thus capital is a historically rooted social relation.

Of vast importance in the scientific explanation of capitalist exploitation is the analysis of the role played by living labour and the means of production in the formation of the value of commodities. The classical bourgeois economists divided capital only into fixed and circulating. Marx did not reject this classification but went on to make a more important one from the standpoint of the role played by capital in the production of surplus-value, namely, as constant (means of production) and variable capital (labour-power). The means of production do not create any new value, living labour alone being the source of new value. In the process of production, living labour transfers the value of the means of production to the new product as these are used up.

Marx's division of capital into constant and variable enabled him to give a profound analysis of the exploitation of wage-labour, and also to find a quantitative expression for the degree of exploitation as a ratio of surplus-value not to the whole of the invested capital, but only to variable capital. Marx called this the rate of surplus-value, or the rate of exploitation. As capitalism develops, the rate of exploitation tends to increase, with the contradictions between the proletariat and the bourgeoisie simultaneously deepening and growing more acute.

In Volume One of *Capital* Marx analyses the ways used by the capitalist to increase the rate of surplus-value. These are two: 1) with the magnitude of the necessary labour-time constant, he increases the surplus working-time by prolonging the working-day (absolute surplus-value); 2) with the length of the working-day constant, he increases the intensity and productivity of labour, thereby changing in his favour the relation between necessary and surplus working-time (relative surplus-value). The former was in the main characteristic of the early stages of capitalist production, chiefly on the basis of handicraft techniques and a relatively primitive organisation of labour, and the latter of the higher stages of capitalist production, when the technical and organisational conditions of production have matured, and the mounting struggle by the working class forces the bourgeoisie to make some reductions in the working-day. Marx used a great deal of factual material to produce a picture of the working-class struggle for shorter working hours.

However, in seeking to obtain an absolute increase in surplus-value, capital in fact always tries to prolong the working-day and to force the worker to expend more labour during every hour of work, that is, to intensify labour. The insatiable craving of capital is limited only by the physical potentialities of the "living machines" and fear of their discontent.

In a number of chapters, mainly based on facts relating to England, then the classic country of developed capitalism, which presented to the less developed countries a picture of their own future, Marx gave a brilliant historical essay on the methods used to produce relative surplus-value, including simple co-operation, manufacture, and large-scale industry, three stages in the development of capitalism itself. He made an especially detailed study of the history, conditions and consequences of the use of machinery under capitalism. The fact that machines and other technical inventions do not lighten the work of the labourer, is determined entirely by the aims to which all the new and latest technical means of labour are geared: to cheapen commodities, to reduce the necessary labour and to lengthen the additional working-time, that is, to serve as a mere instrument for producing surplus-value for the "noble idlers".

The growth in the productivity of labour resulting from the division of labour and the capitalist application of machinery is accompanied by a general deterioration in the condition of the workers. In the capitalist countries, machines cause growing unemployment and a vast number of industrial accidents, labour becomes intensified, monotonous and dull, the despotism of capital is increased, and barrack-room discipline introduced.

In the manufactory, the speed and quality of the work depend directly on the worker, on his skill, his experience, his diligence, etc. At the factory, the speed of the work depends predominantly on the machine and the given technological process. Accordingly, Marx says that the stage of machine production is one of real subordination of labour to capital. In the machine and the machine industry, capitalism acquires a material-technical basis which is adequate to itself.

Having examined the substance of capitalist exploitation and the development of the production of surplus-value, Marx made a thorough analysis of the problem of capitalist accumulation, that is, the conversion of surplus-value into capital.

Every process of production which is repeated again and again is essentially a process of reproduction. In the process of capitalist production, the worker reproduces the advanced capital in the value of the product and creates surplus-value over and above that. If the surplus-value were fully consumed by the capitalist, the process would be one of simple reproduction, that is, a repetition of the process of production on an invariable scale. But it is inherent in capitalism to engage in extended reproduction, to accumulate capital.

By their labour, the workers create surplus-value in considerably larger proportions than the capitalists require for their personal consumption. A part of the surplus-value is converted into capital and used to extend the scale of production. Consequently, the worker creates not only the means of the capitalist's personal consumption, but also the additional means for enlarging the arena of exploitation.

The accumulation of capital, or extended capitalist reproduction, is accompanied by a growth in the organic composition of capital, by which Marx means the relation between the constant and the variable parts of capital, that is, between the value of the means of production and the sum-total of wages. With the introduction of improved machinery and the development of production techniques constant capital tends to grow faster than variable capital, and this results in growing exploitation of the working class and increases the rate of surplus-value.

At the same time, the growth in the organic composition of capital leads to a relative decline in the demand for labour-power, because this demand is determined not by the amount of the total capital, but only of its variable part, which is relatively reduced.

In contrast to the "everlasting" and "natural" law of population, put forward by Malthus, Marx formulates the actual law of population operating under capitalism, a law which is transient and determined exclusively by the nature of capitalism.

A section of the working population is ousted from production, constituting so-called relative over-population, or the industrial reserve army. Unemployment causes extreme instability in the workers' material condition and uncertainty about the future, exerts pressure on the general level of wages, and makes it easier for the capitalists to intensify the labour of the workers employed.

Consequently, as capital is accumulated there is a growth at the one pole of bourgeois society of vast wealth, luxury, parasitism and extravagant spending by the exploiting classes, and at the other, ever-increasing oppression, exploitation, unemployment and an insecure existence for the working people. "The greater the social wealth, the functioning capital, the extent and energy of its growth, and, therefore, also the absolute mass of the proletariat and the productiveness of its labour, the greater is the industrial reserve army. The same causes which develop the expansive power of capital, develop also the labour-power at its disposal. The relative mass of the industrial reserve army increases therefore with the potential energy of wealth. But the greater this reserve army in proportion to the active labour-army, the greater is the mass of a consolidated surplus-population, whose misery is in inverse ratio to its torment of labour.... *This is the absolute general law of capitalist accumulation.*" [1]

The absolute general law of capitalist accumulation, which Marx discovered and formulated, is the theoretical basis for an understanding of the antagonistic contradictions between wage labour and capital.

Marx's researches refuted the notion spread by bourgeois scientists that the primitive accumulation of capital was the result of outstanding industry and thrift by enterprising individuals who gradually amassed great wealth by their labour. In a special chapter dealing with the process of primitive accumulation, Marx showed that it consisted of the complete separation of the direct producers from the means of production, a process which was accelerated by the use of brute force by the ruling classes. On the strength of numerous historical facts, Marx gave a detailed picture of how the small and middle peasants were forcibly deprived of their land, driven from the villages and turned into a reserve of cheap labour-power for developing industry. Wealth was also accumulated in a few hands through fierce plunder and piratical bloodshed in the colonies. Describing the process of primitive accumulation, Marx wrote that "capital comes dripping from head to foot, from every pore, with blood and dirt".[2]

The final part of Chapter 24[3] of Volume One of *Capital* sums up the results of the whole study and draws a conclusion about the future of capitalism and the inevitability of socialist revolution. The development of capitalist accumulation means increasing socialisation of labour, and this tends constantly to aggravate the basic contradiction of capitalism, that between the social character of pro-

---

[1] Karl Marx, *Capital*, Vol. I, p. 603.
[2] Ibid., p. 712.
[3] Chapter XXXII in the English edition.

duction and the private form of appropriation. Marx ends his analysis of the historical tendency of capitalist accumulation by expressing his firm conviction in the triumph of the proletariat: "Along with the constantly diminishing number of the magnates of capital ... grows the mass of misery, oppression, slavery, degradation, exploitation; but with this too grows the revolt of the working-class, a class always increasing in numbers, and disciplined, united, organised by the very mechanism of the process of capitalist production itself. The monopoly of capital becomes a fetter upon the mode of production, which has sprung up and flourished along with, and under it. Centralisation of the means of production and socialisation of labour at last reach a point where they become incompatible with their capitalist integument. Thus integument is burst asunder. The knell of capitalist private property sounds. The expropriators are expropriated." [1]

THE PROCESS OF CIRCULATION OF CAPITAL

In Book II (Volume Two) of his work, Marx continues to analyse the movement of industrial capital, but instead of concentrating on the process of production, as he did in Volume One, he takes a close look at the succession of forms and the metabolism which occurs in industrial capital in the sphere of circulation.

In Part I, Marx analyses the metamorphoses of capital and its circuits, starting with the circuit of money-capital, and then going on to analyse in separate chapters the circuit of productive and of commodity-capital.

A capitalist enterprise in operation involves the use of definite means of production (land, buildings, machinery, tools, raw materials, etc.) by wage-workers and employees to produce definite commodities. Neither the means of production nor the labour-power of the wage-workers are in themselves capital. They become capital only in combination with each other, only by virtue of the fact that the former are the property of the capitalists, while the workers and employees are forced to sell them their labour-power in order to live.

Money-capital, already converted into the means of production and labour-power, the combination of these two material forms of capital in the process of production, constitutes in its aggregate the form of productive capital. If production is carried on continuously, capital is constantly found in this form.

In the process of production the whole of the advanced capital is sooner or later converted into commodities and acquires the form of commodity-capital. In this form, capital also performs a special circuit, the circuit of commodity-capital. At this point, the capitalist is faced with the problem of selling the commodities produced. The

---

[1] Karl Marx, *Capital*, Vol. I, p. 715.

sale of the commodities must ensure that the capitalist recovers all the capital-value he has expended, and in addition yield the surplus-value produced by his wage-workers. An explanation of the conditions and specific features of the sale of commodities constitutes one of the main aspects of Marx's analysis in Book II.

No one before Marx had examined the circuits of capital in all its forms, in their interconnection and in all their details. It was he who first presented capital as a unity of production and circulation, as a continuous movement of capital-value in time and space, from one form to another, from one magnitude to another, greater magnitude. That was extremely important, for, as Marx said, capital could be "understood only as motion, not as a thing at rest".[1]

Another remarkable aspect of Marx's analysis of the circuits of all three main forms of capital (money, productive and commodity), separately and taken together, is that it shows the deep-going contradictions in the movement of capital.

Continuous movement is characteristic of the whole of social capital. However, in this movement there constantly arise general and partial crises and revolutions in the values and the prices of commodities. Some capitalists have an excess of money-capital, others are ruined through lack of it, some feverishly produce and expand their production, others see their idle machines rust away. Masses of commodities find no market, are spoiled and lose value, and are sometimes simply destroyed at the same time as the working people are suffering from unsatisfied demand. Some workers overstrain themselves by excessive work, while others suffer the torments of unemployment. Marx shows that these and other similar phenomena are not accidental but constitute the necessary and natural consequences of the very substance of the movement of capital.

Any circuit of capital takes a definite period of time. Whatever the duration of this period, it falls objectively into two parts: the time of production and the time of circulation.

In Part II Marx makes a detailed study of the turnover of capital. For the capitalist, the turnover time of his capital is the time for which he has to advance capital in order to have it returned not only in its original form, but increased in value. In every case the turnover time for the various individual capitals is equal to the sum-total of the time of circulation and the time of production. Differences in turnover time exert a substantial influence on the magnitude of the advanced capital, on the annual mass of surplus-value, and on the whole course of the capitalist process of production and circulation.

In the process of production, the value of the various parts of constant capital is transferred to the commodities in different ways. Thus, the raw materials are fully consumed, and the whole of their value, even including the value of industrial waste, is added to the value of the commodities produced. By contrast, the value of the

---

[1] Karl Marx, *Capital*, Vol. II, p. 108.

machines used to process the raw materials is added to the value of the commodities produced only to the extent of their wear and tear. Once the commodities have been sold, the capitalist recovers the whole value of the raw materials and only that part of the value of the machines which has been consumed in the process of production. That is why, from the standpoint of circulation and the turnover of capital-value, the whole of constant capital is divided into fixed and circulating capital.

Marx was the first to establish that the means of production become either fixed or circulating capital depending only on whether their value is transferred to the commodity gradually or at once, in part or in full.

The variable capital which the capitalist spends on labour-power does not in any way differ in terms of turnover from that part of the constant capital which constitutes circulating capital. Consequently, circulating capital consists of two parts, which have totally different roles to play in the production of value and surplus-value, but which appear as a single whole in the process of circulation of capital. This helps to conceal the exploitative nature of capitalist production, creating the illusion that surplus-value arises in the sphere of circulation when the produced commodities are sold. Bourgeois economists use this illusion to vindicate the capitalist system.

In his analysis of the turnover of capital as a whole, and the turnover of its fixed and circulating components in particular, Marx gave a scientific explanation of the role which the turnover of capital has to play in the various branches and spheres of capitalist production, and the exact influence which the division of capital into fixed and circulating has on the development of material production and on the position of the capitalists and workers.

Unlike individual production, which for various reasons can be either temporarily or altogether discontinued, the whole of social production is always continuous. An analysis of the conditions in which capital is reproduced constitutes the most important theoretical problem of Volume Two.

The first economist before Marx who tried to analyse the regularities governing social reproduction was the physiocrat François Quesnay. His *Tableau économique* shows how the aggregate annual product of a given country (France) circulates and is finally distributed between the classes of a given society in a way that makes possible simple reproduction, that is, reproduction on the same scale. However, Quesnay considered agriculture alone to be a productive sphere, assuming that only there labour creates value and surplus-value. Quesnay and his school did not analyse capitalist reproduction on the basis of developed industrial production and with the extensive division of all social labour.

Marx begins his analysis of simple reproduction by elucidating the commodity and value structure of the total social product. In its natural form the aggregate of commodities, constituting the annual product of society, falls into two large departments. The first consists of the means of production which must, or at least may, again pass into productive consumption. The second consists of the articles of consumption which pass into the individual consumption of the class of capitalists and the class of workers. Accordingly, the whole of social production falls into two large departments: the production of the means of production, and the production of articles of individual consumption. This division is of great methodological importance, and applies not only to capitalist but to all other social production and reproduction.

In each of the two departments the value of the constant capital consumed is fully transferred to the value of its annual product.

In the course of the year, labour-power produces a new value and adds this to the value of constant capital consumed. The value of the variable capital expended by the capitalists to pay for the labour-power is not only reproduced in the value of the annual product, but is increased by the magnitude of the surplus-value. The total magnitude of the new value created by the wage-workers in the value of the annual product depends on their numbers and the degree of capitalist exploitation.

Consequently, the value of the total annual product in each of the two departments of social production consists of the constant capital consumed (c), the variable capital (v), and the surplus-value (s). In Marx's notation, it consists of the sum: $c + v + s$.

Marx's great scientific achievement is the clarification of the conditions and the proportions of exchange within each of the two large departments of social production, and also between the two. He worked out the schemes of exchange and indicated the relative magnitudes of the component parts of the product in value and in material content in each of the departments of social production which are required for the realisation of the social product, and consequently, for continuous reproduction. Marx was the first to show the way in which both that part of the product which goes into the individual consumption of the workers and the capitalists and that part of the product which is used to form the elements of productive capital are compensated in the process of social production.

Marx determined the ideal proportions required for continuous reproduction, but also showed that under capitalism these proportions cannot be realised and that various disproportions, partial and general crises of overproduction and monetary crises, inevitably arise in practice. The mechanism of capitalist reproduction is such that it cannot help constantly generating disproportions and periodic fluctuations. The internal balance of the capitalist economy exists only as a constantly evanescing moment in its overall process of haphazard and anarchic development.

Marx's researches into the laws governing social reproduction were of tremendous importance for the practical revolutionary propaganda of the working class, and the struggle carried on by his followers against harmful petty-bourgeois theories predicting an "automatic collapse" or "self-strangulation" of capitalism, and also against the apologetic theories claiming "lasting prosperity" and "harmonious development" for the capitalist economy. Relying entirely on the conclusions of Marx's theory of the reproduction of social capital, Lenin gave an especially vivid and clear picture of the formation of the internal market under capitalism, when the mass of people is doomed to poverty. Lenin also repeatedly emphasised the great importance of Marx's theory of social reproduction for building a socialist and a communist society.

THE PROCESS OF CAPITALIST PRODUCTION AS A WHOLE

Volume Three of *Capital* completes the theoretical analysis of the whole of the capitalist mode of production. Here Marx examines the process of capitalist production as a coherent unity of production and circulation.

On the scale of society as a whole, the specific interests of various sections of the capitalist class are expressed in different terms. There is a constant struggle between industry, transport, agriculture, commerce and the banks for a "place in the sun", for a greater share of the surplus-value squeezed out of the wage-workers. It is no easy matter to find one's way in this labyrinthine and many-sided conglomerate of specific interests, in the internal contradictions rending the class of owners of the means of production, and to discover and show the specific place and part belonging to each large group of capitalists with respect to other groups of capitalists and to the working class. Before Marx, bourgeois economists had been unable to do this.

Relying on the content of the first two volumes of *Capital*, Marx shows in Volume Three how the concrete types and forms of capital emerged and constantly continue to emerge, in which it appears on the surface of capitalist society and operates for all to see. This clarified for the first time the natural connection between the various forms and types of capital and capitalists, and the special role and prospective development of each large sphere of production and circulation, and therefore of the whole capitalist mode of production in all its concrete complexity. "The various forms of capital, as evolved in this book, thus approach step by step the form which they assume on the surface of society, in the action of different capitals upon one another, in competition, and in the ordinary consciousness of the agents of production themselves."[1]

Marx starts by showing how the value of commodities is transformed into their market prices, how the whole of the surplus-

---

[1] Karl Marx, *Capital*, Vol. III, p. 25.

value created by the worker is transformed into the profit of the capitalists, how that profit is shared out in definite proportions between the various capitalists and how, as a result of this sharing out, the different rates of profit—the ratio of the mass of surplus-value to the aggregate of the constant and variable capital—are transformed in the different spheres of capital investment into the general average rate of profit for the given capital of any capitalist.

Before Marx, economists had been unable to understand how the law of value operated to produce an equal average rate of profit. It follows necessarily from the operation of this law of value that where two capitals equal in value use the same number of workers and employees, and exploit and pay their labour-power in the same way, these capitals, all other turnover conditions being equal, should yield their owners an equal profit. But if these capitals exploit a different number of workers and employees to a different degree—one more and the other less—they cannot, in accordance with the same law of value, produce and then appropriate an equal profit.

However, day-to-day capitalist practice reveals something quite different. In fact equivalent capitals yield the same profit, regardless of the quantity of living labour they exploit. This creates and constantly maintains the appearance that the value of commodities and their selling-price are determined not by the outlay of living labour-power, not by the socially necessary labour embodied in the commodities. Consequently, if this appearance is taken at its face value, the labour theory of value is wrong and in practice the law of value is being constantly broken.

Marx's studies on the basis of the labour theory of value allowed him to outline a way for solving the question on the formation of equivalent profit from equivalent capitals with different organic compositions.

Each capitalist and each sectoral group of capitalists seek to ensure that a corresponding portion of the total surplus-value (or profit) created in society as a whole falls to each portion of the whole capital invested in this or that enterprise, in this or that branch of production. Marx proved that in the branches of production where the organic composition of capital is identical with the organic composition of the whole of social capital, the selling-price of commodities will coincide with their actual value. In all other branches, the selling-price of commodities necessarily deviates from their value. In some branches with a relatively large share of constant capital (fixed and circulating), the prices of commodities will be higher than their value. In others, with a composition of capital lower than the social average, the prices of commodities will be below their value. The sum-total of all these prices expresses the value of all this social product in terms of money. However, prices are not regulated directly by value in the real sense of the word, but by its modified form, the price of production, which constitutes the sum of the cost of production and average profit.

Volume Three of *Capital* contains a detailed study of the internal mechanism of capitalist competition, and clarifies the reasons why values are transformed into prices of production. The price of production is the magnitude which determines the market price of commodities, and constitutes the centre round which market prices fluctuate.

Bourgeois economists had also dealt with the price of production, but none of them had studied the difference between the prices of production and value, or shown the close kinship between these two categories, which were only outwardly incompatible. It was Marx who achieved this.

Bourgeois economists of various schools had also made futile efforts to explain why the general rate of profit tended to fall with the advance of capitalism.

Marx showed that the rate of profit was only a converted form of the rate of surplus-value. On the scale of the whole of society, the amount of the annual profit coincides with the mass of surplus-value. However, the general annual rate of profit is always lower than the annual rate of surplus-value. All other conditions being equal, the more constant capital that is used and consumed in production, and, by contrast, the less variable capital that is used, the lower the rate of profit will be than the rate of surplus-value. That is why the continuously rising organical composition of the total social capital, a tendency inherent in capitalism, leads to a continually falling general rate of profit.

At the same time, a number of factors counteract the fall in the rate of profit, first and foremost 1) increasing intensity of the exploitation of labour; 2) cheapening of the elements of constant capital; 3) overt and latent unemployment; and 4) the extensive development of foreign trade and the export of capital to the colonies for the exploitation of cheap manpower. That is why the law of the falling rate of profit is only in the nature of a tendency.

Volume Three contains a detailed study of the specific types and forms which capital assumes in commerce, credit and monetary circulation, and agriculture. The reader is given a vivid picture of merchants, bankers, big farmers and landlords in addition to the industrial capitalists presented earlier. Ranged against them are the various sections and contingents of the working class. Marx also analyses the fragmentation of the total social surplus-value into its specific parts and forms corresponding to the specific forms of capital itself.

As Marx showed in Volume Two, a part of capital always remains in the sphere of circulation, either in commodity or in money form. With the development of industrial capital, its commercial activity — the volume of its operations involving the sale and purchase of commodities — grows steadily, and with it that part of the capitalist outlay which goes into the purchase and sale of the mass of commodities, into the circulation of capital in the commodity form. Commercial capital does not produce profit, but because it reduces the costs of circulation and performs a necessary and useful function for industrial capital, it claims a share of the latter's profit. The average profit is shared out between industrialists and merchants in accordance with the amount of their capital, and this produces two types of profit: industrial and commercial.

By selling and buying commodities on credit and lending their ready money to each other, industrial and commercial capitalists act as creditors and debtors. There is a steady growth in the scale of operations and monetary relations within the capitalist class as capitalism advances, and this leads to a separation and development of the credit and banking system of capitalism. In place of the ancient hoarders and petty usurers the modern bankers appear on the scene.

With the development of capitalism a special market arises on which one finds the uncommitted, excess money-capital. The concentration and centralisation of money-capital through the credit and banking system intensifies the processes of concentration and centralisation of capital in industry and commerce, and enables the bankers to control the affairs of active capitalists, their debtors, and when the opportunity arises, to become part or even full owners of their enterprises. The mobilisation and accumulation of money-capital leads to the emergence of large joint-stock companies, the development of the stock-market trading in bonds, stocks and other "securities", turning the stock-exchanges into centres of speculative dealings and places where capitalists cheat each other.

Volume Three also analyses the transformation of a part of surplus-value into land-rent, which is a logical completion of the earlier analysis of the concrete forms of surplus-value and profit in capitalist society. The Marxist theory of rent shows the specific development of capitalism in agriculture, and sheds a true light on the condition of the rural proletariat, showing the industrial proletariat its allies in the struggle to abolish capitalism.

The land, with all its natural wealth, is the universal object of human labour. All social production exists and develops on the land. Any product of labour is no more than a natural substance adapted by man for the satisfaction of his wants. Analysing mainly capitalist agriculture and, in passing, also other branches of production which make direct use of the land, its minerals, waters, forests, etc., Marx condemned the savage exploitation of nature's resources by the capitalists. The emergence and development of capitalism, far from abolishing private property in land, merely changes it. The usurpation of the landed property of the direct producers is a historical prerequisite for the capitalist mode of production.

Marx makes a distinction between two main forms of rent: differential and absolute.

Differential rent is the excess of profit over and above the average profit obtained from farming carried on in more favourable conditions of production.

The surplus-profit of the rural capitalists is connected with their monopoly of land as an object of economic operations. Competition between these capitalists within the same branch leads to the formation of market prices for their commodities which are regulated by the price of production not on the best or average but on the worst areas of cultivated land. This makes it possible to obtain surplus-profit on the more productive plots, which takes the form of differential rent.

Marx was the first theoretically to prove the possibility of the formation of absolute land rent under capitalism. Absolute rent is the tribute society has to pay to the landed proprietors for nothing more than their title of ownership. The landlords and landowners are a type of rentier who clip the coupons of their "own" land, without in any way taking part in organising and carrying on agricultural production. Because of the lower organic composition of capital and the lower productivity of labour in agriculture, the value and the price of its products are on the average higher than the value and the price of industrial products. At the same time, the monopoly of private ownership of land makes it impossible for the prices of agricultural products to be reduced through competition to the given level of the social price of production. The difference between the high value of the agricultural products and the prices of production of other commodities constitutes absolute rent.

The existence of absolute rent is not a necessary condition for capitalist production. On the contrary, by diverting a part of surplus-value and capital into the hands of a parasitic class—the landed aristocracy—it hampers the development of this production. The demand for nationalisation of the land is essentially in the interests of the bourgeoisie, and if the latter refrains from challenging private property in land, it is only because an attack on this type of private property could trigger off a chain reaction of revolts against the principle of private property in all the means of production.

Bourgeois economists had been unable to explain the nature of this gratuitous income of the landed proprietors. Even the best of them, Smith and Ricardo, ultimately reduced the movement of rent to the operation of the laws of nature, thereby flinging the door wide open for an apology of capitalism. The "law of diminishing returns" became one of the most widespread dogmas which were fed by Ricardo's erroneous theory of rent. Marx's theory of rent cut the ground from under the feet of the bourgeois apologists.

Volume Three of *Capital* also shows that under capitalism there is a continuous process in the sphere of agriculture, too, in the course of which some are ruined, and others enriched, and that the much-vaunted "stability" of the small and middle peasantry is only a figment of the bourgeois imagination, for the bulk of the tillers of the soil are doomed to back-breaking toil and not guaranteed against ruin and total penury. The material condition of the bulk of the rural population differs little, if at all, in essence from that of the factory wage-workers, and their only salvation lies in an alliance with the industrial workers for a resolute assault on capitalism.

In the closing pages of Volume Three, Marx says that when the bourgeois form of production and distribution attains a certain stage of maturity it is superseded by a new and higher form. This historical succession of the modes of production and distribution is based on "a conflict ... between the material development of production and its social form".[1] Marx's analysis of the capitalist process as a whole produced fresh and more detailed evidence of the necessity of the socialist revolution.

THEORIES OF SURPLUS-VALUE

Marx never returned to the sections of the 1861-63 manuscript containing his *Theories of Surplus-Value*, because he had no time to polish up this part of his great work.

Marx's *Theories* is an historical study of the interpretation of the laws of the capitalist formation by bourgeois economists, with the evolution of bourgeois political economy seen as reflecting the evolution of bourgeois society itself, the development of its intrinsic contradictions. For a full understanding of the laws of capitalism Marx needed to clarify how the basis influences the superstructure, how capitalist reality is reflected in the ideological sphere, notably, in the sphere of economic science. Marx's critical analysis of the history of political economy is the logical capstone to his theoretical research in the first three volumes of *Capital*.

At the same time, this analysis was necessary for a deeper insight into the essence of the economic relations under capitalism. Marx subsequently wrote: "For myself I began *Capital* in the very opposite way to that in which it is presented to the public (beginning with the third, historical part)."[2] Here Marx was following Hegel's example, who used to say that "in order to master the theory of the subject, one must know its history".

When he started on the *Theories of Surplus-Value*, Marx intended to divide the historico-critical material among the various theoretical parts of his economic work, but by the time he was writing his 1861-63 manuscript he had abandoned the intention and decided to put the whole of the historical part together in a special volume.

The *Theories of Surplus-Value* is, according to Engels, "a detailed critical history of the pith and marrow of Political Economy",[3] a theory of surplus-value. Marx saw the category of surplus-value as

---

[1] Karl Marx, *Capital*, Vol. III, p. 884.
[2] Marx, Engels, *Werke*, Bd. 3, S. 307.
[3] Karl Marx, *Capital*, Vol. II, p. 2.

being of crucial importance in his assessment of any bourgeois economist or school of political economy.

The first part of the *Theories of Surplus-Value* deals mainly with economists, like Smith, whose contribution to the development of the theory of surplus-value was connected in some way or other with the problem of the exchange between capital and labour on the basis of the law of value. Part II discusses questions relating to average profit and the price of production, rent and crises, with Ricardo's theory as the central point. The third part examines bourgeois political economy after Ricardo.

The first part opens with a look at the school of physiocrats, a natural beginning, because Marx valued them highly as the "first methodical (not simply casual, like Petty, etc.) *interpreters of capital and the capitalist mode of production*".[1] They took the first major step in solving the problem of the exchange between labour and capital on the basis of the law of value, and were the first to transfer the question of the origin of surplus-value from the sphere of exchange to the sphere of production.

Smith went much farther than the physiocrats in formulating the theory of surplus-value. According to him, value is created by any social labour, regardless of the kind of use-values it produces. That is why Smith sees surplus-value as taking the form not only of rent, as the Physiocrats did, but also of profit and interest. But although Smith regards surplus-value as a general category, as the product of the workers' unpaid labour (Marx said that Smith "has recognised the true origin of surplus-value"[2]), he confuses it with profit, which means that he did not examine the category of labour-power as a commodity, and consequently was unable to come up with a scientific solution for the problem of the exchange between capital and wage labour. What Smith did, to his credit, was to establish the fact that under the capitalist mode of production, in the exchange between labour and capital, the law of value is in fact transformed into its opposite. However, being unaware of the category of labour-power as a commodity he was unable to solve this problem.

Closely connected with the problem of the exchange between labour and capital was the question of productive and unproductive labour in capitalist society. The approach of the various schools of bourgeois political economy (the Mercantilists, the Physiocrats and Adam Smith) to the question of the criterion of productive labour under capitalism was determined by their view of the origin of surplus-value and the exchange between labour and capital.

The *Theories of Surplus-Value* gives a full substantiation of the view that productive labour in capitalist society and in the capitalist sense is labour producing surplus-value.

In the first three volumes of *Capital*, where Marx sets out his own

---

[1] Marx, Engels, *Werke*, Bd. 34, S. 39.
[2] Karl Marx, *Theories of Surplus-Value*, Part I, Moscow, 1975, p. 80.

theory of surplus-value, he starts by considering surplus-value in its pure form and only then (in Volume Three) goes on to an examination of the converted forms in which surplus-value appears on the surface of capitalist society. In the *Theories of Surplus-Value*, Marx has to proceed from the converted forms of surplus-value, which he finds in the works of other economists, and then go on to show the elements of the theory of surplus-value which they conceal. Thus, in analysing Ricardo's theory, Marx begins by considering Ricardo's theory of rent and the price of production, because for Ricardo surplus-value appears only as rent and average profit.

That is why Marx's own theory of rent, particularly his theory of absolute land-rent, is central to the second part of the *Theories of Surplus-Value*, where he examines Ricardo's theory. Marx's theory of rent was proof that both Smith and Ricardo had been wrong to assume that values and prices of production are identical.

The *Theories of Surplus-Value* is an essential supplement to the analysis of rent in Volume Three of *Capital*. Marx examines two types of monopoly in agriculture (the monopoly of the private landowner and the monopoly of the capitalist farmer) and in this context elaborates the view that under capitalism nationalisation of land is a bourgeois measure which helps to release agriculture from the fetters slowing down its advance along capitalist lines. He goes on to show that the price of agricultural produce, insofar as it includes either absolute or differential rent, is necessarily a monopoly price. Marx devotes much attention to competition within and between branches of agriculture, which tends to undermine, partially or in full, both types of monopoly.

Many pages of the *Theories of Surplus-Value* deal with the causes of economic crises and the conditions in which a potential crisis becomes "reality".

The abstract possibility of crises is latent in the simple commodity form of exchange of products and in the function of money as a medium of payment, but in order for it to be realised the contradictions of a developed, capitalist form of production must come into play. Bourgeois wealth is not an aggregate of use-values, and use-value does not predominate in the bourgeois mode of production. On the contrary, bourgeois wealth is an aggregate of exchange-values, and exchange-value dominates in the bourgeois mode of production. Marx emphasises that "bourgeois production is not production of wealth for the *producers*", that is, the workers, and that "the production of bourgeois wealth is something quite different from the production of abundance, of necessities and luxuries for the men who produce them".[1] As the productive forces are developed, there are growing contradictions between use-value and value, between the commodity produced for the market, and money, between purchases and sales, between production and consumption, between

---

[1] Karl Marx, *Theories of Surplus-Value*, Part III, Moscow, 1975, p. 55.

capital and wage labour. The bourgeois form of production implies a specific limitation of distribution, whereas production on a capitalist basis tends to develop as if there were no such intrinsic limitation. In this contradiction lies "the deepest and most hidden cause of crises",[1] which are a form of its temporary and forcible resolution.

The first and second parts of the *Theories* mainly analyse the advance of bourgeois political economy, from its origins to its peak (Ricardo's theory), while the third part shows how bourgeois economic science was being vulgarised with the sharpening of the class struggle between the proletariat and the bourgeoisie.

Referring to the disintegration of the Ricardian school of bourgeois political economy, Marx analyses, first and foremost, the views of James Mill, who set out Ricardo's theory in formal logical terms in an effort to enshrine it as an absolute. Whereas the contradictions in Ricardo's theory reflected the actual contradiction in capitalist reality, Mill did not deal with reality itself, but with its expression in Ricardo's theory. In order to eliminate the latter's contradictions Mill resorted to purely formal, verbal arguments.

The final part of the *Theories of Surplus-Value* brings out the class and epistemological roots of vulgar political economy, accentuates the essential differences between classical and vulgar political economy, and sharply criticises vulgar socialist views. In contrast to classical bourgeois political economy, which "seeks to grasp the inner connection",[2] without confusing the whole with the diversity of forms in which it is expressed, the vulgar economists usually reproduce the superficial phenomena of capitalist reality. A specific feature of vulgar political economy is that it feeds on the classics and does not create anything itself. Instead of advancing, it retreats, becoming increasingly apologetic, as the class struggle sharpens.

It is true that some bourgeois economists after Ricardo gained a certain understanding of some aspects of the capitalist mode of production, while the socialist followers of Ricardo came out with open criticism of bourgeois society and stood up for the industrial proletariat. However, they were unable to rise above the bourgeois basis of their views.

The *Theories of Surplus-Value* is a remarkable specimen of the profoundly scientific, objective and truly party approach to the various schools and systems of bourgeois economic thinking. Considering that bourgeois political economy today frequently seeks to galvanise the dead dogmas which Marx exploded, his critique of the bourgeois economic theories is in no sense a page of old history, but a sharp-edged weapon for exposing modernised versions of what are essentially the old conceptions of bourgeois apologetics.

---

[1] Ibid., p. 84.
[2] Ibid., p. 500.

PROBLEMS OF COMMUNISM IN *CAPITAL*

In his *Capital*, Marx examined the capitalist mode of production as a living whole, as an historically defined and, consequently, historically transient stage in the development of society, which was sooner or later bound to be superseded by another system, the communist system. In contrast to the utopian socialists, who had sharply criticised capitalism and presented fantastic pictures of a future society, Marx gave a description of communism which stemmed organically from his analysis of the most profound tendencies in the development of capitalism. Marx did not — and could not — produce a detailed picture of the future society, but his views of communism give an idea of some basic features of this formation and are of tremendous interest in this epoch of ours, the focal point of which is the transition from capitalism to socialism.

Limits are placed on the development of the productive forces within the framework of capitalist relations of production by the fundamental contradiction of capitalism (that between the social character of production and the private form of appropriation) and its inevitable manifestations, such as the anarchy of social production, fierce competition, periodic economic crises, and the use of scientific and technical achievements for destructive purposes, instead of for the benefit of mankind.

The productive forces developing within capitalism are incompatible with their social integument, with the capitalist relations of production. The development of the capitalist mode of production itself produces the material prerequisites for its inevitable destruction. However, the transition to communism cannot take place by itself. It requires revolutionary action, the revolutionary overthrow of the rule of the capitalist class, and the winning of political power by the working class. A most important conclusion which Marx drew from his economic theory was the need for a socialist, proletarian revolution to effect the substitution of a communist mode of production for the capitalist one. Marx and Engels observed that, given the right conditions, it was quite possible for the revolution to be carried out "entirely by peaceful and legal means". Such a possibility existed, for instance, in the British Isles although, as Marx said, he hardly expected "the English ruling classes to submit, without a 'pro-slavery rebellion', to this peaceful and legal revolution".[1]

The socialist revolution would establish social property in the principal means of production, thereby restoring the unity between the producers and the conditions of production, which would cease to be alienated from the working people. Production would become organised and planned. The basic principle of communist society and its chief purpose is to provide for the full and free development

---

[1] Karl Marx, *Capital*, Vol. I, p. 17.

of "every individual", which implies "the conscious reorganisation of society".[1]

In Volume One of *Capital*, Marx gave a description of communist society at the stage of development when distribution is still in accordance with work done. Marx characterised it as a "community of free individuals, carrying on their work with the means of production in common, in which the labour-power of all the different individuals is consciously applied as the combined labour-power of the community....The total product of our community is a social product. One portion serves as fresh means of production and remains social. But another portion is consumed by the members as means of subsistence. A distribution of this portion amongst them is consequently necessary. The mode of this distribution will vary with the productive organisation of the community, and the degree of historical development attained by the producers. We will assume, but merely for the sake of a parallel with the production of commodities, that the share of each individual producer in the means of subsistence is determined by his labour-time. Labour-time would, in that case, play a double part. Its apportionment in accordance with a definite social plan maintains the proper proportion between the different kinds of work to be done and the various wants of the community. On the other hand, it also serves as a measure of the portion of the common labour borne by each individual, and of his share in the part of the total product destined for individual consumption. The social relations of the individual producers, with regard both to their labour and to its products, are in this case perfectly simple and intelligible, and that with regard not only to production but also to distribution."[2]

The socialist transformation of society implies that the spontaneous operation of the laws of the capitalist economy will give way to a rational conduct of the economy on the basis of objective economic laws, conscious social control, and purposeful regulation of social production for the benefit of society as a whole.

The conscious and rational distribution of public labour between the branches of production would be a most important function and feature of communist society. "It is only where production is under the actual, predetermining control of society that the latter establishes a relation between the volume of social labour-time applied in producing definite articles, and the volume of the social want to be satisfied by these articles."[3] The establishment of such a relation implies a high standard of accounting of social requirements and outlays of social labour.

In communist society, labour would be "universal", and as a result of that alone the working-day would be reduced, and leisure-time increased. Working-time would be regulated solely by the need

---

[1] Ibid., p. 555; Vol. III, p. 88.
[2] Ibid., Vol. I, pp. 82-83.
[3] Ibid., Vol. III, p. 187.

to carry on extended reproduction for the full satisfaction of the steadily growing requirements of all members of society.

Under communism, surplus-labour — labour over and above individual requirements — would appear as a necessary component part of productive labour. The distinctions between necessary and surplus-labour would become conventional to a certain extent because surplus-labour would be just as necessary for the workers of communist society as their necessary labour. Marx included in the category of necessary labour under the communist mode of production that part of labour which formed "a fund for reserve and accumulation".[1]

Another reason why necessary labour is bound to extend its limits is that the living conditions of the workers would become richer than ever before, and their vital requirements would increase immeasurably.

Marx examined the main features of reproduction in a communist society, and established that the laws governing extended capitalist reproduction, which stem from the material conditions of the process of labour, but not from its social form, in the main would also apply to the communist mode of production.

The fundamental division of social production into two departments — the production of the means of production and the production of the articles of consumption — would remain, as also would the basic relations within these departments and between them. Examining the movement of capital within Department I of social production, Marx emphasised that this movement would also occur "if production were socialised instead of capitalistic".[2] The need to replace the basic funds in kind makes it necessary to accumulate material reserves, or to have what Marx calls a special, relative overproduction. In communist society, "this sort of overproduction is tantamount to control by society over the material means of its own reproduction", because apart from everything else it creates the possibility "to compensate for the extraordinary destruction caused by accidents and natural forces".[3] Marx also gives much attention to long-term capital investments, as an important aspect of social reproduction, and in this context also considers the need for communist society "to calculate beforehand" how much labour, means of production and means of subsistence it can invest, without detriment, in branches of production which are absolutely necessary but which do not yield any useful effect at once.[4]

Communism will change the very nature of labour in material production. In place of the "partial worker", a victim of the capitalist division of labour which mutilates man's personality, there will be the fully developed man. Labour itself, placed under the joint

---

[1] Karl Marx, *Capital*, Vol. I, p. 496.
[2] Ibid., Vol. II, p. 428.
[3] Ibid., pp. 181, 473.
[4] Ibid., p. 318.

control of the producers themselves, will become rational and truly free. Still, the sphere of labour in material production will remain a "realm of necessity". The realm of freedom will arise outside the limits of necessary labour, but only on its basis. "In fact, the realm of freedom actually begins only where labour which is determined by necessity and mundane considerations ceases; thus in the very nature of things it lies beyond the sphere of actual material production. Just as the savage must wrestle with Nature to satisfy his wants, to maintain and reproduce life, so must civilised man, and he must do so in all social formations and under all possible modes of production. With his development this realm of physical necessity expands as a result of his wants; but, at the same time, the forces of production which satisfy these wants also increase. Freedom in this field can only consist in socialised man, the associated producers, rationally regulating their interchange with Nature, bringing it under their common control, instead of being ruled by it as by the blind forces of Nature; and achieving this with the least expenditure of energy and under conditions most favourable to, and worthy of, their human nature. But it nonetheless still remains a realm of necessity. Beyond it begins that development of human energy which is an end in itself, the true realm of freedom, which, however, can blossom forth only with this realm of necessity as its basis. The shortening of the working-day is its basic prerequisite."[1]

A shorter working-day implies growing productivity. High labour productivity producing material values will make it possible to enlarge the framework of leisure-time, and this will for its part exert a substantial influence on the nature of all activity. Leisure is the time the individual spends in rational activity in a sphere that does not necessarily coincide with the sphere of his main professional occupation. Leisure will ultimately become the true measure of the wealth and level of development in a society of associated producers.

Capital contains highly valuable ideas on the education of children and on family relations in the epoch of the future. Marx said that in this epoch, that is, under communism, there will be available "an education that will, in the case of every child over a given age, combine productive labour with instruction and gymnastics, not only as one of the methods of adding to the efficiency of production, but as the only method of producing fully developed human beings". Marx believed that "technical instruction, both theoretical and practical",[2] will take its proper place in the schools of the future. He added: "Modern industry, by assigning as it does an important part in the process of production, outside the domestic sphere, to women, to young persons, and to children of both sexes, creates a new economic foundation for a higher form of the family and of the relations between the sexes."[3] Under capitalism the involvement of the

---

[1] Ibid., Vol. III, p. 820.
[2] Ibid., Vol. I, pp. 454, 458.
[3] Ibid., p. 460.

worker's family into the sphere of social production became a "pestiferous source of corruption and slavery", but in communist society it will of necessity become a source of "humane development".[1]

Thus, in his *Capital*, which deals specially with the laws of capitalism, Marx formulated, with his usual depth and incisiveness, a number of laws of the communist system.

THE METHOD OF *CAPITAL* AND ITS GENERAL IMPORTANCE TO SCIENCE

Marx's greatest work, *Capital*, has stood the ultimate test, the test of time. His main scientific conclusions have been borne out by life. The judgment of long years of history has also shed an even stronger light on the powerful scientific method employed by Marx in his *Capital*, on its logic, i.e., what Marx himself had in mind when he spoke about the "*composition*, the structure" of his vast work.[2]

As early as 1857 and 1858, when Marx was drafting the first coherent exposition of his economic theory, he was faced with the problem of which method to use in processing the empirical material. In his Introduction to the 1857-58 manuscripts, Marx formulated the basic principles of his method of economic research, and in a letter to Engels in early 1858 said that one day he hoped to write a special work on dialectics. "If ever the time comes when such work is again possible, I should very much like to write 2 or 3 sheets making accessible to the common reader the *rational* aspect of the method which Hegel not only discovered but also mystified."[3] Following the publication of Volume One of *Capital*, Marx once again mentioned his intention in a letter to Joseph Dietzgen: "When I cast off the burden of political economy, I shall write a 'Dialectic'."[4] As it turned out, he never found the time to write a special work on his method, on dialectical logic as a special science. But he did leave us the logic of his *Capital*, and this is what Lenin had in mind when he stressed: "If Marx did not leave behind him a '*Logic*' (with a capital letter), he did leave the *logic* of *Capital*.... In *Capital*, Marx applied to a single science logic, dialectics and the theory of knowledge of materialism ... which has taken everything valuable in Hegel and developed it further."[5] This is a most profound assessment of the universal importance of the general methodological principles contained in Marx's chief work.

The method of *Capital* embodies all the main propositions of materialist dialectics and the materialist view of history, which Marx first began to formulate in the 1840s. In an afterword to the second edition of Volume One of *Capital* (January 24, 1873) Marx wrote:

---

[1] Karl Marx, *Capital*, Vol. I, p. 460.
[2] Marx, Engels, *Collected Works*, Vol. 42, p. 232.
[3] Ibid., Vol. 40, p. 249.
[4] Ibid., Vol. 43, p. 31.
[5] V. I. Lenin, *Collected Works*, Vol. 38, p. 319.

"My dialectic method is not only different from the Hegelian, but is its direct opposite. To Hegel ... the process of thinking, which, under the name of 'the Idea', he even transforms into an independent subject, is the demiurgos of the real world, and the real world is only the external, phenomenal form of 'the Idea'. With me, on the contrary, the ideal is nothing else than the material world reflected by the human mind, and translated into forms of thought." [1]

Hegel gave a comprehensive presentation of the universal forms of motion, which is why Marx firmly declared himself to be a disciple of the great philosopher. But Hegel's dialectics was mystified, the object of its analysis being the self-development of the idea, its self-alienation in nature, and its self-cognition in the development of the spirit. Marx realised this fundamental flaw in Hegel's thinking and put Hegel's dialectics the right way up, on the solid material basis of real living relations. Soon after the publication of Volume One of *Capital*, Marx stressed: "My method of exposition is *not* Hegelian, since I am a materialist, and Hegel an idealist. Hegel's dialectic is the basic form of all dialectic, but only *after* being stripped of its mystical form, and it is precisely this which distinguishes *my* method." [2]

However, the method of *Capital* is not a simple application of certain general categories of dialectics to concrete empirical material. The logic of *Capital* is the method of political economy worked out in relation to the tasks of concrete research. Marx relied on materialist dialectics, as the universal methodology of scientific cognition, and produced an exceptionally rich and varied set of concrete methods for dissecting the contradictory substance of the bourgeois system.

Capital is a developed and coherent system of scientific categories correctly reflecting phenomena within the economic system of capitalism which were both visible and invisible to the naked eye. At the same time, the laws and methodological principles of *Capital*'s logic are also applicable in the study of other socio-economic formations. In fact, they are of much wider importance, going well beyond the framework of political economy. In his *Philosophical Notebooks*, Lenin said: "With Marx the dialectics of bourgeois society is only a particular case of dialectics." [3]

The method of research used and developed by Marx in his *Capital* is primarily the specific method of political economy. But being the method of an individual science, it is an expression not only of the specifics of the logical apparatus of the given science but of something much greater, namely, the general features of theoretical thinking as such, of science as one of the principal forms of comprehending reality. *Capital* sets an example for all sciences of the analysis of a subject, the reduction of the subject to its particulars, with

---
[1] Karl Marx, *Capital*, Vol. I, p. 29.
[2] Marx, Engels, *Collected Works*, Vol. 42, p. 544.
[3] V. I. Lenin, *Collected Works*, Vol. 38, p. 361.

their subsequent synthesis into a concrete whole in all its living and complex diversity.

The *historical approach* to capitalism as a whole, and to each category of the capitalist economy, is one of the main expressions of the dialectical method of studying the capitalist mode of production. Marx examines this mode of production and all its elements as being in a process of constant motion, in their origin, development and inevitable destruction. In contrast to his predecessors, the classical bourgeois political economists, who regarded capitalism as something immutable and everlasting, Marx examined it historically. In his Preface to Volume One of *Capital* he emphasised that bourgeois society is not a "solid crystal", but an organism constantly changing. He expressed a similar idea in the Afterword to the volume.

In his *Capital*, Marx consistently applies the historical approach to his analysis of all the categories of bourgeois society, beginning with commodities. For the first time in the history of political economy, he examines the origin and development of the value-form, the genesis of the money-form, and the conversion of money into capital, and clarifies the specific historical nature of the law of value and its varying operation under simple commodity production and under capitalism.

Having brought out the historical character of the categories of bourgeois society, both the elementary and the more complex ones, Marx produces evidence to show that the capitalist mode of production cannot be an everlasting and natural form of social production, that this mode of production is historically transient, and that, consequently, its laws are in no sense equivalent to the laws of nature. It was this historical approach to the study of capitalism that enabled Marx to predict scientifically some of the basic features of the future society.

Analysing the capitalist mode of production in the light of dialectics, Marx applied the whole range of laws and categories of the theory of development: the laws of transition of quantity into quality, the unity and struggle of opposites, the negation of negation, the categories of quality, quantity and measure, of essence, appearance and semblance, of content and form, of the internal and the external, of cause and effect, of necessity and chance, of possibility and reality, of the individual, the specific and the universal, of the abstract and the concrete, of the historical and the logical, and so on. He was faced with the task of showing the objective dialectics of the subject he was studying, that is, the capitalist mode of production, and at the same time of working out a method of research adequate to the subject, that is, dialectics as the logic and theory of cognition. Relying on the cognitive material which he had inherited from Hegel, Marx reworked materialistically all the laws and categories of dialectics which Hegel had formulated and developed. Marx's mastery of the whole range of means made available by the dialectic method enabled him to find his bearings in the concrete economic material. Just as the application of the materialist view of history to the analysis of the bourgeois social formation had completed the process transforming this conception into a scientifically-grounded theory, so the application of materialist dialectics to the analysis of the capitalist mode of production was a decisive scientific substantiation for the universality of this method of research. Without the dialectic method it would have been impossible to make a study of capitalism, because, as Engels said, dialectics is the only method of analysis to be used at the highest instance, that is, in the analysis of the most complex phenomena. In considering the commodity — the basic element of his research — Marx makes a distinction between the qualitative aspect (use-value) and the quantitative aspect (value). From the standpoint of quality and quantity, he then examines money, capital and all the other economic categories, whose development and mutual transformations are subject, in particular, to the law of the transformation of quantity into quality and vice versa; which is why a knowledge of this dialectical law opens up the way to an understanding of real economic processes. A striking example of the operation of the law by which quantity is transformed into quality is the transformation of money into capital and accordingly of the simple commodity producer into the capitalist. Marx shows that there must be a concentration of a definite minimum of values (money) in the hands of one producer for these values to start functioning as capital, and for the producer himself to become a capitalist. He sums up: "Here, as in natural science, is shown the correctness of the law discovered by Hegel (in his *Logic*), that merely quantitative differences beyond a certain point pass into qualitative changes." [1] In a letter to Engels on June 22, 1867, Marx specifically drew his attention to that fact.

Engels subsequently used this example to show the fundamental distinction between Hegel's idealist dialectics and Marx's materialist dialectics. He wrote: "Hegel's distortion of dialectics is based on his assumption that it must be 'self-development of thought' and consequently the dialectics of things is nothing but its reflection, whereas the dialectics in our head is only the reflection of real development which takes place in the world of nature and human society and which submits to dialectical forms.

"Compare for instance what Marx says about the development from the commodity to capital with what Hegel says about development from being to essence, and you have an excellent parallel: on the one hand, concrete development as it takes place in reality, and on the other, an abstract construction in which highly brilliant thoughts and occasionally very important transitions, as for instance of quality into quantity and vice versa, are adapted into an apparent self-development of one concept from another." [2]

Throughout the whole of Marx's economic doctrine runs his anal-

---

[1] Karl Marx, *Capital*, Vol. I, p. 292.
[2] Marx, Engels, *Werke*, Bd. 38, S. 204.

ysis of the contradictory substance of the categories of the capitalist mode of production and bourgeois society as a whole. Every phenomenon of reality is motivated by its internal contradictions, so that the only way to understand developing reality, the only way of consistently applying the historical approach, is to make an analysis of these contradictions.

Marx begins his analysis of capitalism by showing the contradictions of the commodity, and ends it with an examination of the antagonistic contradictions of the capitalist formation as a whole, which inevitably lead it to destruction, showing that transition from capitalism to communism is the only way of resolving the social antagonisms of bourgeois society. This analysis brought out the twofold nature of all economic categories without exception: labour, commodity, money, capital, and so on.

Not only does Marx show the dichotomy of the whole into two opposite parts, but he also traces the development of the contradiction itself, namely, the transition of identity into distinction, transformation into the opposite, resolution of contradictions; he distinguishes between internal and external contradictions, and shows that motion is a mode of realising contradictions, and that the development of contradictions leads to a qualitative transformation of one phenomenon into another.

His method of the logically consistent dialectical analysis of contradictions was already clearly evident in *A Contribution to the Critique of Political Economy*, and in a review of that work Engels gave a classical definition of its substance: "Using this method we begin with the first and simplest relation ... with the first economic relation to be found. We analyse this relation. The fact that it is a *relation* already implies that it has two aspects which are *related to each other*. Each of these aspects is examined separately; this reveals the nature of their attitude to one another, their reciprocal action. Contradictions will emerge which require a solution. But since we are not examining here an abstract mental process that takes place solely in our mind, but an actual event ... these contradictions, too, will have arisen in practice and have probably been solved. We shall trace the mode of this solution and find that it has been effected by establishing a new relation, whose two contradictory aspects we shall then have to set forth, and so on." [1] The theoretical part of *Capital* is also generally structured in accordance with this specific method of Marx's.

Consistently applying the law of the unity and struggle of opposites, Marx criticises Hegel's conception of the "mediation", reconciliation of contradictions, constantly drawing attention to the indissoluble connection between the two sides of the phenomenon expressing the law: the indissoluble *unity* and *struggle* of opposites. This is clearly expressed, for instance, in the economic crises under capital-

---

[1] Marx, Engels, *Collected Works*, Vol. 16, pp. 475-76.

ism in which the unity and struggle of interrelated elements are simultaneously revealed.

Tracing the general tendency in the development of the capitalist mode of production, Marx establishes that it is subject to the general dialectical law of negation of the negation, a law that is manifested in the connection between the capitalist mode of production with earlier social formations, on the one hand, and with the future, communist formation, on the other. It is the discovery of the operation of this law, as applied to the capitalist epoch as a whole, that lies at the basis of Marx's brilliant conclusion about the historical inevitability of the "expropriation of the expropriators". Capitalism develops from petty production based on the labourer's private property in the means of production. The capitalist mode of production, and consequently capitalist private property, is the "first negation of individual private property, as founded on the labour of the proprietor. But capitalist production begets, with the inexorability of a law of Nature, its own negation. It is the negation of negation. This does not re-establish private property for the producer, but gives him individual property based on the acquisitions of the capitalist era: *i.e.*, on co-operation and the possession in common of the land and of the means of production." [1] Under capitalism the initial unity of labour and property is carried to breaking point, but the immanent dialectics of the development of production necessarily leads to the re-establishment of this unity on the higher level created by socialism.

Marx does not, of course, deduce the necessity of the transition from capitalism to communism from this law of negation of the negation, but from his concrete analysis of the law governing the motion of the capitalist mode of production. However once he has arrived at this conclusion on the strength of his purely factual analysis, he goes on to state that the emergence, development and destruction of capitalism proceed in accordance with the law of negation of the negation, and this statement, for its part, helps him to obtain a deeper comprehension of the general logic underlying the whole process, including the specific features of the future society. Therein lies the essential distinction between Marx's materialist view of that law and Hegel's idealist one.

The operation of the law of negation of the negation is revealed in many other processes of economic development under capitalism. A vivid example of the negation of the negation is presented by the general formula of the movement of capital: $M-C-M'$. This law is also manifested in the development of production from the initial union of agriculture and industry through a rupture of that union to a new synthesis on a higher level: "Capitalist production completely tears asunder the old bond of union which held together agriculture and manufacture in their infancy. But at the same time it creates the material conditions for a higher synthesis in the future." [2]

---

[1] Karl Marx, *Capital*, Vol. I, p. 715.
[2] Ibid., p. 474.

Apart from the three basic laws of dialectics and the categories directly connected with them, Marx makes full use in his analysis of capitalism of all the other categories of dialectics.

From the dialectic-materialist view of the categories of form and content follows the important method of drawing a distinction between the material content and social form of every economic phenomenon, something which makes it possible to bring out both the historical character of each economic category and the elements in it which are typical not only of the given stage of historical development. As he analysed the development of economic crises, Marx formulated the categories of possibility and reality, and traced the complex process in which possibility was transformed into reality.

A cardinal problem with which Marx was faced in formulating his system of categories or concepts was to select a starting-point for his study, an initial element the analysis of which would make it possible to unravel the intricate chain of economic relations, and help to recreate the capitalist formation in theoretical terms with faultless logical and historical authenticity.

This starting-point in *Capital* is the commodity, the simplest concrete economic element.

However the commodity is not only the basis and the prerequisite for the capitalist mode of production. It is also its product, and as such "each individual commodity represents a definite portion of capital and of the surplus-value created by it".[1] The commodity is latent with all the main elements of the capitalist mode of production, with all its contradictions. In his *Philosophical Notebooks*, Lenin described Marx's analysis of capital as follows: "In his *Capital*, Marx first analyses the simplest, most ordinary and fundamental, most common and everyday *relation* of bourgeois (commodity) society, a relation encountered billions of times, viz. the exchange of commodities. In this very simple phenomenon (in this 'cell' of bourgeois society) analysis reveals *all* the contradictions (or the germs of *all* the contradictions) of modern society."[2]

Taken all in all, the instruments of scientific research used by Marx in his *Capital* constitute a definite system whose coherence is manifested in the method of ascending from immediate contemplation to abstract thought, from the simple to the complex, from the abstract to the concrete.

This ascent from the abstract to the concrete is expressed and embodied in the logical structure of the whole of *Capital*, in the exposition of the results of research. In Volume One, Marx observes the production of capital abstracted from the sphere of circulation. In Volume Two, he analyses the circulation of capital, viewing production only as an element in the circulation of productive capital. In Volume Three, he examines the capitalist process as a whole, in concrete terms, undertaking to "locate and describe the concrete forms

---

[1] Karl Marx, *Theories of Surplus-Value*, Part III, p. 113.
[2] V. I. Lenin, *Collected Works*, Vol. 38, pp. 360-61.

which grow out of the *movements of capital as a whole*",[1] forms which approximate to the forms appearing on the surface of capitalist society. In the *Theories of Surplus-Value*, Marx makes a special and detailed examination of the history of theoretical conceptions of capitalism.

In probing the deep-seated laws underlying the development of capitalist relations and their specific forms of expression, Marx has constantly to deal with a twofold problem. On the one hand, he reduces the processes taking place on the surface of capitalist society to their essence, a most important, but only the first, stage of analysis, because the next is to show how these most general laws of capitalist production are modified in the sphere of circulation, and outwardly appear in a form which not only conceals their essence, but frequently distorts it, creating a semblance which clashes with the essence.

This specific method of Marx's is based on his dialectical-materialist understanding of the categories of essence, appearance and semblance, above all of the fact that while these categories are interconnected, they are not identical. "All science would be superfluous if the outward appearance and the essence of things directly coincided."[2]

The ascent from the abstract to the concrete, from essence to appearance is shown by Marx to be the process of cognition of essence and the law expressing it, the process of concretisation of a more general law in a number of laws governing particular spheres. Thus, the law of value, the general law of commodity production, was elaborated in the law of supply and demand, the laws of currency, and so on. Marx set out the law of surplus-value in the form of absolute and relative surplus-value, in the laws regulating the rate and mass of surplus-value, the movement of profit, rent and interest, and other laws. In this way, the intricate concatenation of economic relations was presented as a system of laws. A most important characteristic of qualitative analysis, the concretisation of economic laws helped him to bring out the quantitative relations between individual magnitudes and categories.

Of essential importance for the analysis of contradictions between the general law and the outward forms of its appearance was Marx's discovery of the specific action of economic laws of capitalism, which consists in the fact that "under capitalist production, the general law acts as the prevailing tendency only in a very complicated and approximate manner, as a never ascertainable average of ceaseless fluctuations".[3] The absolute realisation of a law, that is, its realisation in each concrete case, is "checked, retarded, and weakened, by counteracting circumstances".[4] Because Marx understood the

---

[1] Karl Marx, *Capital*, Vol. III, p. 25.
[2] Ibid., p. 817.
[3] Ibid., p. 161.
[4] Ibid., p. 235.

specific action of the general laws, and analysed the counteracting circumstances and the extent to which they modified the action of general laws in this or that concrete instance, he was able not only to solve the problems with which the best minds of bourgeois economic science had wrestled in vain, but also to create a reliable instrument for analysing the social organism, which gave a deeper insight into the connection between the activity of individuals in the process of production and the realisation of the general laws within the framework of this activity.

Marx insisted that every science must regard as its fundamental principle the unity of the process of "reducing" appearance to essence, the casual form to regularity, and the reverse process of "deducing" the given phenomenon from the essence, the given, concrete form of appearance from the general law. In Volume One of *Capital* he wrote: "It is, in reality, much easier to discover by analysis the earthly core of the misty creations of religion, than, conversely, it is to develop from the actual relations of life the corresponding celestialised forms of those relations. The latter method is the only materialistic, and therefore the only scientific one."[1]

In his *Capital* Marx made a brilliant application of the most important scientific principle of combining the logical and the historical, which he had formulated in general terms in the introduction to the economic manuscripts of 1857-58.

The gist of what he says is as follows: what is the relation between the scientific, logical analysis of capitalism, which has resulted in the creation of a system of economic categories, ranged in accordance with a definite hierarchy, and the real historical process of the origin and development of the economic forms expressed by these categories? In other words, must the method used in analysing any process repeat all the zigzags of its history to gain a correct understanding of it and to restate its present condition in theoretical terms? Marx argued that in each epoch there exists a predominant system of relations of production which modifies and subordinates to itself the elements of the old relations of production. That is why, the sequence of exposition of any economic categories, notably in analysing capitalism, should not reflect the order in which they played the decisive role before the capitalist epoch, but, on the contrary, should be determined by the relation in which they stand to each other in contemporary bourgeois society. Thus, for instance, although commercial and usurer's capital originated historically earlier than industrial capital, and played a considerable part in the appearance of the latter, they should be examined after an analysis of industrial capital, because under developed capitalism they are no more than subordinate elements, isolated forms of industrial capital.

At the same time the logical method of analysis by no means implies an arbitrary structuring of bonds and relations between phe-

---

[1] Karl Marx, *Capital*, Vol. I, p. 352.

nomena. It is rather a reflection of the historical process in an abstract and theoretically consistent form, a corrected reflection, but one which has been corrected in accordance with the laws yielded by the actual historical process.

Capital contains specimens of profound criticism not only of the conclusions but of the very methodological principles of bourgeois political economy, which made it incapable of producing a consistently scientific analysis of the capitalist system. In setting out his own dialectical-materialist method, Marx gives many examples to show the limited empiricism, the metaphysical character, and now and again the eclecticism and superficiality of the bourgeois economists' method. Apart from social roots, their tendency to act as apologists for capitalism also has epistemological roots, which lie in the defects of the bourgeois outlook itself.

The unhistorical approach is the most vivid expression of the metaphysical character of bourgeois political economy and its hostile attitude to dialectics. In his Afterword to Volume One of *Capital*, Marx revealed the essence and the class roots of this methodological weakness of all the bourgeois economists without exception. He wrote: "In so far as Political Economy remains within that horizon, in so far, *i.e.*, as the capitalist régime is looked upon as the absolutely final form of social production, instead of as a passing historical phase of its evolution, Political Economy can remain a science only so long as the class-struggle is latent or manifests itself only in isolated and sporadic phenomena."[1] With the development of the proletariat's class struggle, objective prerequisites appear for the emergence of a truly scientific, proletarian political economy, in contrast to bourgeois political economy. It is no accident, therefore, that proletarian political economy was founded by Marx, the theorist of this rising class.

The bourgeois economists' line of thought is directly opposed to that of Marx, as can be seen from their approach to economic phenomena, whose dialectical nature they either kill or distort. Marx made a systematic critique of the bourgeois economists' apologetic conception which denies the fact that antagonistic contradictions exist in bourgeois society. Here is what he wrote about the defective method used by James Mill: "Where the economic relation ... includes contradictions, opposites, and likewise the unity of the opposites, he emphasises the aspect of the *unity* of the contradictions and denies the *contradictions*. He transforms the unity of opposites into the direct identity of opposites."[2] Marx observed that one of the most characteristic defects of bourgeois political economy is its neglect of the qualitative aspect of economic phenomena, its failure to understand the dialectics of form and content, essence and appearance, its tendency to confuse appearance and essence, and its inability to see the connection between economic laws and to under-

---

[1] Ibid., p. 24.
[2] Karl Marx, *Theories of Surplus-Value*, Part III, p. 88.

stand the contradictory operation of general laws in concrete conditions.

Even the classical bourgeois economists sought to resolve the contradictions between the general law and the concrete forms in which it manifested itself not by seeking to find the mediating elements, but by directly adapting the concrete to the abstract. Since this did not work, they either denied the law or faced an insoluble contradiction. That is what happened with the contradiction between the law of value and the law of equal profits for capitals of equal magnitude. Marx alone resolved this contradiction, by showing the dialectics of value and price of production.

Capital provides striking evidence of the methodological superiority of Marx's doctrine over bourgeois political economy. But Marx did not regard the development of bourgeois political economy as a succession of misconceptions to be either regretted or condemned. It was the critical analysis of bourgeois political economy that helped to create proletarian political economy. Marx did not reject the legacy of his predecessors, but critically adapted it and presented the vast array of facts in a new light. He wrote: "Political economy can only be turned into a positive science by replacing the conflicting dogmas by the conflicting facts, and by the real antagonisms which form their concealed background." [1]

Capital is a work which is permeated with the party spirit, but this is far removed from subjectivist attempts to anticipate conclusions, or to force empirical material into ready-made schemes. The party spirit of *Capital* is synonymous with scientific objectivity and is its highest form. Marx's method is marked by a faultless analysis of the contradictions within the capitalist mode of production at its every stage. He shows that the development of capitalist relations does not eliminate these contradictions, but creates their form of movement, carries these contradictions to a new level and sharpens them, simultaneously creating the prerequisites for their resolution in a revolutionary way. Marx's conclusion in *Capital* that capitalist production must inevitably be abolished and replaced by communism, a higher form of social organisation, sprang organically from the very course of his scientific analysis of the tendencies and laws of capitalist development.

Capital is a great achievement of the human mind. It helped theoretically to destroy the belief that capitalism was immutable, long before the latter began to fall apart in practice. Consequently, it gave the international working class not only clarity of purpose, but also confidence in the prospects of a victorious struggle against the exploiting system of wage slavery. *Capital* is more than an economic work. It is an invaluable contribution to the development of the other component parts of Marxism: Marxist philosophy and scientific communism.

---

[1] Marx, Engels, *Collected Works*, Vol. 43, p. 128.

CHAPTER ELEVEN

FOUNDER AND LEADER OF THE FIRST INTERNATIONAL

Marx was the heart and soul of this organisation.

V. I. Lenin

INTERNATIONAL MEETING AT ST. MARTIN'S HALL

A large meeting attended by English and French workers and members of proletarian and democratic emigrant organisations was held in London on September 28, 1864, at St. Martin's Hall where workers' and democratic meetings frequently took place. On that occasion, the small hall decorated in the traditional manner with the flags of different countries saw the founding of the International Working Men's Association, the first mass international organisation of the proletariat, known for short as the International.

It was founded by acclamation, and the Committee, elected there and then, was authorised to draft the Rules and submit them for approval by an international workers' congress which was to be held in Brussels in 1865.

Among those present at St. Martin's Hall, Engels subsequently wrote, "there was only one person who was clear as to what was to happen and what was to be founded: it was the man who had already in 1848 issued to the world the call: 'Proletarians of All Countries, Unite!' " [1] Marx's plans for the new organisation were quite different from those of other participants in the meeting. The leaders of the London workers, for instance, wanted an international association of trade unions to regulate wages, reduce working hours, and co-ordinate the strike struggle. The Paris delegates were hoping that the association would help to establish class "harmony" and provide interest-free credits on an international scale to encourage cooperatives. Only Georg Eccarius, who conveyed greetings to the meeting on behalf of the German workers, and had the night before discussed his speech with Marx, spoke as a class-conscious proletarian revolutionary, who regarded the international association of

---

[1] Marx, Engels, *Werke*, Bd. 22, S. 341.

the proletariat as a means of fighting the existing exploitative system.

Marx saw an opportunity to realise his cherished hope: to found an international proletarian association which, as Engels put it, "would demonstrate bodily, so to speak, the international character of the socialist movement both to the workers themselves and to the bourgeois and the governments—for the encouragement and strengthening of the proletariat, for striking fear into the hearts of its enemies".[1]

The International Working Men's Association was set up as a result of the spontaneous urge on the part of the workers of various countries for international unity. Thanks to the leadership provided by Marx and Engels, it played an outstanding role in the history of the proletariat's revolutionary struggle for emancipation.

INAUGURAL ADDRESS AND PROVISIONAL RULES

It was of the utmost importance for the future of the International that its first programme documents were written by Marx. On September 28, 1864, he was elected to its Committee (subsequently known as the Central Council and then the General Council, the name under which it has gone down in history), but learnt belatedly that he had also been appointed to the Sub-Committee to draft the Provisional Rules and Programme (pending their approval by a congress). By then the Committee had already discussed a wordy declaration of principles drawn up by the Owenist John Weston and the draft Rules proposed by a follower of Mazzini, Luigi Wolff. Victor Le Lubez, a young Frenchman, was to combine the two documents. Informing Marx of this in a letter of October 12, 1864, Eccarius urged him to intervene so as to leave the stamp of his "*meaningful brevity* on this first-born of the European workers' organisation".[2]

However, the first meeting Marx could attend was on October 18, when Le Lubez's draft was being discussed. Marx wrote to Engels on November 4: "I went along and was really shocked when I heard the worthy Le Lubez read out a fearfully cliché-ridden, badly written and totally unpolished preamble pretending to be a declaration of principles, with Mazzini showing through the whole thing from beneath a crust of the most insubstantial scraps of French socialism."[3] Following a long discussion in the course of which Marx subjected the declaration to some discreet criticism,

---

[1] Marx, Engels, *Collected Works*, Vol. 24, p. 190.
[2] Central Party Archives of the Institute of Marxism-Leninism.
[3] Marx, Engels, *Collected Works*, Vol. 42, p. 17.

Le Lubez's draft was returned to the Sub-Committee for final editing.

The efforts on the part of Mazzini and his closest followers to get the International Working Men's Association to accept their own programme reflected the general tendency among the republican and democratic-minded members of the bourgeoisie to use the upsurge in the working-class movement for their own political purposes. Many Italian emigrants were on the General Council, and Mazzini himself was also regarded as an authority by its English members. All of this made Marx's position very difficult, because at the time he had no supporters on the Council except Eccarius, although Marx had already won recognition as a revolutionary dedicated to the working-class cause.

A meeting of the Sub-Committee held at Marx's house on October 20 was attended by the English trade unionist William Cremer, Le Lubez and the Italian Giuseppe Fontana. On a motion by Marx, they began by discussing the Rules, but by one o'clock in the morning they had managed to approve only the first of their 40 points. Cremer, with the support of the others, suggested, as Marx had hoped, that approval of this programme document by the General Council should be postponed until November 1, with preliminary consideration of it by the Sub-Committee on October 27. Until then, Marx was asked to put the finishing touches to the documents.

Marx radically rewrote the Rules. He altered the whole preamble and reformulated the organisational principles, discarding all the petty regulations envisaged by the Mazzini draft. In effect all that was left of the old version was the name of the organisation and the point about the convocation of the general congress in Brussels in 1865. In addition, Marx also wrote the Inaugural Address of the Working Men's International Association, something that had not been originally provided for.

Marx's proposals were accepted by the Sub-Committee. On November 1, the General Council unanimously approved the documents he had drawn up. This was a defeat for the attempt to impose a bourgeois-democratic programme on the new organisation. Thus its proletarian class character was safeguarded from the outset.

In the first documents of the International Marx formulated the aims and tactics of the proletariat's emancipation struggle in the most general terms, so as to make them acceptable to the various trends in the working-class movement. The organisation could be made a mass one only through a programme which did not close the door on either English trade unionists, French and Belgian Proudhonists or German Lassalleans. Marx coped brilliantly with this complex task. He wrote to Engels: "It was very difficult to frame the thing so that our view should appear in a form that would make it acceptable to the present outlook of the workers' movement.... It will take time before the revival of the movement allows the old boldness of language to be used." [1] Marx himself described the Inaugural Address as being "*fortiter in re, suaviter in modo*". [2] He anticipated that joint action and exchange of experience in the ranks of the International would subsequently lead the workers to recognise a single theoretical programme based on the principles of scientific communism. Adoption of the Inaugural Address and the Provisional Rules was a most important prerequisite for the subsequent triumph of these principles.

The Preamble of the Provisional Rules held a special place in the documents which Marx drew up, for it formulated the fundamentals of the programme of the proletarian movement. Its first line said: "The emancipation of the working classes must be conquered by the working classes themselves." [3] The goal of the proletariat was to abolish all class rule. Political struggle by the working class against the ruling classes was the means of emancipating the working people from oppression by the capitalist system, which was based on their economic subjection to those who owned the means of production. Unity of forces on class lines and proletarian internationalism were vital principles for the working-class movement.

Engels believed that the Inaugural Address was a "necessary commentary" on this programme. The Inaugural Address opened with a review of the history of the working class from 1848 to 1864. With great accusatory power, Marx described the growing misery of the European proletariat during that "millennium of free trade", which was unrivalled for the development of its industry. He wrote: "No improvement of machinery, no appliance of science to production, no contrivances of communication, no new colonies, no emigration, no opening of markets, no free trade, nor all these things put together, will do away with the miseries of the industrous masses; ... on the present false base, every fresh development of the productive powers of labour must tend to deepen social contrast and point social antagonisms." [4]

Marx noted the successes scored by the working-class movement over that period: the ten-hour working day, and the growing co-operative movement. While the legal restriction of the working day refuted the liberal bourgeois dogma that the state should not intervene in economic relations, the successes of the co-operative movement showed that the workers were quite able to organise production without the capitalists. However, within the framework of capitalist society, co-operative labour could not substantially improve the condition of the working class. It would serve as an instrument of the working people's emancipation only when it developed to national dimensions and was fostered by national means. That was be-

---

[1] Marx, Engels, *Collected Works*, Vol. 42, p.18.
[2] "Strong in deed, mild in manner". Ibid.
[3] Ibid., Vol. 20, p. 14.
[4] Ibid., p. 9.

ing prevented by "the lords of land and the lords of capital", who would "always use their political privileges for the defence and perpetuation of their economical monopolies". Marx suggested this conclusion: "To conquer political power has therefore become the great duty of the working classes." The workers possessed one element of success — numbers, he said, but "numbers weigh only in the balance, if united by combination and led by knowledge".[1]

The Inaugural Address stressed the need for international working-class solidarity. "Past experience has shown how disregard of that bond of brotherhood which ought to exist between the workmen of different countries, and incite them to stand firmly by each other in all their struggles for emancipation, will be chastised by the common discomfiture of their incoherent efforts."[2] Marx urged the workers to fight against the ruling classes' "foreign policy in pursuit of criminal designs, playing upon national prejudices, and squandering in piratical wars the people's blood and treasure."[3] He emphasised that the working class must counter this policy with its own class stand on international issues, based on the principles of proletarian internationalism.

The Address ended with the slogan "Proletarians of All Countries, Unite!", which Marx and Engels had issued 16 years earlier, and which now rang out with fresh force.

In accordance with the Provisional Rules, the International Working Men's Association was built up from the start on the principles of democracy, with all the officers of the General Council (a general secretary, a treasurer, corresponding secretaries for the different countries, and others) being elected, and of centralism, which was expressed in a clear-cut division of the powers vested in the Association's governing bodies: the Congress, the General Council, and the Federal Councils in the different countries.

HEAD OF THE INTERNATIONAL
PROLETARIAN ORGANISATION

It was mainly the central governing body of the Association that determined its activity, so the leading role which Marx soon came to play on the General Council was of tremendous importance. Initially its composition was extremely mixed. Marx, officially fulfilling the functions of the Corresponding Secretary for Germany, worked resolutely to turn the International into a proletarian class organisation, and its Council into a militant and authoritative organ. Accordingly, from the outset he strove to consolidate its proletarian core. Old members of the Communist League, Lessner, Lochner, Pfänder, and Kaub, were co-opted into the Council. Marx met with under-

---
[1] Ibid., p. 12.
[2] Ibid.
[3] Ibid., pp. 12-13.

standing and support from Eugène Dupont, a maker of musical instruments, who had taken part in the June uprising (in the spring of 1865 he became Corresponding Secretary for France), and Hermann Jung, a watchmaker and the Corresponding Secretary for Switzerland. By the spring of 1865 the General Council was quite representative of the various contingents of the European proletarian movement, with members meeting regularly every Tuesday in a small room at 18 Greek Street in Soho.

The Sub-Committee, or the Standing Committee, appointed to draft programme documents, continued to act as a narrower executive body, preparing material for Council meetings and taking decisions on urgent, current business. Marx always attended the weekly meetings of the Sub-Committee, which were usually held on Saturdays. Frequently these meetings were held in Marx's study at 1 Modena Villas, Maitland Park, where he and his family had moved in March 1864, and where he lived for eleven years. Very soon, almost all the members of the General Council and many foreign workers who came to London on the International's business regularly visited the Marx home, which increasingly resembled the combat headquarters of the proletarian movement.

The International owed its success largely to Marx's skill in defining the tasks ahead and issuing timely slogans which secured the broadest support for the General Council among the local sections. His skill sprang not only from a profound understanding of the general laws of social development, but also from his thorough knowledge of the concrete forms of the workers' struggle, their ideological level and the specific features of every national contingent of the international proletariat.

Marx obtained the facts for his strategic and tactical generalisations from the working-class and the socialist press, reports on local congresses and general congresses of the International, his constant contacts with working-class leaders and General Council members, the numerous letters received by the Council from the localities, and his personal correspondence with his associates in Germany, France, Switzerland, Belgium and the United States. He kept in close touch with the working-class movement throughout the world, and was especially pleased when the workers, impelled by their true class instinct, put forward demands which largely coincided with conclusions he had reached on the basis of his theoretical research.

Marx always heeded the voice of the masses with great respect, but never made any concessions to backward attitudes. The line he formulated for the international organisation was based on a sober analysis of the overall situation and was designed above all to strengthen the proletariat's own class movement. In helping the workers to rise above their particular and local demands to an understanding of the more general class tasks, Marx invariably sought to carry forward the development of the proletarian movement.

In the Association the whole of the international proletariat stood to gain from the advance by any contingent of the working class to a higher stage. Mindful of the movement's future, Marx worked to incorporate in its programme documents every important achievement gained in practical struggle. In this sense, the historical development of the International was a consistent formulation of the militant programme of the international proletariat and the gradual assertion of Marxist principles in it. Therein also lay the meaning of the struggle between the trends in the International, which reflected the process by which the working class of Europe and the United States was overcoming its utopian and sectarian views.

In 1871, looking back on seven years of effort, Marx wrote that the history of the International was "*a continual struggle of the General Council* against the sects and attempts by amateurs to assert themselves within the International itself against the real movement of the working class". [1]

The dogmas and the cure-alls suggested by various sects did to some extent reflect the practical experience of some sections of the proletariat, and the specific conditions in each country, but because of a tendency to treat this limited experience as an absolute, the notions deduced from it were subjective and unscientific, and eclectically combined into casual and contradictory propositions. The sect tended to justify its existence not by what it had in common with the class movement, but by the "*particular shibboleth*" which distinguished it from the general movement.[2]

Regardless of the specific features of each trend of petty-bourgeois socialism at the time (Proudhonism, various brands of anarchism in Belgium, Italy, Spain, and so on), they all had one thing in common, namely, that they reflected not only the working people's protest against capitalist exploitation, but also the small producers' protest against the tendency of capitalist development towards centralisation, and their urge to stop the development of capitalism and reverse its advance.

The liberal trade unionists took a different stand. They accepted the progressive nature of large-scale capitalist production, but many of them followed the vulgar economists, the apologists of bourgeois society, by idolising capitalism, believing it to rest on solid foundations, and setting before the working-class movement no other task than that of slightly correcting and "improving" the bourgeois system. The liberal trade unionists were confirmed reformists.

Marx regarded the existence of reformist and sectarian trends within the working-class movement as both the result of influence exerted by bourgeois ideology on some sections of the proletariat and an expression of their backwardness, and was sure that this stage would be inevitably overcome as the class struggle developed. However, he certainly did not believe that one need do no more than

---

[1] Marx, Engels, *Collected Works*, Vol. 44, p. 252.
[2] Ibid., Vol. 43, p. 133.

observe the process taking place. He held that the task of the leadership of the international proletarian organisation was to promote class consciousness as actively as possible, and to use the various forms of ideological influence, together with painstaking educational work and vigorous support for independent working-class action. "In uniting the labour movement of various countries, striving to channel into joint activity the various forms of non-proletarian, pre-Marxian socialism (Mazzini, Proudhon, Bakunin, liberal trade unionism in Britain, Lassallean vacillations to the right in Germany, etc.), and in combating the theories of all these sects and schools, Marx hammered out a uniform tactic for the proletarian struggle of the working class in the various countries." [1]

THE WAY TO THE MASSES

To make the International a mass organisation from the outset, the General Council had to establish the most diverse contacts with the workers of various countries. The strike movement which developed in the countries of Western Europe helped to bring out the most active elements of the working class, and it was to these fine reserves of the emergent proletarian army that Marx turned in the first place. On his initiative, the General Council organised moral and material support for the strikes. The Council's tasks included exposing the employers, who were recruiting workers from abroad to replace the strikers. Marx regarded this as a means helping the workers of the different countries to understand that they had common interests and fostering a sense of class solidarity.

At a meeting of the General Council on April 25, 1865, Marx read a letter which he had received from the Berlin Compositors' Union, reporting on the strike by 500 Leipzig compositors and requesting assistance for them. The letter said: "...Every working-men's movement, every strike has an international significance, that, in fact, the immediately and locally engaged working-men do battle for the whole of their class." [2] The General Council decided to turn for support to the London Compositors' Union, and Marx was among the delegates appointed to visit it. This was the beginning of the practice by the Council and the Association as a whole of regularly organising international mutual assistance in strikes.

It took the International some time to develop a correct attitude to strikes. The French, Swiss and Belgian Proudhonists, like the German Lassalleans, took the sectarian attitude of rejecting strikes. Although the English working-class movement had much experience in staging strikes, not even all the English members of the General Council regarded them in a positive light. One active opponent

---

[1] V. I. Lenin, *Collected Works*, Vol. 21, p. 49.
[2] *The Bee-Hive Newspaper*, No. 185, April 29, 1865.

of strikes was the carpenter John Weston, an adherent of Owen's utopian system. He repeatedly made his views known in the newspaper *The Bee-Hive*. At meetings of the General Council he argued that the workers' demands for better working conditions were futile and that the trade unions which gave a lead in the proletariat's economic struggle were in fact doing it harm instead of good, because any rise in wages would be bound to result in a general rise in the prices of consumer goods.

It was the campaign to refute such views that clearly showed the great importance of Marx's economic research for working out the correct tactics in the class struggle. In this instance, arguments provided by the new economic doctrine were a great help in exploding the false theory that the prices of goods were determined by the level of wages, a theory which tended to undermine the militant spirit of the working class and suggested the need to submit to its fate. By contrast, Marx urged the International to give utmost support to workers who were under the "infection of strikes".[1]

At two General Council meetings, on June 20 and 27, 1865, Marx delivered a special report containing a critical analysis of Weston's views and setting forth the scientific principles of the theory of value, price and wages. The main section of Marx's report, widely known since its first publication in 1898 under the title *Wages, Price and Profit*, was a preliminary and popular exposition of the gist of Volume One of *Capital*.

In clear and simple terms Marx explained the origin of profit from the surplus-value which the owners of capital gratuitously appropriated. The worker's wages and the capitalist's profit were shown to be component parts of the newly created value of the product. Their proportion can change within that value. Wages can be increased at the expense of the surplus-value taking the form of profit, and vice versa. This proportion is also established under the impact of the proletariat's class struggle. The workers can gain a rise in wages, although the general tendency of capitalist production is to reduce the average wage level. The general living conditions in this or that country are also of great importance for the working-class struggle. The working class should not underestimate the potentialities of its day-to-day economic struggle, by following those who shared Weston's ideas, but neither should it overrate these potentialities, as the leaders of the English trade unions were doing. The radical solution for the social problems of bourgeois society lies solely in the abolition of the whole system of wage labour. The trade unions are important, therefore, not only as centres of resistance to the encroachments of capital on the workers' rights and living standards, but also as a school where workers are trained for resolute battles against capitalism.

Marx's report was a great success, and the General Council was

---

[1] Marx, Engels, *Collected Works*, Vol. 42, p. 159.

guided by its theoretical and tactical propositions in its subsequent practical activity.

To strengthen the International Working Men's Association it was essential to draw into its ranks the English trade unions, the only mass organisations of the English proletariat since the disintegration of the National Charter Association. Marx, who had observed the development of the English working-class movement for over twenty years, had no illusions about the ideological level of reformist leaders like George Odger, William Cremer and other trade unionists. However, he was aware that behind them were thousands of rank-and-file members, and so maintained close business contacts with them, while continuing to combat their liberal bourgeois views.

On November 22, 1864, Marx invited the General Council to urge the English workers' societies and trade unions to become corporate members of the International. The organisations in London and its suburbs each possessed the right to have one representative on the Council. These new Council members, who were more closely connected with the mass of workers, now and again gave Marx support in his fight against the reformism of the trade union leaders.

It was Marx who started the practice, continued until the International ceased its activities, of sending General Council members to attend workers' meetings in order to spread the ideas of the Association. The appointment of such delegations and the hearing of their reports soon became part and parcel of the Council's work. Marx himself was frequently a member of such delegations. Among the English members of the Council, Robert Shaw, a house painter, at one time Secretary of the General Council, stood out as an able propagandist and organiser. In 1870 Marx wrote about this fine representative of the English working class who died of tuberculosis at an early age: "It is principally due to his constant efforts that the *Trades Unions* have rallied around us." [1]

Marx attached much importance to involving the trade unions in direct political struggle, and warmly supported Cremer's proposal in January 1865 that the General Council should take part in the broad campaign for electoral reform, which the bourgeois radicals had begun. Marx clearly formulated the terms on which joint action could be taken with the radical bourgeoisie. He expected the workers' participation in the general democratic movement to pave the way for the formation of an independent political party of the English proletariat, with far-reaching consequences for the development of the revolutionary working-class and democratic movement on the continent. On May 1, 1865, he wrote to Engels: "If you succeed in re-electrifying the political movement of the English working class, our Association will already have done more for the European

---

[1] Marx, Engels, *Collected Works*, Vol. 22, p. 92.

working class, without making any fuss, than was possible in any other way."[1]

The Reform League, founded in March 1865 on the General Council's initiative and according to a plan produced by Marx, exerted considerable influence on English political life. It was joined by thousands of workers, and its campaign for democratic electoral reform assumed great scope. However, at the crucial moment the trade unionist leaders who represented the working class on its leadership supported the radicals and prevented the League from taking the General Council's line.

Marx also sought to make use of foreign-policy issues to educate the English workers in the spirit of proletarian internationalism, and on November 29, 1864, on behalf of the General Council, drafted an address to Abraham Lincoln following his re-election as President of the U.S.A. Marx found just the right words to express the attitude of the international proletariat to the struggle being carried on by the progressive forces of the United States against the slave system.

Marx highly appreciated the fact that even before the establishment of the International Working Men's Association a group of French workers, who had been under the strong influence of Proudhon's petty-bourgeois reformist doctrine, had come out in 1863 for the nomination of independent workers' candidates in the election to the Legislative Corps. Representatives of this group—Henri Tolain, Ernest Edouard Fribourg and Charles Limousin—were appointed correspondents of the Association in France. Marx at once entered their Paris addresses in his notebook, and through his friend Victor Schily, a German emigrant, sent them the text of the Inaugural Address and the Provisional Rules.

By then, the first section of the International in France had begun to function in the workshop of the engraver Fribourg, in very modest premises in the backyard of 44 Rue Gravillier in Paris. It was run by a board of three correspondents, whose appointment had been approved in London. The board had already issued a French translation of the Provisional Rules. However, they had omitted the words about the abolition of all class rule as the ultimate goal of the proletariat's liberation struggle in the first paragraph, and the words "as a means" in the third paragraph, which said "that the economical emancipation of the working classes is therefore the great end to which every political movement ought to be subordinate as a means".

Marx was quick to notice these inaccuracies, which distorted the meaning of this key document in a Proudhonist spirit, reflecting above all the Proudhonist failure to understand the importance of political struggle. When the General Council requested an explanation, the board replied that it had to reckon with various difficulties arising from the police regime under the Second Empire.

---
[1] Ibid., Vol. 42, p. 150.

The political tendency of the French translation of the Rules was also noticed by a group of bourgeois republicans who had at one time advocated the idea of setting up the Association and tried to secure control of it. The distorted translation of the Rules gave the bourgeois republicans a pretext for accusing Tolain of deliberately repudiating political struggle against the Bonapartist Empire. This campaign was supported by bourgeois-democratic emigrants in London.

The leaders of the Paris section turned for help to the General Council, which was now to act for the first time as an arbiter on internal matters in the local organisations. It took all of Marx's high principles and organisational experience to bring about a successful solution of the conflict. The attacks by the bourgeois elements, which tended to jeopardise the international and class character of the organisation, were thwarted. Acting through Schily and Dupont, who had specially gone to Paris for the purpose, Marx got the Paris section to hold a general meeting of its members on April 26, 1865, to reorganise its leadership. A commission to help the board included representatives of workers' societies, among them the future Communards Zéphirin Camélinat, a bronze-worker, and Louis Eugène Varlin, a bookbinder, the latter already having shown himself to be an outstanding organiser of the French workers.

Léon Fontaine, a Belgian democrat, was appointed the Association's representative in Belgium, but he had no connections with proletarian circles and in fact delayed the establishment of contacts between the General Council and the Belgian workers. This was discovered in the spring of 1865 when Marx was made Corresponding Secretary *pro tem.* for Belgium. There, as elsewhere, the first steps by the International's sections met with bourgeois attempts to secure control of the international proletarian organisation. These attempts were rebutted by Marx, who started direct correspondence with representatives of the Belgian workers, headed by the socialist César De Paepe.

CORRESPONDING SECRETARY
FOR GERMANY

Marx worked hard to have German workers join the International. He was confronted with great difficulties at first, partly because of the laws, which prohibited German workers' societies from associating with foreign organisations, and partly because of the sectarian stand taken by the Lassallean leadership of the General Association of German Workers. Marx believed that if the necessary changes in its leadership were made, it could be restructured and released from the harmful influence of Lassallean dogmas, so he made efforts to have it join the International. He repeatedly returned to this question at General Council meetings, and wrote about it to Wilhelm Liebknecht, Carl Siebel and other followers of his in Germany.

In order to be able to spread the International's ideas in Germany, Marx and Engels agreed to contribute to the *Social-Demokrat*, a newspaper which one of Lassalle's ideological successors, the Frankfurt lawyer Johann Baptist Schweitzer, began to publish in Berlin on December 15, 1864. Marx regarded the absence in the newspaper's prospectus of any specifically Lassallean slogans as a promising factor, and the fact that Liebknecht was on its editorial board suggested that it might be run on the correct lines.

Marx began by sending the *Social-Demokrat* the German text of the Inaugural Address, which was printed in Nos. 2 and 3 at the end of December 1864. On January 3, 1865, he had the satisfaction of reporting this important event to the General Council.

When Proudhon died in January 1865, Marx wrote an article entitled "On Proudhon", following Schweitzer's insistent requests.

It was a masterful portrait of Proudhon, which brought out the specific aspects of his outlook and activity, and gave a scientifically objective view both of his merits and shortcomings. It was also a brilliant example of a combined blow at the various types of reformism and sectarianism. Marx succeeded in stressing the features which Proudhon had in common with the other spokesmen of petty-bourgeois socialism, particularly Lassalle, although the latter's name was not even mentioned. Inability to use the dialectical method, failure to understand historical materialism, ignorance of political economy, substitution of metaphysical for historical categories—all these methodological shortcomings were common to Proudhon and Lassalle. As Marx pointed out, among men who were consumed with vanity and yearned for a taste of sensational success the tendency towards charlatanism in science had as its corollary vacillation and lack of principle in politics. Marx's criticism of Proudhon's accommodation to the Bonapartist regime was also an outright condemnation of Lassalle's flirtation with the Prussian ruling circles. Thus, Marx unequivocally branded Lassalle in a Lassallean paper.

When Marx was writing his article on Proudhon, he had already learned from Liebknecht of the agreement concluded between Bismarck and Lassalle shortly before the latter's death, and this shed a new light on Schweitzer's behaviour as well. It was clear that Schweitzer had not only known all along about the secret negotiations between Lassalle and Bismarck, but was himself just as closely connected with the Prussian authorities. When Marx demanded that there should be nothing to suggest that the workers' party was flirting with Bismarck, Schweitzer asked him to consider the paper's difficult position and the need for it to establish itself, but in the meantime continued to publish a series of articles entitled *The Bismarck Ministry* praising Prussia's policy.

In early 1865 the Prussian Provincial Diet was debating, at the insistence of the Progressists, a bill to revise the 1845 "industrial charter", which was impeding industrial development. Berlin workers launched a campaign for the abolition primarily of those clauses in the "charter" which prohibited combinations and strikes. Marx and Engels attached much importance to this movement, but despite their advice Schweitzer ignored it and concentrated on a campaign for state assistance to productive societies. In a letter to Schweitzer on February 13, 1865, Marx once again sharply criticised his reformist "cure-all". He wrote: "It is beyond all question that Lassalle's ill-starred illusion that a Prussian government might intervene with socialist measures will be crowned with disappointment... But the *honour* of the workers' party requires that it reject such illusions, even before their hollowness is punctured by experience. The working class is revolutionary or it is nothing." [1]

In their statement "To the Editor of the *Social-Demokrat*" on February 23, 1865, Marx and Engels announced their refusal to work on the paper. They said that the break was due to fundamental political differences: whereas the two men demanded that "the language directed at the ministry and the feudal-absolutist party should be at least as bold as that aimed at the men of Progress", the editors continued to act in the spirit of the "royal Prussian governmental socialism".[2]

There was a strong response to the statement among progressive German workers, and it was approved by some of their organisations, including the Berlin Compositors' Union. Liebknecht and a number of other contributors likewise broke with the Lassallean organ.

However, a full-scale critique of the Lassalleans' political stand was also needed. On a visit to Manchester in January 1865, Marx had asked Engels to write an article for the *Social-Demokrat* on Bismarck's army reorganisation bill. Engels did so and by early February had a work that was too long for a newspaper article. However, since the break with Schweitzer was imminent, it was decided to publish it as a pamphlet entitled *The Prussian Military Question and the German Workers' Party*. It contained an incisive analysis of the alignment of class forces in Germany, argued the need for the establishment of an independent workers' party and outlined the party's tactics at a time when the constitutional conflict in Prussia was yet to come to a head. In contrast to the Lassalleans, Engels urged the need not only for relentless criticism of the inconsistency and cowardice of the bourgeois Progressist Party, but also for an implacable fight against the military-bureaucratic monarchy and exposure of Bismarck's social demagogy. Marx approved of Engels' pamphlet and wrote a number of short notices about it for various German newspapers.

The break with the *Social-Demokrat* meant that for the time being

---

[1] Marx, Engels, *Collected Works*, Vol. 42, p. 96.
[2] Ibid., Vol. 20, p. 80.

Marx had to abandon his efforts to draw the General Association of German Workers into the International, but he continued his intense search for other ways of establishing strong ties between the International and the German working-class movement. In early 1865, in view of the situation in Germany, he suggested that the German workers should join the International individually, thereby formally abiding by the existing laws. This tactic justified itself and helped to consolidate the ties between the German proletarians and the International, but it took some time for it to produce tangible results.

THE POLISH QUESTION

In the first few months following the establishment of the International Working Men's Association, Marx gave much attention to substantiating the internationalist stand on the Polish question, which of all the international problems at the time was of the greatest concern to democrats and proletarians. He continued to attach great importance to the Polish national liberation movement, which he regarded as a revolutionary force that the working class should support in every way. But he also believed it to be necessary for the proletarian organisation to take a stand of its own on the issue, in contrast to that of the bourgeois radicals, who led the British National League for the Independence of Poland, founded in London in 1863. Some of the League's members — Peter Fox, William Dell and Robert Hartwell — were on the General Council of the International. In December 1864 and January 1865, Marx had to deliver reports in connection with the discussion of a message to the Polish people, which had been drafted on behalf of the British members of the Council by Peter Fox, a radical journalist, who had joined the working-class movement. He was an ardent advocate of restoring Poland's national sovereignty, but like many other British radicals was a Francophile and sought to prove that the various French governments had pursued a foreign policy favouring Poland.

In order to refute this idea, Marx summoned a vast array of facts, making use of some of the preparatory material for his pamphlet on Poland which he began in the spring of 1863 but did not finish. He presented, first to members of the Standing Committee and then to the General Council, "a historically irrefutable tableau of the constant French betrayal of Poland from Louis XV to Bonaparte III",[1] and drove home the point that it was the workers and not the ruling circles of the West who were Poland's true friends.

Marx took an active part in preparing the anniversary celebrations of the 1863 Polish insurrection. The meeting held on March 1, 1865 unanimously adopted a resolution proposed on behalf of the

---

[1] Ibid., Vol. 42, p. 55.

International, which said that "an integral and independent Poland is an indispensable condition of democratic Europe".[1] Eccarius, who seconded the resolution, stressed the need to destroy the Prussian monarchy as one of the main obstacles in the way of Poland's restoration and Germany's democratic unification.

The English bourgeois press carried reports of the meeting but said nothing about the International's participation, and this gave Marx the opportunity to publish an appropriate "Correction" in the German-language Swiss newspaper *Der weisse Adler*, hoping that this would inform the German workers of the International's stand on the Polish question. He accentuated the importance of Eccarius' speech, thereby publicly demonstrating the International's hostile attitude to the Prussian government and the Lassalleans' flirtation with Bismarck.

HOLIDAYING AT ZALT-BOMMEL

It took a truly superhuman effort on Marx's part to direct the International and carry on his vast theoretical research. He had to cope with a host of large and small organisational matters, such as meetings and correspondence with working-class leaders, attendance at meetings, drafting of resolutions and speeches, advice to his comrades, etc. In the spring of 1865, he wrote to Engels: "Besides my work on the book, the *International Association* takes up an enormous amount of time, as I am in fact the head of it. And what a waste of time!... E. g. the French shit:

"*28 February*. Tolain and Fribourg here from Paris. Meeting of the *Central Council*, where they state their case and bicker with Le Lubez until 12 o'clock at night. Then reconvene in Bolleter's tavern, where I had another 200 odd cards to sign. (I have now got them to change this stupid practice by having our handwriting engraved on the plate.... Meanwhile, the remaining 1,000 cards ... had to be signed in the old style.)

"*1 March*. Polish meeting.

"*4 March. Subcommittee meeting about the French question* until 1 o'clock in the morning.

"*6 March. Subcommittee meeting* about ditto until 1 o'clock in the morning.

"*7 March. Sitting of the Central Council* until 12 o'clock at night." [2]

Overworked and worn out by another attack of his grave chronic complaint, Marx decided to take a short break and have a change of air. He spent three weeks, from March 19 to April 8, 1865, in Zalt-Bommel with his Dutch relatives, whose old burgher house offered an atmosphere of calm and comfort. But even there his mind was

---

[1] Marx, Engels, *Collected Works*, Vol. 20, p. 97.
[2] Ibid., Vol. 42, p. 130.

constantly turning to the political issues of the day. His uncle, Lion Philips, a Dutch merchant, was a man of broad outlook and democratic cast of mind, and the two men had frank discussions on the outcome of the American Civil War, the prospects for German unification, and the Polish and Italian questions. Old Philips took a sceptical view of the working-class movement, but by no means considered his nephew to be irresponsible, for he realised that the younger man was tackling problems of vast scale and importance.

The three-week break had a beneficial effect on Marx. The pleasure of his stay at Zalt-Bommel was heightened by the presence of his cousin, Nannette, with whom he had established easy, friendly relations earlier. He often jokingly called her the "Dutch Secretary" of the General Council.

An interesting memento of this short "carefree" period of Marx's life is his "Confession", written on April 1, 1865, in response to a half-serious questionnaire which he filled in several times at his daughters' request. Besides the Zalt-Bommel version, there are two other sets of replies which are for the most part identical with the former. The tone is alternately serious and humorous, and reveals his integrity and human warmth. Here is an extract from this questionnaire:

The quality you like best	. Simplicity.
Your chief characteristic	. Singleness of purpose.
The vice you hate most	. Servility.
The vice you excuse most	. Gullibility.
Your idea of happiness	. To fight.
Your idea of misery	. To submit.
Your hero	. Spartacus, Kepler.
Your maxim	. *Nihil humani a me alienum puto.*[1]

During Marx's absence, the contract for the publication of *Capital* had arrived in London from Hamburg, and there was a backlog of urgent matters in the International. It was time he resumed his hard work.

AT THE LONDON CONFERENCE OF 1865

The International's Provisional Rules provided for the convocation of a General Workers' Congress in Belgium in 1865, but Marx believed this to be premature, because the local sections were not yet on a firm footing either organisationally or ideologically. On June 24, 1865, he wrote to Engels that "the time was not yet ripe for it". Engels was of the same opinion.[2]

Meanwhile, the members of the International in France and Swit-

---

[1] Ibid., pp. 567-68.
[2] Ibid., pp. 163, 179.

zerland were urging that the congress should be held. The leaders of the Paris section hoped that it would help them to secure recognition of Proudhonism as the International's official doctrine. On July 7, they forestalled the General Council by issuing an address proposing their own agenda for the congress.

By then, Marx had already succeeded in convincing the General Council that it would be better to call a preliminary conference in London of the leaders of the principal sections to prepare the congress. A plenary meeting of the General Council on July 25, 1865 approved Marx's draft agenda for the congress, which also included the points proposed by the Parisians but reformulated by him in such a way as to bring them more into line with the actual tasks facing the International.

Marx very much wanted to see representatives of the German workers at the conference, particularly Liebknecht, but the latter was unable to come and submitted a detailed report on the state of the working-class movement in Germany. Marx had always opposed, as a matter of principle, any glorification of leaders and had criticised the Lassalleans for doing so. He felt that Liebknecht had put too much accent on his, Marx's, role in advancing the emancipation struggle of the German working class. Accordingly, on November 21, 1865, he wrote to Liebknecht: "As to your report, I could *not* lay it before the conference, because I was too personally introduced in it."[1]

The conference met from September 25 to 29. The morning sessions, held at the Freemasons Arms in Long Acre, were attended by delegates from the continent and members of the Standing Committee, and the afternoon sessions, held in a house in Adelphi Terrace in the Strand, were of a more ceremonial character and were open to the public. In addition to the delegates from the localities, they were also attended by visitors. Marx attended all the sessions, got to know the delegates and had long talks with many of them. On September 28, 1865, a soirée was held at St. Martin's Hall to mark the anniversary of the founding of the International, which ended with a tea also attended by members of the delegates' families. While Varlin and Limousin danced with Marx's daughters, Laura and Jenny, Marx described his differences with Proudhon to Tolain and Fribourg. On October 1, a few delegates, among them Becker, Jung and De Paepe, came to dinner at the Marx home.

The London Conference was an important stage in Marx's efforts to constitute the International, and helped considerably to consolidate the leading role of the General Council and Marx's own authority in the Council, and to establish contacts between its most active members — Eccarius, Lessner, Dupont and Jung — and delegates from the continent — Varlin, De Paepe and Becker. The way Marx had used the proposals of the Paris section in drafting the agenda

---

[1] Marx, Engels, *Collected Works*, Vol. 42, p. 201.

for the congress had also fully justified itself. At the conference this draft was discussed as a joint motion by Marx and Fribourg and received general approval.

The conference rejected the French demand that any worker should be allowed to attend the congress, and came out strongly for strict observance of the principle of representation: it decided that the congress should be attended only by delegates empowered to do so by sections which had been duly formalised and had paid their membership dues.

The discussion of the Polish question at the conference showed that most members of the General Council, particularly the Germans and the English, backed Marx's line for support by the working class of the struggle for Poland's independence. However, almost all the French delegates opposed placing the Polish question on the congress agenda. In line with Proudhon's views, they argued that this was a "political" question, which was out of place in the programme of an "economic" workers' congress. The petty-bourgeois democrats accused the General Council of insisting on the "principle of nationalities" and following in the wake of the Bonapartists.

Bearing in mind that the Proudhonists' nihilist attitude to the national question sprang in part from their protests against its demagogic use by Napoleon III, Marx urged Engels to explain the Polish problem in the press, the result being a series of articles, entitled *What Have the Working Classes to Do with Poland?*, showing that the Bonapartist "principle of nationalities" and proletarian recognition of the right of nations to self-determination were diametrically opposed.

On various subsequent occasions in the course of their activity in the International, Marx and Engels defended the internationalist stand on the Polish question. On January 22, 1867, Marx delivered an impassioned speech at a meeting in Cambridge Hall in London, which the General Council, together with Polish revolutionary exiles, held to mark the anniversary of the 1863 Polish insurrection.

INTERNATIONAL'S SECTIONS SET UP IN GERMANY. AUSTRO-PRUSSIAN WAR AND THE GERMAN WORKING CLASS

The tireless propaganda of the International's principles by Marx and Engels began to produce results in the German working-class movement in the winter of 1865 and 1866. Illegal sections of the International were set up in various German towns, primarily by members of the General Association of German Workers, who cherished the traditions of the Communist League and opposed the

Lassallean leadership. These sections frequently operated under the cover of consumers' and producers' co-operatives, educational societies, mutual aid funds, and other forms of organisation allowed by the authorities. Although their membership was not numerous, they helped to spread the International's ideas in Germany, and to involve the German working class in joint action with the international proletariat.

Meanwhile, the revolutionary forces within the Union of the German Workers' Educational Societies founded by the liberals in 1863 were being consolidated, as the Union gradually shed the liberals' tutelage and the influence of Schulze-Delitzsch's co-operativist ideas, and moved closer to the International. Among those who best expressed these revolutionary proletarian tendencies was August Bebel, a young turner, under whose chairmanship 29 workers' societies had united in Saxony in July 1865. Bebel was on the board of the Union and exerted an active influence on its evolution.

The firm alliance between Liebknecht, a disciple of Marx's, and Bebel played an important part in the development of the German working-class movement. Following his expulsion from Berlin in April 1865, and his wanderings all over Germany, Liebknecht settled in Leipzig. In August 1865 he met Bebel and helped him to understand Marxism. Despite the difference in age—Liebknecht was 39 and Bebel only 25—the two men worked together for many years. Both the veteran of the 1848 revolution and the young worker, who already commanded authority as organiser and proletarian orator, understood clearly that the German workers were faced with the task of setting up a truly proletarian party.

In the summer of 1866, the attention of Marx and Engels was riveted to Germany, which was on the brink of war. They sought to help the revolutionary wing of the German working-class movement stand the test of the imminent conflict. Bismarck was preparing to settle with "blood and iron" the long-standing feud between Prussia and Austria over supremacy in Germany. Anti-Prussian feeling among the masses and fear of war spurred the revolutionary elements in the working class to activity. It was important for Bismarck, therefore, to create the semblance of a defensive war, and he was trying hard to provoke Austria into attacking.

Marx, Engels and the German proletarian leaders who associated with them saw German unification in the revolutionary way as the solution to the crisis. A mass movement, in which the Union of the German Workers' Educational Societies played the leading role, spread across Germany in the spring of 1866. At a popular meeting in Leipzig, Bebel proposed a resolution formulating the militant demands of the proletariat as the leading force in the bourgeois-democratic revolution which appeared to be imminent. The demand for a united German democratic republic was also supported by the Geneva Committee of the German sections of the International, which had been founded in January 1866 by Johann Philipp Becker, one of its leading members.

War broke out between Prussia and Austria in mid-June. Expecting the Austrian troops to make a rapid advance, Marx and Engels were hoping that Prussia's military defeat would lead to a democratic revolution. However, events took a different turn. Bismarck's military reform had made the Prussian army much stronger than the Austrian, and the latter was dealt a crushing defeat at Sadowa. Prussia's victory had far-reaching consequences. The German Confederation was dissolved, and Austria was deprived of a say in deciding on the national unification of Germany. By annexing a number of small German states and setting up the North German Confederation, dominated by the Prussian monarchy, Prussia in fact secured control over the whole of Germany. The military victory also put an end to the constitutional conflict in Prussia proper, where the liberal bourgeoisie, swayed by chauvinism, completely gave in to Bismarck. Germany was being unified in the worst possible way, "from above". The Prussian militarists and Junkers exerted a growing influence in Germany. A hotbed of new military gambles had emerged in the heart of Europe, next to Bonapartist France.

On the other hand, it was also quite evident that many of the obstacles to the working-class movement arising from Germany's political fragmentation were now removed. Marx wrote: "For the workers, of course, everything that centralises the bourgeoisie is to their advantage."[1] However, in contrast to Schweitzer and the other Lassallean leaders, who gave Bismarck unconditional support, Marx and Engels saw the formation of the North German Confederation only as preparing the ground for a further and even more intense revolutionary struggle against a much stronger enemy. Engels said that the German workers and their leaders were now faced with the immediate task of making the most extensive use of the opportunities that were now available for the organisation and unification of the German proletariat *"nationally"*,[2] and for the establishment of its own political party.

INTERNATIONAL PROLETARIAT'S ECONOMIC PLATFORM

As the International grew in the various countries, the range of Marx's activities increased together with the time he had to devote to its affairs. Meanwhile, he was once again confronted with attempts to turn the International into a petty-bourgeois democratic organisation, similar to those that had been made when its first programme documents were being framed.

The opponents of the International's revolutionary proletarian

---

[1] Marx, Engels, *Collected Works*, Vol. 42, p. 300.
[2] Ibid., p. 298.

wing had ensconced themselves in the French section founded in London in the autumn of 1865. They were led by a French journalist, Pierre Vésinier, who had close ties with the emigrant followers of Mazzini and who had already attacked the General Council in the press. The French section published a new set of draft rules for the Association under which the General Council was to be abolished and replaced by a purely technical secretariat. This was only one element of the elaborate intrigues aimed at keeping Marx away from the leading role in the International. On March 6, 1866, in the absence of Marx and his closest associates, members of this group of petty-bourgeois democrats got the General Council to pass a resolution harking back to "old Mazzinism" and expressing thanks to Mazzini and Louis Wolff for their alleged services.

On March 10 the Council's Corresponding Secretaries, Dupont, Jung, Longuet, Lafargue and Bobczyński, assembled at Marx's home for a regular meeting of the Standing Committee, resolved that it was his duty to protest against that resolution at the next meeting of the Council. On March 13, despite another acute attack of his chronic complaint, Marx delivered a speech before the General Council, explaining the fundamental difference between the International's principles and those of Mazzini. The March 6 resolution was annulled. This episode showed that Marx enjoyed the support of the best representatives of the working-class movement on the continent of Europe, as well as in England.

Meanwhile, his chronic ailment had taken a turn for the worse and his doctors were adamant: they insisted on his immediate departure from London, away from its noxious fogs, away from his writing desk, and the noisy atmosphere of workers' meetings. Engels, too, firmly insisted that Marx should leave London as soon as possible and receive medical treatment.

Towards nightfall on March 15, Marx arrived at Margate, a resort on the east coast of England, which is famous for its invigorating air. This was an off-season period and the resort was deserted. He found accommodation in a private house so as to avoid the casual meetings and tiresome conversations that were inevitable in hotels and boarding-houses. He went to bed early, read as little as possible, and took long walks, working his mind up "to that state of nothingness which Buddhaism considers the element of human bliss".[1]

It did Marx good to spend almost a month at the seaside, but he kept worrying about the International. It was now April and the congress was scheduled to be held in Geneva at the end of May. The future of the International, its strategy and tactics, and the composition of its General Council depended largely on the outcome of this first congress, which was to adopt the Rules and determine the direction of its future activities.

---

[1] Marx, Engels, *Collected Works*, Vol. 42, p. 244.

The French were insisting, as they had the year before, that the congress should be held as soon as possible. Meanwhile, the English were engrossed in the reform movement, and the German sections were just being formed. Marx feared that the Paris Proudhonists would have things very much their own way in Geneva, and might be supported by some of the Swiss artisans. He was prepared to go to Paris to dissuade the local leaders from insisting on an early congress. Engels felt that, in view of the Bonapartist authorities' hostile attitude to the Association, such a trip would be too risky, and did his best to reassure his friend. But the leaders of the Geneva sections, who were to play host to the congress, had already asked the General Council to postpone the congress, because they were behind with the organisational side of the preparations. On April 10 Marx resumed his attendance of Council meetings, and was present at the meeting of May 1, when the Council decided that the congress would open on the first Monday in September 1866.

Preparations for the congress began in the summer of 1866. Marx refused to attend it. On April 23 he wrote to Engels: "I have resolved to do all that I can here to promote its success, but not to attend it in person."[1] The main reason was that Marx decided he could not possibly interrupt, for however short a period, his preparation of *Capital* for the press. On August 23, 1866, he wrote to Kugelmann: "I consider that what I am doing through this work is far more important for the working class than anything I might be able to do personally at any *congrès quelconque* [congress whatsoever]."[2] Moreover, he had already had several occasions to see that his tactics were correct: having in advance got a majority on the General Council to adopt a common stand on the matter in question, he then left them to take action by themselves in public.

Marx was also very busy preparing the organisational side of the congress. He gave final instructions to Dupont and Jung, who were leaving for Geneva, and wrote a detailed letter to Becker, strongly urging that Jung, who had a good knowledge of three languages, should be elected chairman of the congress.

A special set of Instructions drawn up by Marx on the different questions helped to prepare the London delegates ideologically for the forthcoming polemics against the petty-bourgeois spokesmen. This document was read out at the congress point by point as the General Council's report, and much of it was incorporated in the text of the congress resolutions.

In drawing up the Instructions, Marx's first concern was to encourage the workers who had joined the International to act together, stressing that the question of international combination of efforts in the struggle between labour and capital, which was on the congress agenda, essentially embraced all the activities of the International Association, which aimed at uniting the efforts of the vari-

---

[1] Ibid., p. 268.
[2] Ibid., p. 312.

ous contingents of the working class. Marx referred to a "particular function" which the Association had performed with success, namely, support of the strike movement and resistance to strike-breaking. "It is one of the great purposes of the Association to make the workmen of different countries not only *feel* but *act* as brethren and comrades in the army of emancipation." [1]

Marx also formulated proposal to institute a statistical inquiry into the condition of the working class, and his scheme of inquiry was a fine model of the methods used in obtaining social statistics. It dealt not only with the level of wages and salaries in different countries, the only thing the English trade unionists were concerned with in their projects for labour statistics, but with many other aspects, like the nature of production and the working and living conditions of various categories of workers.[2] The inquiries were to be carried out by the workers themselves (to prevent any falsification by the bourgeoisie); they were to help the workers establish their own status within the capitalist economy and consolidate international ties. The point on labour statistics was subsequently included in the General Rules, and many sections in France, Germany and Britain began to put it into practice.

With the General Council's approval, Marx included in the Instructions the demand for an eight-hour working day. In August of that year, an American Workers' Congress in Baltimore had come out in favour of the eight-hour working day. The incorporation of this demand in the International's programme turned it into a general platform for the working class of the whole world.

The item on the trade unions was the central one in the Instructions. The trade union movement, in the true sense of the term, was then just taking shape, and very few people at the time saw the fundamental distinction between such widespread forms of workers' organisation as mutual-aid and insurance societies, educational societies, choirs and sports clubs, etc., and trade unions, like those in England, which emerged on the basis of the proletariat's economic struggle against capitalist exploitation, and for that reason had an explicit class character. This matter had to be clarified, and that is precisely what Marx did in the item entitled "Trades' Unions. Their Past, Present and Future".

In drawing up the Instructions, Marx not only took account of the positive experience of the English trade unions, but also criticised their reformist leaders' limited view of their tasks, such as the narrow pragmatism which made them confine themselves to fighting for minor concessions while keeping too much aloof from "general social and political movements". In future trade unions in general must "learn to act deliberately as organising centres of the working class in the broad interest of its *complete emancipation*".[3] They

---

[1] Marx, Engels, *Collected Works*, Vol. 20, p. 186.
[2] Ibid., pp. 186-87.
[3] Ibid., pp. 191, 192.

must involve in the struggle ever broader masses of unorganised, unskilled, and the lowest paid workers, including agricultural labourers.

Lenin gave a high assessment of the resolution on the trade unions adopted by the Geneva Congress on the basis of Marx's Instructions. "The resolution adopted at that congress spoke explicitly of the importance of the economic struggle and warned the socialists and the workers, on the one hand, against exaggerating its importance (which the English workers were inclined to do at that time) and, on the other, against underestimating its importance (which the French and the Germans, particularly the Lassalleans, were inclined to do)."[1] He stressed that thanks to Marx the conviction that the class struggle must necessarily combine the political and the economic struggle into one integral whole has entered into the flesh and blood of the international proletarian movement.

While preparing for the Geneva Congress, Marx also returned to the question of co-operative societies, an important point, in view of the popularity among the workers of diverse petty-bourgeois co-operative doctrines, including Proudhon's mutualism, Lassalle's ideas of state assistance to co-operatives, and Owen's utopian co-operative recipes.

In the Instructions, Marx gave a fresh reminder that social production could be converted into "one large and harmonious system of free and co-operative labour" only as a result of the "transfer of the organised forces of society, viz., the state power, from capitalists and landlords to the producers themselves".[2] Bearing in mind, however, that numerous co-operative societies in France and Germany had already joined the International, and that participation in them was helping the workers to acquire useful organisational and economic skills, Marx included in his Instructions a number of concrete recommendations designed to prevent the workers' co-operative societies from degenerating into "ordinary middle-class joint-stock companies". He advised the workers to "embark in *co-operative production* rather than in *co-operative stores*".[3]

The points in the Instructions on juvenile and child labour were of great importance, for they called on the workers to do their utmost to safeguard the rising generation from the destructive, physical and moral, effects of the contemporary capitalist system. However, in contrast to the Proudhonists who urged that women and children should not be allowed to leave the "beneficial" influence of hearth and home, Marx argued that it was highly important for children and juveniles to take part in social production, within reasonable limits, to help them grow up as active members of society. The In-

---

[1] V. I. Lenin, *Collected Works*, Vol. 4, p. 176.
[2] Marx, Engels, *Collected Works*, Vol. 20, p. 190.
[3] Ibid.

structions substantiated the principle of polytechnical education, which combined mental, physical and technological training.

The Geneva Congress was a success. This first international workers' forum adopted the programme documents submitted by the General Council, approved its activities of the past two years, and re-elected the Council *in toto* for another term. The congress showed that in its two years the International had struck deep roots among the leading members of the European working class. This success was noted both by the bourgeois press and government circles, who now had to pay special heed to the International. Thus, in France, the congress was used by the police as a pretext for harassing members of the Association, which went on until the fall of the Second Empire.

DIFFERENCES WITH ENGLISH TRADE UNION LEADERS. THE IRISH QUESTION

After the Geneva Congress, the International consolidated its positions in all the countries, including England. This was to some extent due to the effect of the 1866-67 economic crisis, which induced the workers to look for support to the international proletarian organisation.

In the autumn of 1866 talks were started regarding the possible affiliation with the International of the London Trades Council, then at the head of the trade unions in the capital, whose membership ran to thousands. The L.T.C.'s influence on the organised proletariat extended well beyond the boundaries of London. Marx took an active part in these talks, believing that their success would be a way of revolutionising the English working class. On October 13, 1866, he wrote to Kugelmann that if the L.T.C. declared itself to be the British section of the International Association, "the control of the working class here will in a certain sense pass into our hands, and we shall be able to give the movement a good 'push on'".[1]

Although the local branches were in favour of joining the International, the decision taken under the reformist leaders' pressure was to continue co-operation with the International, but to refrain from formalising these relations organisationally.

In the spring of 1867 growing unemployment and discontent among the English workers coincided with a fresh tide in the mass movement for universal suffrage and a more vigorous struggle by the Irish for national liberation. Marx's friends on the General Council believed that a revolutionary explosion was at hand. Dupont wrote that "over 200,000 men in the provinces were merely waiting for a signal to move on London arms in hand to help the reformers".[2]

---

[1] Marx, Engels, *Collected Works*, Vol. 42, p. 329.
[2] *Procès de l'association internationale des travailleurs. Première et deuxième Commissions du Bureau de Paris*, Paris, July 1870, p. 106.

However, most of the Reform League leaders, mainly bourgeois radicals and Right-wing trade unionists, were terrified at the growth of revolutionary feeling among the masses, and accepted a curtailed Reform Bill, which gave the franchise only to the top section of the working class. The League's refusal to back up the national demands of the Irish likewise had unfavourable consequences, and reduced its support among the masses. Shortly afterwards the second Reform Bill, introduced by the Tory government, was passed by Parliament.

By means of partial concessions, the ruling classes managed to split the mass movement of the English workers. At the same time, they brutally suppressed the Irish struggle for independence: 169 participants in the March 1867 uprising were put on trial, and half of them were sentenced to hard labour. The arrests and harsh sentences continued and aroused growing resentment among the democratic-minded public. The Irish question became the central political issue in the country.

The Irish liberation movement was organised by a secret Fenian society, known as the Irish Revolutionary Brotherhood. It primarily reflected the interests of the Irish peasantry and its members came mainly from the urban middle classes and working intellectuals. Marx did not approve of the Fenians' conspiratorial tactics, and pointed out their sectarian and bourgeois-nationalistic mistakes, but greatly admired their revolutionary courage, as did Engels.

In September 1867, a group of Irish revolutionaries attacked a prison van in Manchester to release two Fenian leaders, and a policeman was killed in the clash. Five men apprehended on the spot were accused of murder and faced the death penalty. The General Council actively joined in the campaign started in England and Ireland in defence of the accused.

Marx believed that a broad discussion of the Irish question in the Council itself would help to work out a single proletarian tactical line on the national question and to spread the ideas of proletarian internationalism among the English workers. The discussion was arranged for November 19, 1867, and representatives of the English and the Irish press were invited to attend. At its special meeting on November 20 (by that time the verdict of the Manchester jury which had passed the death sentence on four of the five accused was known), the Council adopted a memorial drafted by Marx to the Home Secretary, describing the sentence as an act of political vengeance and demanding that it be commuted.

The lessons of the reform movement, the talks with the London Trades Council, and the equivocal stand of the trade union leaders, among them Odger and Lucraft, on the Irish question (for all practical purposes they shared the anti-Irish feelings of the bourgeois radicals in the Reform League, and condemned the Fenians) made it clear to Marx that although the mass of workers in England had some traditions of internationalism and proletarian solidarity they were on the whole in the grip of the reformist ideology. There was no reason to expect any revival of Chartist fervour in the near future. Meanwhile, the Irish national liberation struggle was gaining in strength, and in this context Marx modified his views of the relation between the Irish national liberation and the English working-class movement. He had formerly assumed that Ireland would be liberated as the result of a victorious proletarian revolution in England, but was now growing increasingly convinced that in the existing circumstances only a collapse of English rule in Ireland could give the English working class the necessary revolutionary impetus to make it escape from reformist influence and do away with its own bourgeoisie.

Marx was to speak in the November 26 debate, but three days earlier three of the accused had been executed, and in view of this Marx felt that solidarity with the fighters for Ireland's independence should be voiced by an Englishman. He therefore asked Peter Fox to speak.

There are notes of the speech Marx was to have delivered that day. They began by restating the right of an oppressed people to insurrection, a question of principle that had been debated on November 19. Marx had no intention at all of appealing merely to a sense of "humanity and right". Although his audience would consist of unsophisticated workers, he proposed to sketch Ireland's history using a strict economic analysis and show that since 1846 Ireland's colonial exploitation had entered a new phase—a fact that even Englishmen who, like Fox, were ardent supporters of the Irish people, had failed to understand. Behind the dry statistical data lay the tragedy of a whole nation: wholesale eviction of small tenant-farmers from the plots they had been tilling for generations; conversion into pastures of the lands seized by English landlords in the 16th and 17th centuries to meet capitalist England's demand for low-cost animal products; mass emigration of the most viable section of the Irish peasantry; a drop in population (of 2 million in 20 years); the physical degeneration of the inhabitants of Ireland, and an unprecedented growth of poverty.

As Marx put it, the new system was a "quiet business-like extinction".[1] It is not surprising, therefore, that the Irish people's struggle for independence had also assumed such acute, revolutionary forms. For the Irish the winning of independence had become a vital necessity and the only means of preventing the consequences of the destructive colonial policy conducted in the interests of the landlords and the English bourgeoisie.

The petty-bourgeois revolutionary Fenians expressed the peasants' spontaneous protest against eviction from their lands, and their struggle against the landlords. In this sense, the Fenian movement

---

[1] Marx, Engels, *Collected Works*, Vol. 21, p. 192.

had a socialist aspect. They acted as anti-clericals and republicans. All this made them natural allies of the proletariat.

What then was to be the attitude of the English working class to the Fenians? Marx's answer was quite definite. Ireland's independence would be an unmixed blessing for the English workers. Ireland's oppression helped to strengthen the position of the landlords, the ruling classes as a whole, in England itself and was used to justify the existence of a regular army which could always be turned against the workers. The low living standards of the Irish working people had an indirect effect on wages in England. The national strife, which was being fanned by the capitalists, tended to split the English proletariat and to undermine its strength. That is why, he wrote in conclusion, Ireland's independence must be "one of the articles of the English Democratic Party".[1]

The members of the General Council learned of the content of this undelivered speech, because Marx always made a point of sharing his ideas generously with his comrades. This can be seen from the speeches by Jung, Lessner and Dupont which they made on the first day of the debate at the Council meeting on November 19. A few weeks later, Marx was given an opportunity of expounding his views on the Irish question before a sizable audience of over 100 members of the German Workers' Educational Society at a meeting on December 16. Marx went into the history of Ireland's enslavement and centuries of oppression by the English. Eccarius, who was making notes of Marx's report, recorded one of the closing passages: "The Irish question is ... not simply a question of nationality, but a question of land and existence. Ruin or revolution is the watchword."[2]

WORKING FOR THE INTERNATIONAL'S SOCIALIST PROGRAMME

In guiding the International, Marx invariably linked the workers' separate demands and their diverse forms of struggle with the main aim of the proletarian movement, namely, the overthrow of capitalism and the building of a new, communist society. However, until 1868 the cardinal point of any socialist programme — the question of property relations — was not dealt with explicitly in any of the Association's documents. For the time being it was found necessary to give consideration to the illusion of the semi-artisan elements of the working class, who regarded individual ownership of the instruments of production and the land parcel as a guarantee of the petty producers' independence. But Marx expected that the way would soon be paved for an open declaration of socialist principles in the

---

[1] Ibid., p. 193.
[2] Ibid., p. 319.

International's programme, and he was sure that he could rely on the forward-looking workers.

The spread of socialist ideas among the members of the International was demonstrated by a debate on landed property, which began unexpectedly at the Lausanne Congress in September 1867. It was opened by De Paepe, who put forward the view that only radical measures, such as the conversion of land into the common property of society, could eliminate the evils of the existing economic system. Tolain and other Proudhonists came out in defence of the private ownership of land, while De Paepe was supported by the London delegates Lessner and Eccarius, Becker of Geneva, Ladendorf of Berlin, and Stumpf, an old member of the Communist League, from Mainz.

Eccarius was well prepared for the debate. In the winter of 1866-67 he had contributed a number of articles to *The Commonwealth*, which he had written with Marx's assistance and which criticised the views of the vulgar economist John Stuart Mill, including his proposal to re-establish a class of small-holders by parcelling out the communal lands.

Marx was able to take only a small part in preparing the Lausanne Congress. In April and May 1867 he was in Germany, where he had gone to deliver the manuscript of his *Capital* to the publisher, and was later engaged in reading the page-proofs. The results of the congress testified to a considerable polarisation of forces within the ranks of the International. In face of the uniting socialist elements, the Paris Proudhonists had come out as bellicose spokesmen for petty-bourgeois ideas in the working-class movement. Determining the direction of the main blow at that stage, Marx wrote to Engels: "I shall personally deliver the coup de grâce to those Proudhonist jackasses at the next congress."[1]

The publication in September 1867 of Volume One of *Capital* was highly instrumental in paving the way for a spread of socialist ideas among the workers and overcoming the influence of petty-bourgeois utopian ideas. Large-scale activity by forward-looking workers in organising the study of *Capital* and explaining its content, reviews of the book in the proletarian and democratic press—all helped to infuse a vivifying spirit into the International's ideological life. The ideas of *Capital* were best explained to working-class readers by Engels' review which appeared in March 1868 in the German working-class organ, *Demokratisches Wochenblatt*. Marx himself lectured on *Capital* at the London German Workers' Educational Society in 1867 and 1868, and quoted from it in his speeches in the General Council. Among those who helped to popularise the great work in one form or another were Johann Becker, Sorge, Dietzgen, Kugelmann, Lafargue, Schily, Lessner and Eccarius. The importance of *Capital* was explained at workers' meetings, and circles were set up

---

[1] Marx, Engels, *Collected Works*, Vol. 42, p. 423.

to study it. Liebknecht even used the rostrum of the North German Reichstag to disseminate its ideas.

The spread of the ideas of *Capital* among the proletarian masses united in the International helped them to understand scientific communism and accelerated the development of the class consciousness without which socialist principles could not have triumphed at the Brussels and subsequent congresses. A year after the appearance of *Capital*, Dietzgen wrote to Marx: "Even in the short space of time I am surveying, your ideas have had an immense influence." [1]

Early in 1868, Marx began to give considerable attention to preparations for the Brussels Congress, which was arranged for September 6-13 of that year. He strove to persuade all the members of the General Council to accept a socialist programme and to take a scientific approach to questions of socialism, the transition to which, as he pointed out, demanded definite objective economic prerequisites. At a General Council meeting on July 28, 1868, in a speech on the consequences of the use of machinery under capitalism, he said that, for all negative features of the capitalist factory system, one of the great results of machinery was the emergence of an "associated organised labour", which heralded the approach of the new social system. The draft resolution he proposed at the General Council meeting on August 11, 1868 said, in part: "The development of machinery creates the material conditions necessary for the superseding of the wages-system by a truly social system of production." [2] Marx returned to this question of the material and technical basis of the socialist system and the conditions for the transition to social labour organised on socialist lines when supporting, at this meeting, the demand for shorter working hours.

Through the letters of Eccarius, Lessner and Dupont, echoes of the London debates reached Geneva, Paris and Brussels. This was all the more important because the members of the International advocating public ownership had yet to agree on its most appropriate form. While Marx and his associates realised that property owned collectively on a national scale could ensure the conditions for the most rational, planned organisation of production, many other members, even those who professed socialist views, saw the socialisation of land and all the means of production in terms of their transfer either directly to separate groups of co-operated workers and peasants, or to rural and urban municipal councils or communes.

At first, Marx planned to deliver a report on the ownership of land at the Brussels Congress, but he soon abandoned the idea, and it was taken over by De Paepe. When preparing his report, he wrote to London for advice and various factual data. Marx's associates tried to exert an influence on De Paepe, who at the time favoured

---

[1] Dietzgen to Marx, September 12/24, 1868 (Central Party Archives of the Institute of Marxism-Leninism).
[2] Marx, Engels, *Collected Works*, Vol. 21, p. 9.

the municipalisation of land. Characteristic in this respect was a letter which Dupont wrote to De Paepe in May 1868: "I believe that the commune will disappear in the general association. Karl Marx says that what needs to be established is *economic centralisation*. I am inclined to agree with him for otherwise how is it possible to establish the harmony which must exist between all the branches of production?" [1]

In his report at the Brussels Congress, De Paepe said that capitalist development tended to bring about production on a large scale, both in industry and agriculture, and drew the conclusion that the parcel was historically doomed, and that the large-scale economy offered definite advantages. However, he left open the question about the forms of collective ownership, apparently with a view to rallying all those who favoured it in any form for a decisive battle against the advocates of small-scale private property. He said: "Time will decide the issue." Nevertheless, in his summing-up speech, voicing his personal view, he came out against municipalisation, which he had earlier advocated, and restated Dupont's line of argument almost word for word.

Despite resistance from the French Proudhonists—Tolain was again De Paepe's chief opponent—the congress declared, by a majority of 30 to 4, that "the economical development of modern society will create the social necessity of converting arable land into the common property of society". [2] The land was to be handed over for cultivation to agricultural co-operative societies on terms guaranteeing the interests both of society and of the agricultural workers. The arable land resolution was only one of the points of a general decision adopted by the congress almost without debate on turning the forests, quarries, collieries, and other mines, as well as railways and highways, canals, posts and telegraphs into the common property.

This was a major triumph for Marx's line in the International, and an important step forward towards uniting the international proletariat on a socialist platform.

QUESTIONS OF WAR AND PEACE

The question of war and peace was a central item on the agenda of the Brussels Congress. In view of the mounting danger of war in Europe in the 1860s, this question was constantly within the field of vision of the International's leaders, and was debated at its congresses, in the General Council, at workers' meetings and in the working-class press.

Marx had to work hard to help the members of the International adopt a proletarian class approach to war. It was important not

---

[1] Central Party Archives of the Institute of Marxism-Leninism.
[2] *The General Council of the First International. 1868-1870*, p. 296.

House in Brussels, 42 Rue d'Orléans, where Marx lived
(October 1846-February 1848)

Amigo prison in Brussels where Marx was incarcerated in March 1848

Letter of Flocon, member of the Provisional Government of the French Republic, inviting Marx to France

Manifest

der

Kommunistischen Partei.

Veröffentlicht im Februar 1848.

Proletarier aller Länder vereinigt euch.

London.
Gedruckt in der Office der „Bildungs-Gesellschaft für Arbeiter"
von J. E. Burghard.
46, LIVERPOOL STREET, BISHOPSGATE.

Cover of the *Manifesto of the Communist Party* (1848 edition)

Leaflet with the text of *Demands of the Communist Party in Germany*

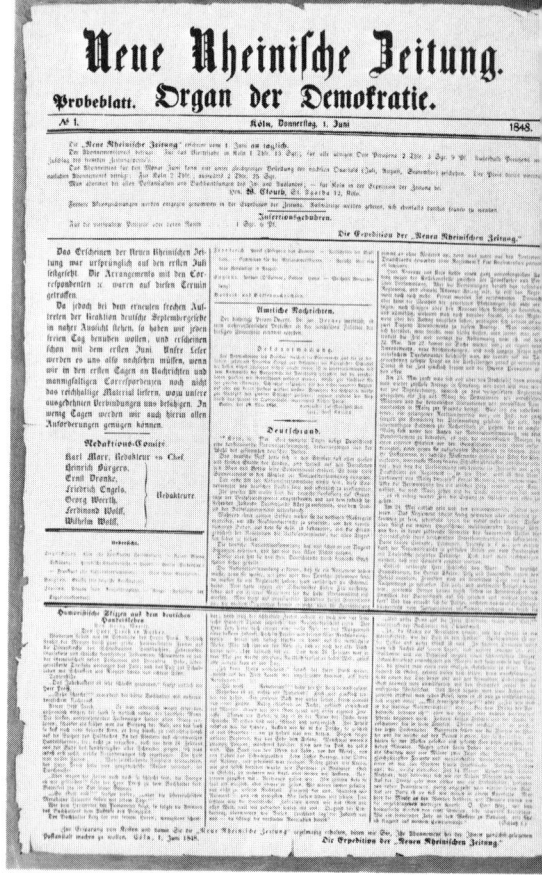

Page of the first issue of the *Neue Rheinische Zeitung*

Unter-Hutmacher Street in Cologne where the editorial office and the printing shop of the *Neue Rheinische Zeitung* were situated

Page of the last issue of the *Neue Rheinische Zeitung*

House in London, 28 Dean Street, where Marx lived from December 1850 to 1856

Jenny Marx in the 1840s

 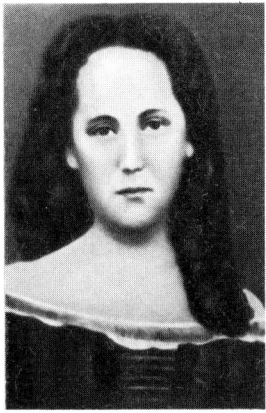 

Marx's daughters: Jenny and Laura in the 1850s and Eleanor in the 1860s

Marx's son, Edgar (Musch)

Hélène Demuth

House in London, 9 Grafton Terrace, Maitland Park, Haverstock Hill, where Marx lived from October 1856 to 1864

Reading-room of the British Museum

Joseph Weydemeyer in the 1860s

Title-page of the magazine *Die Revolution* containing Marx's work *The Eighteenth Brumaire of Louis Bonaparte*

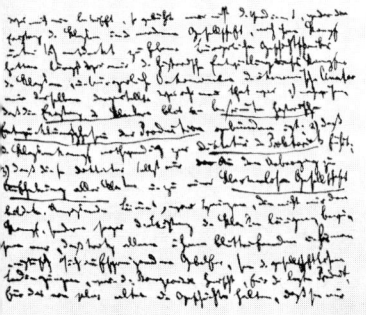

Page from Marx's letter to Weydemeyer of March 5, 1852

Page of the economic manuscripts of 1857-58

Title-page of Marx's book
A Contribution to the Critique of Political Economy

Zur Kritik

der

Politischen Oekonomie

von

Karl Marx.

Erstes Heft.

Berlin.
Verlag von Franz Duncker.
(W. Besser's Verlagshandlung.)

1859.

Marx in 1861

First editions of Volume One of *Capital* in German, Russian and French

Marx, Engels and Marx's daughters in the 1860s

only to realise clearly the need to work consistently for peace and be ready to do so, but also to be able to understand the nature of various armed conflicts, and take a tactical stand accordingly. The workers had to be warned against the pacifist illusions of the petty-bourgeois and bourgeois circles, and helped in overcoming the one-sided pacifist attitude which induced them to see any war — even a war of liberation — as an absolute evil.

The International first had a heated debate on military problems during the Austro-Prussian War of 1866. This had revealed that many members of the General Council failed to understand the dialectics of social development, notably, the need for the national unification of fragmented countries and establishment of national independence, over which many of the wars of the period had been fought. The attitudes of two men who had been the most active members of the General Council since 1866 — the journalist Charles Longuet and the medical student Paul Lafargue — were highly indicative. Both supported Marx on many issues, and Lafargue soon became one of his true disciples. However, both were under the influence of Proudhon's ideas. During the debate, Lafargue argued that nations were antiquated prejudices, that workers and socialists had no business making political demands, and that attention should be totally concentrated on countries which were already "ripe" for a social revolution. At a meeting on June 19, 1866, Marx criticised Proudhonist nihilism on the national question and in a friendly way showed Lafargue that "by his denial of nationalities he seemed quite unconsciously to imply their absorption by the model French nation".[1]

On questions of foreign policy especially, Marx insisted on a sober assessment of the situation, urging the leaders of the International to refrain from issuing loud declarations which impelled the masses to take unprepared action, and from reckless calls for importing revolution. In a letter to Engels, Marx stressed that "one must ... above all prevent any demonstration which would involve our Association in a one-sided course".[2] That was, in fact, the tenor of the resolution which the Council adopted on July 17, 1866, following the debate in which Marx was one of the main speakers. The resolution placed the responsibility for the war entirely on the governments, and the international proletariat's independent stand in this instance was expressed in its refusal to take sides. By urging the workers to "acquire strength by unity and to use the strength so acquired in working out their social and political emancipation",[3] the General Council resolution encouraged them to consolidate their class organisation as the only real means of resisting the policy of the ruling classes.

In the summer of 1867, the General Council was faced with the

---

[1] Marx, Engels, *Collected Works*, Vol. 42, p. 287.
[2] Ibid.
[3] *The General Council of the First International. 1864-1866*, p. 213.

question of what attitude the International should adopt to the League of Peace and Freedom, an international pacifist organisation then being established. The League's Organisation Committee, on which French democrats held sway, had secured the support of prominent radical and democratic leaders — Mill, Hugo, Garibaldi and Bakunin — and Marx also received a personal invitation to attend the League's constituent congress in Geneva.

Marx opposed on principle the sectarian tendency to isolate the mass of workers from general democratic movements, for he believed that participation in such movements helped them to become aware of their role as the leading class and the vanguard force of social progress. However, it must also be clearly understood that the proletarian and the bourgeois democrats had both common and different class purposes. Joint action with bourgeois democrats should never jeopardise the proletariat's independent class organisation.

Accordingly, on August 13, 1867, Marx took a resolute stand in the General Council against the International's official participation in the League's congress, believing that it would help to strengthen the authority of the bourgeois pacifists and to confirm the illusion that war could be abolished under the capitalist system. He said: "Those who declined putting their shoulders to the wheel to bring about a transformation in the relations of labour and capital ignored the very conditions of universal peace." [1] But taking account of the fact that the establishment of the League reflected the anti-war mood of broad masses of people and the bourgeois intelligentsia, Marx proposed that the Council should, without sending its official delegates to the League congress, recommend that members of the International should attend the congress in their individual capacity, to demonstrate the workers' readiness to fight against militarism, while taking a firm stand for the proletarian line on this question.

Marx's proposed tactics with respect to the League of Peace and Freedom were confirmed by the decisions of the Brussels Congress, which rejected the League's claim to unite all the anti-war forces, including the working class, under the banner of bourgeois pacifism and sentimental cosmopolitan talk about a brotherhood of nations. The congress reaffirmed the International's leading role in the struggle for peace and said in its resolution that the League of Peace and Freedom "has no *raison d'être* in the presence of the efforts of the International Working Men's Association". [2] Members of the League were invited to join the International's sections in their respective countries. On the other hand, a readiness was expressed on the part of the members of the International to collaborate with other progressive organisations.

Another important resolution adopted by the Brussels Congress concerned the attitude the proletariat was to take in the event of

---

[1] *The General Council of the First International. 1866-1868*, p. 152.
[2] *The General Council of the First International. 1868-1870*, p. 297.

a European war. In his instructions to Eccarius and Lessner, who were attending the Congress in Brussels, Marx wrote: "The decision to be taken ... would seem to be simply that the working class is not yet sufficiently organised to throw any decisive weight on to the scales; that, however, the congress protests in the name of the working class, and denounces those who instigate war; that a war between France and Germany is a civil war, ruinous for both countries and for Europe as a whole." [1]

The resolution adopted by the Brussels Congress for the most part directed the workers along correct lines and reflected the ideas of Marx and his followers. Proceeding from the fact that the exploitative system was a constant source of wars, the congress recognised that these could be eliminated for good only by thorough social reform. But even with the existing state of things, the number of wars and the scale of the disasters caused by wars could be diminished if the peoples, particularly the workers of the various countries, used all the real means at their disposal to resist the governments and to expose their policy of aggrandisement.

This section of the resolution summed up the results of the three-year debate within the International on the question of war and peace. However, at the insistence of the Belgian delegates, the resolution included a recommendation that if a war broke out, the workers should declare a general strike, a proposal which substituted a declarative and virtually unrealisable slogan that could only confuse the workers for a concrete analysis of any armed conflict. Marx called this proposal an "absurdity". [2]

However, the fact that the documents of the International contained some immature propositions did not in any sense detract from its historic, pioneering role in the struggle for peace. This struggle sprang from the very nature of the system the proletariat sought to establish, and was adopted as a point in the programme of the international working-class movement. A General Council Address to the National Labour Union of the United States, which Marx wrote on May 12, 1869, foresaw a time when "the working classes are bestriding the scene of history no longer as servile retainers, but as independent actors, conscious of their own responsibility, and able to command peace where their would-be masters shout war". [3]

THE BIRTH OF THE FIRST MASS MARXIST PARTY

Marx and Engels were always pleased when their conclusions and tactical plans coincided, and this was particularly evident when they were dealing with the problems of the German working-class movement. To ease Marx's heavy burden, Engels took over some of the

---

[1] Marx, Engels, *Collected Works*, Vol. 43, p. 94.
[2] Ibid., p. 102.
[3] Ibid., Vol. 21, p. 54.

work involved in establishing contacts with proletarian leaders in Germany. Now and again, his personal letters to them contained advice and remarks couched in highly outspoken terms that would have been inconceivable in the official correspondence of a General Council Corresponding Secretary.

In 1867, forward-looking German workers won a major success when two of their best men, Liebknecht and Bebel, were elected deputies to the North German Reichstag, thus giving the German working class a national rostrum. On October 17, 1867, Liebknecht declared to the ranting Right-wing deputies: "As I speak from the only place where freedom of speech exists in the whole of Prussia, I am not addressing you.... I am addressing the people outside." [1]

Liebknecht's speeches and his bold criticism of Bismarck's regime and its constitutional guise, the "fig-leaf of absolutism", gave Marx much pleasure, and on October 4 he wrote to Engels that Liebknecht "has done us proud with his first intervention in the Reichstag". [2] However, Marx observed that while attacking the Lassalleans, who acted as apologists for Bismarck's policy, Liebknecht was occasionally inclined to go to the other extreme: his anti-Prussian feeling impelled him to make considerable concessions to the petty-bourgeois democrats of the central and southern German states, which could cause him to deviate from his class line. At Marx's request, Engels advised Liebknecht in a letter that he should attack not only the Prussians, but also their opponents, the Austrians, the Federalists and all the other supporters of the small states.

The International's influence on the German workers and their urge for international unity led to growing discontent with the leadership within the General Association of German Workers. This induced Schweitzer to make fresh efforts to establish contacts with Marx. In the *Social-Demokrat* he published articles about *Capital* and wrote to London for advice on the forthcoming discussion in the Reichstag of the protective duties on German iron and steel products. As Schweitzer was a deputy from Berlin, one of the most developed industrial areas, Marx felt it necessary to reply. On the substance of the matter, he believed that the German iron and steel industry was strong enough to do without protectionist tariffs, but the acceptance of lower tariffs should be made conditional on the demand for a parliamentary inquiry into enterprises in the industry, including the condition of the workers. That is exactly what Marx advised Schweitzer to do in a letter written in a deliberately business-like tone so as not to give the recipient any pretext for boasting of his "intimacy" with the author of *Capital*.

The next step Schweitzer took was to place on the agenda of the congress (general meeting) of the General Association of German Workers, which was to be held in Hamburg, an item about the atti-

---

[1] *Die I. Internationale in Deutschland*, Berlin, 1964, S. 186.
[2] Marx, Engels, *Collected Works*, Vol. 42, p. 433.

tude to be taken to the International, and a report on Volume One of *Capital*. On July 6, 1868, the governing body of the Association, headed by Schweitzer, sent Marx an official invitation to attend the congress as a guest of honour, in view of the "outstanding services which you have rendered to the workers' cause by your book".[1] In his reply to Schweitzer, Marx said urgent business in the General Council did not allow him to leave London, and expressed his satisfaction over the inclusion in the agenda of the congress of an item on the international co-operation of the working class and other important "points from which, in fact, any serious workers' movement must proceed".[2] This was an indirect way of congratulating the Association's leaders for repudiating many Lassallean dogmas. The letter, which Marx had expressly written for publication, appeared in the *Social-Democrat* on August 28, 1868.

The Lassallean congress was held from August 22 to 26. Reports were given on *Capital* by the Brunswick publisher Wilhelm Bracke, and on the attitude to the International, by Leonhard von Bonhorst and Karl Hirsch. All three speakers were among the leaders of the opposition to Schweitzer. Within a few months, they had broken with the General Association of German Workers and had adopted Liebknecht's and Bebel's platform. But at the time they were still hoping to isolate Schweitzer and to direct the Association along a new path. However, Schweitzer skilfully manoeuvred between the opposition and the orthodox Lassalleans. With the help of the latter, he managed to get a resolution passed on the international character of the working-class movement which was nothing but a general declaration.

Within a few days, on September 5, 1868, the League of German Workers' Societies, headed by Bebel, met at Nuremberg, marking the break between the majority of the League's members who firmly adopted a proletarian class stand and the liberal bourgeoisie. By 69 votes to 46, the delegates adopted the platform of the International as briefly formulated in the new programme of the League put before the congress.

Robert Schweichel, who reported on the main question, gave the gist of this platform with references to *Capital* and declared that the workers could secure their emancipation only by winning political power and only by taking "a firm stand with the workers of all countries".[3]

The debate revealed that the delegates were familiar with the International's programme documents. This was largely the result of a pamphlet entitled *The International Working Men's Association* written by the Berlin socialist Wilhelm Eichhoff, which had appeared shortly before. Marx had not only supplied the author with facts and original sources, but had thoroughly edited many pages of his

---

[1] *Die I. Internationale in Deutschland*, S. 742.
[2] Marx, Engels, *Collected Works*, Vol. 42, p. 433.
[3] *Die I. Internationale in Deutschland*, S. 243.

pamphlet. Eichhoff was present at the Nuremberg Congress and was the first to report to London on the triumph of the International's principles.

Marx made haste to formalise the League's affiliation with the International. The General Council's first meeting, after the Brussels Congress, on September 22 appointed the governing body of the League to act as the International's Executive Committee for Germany, and also officially empowered Liebknecht in Leipzig and Eichhoff in Berlin to spread the International's ideas and set up its sections.

Ahead lay more struggle to overcome Lassallean influence among the workers. But it was also necessary to protect them from the influence exerted by the petty-bourgeois People's Party of Saxony. This had been set up in August 1866, with the direct participation of Bebel and Liebknecht, and its members included many workers, but it had a bourgeois-democratic programme. Liebknecht also enjoyed the support of the Saxony democrats in his journalistic activities: his weekly, the *Demokratisches Wochenblatt*, bore the words "Organ of the People's Party". Now and again he found his freedom of action limited because of a certain ideological and political dependence on the People's Party.

In a letter to Kugelmann, Engels gave this analysis of the state of affairs in the German working-class movement: "The dissolution of the Lassallean sect and, on the other hand, the severance of the Saxon and South German workers from the leading-strings of the 'People's Party' are the two fundamental conditions for the new formation of a genuine German workers' party." [1]

Marx soon sharply criticised Schweitzer's tactics. At the end of September 1868, Schweitzer called a congress in Berlin to set up trade unions. He was seeking to forestall Bebel and Liebknecht in establishing trade unions, so as to give the Lassallean organisation support among the workers. However, delegates from the Lassallean trade unions alone were admitted to the Berlin Congress, and this was evidence that Schweitzer was pursuing his old sectarian line.

In a letter addressed to Schweitzer on October 13, Marx frankly stated his views on the difference between the sectarian movement and the class movement. He criticised Schweitzer's plan for a strictly centralised trade union organisation subordinate to a presidential dictatorship — very much in Lassallean style. Such a structure clashed with the essence of the trade union movement, and was least of all desirable in Germany. "Here, where the worker is regulated bureaucratically from childhood onwards, where he believes in authority, in those set over him, the main thing is *to teach him to walk by himself*." [2] Marx stressed that the working-class movement could not develop without democracy.

---

[1] Marx, Engels, *Collected Works*, Vol. 43, p. 313.
[2] Ibid., p. 134.

In the course of the spring and summer of 1869, ever more numerous groups of rank-and-file members of Lassallean organisations joined the opposition and supported its leader, Wilhelm Bracke. On the initiative of Bebel and Liebknecht, a general congress was to be held in Eisenach in August of representatives of the Nuremberg majority of educational societies, trade unions, delegates of the German sections of the International and delegates of the branches of the General Association of German Workers which had broken with Schweitzer.

Marx had no intention of going to Eisenach, although Liebknecht insisted that he and Engels should "show themselves to the German workers". Marx believed that the break with Lassallean doctrine and organisational principles should come as "a free action by the workers".[1] Moreover, the platform on which the unification was to take place gave Marx cause for concern, because it showed a residual influence of petty-bourgeois ideas. Indeed, the programme adopted by the Eisenach Congress, held from August 7 to 9, 1869, was not free from vulgar-democratic views and also showed traces of Lassallean dogmas. But in the main it was based on the principles written into the International's programme documents. That was the first occasion on which a basically Marxist programme was adopted by a mass working-class party emerging on a country-wide scale. The publication of the Eisenach programme and the establishment of the Social-Democratic Workers' Party marked a major victory for the ideas of scientific communism, and opened a new page in the history of Marxism and the international working-class movement.

In other countries too there was evidence of a tendency for the working class to consolidate itself on a national scale and unite under the banner of Marxism. This was promoted by the Rules of the International Working Men's Association, which set the task of uniting workers' societies into national organisations. Marx worked tirelessly to help the leaders of the working-class movement become aware of this objective process and promote its success.

START OF STRUGGLE AGAINST BAKUNINISM

The Brussels resolutions on common property showed that in the four years of their joint activity a majority of the International's members had forged a common view of the goal of the proletariat's struggle, namely, the creation of a socialist society. Marx was now faced with the task of getting them to accept a common view on the ways of achieving this goal. However, on the question of the motive forces of the socialist revolution, the hegemony of the proletariat, its dictatorship, and the proletarian party, he inevitably faced even

---

[1] Ibid., p. 304.

more acute clashes with the representatives of the petty-bourgeois trends, anarchism in particular.

Anarchist and individualistic attitudes among the workers were encouraged by the small-scale production which still prevailed in some industries in many countries. That was the soil from which there spread among members of the International in Switzerland, Spain and Italy a rebellious anarchism, or "revised Proudhonism", which was connected with the name of Mikhail Bakunin, a Russian revolutionary Narodnik and a man of many talents who had taken part in the revolutionary battles of 1848-49. He had been imprisoned in Austrian and tsarist gaols, and had but recently escaped from exile in Siberia. His reappearance on the international scene intensified the internal struggle within the International.

When in the autumn of 1864 Marx learned from Lessner that Bakunin had arrived in London, he expressed a desire to see him. The two men met on November 3, 1864, and the following day Marx wrote to Engels: "I liked him very much, more so than previously.... On the whole, he is one of the few people whom after 16 years I find to have moved forwards and not backwards." [1] Bakunin was going to Italy and promised Marx that he would establish contacts with Italian workers who could be relied upon in an acute struggle against the Mazzini group. At the end of November, Marx sent Bakunin several copies of the Inaugural Address and the Provisional Rules, and continued to count on Bakunin's support. In 1867 he asked for Bakunin's address from Johann Becker to send him a copy of Volume One of *Capital*. All this shows that for a long time Marx sincerely liked Bakunin and regarded him as an ally and possible associate.

Meanwhile, Bakunin's stay in Italy from 1865 to 1867 was a period in which his anarchist views crystallised. They were a reflection of the economic backwardness prevailing in Russia after the 1861 Reform, and were given a fresh impetus by life in Italy, where the working people were growing poorer, and where the proletarian movement was in the process of branching off from the general democratic tide. Bakunin moved among radical-minded bourgeois intellectuals, mainly young people, from among whom he recruited his first followers and united them in his secret International Brotherhood.

Bakunin's anarchism—a brand of petty-bourgeois socialism— expressed the despair of the downtrodden and oppressed masses of people, the peasantry and the petty bourgeoisie, who had lost faith in the bourgeois political leaders and were incapable of finding their own way to an organised class struggle. Hence, his lashing criticism of social inequality and exploitation, his impassioned advocacy of socialism, his calls for world revolution which went hand in hand with extreme individualism, his demands for "absolute" freedom

---

[1] Marx, Engels, *Collected Works*, Vol. 42, pp. 18, 19.

and autonomy, and his denial of all discipline and all authority. Bakunin was familiar with some of Marx's writings and in 1869 translated the *Manifesto of the Communist Party* into Russian. However, he ignored the historico-materialist view of social development, the regularities underlying the succession of socio-economic formations, the proletariat's role in the socialist revolution, the whole range of concepts which, through Marx's tireless efforts, were being accepted by progressive European workers in the ranks of the International.

It was the state, and not capital or the system of wage labour, that Bakunin designated as the main evil to be fought. He saw the state as the root of all inequality and exploitation. In contrast to socialist revolution, prepared by the whole course of capitalist development and proletarian struggle, Bakunin advocated spontaneous "social liquidation", "the destruction of all the states, national and territorial".[1] He declared that the motive force behind this "liquidation" was to be provided by the *déclassé* elements: the lumpenproletariat and the Bohemian intellectuals. He saw the future social order as a conglomeration of isolated, autonomous communities, set apart from each other and free from any obligatory bonds.

Bakunin also opposed any mass organisation of the revolutionary forces, insisting that an uprising could be started by the efforts of individual revolutionaries who would fire the people with the spirit of rebellion. However, to co-ordinate their efforts he allowed the existence of a strictly secret organisation consisting of a handful of revolutionary conspirators. While urging instant revolutionary action, Bakunin declared any political activity to be harmful if it did not lead directly to revolution. This was merely a revival in a new form of Proudhon's dogma of abstaining from political struggle.

Bakunin regarded a fully-formed international organisation like the Working Men's Association as a suitable field for spreading his anarchist views and set himself the aim of securing control of it. In 1867 he was one of those who suggested the merger of the International and the bourgeois pacifist League of Peace and Freedom. When this project fell through, Bakunin established an International Alliance of Socialist Democracy in Geneva in the autumn of 1868, and asked the General Council to admit it to the International. Its muddled programme and rules declared the Alliance to be a branch of the International and simultaneously its ideological leader, while continuing as an autonomous entity outside its ranks. Alongside such points as the abolition of religion, liquidation of the state and so on, they contained two demands which soon became the focus of the proletarian revolutionaries' struggle against Bakuninism. These were the abolition of the right of inheritance, which the Bakuninists regarded as a means of transferring land into common property, and rejection of political action.

Marx proposed that the General Council should, without allow-

---

[1] *La première Internationale. Recueil de documents*, t. II, *Le Congrès de Bâle*, Geneva, 1962, p. 67.

ing itself to be drawn into polemics on the various points, refuse admission on the grounds that, in accordance with the International's Rules, membership was open only to local and national organisations, not international ones.

On February 27, 1869, the Alliance again wrote to the General Council expressing readiness to disband its international organisation if the General Council admitted its individual sections as members.

The scheme was a transparent one. On March 5, 1869, Marx wrote to Engels: "Bakunin thinks: if we approve his 'programme radical' he can trumpet it forth and compromise us *tant soit peu*. [1] If we declare ourselves against it, we shall be denounced as counter-revolutionaries." [2]

The reply written by Marx to the Alliance is a fine specimen of principled tactics in the struggle for working-class unity. It said that since the International admitted all workers' societies aiming at "the protection, advancement and complete emancipation of the working classes", it was not within the functions of the General Council to make a detailed examination of the programmes of prospective members. It only had the duty to find out whether or not they contained anything running counter to the General Rules. In the Alliance programme, this was the demand for the "political, economical and social *equalisation... of classes*", which was tantamount to the bourgeois slogan of the *"Harmony of Capital and Labour"*. Marx wrote: "It is not the logically impossible 'equalisation of classes', but the historically necessary, superseding 'abolition of classes', this true secret of the proletarian movement, which forms the great aim of the International Working Men's Association." [3] The sections of the Alliance, following the dissolution of its international organisation, could join the International under the General Rules, provided they duly amended their programme.

The terms Marx put forward on behalf of the General Council were officially accepted by the Alliance leaders but, as subsequent events showed, these were never observed. Following the formal dissolution of the Alliance in May 1869, its Geneva group was constituted as a section of the International under the title of "Alliance of Socialist Democracy. Central Section". It included the most prominent Bakuninists, and it was this section that, for all practical purposes, exercised leadership of the international Alliance, which the Bakuninists maintained as a secret organisation within the International.

At the time Marx had no knowledge either of the existence of the secret, conspiratorial Bakuninist International Brotherhood, or of the fact that the international Alliance was still functioning. Nevertheless, he saw through Bakunin's subversive tactics, and expected

---

[1] However little.
[2] Marx, Engels, *Collected Works*, Vol. 43, p. 235.
[3] Ibid., Vol. 21, p. 46.

a serious clash with him at the next congress of the International at Basle. Marx's speeches in the General Council show the lines along which he believed it necessary to orient the delegates to the future congress.

When the agrarian question was discussed on July 6, 1869, Marx resisted the attempts to support the idea of land nationalisation by references to the peasants' "natural right", as opposed to the usurpation of the landlords. In contrast to these idealistic concepts typical of petty-bourgeois socialist doctrines, Marx gave a historico-materialist substantiation of the International's programme demands, equipping the General Council delegates with the necessary arguments for the polemic against Bakunin. Marx showed that the agrarian programme of the working class should be based not on some abstract "natural right", but on consideration of the real processes of social development which tended to convert the peasant into nothing more than a nominal proprietor, leaving him only one way of escaping poverty and ruin, namely, the socialist transformation of society on the basis of co-operated labour and large-scale social production, both industrial and agricultural.

Marx saw a close connection between the peasant question and the abolition of the right of inheritance, an item included in the agenda of the congress on a proposal by the Geneva Bakuninists. At a General Council meeting on July 20, 1869, Marx made a critical analysis of the Bakuninist claim that the abolition of the right of inheritance was a starting-point for the social revolution. He explained that the laws of inheritance, like all juridical institutions, are not the cause but the effect of the social order. The task of the proletariat is first and foremost to work for the abolition of private property in the means of production, which constitutes the economic basis of capitalist society, and not merely for the abolition of its juridical superstructure. He said: "If the working class had sufficient power to abolish the right to inheritance, it would be powerful enough to proceed to expropriation which would be a much simpler and more efficient process." [1]

Having shown the Bakuninist thesis to be theoretically untenable, Marx drew attention to the danger and harm it could cause in the light of the proletarian organisation's tactics. Just when the International was faced with the urgent task of securing influence in the countryside, Bakunin was putting forward a sectarian slogan which would merely alienate the peasantry and throw it into the arms of the enemies of the working class. Marx subsequently wrote to Lafargue: "The proclamation of the *abolition of inheritance* would be not a serious act, but a foolish menace, rallying the whole peasantry and the whole small middle class round the reaction." [2]

At the request of the General Council, Marx put the gist of his speech in writing to be read at the congress. In preparing the Gene-

---

[1] Ibid., pp. 395-96.
[2] Ibid., Vol. 43, p. 490.

ral Council report on the right of inheritance, Marx concentrated on criticising Bakunin's idealistic views, and by way of contrast stated the principal concepts of historical materialism and the theory of proletarian revolution. That was the first time that a document of the International had formulated revolutionary ideas in the light of materialist philosophy. It is highly indicative that at this stage Marx found it useful to introduce the leaders of the International to the philosophical substantiation of the concept of the proletarian revolution, the need for which he had argued earlier on the strength of more commonplace economic facts.

BASLE CONGRESS. INTERNATIONAL'S TACTICS ON THE PEASANT QUESTION

The followers of Marx and Bakunin clashed openly at the Basle Congress, held September 6-11, 1869, especially over the question of the state and the related question of political struggle. Thus, during the debate on the agenda, Bakunin and the Belgian delegate Eugen Hins attacked the idea of workers' participation in parliamentary activity as being anti-revolutionary in principle. This view was resolutely opposed by Liebknecht. Informing Marx of this episode, Lessner wrote: "Yesterday afternoon a heated debate ensued ... and in the course of it *Bakunin* displayed his antipathy for any political action. However, *Liebknecht, Rittinghausen* and others gave him a good drubbing; even after the meeting he continued to roar like a wild lion. Most of the French came out against him."[1] In their polemics with Bakunin, Marx's associates insisted that the proletariat should fight to win state power.

The Basle Congress, which once again supported the abolition of private property in land, fully reaffirmed the International's socialist platform. This decision caused a real storm in the bourgeois press, but was the source of much satisfaction in the International's sections. The Basle resolutions began to be popularised in all countries. In England, for instance, a Land and Labour League was set up with the participation of the General Council. Its programme was drawn up by Eccarius, who had the benefit of Marx's advice.

The polemics in the German press over the Basle resolutions helped the young Social-Democratic Workers' Party to formulate the correct tactics with respect to the peasantry and the petty-bourgeois People's Party. In the course of this, Marx and Engels discovered that Liebknecht and his comrades were not quite clear on the importance of socialist propaganda in the countryside. Accordingly, Engels decided to write a special preface for the second edition of his work *The Peasant War in Germany*. This he did in early February 1870, and it was published separately in the Party's central organ,

---

[1] Friedrich Lessner to Karl Marx, September 7, 1869 (Central Party Archives of the Institute of Marxism-Leninism).

Volksstaat, in April. Engels had dicussed the main points of his preface in his correspondence with Marx. In the preface he explained the importance of the Basle resolutions for a country like Germany, where rural producers made up a sizable part of the population. He warned that under capitalism it was wrong to regard the peasantry as a homogeneous mass, and stressed that it consisted of different strata each of which required specific consideration, if a firm alliance were to be established with the toiling majority in the countryside in contrast to its wealthy capitalist elements.

INTERNATIONAL IMPORTANCE OF THE IRISH QUESTION

The differences between the Marxist wing of the International, on the one hand, and the Bakuninist sectarians and the reformist elements on the General Council, on the other, spread to the International's tactics on the national question, in particular, the attitude to the Irish national liberation movement. A broad movement demanding an amnesty for the imprisoned Fenians started in Ireland and England in the summer of 1869. A mammoth protest demonstration and meeting took place in London's Hyde Park on October 24 and Marx attended it. In the General Council, he had again brought up the Irish question for discussion, accentuating two of its aspects: 1) the attitude of the British government to the Irish amnesty question; and 2) the attitude of the English working class towards the Irish question in general.

The new discussion on the Irish question on November 16, 23 and 30, 1869 was held in a different atmosphere from the one which had prevailed in 1867. The opponent was no longer a Tory government, with which everyone was dissatisfied, but the liberal Gladstone, a more subtle adversary who flirted with the trade unions and in Ireland combined a policy of reprisals with partial reform. In a long speech opening the discussion on the first point, Marx exposed Gladstone's hypocrisy and proved that his policy was in blatant contradiction to his lavish declarations during the election campaign.Gladstone's terms for an amnesty demanded of the Fenians complete and humiliating surrender.

The resolution proposed by Marx said that "Mr. Gladstone deliberately insults Irish Nation".[1] Attempts to vindicate Gladstone were made by Odger and other reformist trade union leaders, but all they managed to do was to have the word "deliberately" deleted from the final text.

The trade union newspaper, *The Bee-Hive*, stubbornly refused to report the General Council's statements, but the debate and Marx's speeches were given wide coverage in the International's press in

---
[1] Marx, Engels, *Collected Works*, Vol. 21, p. 83.

Switzerland, Belgium and Germany. On November 29, 1869, Marx wrote to Kugelmann: "You will probably have seen in the *Volksstaat* the resolutions I proposed regarding Gladstone on the Irish amnesty question. I have now attacked Gladstone—and this has attracted attention here—just as I attacked Palmerston earlier. The demagogic refugees here love to attack the continental despots from a safe distance. I find this only attractive if it is done *vultu instantis tyranni* [in the face of the tyrant]." [1]

To help expose British policy in Ireland, Marx sent material to De Paepe in Brussels which he published in the newspaper *L'Internationale* on February 27 and March 6, 1870. With the same end in view, Marx's daughter, Jenny, wrote with his help eight articles for the Paris *La Marseillaise* in February, March and April 1870. The General Council's steps in support of the Irish independence movement drew the Irish workers' attention to the International and paved the way for the establishment of Irish sections.

The second point—the attitude of the English working class towards the Irish—was not discussed because Marx fell ill and was unable to attend Council meetings for almost three months, from mid-January 1870 onwards. However, he had given a profound substantiation of the International's stand on this question in a confidential circular letter which the General Council wrote in view of the Bakuninists' attacks.

After the Basle Congress, Bakunin and his supporters launched an open war against Marx and the General Council. In November and December 1869, they started a campaign against the Council in the Geneva *L'Egalité*, which had the Bakuninist, Paul Robin, on its editorial board. The Council was accused of breaking the Rules, refusing to set up a special Federal Council for England, and imposing on the international working-class movement "irrelevant" issues, like the Irish question, in detriment to the proletariat's international interests.

The Council discussed the *Egalité* articles on December 14, 1869 and decided to issue a refutation in a circular letter to the Federal Council of Romance Switzerland, which was written by Marx and adopted by the Council at a special meeting on January 1, 1870. It contained a rebuttal of all the Bakuninists' inventions and explained above all that the proposal to set up a Federal Council in England, like those in other countries, had been repeatedly put forward in the General Council, but had invariably been judged untimely in view of the existing conditions. In fact, Marx wrote, a Federal Council in England would find itself somewhere between the General Council and the London Trades Council, and would enjoy no authority at all, while preventing the General Council from exerting a direct influence on the English working class. With revolutionary events coming to a head in Europe, it was necessary to consider Eng-

---

[1] Marx, Engels, *Collected Works*, Vol. 43, p. 390.

land's specific position as the metropolis of capital, as a country virtually without any peasantry and with wage-workers constituting a vast majority of the population, a fact that turned her into a *"great lever of the proletarian revolution"*. It would be more than folly, it would be a crime to lose control of this lever.[1]

The special role which the strategy of the proletariat's international struggle then assigned to the English working-class movement also added international importance to the Irish people's liberation struggle. Marx dealt in detail with this aspect of the question, emphasising that the liberation struggle of oppressed peoples played a highly important role as an element in the overall revolutionary process. The Irish national liberation movement was an ally of the English and consequently of the international proletariat. A revolutionary solution of the Irish question would also be a precondition to the emancipation of the English working class, which for its part would hasten the proletarian revolution in the other countries as well. That was why the International's watchword on the Irish question should be "to transform the present *forced union* (i. e., the enslavement of Ireland) into *equal and free confederation* if possible, into *complete separation* if need be".[2]

The circular ended with a request that the Romance Federal Council should make its content known to all its sections. The text of the letter was also conveyed by Marx to Belgium and by Dupont to France. On March 28, 1870, Marx, having added a preface and a conclusion, sent it as a "Confidential Communication" to Germany for the members of the Committee of the Eisenach Party. Marx also gave a detailed summary of this most important document in his letters to Paul Lafargue, and to Sigfrid Meyer and August Vogt, members of the International in New York, where its sections had been taking shape since 1869, involving considerable numbers of Irish emigrant workers.

Before the circular letter arrived in Geneva, the editorial board of *L'Egalité* had been reorganised, and no longer included Bakunin's supporters. Becker, who had earlier supported the Bakuninists on some points, before he fully understood their doctrine and tactics, finally broke with them, and Bakunin himself, having lost his hold on the local workers, left Geneva. From then on, the mountain area of the Swiss Jura became the citadel of Bakuninism.

GENERAL COUNCIL CORRESPONDING SECRETARY FOR RUSSIA

During his work in the International, Marx continued to keep a close watch on the foreign policy of tsarist Russia, which even after her defeat in the Crimean War continued to exert considerable

---

[1] Ibid., Vol. 21, p. 87.
[2] Ibid., p. 89.

influence on international affairs. Marx also felt a growing need to know more about life in post-Reform Russia. As an economist, he took a great interest in the socio-economic relations of this vast peasant country, which had embarked on the road of capitalist development.

When studying the Russian countryside, Marx concentrated on the various facts and features of everyday life, which refuted the view about the exclusive nature of the Russian village commune, a view which the Western press then connected chiefly with the name of Alexander Herzen, the great Russian revolutionary writer. Marx treated Herzen with suspicion because of the latter's inclination towards liberalism, his intimacy with West-European bourgeois democrats, who were then opposed to any independent working-class movement, and his friendly relations with Bakunin. Marx was not aware that in 1869, towards the end of his life, Herzen had "turned his gaze, not to liberalism, but to the *International*",[1] as Lenin subsequently observed; that he spoke with deep respect and hope about the international proletarian organisation, and expressed doubts about the views of his old friend Bakunin, complaining that the latter had set him at odds with the "Marxides".

For a long time Marx and the men around him were aware of no other trend in revolutionary Russian circles except Herzen's. Marx did have a general knowledge of the peasant disturbances, the rise of the Russian revolutionary movement in the late 1850s and early 1860s, and its suppression by the tsarist government. In his speech at the London Conference of the International in 1865, De Paepe referred to the struggle which had started in Russia under the slogan of "land and freedom". But it was unlikely that either of the two men had any detailed knowledge about the activities of the secret revolutionary society set up in St. Petersburg in the early 1860s under that name, or about the men who led and took part in it. At the time, Marx appears to have been unaware of Chernyshevsky's name, his arrest, his public punishment in the spring of 1864, and his exile to Siberia. Nor had he then received — or taken note of — the reports about the serious disagreements between Herzen and a group of young emigrants, including Nikolai Utin, later a member of the International, and Alexander Serno-Solovyevich, a talented organiser and journalist, which had started in the winter of 1864-65. At one time, both men had been among the leaders of the Land and Freedom organisation and followers of Chernyshevsky. They had been connected with Herzen and his group, but had not seen eye to eye with him on the tasks of the revolutionary struggle. Serno-Solovyevich came to live in Geneva, took an active part in the local working-class movement, and in 1866 issued a pamphlet in Russian, entitled *Our Domestic Affairs*, describing the controversy between the two generations of Russian revolutionaries.

---

[1] V.I. Lenin, *Collected Works*, Vol. 18, p. 27.

It was something of a revelation when Sigismund Borkheim, a German journalist who knew Marx well, stopped over in Geneva in September 1867 and was told by a casual companion about the existence of the "Russian republicans and socialists". Marx wrote to Engels that Borkheim had "discovered Serno".[1] Upon his return to London, Borkheim told Marx about the Russian pamphlet. On October 14, he sent a copy of it to Engels in Manchester, and the same day wrote to Serno-Solovyevich suggesting that he translate it into German and requesting additional information about Russian revolutionaries and their writings. This meant Nikolai Chernyshevsky and Nikolai Dobrolyubov, as Serno-Solovyevich's reply, dated October 18, 1867, makes clear. Serno-Solovyevich's pamphlet and letter to Borkheim appear to have been the sources from which Marx and his friends first learned about Chernyshevsky, the great Russian revolutionary democrat. On November 24, Borkheim gave Marx a written résumé of this pamphlet and included some new information which he got from the young Russian correspondent about Chernyshevsky's work on the journal *Sovremennik*, his knowledge of German philosophy, his novel *What Is to Be Done?*, and the publication of his and Dobrolyubov's works.

The German translation of the pamphlet *Our Domestic Affairs* was not printed until 1871, but Marx having learned of its content from Borkheim's account and résumé, took such an interest in the author that in December 1867 he sent him, through Becker, a copy of Volume One of *Capital*. A year later, Serno-Solovyevich was on a commission set up to prepare the publication in Geneva of a newspaper of the International and wrote to Marx, inviting him to be a contributor. "I appeal to you for your services in this instance in a cause for which you have stood all your life."[2] Marx's reply is not extant, but he is known to have refused to act as a permanent contributor because he was too busy, though he promised to give all the help he could. Serno-Solovyevich was the first representative of the young generation of Russian revolutionaries with whom Marx had direct contacts, but these were soon broken off when Serno-Solovyevich fell gravely ill and died.

Subsequently, Marx extended his contacts with leaders of the Russian revolutionary movement, to the development of which he attached much importance. He was helped in this by his study of the Russian language, Russian revolutionary writings, the works of Chernyshevsky and Flerovsky.

It the 1860s conditions in Russia were still just forming for the development of a mass working-class movement, and the ideas of scientific communism could not yet have had any extensive appeal. However, forward-looking social thinkers displayed a keen interest not only in Marx's theory, but also in Marx's practical activities and in the International. Lenin remarked that it was towards the end of

---

[1] Marx, Engels, *Collected Works*, Vol. 43, p. 189.
[2] *K. Marx and F. Engels and Revolutionary Russia*, pp. 161-62 (in Russian).

the 1860s that "the Russian Narodnik socialists were trying to introduce into Russia the most advanced and most important of 'European institutions' — the International".[1]

A Russian section of the International was set up in Geneva in the spring of 1870. It consisted of a group of Chernyshevsky's followers, revolutionary emigrants who had broken with Bakunin and who were publishing in Geneva a journal called *Narodnoye Dyelo*. Among the members, apart from Utin, there were Anton Trusov, who had commanded a rebel detachment in Byelorussia during the Polish insurrection, Yelizaveta Dmitriyeva-Tomanovskaya, the outstanding Russian revolutionary who was to take an active part in the Paris Commune, Anna Korvin-Krukovskaya (Mrs. Jaclard) who was also to take part in the Commune, Victor Bartenev (Netov), and other revolutionaries. The section was exerting a considerable influence on leading circles among the Russian emigrants, and was linked with the Narodnik underground movement in Russia, and with the revolutionary movement in other Slav countries. Thus, one of its correspondents was the Serbian revolutionary and socialist, Svetozar Markovic.

On March 12, 1870, the Committee of the Russian section asked Marx to act as its representative on the General Council. The letter said: "Today, Russian democratic youth has the opportunity to express, through its exiled brothers, its profound gratitude to you for the services you have rendered to its cause by your theoretical and practical propaganda."[2]

What Marx liked about the letter from the young Russian revolutionaries was their rejection of Slavophile illusions, their realisation that Russia and Western Europe had a common historical destiny, and their repudiation of Bakunin and his associates. He readily agreed to the Committee's request. In his reply to the Russian section on March 24, he spoke with approval about the internationalist ideas in its programme, which declared Poland's oppression to be a fetter equally hampering the political and social freedom both of the Polish and of the Russian people. Marx ended his letter with these words: "Such works as Flerovsky's and those of your teacher Chernyshevsky do real honour to Russia and prove that your country is also beginning to take part in the movement of our age."[3]

In his capacity as Corresponding Secretary for Russia, Marx constantly helped the Russian revolutionaries, regularly corresponding with them, informing them of the state of affairs in the International and the decisions of its Council, and sending them the necessary documents. He strove to influence the evolution of their thinking and get them to accept the ideas of scientific communism, thereby helping them to overcome their Narodnik views of the village commune as the most reliable obstacle to capitalist development. He sought to

---

[1] V. I. Lenin, *Collected Works*, Vol. 1, p. 278.
[2] *K. Marx and F. Engels and Revolutionary Russia*, p. 169 (in Russian).
[3] Marx, Engels, *Collected Works*, Vol. 21, p. 111.

help them to understand the leading role in society's transformation of the industrial proletariat, which they did not distinguish from the mass of working people.

Members of the Russian section translated and published in Russian the International's most important documents written by Marx, including the Inaugural Address and the General Rules. Through his contacts with the Russian section, Marx extended his circle of friends in the Russian revolutionary movement. Among the members of the section who became Marx's particular friends were Utin and Yelizaveta Dmitriyeva-Tomanovskaya, both of whom were later warmly received by Marx in London.

Something that also redounded greatly to the credit of the small but highly active Russian section was that at the time when an acute struggle was being launched in the international working-class movement against anarchism, it took a resolute stand against Bakunin, and supported the Marxist revolutionary wing of the International. Almost from its very inception it had carried on an active fight against Bakuninism in Switzerland. At a congress of the Federation of Romance Switzerland, held at La Chaux-de-Fonds on April 4, Utin denounced Bakunin. As a result of the ensuing split, the Jura sections which adopted the Bakuninist platform of abstaining from political struggle elected another Federal Council that claimed to be the Romance Council. Both councils appealed to London, and on June 29 the General Council decided that the designation of the Romance Federal Council and the corresponding functions were to remain with the old council at Geneva, while the new, Bakuninist council at La Chaux-de-Fonds was invited to choose another name for itself.

CRISIS OF THE SECOND EMPIRE AND PROSPECTS FOR A EUROPEAN REVOLUTION

Towards the end of the 1860s, Marx noted with satisfaction the changes that had taken place in the French working-class movement. The International was coming to play a growing part in French socio-political life. The sympathies of the anti-Bonapartist workers and democratic elements had been drawn to it by two trials in 1868 and the systematic reprisals against it by the imperial police. Marx sought every opportunity to help the French proletariat adopt a revolutionary form of struggle and discard its Proudhonist views.

Marx's second daughter, Laura, who married Paul Lafargue on April 2, 1868, arrived in Paris with her husband in October 1868. Lafargue had qualified as a doctor, but was in no hurry to set up in practice, for he had long since had other preoccupations. It was in Paris that he fully revealed himself as a talented journalist and began his activity as an outstanding propagandist of Marxism in France.

When his daughter and son-in-law were leaving for Paris, Marx had given them a full list of the addresses of the International's French sections. Before their departure they must have had many discussions on one of the vital problems of the French working-class movement, namely, the need to establish its unity, a process which was being hampered by the sectarian attitude of both the Proudhonists and the Blanquists, the two main trends. The task was to overcome the reformist illusions and the conspiratorial tactics, and to rally all the proletarian forces in the fight against the Empire and in defence of the economic and political interests of the proletariat and all the other working people.

Among Lafargue's friends and comrades in Paris were Eugène Varlin, the Hungarian socialist Leo Frankel, and former members of the General Council Amédée Combault and Jules Johannard. He was also constantly in touch with Blanqui's closest associates— Edme Tridon, the future general of the Commune Emile Eudes, Germain Casse and Théophile Ferré. In the spring of 1869, when the Blanquists started preparations for publishing their newspaper the *Renaissance*, Lafargue joined the editorial board and got Marx to promise his support and cooperation.

In that period, Lafargue frequently met Blanqui, who used to travel incognito from Brussels to Paris to inspect his combat organisations and call on Paul and Laura at their home in the Rue Cherche du Midi. At the end of May 1869, Lafargue wrote to Marx: "Le Petit [Blanqui's nickname in party circles] has a particular affection and respect for you." [1] Blanqui warmly welcomed the idea of asking Marx to write a number of articles on the socio-political situation in Germany for the proposed paper. However, at the time its publication had not yet materialised.

In January 1869, a son, Marx's first grandchild, was born to the Lafargues, and in early July Marx went to visit them because he was worried by the state of Laura's health. He wrote to Engels: "Arrived in Paris last Tuesday evening, left again Monday (12 July). I managed to remain completely *incognito*." [2]

Elections to the Legislative Corps had just been held in France, showing a considerable growth of opposition to the regime of the Second Empire. In May 1869, Varlin and his comrades issued the Electoral Programme of a Group of Paris Workers, which proved that the leading French workers had moved even farther away from Proudhonist dogmas. In the capital, the elections were accompanied by disturbances (some barricades were even put up) and arrests. What Marx had seen and heard in Paris and what he had learned from the accounts and letters of the Lafargues, from Dupont's correspondence with the French sections, and from the press testified to an ever deepening crisis of the Second Empire. Considering the prospects for a European revolution, Marx wrote in January

[1] Central Party Archives of the Institute of Marxism-Leninism.
[2] Marx, Engels, *Collected Works*, Vol. 43, p. 315.

1870 that the "revolutionary *initiative* will probably come from France".[1]

Publication of the daily, *La Marseillaise*, was started in Paris in December 1869, and its editorial board included socialist-minded workers, members of the International, Blanquists and Left-wing republicans, who had banded together in the fight against the Second Empire. Marx and Engels kept a close eye on the paper, which at once assumed the functions of an organ of the International. A further step in the cohesion of the proletarian socialist elements was the establishment, in April 1870, of the Paris Federation of the International's sections, in which Lafargue and Varlin played a big part.

This consolidation of the politically most active workers round the International reduced the Bakuninists' influence to the south of France. In view of the situation and the growth of revolutionary feeling among the masses, some members of the International suggested that the General Council should be moved to Paris. Marx must have taken a positive view of the proposal, which was, however, never realised.

To strengthen his unstable position Napoleon III resorted to another demagogic manoeuvre, by appointing a plebiscite for May 8, 1870. On the eve of it, the leaders of the International's sections were arrested all over France on the trumped-up charge of being involved in a conspiracy to assassinate the Emperor. On May 3, Marx proposed that the General Council should issue in English and French a declaration on the persecution of members of the French sections. Brushing aside the absurd charge that the International engaged in conspiratorial activity, Marx wrote: "If the working classes, who form the great bulk of all nations, who produce all their wealth, and in the name of whom even the usurping powers always pretend to rule, conspire, they conspire publicly, as the sun conspires against darkness, in the full consciousness that without their pale there exists no legitimate power."[2]

At the same time, Marx suggested that the General Council should publicly disavow the reckless statements being made by the so-called French branch in London, which consisted of a few dozen petty-bourgeois democrat emigrants, who had been out of touch with the International since 1868. The manifestos issued by Félix Pyat, the leader of this branch, and his men, which abounded in provocative and pseudo-revolutionary catchwords and calls for individual terrorist tactics, were being used by the Public Prosecutor's office in Paris as evidence to support its charges against members of the International. A resolution, proposed by Marx, in which the International disclaimed all responsibility for the acts of Pyat's group, was passed by the General Council on May 10, 1870.

---

[1] Ibid., Vol. 21, p. 86.
[2] Ibid., p. 127.

The persecutions did not daunt the French members of the International, and in a letter to Engels on May 18, 1870, Marx noted with satisfaction that in place of the International's organisations and committees dispersed by the authorities, new ones were being established in even greater numbers all over the country. The Blanquists also began to establish sections of the International. The French working class was advancing towards unity on the International's platform, but before this important process had time to yield tangible results there came events of momentous importance.

CHAPTER TWELVE

THE PARIS COMMUNE

> *Working men's Paris, with its Commune, will be for ever celebrated as the glorious harbinger of a new society.*
>
> Karl Marx

ON THE THRESHOLD OF A NEW HISTORICAL EPOCH

The years of 1870 and 1871 witnessed epoch-making events. The Franco-Prussian War was started by the ruling circles of the two countries. France's military defeat not only led to the downfall of the long-since bankrupt regime of the Second Empire, but also aggravated to an extreme the class antagonisms in the country.

On March 18 a proletarian revolution broke out in Paris, and for the first time in history a proletarian state was set up in the form of the Paris Commune. It was the culminating point in the development of capitalist society and the close of the epoch of the bourgeoisie's rise, of progressive bourgeois change, and of the break-up of absolutist feudal institutions. It opened the epoch "of the full domination and decline of the bourgeoisie, one of transition from its progressive character towards reactionary and even ultra-reactionary finance capital".[1] It was also a historical milestone in the development of the working-class movement and of socialist thought. For the first time in history, the Commune, an epoch-making achievement of the working class, provided evidence that the conclusion concerning the inevitability of socialist revolution and the winning of power by the proletariat was more than the fruit of theoretical analysis by the ideologists of the working class: it was an imperative of the time, a practical necessity, an issue which historical development itself placed on the order of the day.

The lessons of the Commune shed a strong light on the pressing tasks of the working-class movement, and showed that it was essential to write into the programme of the international proletariat a number of principles of scientific communism as being fundamental and generally accepted. The events in Paris revealed the flimsi-

---
[1] V. I. Lenin, *Collected Works*, Vol. 21, p. 146.

ness of the sectarian and reformist theories of petty-bourgeois socialism, and gave clear confirmation of the great viable power of scientific communism.

Although the workers of various nationalities had great sympathy for the Commune, they were unable at once to grasp its lessons, which required profound theoretical comprehension. Only a great thinker and theoretician of the fighting proletariat could give a full picture of what had taken place in 1870 and 1871 and draw the right conclusions. It was to Marx that this task fell once again, as it had in the big class battles in the past. It was he who saw these events as marking the threshold of the future, as ushering in a new historical epoch. Marx, the Commune's first historian and chronicler, placed the experience of the proletarian revolution in France within the reach of the broad masses, and put it on record for coming generations of proletarian fighters.

But Marx did much more. He was a direct participant in the mass revolutionary struggle. He led the international proletarian organisation through the turbulent stream of events, helping it to follow its revolutionary course, and preventing the slightest departure from the principles of proletarian internationalism. It was he who mainly inspired the working class to independent action during the war, formulated the International's general tactics in that period, and helped to work out the tactical line of the proletarian forces both in the belligerent and the neutral countries.

During the Paris Commune, Marx's role as participant in these events was expressed above all in his direct contacts with its leaders and in his sound advice to the Communards. Together with Engels, he strove hard to co-ordinate, and now and again to generate, the movement in support of the Commune among the workers of various countries, and to give it the right orientation. When the proletarian state was suppressed, Marx worked vigorously to organise assistance to the Commune's refugees, who fell victim to the reign of terror unleashed by the men of Versailles.

FIRST ADDRESS
ON THE FRANCO-PRUSSIAN WAR

It was in the course of these events that Marx worked out his objective assessment of the historical process, which led up to the revolutionary situation in Paris. The Franco-Prussian War, which broke out in July 1870, was a major link in the chain of events. Germany's final unification was seriously hampered by the unceasing sabre-rattling of the Bonapartists, their encroachments upon the left bank of the Rhine, and their support of the separatist tendencies of some German states. At the same time, the existence of the aggressive Bonapartist Empire, a constant seedbed of war, also intensified the militaristic urges of the Prussian Junkers and the bellicose circles of the

German bourgeoisie, who sought to realise their own predatory and dynastic plans — to spread the power of the Hohenzollerns to the southern German states as well — on the pretext of defending Germany's national interests. Bismarck made skilful use of the chauvinistic statements by Napoleon III and his clique to reduce anti-Prussian feeling at home and provoke France into acting as the aggressor in the armed conflict. In these circumstances, the war, objectively begun for the purpose of preventing Napoleon III from perpetuating the dismemberment of Germany, threatened to develop into a campaign of territorial aggrandisement against France.

Marx was quite clear on all these points already on July 19, 1870, the day war was declared, when the question of issuing an address on the war was raised at the General Council meeting. There was no unanimity on the Council, some members condemning war in general, others branding the French or the German rulers, who had unleashed it, or complaining that the workers were not yet strong enough to stop the war. Marx gave a reminder that the Council "could not entertain the general war question, only the special case". [1] As always, he insisted on taking the concrete historical approach to events. A correct line for the international proletariat could be formulated only by determining, on the basis of a scientific analysis, the character of the war in question, its causes and probable outcome. The Council asked Marx to draw up the address and at its next meeting on July 26 it unanimously approved the text which Marx had written and read out. This important document was issued as a leaflet, and was published by many of the International's periodicals. It was also reproduced by the bourgeois press.

Marx concentrated on exposing the Bonapartist regime and showed that a military defeat of the Second Empire could rejuvenate France and eliminate one of the main obstacles to Germany's genuine unity. That is why, at that stage the war on the German side should be regarded as being defensive. In so doing, Marx drew a sharp distinction between the German people's national interests and Prussia's dynastic interest, and warned the German workers that a war under the Prussian militarists could well develop into a war against the French people. He urged the German members of the International to display vigilance, and welcomed the sentiments of proletarian internationalism expressed in the messages of peace and goodwill which they had exchanged with French workers just when their governments were plunging them into a fratricidal war.

"This great fact, unparalleled in the history of the past, opens the vista of a brighter future," wrote Marx. "It proves that in contrast to old society, with its economical miseries and its political delirium, a new society is springing up, whose international rule will be *Peace*, because its national ruler will be everywhere the same — *Labour*!" [2]

---

[1] *The General Council of the First International. 1870-1871*, Moscow, 1974, p. 31.
[2] Marx, Engels, *Collected Works*, Vol. 22, p. 7.

HELPING THE GERMAN SOCIAL-DEMOCRATS FORMULATE REVOLUTIONARY TACTICS

The war proved to be a severe trial for the workers, particularly in the belligerent countries. A great deal—the authority of their international organisation, with the principles of proletarian internationalism inscribed on its banner, and the subsequent development of the working-class movement—depended on the stand they took, on whether they remained true to the principles of proletarian internationalism or whether they succumbed to the chauvinist hysteria. Marx did his utmost to help both the French members of the International and the German Social-Democrats follow a revolutionary internationalist line throughout the war. He attached exceptional importance to the behaviour of the German proletariat and its party, the most organised contingent of the international working-class movement.

Marx was happy to learn of the stand taken by Liebknecht and Bebel in the voting of the war credits in the North German Reichstag on July 21. Both abstained, saying in a written declaration that support for the credits implied a vote of confidence in the Prussian government, while a vote against them could be interpreted as favouring Bonaparte's criminal designs. Marx regarded this declaration as an act of courage and translated it into English; it was read out in the General Council, and then published in the English press.

The changing military situation required that the proletariat's tactical tasks should be constantly concretised and brought up to date. The war was correctly seen by the people of Germany as a national one, and there was no reason to try to cushion the blow against the Bonapartist army. At the same time, the heavy defeats inflicted on the latter changed the situation and carried the war to its turning point. Success had gone to the heads of Prussia's rulers, and they were already clamouring for Alsace and Lorraine. On August 17, Marx wrote to Engels that such an outcome of the war would be the "greatest misfortune that could befall Europe and above all Germany".[1]

Serious differences arose between Liebknecht, who headed the party's organ *Volksstaat*, and the Committee of the Social-Democratic Workers' Party, which had its seat in Brunswick. Liebknecht failed to take full account of the defensive nature of the war at its first stage, whereas some members of the Brunswick Committee had succumbed to nationalistic feelings. A note of alarm was sounded in a letter which arrived from Brunswick asking Marx for advice.

At the time, Marx was in Ramsgate, where he had gone with his

---

[1] Marx, Engels, *Collected Works*, Vol. 44, p. 51.

family in early August. He felt that it was not enough to have an exchange of views with Engels by letter and so made a special trip to Manchester to discuss the plan of action. The full reply drawn up by Marx and Engels is not extant, but large extracts from it were reproduced in the Brunswick Committee's Manifesto of September 5.

In the General Council's July Address, Marx had predicted the collapse of the Second Empire, and in his reply to the Brunswick Committee written in late August he said this was now inevitable. Anticipating a change in the nature of the war, Marx and Engels urged the German workers to resist in every way the annexationist plans of the Prussian militarists and the German bourgeoisie. They described in detail the baneful consequences for the future of Europe of the annexation of Alsace and Lorraine, and showed that a peace concluded on such terms would be plunderous and latent with fresh wars. They said the task of completing Germany's unification had been solved even if, "to begin with, it is finding its *unity* in the *Prussian barracks*". It was up to the German workers to see that an honourable peace treaty was signed with France, which would open up totally different prospects: the possibility of peaceful development in the western continent, Prussia's dissolution in Germany, and, in the event of a war against tsarism and its defeat, a social revolution in Russia the elements of which "only need such an impulse from without for their development".[1]

In that period, the forward-looking German workers and their leaders, fostered by Marx and Engels, did their duty to the international working-class movement. In contrast to the Lassallean leaders, who supported the chauvinist policy of Germany's rulers, the Eisenach leaders, acting entirely on Marx's advice, centred their tactics on a struggle against the annexation of Alsace and Lorraine, and for an end to the war and an honourable peace with the French Republic established on September 4. The leaders sank their differences and the party closed its ranks round the banner of proletarian internationalism. Despite the hardships of wartime, the state of siege, the confiscation of party periodicals, and other police persecution, the Eisenachers protested, at mass meetings and in the press, against the continuation of the war and plans to annex Alsace and Lorraine.

The authorities started reprisals against the party, and all the members of the Brunswick Committee, headed by Wilhelm Bracke, were sent to a Prussian fortress. For their accusatory speeches in the Reichstag Bebel and Liebknecht, who had voted against credits for a continuation of the war, were also thrown into prison, when the session ended, on December 17, 1870.

Marx worked hard to expose the acts of violence and lawlessness perpetrated under Bismarck and to ease the lot of his party friends. He sent a number of items to English newspapers concerning the ar-

---

[1] Ibid., Vol. 22, p. 261.

rest of the Brunswick Committee. In a letter to the editor of *The Daily News*, he condemned Bismarck's police action against Bebel and Liebknecht, and the gross breach of their parliamentary immunity. Marx took pride in his German comrades' heroic stand and set them up as an example to the members of the International in other countries. A collection of funds was organised in the International in aid of the arrested Social-Democrats and their families.

COLLAPSE OF THE SECOND EMPIRE.
SECOND ADDRESS ON THE FRANCO-PRUSSIAN WAR

A telegram from Charles Longuet (from Paris), which arrived in London at dawn on September 5, 1870, informed Marx that the French Republic had been proclaimed the day before. This did not come as a surprise to Marx and Engels who had been aware of the rottenness of the Bonapartist regime and had observed the growing unity of the proletarian and democratic forces in the country. They had expected a revolution in France long before the war, and quite independently of the impending armed conflict. The only thing they had feared was that it would break out before the proletarian party was formed there. Considering the possible lines along which a European revolution could run, Marx suggested: "The first blow will come from France."[1] The denouement was precipitated by the war, the prologue to the explosion being the Sedan disaster of September 1-2, when one of the French armies capitulated and the Emperor himself was taken prisoner.

The collapse of the Empire paved the way in France for a democratic system and truly national resistance to the aggressor. But the most experienced leaders of the French workers were then either imprisoned or abroad, while members of the International were out of touch with their sections because of the mobilisation. The proletariat's organisational weakness and the hesitance of its petty-bourgeois allies led to the establishment on September 4 of a provisional government of Right-wing republicans and avowed monarchists. Marx at once realised their intention of making a secret deal with Bismarck, heaping the disgrace of a surrender on the young republic and so paving the way for a restoration of the monarchy.

With the collapse of the Second Empire, the war entered a new stage. This made it necessary not only to reaffirm the line followed by the German Social-Democrats, but also to formulate the new tasks of the proletariat united in the ranks of the International. Marx did so in the Second Address on the Franco-Prussian War, which the Council approved on September 9. In order to expose Prussia's annexationist plans, Marx had to analyse and refute the arguments of Prussia's military specialists in favour of annexing Al-

---

[1] Marx, Engels, *Collected Works*, Vol. 43, p. 429.

sace and Lorraine. He made use of considerations which Engels had sent him at his request.

The Address urged the proletariat of all countries to struggle resolutely against the dismemberment of France and seizure of the French provinces, and against the policy of territorial conquest being pursued by the Prussian Junkers and the German militarists. With rare insight, Marx described the inevitable consequences of Bismarck's aggression and the alignment of rival forces in Europe which it determined for decades ahead; he predicted the inevitable revanchist attempts, the formation of a Franco-Russian alliance, and its clash with Germany and her potential allies. The International's sections, the Address said, should urge the workers to take vigorous action against the plans of the Prussian invaders. "If they forsake their duty, if they remain passive, the present tremendous war will be but the harbinger of still deadlier international feuds, and lead in every nation to a renewed triumph over the workman by the lords of the sword, of the soil, and of capital." [1]

In formulating the tasks of the French workers, Marx stated frankly that they were faced with an extremely difficult situation. It was their duty to take part in defending their country, but in so doing they should beware of chauvinistic bourgeois catchwords and illusions. At the same time, he warned that any attempt to overthrow the government at a moment when it still had reason to claim to be a bona fide organiser of defence was bound to fail. The workers would do well to make use of their republican freedoms to strengthen their class organisation, which would "gift them with fresh Herculean powers for the regeneration of France, and our common task—the emancipation of labour". [2]

The Address was issued in London as a separate leaflet on September 11-13, 1870, and among the members of the Council who signed it was the Russian revolutionary Hermann Lopatin. He had joined the International in Paris in 1870, before his arrival in London. On September 6, Marx and Auguste Serraillier, a French worker and a member of the General Council, proposed Lopatin's co-option to the Council, and this was subsequently approved.

The Paris members of the International did not manage to avoid the danger of which Marx had warned in the Address. Their September 4 manifesto repeated the bourgeois politicians' chauvinistic catchwords. On September 14 Marx wrote to De Paepe: "The whole tone of the manifesto is absurd and contrary to the spirit of the *International*." [3] This had resulted from the theoretical backwardness of most leaders of the French proletariat, who for a long time failed to see through the ruling circles' capitulationist plans. It was only in the harsh trial of the blockade and the fierce fighting against the bourgeoisie that the progressive workers of Paris began to ac-

---

[1] Ibid., Vol. 22, p. 270.
[2] Ibid., p. 269.
[3] Ibid., Vol. 44, p. 80.

quire a mature class-consciousness and to shed their harmful illusions.

CAMPAIGN FOR RECOGNITION OF THE FRENCH REPUBLIC

The Second Address called upon the workers, especially those in England, to urge their governments to give official recognition to the French Republic, an act, Marx believed, that would moderate both the Prussians' annexationist aspirations and the French monarchists' desire for restoration. In September 1870, with the help of the English members of the General Council, and Eccarius, who had by then established close contacts with the trade unions, Marx succeeded in mounting a broad campaign of solidarity with the French Republic. Within a short time, over 20 meetings and rallies had been held in London, and the workers of Manchester, Birmingham and Newcastle were involved in the movement. Marx prompted the English workers to resort to their traditional means, "a wholesale pressure from without", to induce their government to give diplomatic recognition to the French Republic.

It was necessary to overcome resistance from the bourgeois pacifists in the Peace Society, who urged that England should remain strictly neutral. The timely arrival of a group of members of the International, Marx among them, at a workers' meeting at Lincoln's Inn on September 13, helped, despite the efforts of the advocates of neutrality, to get a resolution passed demanding recognition of the Republic and an honourable peace without annexations.

A highlight of the campaign for recognition of the Republic was the call paid on the Prime Minister, Gladstone, on September 27 by a large delegation representing over 100 workers' societies. When the General Council met again on October 4, Marx exposed the hypocrisy of Gladstone, who had not given the workers any straightforward answer on the plea that it was necessary to wait for the Provisional Government to be approved by the French National Assembly.

At the height of the campaign, the Marxist nucleus of the General Council was immensely strengthened: on September 20, 1870, Engels arrived in London and settled not far from the Marx home. At the end of 1869, he had had an opportunity of resigning from the trading company on terms which left him an independent income. With great enthusiasm he began withdrawing from the commercial affairs, which had become such a burden, to have more time for his scientific pursuits and party work. Engels' arrival also made a great deal of difference for Marx. The two friends now met almost daily, and Engels willingly took over a large part of Marx's practical duties in the International. On October 4 he was unanimously co-opted to the General Council. In view of his prestige in the working-class movement and his excellent knowledge of most European languages, he was appointed Corresponding Secretary for Belgium and then also for Italy and Spain. Thus, at a critical and intense period of history, Marx found his best and most reliable friend next to him at the helm of the international proletarian organisation.

Among Marx's allies in the campaign for recognition of the French Republic were the English bourgeois radicals, professing the positivist philosophical and sociological views of Auguste Comte who had denied the class struggle and had seen social progress as lying only in a gradual evolution, primarily in the advance of human knowledge. Marx also thought it important to dispel the English Comtists' political illusions, for they idealised the French Provisional Government and in all seriousness regarded it as a "Government of National Defence" and the French bourgeoisie as truly patriotic. Marx wrote to Edward Spencer Beesly, a Professor of History and prominent British positivist: "I must tell you that according to all information I receive from France, the middle class on the whole prefers Prussian conquest to the victory of a Republic with Socialist tendencies."[1]

The London positivists and the reformist trade union leaders closely associated with them were preparing to give a triumphant reception to the French Foreign Minister, Jules Favre, who was expected to arrive in England. This was all the more inappropriate, since the French people were beginning to realise the traitorous role played by the members of the government. Accordingly, on January 17, 1871, Marx delivered a speech at the General Council exposing Favre, in particular, his improper behaviour during the 1848-49 revolution.

A great contribution to exposing the treacherous conduct of the war by the "Government of National Defection", and the capitulationist stand of the French bourgeoisie as a whole, was made by Engels in a series of articles entitled *Notes on the War* in the London *Pall Mall Gazette*. The purely military aspect of these articles did not prevent Engels from giving a systematic account of the International's standpoint at the various stages of the war.

MARCH 18 REVOLUTION

The proletarian revolution of March 18, 1871 led to the proclamation of the Paris Commune. It stemmed from the whole development of the French and the international working-class movement in the 1860s, which had been profoundly enhanced by the International. Lenin said that the main role in the Commune was played by the Paris workers, "among whom active socialist propaganda had been carried on during the last years of the Second Empire and many of whom even belonged to the International".[2] That is the

---
[1] Marx, Engels, *Collected Works*, Vol. 44, p. 89.
[2] V. I. Lenin, *Collected Works*, Vol. 17, p. 140.

context in which one should read Engels' statement that the Commune was "beyond doubt the child of the International intellectually, though the International did not lift a finger to produce it".[1] From its very outset, the workers of various countries identified the cause of the Commune with that of the International, and stood up in its defence.

On the eve of the March 18 events, the situation in France was discussed at each General Council meeting. On March 14, Marx objected to the proposal by the Bakuninist, Paul Robin, for the immediate convocation of a conference of the International — the Congress which was to be held at Mainz in September 1870 did not, of course, take place because of the war — and argued that "Paris was in a very unsettled state".[2]

Marx feared that the Paris workers would take premature action in an unfavourable situation. However, when the proletarian revolution did break out, he gave it full and utmost support with all the fervour of the proletarian revolutionary.

News of the March 18 revolution arrived in London at the height of the Council's struggle against the bourgeois slander which was being spread about the International in view of the sharpening situation in Paris. At its ordinary meeting on March 21, the General Council discussed the Paris events and, on Marx's motion, decided to send delegations to attend workers' meetings to explain the essence of the revolution in Paris and urge them "to express sympathy with the Paris movement".[3] Marx and Engels believed there was some chance of success, although they were fully aware of the great complexity of the situation: the main danger was a possible deal between the Versailles counter-revolutionaries and the Prussian invaders.

Until the very end of March, Marx continued to believe that the revolutionary movement could spread throughout the country. The insurgents could consolidate their victory and assure themselves of support from the revolutionary elements in the provinces by resolutely suppressing the counter-revolution in Paris and advancing on Versailles, where the reactionary National Assembly and the Thiers government were entrenched.

Meanwhile, the Parisians' defensive tactics were tending to isolate the capital. Marx was quick to note the fatal consequences of the mistake which the Central Committee of the National Guard had made. Until March 26, the day the Commune was elected, power had been in the hands of the Central Committee. On April 6, Marx wrote to Liebknecht: "The Central Committee and later the Commune gave that mischievous *avorton*,[4] Thiers, time to consolidate hostile forces, in the first place by their folly of not wanting to start a civ-

---

[1] Marx, Engels, *Werke*, Bd. 33, S. 642.
[2] *The General Council of the First International. 1870-1871*, p. 151.
[3] Ibid., p. 162.
[4] Degenerate.

il war — as if Thiers had not already started it by his attempt at forcibly disarming Paris, as if the National Assembly, summoned merely to decide the question of war or peace with the Prussians, had not immediately declared war on *the Republic*! Secondly, in order that the appearance of having usurped power should not attach to them, they lost precious moments (they should immediately have advanced on Versailles...) by the election of the Commune, the organisation of which, etc., cost yet more time."[1]

In early April, taking a realistic view of the balance of forces, Marx saw that the revolution's chances for success were dwindling, but that was precisely when, with the profound insight of the revolutionary scientist, he came to see the full historic greatness of what the Paris workers had done. Marx was the first to realise that this was an unprecedented expression of creative revolutionary initiative by the people. He discerned in the Paris events a titanic clash between the old and the new forces of contemporary society, which brought out the proletariat's unequalled heroism. Marx's understanding of the true nature of the events in France was evident from his letters to Kugelmann.

The first one, dated April 12, was in reply to Kugelmann's quibbling comment on the Paris revolution. On April 5, he had written to Marx: "One can't expect the muddle-headed French to bring about a revolution in the mode of production, and in general this is something that no nation can do by itself."[2] Marx's letter was a rebuttal to anyone who applied the common yardstick to the Commune and saw nothing but miscalculations and mistakes in its activity. By then, Marx was already in possession of information about the Commune's first measures, including the abolition of the standing army and political police, the separation of church from state, the introduction of a consistently democratic suffrage, the accountability and removability of persons in office, and the equalisation of their wages with those of the workers. Marx said that the great historical importance of the Commune's activity lay in the fact that it had made the first practical attempt in history to break up the bourgeoisie's military-bureaucratic state machine, which was an essential condition for the victory of the socialist revolution, in the continental countries of Europe at any rate. Marx greatly admired the Communards' heroism and dedication, and he wrote: "What resilience, what historical initiative, what a capacity for sacrifice in these Parisians!... However that may be, the present rising in Paris — even if it be crushed by the wolves, swine and vile curs of the old society — is the most glorious deed of our Party since the June insurrection in Paris."[3] Lenin said this letter contained "words of the highest praise" to the heroic Paris workers.[4]

---

[1] Marx, Engels. *Collected Works*, Vol. 44, p. 128.
[2] Central Party Archives of the Institute of Marxism-Leninism.
[3] Marx, Engels, *Collected Works*, Vol. 44, pp. 131-32.
[4] V. I. Lenin, *Collected Works*, Vol. 12, p. 109.

Marx wrote a second letter five days later as something of a continuation of his reply to Kugelmann's doubts. He said: "World history would indeed be very easy to make if the struggle were taken up only on condition of infallibly favourable chances."[1] Marx stressed that the presence of the Prussian army of occupation in France was the decisively unfavourable factor for the Paris workers, and that the counter-revolutionary government had made base use of it to confront the workers with the alternative of either starting an uprising or surrendering without a fight. In the event of the latter, the demoralisation of the working class would have been a worse misfortune than the defeat of the insurgents. Marx added: "The struggle of the working class against the capitalist class and its state has entered upon a new phase with the struggle in Paris. Whatever the immediate results may be, a new point of departure of world-historic importance has been gained."[2]

Thus, already by mid-April Marx saw the Paris Commune as the first attempt to set up a proletarian dictatorship, and as an event of epoch-making importance which opened a new page in the history of the great liberation struggle of the working class.

CONTACTS WITH THE COMMUNARDS

Marx took every opportunity to keep in touch with the leaders of the Commune and to help them to work out the correct policies. By decision of the General Council, Auguste Serraillier was sent to Paris, and his letters provided Marx with valuable information. Very soon, however, the Versailles and Prussian police set up a blockade round Paris, and letters had to be smuggled out of the city and posted in the suburbs. A more reliable procedure was to send them with someone travelling to London, but then they arrived after considerable delay. Several letters for the General Council were brought by Lafargue, who had travelled to Paris from Bordeaux in early April. The letters reached London after April 20. In early May, Marx received another batch of letters through the Russian Narodnik, Pyotr Lavrov. The General Council also kept in touch with the Communards through Yelizaveta Dmitriyeva, who corresponded with Jung.

For reasons of secrecy, Marx preferred to convey his advice to the Commune either orally or through men he could trust. Apart from Serraillier, he maintained contacts with Frankel and Varlin, through whom he sought to induce the Commune to take more vigorous action against the counter-revolutionaries in Paris and insistently advised it to launch an attack on Versailles. Fearing a deal between Bismarck and the men of Versailles, Marx advised the Communards

---

[1] Marx, Engels, *Collected Works*, Vol. 44, p. 136.
[2] Ibid., p. 137.

to fortify the northern side of the heights of Montmartre, which faced the deployed Prussian troops. Later, he wrote with bitterness: "They still had time to do this; I told them beforehand that they would otherwise be caught in a trap."[1] Marx warned the truly proletarian elements in the Commune about the petty-bourgeois leaders' intrigues. On May 13, 1871, he wrote to Frankel and Varlin: "I believe that the Commune wastes too much time over trifles and personal squabbles. One can see that there are influences at work other than those of the working men."[2]

Frankel, a member of the Labour Commission, consulted Marx on how best to "implement a radical transformation of social relations",[3] as he says in one of his extant letters. Marx advised the Commune to secure the support of the provinces, in the first place, so as to break the fatal isolation of Paris, and this meant in fact confronting the Communards with the question of the proletariat's allies in the socialist revolution. From the outset Marx had insisted on the need to draw the French peasantry to the side of the proletarian revolution. In order to do this the small peasant's anti-socialist preconceptions had to be dispelled, and he had to be made to feel that his true interests could be secured only with the victory of the working class.

Marx approved of the measures taken by the Commune in the interests of the urban petty bourgeoisie: the cancellation of rent arrears, the moratorium on commercial bills and the cancellation of interest on them. "The decrees about rent and commercial bills were two master strokes."[4]

In early May, Marx felt a growing alarm over the Commune's military position.

A fortnight before the fall of revolutionary Paris, he gave the Communards the details of a secret treaty signed by Bismarck and Favre against the Commune, and warned that they should expect their enemies to deliver the decisive blow on or about May 26. He wrote: "It is very necessary to do quickly what you intend to do outside Paris, in England or elsewhere."[5] Anticipating the Commune's defeat, Marx believed that by sequestering the funds of the French bank and secreting documents discrediting the Versailles leaders, the Commune could hope to exert an influence on Thiers and compel him to make some concessions.

---

[1] Ibid., p. 151.
[2] Ibid. p. 149.
[3] *The First International and the Paris Commune. Documents,* Moscow, 1972, p. 453 (in Russian).
[4] Marx, Engels, *Collected Works,* Vol. 22, p. 591.
[5] Ibid., Vol. 44, p. 149.

MOVEMENT OF SOLIDARITY WITH THE COMMUNE

The Thiers government was doing its utmost to isolate the Commune from the French provinces and the international proletariat, a policy which was described by Marx as follows: "To keep the provinces down, to prevent their general rising for Paris, by *a wall of lies*." [1] The official and Right-wing press in all countries followed the Versailles counter-revolutionaries in spreading the most monstrous fabrications about the communards. On April 6, Marx wrote to Liebknecht: "You must not believe a word of all the stuff you get to see in the papers about the internal events in Paris. It is all lies and deception. Never has the vileness of the reptile bourgeois newspaper hacks displayed itself more splendidly." [2] It was of the utmost importance in these circumstances that the working people of France and the other countries should be told the truth about the Paris revolution, and that the bourgeois slander of the Commune should be exposed. To this end, the General Council made use of the whole organisational network, which the International had built up in its six years, the whole system of contact with local branches, their periodicals and leaders. Marx informed Frankel: "The true character of this grand Paris revolution has been explained to workers everywhere in letters from various secretaries to sections on the Continent and in the United States." [3]

In many countries, Marx succeeded in starting a broad campaign in support of the Commune, which assumed especial proportions in Germany, evidence of Marx's profound influence on the leading representatives of the German proletariat. Bebel's speech in the Reichstag on May 25 was a remarkable expression of international solidarity. In that citadel of the Junkers and the bourgeoisie, Bebel courageously declared — to wails and catcalls from the Right-wing deputies — that the proletariat of Europe regarded the Commune as its own cause and would carry it forward to full victory.

Under the guiding influence of the General Council, the international movement of solidarity with the Commune assumed immense proportions, reflecting the growth everywhere of the activity and organisation of the proletarian masses. Even in the economically backward countries, where the proletariat was just taking its first steps along the way of independent struggle, the Commune aroused a lively response among the workers, generating a tide of sympathy and an urge for cohesion. It helped to bring out the revolutionary tendencies among the working class and to sift the revolutionaries from the reformists. Despite resistance from the latter, despite the police obstacles and bans, and the overt hostility of the official bourgeois world, the revolutionaries selflessly came out in support of the Commune. The remarkable thing was that the demonstra-

---

[1] Marx, Engels, *Collected Works*, Vol. 22, p. 466.
[2] Ibid., Vol. 44, p. 128.
[3] Ibid., p. 142.

tions of solidarity with the Communards and condemnation of the Versailles counter-revolutionaries everywhere acquired the nature of protests against local political regimes, becoming a form of anti-government struggle. These actions in defence of the immortal cause of the Paris Commune continued even after its fall.

Thanks to the International, which was led by Marx, it has become a working-class tradition in many countries to mark the anniversary of the Commune, to stage meetings and rallies in its honour and to send messages of greetings to the French workers. On the first anniversary of the proletarian revolution in Paris, the Spanish socialist newspaper *Emancipación* wrote: "The Commune, which some believe to be dead for ever, is alive in the great heart of the working class." [1] On March 18, 1878, the workers of Odessa, a trading and industrial centre in the south of Russia, wrote to the proletarians of France: "In our native land we are working for the same great goal for whose achievement so many of your brothers, sisters, fathers, sons, daughters and friends died on the barricades of Paris in 1871." [2]

There were considerable difficulties in organising demonstrations of support in England, where any mass attempt to do so was frustrated by the leaders of the Right wing of the democratic republican movement, with covert support from the Right-wing trade unionists. At the same time, the campaign was also harmed by the loud and pseudo-revolutionary manifestations in defence of the Commune by the petty-bourgeois emigrants in London, who now and again claimed to represent the International. The General Council had to display great caution in view of the strident charges of the bourgeois press that the revolution in Paris had been "engineered" by the International from London.

In face of all these obstacles, but helped by the sympathy of the forward-looking workers and the Left-wing republicans, who were honest supporters of the working class, Marx worked to enlist the English workers and progressive circles in the solidarity campaign. Through his personal connections, he even succeeded in getting the bourgeois and trade union press to carry objective reports on the Commune and articles in its defence. Speeches were delivered and resolutions adopted in support of the Communards at workers' rallies and meetings of republican clubs.

As the denouement in Paris drew nearer, it was of the utmost importance that the English working class should give assistance to the Commune. The ailing Marx had been unable to attend a number of General Council meetings, but on May 23 he delivered a long speech opening a debate on this question. He made no secret that the end of the Commune was near, but insisted that this was a temporary defeat for the proletariat. "The principles of the Commune were eternal and could not be crushed; they would assert themselves again and

---

[1] *The First International and the Paris Commune*, p. 386 (in Russian).
[2] Ibid., p. 417.

again until the working classes were emancipated."[1] In the course of the debate, he proposed that the English members of the Council should arrange a public meeting and send a deputation to the British government to demand that it should act against the Versaillese's bloody reign of terror.

Following the publication of Favre's May 26 circular declaring the Communards to be criminals who were to be handed over to the Versailles government, the question of securing asylum in England for the Commune's refugees was of the utmost importance. In support of this demand representatives of various democratic and republican organisations met on May 31 on the General Council's premises at 256 High Holborn (the Council held its meetings there from June 1868 to February 1872).

Gladstone was forced to reckon with the workers' mood and the country's democratic traditions and in reply to a preliminary inquiry by the French government concerning the extradition of Communards said that there would have to be an English court ruling in each individual case. This, of course, gave the refugees some guarantee of safety.

Marx had to work with exceptional vigour to organise support for the Commune's refugees who began to arrive in England, many with their families, in the early days of June. It took much effort to provide them with housing and employment, and to collect the necessary funds to cover the cost of helping them to settle down, which included the provision of clothes and household utensils. Marx saw all this as his internationalist duty, and was not irked by any of these chores, however petty. For a long time, the General Council functioned concurrently as a committee in aid of the Commune's refugees. Members of the Marx family also took an active part in the raising of funds.

Marx sought to hearten the men and women who arrived in London and see to it that they were well cared for. Those who had taken part in the great revolutionary battles in Paris always met with warm hospitality in the Marx home. Walery Wróblewski, a Polish revolutionary and a hero of the Paris Commune, wrote to Engels from Geneva on October 9, 1878, recalling with gratitude the consideration Marx and Engels had shown him in that trying period. He said: "During my exile in London, your home and that of Marx offered a sole and truly fraternal refuge where so much friendship and kindness was shown to me on your part."[2]

The highly secret operation to rescue the Communards who were in hiding from the Versailles police in France called for particular caution and entailed great risks. On many occasions, Marx supplied them with British and German passports, which helped them to travel abroad.

---

[1] Marx, Engels, *Collected Works*, Vol. 22, p. 595.
[2] J. W. Borejsza, *W knegu wielkich wygnańców (1848-1895)*, Warsaw, 1963, p. 278.

Marx felt that the most important task with respect to the Paris Commune was to make a theoretical analysis of its lessons which would help to transform spontaneous sympathy for the Commune into a conscious desire on the part of the mass of proletarians to continue its cause and carry it through to the end. He sought to disseminate the truth about the Commune so as to explode the slanders being spread by the hack writers in the bourgeois press and to correct the distorted picture of its activity presented by the sectarians. In addition there was the task of exposing the hangmen of Versailles, the counter-revolutionary band of Thiers and Favre, which was also highly important in assuring the future of those who had survived the massacre. All of this induced the ailing Marx to work on a General Council address on the Commune, especially after the Council finally decided on April 18, 1871 to put out such an address and asked Marx to write it.

ANALYSIS OF THE COMMUNE'S ACTIVITY.
WRITING THE GENERAL COUNCIL'S ADDRESS

Marx got down to writing the address with his usual thoroughness, by seeking out and studying the factual material about the events he was considering. Evidence of this vast and painstaking work is provided by a notebook containing extracts from the press, which fully reveal Marx's skill in discerning any new historical development at its very inception. From underneath layers of newspaper lies and tittle-tattle, Marx dug out the original fact, figure or typical statement by some political leader to recreate the pattern of events, to trace their development and get to their social and political roots. Alongside references to the bourgeois press, the extracts contained a growing number of references to the periodicals of the Commune which Marx had received from Paris. Step by step, he put on record the Commune's political and social measures, and revealed its substance as the first working-class government. There followed reports on the fighting between the Communards and the men of Versailles.

In the second half of April, while continuing to collect the facts, Marx began to write the first outline of the address. In early May, he started to work on his second outline, before getting down to write the final text.

These two preliminary versions set out a number of important points much more circumstantially, which suggests that Marx was trying to clarify them for himself. This applies to his description of the historical situation which led to the emergence of the Commune, his analysis of the socio-economic measures taken by the first proletarian government and its policy towards the middle sections, the criticism of its mistakes, and also some theoretical generalisations on the tasks and distinctive features of the proletarian dictatorship.

In formulating the fundamentals of his doctrine of the transition period between capitalism and socialism, Marx expressed some profound considerations on the nature of the class struggle at that stage, and on the proletariat's economic policy. The workers' advent to power does not do away with the class struggle but "affords the rational medium in which that class struggle can run through its different phases in the most rational and humane way".[1] Marx stressed that in the period of building the classless society increasing importance would attach to the economic activity of the proletarian state, whose task would be to restructure the whole economic organisation on new principles, to do away with the haphazard, anarchic character of development, and to secure the "harmonious national and international co-ordination" of the social forms of production.[2]

In the latter half of May, Marx was already working on the final version of his address, which he entitled *The Civil War in France*. On May 23, he set out some of its points before the General Council, and on May 30 read the full text, which the Council unanimously approved.

THE CIVIL WAR IN FRANCE

The General Council's Address on the Civil War in France, written by Marx, is among the fundamental programme documents of Marxism, a classic work which shows, with remarkable clarity and scientific precision, the epoch-making significance of the Paris Commune as the first attempt to establish the dictatorship of the proletariat, the prototype of the future socialist state. Lenin wrote that Marx's assessment of the Commune was that of a revolutionary, "profound, clear-cut, brilliant, *effective*".[3] It is written in a vigorously revolutionary style. The proletariat's ideological growth and the profound changes that had taken place in the International since its foundation enabled Marx to discard the moderate form of exposition which he had felt obliged to adopt for tactical reasons, when setting out the ideas of scientific communism in the International's early periods. Once again he could and did use the style of the *Manifesto of the Communist Party*.

He emphasised that the Commune's great historical act was the destruction of the bourgeois state bureaucratic apparatus, of the old army and the police, and of the administrative and judicial bodies. In a letter to Kugelmann he said that the Commune provided a practical and visual confirmation of the conclusion drawn in *The Eighteenth Brumaire of Louis Bonaparte* (1852) concerning the need to smash the bourgeoisie's state machine as the most important condition for the emancipation of the proletariat and all the working people. Marx attached special importance to this key tenet of revo-

---

[1] Marx, Engels, *Collected Works*, Vol. 22, p. 491.
[2] Ibid.
[3] V. I. Lenin, *Collected Works*, Vol. 21, p. 49.

lutionary theory which followed from the whole experience of the Paris Commune. As well as in *The Civil War in France*, he formulated it clearly in the Preface to the 1872 German edition of the *Manifesto of the Communist Party*, which he wrote shortly afterwards together with Engels.

The Civil War in France dispelled reformist illusions about the possibility of using the bourgeois state as such for socialist purposes, and showed that it remains exploitative whatever its form — monarchy, Bonapartist regime, or parliamentary republic.

In considering the working-class attitude to the bourgeois state, Marx displayed his usual dialectical and concrete historical approach, once again objecting to the dogmatic setting up of any propositions as absolutes. While criticising bourgeois parliamentarism and emphasising the limitations of bourgeois democracy, he did not in any way suggest rejecting the use of democratic freedoms and parliament in the interests of the working class and the other working people. The destruction of the bourgeois state by no means ruled out the possibility of preserving the traditional democratic institutions, like universal suffrage, which could well be remodelled in a truly popular spirit. He wrote that "while the merely repressive organs of the old governmental power were to be amputated, its legitimate functions were to be wrested from an authority usurping pre-eminence over society itself, and restored to the responsible agents of society".[1]

Another characteristic feature is that Marx backed up his idea of the forcible destruction of the old state machine with facts taken mainly from the history and contemporary state of continental Europe, believing that in the historical conditions then prevailing this was a necessity for most countries, though not for all. In a letter to Kugelmann dated April 12, 1871, he made it quite clear that what he had in mind were proletarian revolutions on the continent of Europe. At the same time, in countries like England, where no ramified military-bureaucratic machine had yet taken shape, Marx believed the working class could win power and transform the state system on revolutionary lines without an armed uprising, by peaceful means.

One of Marx's greatest achievements as a revolutionary scientist was that he discerned in the Commune the features of an emergent proletarian state, a form of proletarian power which was to replace the broken state machine of the bourgeoisie. He said that the Commune was "the political form at last discovered under which to work out the economic emancipation of Labour".[2] Marx did not confine himself to this general conclusion, but went on to pinpoint the characteristic features of the Paris Commune type of state. He stressed that the very fact that the proletarian revolution combined the break-up of the old bourgeois state with the construction of a new

[1] Marx, Engels, *Collected Works*, Vol. 22, pp. 332-33.
[2] Ibid., p. 334.

state witnessed to its creative character. In this sense, the Commune revealed the ridiculousness of the Bakuninist ideas of a socialist revolution as amounting to total destruction and liquidation of any form of state. The Commune was a practical refutation of the anarchist denial of the dictatorship of the proletariat.

Marx said that the Commune was the first state in history which truly expressed and championed the interests of the working people, and which relied in everything it did on the exploited majority of the people. From the proletarian nature of this state sprang its consistently democratic character: the electivity, removability and accountability to the people of all organs of power and persons in office, the genuinely democratic principles underlying the formation and organisation of the armed forces (National Guard), the new administrative and judicial system, and the public safety system. Everywhere it strove to eradicate the bureaucratic spirit and to do away with the privileges which placed officials above the people.

At the same time, Marx said that the new proletarian power must be sufficiently centralised and solid, for it has to serve as the proletariat's weapon in the class struggle against the bourgeoisie, and to suppress the "slaveholders' insurrections". One mistake the Communards made because of their inexperience was their less than vigorous use of this weapon against the Versailles counter-revolutionaries. However, in contrast to the bureaucratic police methods of centralisation used by the bourgeois state, the proletarian state of the Paris Commune type carried out its centralisation in a truly democratic way.

Another reason why the victorious proletariat had to have a sufficiently centralised power was the great work it had to do in transforming social relations. The Commune, which existed for only 72 days, did not have the time or opportunity to commence this work on the required scale. But the social measures it managed to introduce (transfer to workers' associations of workshops and factories belonging to the capitalists who had absconded from Paris, etc.) were highly valued by Marx as the first steps indicating the lines on which the proletarian state was to pursue its economic policy for the purpose of transforming the means of production, land and capital into "instruments of free and associated labour". Marx warned against a reckless approach in introducing economic and social changes, stressing that these could not be implemented at one stroke, and that neither the Commune nor any other proletarian government could be expected to work such miracles. This was a task for a whole transition period, a relatively drawn-out process, in the course of which both the circumstances and the people themselves were bound to change. In this context, Marx believed the proletarian state's cultural and educational work to be highly important to make education "accessible to all",[1] thereby enriching the mass of people with the achievements of world science and culture.

---

[1] Marx, Engels, *Collected Works*, Vol. 22, p. 332.

Marx used the experience of the Commune to reveal the proletariat's role as the true champion of the interests of the toiling peasantry and the urban petty bourgeoisie — its natural allies — as the fighter for the nation's genuine interests. The Commune clearly showed the internationalist essence of the proletarian revolution and took an implacable attitude to bourgeois chauvinism and nationalism. The first workers' state identified its tasks with the cause of the working people's international emancipation movement. Revolutionaries of various nationalities fought in the Communard ranks. The whole activity of the Commune was a convincing demonstration of the unity of the proletarian revolution's democratic and socialist tasks, and of its national and international goals.

One of the most important lessons of the Commune stemmed not so much from its positive as from its negative experience. The main cause of its defeat was that the workers' power did not have at its head a well-tried leader, a revolutionary proletarian party clearly aware of its tasks. As Engels subsequently wrote in his comments on *The Civil War in France*, neither the Blanquists, who commanded the greatest influence in the Commune, nor the Left-wing Proudhonists, to say nothing of the petty-bourgeois neo-Jacobins, were capable of playing this part. It is true that the course of the revolutionary developments and the class instinct of the masses induced the Communards who were loyal to the revolutionary cause to seek and frequently find the right mode of action. But this was at variance with their own petty-bourgeois doctrines, whose influence they had not yet overcome. This kind of leadership, spontaneous, groping and frequently going against one's own convictions, could not provide consistent revolutionary policies or prevent fatal mistakes. Moreover, the dissent among the various trends frequently disrupted the Commune's own work. The proletariat needed a well-knit militant vanguard, equipped with a knowledge of the laws of social development. Such was the conclusion which Marx had long since drawn, and which the experience of the proletarian revolution in Paris had now fully confirmed. Without a revolutionary party, the working class was unable to retain the power it had won and to carry out social transformations. The whole content of *The Civil War in France* led up to this cardinal point.

With the fervour of the proletarian journalist and without in any way idealising the Commune or glossing over its mistakes, Marx gave a full picture of the great work of the Paris Communards. He was filled with admiration for the genuine humanism displayed by the ordinary workers of Paris, who had made a heroic start on building a new society amid the ruins of war and after a four-month blockade. He was enchanted with the modesty, industry and genuine selflessness with which they fulfilled their historic mission. The protagonist of Marx's immortal work is "working, thinking, fighting, bleeding Paris ... radiant in the enthusiasm of its historic initiative". It was contrasted with the hypocrisy, the class egoism and the brutal savagery of the bourgeois world, personified by the executioners of the Communards, the leaders of the Versailles government, these "bloodhounds of 'order'",[1] who had lost all human semblance.

The revolutionary proletarian wing of the International saw *The Civil War in France* as its programme document and did its utmost to circulate it. The first English edition of 1,000 copies appeared on June 13, followed by another of 2,000 copies at the end of June, and a third in August. Steps were taken at once to issue it in German, French, Flemish, Danish, Dutch, Spanish, Italian, Russian, Serbo-Croatian and other languages. None of Marx's other works had been so widely circulated in such a short period. This soon produced the required results — it was being discussed all over the world. The English bourgeois press failed to kill it by a conspiracy of silence. Already by mid-June, the bourgeois newspapers began to carry extracts from Marx's work supplied with hostile comments, or leaders containing biased attacks against the International. *The Times* had two items, and one of Marx's friends wrote to him in this connection: "Judging by the rage of the English philistine, the world philistine must be in a towering rage over your *Civil War in France*."[2]

Marx and Engels took up the challenge issued by the bourgeois press. In a short time they wrote more than twenty letters, statements and refutations to the editors of the various newspapers, mostly on behalf of the General Council. They were hoping to use the traditions of the English bourgeois press which prescribed the publication of all letters to the editor. However, these traditions did not seem to apply to the advocates of the proletariat, and only a few of the statements were printed in *The Times, The Daily News*, and other newspapers. The rest were published in the International's periodicals in the various countries, while some remained in manuscript form and were published later.

At the height of the malicious campaign against the Commune and the International, Marx, who as a rule did not allow the publication of any matter which indicated that this or that General Council document had been written by him, now assumed personal responsibility for the International's action in defence of the Commune. In a letter to the editor of *The Daily News* on June 26 he declared that he was the author of the Address, *The Civil War in France*, and that he was prepared to appear in court to testify to the authenticity of the facts quoted by him in relation to Thiers, Favre and their henchmen.

The clear-cut statements of the International's revolutionary platform in *The Civil War in France* caused the vacillating elements, many reformists in particular, to withdraw from it. Thus, in June 1871, the General Council had to make an open break with the En-

---

[1] Marx, Engels, *Collected Works*, Vol. 22, pp. 341, 350.
[2] *The First International and the Paris Commune*, p. 524 (in Russian).

glish Right-wing trade union leaders, Odger and Lucraft, who had attacked the Address in the bourgeois press, thereby repeating the treacherous act of the Right-wing Proudhonist Tolain, who deserted to the camp of the Versailles bourgeoisie during the period of the Commune. There were also growing contradictions with the anarchist sectarians.

At the same time, the wide circulation of the official document in which, as Engels put it, the General Council openly took a stand "in favour of communism"[1] was a great help in rallying all the truly proletarian forces within the International. Adoption of Marxist views by the forward-looking proletarians was accelerated. Under the International's revolutionary banner the consolidation of the proletarian masses was considerably advanced.

---

[1] Marx, Engels, *Collected Works*, Vol. 44, p. 184.

CHAPTER THIRTEEN

FIGHTING FOR THE PURITY OF THE INTERNATIONAL'S IDEOLOGICAL PRINCIPLES

Without the International Moor's life would have been a diamond ring without the diamond.

Frederick Engels

PREPARATIONS FOR THE LONDON CONFERENCE

The publication of *The Civil War in France* was only the first step in giving the working class the benefit of the lessons of the Paris Commune. Ahead lay a stiff fight and a great deal of explanatory work so as to secure the official adoption, as the International's programme principles, of the propositions—confirmed and enriched by those lessons—on the socialist revolution, the proletarian state, and the need to establish a revolutionary party of the working class in each country.

Meanwhile, the savage reprisals against the Communards were developing into a world-wide reactionary campaign against the International, increasingly taking the form of concerted action by the European governments aimed at suppressing the working-class movement. The governments of Germany, Austria-Hungary, Spain, Italy, Belgium, Denmark and tsarist Russia joined in the police action of the Versailles government. Even in such "free" countries as England and Switzerland, the reactionary forces clamoured for reprisals against the Communards and members of the International.

The slander campaign against the International assumed unprecedented proportions. In a report to the Hague Congress of 1872 Marx wrote:"This war of calumny finds no parallel in history for the truly international area over which it has spread, and for the complete accord in which it has been carried on by all shades of ruling class opinion." [1] A characteristic feature of this campaign was that the attacks were being increasingly directed against Marx personally.

Following the publication of *The Civil War in France*, Marx became ever more widely known as the leader of the International. As

---

[1] Marx, Engels, *Collected Works*, Vol. 23, p. 226.

his popularity among the workers and progressive circles grew, the enemies of the proletarian movement intensified their fierce attacks on "the supreme chief of the International", as the hostile press called him. The bourgeois press resorted to the old trick of trying to discredit the movement by slandering its leader, and began to spread all sorts of lies about Marx. As in the past, Marx generally refrained from rebutting any personal attacks, but he publicly exposed the slanderers whenever they were likely to harm the International.

The situation was made more complicated by the influx of fresh strata of the proletariat into the working-class movement. Sections of the International were set up and enlarged in Spain, Portugal, Italy, Denmark, Holland and Latin America, then all backward countries. Many of their members were still under the influence of various petty-bourgeois socialist trends, notably Bakuninist anarchism. At the same time the reformists, alarmed by the glow of the Commune, also intensified their attacks on the International's revolutionary principles.

All this made it necessary to clarify further the ideological and political tasks of the proletarian movement and to improve its forms of organisation. However, it was quite impossible in the near future to convene an authoritative general congress to deal with these matters. In view of this, and referring to the precedent of 1865, Marx and Engels proposed to the General Council on July 25, 1871 that a private conference of the Association's delegates should be called in London in September.

The whole burden of preparing the conference fell on Marx and Engels, who had to draft the resolutions laying down the International's political programme in the light of the requirements of the working-class movement after the Commune, and to rally a majority of the General Council in support of these resolutions.

On August 15, Marx motioned in the General Council that the conference should be "confined exclusively to questions of organisation and policy".[1] At the same meeting, the Council instructed the Standing Committee (the Sub-Committee) to draft the resolutions. This made matters much easier for Marx, because his supporters were in a majority on the committee. Marx and Engels informed the local organisations of the International about the convocation of the conference, and in his capacity as Corresponding Secretary for Russia, Marx sent a special communication to Utin, also informing him that the conference was to consider the conflict with the Bakuninists in the Swiss Romance Federation.

By the latter half of August, Marx was so overworked that he was forced to take a rest. He allowed himself a fortnight in Brighton, but even from there he wrote almost daily to Engels about the International's business.

Marx returned to London in early September and devoted all his

---

[1] *The General Council of the First International. 1870-1871*, p. 259.

energy to the preparations for the conference. On September 5, he proposed in the General Council that its members should attend the conference with power to speak on all questions; in the event of any country's delegates being unable to attend, it was to be represented by its corresponding secretary. The Sub-Committee, meeting at Marx's home on September 9 and 11, made a preliminary examination of the draft resolutions. On September 12 and 16, they were discussed and approved by the General Council. As a result, the agenda for the conference was compiled.

Delegates began to arrive in London in mid-September. Marx and Engels met them and helped them to find accommodation.

Marx's home had long been a meeting-place for proletarian revolutionaries arriving in London, who were always given the warmest welcome and the greatest hospitality by every member of the family. Even Anselmo Lorenzo, the Spanish delegate, who had anarchist sympathies, recalled 30 years later the cordial welcome Marx gave him on the eve of the London Conference. In his reminiscences he wrote: "In a short time we stopped before a house. Framed in the doorway appeared an old man with a venerable patriarchal mien.

"I approached him with shy respect and introduced myself as a delegate of the Spanish Federation of the International. He embraced me, kissed me on the forehead and showed me into the house with words of affection in Spanish. He was Karl Marx.

"The family had already retired and he himself served me an appetising refreshment with exquisite amiability. Then we had tea and spoke for a long time of revolutionary ideas, propaganda and organisation. Marx showed great satisfaction with what we had achieved in Spain." They then began to discuss Spanish literature, and the Spaniard was amazed at the depth and competence with which Marx commented on the works of Calderón, Lope de Vega and Tirso de Molina. They talked into the small hours, and Lorenzo stayed for the night. In the morning, Marx took him to the room reserved for him.[1]

MILESTONE IN THE HISTORY OF THE INTERNATIONAL

The London Conference of the International opened at the Artisans' Club in Tottenham Court Road on September 17, 1871. Marx represented Germany, and Engels Italy.

In his opening speech at the conference, Marx formulated its main task, which was to "set up a new organisation to meet the needs of the situation".[2] Accordingly, he focussed the work of the conference

---

[1] *Reminiscences of Marx and Engels*, pp. 289-90.
[2] Marx, Engels, *Collected Works*, Vol. 22, p. 613.

on the question of the proletarian party, the pivotal point in the fight against the anarchist and trade unionist ideologists. A heated debate naturally developed over the main resolution on this question: "Political Action of the Working Class." The initial draft, proposed by Edouard Vaillant, a Blanquist and a prominent member of the Paris Commune, on September 20, said that for the triumph of their cause the workers had to "coalesce their forces as much on the political as on the economic terrain". [1] Despite the vague wording, Vaillant's draft provoked sharp objections from the anarchist delegates, who supported Lorenzo's proposal that an international association of trade unions aloof from politics should be set up in place of the International. A similar idea was proposed by Pierre Delahaye, a French worker and a former member of the Commune, who suggested that an international trade union federation should be regarded as the prototype of the future social order ("Commune of the Future") which, he urged, should be based on the principles of decentralisation and autonomy. Delahaye believed that the International's sections should confine their activities to propaganda. Both draft resolutions were essentially anarcho-syndicalist.

Speaking in defence of Vaillant's draft and elaborating on it, Marx showed that the type of organisation proposed by the anarchists was similar to the one which already existed in the form of the trade unions. In contrast to the anarchist approach, Marx, relying on the experience of the Commune, urged the need for the working class to carry on the political struggle, with the proletarian revolution as its highest form. The success of this revolution, the gaining of political power, was inconceivable without the proletariat being organised into a political party. The trade unions were incapable of playing the proletarian party's role of political educator and leader of the working class.

Marx pointed out the great importance of the trade unions in the proletariat's organisation, but showed their activity to be somewhat narrow and limited. He also brought out the specific defects of the English trade unions of the period, which represented mainly the labour aristocracy, a privileged minority of the English working class, and ignored the interests of the low-paid mass of workers.

Referring to the revolutionary tactics, forms and methods in the political struggle of the working class, Marx said: "We must tell them [the governments] — we know that you are the armed force opposing the proletariat — we shall act against you peacefully wherever possible — and take up arms when that is necessary." [2]

Engels also spoke in support of Vaillant's proposal, his speech being directed both against the anarchist slogan of abstention from political activity and against the trade unionist interpretation of

---

[1] *La Première Internationale. Recueil de documents*, t. II, p. 192.
[2] Marx, Engels, *Collected Works*, Vol. 22, p. 618.

"working-class politics" which meant adapting the proletariat's interests to those of the bourgeoisie. Engels said: "The workers' party must be constituted not as the tail of some bourgeois party, but as an independent party with its own objective, its own politics."[1]

The delegates were strongly impressed by the arguments set out by Marx and Engels, which were logically faultless and based on practical experience in revolutionary struggle. Most of them voted for the resolution "Political Action of the Working Class", the General Council — its leaders Marx and Engels, for all practical purposes — being instructed to produce the final text. The two men fundamentally revised the initial draft taking into account what had been said at the conference in its support. Its final text read in part: "...Against this collective power of the propertied classes the working class cannot act, as a class, except by constituting itself into a political party, distinct from, and opposed to, all old parties formed by the propertied classes."[2]

The other conference resolutions also showed concern for introducing the proletarian party spirit into the International and developing its tactical and organisational principles: alliance between the working class and the peasantry, promotion of the international ties of the working class, including trade union ties, prohibition of conspiratorial and sectarian groups within the International, and so on. Many of these were proposed by Marx. Thus, on a proposal by Marx and several other delegates the conference authorised the General Council to issue a new edition of the Rules, including all the amendments introduced by the congresses and deleting all the points which had become invalid. Thanks to the efforts of Marx and Engels, a revised edition of the General Rules was issued in English and French at the end of 1871, and in German in February 1872. A documentary substantiation of all the amendments was given in the Appendix. The publication of the new Rules, together with the conference resolution requiring every member of the International to have a copy of the Rules — in many countries acknowledgement of paid-up contributions was recorded on it, which made it something of a membership card — helped to consolidate the International's ideological unity and discipline in its ranks.

The conflict between the General Council supporters and the Bakuninists in Switzerland was one of the important items on the conference agenda. Marx was on the commission appointed to inquire into the matter. It met at his house in the evenings, usually after the conference meetings. Marx was more fully informed than the other delegates about the Bakuninists' activity, and from the Swiss members of the International — Utin, Perret and Becker — knew of the circumstances of the split within the Romance Federation at the Chaux-de-Fonds Congress in April 1870. He knew that the Bakuninists' subversive activity had extended beyond the boundaries of

[1] Marx, Engels, *Collected Works*, Vol. 22, p. 417.
[2] Ibid., p. 427.

Switzerland and that they were also engaged in their intrigues in Spain and Italy. He had been informed by Lopatin and other Russian friends about Bakunin's contacts with the revolutionary conspirator Sergei Nechayev, and the harm of the latter's methods—terrorism, provocation and fraud—especially when applied to those who were taking part in the revolutionary struggle. But neither Marx nor his associates were then aware of the existence of a secret Bakuninist organisation within the International itself, nor did they fully realise the scale of this disruptive activity.

All of this determined the tenor of the resolutions drafted by Marx: they reaffirmed the General Council's decision leaving the designation of "Romance" with the old Federal Council, thereby thwarting the Bakuninists' attempt to take over the leadership of the Romance Federation.

Marx was satisfied with the results of the conference, even though success had not come easy. He had to speak 97 times. On September 23, he wrote to his wife in Ramsgate: "The conference is at last coming to an end today. It was hard work. Morning and evening sessions, commission sessions in between, hearing of witnesses, reports to be drawn up and so forth. But more was done than at all the previous Congresses put together." [1]

A meeting was held in London on September 25 to mark the seventh anniversary of the International. It was attended by the conference delegates, members of the General Council and the Commune's refugees. In a long speech, Marx dealt with the historical lessons of the Commune and the importance of the conference resolutions. Emphasising the Commune's epoch-making role as the first attempt by the working class to win political power for the purpose of abolishing all class rule, Marx said: "But before such a change could be effected a proletarian dictature would become necessary, and the first condition of that was a proletarian army. The working classes would have to conquer the right to emancipate themselves on the battlefield. The task of the International was to organise and combine the forces of labour for the coming struggle." [2] In this form, Marx once again emphasised the significance of the highly important conclusion which followed from the lessons of the Commune, the conclusion about the need to establish proletarian political parties.

FIGHT FOR RECOGNITION OF THE LONDON CONFERENCE RESOLUTIONS

Marx realised full well that there would be resistance to the conference resolutions from the anarchist and reformist elements, which made it all the more important to explain their meaning and to sec-

[1] Marx, Engels, *Collected Works*, Vol. 44, p. 220.
[2] Ibid., Vol. 22, p. 634.

ure their full approval by the General Council and the local organisations.

Despite his failing health, Marx tackled this task with the utmost vigour. He was given great assistance by Engels, and all the key documents and decisions of the General Council in that period and all the plans for practical measures were the product of their joint effort.

Marx also received much help from his daughters. Laura and her husband, Paul Lafargue, were doing a great deal to spread the ideas of scientific communism in France and Spain while Jenny and Eleanor handled part of his daily correspondence.

As in the past, Marx and Engels continued to rely on prominent participants in the working-class movement in the various countries, among them their old associates Liebknecht and Bebel in Germany, Becker in Switzerland, General Council members Serraillier, Dupont, Lessner, Lochner and others. They also made new contacts.

In the first few months after the London Conference, Marx and Engels had to devote much time to preparing for the press its resolutions and the new edition of the General Rules and Administrative Regulations, and their dispatch to the various countries. In their letters to working-class leaders they explained how important it was for the local sections of the International to accept these conference resolutions. Some federations held special meetings to discuss them. They were approved by the German sections and the Romance Federation in Switzerland, the Spanish Federal Council, the English sections, and the sections of the International in the U.S.A. and Belgium.

The results of the London Conference were also approved by the German Social-Democratic Workers' Party, notably, by the congress of its Saxony organisation, which was held in Chemnitz on January 6 and 7, 1872, as Marx informed the General Council on January 23. The attitude taken by the Eisenach Party to the London Conference reaffirmed its determination to follow the line laid down by the leaders of the International. In the complicated situation, with reaction carrying on its offensive and sectarian and reformist trends intensifying their activity, it became the main force within the International supporting the struggle of Marx and Engels for ideological purity and for the principles of scientific communism. In the course of this struggle, the revolutionary-minded majority of the international proletarian organisation rallied ever closer round the founders of Marxism.

INTENSIFIED STRUGGLE AGAINST THE BAKUNINISTS. *FICTITIOUS SPLITS IN THE INTERNATIONAL*

At the end of November 1871, Marx learned from an issue of the Bakuninist newspaper, *La Révolution Sociale*, about the congress of the Bakuninist Swiss sections which had been held at the small Swiss town of Sonvillier on November 12. It had declared that the London Conference resolutions ran counter to the principles of the International, proclaimed "complete autonomy" for its sections and refusal to participate in political struggle, and demanded the dissolution of the General Council as a first step towards the abolition of "all authority". It also announced the establishment by the Bakuninist sections in Switzerland of the Jura Federation.

Upon receipt of the Sonvillier Circular, Marx and Engels began writing a reply circular on behalf of the General Council, which they believed should broadly expose the Bakuninists' subversive, splitting activities. At the same time, the leaders of the International took steps to unite the forces capable of rebuffing the Bakuninists. In their letters to representatives of the International in the various countries, Marx and Engels gave a comprehensive critique of the doctrine and tactics of anarchism, exposed the dogmas of denying "all authority" and repudiating working-class participation in political struggle. Marx provided Lafargue and other comrades-in-arms with a detailed explanation of the role and importance, for the International's successful activity, of a central governing body which had authority and was responsible to the whole organisation.

Marx and Engels established direct contacts with representatives of the proletarian masses in Italy and Spain, which the Bakuninists regarded as their citadels. With the help of the International's leaders, groups of General Council supporters were formed in these countries, overcoming the influence of the anti-proletarian ideology and intensifying their fight against Bakuninism. Among those who sided with Marx and Engels was Enrico Bignami, the publisher of a popular Italian newspaper, *La Plebe*. The active fighter against Bakuninism in Italy and later in Belgium was the German socialist, Theodor Cuno.

The stay of Paul and Laura Lafargue in Spain helped Marx and Engels to establish closer ties with the founders and leaders of the Spanish sections, José Mesa, Francisco Mora and Pablo Iglesias.

The fight carried on by Marx's followers against the influence of the Bakuninists led to the establishment, in the summer of 1872, of the New Madrid Federation, the General Council's mainstay in Spain. Through Lafargue and their Spanish friends, Marx and Engels also established contacts with the Portuguese Federation, one of whose leaders, José Nobre-Franca, first brought to the knowledge of the Portuguese workers the *Manifesto of the Communist Party* and other works of scientific communism.

Work on the anti-Bakuninist circular was also advancing. On March 5, 1872, Marx informed the General Council of the gist of a pamphlet entitled *Fictitious Splits in the International*, which he and Engels had written in French. It was unanimously approved by the General Council, which authorised the Sub-Committee to publish it.

This was a fine example of the defence of proletarian party principles and exposure of anarchist sectarianism operating behind a barrage of ultra-Leftist catchwords. It exposed the nature and historical roots of sectarian trends, and proved the anarchists' dogmas to be untenable and their practical activities defective.

The latter point, backed up with irrefutable facts and documents, was of great importance, because most members of the International had not been aware of the Bakuninists' intrigues, or the schismatising and double-dealing methods they were using against the General Council. Nor did everyone fully realise their true aim, which was to take over the leadership of the International. That is why Marx and Engels put on record the whole history of the relations between the Bakuninist official Alliance and the General Council, revealing the underlying purpose of the Bakuninists' slanderous attacks on the Council and their campaign against the London Conference resolutions. Marx and Engels made a detailed examination of every point in the Sonvillier Circular, and showed it to be slanderous and disruptive.

Marx and Engels stressed that all the Bakuninists' activities were inspired by a bellicose sectarianism and aimed at substituting sects for the International, a genuine and militant organisation of the proletariat of all countries united in their common struggle against the capitalists and the landowners and their class rule.[1] They showed that socialist sectarianism was a characteristic feature of the early, immature stage of the working-class movement, of its infancy, much as astrology and alchemy were of the infancy of science. Initially playing a positive part by awakening the workers' interest in socialism, the sects became a hindrance to the working-class movement as soon as it grew out of its early stage. By seeking to revive sectarianism, the Bakuninists stood for a past stage of the working-class movement and were dragging it back.

Analysing the Bakuninists' programme, Marx and Engels showed that it was nothing "but a heap of pompously worded ideas long since dead and capable only of frightening bourgeois idiots or serving as evidence to be used by the Bonapartist or other prosecutors against members of the International".[2] They proved anarchism to be untenable and hostile to the working-class movement and the

---

[1] Marx, Engels, *Collected Works*, Vol. 23, p. 107.
[2] Ibid.

truly revolutionary theory of the working class. By proposing to start with the destruction of any state, the anarchists turned inside out all the fundamental tasks of the proletariat's liberation struggle: the winning of state power and its use to build the classless society in which the state was to wither away. The most harmful thing about their activity was their attempt to inject anarchy into the ranks of the proletariat, which was tantamount to seeking to disarm it in its fight against the exploiters, who wielded powerful political weapons.

When working on the pamphlet, Marx regarded the preservation of the International's unity and the Bakuninists' ideological defeat and isolation as the central task. He took account of the fact that the anarchists' action had been used by the reactionaries, who hastened to announce a split and a crisis within the International. The very title of the pamphlet was a rebuttal of the reports circulated by the bourgeois press. Marx and Engels emphasised that, apart from a handful of schismatics, the International was united in face of the reprisals, and that consolidation of its unity was a pledge of the proletariat's strength and success. To deprive the enemies of the working-class movement of any further pretext for their slanders, the pamphlet was issued as a private circular available only to members of the International.

However, by the time the pamphlet was published — in Geneva in May 1872 — the fight against the Bakuninists had entered a new phase. By the end of April 1872, Marx and Engels received their first information from Lafargue that the Alliance of Socialist Democracy, which the Bakuninists had ostensibly dissolved, had been preserved as a secret society. This naturally put the struggle in a new context. The existence within the International of a secret international Bakuninist organisation, with its own rules and programme, meant that the Bakuninists, who had been undermining the International's ideological unity by their public statements, had in practice already been working for its organisational split. It was now a matter not only of carrying on the ideological fight against them, but also of taking organisational measures to remove this foreign body from the International.

AGAINST REFORMISM

After the Paris Commune, English liberal trade unionism became the main ideological opponent of scientific communism in the International. The trade unionist ideology was voiced in the General Council by the reformists who, while pretending to accept the London Conference resolutions, interpreted them in the spirit of a Liberal Labour policy. The reformists saw the workers' party in England as one which would co-operate with the Liberals, and which with their assistance would put "labour leaders" in Parliament.

Marx realised that a shift to the right was taking place in the English working-class movement, and this made it especially important to prevent English reformists from distorting the International's principles and to lay the ideological foundations for an independent working-class party in England. Marx was hoping that the establishment, in accordance with the London Conference resolution, of an independent British Federal Council (whose functions were earlier performed by the General Council) would promote the solution of these tasks in the post-1871 situation. With the help of the Federal Council, the International could enlist the mass of unionised and non-unionised proletarians in England.

However, many members of the British Federal Council turned out to have connections with the bourgeois radicals. Leadership of the Council was claimed by John Hales, a man of outstanding talent and great vigour, who had at one time supported Marx in the General Council on a number of issues. However, his opportunist tendencies gained the upper hand, and he also strove to align the British Federation's leadership against the General Council. In order to assure himself of a majority on the British Council, Hales brought in representatives of the semi-working-class, semi-radical societies in London with which he was connected.

At the General Council's meeting on January 16, 1872, Marx secured the removal from the Federal Council of all the members of petty-bourgeois organisations, particularly the Universal Republican League. Amendments were introduced into the British Federation's Rules which to some extent prevented petty-bourgeois elements from penetrating into its governing body. Marx succeeded in rallying the revolutionary forces—Lessner, Dupont, and former participants in the Chartist movement, Milner, Murray, Boon and others—with whose help he could carry on the fight against Hales and his supporters.

Of great importance in the struggle against the opportunist trade unionist ideology, which revealed bourgeois-nationalistic tendencies, was the debate on the Irish question which took place in the General Council in the spring of 1872. It was sparked off by the chauvinistic attitude taken by Hales and several other English members of the British Federal Council and the General Council to the Irish sections which were being set up in England and Ireland. Hales opposed the formation of independent Irish sections, an attitude which Marx and Engels exposed as a departure from the principles of proletarian internationalism, stressing once again that one of the key tasks of the English working class was to support the Irish national liberation movement.

Marx took every other opportunity to attack the reformist ideology. On March 3, 1872, Dupont, head of the Manchester foreign section, a part of the British Federation, asked Engels to help him arrange a discussion on the agrarian question. In response Marx wrote in March and April an article entitled "The Nationalisation of the Land" and sent it to Dupont, who presented it as a report in his section on May 8. On June 15, it was published by *The International Herald*, an organ of the British Federal Council. In contrast to the English reformists, who said that the nationalisation demand was an exclusively bourgeois-democratic measure, in this document, which contained important theoretical points, Marx considered the problem in the context of the tasks of the proletarian revolution and the socialist transformation of society. The working class, he said, should not regard as an aim in itself a type of nationalisation that would involve letting out the land, which had become the property of the bourgeois state, "in small plots to individuals or working men's societies".[1] That kind of nationalisation would intensify competition between individual farms and would result in the enrichment of the largest of them at the expense of the producers. The true, "humanitarian goal" of the great working-class movement is to secure the conversion of the land and of all the other means of production into common property, into the property "of the whole nation". That is the only basis on which it would be possible to "work a complete change in the relations between labour and capital", to organise all the branches of production, including agriculture, on rational and efficient lines, making extensive use of the advantages offered by collective socialist labour. "*National centralisation of the means of production* will become the national basis of a society composed of associations of free and equal producers, carrying on the social business on a common and rational plan".[2] Marx stressed, however, that this could be achieved only by means of a deep-going social revolution, as a result of the workers gaining power from the bourgeoisie.

The disagreements between Marx's followers and the opportunist trade unionists developed further in connection with the conflict in the American sections over the bourgeois reformists' attempts to use the International's organisations in the U.S.A. to promote their own ends. Some radical American leaders set up sections with a bourgeois membership in New York and elsewhere, laid claim to the leadership of all the International's organisations in the U.S.A., challenged the powers of their federal organ, and tried to replace the International's programme by the demand for bourgeois reforms. The struggle of the truly proletarian forces against them became highly acute.

In his letters to Sorge, Bolte and other leaders of the International in the U.S.A., Marx laid down the main line of action, which was to prevent the bourgeois radicals from securing leadership of the American working-class movement at all costs. He also urged the need to overcome sectarianism and to draw into the International native-born American workers, particularly those who were members of trade unions. In the U.S.A., where the International's sections were composed mainly of immigrant workers (Germans, French, Irish,

---

[1] Marx, Engels, *Collected Works*, Vol. 23, p. 135.
[2] Ibid., p. 136.

Czechs), the tasks set by Marx expressed the fundamental need of the struggle to establish an independent proletarian party in the country.

Marx kept a close watch on developments in the American sections. A large notebook has survived containing his extracts from American newspapers, pamphlets and other printed matter. On March 5 and 12, 1872, summing up the facts he had assembled, he informed the General Council of the split in the U.S.A. and proposed a number of specific measures to strengthen the proletarian composition of the American sections.

On Marx's proposal, the General Council expelled from the International New York's Section No. 12, the main centre of bourgeois influence.

Seeking to protect the International from being penetrated by "bogus reformers, middle-class quacks and trading politicians", the General Council passed a resolution under which at least two-thirds of the membership of each section was to consist of wage-labourers.[1] On May 28, 1872, the Council recognised the Provisional Federal Council, constituted by the proletarian sections, as the sole governing body of the International in the United States.

The discussion of the split in the American sections revealed that some General Council members gave an opportunist, reformist interpretation to the London Conference resolution on political action by the working class, something that was most pronounced in the speeches of Hales and Eccarius, who urged unity with the bourgeois reformists. A rift developed between Marx and Eccarius, and their long friendship did not prevent Marx from strictly censuring his behaviour. On May 3, 1872, he wrote to Eccarius: "You appear to imagine ... that when you make blunders others must pay you compliments in return, instead of telling you the truth as one would to anyone else."[2] Eccarius failed to understand the key tenets of scientific communism and the true meaning of the London Conference resolutions, went over to the English reformist camp, and became an avowed opponent of Marx and his revolutionary line.

CONTACTS WITH THE COMMUNE'S REFUGEES

The sharpening struggle within the General Council and the growing opportunist tendencies among its English members made Marx take steps to strengthen the revolutionary wing of the Council by enlisting new members. One of the sources on which he drew were the Commune's refugees. Marx's efforts to organise aid to the refugees had brought him into closer contact with the proletarian sections of the French emigrants. Many of those who had been schooled in the Paris Commune, whether Blanquists or Proudho-

---

[1] Marx, Engels, *Collected Works*, Vol. 23, p. 126.
[2] Ibid., Vol. 44, p. 363.

nists, gradually overcame their old utopian views and adopted some principles of scientific communism.

Among those who came closest to accepting Marx's ideas on the socialist revolution were the Blanquists, who stood for the establishment of independent political parties of the working class. They were profoundly influenced by their personal contacts with Marx and such works of his as *The Poverty of Philosophy* and *Capital*.

The best men among the refugees grouped round Marx, including old members of the International — the Hungarian revolutionary Leo Frankel, the French socialist Charles Longuet, the Polish national liberation fighter and a General of the Commune, Walery Wróblewski, and other prominent Commune members. Many of them were co-opted to the General Council.

One of the ways in which Marx exerted an influence on the refugees was by taking part in their Social Studies Circle, which they set up in early 1872. It discussed reports on the Commune and the theoretical and historical problems it had involved. This gave Marx the opportunity to spread the ideas of *The Civil War in France*, and most participants in the circle accepted its truly scientific assessment of the revolution in Paris.

On March 12, Marx was appointed by the General Council as one of the speakers at a meeting to mark the first anniversary of the Paris Commune, which was being arranged together with the Social Studies Circle. On March 18, over 5,000 persons gathered near St. George's Hall, but the meeting was banned by the authorities. Those present elected 150 delegates who then held a meeting in the small hall of the Social Studies Circle, which adopted the resolutions Marx had drafted. One of these hailed "the glorious movement inaugurated upon the 18th March" as "the dawn of the great social revolution which will for ever free the human race from class rule".[1]

PREPARING FOR THE HAGUE CONGRESS

On May 28, 1872, Marx proposed in the General Council that preparations should be started for the International's next congress. An extremely complex situation was being created by the reprisals against the working-class movement, and the Bakuninists' increased subversive activity. The International's political programme, which had been proclaimed by the London Conference, was also being attacked by the reformists. "The period was the most critical one," as Marx said.[2]

Vigorous preparations were started in June. Marx was aware that the congress would have a decisive role to play in establishing the principles of scientific communism. He wrote to Sorge: "*At this Congress the life or death of the International will be at stake.*"[3] It

---
[1] Marx, Engels, *Collected Works*, Vol. 23, p. 128.
[2] *The General Council of the First International. 1871-1872*, p. 206.
[3] Marx, Engels, *Collected Works*, Vol. 44, p. 398.

was hard to choose the venue for the congress. Marx proposed The Hague, because the Dutch government had not openly attacked the working-class movement and in Holland the Bakuninists, to say nothing of the English reformists, had no strong ties.

The main content of the agenda for the congress was determined by the General Council. A circular sent to the sections said that the Council placed "on the order of the day as the most important question to be discussed by the Congress of The Hague, the revision of the General Rules and Regulations".[1] But in contrast to the Bakuninists and their followers, who wanted the Rules to be revised in anarchist terms, Marx and Engels wished the Rules to contain the principal resolutions of the London Conference. Under Marx's guidance, the General Council reviewed the General Rules, article by article. There is an extant copy of the Rules showing Marx's amendments, all aimed at strengthening the proletarian party spirit. He sought to improve the Rules as a basis for formulating the programme documents and organisational principles of proletarian parties to be set up in the future.

On July 23, the Council adopted a proposal to have the London Conference resolution, "Political Action of the Working Class", incorporated in the Rules. Speaking for the motion, Marx showed that it was aimed against both the anarchists and the reformists. He said: "We have two classes of enemies: the abstentionists, and they have attacked that resolution more than any other; the working classes of England and America let the middle classes use them for political purposes; we must put an end to it...."[2]

Assembling the facts about the secret Bakuninist Alliance was another key task, for it was necessary to back up with documents the available information about its subversive activity, to give weight to the proposal to expel the Alliance from the International, as an alien and hostile organisation.

While preparing for the congress, Marx and Engels carried on an extensive correspondence with International leaders in Germany, Spain, Italy, Switzerland and the U.S.A., requesting the necessary documents, insisting on the dispatch of delegates to the congress, and explaining that there was bound to be a decisive clash with the Bakuninists, who would try to pack the congress with their own delegates.

Marx attached special importance to Germany's representation, for he was aware that after the 1871 events the centre of the continental working-class movement had shifted to Germany. Together with Engels, he sought in every way to help German revolutionary Social-Democracy consolidate theoretically and organisationally.

Marx was sure that the participation of the German party, then the only independent proletarian party, in the work of the congress was very important. Under his influence, despite the fact that the

---

[1] Marx, Engels, *Collected Works*, Vol. 23, p. 173.
[2] *The General Council of the First International. 1871-1872*, p. 263.

party's leaders, Liebknecht and Bebel, were then in prison, and the German Social-Democrats were holding in August their own congress in Dresden, Germany sent a highly representative delegation.

Having done his utmost to secure victory for revolutionary principles at the congress, Marx decided not to stand again for election to the General Council because of his failing health and the fact that his vast organisational activity on the Council was hampering his theoretical studies. He informed his close friends of this decision.

On the morning of August 20, he was visited by Friedrich Sorge, who had arrived in London as an American delegate. This meeting and their close association during and after the congress strengthened the friendship between Marx and this talented organiser and propagandist, a veteran of the revolutionary struggle and a man with a rare sense of responsibility and unusually high standards for his own activity.

THE HAGUE CONGRESS

On September 1, Marx, his wife Jenny, Engels, Sorge and the British delegates arrived at The Hague. Marx had a mandate from New York's German Section No. 1 and the Leipzig Section. At The Hague, a letter was received from the Italian workers' society in Porto Maurizio, saying that it had also elected Marx as its representative.

The same day the delegates held a preliminary conference, at which Marx met many of his associates. Paul and Laura Lafargue arrived from Portugal, Becker from Switzerland, and Kugelmann, the worker-philosopher Dietzgen, and one of the editors of *Volksstaat*, Adolf Hepner, from Germany. Among the delegates were also Cuno, Longuet, Wróblewski and Frankel.

The reactionaries of Europe were alarmed by the convocation at The Hague of the International's most representative congress, which was attended by 65 delegates from 15 countries. Spies from various countries flocked to The Hague, as did bourgeois press correspondents. As the recognised leader of the International, Marx was the central figure at the congress. To him, the great proletarian scientist and revolutionary, the author of *Capital, The Civil War in France* and other outstanding works, looked most of the delegates, representatives of the local workers, and democratic circles sympathising with the International. An English participant in the congress, Maltman Barry, wrote that Karl Marx was attracting "special attention, his name on every lip".[1]

The meetings were held in the small Schraifer café at 109 Lombard Straat. The congress aroused great interest among the working

---

[1] M. Barry, *Report of the Fifth Annual General Congress of the International Working Men's Association, held at The Hague, Holland, September 2-9, 1872*, London [1873], p. 6.

people of The Hague, and there was always a crowd to greet the delegates with shouts of welcome and the *Marseillaise*. However, soldiers were posted along the street, and this made organised demonstrations impossible.

The congress was directed by Marx, who spoke on all the main items on the agenda and met with his associates after the meetings.

During the debate on the agenda at the preliminary conference of the delegates, it was decided, on a proposal by Marx, to start with a verification of the credentials. At the first meeting of the congress on September 2, Marx was elected to the Credentials Committee. Just as he had expected, there was a heated debate on the Committee's report, which lasted for three days. On September 3, speaking in defence of Lafargue's credentials, which the Bakuninist delegates had challenged, Marx declared that the existence of a secret international Bakuninist organisation within the International was incompatible with its principles. He told the delegates, in the most general terms for the time being, about the existence of the secret Alliance, and proposed its expulsion from the International.

Marx also spoke in defence of Barry's credentials, challenged by several English reformists on the ground that he was not among the "recognised leaders" of the English working-class movement. In response, Marx said that the official English working-class leaders had "all more or less sold out to the bourgeoisie and the government".[1] The reformist clique of the British Federal Council reacted sharply to his statement. Lenin wrote: "In the Federal Council, in 1872, a vote of censure was passed on Marx for saying that the British leaders had been bribed by the bourgeoisie. Of course, Marx did not mean this in the sense that certain people were traitors. That is nonsense. He spoke about a bloc of a certain section of the workers with the bourgeoisie. The bourgeoisie supports this section of the workers directly and indirectly. That is the way in which it bribes them."[2]

The resolutions adopted in the course of the debate and sanctioning the General Council's actions signified approval by a majority of the delegates of its activity and of its fight against elements hostile to the International. The debate also revealed the balance of forces at the congress. The opponents of the General Council turned out to be in a minority. However hard they tried, the Bakuninist leaders — the Swiss anarchist James Guillaume and his men — could not rally more than 16 delegates.

At the first public meeting on the morning of September 5, Marx read out in German his "Report of the General Council to the Fifth Annual Congress of the International Working Men's Association", which was also reproduced by the various delegates in English, French and Dutch, and approved by the congress. Marx described

---

[1] *The First International. Minutes of the Hague Congress of 1872*, Madison, 1958, p. 186.
[2] V. I. Lenin, *Collected Works*, Vol. 30, p. 512.

how the International was being harassed by world reaction, and gave a general account of the successes and the growing influence of the International. For reasons of secrecy and in view of police persecution, he was unable to provide any concrete data on these points.

His report emphasised the importance of organisation for the workers' struggle. He wrote: "The difference between a working class without an International, and a working class with an International, becomes most evident if we look back to the period of 1848. Years were required for the working class itself to recognise the Insurrection of June, 1848, as the work of its own vanguard. The Paris Commune was at once acclaimed by the universal proletariat."[1]

There was a sharp clash over the question of amending the Rules. Most delegates rejected the anarchist idea of abolishing the General Council and completely decentralising the Association, because in practical terms this meant disorganising the working-class movement. Marx delivered an eloquent speech in favour of extending the Council's powers, but laid special stress on its responsibility to the Association, observing that its authority rested on the approval and support of the whole International. His speech was aimed against the claims to infallibility and dictatorial methods of the trade union leaders, many of whom ran their organisations without being accountable to anybody, and also against the anarchist denial of any authority. Lafargue, Hepner, Sorge and other associates of Marx's spoke in defence of the International's organisational principles, which combined democracy and centralism. Rebutting the Bakuninist arguments, Hepner declared that if the opponents of any authority managed to impose their principles on the working-class movement, "they must establish absolute anarchy everywhere, that is, they must turn the militant International into a petty-bourgeois party in a dressing-gown and slippers".[2]

On September 6, the congress adopted a number of resolutions, drafted by the General Council, amending the General Rules and Administrative Regulations. Amendments to Article 6 of the Regulations empowered the General Council to expel from the Association, pending the next congress, not only sections but also local federations, adding, however, that the extraordinary measure of expulsion had to be approved by the whole International.

By a substantial majority the congress approved the proposal to include in the Rules a somewhat modified text of the London Conference resolution, "Political Action of the Working Class". It read in part: "This constitution of the working class into a political party is indispensable in order to ensure the triumph of the Social Revolution and its ultimate end—the abolition of classes.... To conquer political power has therefore become the great duty of the working classes."[3]

---

[1] Marx, Engels, *Collected Works*, Vol. 23, p. 226.
[2] *The Hague Congress of the First International, September 2-7, 1872. Minutes and Documents*, Moscow, 1976, p. 161.
[3] Marx, Engels, *Collected Works*, Vol. 22, pp. 427, 426.

A special resolution authorised the General Council to initiate the establishment of a mass international organisation of trade unions, thereby stressing that political-party type organisations, like the International, were to play the directing and guiding role in founding mass trade union associations of the working class. In this way, the resolution paved the way for developing the principles of correct relations between the proletarian party and the trade unions.

On its final day, September 7, the congress considered the question of the secret Alliance. On a proposal by Marx, a special commission of inquiry into the matter had been appointed on September 5. Marx and Engels presented it with vast material they had collected, which proved that a secret Bakuninist organisation, with its own programme and rules, clashing with the spirit and principles of the Association, did in fact exist within the International and engage in subversive activity against it.

The vast volume of the documents which were in Russian, French, Spanish and Italian, and the limited time at the commission's disposal made a detailed study and collation of the material impossible. The report on the Alliance, presented by Engels on behalf of the General Council, was only the first effort to summarise all the documents because many of them had been received by Marx and Engels almost on the very eve of the congress. What is more, the members of the commission were misled to a considerable extent by the Bakuninists' false testimony. Guillaume and his friends declared that no secret Alliance existed at all, while the Spanish Bakuninists insisted that it had operated only in Spain and had since been disbanded.

All of this naturally had an effect on the report which the commission submitted to the congress on September 7. Nevertheless, it reached the conclusion that the existence of a secret Alliance was in principle contrary to the International's Rules, and that its programme was basically at variance with the programme of the Association. Acting on the commission's proposal, the congress resolved to expel Bakunin and Guillaume from the International, and also to publish the documents relating to the Alliance.

On the eve of this decision, September 6, Engels proposed, on behalf of Marx, Serraillier, Dupont, Wróblewski and several other members of the General Council, that the General Council should transfer its seat to New York. In proposing such a step, Marx and Engels took account not only of the unfavourable situation on the European continent for the General Council's activity, but also of the danger that, if it remained in London, the British reformists or Blanquists would gradually secure a majority on it. Despite resistance from the Blanquist delegates, the congress passed a resolution on a new membership of the Council and on the transfer of its seat.

The Hague Congress was of exceptional importance for the development of the international working-class movement. Its resolutions were a victory for the theoretical and organisational principles of Marxism over sectarian and reformist doctrines, and dealt a crushing blow at anarchist ideology. The inclusion in the Rules of the main resolutions of the London Conference was of great importance. A new basis was laid for establishing independent political parties in each country and structuring them organisationally in a spirit of democracy and necessary centralism.

AFTER THE CONGRESS. MEETING AT AMSTERDAM

On September 8, 1872, most delegates to the Hague Congress, led by Marx, went to Amsterdam at the invitation of the local section of the International, where a meeting was held in a small hall to mark the end of the congress. Marx was the principal speaker. His address showed a profound understanding of the historical situation and the tasks of the working-class movement. Explaining the main points of the resolutions just adopted at The Hague, Marx pointed out that the congress "proclaimed the necessity of the working classes to fight the old disintegrating society in the political as well as the social field ... One day the worker will have to seize political supremacy to establish the new organisation of labour".[1]

Marx provided a scientific basis for the proletarian movement's tactics. Rejecting the reformist approach and the sectarian-dogmatic attempt to fit these tactics into a set pattern, which allegedly applied equally to all periods and all conditions, Marx elaborated and substantiated the proposition, which he had first put forward in the 1850s, concerning the possibility of the proletarian revolution developing along different lines — peaceful and non-peaceful — in the various countries. He spoke of the need to take into account the concrete historical situation and specific conditions in each country, when selecting the tactical forms and methods of struggle for establishing the proletarian dictatorship and carrying out socialist transformations on the basis of general principles. "We know that the institutions, customs and traditions in the different countries must be taken into account; and we do not deny the existence of countries like America, England, and if I knew your institutions better I might add Holland, where the workers may achieve their aims by peaceful means." However, in view of the historical conditions prevailing at the time, there was very little likelihood of a peaceful revolutionary process, and so "in most countries on the Continent it is force which must be the lever of our revolution; it is force which will have to be resorted to for a time in order to establish the rule of the workers".[2]

---

[1] Marx, Engels, *Collected Works*, Vol. 23, pp. 254, 255.
[2] Ibid., p. 255.

Anticipating false interpretations, Marx made it clear to the audience that the change in the membership of the General Council in view of its transfer to New York did not mean that the old members of the Council, including himself, would no longer take any part in the affairs of the International. "No, I am not withdrawing from the International, and the rest of my life will be devoted, like my efforts in the past, to the triumph of the social ideas which one day, be sure of it, will bring about the universal rule of the proletariat." [1]

After the meeting, Marx and a group of congress delegates went sightseeing in picturesque Amsterdam with its many canals and museums. The following day, Marx and Engels gave a dinner at a small restaurant in Scheveningen, a seaside resort near The Hague, to mark the end of the congress. Among those present were members of the Marx family, Longuet, Cuno and several other delegates. At the dinner, a friendly, convivial affair, Marx said good-bye to the delegates whose way home did not take them through London. Marx returned to London in mid-September and began work on the commission for publishing the congress resolutions to which he had been elected at The Hague. He was also faced with the immediate task of counteracting the distorted accounts of the congress resolutions by the bourgeois and the anarchist press. He wrote to the *Corsaire, Daily News*, and *Volksstaat* refuting their slanderous fabrications, especially the rumour that the Alliance leaders had been expelled from the International not over questions of principle, but because of personal rivalry.

THE INTERNATIONAL'S LAST YEAR

Marx helped the new General Council as soon as it began to function. At his insistence Sorge joined the Council, which then elected him General Secretary. In order to facilitate the Council's difficult task of establishing and maintaining contacts with local organisations in Europe, some of which operated underground, Marx proposed that the General Council should appoint agents for the various countries, mainly from the former Corresponding Secretaries. Naturally enough, the activities of Marx and Engels went well beyond the functions of such agents. They acted as the connecting link between New York and European sections of the International, and also directed the work of other agents. They continued to handle much of the International's business, to formulate its general line, to stand up for its principles in the fight against its opponents, and to carry on an extensive correspondence. Sorge made a point of consulting Marx on key decisions taken by the General Council.

Meanwhile, the situation within the International was growing increasingly complicated, and the struggle between the trends within it

---

[1] Marx, Engels, *Collected Works*, Vol. 23, p. 256.

was sharpening. The transfer of the General Council to New York evoked a protest from the French Blanquist emigrants, and at the end of 1872 they put out a pamphlet entitled *The International and the Revolution*, stating that those who had backed the change had "fled from the revolution". The pamphlet was contradictory: on the one hand, it reflected the influence exerted on the Blanquists by scientific communist views, notably, the idea of establishing a proletarian party, and on the other, paid tribute to adventurist, conspiratorial and voluntarist tactics and betrayed a lack of understanding that revolutionary action required the necessary objective conditions, and that calls for instant action were fatal in the present situation. This, in fact, showed that Marx and Engels had been quite right in anticipating a Blanquist attempt to use the International as an instrument of adventurist policy, and that the Hague Congress had been justified in transferring the General Council from London in order to prevent its seizure by the Blanquists.

It was, however, the Bakuninists who presented the greatest threat to the International. At the time of the Hague Congress and immediately after it, Marx received information that they were establishing contacts with the English reformists and forming a bloc against the revolutionary wing of the International. He soon received news of an international congress held by the anarchists at Saint-Imier in Switzerland on September 15 and 16, 1872, which rejected all the resolutions of the Hague Congress and the powers of the new General Council, proclaimed anarchist principles in defiance of the Rules, and called for an alliance of all trends hostile to scientific communism. The Spanish and Belgian anarchists and the reformist group of the British Federation followed in the wake of the Bakuninist Jura Federation, which had convened the Saint-Imier congress. At their local congresses in December 1872 and January 1873, they likewise denounced the Hague resolutions. The split in the International had become a fact.

Marx and Engels had been aware for some time that organisational separation from the "Left" splitters was inevitable and that the main thing in the given situation was to prevent them from making use of the International's banner. That is precisely what the Bakuninists were seeking to do: they claimed to be the revolutionary wing of the International and tried to isolate Marx's followers from the working-class movement in Europe. Any continuation of unity with the sectarian elements would have meant the destruction not only of the International, but of all its achievements. Accordingly, bringing about an organisational break with the Bakuninists and exposing fully the secret Alliance became the central task.

Marx and Engels reached the conclusion that the point in the Regulations on suspension (until the next congress) was inapplicable to sections and federations which totally ignored the resolutions of the Hague Congress and the Rules of the International, thereby in fact placing themselves outside its ranks. Engels expressed this view in a letter to Sorge on January 4, 1873. On February 12, 1873, Marx substantiated this view in a letter to Friedrich Bolte, a member of the General Council. He wrote: "Everyone and every group has the right *to withdraw from the International,* and when that happens the General Council has only to *record* their *departure* officially; it is not in any way its function to *suspend* them. *Suspension* is provided for where groups (sections or federations) merely dispute the authority of the General Council, or infringe one or another of its Rules or Regulations. However, the Rules have no article concerning groups which reject the organisation in its entirety—for the simple reason that, according to the Rules, it is *self-evident* that such groups no longer belong to the International."[1]

Marx's letter, containing profound ideas on party organisation and on the obligation of all the members of the organisation and its local sections to abide by the decisions of the higher bodies and the Rules was of great practical importance. It became the basis of one of the key resolutions adopted by the New York General Council, which on May 30 resolved that all national or local federations, sections and individuals attending break-away congresses, which rejected the resolutions of the General Congress at The Hague, or expressing approval of these congresses, "*have placed themselves outside the International Working Men's Association and ceased to be members of it*".[2]

For all practical purposes, this meant the expulsion from the International of the Bakuninists and reformists who had taken the path of dissidence. This signified the triumph of the line taken by Marx and Engels to effect an organisational separation with the forces alien to the international proletarian organisation, which enabled the International to keep unsullied its ideological banner and the programme and organisational principles of the proletarian party, that it had formulated.

It was also necessary to expose fully the Bakuninists' secret subversive activity. In accordance with a resolution of the Hague Congress, all the documents collected by Marx and Engels on the secret Bakuninist Alliance were to be published. Since the commission which inquired into the Alliance's affair had been unable to do this, the task was undertaken by Marx and Engels, who decided to issue a special pamphlet on the basis of the available material. Another of Marx's projects, which was largely connected with the fight against Bakuninism, was to write a biography of Chernyshevsky, the material for which he had received from Danielson in April 1873. Marx realised that Bakunin's authority rested on the revolutionary role he had played in the fight against tsarism, and the pamphlet was to present a contrast between Bakunin and Chernyshevsky, another Russian revolutionary fighter and thinker, who was much more consis-

---

[1] Marx, Engels, *Collected Works,* Vol. 44, p. 475.
[2] Marx, Engels, *Werke,* Bd. 18, S. 693.

tent, whose materialist and socialist views were highly superior to Bakunin's idealistic concepts, and whose influence on revolutionary youth — in Russia and elsewhere — was highly fruitful and helped it to draw closer to the working-class movement, something that could not be said about Bakunin's influence.

Marx was unable to realise his project because of bad health, and this also explains his relatively modest participation in preparing the pamphlet against the Alliance, which was written mainly by Engels and Lafargue. Marx himself wrote only the concluding section, but he did help to formulate the plan and the basic ideas of the pamphlet.

The pamphlet entitled *The Alliance of Socialist Democracy and the International Working Men's Association* was published in August 1873. Its authors were right in thinking that there was only one means of combating the Bakuninists' intrigues, "but it will prove astonishingly effective; this means is complete publicity.[1] Marx and Engels employed this means brilliantly. Their pamphlet gave documentary evidence of the existence of Bakunin's secret Alliance, exposed the unsavoury side of its disruptive work and the web of intrigue it had woven in its drive to secure control of and impose its anarchist doctrines on the International.

The analysis of the Alliance's programme showed it to be fundamentally opposed to the revolutionary principles of the International. Marx and Engels revealed the pathetic and primitive nature of the Bakuninists' ideological armoury: their petty-bourgeois egalitarian ideas about the future society in the spirit of "barrack-room communism", their wild calls for rebellion and wholesale destruction, which compromised the revolutionary movement, their use of ultra-revolutionary catchwords, their fanatical hatred for those who did not share their views, and their reliance on the *déclassé* elements, which they claimed to be the most revolutionary force. Marx and Engels defended proletarian party principles, dealt a blow at all forms of petty-bourgeois sectarianism, and showed the harm which factional activity was doing to the working-class movement.

In this extremely complicated situation, with reaction rampant in all the countries of Europe, and the International divided, Marx and Engels began preparations for the following congress which, according to the resolution passed at The Hague, was to be held in Switzerland in September 1873. However, by the second half of August it became quite clear, as Marx and Engels had feared, that the congress could in no sense be a representative one. An extremely unfavourable situation had been created by the bourgeois governments' savage persecution and reprisals and a temporary decline in the working-class movement in many countries.

Marx and Engels discussed the question of their own participation in the forthcoming congress in Geneva, and decided not to go.

---

[1] Marx, Engels, *Collected Works*, Vol. 23, p. 459.

The Sixth Congress of the International Working Men's Association opened at Geneva on September 8, 1873, and, as Marx and Engels had foreseen, was attended mainly by Swiss delegates. Only two delegates were present from other countries. The majority at the congress, led by Becker, had to carry on a difficult fight against the delegates who were inclined to compromise with the anarchists and have the General Council transferred to Geneva, which would have posed a direct threat of its take-over by the Bakuninist sectarians. Thanks to the efforts of Becker and his supporters, the congress overcame the resistance of the vacillating delegates and confirmed the resolutions passed at The Hague. Consequently, the International's last congress remained true to its revolutionary proletarian principles.

DISSOLUTION OF THE INTERNATIONAL WORKING MEN'S ASSOCIATION

While preparing for the Geneva Congress, Marx became convinced that the International had fulfilled its historical mission, and that the post-1871 developments required a change in the organisational form of the working-class movement. The central task now was to unite the proletarian forces within the framework of each country and to set up national socialist workers' parties on the basis of the International's programme. In its old form, the existing international association of the proletariat, whose activity as a legal mass organisation had become virtually impossible in many European countries because of police reprisals, no longer accorded with the changed requirements of the proletarian struggle. On September 27, 1873, Marx wrote to Sorge. "As I view European conditions it is quite useful to let the formal organisation of the International recede into the background for the time being." [1]

Marx was never dogmatic about the organisational forms of the proletarian struggle and believed that in the various periods the need for a change inevitably sprang from the development of the working-class movement itself. He stressed that the end of the International's activity by no means signified a weakening of fraternal international ties between the forward-looking proletarians in various countries. The principle of international unity of the working-class movement, introduced by the International Working Men's Association, remained immutable, and only the forms in which this unity was expressed tended to change. In 1875, he wrote: "The international activity of the working classes does not in any way depend on the existence of the *International Working Men's Association*. This was only the first attempt to create a central organ for that activity; an attempt which was a lasting success on account of the im-

---

[1] Marx, Engels, *Collected Works*, Vol. 44, p. 535.

pulse which it gave, but which was no longer realisable in its *first historical form* after the fall of the Paris Commune." [1]

Marx and Engels did not rule out the possibility of the future development of the socialist movement leading to the establishment of another international association of the proletariat. They hoped that such an association would be based from the outset on the theory of scientific communism and would rely on socialist parties in each country.

By the end of 1873 the International had virtually left the historical scene, and the activity of its organisations had ceased almost everywhere, although the final decision on its dissolution was taken by a conference in Philadelphia on July 15, 1876. This marked the end of one of the most brilliant pages of Marx's activity. Recalling the period on a subsequent occasion, Engels wrote that the International "was indeed an achievement of which its founder might well have been proud even if he had done nothing else". [2]

For nine years, neglecting his scientific research and sacrificing his health, Marx put everything he had into guiding the proletariat's first mass international organisation. The results of its activity were truly majestic. Thanks to the International, the proletariat's revolutionary struggle passed through one of its most important stages and reached a new and considerably higher one.

In the period of the First International, tens of thousands of workers in Europe and America rallied to the banner of proletarian internationalism and became aware of themselves as fighters in the united army of labour. For the first time, the working-class movement appeared on the international scene as a powerful factor of social development. As a result of Marx's guidance of the International, a great advance was made in carrying the great ideas of scientific communism to the broad masses of the working people. Pre-Marxian petty-bourgeois socialism of every type was defeated and on the retreat, a Marxist proletarian party was set up in Germany, and the prerequisites were created for the formation of similar parties in other countries.

Under the International, the working class gained vast experience in fighting for its interests. The Paris Commune, whose establishment had been prepared by the International's whole activity, and Marx's theoretical generalisation of the lessons of the Commune were of exceptional importance for the proletarian movement in the subsequent period. Under Marx's direct influence, a brilliant group of proletarian revolutionaries, organisers, journalists and propagandists emerged in the ranks of the International, whose ideas spread to many parts of the world, including the then backward countries of Eastern Europe and Latin America.

The International guided by Marx "laid the foundation of the

---

[1] Marx, Engels, *Collected Works*, Vol. 24, p. 90.
[2] Ibid., p. 468.

proletarian, international struggle for socialism".[1] Its services to the international working-class and communist movements, and to subsequent generations of staunch fighters against the tyranny of capital for social progress and communism, will never be forgotten. "It is unforgettable, it will remain for ever in the history of the workers' struggle for their emancipation."[2]

---

[1] V. I. Lenin, *Collected Works*, Vol. 29, p. 307.
[2] Ibid., p. 240.

CHAPTER FOURTEEN

FURTHER DEVELOPMENT OF THE THEORY AND TACTICS OF THE WORKING-CLASS MOVEMENT

> *Karl Marx was one of the rare men who could be leaders in science and public life at the same time; these two aspects were so closely united in him that one can understand him only by taking into account both the scholar and the socialist fighter.*
>
> Paul Lafargue

The period after the Paris Commune of 1871 was marked by substantial changes in the economic and political life of the capitalist countries. In 1873 the industrial boom of the beginning of the decade gave way to a world economic crisis of unprecedented duration, which hit Germany and the U.S.A. hardest of all. The industrial and commercial crisis coincided with the start of a prolonged agrarian crisis. Marx had predicted the severity of the crisis from its first symptoms. In January 1873 he wrote in his afterword to the second German edition of Volume One of *Capital*: "That crisis is once again approaching, although as yet but in its preliminary stage; and by the universality of its theatre and the intensity of its action it will drum dialectics even into the heads of the mushroom-upstarts of the new, holy Prusso-German empire." [1]

The role of the various countries in the world economy had begun to change. Britain had reached the zenith of her commercial and industrial monopoly. There were signs of much faster economic development in the U.S.A. and Germany. It became evident that premonopoly capitalism was gradually growing into monopoly capitalism, a process which was completed at the turn of the century. Joint-stock capital was gaining ground, though in the 1870s cartels were still "a transitory phenomenon". [2]

In political terms, the 1870s, like the two following decades, were relatively peaceful and were not marked by any large-scale revolutionary storms. This period was described by Lenin as follows: "The West had finished with bourgeois revolutions. The East had not yet risen to them." [3] In Europe there was some stabilisation of the po-

---

[1] Marx and Engels, *Selected Works*, Vol. 2, p. 99.
[2] V. I. Lenin, *Collected Works*, Vol. 22, p. 202.
[3] Ibid., Vol. 18, p. 583.

wer of the counter-revolutionary bourgeoisie and the big landowners either in the form of a conservative bourgeois republic, as in France, or of a reactionary monarchy, like the one established in the German Empire in January 1871, which Marx said was "nothing but a police-guarded military despotism, embellished with parliamentary forms, alloyed with a feudal admixture, already influenced by the bourgeoisie and bureaucratically carpentered".[1] By the end of the 1870s revolutionary situation had begun to take shape in Russia alone of all the European states, and the national liberation struggle against Turkish rule continued in the Balkans.

As Marx had foreseen, the outcome of the Franco-Prussian War paved the way for fresh international conflicts. In 1873, 1875 and 1877 war appeared to be imminent because of the chauvinistic, aggressive policy pursued by the ruling classes of the German Empire and the revanchist aspirations of the bellicose circles of the French bourgeoisie. Colonial expansion was being intensified, with the African continent as one of its main areas.

In these circumstances, the working class was faced with the task of rallying its forces and preparing for fresh revolutionary battles, the question of establishing proletarian parties in some countries being well in the foreground. Lenin wrote: "The First International had played its historical part, and now made way for a period of a far greater development of the labour movement in all countries in the world, a period in which the movement grew *in scope*, and *mass* socialist working-class parties in individual national states were formed."[2]

However, the formation of socialist parties was slowed down by a growth of reaction, a certain decline in the political activity of the working class in a number of countries and the activity of sectarian trends, which had collapsed but not yet disappeared entirely. The influence of reformed ideology was still felt, especially in Britain and the U.S.A. The extensive spread of Marxism had its negative aspects as well: Marxist ideas were frequently adopted quite superficially, and this led to opportunist vacillation among inconsistent elements.

Nevertheless, the working-class movement made steady headway. Thanks to the International's activity, Marxism was firmly entrenched in a number of countries and was exerting a decisive influence on the formation of proletarian parties.

The consolidation and cohesion of the proletarian elements on the basis of Marxism were promoted by the theoretical and practical activities carried on by Marx and Engels in this period, their tireless propaganda of revolutionary theory, and their constant assistance to working-class leaders in many countries.

---

[1] Marx, Engels, *Collected Works*, Vol. 24, p. 96.
[2] V. I. Lenin, *Collected Works*, Vol. 21, p. 49.

THE MID-1870s

Relieved of the pressure of organisational work in directing the International, Marx now devoted most of his time to scientific research. The first thing he had to do was to complete *Capital*. As usual he worked with great enthusiasm and intense concentration. He worked even when resting: on his walks he either talked his ideas over with companions or turned over various problems in his mind. Scientific and political matters were most intensively discussed during his almost daily meetings with Engels, when the two men either took a stroll or talked in Marx's study, as they paced diagonally across the room, Marx from one corner to another and Engels at right angles to him. Now and again their conversation developed into a scientific debate, something the two men frequently prepared for in advance.

Marx's health again gave way under the strain of overwork: in the spring of 1873, he developed acute headaches and insomnia. He was faced with the threat of disablement, a most horrible prospect for a man of his temperament. Later he wrote to Sorge that "being *unable* to work is indeed a death sentence for any man who is not a beast". [1] His doctors gave him strict orders to work no more than four hours a day and take holidays outside London as frequently as possible. Engels undertook to see that Marx carried out his doctors' orders and set himself the task of rescuing him from this "work routine". [2]

However, Marx's stay at Harrogate in the late autumn of 1873 and at Ramsgate on the coast in the spring of 1874 did not markedly improve his condition. Moreover, in the summer of 1874, his chronic liver complaint grew more acute.

On the advice of his doctors, Marx went to Karlsbad (Karlovy Vary) in mid-August 1874, accompanied by his daughter Eleanor (Tussy), where he stayed from August 19 to September 21. On this and subsequent visits to the spa he stayed at the Hotel Germania, registering as Charles Marx, rentier, so as not to attract undue attention.

The waters of Karlsbad had a beneficial effect, and his general state improved after two visits—from August 15 to September 11, 1875, and from August 15 to September 15, 1876 (when he was again accompanied by Eleanor).

He was feeling so much better that on his way back, in September 1874, he stopped at Dresden, Leipzig, Berlin and Hamburg, and saw many of the German Social-Democratic leaders, including Wilhelm Liebknecht, August Geib and Theodor Yorck, and the publisher Otto Meissner. In 1875, at the invitation of Max Oppenheim, a relative of Kugelmann's, who lived in Prague and was a great admirer of

---

[1] Marx, Engels, *Werke*, Bd. 33, S. 634.
[2] Ibid., S. 594.

its historical and revolutionary traditions, Marx visited "the old Hussite city". [1] On September 15, 1876, he again visited Oppenheim in Prague and then, accompanied by Eleanor, travelled to Bingen and Kreuznach where he showed his daughter the spots where 33 years ago he and Jenny had spent their first few months of married life. Before returning to London, Marx went to Liège, where he saw Utin, a former leader of the International's Russian section.

Although his stay in Karlsbad had been highly beneficial from the medical point of view, Marx was less than pleased at having to associate with the people at the spa. He was extremely irritated by the "gang of Hamburg-Bremen-Hanover philistines, male and female alike, who simply refused to leave him in peace". [2] He was also disappointed with Kugelmann, whom he met often during his first stay at Karlsbad. From the very first, Kugelmann annoyed Marx with his advice to drop politics and concentrate on science. Marx was also indignant at Kugelmann's high-handed treatment of his wife and daughter. One day, he could stay it no longer and told Kugelmann what he thought of him. They fell out and did not make up until just before Marx's departure from Karlsbad, but the old cordial relations were never resumed. Marx never forgave his old friend for his narrow-mindedness and selfishness.

However, Marx did meet some interesting people in Karlsbad, among them doctors, artists and scholars who stood out from the crowd because of their broad-mindedness and education. In the autumn of 1875, Marx made friends with the eminent Russian ethnographer, historian and lawyer, Maxim Kovalevsky, whom he had earlier met in London. They frequently went for long walks together in the countryside.

In Karlsbad, Marx was soon under surveillance by the local authorities. The name of the "Red doctor" had long struck fear into the hearts of the officials and the bourgeois public, who hated him and associated his name with all sorts of revolutionary events, including anarchist *putsches* in Italy. The German Social-Democrat, Wilhelm Blos, was told by an eyewitness that the arrival in Milan in 1873 of a German called Max Karl alarmed the police authorities because his name had been erroneously put down in the foreigners' register as Karl Max. The house where he was staying was surrounded by the police, everyone present was searched, and he himself taken to the police station, where it required some effort on his part to prove that even his surname was different.

Marx had been living in democratic England for over two decades but even there he met with hostility on the part of official circles. When in August 1874, on the eve of his first trip to Karlsbad, he filed his application for British citizenship with the Home Secretary, it was rejected, the reason being a special report from the London Police Office describing Marx as an advocate of dangerous "Commun-

---

[1] Marx, Engels, *Werke*, Bd. 33, S. 646.
[2] Ibid., S. 117.

istic principles" and a man who "has not been loyal to his own King". [1]

Naturally enough, Marx could expect an even cooler reception on the territory ruled by the Hapsburgs. At first, he was not identified, but on August 30, 1874, the local *Der Sprudel*—a tittle-tattle, as Marx called it—reported the arrival of the "leader of the International". When Marx came to Karlsbad the second time, the police authorities were fully alerted. On September 1, 1875, the chief of the Karlsbad district reported to his superiors in Prague that "an outstanding leader of the Democratic-Social party" was visiting the spa. The Governor of Bohemia sent a corresponding report to the Minister of the Interior in Vienna. But since Marx's behaviour did not give the government officials any pretext for open harassment, they had to confine themselves to issuing orders for him to be kept under "constant secret surveillance".

In August 1877, Marx, his wife Jenny and Eleanor took a holiday at Neuenahr, a lesser known spa in Rhenish Prussia, whose mineral waters were not as effective as those of Karlsbad. He wrote to Engels that he was keeping the Karlsbad waters in reserve, in case his ailment took a dangerous turn. "One has to treat his phisique with as much diplomacy as everything else," [2] he added. But Marx never had another opportunity to take the Karlsbad waters, which were so good for him, because police persecution of Social-Democrats started in Germany and then in Austria-Hungary, and the introduction of Bismarck's Anti-Socialist Law made it impossible for him to travel to Central Europe.

The illness which had been eroding Marx's physical strength for years could not quench the energy of his brain, the tireless spirit of the researcher and the temperament of the fighter. In the second half of the 1870s, his health slightly improved and he threw himself into his scientific studies with fresh zeal. Everyone who met him in that period was amazed by the clarity and depth of his judgments, the scope of his scientific knowledge and interests, and his remarkable grasp of the international situation and the state of affairs in the various countries. A correspondent of *The Chicago Tribune*, who interviewed him in December 1878, "was struck with *his intimacy with American questions* which have been uppermost during the past twenty years". [3] Another American journalist and socialist, John Swinton, had a talk with Marx at Ramsgate in the autumn of 1880, and recorded his impressions as follows: "His dialogue reminded me of that of Socrates—so free, so sweeping, so creative, so incisive, so genuine—with its sardonic touches, its gleams of humor, and its sportive merriment. He spoke of the political forces and popular movements of the various countries of Europe—the vast current of the spirit of Russia, the motions of the German mind, the action of

---

[1] Marx, Engels, *Collected Works*, Vol. 24, p. 564.
[2] Marx, Engels, *Werke*, Bd. 34, S. 59.
[3] Marx, Engels, *Collected Works*, Vol. 24, p. 569.

France, the immobility of England. He spoke hopefully of Russia, philosophically of Germany, cheerfully of France, and sombrely of England — referring contemptuously to the 'atomistic reforms' over which the Liberals of the British parliament spend their time." [1]

Marx continued to be a great lover of belles-lettres and the arts, as we are told by all of the many visitors to his house at 41 Maitland Park Road — his last place of residence, to which he had moved in March 1875. Marian Comyn, a friend of Eleanor's, said that on his writing-desk lay the books of many poets and prose writers, including the novels of Edward Bulwer-Lytton. *The Chicago Tribune* correspondent reported seeing on the shelves in Marx's study, alongside a great range of scientific books in different languages, the works of Shakespeare, Dickens, Thackeray, Molière, Racine, Voltaire, Goethe, and many others. The family constantly discussed literary topics, the Victorian writers, the Brontë sisters, and the latest fiction in the various countries. Marx frequently attended musical soirées at Karlsbad and loved choir recitals. He had long talks with the painter Otto Knille about the fine arts.

In London Marx often went to see plays, especially Shakespeare's plays. Like other members of his family he had a profound understanding of the talented rendering of Shakespeare's plays by the outstanding English actor and director Henry Irving. With Marx's approval his wife campaigned in the German press in support of the efforts of Irving and his fellow-actors to rekindle an interest in the work of the great playwright. In a series of articles on theatrical life in London, which was published in the democratic *Frankfurter Zeitung und Handelsblatt* from November 1875 to May 1877, Jenny Marx gave a discriminating description of Irving's realistic manner in performing the leading roles in Shakespeare's tragedies *Hamlet, Macbeth* and *Richard III*. She had some caustic remarks, which were very much to the point, about the snobbishness and philistine tastes of the English bourgeois public which delighted in banal melodrama. Jenny said that was the reason for its indifference to Shakespeare and its ill will to such forward-looking intellectuals as Irving. The thrust of her articles was that the proletarian public was alone able truly to appreciate Shakespeare, whose humanistic traditions it would carry on. Marx subscribed to these and other statements, including those relating to the actor's craft.

In 1880 and 1881 Shakespeare play-readings were held at his home by a group of amateurs, who jokingly called themselves the Dogberry Club.

Marx still enjoyed playing chess. His most frequent partner was now Tussy.

---

[1] Marx, Engels, *Collected Works*, Vol. 24, pp. 583-84.

IN THEIR FATHER'S FOOTSTEPS

For Marx, his grown-up daughters were not only loved and loving children, but also comrades-in-arms. By the end of the 1860s, Jenny and Laura, and in the 1870s, Eleanor all became active fighters for the working-class cause. Marx had involved them in his scientific and party work in one form or another. He had good reason to be proud of his daughters and was quite sure that they would never swerve from their chosen path.

At an early age, the three girls insisted on contributing to the family budget. Jenny began to give private lessons in 1869. The 18-year-old Eleanor went to teach at a school at Brighton in 1873, but had to give up her work for reasons of health.

All three had a broad outlook, were well read, knew many foreign languages well, and expressed themselves fluently in writing. Apart from the social science, and the history of the working-class and the revolutionary movement, Jenny enjoyed studying the natural sciences and was familiar with Darwin's theory. Laura was a first-rate translator, and subsequently translated the *Manifesto of the Communist Party* and several other Marxist works into French, and songs by Béranger, poems by Chamisso, Eugène Pottier (the author of the *Internationale*), Baudelaire and other poets into English. Eleanor was widely read in English and world literature, and also had an artistic talent, which enabled her to try her hand at Shakespearean criticism and to act on the stage. She continued to write and take a great interest in the theatre in later years, but participation in the working-class movement always came first.

From childhood, the three girls had a whole-hearted sympathy for the liberation movement. Jenny's favourite hero was Gracchus, the famous tribune of the people in ancient Rome, Laura's the revolutionary poet Shelley, and Eleanor's Garibaldi. As they grew up, their romantic revolutionary frame of mind developed into a conscious urge to make a personal contribution to the cause of emancipating the oppressed. All three were internationalist-minded and rejoiced at the news of revolutionary events in any country. As a mark of solidarity with the fighters in the Polish insurrection of 1863-64, Jenny wore an insurgent cross which she had been given. She hung it on a green ribbon — the national emblem of the fighters for Ireland's independence — following the British government's execution of the Fenians. The three girls had a great many friends among the leaders of the International and the heroes of the Paris Commune. They warmly supported the selfless struggle of the Russian revolutionaries against tsarist autocracy, and Lopatin, Lavrov, Yelizaveta Dmitriyeva, Hartmann and subsequently Stepnyak-Kravchinsky were among their friends.

In 1868 Laura married Paul Lafargue and became his true aide in the revolutionary struggle, remaining by his side wherever duty took him. With her young child, she followed Paul to Spain, where he had sought refuge from the Thiers police, who were hounding him for helping the Paris Communards in his capacity as leader of the International's Bordeaux section. Laura helped Paul to spread the International's ideas in Spain and Portugal, and together with him attended the Hague Congress.

Jenny, who took an active part in the International's affairs, was likewise to have her revolutionary steadfastness put to a stern test. In the summer of 1871 she and Eleanor were taking a cure at Bagnères-de-Luchon, a health resort in the south of France, when she was arrested and interrogated hard by Kératry, the Prefect of the Upper Garonne Department. Kératry was trying to get some information about Lafargue, who had fled to Spain. But all his wiles and threats foundered on Jenny's self-possession and sangfroid, and he was forced to pay an angry tribute to the vigour of all the women in the Marx family. Upon her return to London, Jenny exposed the ringleaders of the Thiers republic in the press.

In the autumn of 1872, after the Hague Congress, the Marx family reassembled in London, with Paul and Laura settling down in Hampstead, not far from the Marx home. In October 1872, Jenny married Charles Longuet, a prominent leader of the International. Like Laura, Jenny had to lead a life of hardship as the wife of a political refugee. Charles sought without success to find permanent employment in Oxford, and soon had to return to London. Only towards the end of 1874 was he able to find a permanent post as a teacher of French. Many trials also fell to the lot of the Lafargues. Despite their daughters' constant uphill fight against privation, Karl and Jenny were happy to see them married to men who were on their side. During Jenny's engagement, her mother wrote to Liebknecht that "the harmony of opinions and convictions between the young couple" was "a guarantee of their future happiness".[1] This was particularly true of the Lafargue family.

Following the 1880 amnesty, Longuet returned to France, and was shortly followed by Lafargue, while Jenny and Laura stayed behind in London for some time with their ailing parents. Jenny supplied Charles with the background material for his articles in the newspaper *Justice*. Her letters showed an acute response to the struggle within the French working-class movement over the establishment of the French Workers' Party and its programme. Much as she loved Charles, she nevertheless resolutely condemned his ideological vacillations at the crucial moment, and frankly told him that she disagreed with his opposition to the Marxist programme and his growing contacts with bourgeois radicals. Upon her return to France, Laura became an active member of the Workers' Party.

Eleanor, the youngest of the three, also began to spread socialist ideas at an early age. In 1874, the French emigrant journal *Rouge et Noire* published her translation of speeches by German Social-

---

[1] Marx, Engels, *Werke*, Bd. 33, S. 703.

Democrats. She also took an active part in English public life and in organising support for the Irish national liberation movement. In 1873, the Marx family became acquainted with Edward Aveling, a doctor of natural sciences and a Darwinist. Eleanor married Edward in 1884, after her father's death, and in the 1880s the two began to play a prominent part in the British and the international working-class movement.

Marx felt profoundly the misfortunes which now and again fell to the lot of his daughters. In August 1874, he wrote to Kugelmann: "I am in this respect less stoical than in others, and family afflictions always hit me hard." [1] One of the cruellest blows for Marx was the death of the Lafargue's three small children and of Jenny's firstborn. On August 14, 1874, he wrote to Jenny: "My heart bleeds when I think of him and how can one get such sweet, lovable little chap out of one's mind! But I hope, my child, that you will be brave for your old man's sake." [2]

Marx loved his grandchildren as he did his own daughters. Jenny had four other sons—Jean (1876), Henri (1878), Edgar (1879), and Marcel (1881), and a girl, Jenny (1882)—and it gave Marx real pleasure to romp with the children and take part in their games. Edgar Longuet, one of Marx's small favourites at the time, subsequently recalled: "He would play with children as though a child himself, without any thought of compromising his dignity." [3] The grandchildren were always treated as equals by their grandfather.

By "a fitting fulfilment of the duties of grandfather", as Marx himself put it in a letter to his eldest daughter, he meant much more than the mere ability to entertain the children, give them nice presents, and so on. He believed this implied above all concern for their development and education, and so attached much importance to reading and giving the children an idea of the great literary classics from an early age. He saw to it that there was sincerity, mutual respect and friendship in the family. He himself was an unquestioned authority even for the most unruly of the children.

POLEMICS AGAINST THE ANARCHISTS ON THE THEORY OF SOCIALIST REVOLUTION

Marx's theoretical activity in this period was mainly concerned with *Capital*, but now and again the needs of the growing working-class movement and the ideological fight against anti-Marxist trends impelled him to deal with other aspects of revolutionary theory, and to develop and concretise the theoretical and tactical propositions of scientific communism. Accordingly, he took an active part in the po-

---

[1] Marx, Engels, *Werke*, Bd. 33, S. 637.
[2] Ibid., S. 640.
[3] *Reminiscences of Marx and Engels*, p. 264.

lemics against the anarchists in the Italian socialist press and also made a general critical analysis of anarchist methods and views.

In January 1872, Marx sent the Italian annual *Almanacco Repubblicano* an article entitled "Indifference in Political Matters". The publication of the almanac was delayed, and it did not appear until the end of 1873. Together with Marx's article it contained one by Engels entitled "On Authority".

Marx's article showed the harm of the anarchist doctrine of working class abstention from political activity, from participation in the democratic movement, establishment of an independent political party, and so on. Consistent implementation of this doctrine, behind a façade of pseudo-revolutionary talk about "social liquidation", which allegedly alone could benefit the workers, inevitably made the proletariat inactive, demoralised it and led to the perpetuation of wage-slavery. "In expectation, therefore, of this famous social liquidation, the working class must behave itself in a respectable manner, like a flock of well-fed sheep; it must leave the government in peace, fear the police, respect the law and offer itself up uncomplaining as cannon-fodder." [1]

The main point Marx made in the article was that the proletarian state was a necessary instrument in the socialist transformation of society. The anarchists insisted that to substitute a revolutionary proletarian dictatorship for the bourgeois dictatorship was a "horrible crime and an affront to every principle", and in his polemics with them Marx emphasised that in historical terms the proletarian state was transient. Lenin commented: "To prevent the true meaning of his struggle against anarchism from being distorted, Marx expressly emphasised the 'revolutionary and *transient* form' of the state which the proletariat needs." [2]

Marx put his views of the laws governing the socialist revolution into a system and gave them greater depth when making a critical study of Bakunin's book *Statehood and Anarchy*, which appeared in Zurich-Geneva in October 1873 and which was hailed by Bakunin's followers as the anarchist movement's programme. Naturally, Marx was unable to ignore this work by one of his main ideological opponents in the International. Between April 1874 and early 1875 he wrote a synopsis of the book, consisting of extracts from it and his comments, entitled "Konspekt von Bakunins Buch *Staatlichkeit und Anarchie*"[3], which was first published in the Soviet Union in 1926. It amounted to a critical analysis of Bakunin's principal historical and social views and an elaboration of his own ideas on the main aspects of the proletariat's revolutionary theory.

Marx showed that the characteristic features of Bakunin's outlook were voluntarism, failure to see the need for objective socio-economic prerequisites for revolution, orientation on the *déclassé*

---

[1] Marx, Engels, *Collected Works*, Vol. 23, p. 393.
[2] V. I. Lenin, *Collected Works*, Vol. 25, p. 441.
[3] "Notes on Bakunin's Book *Statehood and Anarchy*".

sections, and contrasting the "farming and stockbreeding" peoples of Eastern Europe, who were allegedly the most prepared for socialism, with the West-European peoples, who had been corrupted by civilisation. Marx wrote: "*Willpower*, not economic conditions, is the basis of his social revolution."[1]

Marx showed that behind the anarchist leader's loud talk about abolition of the state lay the highly primitive ideals of a future "anarchist society", based on a "levelling off" of economic and cultural standards in the advanced and the backward countries. These ideals fully reflected Bakunin's neglect of the role played by the development of the productive forces, the historical mission of the working class, its political power as an instrument of social change, and the importance of the proletarian party. Marx wrote that Bakunin "understands absolutely nothing of social revolution, only its political rhetoric".[2]

Marx countered Bakunin's views with profound ideas on the substance of the proletarian state. When the working class takes power, it is faced with the need to suppress the resistance of its class enemies and to destroy the old organisation of society. To substitute for the latter a "new social" organisation is the main task which arises before the working-class state. Marx saw this state as the main instrument of social transformation in the period of transition from capitalism to communism, as the main force exerting an active influence on and accelerating objective, social processes.

Marx also formulated much more clearly than in his earlier writings the question of the historically transient character of the proletarian dictatorship, and of the social basis for the disappearance of the state as such. "As long as the other classes, above all the capitalist class, still exists, and as long as the proletariat is still fighting against it (for when the proletariat obtains control of the government its enemies and the old organisation of society will not yet have disappeared), it must use *forcible* means, that is to say, governmental means; as long as it remains the class itself, and the economic conditions which give rise to the class struggle and the existence of classes have not vanished, they must be removed by force or transformed and the process of transforming them must be accelerated by force."[3] Marx held that deep-going social change would create the prerequisites for the disappearance of the state and pointed out that "when class rule has disappeared there [will] be no state in the present political sense."[4]

Marx also reached some important conclusions on the policy the proletariat would have to adopt on the peasant question once it took power. He formulated the proposition about an alliance between the working class and the peasantry not only as an indication

---

[1] Marx, Engels, *Collected Works*, Vol. 24, p. 518.
[2] Ibid.
[3] Ibid., p. 517.
[4] Ibid., p. 519.

of the need to win the mass of peasants to the side of the proletarian state by taking effective measures in their interest. He supplemented this with highly fruitful ideas about involving the toiling peasantry in the socialist transformation of society, and about the methods to be used in carrying out the switch from private peasant ownership to social ownership, from small-scale individual farming to large-scale collective farming. He stressed that any coercive, violent measures, artificially accelerating the process, were unacceptable, and that the peasant should "arrive at this economically of his own accord". It was intolerable "to get the peasant's back up, e.g. by proclaiming the abolition of the right of inheritance or the abolition of his property".[1]

The policy with respect to the peasantry has to be flexible and take into account the specific social composition, traditions and customs of the rural population in the various countries. Where the capitalist tenant has ousted the peasant and the actual tiller of the soil has become for all practical purposes a proletarian, the switch to socialist ownership can be effected much more quickly. But where the small peasant holding predominates, excessive haste in this matter can spoil everything and will be just as inappropriate as the measures proposed by the Bakuninists, which were in effect designed to bring about an even greater parcelling of the land.

IDEOLOGICAL LEADERSHIP
OF THE INTERNATIONAL WORKING-CLASS MOVEMENT

After the International ceased its activity, Marx remained the ideological leader and teacher of the socialists. Without holding any official posts, he and Engels played a leading role in the working-class movement. Respect for Marx in working-class and socialist circles grew with their understanding of the need for a scientific approach to various aspects of the proletariat's revolutionary struggle. As the leading workers shed their narrow doctrinaire and practical approach, the product of the reformist ideology, they became increasingly convinced that the "working-class cause", as the Italian Socialist Gnocchi-Viani wrote to Engels on March 29, 1877, "is not an ecclesiastical dogma but a scientific theory".[2] That is why, with every fresh success of the scientific socialist outlook, the name of the man who had given socialism its scientific grounding commanded ever greater authority. Even his enemies, as an American journalist told Marx in 1878, regarded him as the "head and front of socialism".[3]

"By theoretical and practical achievements," wrote Engels,

---

[1] Marx, Engels, *Collected Works*, Vol. 24, pp. 517-18.
[2] Central Party Archives of the Institute of Marxism-Leninism.
[3] *The Chicago Tribune*, January 5, 1879.

"Marx has gained for himself such a position that the best people in all the working-class movements in many countries have full confidence in him. At *critical junctures* they turn to him for advice and then usually find that his counsel is the best.... And it is upon this that Marx's peculiar influence, so extremely important for the movement, reposes."[1]

Marx frequently met and had long talks with the socialists who came to London. Among his guests in that period were the Spaniard José Mesa (summer 1875), the Danish socialist Louis Pio, who had set up the International's sections in Denmark (autumn 1876), and the Russian revolutionary Pyotr Lavrov. Marx carried on an extensive correspondence. He was asked for advice not only by the tried and tested leaders of the proletarian movement, but also by men who had only recently embarked on the path of revolutionary struggle.

Among those with whom Marx and Engels corresponded regularly were the German Social-Democrats Bebel, Liebknecht, Bracke, Hepner, Geib, Eichhoff, Dietzgen, and Blos. Marx also corresponded with the French socialist Just Vernouillet. In early 1877, he established friendly relations with Gabriel Deville, a spokesman for socialist student youth in France. The German Social-Democrat Karl Hirsch, who lived mainly in Paris, carried on a lively correspondence both with Marx and with his daughter Eleanor. Marx received letter from Becker and a member of the International, Perret, in Switzerland, Glaser de Willebrord in Belgium, and Pio in Denmark. Leo Frankel, who in 1875 moved from London to Vienna and then on to Budapest, sent Marx detailed reports of his activity in Austria-Hungary. Among those who kept Marx informed of their activities were his Russian and Polish friends, Lopatin and Wróblewski, and the Italian Bignami. Detailed reports about the situation in Russia came from Danielson.

Apart from their close friend Sorge, Marx and Engels had many other correspondents in the U.S.A., including Klings, Cuno, Bolte, the Irishman MacDonnel and Eugène Dupont, who had gone to live in the United States. As the working-class movement developed, more people wrote to Marx and Engels.

Marx tried in every way to help the leaders of the working class spread the ideas of scientific communism, and had constantly to deal with matters concerning new editions and translations of *Capital*, the *Manifesto of the Communist Party*, and other works. There was an acute need for popular aids. Marx was well aware of the importance of a popular presentation of economic theory for the people. But he was just as exacting with the populariscrs as with the translators of *Capital*. He was altogether dissatisfied with the résumé of Volume One in a pamphlet entitled *Capital and Labour*, which the German Social-Democrat Johann Most—subsequently

---

[1] Marx and Engels, *Selected Correspondence*, pp. 324, 325.

an anarchist—put out at Chemnitz in 1873. Since no other popular account was available, Marx conceded to Liebknecht's request and in August 1875 agreed to revise the pamphlet for a second edition. It defied any fundamental improvement, but Marx did eliminate all the flagrant mistakes and made a number of amendments and additions. In this corrected form the pamphlet was issued in 1876.

Marx believed the education of the workers in a spirit of revolutionary tradition and reliance on the experience of the proletariat's past struggles to be highly important, and in particular saw to it that the history of the International was presented in a truthful light. He was sharply critical of the writings about the International by bourgeois, reformist and anarchist authors, who distorted the historical truth. Thus, he said that a book by the Proudhonist Fribourg was "totally unreliable".[1]

He was especially incensed by deliberate distortions. In 1878 he issued a sharp rebuttal in the progressive English press to George Howell, a liberal trade unionist and a former member of the General Council, who had published a grossly biased article about the International in the journal *The Nineteenth Century*. Howell's inventions were due not to his ignorance, but to his hostile attitude to the truly revolutionary proletarian movement. Marx pointed out that the attempts to discredit the revolutionary wing and to declare the idea of the proletariat's international cohesion to be ineffective fitted in with the outlook of the "labour leaders" who had been corrupted by the English bourgeoisie and who had developed the habit of "being but imitative of the manner of thought and style 'natural' to the English moneyed man of sated virtue and solvent morals".[2]

Marx was hoping to find someone who would write a truthful history of the International, something he himself had no time to do, and he made a point of preserving the International's documents at his disposal as an important source for such a work.

Marx considered it of prime importance for the participants in the working-class movement to learn the lessons of the Paris Commune, and believed that this could be promoted by the writing of a true history of the Commune. He considered a book on the Commune by the former Communard Prosper-Olivier Lissagaray, published in Belgium in 1876, to be a very good one. When working on the first and subsequent editions, the author had made use of some of Marx's observations. Marx warmly advised Bracke and other Social-Democrats to get on with the publication in German of "this work which is of importance to our party and of interest to the German reading public at large".[3] He helped to find a translator for it and checked the translation for the German edition of 1878.

In this period Marx continued to devote much attention to educating the working class and the socialists of various countries in

---

[1] Marx, Engels, *Werke*, Bd. 34, S. 147.
[2] Marx, Engels, *Collected Works*, Vol. 24, p. 238.
[3] Marx, Engels, *Werke*, Bd. 34, S. 203.

a spirit of proletarian internationalism. In contrast to the bourgeois and reformist ideologists, who spoke of the collapse of the International and the disintegration of the international working-class movement, Marx kept stressing that the International had ceased to function only as a specific organisation, while the unification and strengthening of the workers' solidarity in each country and in the international arena was inexorably advancing. This was thanks to the mass of workers themselves, who were "in continuous, active, direct intercourse, cemented by exchange of thought, mutual services, and common aspiration".[1]

Marx strove to have the socialists of various countries adopt and continue the International's traditions of selfless and consistent support for the oppressed peoples' struggle for freedom. He took part in an international meeting in London on January 23, 1875, to mark the twelfth anniversary of the Polish insurrection of 1863-64. Among those who delivered speeches were Marx, Engels, Frankel, Lissagaray and Lavrov. Marx's speech was heard with exceptional attention, as he paid a tribute of profound respect to the Polish people—"a cosmopolitan soldier of the revolution"—for the outstanding role its sons were playing in the international liberation movement and for their participation in the Paris Commune. The working class took a stand for Poland's liberation because it opposed national oppression in principle, for such oppression retarded social development and slowed down the working people's struggle for emancipation from the social bondage. Poland's liberation would be a blow at the three despots—Russia, Prussia and Austria-Hungary—and would accelerate the movement for social emancipation throughout Europe.

Marx thought it highly important for the socialists of various countries to establish contact with each other. However, he was wary of calls for socialist congresses to set up new international associations, for he realised that this was inopportune and impracticable for the time being. He also feared that the very idea of founding a new International might be discredited by the intrigues of the anarchists, who were seeking in this way to salvage their own international organisation, and also the acts of the reformists, who were trying to take the initiative in setting up an international association. All this would make it much more difficult to establish such an organisation when the need for it actually arose.

Accordingly, Marx was satisfied with the results of the international socialist congress held at Ghent from September 9 to 15, 1877, which thwarted an attempt by the anarchist leaders, Guillaume and Kropotkin among them, to saddle the international socialist movement with Bakuninist principles. In spite of their resistance, the congress adopted a resolution on the need for workers to participate in political struggle and to set up proletarian parties.

---

[1] Marx, Engels, *Collected Works*, Vol. 24, p. 239.

Even the anarchists' former supporters, like the Belgian socialists, would have nothing to do with them. Marx believed that the Ghent Congress, as he wrote to Sorge on September 27, 1877, "at least had the advantage that Guillaume *et cie.* were totally abandoned by their former allies. It was only with difficulty that the Flemish workers were restrained from lambasting the great Guillaume." [1]

Although he was sure of the working-class movement's future successes, Marx by no means idealised it or glossed over the difficulties it faced in the various countries. He wrote bitterly about the Proudhonist and other utopian illusions which the French workers had not yet discarded, and the theoretical backwardness they were still to overcome. At the same time Marx saw the establishment of workers' syndicates in France as a positive development. In a letter to Sorge of August 4, 1874, he observed that although these were still largely under the influence of the bourgeois republicans and the co-operativists and took an extremely narrow view of the tasks before the working-class movement, their emergence testified to the growing organisation of the French proletariat. The syndicalist movement opened up some prospects in the struggle for a mass working-class party in France.

Then, too, the International's revolutionary traditions were being continued in France with the support of socialist circles and Left-wing groups in the syndicates. There was evidence of strong gravitation towards Marxism among the best elements of the working-class movement.

Marx pointed out that anarchist elements had driven the working-class movement into an impasse in Italy, Spain and in some respects also in Belgium, but he believed this to be temporary, for the practical barrenness of anarchists' activity was bound to spread disillusion among the workers with their "super-socialism". [2] He expressed his satisfaction in a letter to Engels in March 1877 over the statement issued by the Upper Italian Federation, repudiating "any actual federative link with the Italian Bakuninist groups". [3] Similar processes were under way in Spain and Belgium.

Marx said that a certain decline in the working-class movement in England was due to the growing influence of reformism, whose main vehicles were the trade union leaders, the Liberal Party's political ragtag and bobtail, who crawled to the bourgeoisie to secure their support in parliamentary election. If the industrial workers were to change to an independent class policy, they had first of all "to get rid of their present leaders". [4]

Marx believed that what was hampering the development of the working-class movement in the U.S.A., apart from such objective causes as the changing and multi-national composition of the work-

---

[1] Marx, Engels, *Werke*, Bd. 34, S. 295-96.
[2] Ibid., Bd. 33, S. 635.
[3] Ibid., Bd. 34, S. 34.
[4] *Letters to Dr. Kugelmann* by Karl Marx, Moscow-Leningrad, 1934, p. 135.

ing class, the strife between native and immigrant workers, and so on, was the dependence of a large section of the workers on bourgeois "professional politicians". Sectarian elements were also strong in the workers' organisations and this prevented the launching of a struggle to win the support of the masses. However, the deepening class antagonisms were a powerful factor promoting the development of the proletarian movement. The great railroad strike of 1877, a flare-up of the class struggle, was characterised by Marx as the "first outbreak against the associated capital oligarchy that has arisen since the civil war". He stressed that the upswing in the strike movement in the U.S.A. could well serve as a "point of departure for the constitution of a serious workers' party".[1]

The Neudorfl Constituent Congress held on April 5 and 6, 1874 to set up the Social-Democratic Workers' Party in Austria-Hungary was regarded by Marx as a great success for the workers, and he was especially pleased at the participation in the congress of representatives of the Czech proletariat, an indication that the Slav workers were beginning "to act together with the German workers".[2] He saw as the most important task before the Social-Democrats the further international cohesion of the working class in the various territories of the Hapsburg Empire, whose ruling classes based their policy on fanning national strife.

Marx derived particular satisfaction from the development of the working-class movement in Germany, whose Eisenach Party was the strongest and most organised national contingent of the international socialist movement. Its internationalist stand during the Franco-Prussian War and courageous defence of the Paris Commune had earned it respect among the workers of various countries, and it was almost generally recognised as the vanguard of the international proletariat. Lenin pointed out that from 1871 and "for almost half a century the German working class was a model of socialist organisation for the whole world".[3]

TEACHER OF THE GERMAN SOCIAL-DEMOCRATS

Marx and Engels attached prime importance to the international role of German Social-Democracy, making especially high demands on its leaders, closely watching that they followed the revolutionary line, and refusing to tolerate any deviations. They worked tirelessly to transform German Social-Democracy into an ideologically seasoned party of the masses. Marx gave it every support in its struggle against the Bismarck regime, police arbitrary rule and militarism. He was mindful of the difficult conditions in which the members of

---

[1] Marx, Engels, *Werke*, Bd. 34, S. 59.
[2] K. Marx and F. Engels, *Letters to Americans. 1848-1895. A Selection*, New York International Publishers, 1953, p. 113.
[3] V. I. Lenin, *Collected Works*, Vol. 27, p. 484.

the Eisenach Party had to work and the constant persecutions to which they were subjected. In March 1872, the Party's leaders, Bebel, Liebknecht and Hepner, were each sentenced by a Leipzig court to two years' imprisonment in a fortress. However, police reprisals merely helped the Social-Democrats to win greater prestige among the masses. Marx wrote: "In Germany, Bismarck is working for us." [1]

Marx praised the organisational work of the German workers' party, its activity in the trade unions, and its effort to start party publications. It enjoyed considerable success in the Reichstag elections of 1874, winning six seats, with Bebel and Liebknecht among the deputies elected. There was warm approval in London of the skilful use the Eisenachers made of the Reichstag rostrum to expose Bismarck's policies and spread revolutionary socialist ideas.

Marx derived great satisfaction from the important assistance which Engels gave in that period to the leaders of the Eisenach Party. Engels' publicistic writings in the *Volksstaat*, his work *The Housing Question* (aimed against the German Proudhonist Mülberger), his series of articles entitled *The Bakuninists at Work* and *Refugee Literature*, his preface to the third edition of *The Peasant War in Germany* and others, expressed the two men's common views.

In that period, Marx did not write as often in the Party press as Engels did but he, too, took advantage of the re-edition of his old works to write a preface or an afterword so as to draw the attention of his German associates to questions which bore importantly on the Party. Thus, in view of the atmosphere of police reprisals in Germany, he found it appropriate to reprint in the *Volksstaat* in October-December 1874, and then as a separate pamphlet in early 1875, his *Revelations Concerning the Communist Trial in Cologne* and wrote an epilogue to the latter, pointing out that as in Prussia in 1852, at the time of the Cologne Trial, so in Bismarck's Germany, the political police had "unrestricted rule". He said it was ridiculous for Bismarck and his henchmen to try to "drive the Workers' Party out of existence", [2] and no amount of effort by the reactionaries could stop the advent of the socialist revolution. "Society simply does not find its equilibrium until it revolves around the sun of labour." [3] While sincerely rejoicing in the successes of the German working-class movement, Marx did not shut his eyes to its negative aspects. The Eisenach Programme still had traces of Lassallean views. A section of former Lassalleans who had joined the Eisenach Party had not yet quite abandoned their admiration for Lassalle's person and ideas. Not all the Social-Democratic leaders realised the importance of the struggle to overcome the survivals of Lassalleanism in the minds of the German workers. This induced Marx and Engels to raise the question with Bebel and Liebknecht in 1873. In

---

[1] K. Marx and F. Engels, *Letters to Americans. 1848-1895*, p. 113.
[2] Marx, Engels, *Collected Works*, Vol. 24, p. 53.
[3] Ibid., p. 54.

his reply, Bebel admitted that the "cult of Lassalle must be eradicated root and branch",[1] and in fact proposed that Marx himself should undertake a critique of Lassalle's works. He wrote to Engels: "Marx's scientific authority in the economic sphere is so incontestable that the effect of such a work would be colossal."[2]

The Party leaders' inadequate theoretical training occasionally prevented them from realising the vulgar and anti-revolutionary nature of statements by various petty-bourgeois writers who claimed to be socialists, and such writings now and again got into the Party press. On August 4, 1874, Marx wrote to Sorge: "You must have noticed that from time to time the *Volksstaat* contains half-baked philistine fantasies. This rubbish comes from schoolmasters, doctors and students. Engels has given Liebknecht a dressing down, something he seems to need from time to time."[3]

The attempts to overcome the split within the German working-class movement focussed attention on the question of keeping the Party's ideological principles pure. The strength of the working class vis-à-vis the bourgeoisie and the Junkers was being dissipated because of the existence of two rival political organisations: the Social-Democratic Workers' Party and the Lassallean General Association of German Workers. The main political differences between them over the ways of unifying Germany had lost their practical significance after the formation of the German Reich in 1871. There was a growing urge for unity among the rank-and-file members of both organisations.

Marx and Engels were clearly aware of the damage this split was doing to the German working class, but they said on many occasions that true unity could be achieved only on a consistent ideological basis, which meant recognition of the principles of scientific communism. They believed that condemnation of the retrograde Lassallean dogmas was a necessary condition for unification. Because this would take time, Marx and Engels advised their associates in Germany not to display excessive haste over organisational unification, but to take real steps towards unity of action. They feared that a merger of the Eisenach Party and the Lassallean Association carried out without due ideological and political preparation would strengthen the opportunist elements in the Party, lower its ideological level, and do more harm than good. They held that an all-round strengthening of the Social-Democratic Workers' Party and expansion of its ties with the masses was the main way to unity, for this would compel the Lassalleans to accept the necessary terms.

Initially the German Social-Democratic leaders abided by these recommendations. The Party's Coburg Congress in July 1874 endorsed, thanks mainly to Liebknecht's effort and in spite of calls for instant unification, a line providing, on the one hand, for practical co-

---

[1] August Bebel, *Aus meinem Leben*, 2 Teil, Berlin, 1953, S. 258.
[2] Ibid., S. 258-59.
[3] Marx, Engels, *Werke*, Bd. 33, S. 636.

operation with the Lassallean organisation, and on the other, cautioning against any merger on the basis of a haphazard mixture of Lassallean dogmas and the Party's Programme and Rules. The congress formulated this line as follows: "Unity but not unification."

Liebknecht was unable to keep to this line, however, and in the course of his negotiations with the Lassalleans he began to put through unification at any price, having decided that its advantages would compensate for any concessions. In February 1875, Liebknecht, Bernstein and other leaders agreed to a compromise with the Lassalleans on key points of the Programme.

The draft unification programme was published in the Party press on March 7, 1875, and as soon as Marx and Engels read it they realised that the Eisenachers were making a big mistake threatening grave consequences for the Party. The draft meant a surrender to the opportunist trend, a step back as compared with the Eisenach Programme of 1869, which itself had been far from perfect. Describing the Programme in its final, somewhat amended version, Engels subsequently wrote that it was an eclectic compilation consisting of "1. Lassallean dicta and slogans which ought in no circumstances to be adopted... 2. a series of vulgar democratic demands, drawn up in the spirit and style of the People's Party; 3. a number of would-be communist propositions, for the most part borrowed from the *Manifesto*, but so reworded that, looked at in the light of day, every one without exception contains hair-raising balderdash".[1]

Marx and Engels strove to induce the Eisenach leaders to correct their mistake. In a letter to Bebel of March 18-28, 1875, Engels criticised the draft Programme, notably, the inclusion of the Lassallean dogmas on the "iron law of wages" and on "state aid to producers' associations", the vulgar view of the state, the ignoring of the international duties of the workers' party. He resolutely condemned the readiness of Liebknecht and the other Party leaders to sacrifice the basic interests of the working-class movement for the sake of unification. He warned that unification on the wrong terms could not be stable and could not ensure true Party unity. It would inevitably give rise to contradictions and dissent, and play into the hands of those who were corrupting the Party.

There was considerable dissatisfaction with the draft Programme among the Party membership as well. In his letters, Bracke declared that it was unsuitable even as a basis for discussion because it defied improvement. On May 10, 1875, he wrote to Marx: "The only way to get out of this morass is by leaving it altogether."[2] Bebel had been in prison during the negotiations with the Lassalleans and was released only on April 1, 1875. He too expressed dissatisfaction with the draft Programme, but neither he nor Bracke had enough determination to take a stand against the majority of Party leadership.

---

[1] Marx, Engels, *Werke*, Bd. 34, S. 155-56.
[2] Karl Marx, Friedrich Engels, *Briefwechsel mit Wilhelm Bracke (1869-1880)*, Berlin, 1963, S. 72.

Marx thoroughly prepared his critical remarks on the draft Programme. When completed, they were sent with a letter dated May 5, 1875 to Bracke in Germany, who was to pass them on to Geib, Auer, Bebel and Liebknecht. The remarks subsequently came to be known as the *Critique of the Gotha Programme*. Marx's letter contained important ideas on how to overcome the split in the working-class movement. Unity, he wrote, is of great benefit to the working class, but it should not be secured at the price of concessions on ideological principles. "Every step of real movement is more important than a dozen programmes. Hence, if it was impossible to advance *beyond* the Eisenach Programme—and circumstances at the time precluded this—they should simply have come to an agreement about action against the common foe. But to draw up programmes of principles (instead of waiting till a longish spell of common activity has prepared the ground for that sort of thing) is to set up bench marks for all the world to see, whereby it may gauge how far the party was progressed." [1]

In his letter, Marx brought out the central idea that compromise on ideological matters is intolerable, but added that tactical agreements and even temporary political concessions are possible and advisable. Marx, Lenin emphasised, "*sharply condemns* eclecticism in the formulation of principles. If you must unite, Marx wrote to the Party leaders, then enter into agreements to satisfy the practical aims of the movement, but do not allow any bargaining over principles, do not make theoretical 'concessions'." [2]

The warnings issued by Marx and Engels did not have the necessary effect on those who organised the unification congress held at Gotha from May 22 to 27, 1875, which proclaimed the establishment of a United Socialist Workers' Party of Germany. Only a few of the remarks on the draft Programme which came in from London were fully reckoned with, and the congress approved it without essential amendments. It is true that one important addition—that on the recognition of the international character of the working-class movement and the consequent international duties of the German party—was introduced in accordance with the remarks made by Marx and Engels. On the whole, the Gotha Programme marked a departure from the scientific programme and tactical principles of the proletarian movement. At first, Marx and Engels intended to publicly dissociate themselves from the document, but subsequently decided not to do so in view of the fact that it was curiously interpreted both by friends and enemies. In a letter to Bracke on October 11, 1875, Engels wrote: "Working men, bourgeois and petty-bourgeois alike, read into it what it ought, in fact, to contain but doesn't contain... That's what has made it possible for us to say nothing about this programme." [3] Marx and Engels also took into account the pos-

---

[1] Marx, Engels, *Collected Works*, Vol. 24, p. 78.
[2] V. I. Lenin, *Collected Works*, Vol. 5, p. 369.
[3] Marx, Engels, *Werke*, Bd. 34, S. 156.

itive aspect that the split within the German working-class movement had been healed.

The German Social-Democratic leaders failed to see the theoretical importance of the *Critique of the Gotha Programme*, and it was published, on Engels' initiative and thanks to his efforts, only in 1891, when the Programme came up for review.

CRITIQUE OF THE GOTHA PROGRAMME

This is a most important programme document of scientific communism, in which Marx once again displayed his remarkable power of scientific prediction and his capacity to see not only the general line of future social development, but also the many concrete ways along which it was to run. He gives a penetrating analysis of utopian socialism, and formulates his own ideas about the period of transition from capitalism to socialism, the role and evolution of the proletarian state, and the two phases of communist society.

The full meaning of this work by Marx was revealed later, when the working class was faced with the immediate prospect of a socialist revolution and the practical tasks of transforming society. In the autumn of 1917, on the eve of the October Socialist Revolution in Russia, Lenin wrote: "The polemical part of this remarkable work, which contains a criticism of Lassalleanism, has, so to speak, overshadowed its positive part, namely, the analysis of the connection between the development of communism and the withering away of the state." [1]

Marx gave a general critique of the mistakes in the Gotha Programme, in a sense summing up his polemics with petty-bourgeois socialist theories. Above all he revealed their common methodological flaw: the failure to understand the crucial role of social production, and the urge to base the critique of the existing system and the planning of a future society on the distribution of material value. Marx wrote: "The vulgar socialists (and from them in turn a section of the Democrats) have taken over from the bourgeois economists the consideration and treatment of distribution as independent of the mode of production and hence the presentation of socialism as turning principally on distribution." [2]

Marx gave an exhaustive description of Lassalleanism as an opportunist petty-bourgeois trend, and his attack on Lassalle's dogmas was aimed in general against the opportunist trends in German Social-Democracy, of which these dogmas were an ideological source.

Marx showed that Lassalle's famous "iron law of wages" thesis was theoretically untenable and reactionary in practice. This law declared that it was fundamentally impossible for the workers to se-

---

[1] V. I. Lenin, *Collected Works*, Vol. 25, p. 457.
[2] Marx, Engels, *Collected Works*, Vol. 24, p. 88.

cure an improvement of their working conditions, and was a vulgar attempt to explain the social antagonisms of capitalist society by the "eternal laws of population", whose growth, Lassalle insisted as Malthus had, inevitably reduced the level of wages. This dogma obscured the capitalists' exploitation of the workers, disarmed the latter, and suggested to them the false conclusions that it was futile to mount organised resistance to capitalist oppression, to set up trade unions and stage strikes. Marx said that another big mistake in the Programme was the Lassallean demand for assistance to producers' co-operative societies on the part of the existing state, which was presented as a peaceful means of achieving socialism.

Marx resolutely condemned the Lassallean assertion that in relation to the working class all the other classes constituted "*only one reactionary mass*", an idea which denied the importance of an alliance between the working class and the peasantry. In Marx's opinion this also accounted for the fact that the Programme said nothing about fighting the big landowners, for this was in line with Lassalle's profoundly erroneous idea of an alliance between the working class, the Junkerdom and the Prussian monarchy against the bourgeoisie. Marx branded as especially harmful the narrow Lassallean nationalism, which also left its mark on the draft Programme, for the latter said nothing about the international character of the working-class movement. This mistake was only partially corrected in the final text of the Programme.

But perhaps its greatest failing in Marx's eyes was the neglect of the principles of proletarian internationalism. Recognition of the fact that the proletariat was primarily to organise itself as a class at home, and that "its own country is the immediate arena of its struggle", did not in any sense justify neglect of one of the main conditions for the proletariat's emancipation: international proletarian solidarity, the unity and cohesion of the working class of various countries.[1]

Marx directed his main criticism at the Programme's distortion of the question of the ways in which the working class was to be emancipated, of the role of the state. He rejected most vigorously the idea of a people's state in a society divided into hostile classes, and the very concept of the supra-class nature of the state. The Programme's vulgar-democratic utopian statements about the "free basis of the state", and its moderate political demands—it did not even contain a demand for a democratic republic—created the illusion that the German Empire or any other modern bourgeois state could be made genuinely free and popular and used as an instrument for democratic and even socialist change. Marx was quite clear as to the source of this highly vulgar and unscientific view of the state. He wrote that the Gotha Programme was "tainted through and through by the Lassallean sect's servile belief in the state, or, what is no better, by

---

[1] Ibid., pp. 89-90.

a democratic belief in miracles, or rather it is a compromise between these two kinds of belief in miracles, both equally remote from socialism".[1]

Marx showed that the bourgeois state was by its very nature hostile to the proletariat and elaborated the theoretical propositions on the proletarian state, once again connecting the need to set up a working-class state with the vast revolutionary social transformations it would have to carry out so as to move on from capitalism to a new social system free from class antagonisms. Moreover, the proletariat would exercise state leadership of this gigantic work of transformation, for the state of the transition period "can be nothing but *the revolutionary dictatorship of the proletariat*".[2]

Lenin said that this thesis of Marx's was something of a summing-up of his whole revolutionary doctrine of the state and the socialist revolution.[3] Commenting on this idea, Lenin stressed that proletarian dictatorship can by no means be reduced to the use of revolutionary coercion against the resisting exploiting classes, but consists above all in diverse organisational and economic activities to lay the foundations of a society without exploiters, in gradually overcoming the power of inertia, customs and morals of the old society, and in re-educating the petty-bourgeois mass and the working class itself in a socialist spirit. "That is why Marx spoke of an entire period of transition from capitalism to socialism."[4]

Marx's formulation of his doctrine of the future communist society is an exceptionally important contribution to revolutionary theory, for in it he generalised his earlier scientific conclusions and supplemented them with new ones, as he applied his theory of development "to the *forthcoming* collapse of capitalism and to the *future* development of *future* communism".[5] Lenin noted Marx's strictly scientific approach in defining the substance of communism and its socio-economic principles. "There is no trace of an attempt on Marx's part to make up a utopia, to indulge in idle guess-work about what cannot be known. Marx treated the question of communism in the same way as a naturalist would treat the question of the development of, say, a new biological variety, once he knew that it had originated in such and such a way and was changing in such and such a definite direction."[6]

A most important aspect of Marx's view of the problems of communism — a highly developed social system based on social ownership of the means and instruments of production — is that he saw it as a developing social formation, whose emergence and growth are governed by definite objective laws. Everything Marx said showed

---

[1] Marx, Engels, *Collected Works*, Vol. 24, p. 97.
[2] Ibid., p. 95.
[3] V. I. Lenin, *Collected Works*, Vol. 28, p. 233.
[4] Ibid., Vol. 29, p. 388.
[5] Ibid., Vol. 25, p. 463.
[6] Ibid.

that there can be no instant communism, that it cannot be introduced by decree. Communist society is the outcome of deep-going revolutionary change, which calls for definite conditions and considerable time. Communist society itself has to pass through two phases: the lower, at which a social order is established, "usually called socialism, but termed by Marx the first phase of communism",[1] and the higher, communism in the proper sense of the word. The transition from capitalism to the first phase of communist society and then to the second, higher phase, should be gradual, constituting a great process of transformation embracing the sphere of production and relations of production, the distribution of material wealth, and men's politics, thinking and morals. However, Marx drew a distinction between the changes to be effected during the transition from bourgeois society to the lower phase of communism, and those to be carried out during the transition to the higher phase. In the first instance, it is a society which "*emerges* from capitalist society, which is thus in every respect, economically, morally and intellectually, still stamped with the birthmarks of the old society from whose womb it emerges".[2] At the subsequent stage, communist society develops in its advance to the higher phase "on its own foundations".[3] The task, therefore, is to develop and improve these foundations in every way, to ensure a growth of material production and culture, which will make it possible finally to eradicate the "birthmarks" of capitalism and to apply communist principles in every sphere of life.

Marx showed the main distinguishing features of the two phases of communist society. In the first phase, private ownership of the means of production and exploitation will be eliminated, but the members of society will not all enjoy the same material standards. To each according to his work will be the principle in satisfying the requirements of those who work, and in distributing material wealth among them. But since men differ in their natural endowments, capacity for work, and so on, and since other distinctions (family status, etc.) are bound to remain, the "equal right" to receive a product in accordance with the input of socially necessary labour will not ensure genuine equality in these conditions. This actual inequality in distribution — Marx called it "the narrow horizon of bourgeois right" — can be overcome only through a powerful development of the productive forces yielding an abundance of material and spiritual values and making it possible to proceed to a new and more perfect system of distribution.

Marx refuted the vulgar views of the petty-bourgeois socialists, including the Lassalleans, that in socialist society every member was to receive "undiminished proceeds of labour", "the total product of labour". Marx said it had been a gross error to insert this Lassallean

---

[1] Ibid., p. 465.
[2] Marx, Engels, *Collected Works*, Vol. 24, p. 85.
[3] Ibid.

proposition into the Gotha Programme, and showed that even under communism the aggregate social product cannot go entirely into individual consumption. First and foremost this product must provide the funds to compensate for the means of production used up in the process of production, and to ensure extended reproduction. A reserve fund also must be set up for the eventuality of natural disasters, for insurance, etc. But even that part of the product which is earmarked for consumption can be distributed between the individuals only after a deduction of funds to cover the cost of administration, to provide for the disabled, and finally to meet the collective requirements of the members of society (education, public health, etc.). Whereas the part allocated for administration will gradually decrease with the development of the new society, the part of the product earmarked for social consumption will grow steadily.

Marx predicted that radical changes in men's material standard of living, in their working conditions and in their thinking will occur at the higher phase of communist society. Work will become a prime human need and a source of creative joy. The flourishing productive forces and universal abundance will make it possible to satisfy fully the diverse material and spiritual requirements of the members of society. This makes it quite obvious that Marx never envisaged communist society as based on ascetic principles, general restrictions and the levelling of individuals and their requirements. Under communism, man will live in plenty and be released from material cares for ever. Every member of society will have an opportunity for all-round development.

"In a higher phase of communist society, after the enslaving subordination of the individual to the division of labour, and thereby also the antithesis between mental and physical labour, has vanished; after labour has become not only a means of life but life's prime want; after the productive forces have also increased with the all-round development of the individual, and all the springs of cooperative wealth flow more abundantly — only then can the narrow horizon of bourgeois right be crossed in its entirety and society inscribe on its banners: From each according to his abilities, to each according to his needs!" [1]

Marx also dealt with the evolution which the proletarian state will undergo in the transition to communist society. He saw the proletarian dictatorship as a form of state in the transition period, the length of which will depend on the time needed for the revolutionary transformation of capitalist society into a communist one. In the most general terms, he dealt with the problem of what would happen to the state in the subsequent period. He wrote about "the future state system of communist society" and drew a distinction between it and the proletarian dictatorship, adding that with the establishment of the communist system the state will undergo "transfor-

---

[1] Marx, Engels, *Collected Works*, Vol. 24, p. 87.

mations" but that some of its social functions, "analogous to present state functions", will remain. [1]

These statements make it clear that the withering away of the state in the future communist society was not seen by Marx as the mere disappearance of every form of state on the day after the victory of the new social system. He insisted on a scientific approach to this question, but did not himself have the facts at his disposal to produce an answer to it. Even then, Marx realised that at this stage the process will be one of gradual transformation of the old state system into new forms of social administration, in accordance with the changing social conditions and requirements of society.

Marx's brilliant scientific prediction concerning the future communist society and its two phases was an invaluable contribution to the development of the theory of scientific communism.

HELPING TO WRITE *ANTI-DÜHRING*

The inadmissible theoretical concessions to the Lassalleans contained in the Gotha Programme created within the Socialist Workers' Party of Germany an atmosphere of conciliation in respect to non-proletarian, petty-bourgeois ideology. In a letter to Sorge in October 1877, Marx observed: "The compromise with the Lassalleans has led to further compromise with other waverers." [2] Among a section of the Party membership, above all civil servants, office employees, writers, students, and other bourgeois intellectuals, there was growing evidence of enthusiasm for diverse petty-bourgeois utopias and fashionable bourgeois philosophical and economic theories, an urge to combine these eclectically with Marxism, and now and again to set them up in its stead altogether. All of this was a source of alarm to Marx and Engels.

One instance of these ideological vacillations was the acceptance by a sizable part of the educated top section of the Party of the views propounded by Eugen Dühring, a German vulgar philosopher and economist. An assistant professor at Berlin University, Dühring claimed in his lectures and numerous writings, which virtually flooded the book market from 1869 onwards, to be the architect of a new "universal science". He advertised his views as the peak of human knowledge, arrogantly declaring all earlier philosophy, political economy and socialist doctrines to be invalid. His attacks on Marxism were especially impertinent and vulgar. His abovementioned review of Volume One of *Capital* in late 1867, in which he tried to ascribe various mistakes to the author, was still couched in more or less moderate tones, but his subsequent writings — the second edition of *A Critical History of Political Economy and Socialism* (published in November 1874), *A Course of Philosophy as*

---

[1] Ibid., p. 95.
[2] Marx, Engels, *Werke*, Bd. 34, S. 303.

a Strictly Scientific Outlook and the Origin of Life (1875)—contained gross attacks on all the component parts of Marx's doctrine. In place of Marxism, Dühring suggested an eclectic mixture of doctrines of primitive mechanical materialism, idealistic and evolutionist views of society, produced by bourgeois positivist sociologists, and petty-bourgeois socialist ideas.

This attempt to revive social utopias at a time when scientific communism had already struck deep root in the working-class movement was highly retrograde. Marx wrote that utopian socialism in its Dühringian form could be nothing but "silly, stale and thoroughly reactionary".[1] Meanwhile, Dühring's followers among the German Social-Democrats strove to enshrine Dühringianism as the official doctrine of the German working-class movement. Misled by Bernstein's ecstatic comments, Bebel published a favourable comment on Dühring in the *Volksstaat* in March 1874. Liebknecht assured Engels that Dühring, even if a muddled thinker, was "totally honest and resolutely on our side".[2]

However, under the influence of Marx and Engels, the Party leaders soon realised the need to rebuff Dühringianism as a trend which presented a threat to the theoretical and ideological principles of the working-class movement. In August 1874, Blos wrote to Engels: "You are quite right about Dühring."[3] Liebknecht also admitted that the spread of Dühring's ideas in the Party was a serious hazard. Bracke and Dietzgen also wrote to Marx and Engels about the need for a public critique of Dühring's ideas.

At first, Marx and Engels did not consider it necessary to engage in polemics with this, generally speaking, mediocre petty-bourgeois socialist. But the fact that his ideas spread widely among the German Social-Democrats, especially after the merger with the Lassalleans, made them reconsider the question of taking a public stand against Dühring. There was no one in the Party itself with enough theoretical grounding to join battle with the "universal systematiser". Moreover, Liebknecht vacillated, now urging Engels to send in articles criticising Dühring's ideas, now printing, under the pressure of Dühring's followers, extracts from Dühring's works in the *Volksstaat*.

All of this made Engels decide to attack Dühring. From January 3, 1877 to July 7, 1878, he published in the *Vorwärts* (started in October 1876), the new organ of the Socialist Workers' Party of Germany, a long series of critical articles. Some parts of this work were also published as pamphlets, and in 1878 a book was issued entitled *Herr Eugen Dühring's Revolution in Science. Philosophy. Political Economy. Socialism* or *Anti-Dühring* for short.

With brilliant wit, youthful polemical fervour and the skill of

---

[1] Marx, Engels, *Werke*, Bd. 34, S. 303.
[2] Wilhelm Liebknecht, *Briefwechsel mit Karl Marx und Friedrich Engels*, Haag, 1963, S. 190.
[3] Central Party Archives of the Institute of Marxism-Leninism.

a highly experienced ideological fighter, Engels revealed the full poverty and banality of Dühring's pseudo-novel views. He showed that these vulgar views were in absurd contradiction to the author's claims to be absolutely infallible, and to his arrogantly nihilistic attitude to all preceding knowledge. Engels also took the occasion to expound the basic content of the three component parts of the Marxtist theory. Lenin said that *Anti-Dühring* "analysed highly important problems in the domain of philosophy, natural science and the social sciences".[1] Engels' encyclopaedic work set out in popular terms the achievements of Marxist thinking and reflected Engels' own creative contribution to the development of Marxism, especially in the philosophical generalisation of material from natural science, history and military science.

Marx did his utmost to help produce this outstanding book. Earlier, on May 25, 1876, he wrote to Engels: "I consider that, if one is to adopt a 'position vis-à-vis these gentlemen', one can do so only by criticising Dühring without any compunction."[2] Marx was fully informed of Engels' plans and helped him in every possible way. Thus, he reread Owen's writings, drew up a bibliographical list of his works, and in a letter to Engels of August 8, 1877, indicated which of them were most important for criticising Dühring's distortions of the history of socialist thought. He also helped Engels to find other material.

Marx took a hand in writing the second part entitled "Political Economy", making a critical analysis of Dühring's view of the history of economic theories. By early March 1877, he had sent Engels the relevant material, supplementing it in August with an analysis of the physiocrat Quesnay's *Tableau économique*. All this went to make up Chapter X of Part II, entitled "From the *Critical History*". Upon receiving the first part of the chapter, Engels wrote to his friend: "Very many thanks for the long opus re. 'Critical History'. It is more than I need in order to destroy the fellow utterly in this field."[3]

The chapter written by Marx accorded strictly with the general scheme of the whole work, which was to thwart Dühring's attempts to minimise the importance of scientific communism and the achievements of its ideological predecessors. In contrast to Dühring, Marx gave a scientific assessment of the contribution made to economic thought by representatives of the classical school of political economy, from Petty and Boisguillebert to Ricardo. Marx showed that, while slighting the classics, Dühring himself plagiarised from the theories of their minor followers and vulgarisers, among them the German List and the American Carey. At the same time, Marx showed the limitations of bourgeois economic science. He also exposed Dühring's attempts to distort Marxist political economy by

---

[1] V. I. Lenin, *Collected Works*, Vol. 2, p. 25.
[2] Marx, Engels, *Werke*, Bd. 34, S. 14.
[3] Ibid., S. 37.

identifying it with totally alien petty-bourgeois and bourgeois doctrines.

The publication of *Anti-Dühring* promoted the ideological growth of German Social-Democracy and the spread of Marxism in other countries. It helped working-class readers to overcome the influence of non-proletarian trends and to learn the principles of Marxist philosophy, political economy and scientific communism.

CHAPTER FIFTEEN

THE STRUGGLE TO ESTABLISH AND STRENGTHEN PROLETARIAN PARTIES. MARX AND REVOLUTIONARY RUSSIA

> What Marx created as a man of science, as a champion of the working class, does not require either wrought-iron monuments or fiery speeches. It is not bronze or granite monuments that speak of Marx's deeds, but the countless ranks of workers in all parts of the globe who follow Marx's immortal battle-cry: "Workers of the World, Unite!"
>
> F. A. Sorge

THEORETICAL RESEARCHES OF THE LAST FEW YEARS

In the last few years of his life, despite failing health, Marx remained a truly devoted scholar. In old age, he retained his youthful enthusiasm for science and his unquenchable passion for new books, which he covered with notes and underlining, turning them into "his slaves", as he put it.

Marx's scientific interests continued to be wide-ranging, with *Capital* as his central concern in this period as well. As he worked on the unfinished sections he sought to study the new economic and political phenomena of capitalism and to take account of the most recent achievements in the related areas of the social and the natural sciences. The requirements of the growing working-class movement also induced him to keep abreast of political and ideological developments.

Marx had already clarified for himself the theoretical content of most problems in Volume Two and Volume Three of *Capital*, but his conscientiousness as a scholar knew no bounds. Engels wrote that a mere enumeration of the manuscripts written by Marx testified to the "strict self-criticism with which he endeavoured to elaborate his great economic discoveries to the point of utmost completion before he published them".[1] It was in this period that Marx again turned to the reproduction and circulation of the aggregate social capital. He made a thorough study of the latest works on commerce, finance, banking and agrarian relations.

When analysing the problems of Volume One of *Capital*, Marx concentrated on England, the classic country of industrial capitalism, but in his new studies for Volume Two and Volume Three he was increasingly concerned with the economic development of Russia and the U.S.A.

---

[1] Karl Marx, *Capital*, Vol. II, p. 2.

There are over 120 titles in Marx's list entitled "Russian books on my shelf", which he compiled in 1881, but even this does not include all the sources he used in his work. Among those who actively helped Marx to collect books for his Russian library were Nikolai Danielson, Pyotr Lavrov, Nikolai Sieber, Illarion Kaufmann, Nikolai Kablukov, Minna Gorbunova, and Vera Zasulich. Among the sources he studied were various documentary and statistical works, including Zemstvo statistics and collections of articles published in Russia after 1861. Marx also read works by Russian historians and scientists on general history, political economy and sociology, prominent among which were the scientific and publicistic writings of Russian revolutionary democrats, notably those of Chernyshevsky.

Marx devoted exceptional attention to agrarian relations in Russia, and the intensity of his studies in this field can be seen from his entries in four notebooks running to over 40 printed sheets, from the various volumes of the *Transactions of the Tax Commission*. He obtained much information from the *Military Statistical Review* and from various special publications. Thus, in the autumn of 1882, he read a work by the prominent Russian scientist and Narodnik publicist, Alexander Engelhardt, entitled *From the Countryside*, in which he made numerous notes. That these studies were connected with his formulation of theoretical economic questions will be seen from the following note which he made during a study of other writings by Engelhardt: "*Situation in Russia. Labour, formation of the bourgeoisie, capital, rent* (with Russia as an example)." [1] Subsequently, in a preface to Volume Three of *Capital*, Engels wrote: "Owing to the variety of forms both of landownership and of exploitation of agricultural producers in Russia, this country was to play the same role in the part dealing with land rent that England played in Book I in connection with industrial wage-labour. He was unfortunately denied the opportunity of carrying out this plan." [2]

Marx also obtained a considerable amount of material on the American economy and social structure from various collections of statistics and documents published by Federal and State agencies, which were sent to him by Sorge, Harney and other friends in the U.S.A., and articles from American and British periodicals. As a result, he assembled important information on the rapid development of industry, the settlement of the West, the state of the farms, working conditions, labour immigration, etc. In his extracts, he remarked on the formation of large joint-stock companies, and the rise of financial and industrial magnates like Vanderbilt, Gould and Rockefeller. In an outline which he drew up at the end of 1878 on the plunder of public lands by joint-stock companies, he pointed out that a number of multimillionaires had made their fortunes by speculating in real estate. As an example he quoted the "railway baron" James

---

[1] Central Party Archives of the Institute of Marxism-Leninism.
[2] Karl Marx, *Capital*, Vol. III, p. 7.

Joy, who had established control over thousands of small homesteaders in the West and had become their "master and king".[1]

Marx also followed the economic situation in Western Europe, the consequences of the 1873 crisis, and the agrarian crisis. In the spring of 1877, making extracts from a book by Rudolph Meyer, entitled *Political Jobbers and Corruption in Germany*, he summed up his view of recent economic developments in Germany as follows: "*Industrial production and large-scale commerce have become increasingly dependent on the banks, on the big capitalists.*"[2] In 1880, he advised Paul Lafargue, who was studying French banking, to pay special attention to the "export of capital". In his "Notes and Extracts on the Distribution of Landed Property in France", he remarked on the extensive ruination of the French peasantry.

Marx kept in touch with new developments in economic thinking, and was confirmed in his view that bourgeois political economy was being vulgarised on an ever-growing scale and in increasingly diverse forms. This was also reflected in the so-called "Katheder-Socialist" writings by bourgeois economists, who were aware of the widespread interest of the masses in socialism and sought to present their apology of capitalism in socialist colours. In 1877, Marx said that the future society depicted in a pamphlet entitled *The Quintessence of Socialism* by Albert Schäffle, a leading spokesman of this trend, was "an ideal realm of good-natured petty bourgeois".[3]

Between mid-1879 and November 1880, Marx wrote detailed critical comments on Volume One of a *Manual of Political Economy* by Adolph Wagner, a German professor. Taking this work as an example, he revealed the defects of the entire Katheder-Socialist trend and Wagner's predecessor, Karl Rodbertus-Jagetzow, a Junker-bourgeois economist and a theorist of "state socialism". Marx stressed, among other things, that Wagner and other exponents of the "socio-legal conception" adopted a vulgar idealistic approach to the main problems of the national economy, and sought to substitute a simple description of economic phenomena for an analysis of economic laws, and to present these phenomena as reflecting the evolution of legal and moral norms. Thus, referring to Wagner's view of the origin and development of exchange, Marx made this critical remark: "Here the *vir obscurus* [obscurantist] places mine and his on their heads. For him the law is first, and then comes commerce."[4] Wagner and his learned colleagues took the straightforward evolutionary approach, denying the role of revolutions, seeking to present the capitalist system as something immutable, and reducing the solution of the social question to the elimination of various abuses, to a reform of the tax system, social security for workers, and so on.

Like Rodbertus, Wagner and the other Katheder-Socialists main-

---

[1] Central Party Archives of the Institute of Marxism-Leninism.
[2] Ibid.
[3] Marx, Engels, *Werke*, Bd. 34, S. 243.
[4] Marx, Engels, *Collected Works*, Vol. 24, p. 553.

tained that the bourgeois state had a special social mission. Marx observed that Wagner's admiration for the state caused him slavishly to extol Bismarck's police-bureaucratic Reich and even to justify the continued existence of Junker landed estates. Marx said that Wagner and his associates "still had one foot in the old muck" and contemptuously called them "serfs" of the existing state.[1]

Marx showed that Wagner took a vulgar view of the principal categories of political economy. In a spirit "traditional for German professors" he confused use-value and value, and apologetically presented profit as a "constituent" element of value. Marx also pointed out the dishonest methods used by bourgeois apologists like Wagner in "criticising" his economic doctrine, and ascribing to him various absurdities and views he did not hold.

In this period, Marx's work in elaborating his political economy was closely connected with his studies in the natural sciences. In considering the problems of rent, he felt obliged to master the latest advances in agronomy, and this induced him to go deeply into the relevant branches of chemistry, agro-chemistry, biology, geology and other sciences. In 1875, he wrote a summary of Engelhardt's *Chemical Principles of Agriculture*, and in 1878 reread James Johnston's *Catechism of Agricultural Chemistry and Geology*. He also extended his knowledge of organic chemistry. In 1882, he thoroughly read a textbook on chemistry by Roscoe and Schorlemmer, and a book on the latest theories in chemistry by Julius Meyer. He wrote out numerous extracts from books on geology and mineralogy (including the works of the English geologists Joseph Jukes and Grant Allen) and on the physiology of plants, animals and man (the works of Matthias Schleiden, Johannes Ranke and others). He took a great interest in the attempts to find ways of wedding chemistry and biology, notably, the experiments by the German scientist, Moritz Traube, to synthesise the cell.

In the early 1880s, Marx read a work by the French engineer, Edouard Hospitalier, on the results of an international electrical congress in Paris in September 1881 which discussed the use of electricity in various fields. On November 2, 1882, he wrote Engels about the remarkable prospects opened up by the invention of the Frenchman, Marcel Deprez, who had demonstrated a long-distance electric transmission line at the Munich Electro-Technical Exposition of 1882.

Marx warmly welcomed scientific discoveries of direct benefit to mankind, which promoted the development of technology and production and helped to improve living conditions. Engels wrote: "However great the joy with which he welcomed a new discovery in some theoretical science whose practical application perhaps it was as yet quite impossible to envisage, he experienced quite another kind of joy when the discovery involved immediate revolutionary

---

[1] Marx, Engels, *Collected Works*, Vol. 24, p. 547.

changes in industry, and in historical development in general."[1]

In this period, higher mathematics occupied special place in Marx's studies. His interest in the mathematical sciences sprang from his economic research, which frequently required complex calculations. In Marx's notebooks containing preparatory material, which he compiled at various periods, especially from 1858 onwards, we find many entries reflecting his studies in the history of mathematics, commercial arithmetic, analytical geometry and algebra. Earlier on, Marx developed the habit of devoting his leisure hours to the solution of mathematical problems, including problems of higher mathematics.

He had begun to study mathematics for applied, ancillary purposes, but he soon advanced to independent research in this branch of knowledge. This was largely due to the fact that there were many points of contact between mathematics, philosophy and dialectical logic, to which Marx attached primary importance. His mathematical research coincided with the decisive stage of Engels' work on *Dialectics of Nature*, a dialectico-materialist generalisation of data provided by the natural sciences. Accordingly, his manuscripts of the early 1880s—"On the Concept of the Derived Function" and "On the Differential"—are marked "For the General" (Engels' nickname) and "For Fred".

Marx studied the classical writers on the mathematical sciences— Descartes, Leibniz, Newton, Euler and Maclaurin—and numerous university textbooks on mathematical analysis and higher algebra. On the basis of this material, he produced a cycle of works comprising the two above-mentioned manuscripts on differential calculus, and also preparatory versions and additions to them, a number of rough drafts of treatises on the history of differential calculus and fragments containing an analysis of Taylor's and Maclaurin's theorems, Lagrange's theory of derived functions, and so on. Marx must have been hoping to assemble these various drafts into a coherent work, but he did not succeed in putting the finishing touches to his mathematical manuscripts.

In these works, Marx sought to bring out the dialectical connection between the basic concepts and methods of differential calculus and elementary algebra and gave these concepts a dialectical interpretation. When dealing with the history of mathematical science, Marx explained the role played by Newton, Leibniz, Euler, d'Alembert and Lagrange in producing and developing differential calculus. He stressed that only the higher, truly dialectical stage in the development of scientific thinking can lead to an adequate view of the essence of the phenomena being studied.

Engels found Marx's first few works on mathematics highly original and congratulated his friend warmly in a letter dated August 18, 1881. After Marx's death, Engels intended to publish his mathemat-

---

[1] Marx, Engels, *Collected Works*, Vol. 24, p. 468.

ical writings, but a host of other important tasks prevented him from doing so.

Marx's *Mathematical Manuscripts* provide yet another example of his highly diverse scientific interests. Lafargue had good reason to say that "his brain was like a man-of-war in port under steam, ready to launch into any sphere of thought". [1] Marx's study, with its many bookcases, was like a captain's bridge from which he charted the course in the sea of human knowledge, to which he made such an invaluable contribution.

STUDIES IN WORLD HISTORY

Marx's studies in world history figured prominently among his scientific pursuits, and his interests in this field were very wide-ranging.

His historical research was sometimes closely interwoven with his work on the problems of Volume Two and Volume Three of *Capital*, reflecting his intention to formulate a theory of political economy in the broad sense of the word, and to bring out the economic regularities of the precapitalist formations as well. Sometimes it was independent of *Capital*. For Marx the important thing was to comprehend the latest advances in historical science for the purpose of deepening and developing the materialist view of the historical process as a whole.

In considering agrarian relations and the formation of rent, Marx made a comprehensive study of the origins and development of landed property among the various peoples. In the 1870s, this led him to a new stage in the study of communal landownership, as a form antecedent to private property. Earlier on, the facts he assembled about the countries of the East showed that closed social organisms, like the village commune, had exceptional resilience and stability. Among some ancient peoples, this was the basic unit in the system of production relations of the type which, in an introduction to *A Contribution to the Critique of Political Economy* (1859), Marx designated as the Asiatic mode of production. He believed that this type of production relations had been maintained in the countries of the East even in the Middle Ages. The existence of the despotic states of the ancient and medieval East depended on the exploitation of such isolated microcosms (Marx called the village commune a "*localised microcosm*" [2]).

Marx's profound study of the history of communal landownership not only in Asia but also in Europe, Africa and America confirmed him in his conviction that the commune was a universal social form. He gleaned extensive information on this subject from the writings of the outstanding German scientist Georg Maurer, which he

---

[1] *Reminiscences of Marx and Engels*, p. 77.
[2] Marx, Engels, *Collected Works*, Vol. 24, p. 353.

had read in the late 1860s. In 1876, Marx made detailed summaries of his works, among them *Introduction to the History of the Mark, Household and Urban Systems*, and *A History of the Mark System in Germany*. He also reread these books in 1881.

Marx obtained a great deal of material about communal landownership from other German, English, Italian and Spanish writings, including those of Hannsen, Maine, Green, Jacini and Càrdenas. He attached much scientific importance to a book by his Russian friend, Kovalevsky, entitled *Communal Landownership, and the Causes, Course and Cosequences of Its Disintegration*, which he received from the author upon its publication in 1879. It described the communal system among the North-American Indians and the natives of the Spanish colonies in the West Indies, and the peoples of India and Algeria. He supplemented his earlier knowledge of the Indian community from a book by John Phears, *The Aryan Villages in India and Ceylon*, which was published in 1880. Earlier, Marx had read a study, in a French special publication, on customary law among the Southern Slavs by the outstanding scholar Valtasar Bogišić, and the work on the Southern Slav household commune (*zadruga*) by Ognieslav Utiešenović.

The communal system in Russia figured prominently in Marx's researches. Apart from his extracts from a book by a Prussian official, August von Haxthausen, entitled *On the Rural System in Russia*, and from a work on the subject by the French bourgeois historian, Leroy-Beaulieu, Marx also made copious notes on the writings of Russian scholars, among them Sokolovsky, Vasilchikov, Belyayev, Koshelev, Semyonov, Chicherin and Gerye. His views on this subject were considerably influenced by his extensive knowledge of the Russian commune and its historical evolution, together with his study of the history of communal landownership in other countries. He set out these views in three drafts of a letter to the Russian revolutionary, Vera Zasulich, and gave a concise statement of them in the final version of the letter dated March 8, 1881 (of which the draft and the fair copy are intact).

Marx regarded the commune as one of the most ancient social institutions, a product of primitive social relations resting on consanguinity and common ownership of the means of production. As primitive society disintegrated, the commune underwent considerable transformation: it evolved from a tribal into a territorial institution, its members going over to individual cultivation of land and private ownership of houses and livestock. However, communal ownership of land remained, subject to periodical reallotment between the individual households. Communal lands continued to be used collectively. The subsequent evolution of the commune among the different peoples depended on differences of "historical surroundings", as Marx put it.[1] Two historical tendencies were inherent in the com-

---

[1] Marx, Engels, *Collected Works*, Vol. 24, p. 352.

mune itself: one led to strengthening the private ownership principle and eroding the commune itself, the other to preserving the collective principle, which made the commune a viable organism capable of surviving in one form or another in the feudal epoch and remaining intact in the economically backward countries even in the capitalist epoch.

Marx maintained that the future of the commune in countries where it still existed, Russia above all, depended largely on the prospects for non-capitalist development. He believed the latter to be quite possible in principle, while emphasising that the necessary condition for it was a victory of the socialist revolution in the advanced capitalist countries. In that event, given favourable domestic conditions and the release of the commune from oppression by a despotic state and semi-feudal exploitation — which in Russia could be achieved only through a popular revolution — the surviving communal forms could be a starting point for socialist transformations. Given such a course of social development, the commune could escape the destruction inevitable under capitalism and could, on the basis of the new productive forces already generated by bourgeois society, be restructured into a form for co-operative labour, and so "turn over a new leaf". [1]

Marx's study of the history of communal landownership confronted him with the need to clarify the specific features of ancient society itself. In the 1840s, when they began working out the principles of historical materialism, Marx and Engels formed a definite view of primitive society as a classless system without private property or state power. In the course of their subsequent research, they were confirmed in these views, as they discovered various features in the customs of the ancient peoples, notably the Celts in Ireland and Wales, and the Germanic tribes, which could be explained only by the hypothesis that the earliest form of society had been a primitive communist one.

However, this hypothesis could be turned into a scientifically grounded theory only on the strength of new discoveries in archaeology, palaeontology, anthropology and ethnography. By the 1870s, considerable advance had been made in all these fields. A scientific classification had been made of ancient stone tools, and Neanderthal man, an ancestor of modern man, had been discovered. The fundamentals of scientific anthropogenesis had been laid by Charles Darwin's *The Descent of Man*, which appeared in 1871. Darwin's conclusions were creatively elaborated by Engels in his article "The Part Played by Labour in the Transition from Ape to Man".

In 1877, the American ethnographer, Lewis Henry Morgan, published his *Ancient Society*, which proved, on the basis of long years of research into ancient customs, mainly those of North-American tribes, that the social unit of primitive society was the tribe, and that

[1] Marx, Engels, *Collected Works*, Vol. 24, p. 368.

marital relations took the form of group marriage, or various forms of polygamy, as reflected in the archaic systems of kinship. Morgan confirmed the hypothesis of the Swiss anthropologist, Johann Bachofen, that women's predominant status in primitive tribes sprang from matrilineal descent under group marriage. He put Bachofen's theory of matriarchy, as set out in his book *Das Mutterrecht* (1861), into the context of his theory of the tribal organisation of ancient society, proving that the patriarchal system had been historically preceded by a matriarchal one.

While official scientific opinion in Europe, and to some extent in the U.S.A., was virtually ignoring Morgan's discoveries, Marx and Engels considered his book an outstanding scientific event, providing fresh concrete evidence of the correctness of their own materialist view of history.

Marx decided to write a special work on Morgan's discovery, made a detailed summary of *Ancient Society* (apparently in late 1880 and early 1881) and did a thorough study of the available literature on the history of primitive culture.

The summary shows that Marx adopted a creative approach to Morgan's conclusions, and that he intended to expound them in the light of his own studies of precapitalist formations. Marx's critical remarks, which Engels subsequently used in *The Origin of the Family, Private Property and the State* (1884), show that he by no means agreed with everything in this work by Morgan who was a spontaneous materialist. Marx rearranged the material, in order to present the evolution in social institutions in the right order: Morgan examined the emergence of private property after the emergence of the state, and Marx, the other way round. He corrected some of Morgan's views, such as his assertion that in the primitive epoch man had already "an *absolute control* over *production of food*".[1] Now and again, on the basis of Morgan's facts, Marx made broader generalisations. Commenting on Morgan's idea that the evolution of the family entailed changes in the system of kinship, he stressed that this was an expression of the general law that secondary, superstructural phenomena depend on primary, basis phenomena. "This applies exactly to *political, religious, juridical and philosophical* systems in general."[2]

Marx went much deeper than Morgan into the ideological causes behind the distorted view of many bourgeois scientists (among them George Grote and Theodor Mommsen) on the nature of tribal relations, and their idealistic attempts, for instance, to explain these relations in terms of the specific features of ancient religions, or to derive them from mythology. Marx stressed that this was due to the limitations of the bourgeois outlook, and frequently to conservative political views. Referring to the modernised presentation of the power of military commanders in Homer's Greece, Marx wrote: "The European savants, most of them born servants of princes, represent

---
[1] *Marx-Engels Archives*, Vol. IX, p. 4.
[2] Ibid., p. 21.

the *basileus* as a monarch in the modern sense. The Yankee republican Morgan objects to this." [1]

Marx rated other works on primitive history, such as those by Maine, Lubbock, Tylor, well below Morgan's book, although he did find some useful facts in them as well. He made a particularly large number of critical remarks on Maine's *Lectures on the Early History of Institutions*, and rejected the scheme, accepted by the author and current among bourgeois sociologists, according to which the patriarchal family, the family commune, antedated the tribe as the initial social form. "It is exactly the other way round," [2] said Marx. While Maine accepted the existence of communal property in the earliest period, he saw it in the light of bourgeois individualism, depicting the commune as the embodiment of the coercion of the individual. Marx regarded this attempt by Maine to present contemporary bourgeois society as a haven of personal freedom, in contrast to the communal way of life, as a typical specimen of bourgeois apologetics and hypocrisy. He also sharply criticised Maine's attempt to present state power as an independent and eternal social institution. The state appears at a stage in the social development when society finds itself split into hostile classes, and as an instrument of definite class interests. "Just as its *emergence* is possible only at a given stage of social development, so it disappears again as soon as society attains a stage which it has not yet reached." [3]

When reading John Lubbock's *The Origin of Civilisation and the Primitive Condition of Man*, Marx noted the author's rational ideas on group marriage and matriarchy, and also his highly vague ideas about the social organisation of early society. His conclusion was: "Consequently, Lubbock knows nothing about its basis — *the gens*." [4]

Marx's studies of early history helped to give depth to his theory of social development and to back up historical materialism with fresh data. Marx also found confirmation of his ideas in other fields of historical research.

He devoted much attention to the history of liberation movements and the struggle of the oppressed peoples. Using a book by Karl Bücher entitled *Risings of Enslaved Workers* (1874), he compiled a chronological table of early slave uprisings in Ancient Rome. From a work by the Russian historian, Nikolai Kostomarov, *Stenka Razin's Mutiny*, he made notes on the history of the peasant movement in 17th-century Russia. Summarising Gino Capponi's *History of the Florentine Republic*, Marx dealt specially with the Florentine wool carders' (*ciompi*) riot in 1378, as one of the first revolutionary actions by the industrial pre-proletariat in history.

Marx was invariably drawn to the history of the French Revolu-

---

[1] Marx and Engels, *Selected Works*, Vol. 3, p. 273.
[2] Central Party Archives of the Institute of Marxism-Leninism.
[3] Ibid.
[4] Ibid.

Marx in 1867

Ludwig Kugelmann

N. F. Danielson

Friedrich Lessner

Johann Philipp
Becker

Louis Eugène Varlin

P. O. Lissagaray

H. A. Lopatin

Georg Jung

Georg Eccarius

A. Serno-
Solovyevich

Charles Longuet

P. L. Lavrov

House in London, 256 High Holborn, where the General Council of the International met (June 1868-February 1872)

First editions of the Inaugural Address of the International Working Men's Association in English, French, German and Russian

ADDRESS

AND

PROVISIONAL RULES

OF THE

WORKING MEN'S INTERNATIONAL ASSOCIATION,

Established September 28, 1864,

AT A PUBLIC MEETING HELD AT ST. MARTIN'S HALL, LONG ACRE, LONDON.

PRICE ONE PENNY.

PRINTED AT THE "BEE-HIVE" NEWSPAPER OFFICE,
10, BOLT COURT, FLEET STREET.
1864.

MANIFESTE

DE

L'ASSOCIATION INTERNATIONALE

DES TRAVAILLEURS

SUIVI

DU RÈGLEMENT PROVISOIRE.

Prix : 10 centimes.

BRUXELLES
ALLIANCE TYPOGRAPHIQUE. — M.-J. POOT ET COMPAGNIE
Rue aux Choux, 55.
1866

Der Social-Demokrat

Organ des Allgemeinen deutschen Arbeiter-Vereins.

Nr. 2. Probe-Nummer.

Berlin, den 21. Dezember 1864.

ПЕРВЫЙ МАНИФЕСТЪ

МЕЖДУНАРОДНАГО ТОВАРИЩЕСТВА РАБОЧИХЪ

(1864 года)

ИЗДАНІЕ
ПЕРВОЙ РУССКОЙ СЕКЦІИ
МЕЖДУНАРОДНАГО ТОВАРИЩЕСТВА
РАБОЧИХЪ

ЖЕНЕВА
Типографія Народнаго Дѣла
Pâquis, rue du Nord; 15
1871

N. I. Utin

Yelizaveta Dmitriyeva

Letter of the Russian Section of the International to Marx, March 12, 1870

Title-pages of *The Civil War in France* in English, German and French

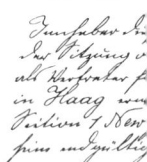

Leo Frankel

Walery Wróblewski

Friedrich Adolf Sorge

Theodor Cuno

Germania Hotel in Karlsbad (Karlovy Vary) where Marx put up

Marx's credentials for the Hague Congress issued by the German Section No. 1 of New York

August Bebel

Wilhelm Liebknecht

Paul Lafargue

Wilhelm Bracke

N. G. Chernyshevsky. Page of Marx's synopsis of Chernyshevsky's manuscript "Letters Without an Address"

V. V. Bervi (N. Flerovsky). Page of Flerovsky's book *The Condition of the Working Class in Russia* with Marx's remarks

Jules Guesde Ferdinand Domela Nieuwenhuis

se in London, 41 Maitland
k Road, where Marx lived
(March 1875-March 1883)

Jenny Marx

Jenny Longuet

Laura Lafargue

Eleanor Marx

G. V. Plekhanov

Vera Zasulich

MANIFESTE DU PARTI COMMUNISTE
par Karl MARX et Fr. ENGELS

РУССКАЯ СОЦІАЛЬНО-РЕВОЛЮЦІОННАЯ БИБЛІОТЕКА

Книга Третья

МАНИФЕСТЪ

КОММУНИСТИЧЕСКОЙ ПАРТІИ

Карла Маркса и Фр. Энгельса

ПЕРЕВОДЪ СЪ НѢМЕЦКАГО ИЗДАНІЯ 1872.

СЪ ПРЕДИСЛОВІЕМЪ АВТОРОВЪ

Prix 1 Fr.

ЖЕНЕВА

Вольная Русская Типографія.

1882

Title-page of the Russian edition of the *Manifesto of the Communist Party*, 1882

Engels in the late 1870s

tion. In 1879, he read a book by the Russian historian Nikolai Kareyev, entitled *The Peasantry and the Peasant Question in France in the Last Quarter of the 18th Century*, on which he commented very favourably in a letter to Kovalevsky. His copious extracts from the book by the French democrat historian, Georges Avenel, *Revolutionary Mondays* (1875) likewise showed Marx's strong interest in the social and political processes in France during the revolution, her international relations, the history of the fight against counter-revolutionary plots, the Vendée rising, the struggle of trends within the revolutionary camp itself, and the democratic-revolutionary, egalitarian and socialist ideas which emerged in the years of the revolution.

The colonial rivalry between the capitalist states to seize still unpartitioned territories induced Marx to devote more and more time to the history and liberation movements of the colonial peoples.

In 1880 and 1881, he resumed his study of agrarian relations in Ireland, Britain's first colony, and a year earlier had read William Carleton's realistic account of the plight of the Irish peasants. The writings of radical publicists and other material suggested that no change for the better had taken place in the condition of the Indian working people either. Concerning the colonial plunder of the Indian people and its grave consequences — the terrible poverty of the inhabitants, the recurring famines on a scale "not yet suspected in Europe" — and the steady extraction of vast wealth from the country by the colonialists, Marx wrote to Danielson on February 19, 1881: "This is a bleeding process, with a vengeance!" [1]

Marx took a fresh look at India's history. From 1879 to 1881 he drew up on the basis of material taken from a number of books his extensive *Notes on Indian History*, covering several centuries, from the Moslem conquest and the establishment of the empire of the Great Moguls to the suppression of the national liberation uprising by the British in 1859. This work is shot through with an impassioned protest against colonial oppression. Marx wrathfully condemned the colonialists — "the British 'brutes'" [2] — and also the traitors among the Indian aristocracy who worked hand in glove with them. He remarked on the great scope of the national liberation uprising of 1857-59 and showed the causes of its defeat.

Marx studied the history of Dutch and British colonial rule in Indonesia, the penetration of Europeans and Americans into Japan in the mid-19th century and works on China. In his extracts in the autumn of 1882 from Mulhall's "Egyptian Finance", which appeared in the *Contemporary Review* for October of that year, he noted a new feature of colonial policy, namely, the growing role of joint-stock companies in the seizure and plundering of economically backward countries. The establishment of control over Egypt's finances, and its enslavement by the European banks paved the way for

---

[1] Marx and Engels, *Selected Correspondence*, p. 317.
[2] Marx, *Notes on Indian History*, Moscow, 1960, p. 89.

the armed invasion by Britain and France. In a letter to his daughter Eleanor on January 9, 1883, Marx said that the British colonial conquest of Egypt was the most ignominious of all the acts of aggrandisement.

Towards the close of his life, Marx made an effort to, as it were, summarise his historical knowledge and reproduce a general picture of the historical development of all countries in a synchronic sequence. He realised his plan only in part and mainly in respect of the history of Europe and some Asian and African peoples (the Arabs, Mongols, Turks, and Khwarizmians), but even this work contains an amazing wealth of facts. From the end of 1881 to the end of 1882, he filled four large notebooks with entries on world history, covering events from the early first century B. C. up to the mid-17th century. When Engels sorted out Marx's papers after his death he called this work the *Chronological Notes*.

Marx's main source was Schlosser's nine-volume *Universal History*. For some periods he used Carlo Botta's *History of the Italian People*, the radical William Cobbett's *A History of the Protestant 'Reformation' in England*, David Hume's *Short History of England*, Niccolò Machiavelli's *History of Florence*, Nikolai Karamzin's *History of the Russian State*, and Comte de Ségur's *History of Russia and of Peter the Great*. In addition to his extracts, Marx also made a summary of John Richard Green's *History of the English People*. In assessing events and personalities, Marx was highly independent of his sources, and his notes did not merely reproduce the facts from the works he was studying, but expressed his own view of the various historical events.

In his *Chronological Notes*, Marx concentrated on political events, but now and again he went to their social and class roots. His exposition shows history not as a casual kaleidoscope of facts but as a law-governed chain of events, reflecting the general trend of the historical process and its specific features in the various countries. On the whole, this is a picture of the history of feudal society from the emergence of feudal relations to the epoch of the disintegration of feudalism, absolute monarchies and early bourgeois revolutions.

The *Chronological Notes* provide fresh evidence that Marx saw history as a living process abounding in dramatic situations, in which the general laws operate not as fatal levelling forces, but as forces which make their way through a thousand fortuitous events and aberrations, manifesting themselves differently in different conditions.

Marx loathed the feigned impartiality with which bourgeois historians so frequently tried to cover up their vindication of the policies of the ruling classes. His manuscript abounds in wrathful epithets against the oppressors and invaders, power-thirsty feudal lords, crowned despots, self-seeking popes and bishops, and religious fanatics and obscurantists. Thus, he called the crusaders who plundered the countries of the East, "*crusading blockheads*", the German Prince Heinrich der Löwe, who organised the conquest of the Slav lands, a "perfidious and savage sloven", the knights of the Livonian Order, savage conquerors of the Baltic peoples, who also invaded the Russian lands, "scoundrels" and "*knight-curs*", and the mercenary lansquenets of the 15th and 16th centuries, "international piratical riff-raff".[1] Marx's sharp words reflected his attitude to the exploiters, but he never oversimplified history or presented it in black and white. He was also adept at observing the contradictory features and the progressive aspects of the policies of various statesmen. Thus, in the policy of the French King Louis XI, "who got on with the townsfolk and with the peasants, and was cruel and perfidious only with respect to the higher aristocracy",[2] Marx discerned the progressive centralising role of the royal power during the rise of national states. He took the same approach to the "great Machiavellian", Ivan III.

Marx had great sympathy for popular resistance to feudal oppression. His extracts record all the facts characterising the class struggle in the feudal epoch. He remarked on the deepening of the class conflicts in the European countries beginning in the 14th century: "In France and England ... *civil wars between the big feudal lords and the knighthood, uprisings by townsfolk against the big feudals and the knights, and the wild fury of the lower classes of the people groaning under unrestrained oppression.*"[3] Marx dealt in detail with the peasant uprising in Italy under the leadership of Fra Dolcino, the French Jacquerie, the uprisings led by Wat Tyler and Jack Cade in England, the Hussite movement in Bohemia, the great peasant war of 1524-25 in Germany, and the bourgeois revolution of 1566-1609 in the Netherlands. He did not ignore the weakness of the peasant movements, their ideological backwardness and political short-sightedness, but he invariably stressed that despite their defeats the peasant uprisings always dealt the heaviest blows at the feudal system.

Marx saw the struggle of the peoples against foreign invaders as a highly progressive factor. His extracts show his admiration for the French peasant girl, Joan of Arc, who rallied popular resistance to the English invasion during the Hundred Years' War. He made special mention of the importance for the Russian people's liberation from the Tartar yoke of the defeats sustained by the Tartars from the Moscow Grand Prince Dmitry Donskoi by the Vozha in 1378 and on "the broad *field at Kulikovo*" in 1380.[4]

The *Chronological Notes* as a whole are a reflection of Marx's extensive work on the problems of world history.

---

[1] *Marx-Engels Archives*, Vol. V, pp. 197, 144, 344; Vol. VII, p. 169.
[2] Ibid., Vol. VI, p. 387.
[3] Ibid., p. 64.
[4] Ibid., Vol. VIII, p. 151.

STRUGGLE TO SET UP PROLETARIAN PARTIES IN VARIOUS COUNTRIES

To the end of his days, Marx constantly combined scientific research with practical guidance of the working-class movement. Engels stressed: "The struggle for the emancipation of the class of wage-labourers from the fetters of the present capitalistic system of economic production was his real element. And no more active combatant than he ever existed."[1]

In the last years of Marx's life, the task of establishing proletarian parties in the countries of Europe and America was increasingly coming to the fore within the working-class movement. Until the mid-1870, only two organised working-class parties—the Social-Democrats in Germany and in Austria-Hungary—were active in the historical arena, but in the following years the formation of party organisations in the individual countries was accelerated.

A workers' congress in Marseilles in October 1879 set up the French Workers' Party, which rose to prominence in the international working-class movement. The Socialist Party of Belgium emerged in 1879. In neighbouring Holland, a former pastor, Ferdinand Domela Nieuwenhuis, began to publish a socialist newspaper, *Recht voor Allen*, in 1879. In 1882 the General Netherlands Social-Democratic Union was set up with his active participation. Earlier, in 1876, the Social-Democratic Union had emerged in Denmark, and in 1881 a committee for the spread of socialism in Sweden was set up at Malmö. Former leaders of the International played a prominent part in establishing these organisations.

The activity of Mesa, Iglesias and other Spanish socialists led to the founding of the Spanish Socialist Workers' Party in Madrid in 1879. The men who had earlier set up the Portuguese section of the International made efforts, as early as 1875, to found a Socialist Party in Portugal. At the end of 1877, a Social-Democratic Party was set up in Switzerland, but it proved to be unstable because it had a very mixed membership.

In Italy, where anarchism had struck especially deep roots in the working-class movement, the formation of the Socialist Party encountered much difficulty, but the leading elements of the working class and the revolutionary intelligentsia, united in the Upper Italian Federation (founded in 1876) and the Revolutionary-Socialist Party of Romagna (founded in 1881), overcame the anarchist dogmas and came out in favour of participating in the political struggle.

The tendency towards the establishment of independent national parties was also evident in the non-Austrian lands of the Hapsburg Empire. The Czechoslavonic Social-Democratic Party arose in 1878. Thanks largely to the activity of Frankel, the foundation of the General Workers' Party of Hungary was formalised in 1880.

---

[1] Marx, Engels, *Collected Works*, Vol. 24, p. 464.

Marxism spread its influence to the east. In 1878, leaders of the Polish revolutionary movement (among them Ludwik Waryński) drew up the socialist Warsaw Programme, and the first Polish socialist party — Proletariat — emerged in 1882.

This period saw a gradual transition from Narodism to Marxism in the Russian revolutionary movement. The founders of the early workers' associations in Russia — the Workers' Union of South Russia (1875) and the Northern Union of Russian Workers (1878) — had sought to assimilate the experience of the West-European working-class movement. The men who set up these early workers' organisations — Yevgeny Zaslavsky, Victor Obnorsky and Stepan Khalturin — were moved by the ideas of the International, and had read the works of Marx. In the early 1880s, the prerequisites also emerged for the formation of the first Russian Marxist organisation, the Emancipation of Labour group.

Socialist organisations began to emerge on the American continent. At a congress in Philadelphia in 1876, various socialist groups joined to form the Workingmen's Party. French and German emigrants, members of the International, among them Raimond Vilmart, a participant in the Paris Commune, who knew Marx and was a friend of Lafargue, played a major part in spreading socialist ideas in Argentina, Uruguay and Chile. A revolutionary propaganda society, La Vanguardia, was set up in Argentina in 1879, and in 1878 a Socialist Party in Mexico.

The emergence of socialist parties and organisations everywhere testified to the correctness of the course which Marx and Engels had mapped out when still working in the International. But the emergent parties needed ideological and organisational consolidation. Their leaders, frequently former bourgeois democrats, were not always consistent Marxists, while some programmes (like those in the Netherlands, Denmark and Sweden) repeated the Lassallean mistakes of the Gotha Programme. Sectarian tendencies within the leadership often hampered the establishment of strong ties with the masses.

Ahead lay a long and stiff struggle for the revolutionary education and training of the emergent workers' parties.

As leaders of the international proletarian movement, Marx and Engels helped the socialists of all the countries, and strove constantly to ensure that their activities were co-ordinated on an international scale. Shortly before Marx's death, Engels wrote: "We lay stress upon this special status of ours as representatives of *international* socialism."[1] In view of the specific features of socialist activity in the various countries, the two men made great efforts to channel it into the mainstream of international struggle for socialism, and to strengthen and develop the international unity of the working class in other forms. Lenin wrote that with the dissolution

---

[1] Marx, Engels, *Werke*, Bd. 35, S. 442.

of the International, "the unifying role of Marx and Engels did not cease. On the contrary, it may be said that their importance as the spiritual leaders of the working-class movement grew continuously, because the movement itself grew uninterruptedly." [1]

Marx taught the socialists to pursue a consistent revolutionary policy and make a sober assessment of given situations. He resolutely opposed pipe-dreaming, the substitution of abstract and groundless discussion and reasoning for actual revolutionary work. He warned against regarding scientific communism as a sum-total of ready-made recipes which were applicable in any circumstances, and stressed that concrete socialist policy "depends, of course, wholly and entirely on the actual historical circumstances in which action is to be taken".[2]

While doing his utmost to promote the development of international ties between representatives of the socialist movement, Marx continued to believe that it was still premature — before the socialist parties were firmly on their feet in the individual countries — to establish another international organisation of the proletariat. He wrote to Nieuwenhuis: "My own conviction is that the critical conjuncture for a new international workers' association has not yet arrived." [3]

The truth of this was realised by the delegates at a socialist congress in 1881, the last international congress of socialists in Marx's lifetime. It was held in the Swiss town of Chur in the first half of October and was attended by socialists from twelve countries, including Russia (Pavel Axelrod). The congress did not even consider the question of founding an international socialist association, and the debate and the decisions showed that, for all the immaturity they revealed on some issues, the true representatives of the international working-class movement took a firm stand for scientific communism. After the congress, Becker wrote to Engels that this had been "an international party congress, free from any socialist doctrinaire, anarchist, sectarian and other inventors of the happiness of mankind".[4]

Marx saw the struggle against the aggressive foreign policy of the ruling classes and the threat of war as one of the most important international tasks facing the socialist parties. On September 12, 1880, he wrote to Danielson: "I hope there will be no general war in Europe. Though, ultimately, it could not check, but would rather intensify, the social, I mean thereby the *economical*, development, it would certainly produce a useless exhaust of forces for some longer or shorter interval." [5] Marx regarded resistance to militarism as an

---

[1] V. I. Lenin, *Collected Works*, Vol. 2, p. 26.
[2] Marx, Engels, *Werke*, Bd. 35, S. 160.
[3] Ibid., S. 161.
[4] Central Party Archives of the Institute of Marxism-Leninism.
[5] Marx, Engels, *Werke*, Bd. 34, S. 464.

important tradition of the International which had to be developed in every possible way.

AGAINST BISMARCK'S ANTI-SOCIALIST LAW. CRITIQUE OF OPPORTUNISM

By 1878 there was evidence of a sharp shift to the Right in the policy of the ruling circles of the German Reich, which was caused primarily by the ruling classes' fear of growing Social-Democratic influence, and also by the aims of the landowner and big bourgeoisie bloc who wanted their government to pursue a policy of active struggle to acquire foreign markets through protectionist tariffs, colonial conquest and expansion. To meet the costs involved in the attainment of these goals and to cover the ever-growing military expenditure, it was necessary to increase taxes, and that is precisely what Bismarck decided to do. Whereas earlier on he had hoped for an alliance with the national liberals, now he turned to Right-wing forces, with whose support he hoped to strengthen the despotic militarist regime, suppress the working-class and democratic movement and intimidate the liberal opposition.

Bismarck and his supporters prepared to strike the main blow at the Socialist Workers' Party, which they rightly regarded as the main obstacle to his new economic and political course. In their fight against the workers' party, the ruling circles made use of two attempts to assassinate Emperor William I: on May 11, 1878, he was fired at by Max Hödel, an unemployed tin-smith, and on June 2 of the same year, he was gravely wounded by Karl Nobiling, a former student of the Agricultural Academy and an anarchist. Neither had any connection with the Social-Democrats, but the latter were held responsible for these terroristic acts.

On October 19, 1878, the conservative majority in the Reichstag passed a law against the harmful and dangerous aspirations of the Social-Democrats, which was to have effect for three years, but which Bismarck subsequently managed to extend for several further terms. It banned all workers' societies, periodicals and campaigns involving the spread of socialist ideas. The authorities were empowered to introduce a "minor state of siege" in various localities and towns, under which the police had the right, at its own discretion, to disperse any rallies, to extradite any undesirable persons together with their families, etc. During the debate of the bill, Marx observed: "The exceptional law is being issued to deprive the Social-Democratic movement of any semblance of legality."[1]

Bismarck's policy was followed in other countries. In Austria-Hungary, measures were taken virtually banning the Social-Democratic Party. In September 1878, the French government pro-

---

[1] Ibid., S. 77.

hibited the holding of an international workers' congress in Paris. In late 1878, Pope Leo XIII issued a special encyclical against the socialists.

At this difficult period for the German workers' party, Marx and Engels championed its interests in the international arena. Having received from Bracke a verbatim report of the Reichstag's sittings, on September 16 and 17, 1878, at which the bill was debated, Marx at once began writing an *exposé* for *The Daily News*, which he does not seem to have completed. He may have realised, perhaps, that there was no chance of its being published in the English bourgeois press. His rough draft shows the lines along which Marx believed the counter-offensive against German reaction should be launched. He attached much importance to exposing the reactionary attempts to identify Social-Democracy with the anarchist trends, and also to refuting the false thesis that the Social-Democratic doctrine as such impelled men to excesses and terroristic acts. He argued that the liberation struggle of the working class does not imply wholesale armed clashes and uprisings. Before it takes the shape of a violent revolution, it inevitably goes through a stage of peaceful development. The transition from the peaceful to the non-peaceful phase does not depend on the subjective intentions of the revolutionaries, or on their doctrines, but above all on the behaviour of the ruling classes themselves. "Historical development can remain 'peaceful' only so long as those who wield the power in a given society do not resort to force to prevent such development." [1]

Marx showed that it was hypocritical of those who themselves resorted to terrorism against the developing working-class movement to accuse the Social-Democrats of using force. The draconian exceptional law was "a *violent response* on the part of the powers that be to *development* which was *running through* a 'peaceful stage'". [2]

In an interview with the American bourgeois newspaper, *The Chicago Tribune*, published on January 5, 1879, Marx made a public statement about the Exceptional Law, the reasons for its introduction and the Bismarck government's counter-revolutionary schemes. He gave a withering description of Bismarck's policy, showing its Bonapartist nature and its urge to intensify the military police dictatorship. Marx declared: "Bismarck will follow in his (Napoleon's — *Ed.*) wake. He began by building up a despotism under the plea of unification.... Under a sham Constitution he has taxed the people for his military and unification plans until he can tax them no longer, and now he seeks to do it with no Constitution at all. For the purpose of levying as he chooses, he has raised the ghost of Socialism, and has done everything in his power *to create an émeute*." [3]

Marx pointed out that the German Chancellor had been unable to realise his provocative plans fully because of the steadfastness

---

[1] *Marx-Engels Archives*, Vol. I (VI), Moscow, 1932, p. 397.
[2] Ibid.
[3] *The Chicago Tribune*, January 5, 1879.

and cool-headedness of the German proletariat. Elsewhere Marx also noted the failure of the attempts to disgrace the names of men with a revolutionary reputation by associating them with such a "wretched man" as Nobiling.[1] Bismarck's dictatorial action, which was tantamount to a coup d'état, was bound to fail. Marx's predictions were borne out. In 1890, twelve years later, the Anti-Socialist Law was revoked and German Social-Democracy became an impressive force.

Marx called on working-class leaders in the various countries to voice solidarity with the German Social-Democrats. He strove to organise the collection of funds for the victims of the Anti-Socialist Law.

Marx was sure that the German workers would display the necessary steadfastness in the fight against the Anti-Socialist Law, and the revolutionary vanguard of the German proletariat lived up to his hopes. The mass of party members faced the police measures with a rare self-possession and determination to continue the struggle. Their class instinct suggested new forms of revolutionary work. In place of the dispersed party organisations, new, illegal ones gradually began to appear, underground propaganda and contacts were established, and legal channels were also used for party activity.

But in contrast to the true revolutionary instinct displayed by the masses, the Exceptional Law gave rise to confusion among some party leaders. Even before it was passed, the Central Electoral Committee in Hamburg, which functioned as the party's Executive, announced, despite Bebel's resistance, that it was disbanding itself and called on the local party bodies to follow suit. This was a course which would ultimately have led to the liquidation of the party. To say nothing of the patently reformist elements, many vacillating Social-Democratic leaders were impelled by the changing situation to abandon revolutionary methods of struggle. Among them was Wilhelm Blos, who, together with other opportunists contaminated by petty cowardice and lack of faith, was prepared to sacrifice revolutionary principles in order to maintain the legal party, and sought to set up a new party adapted to the Bismarck regime. They urged support for Bismarck's measures, notably, the workers' insurance bill, announced in 1881 for demagogic purposes. On May 17, 1879, the Social-Democratic deputy, Marx Kayser, with the consent of the parliamentary group, spoke in support of the government bill to introduce protectionist tariffs in the interests of the big capitalists and landowners. Marx said Kayser's speech was disgraceful.

Another danger also appeared within the party ranks. Sectarian-anarchist elements were becoming active in Germany and Austria-Hungary. This "Left-wing" deviation was fed by the vacillations of the petty-bourgeois elements which had made their way into the

---

[1] *The Times Literary Supplement*, July 15, 1949, p. 464.

party, and by the influence of non-proletarian ideology. It was not accidental, therefore, that sectarian-anarchist views were being spread by many supporters of Dühring, notably Johann Most, and the former Lassallean, Wilhelm Hasselmann.

In late 1878, Most was expelled from Berlin with a number of other Social-Democrats, and made his way to London, intending to emigrate to the U.S.A. However, he stayed on in London, having undertaken, at the request of the London German Workers' Educational Society, the editing of the weekly *Freiheit*, first issued in early January 1879. At first the newspaper attacked Right-wing opportunism, but later became a mouthpiece for ultra-Left anarchist views. It accused all the party leadership of opportunism, and did not stop short of the grossest insinuations. Most and his associates opposed legal forms of party activity, like participation in elections, use of the Reichstag rostrum, etc. They urged open clashes with the authorities and preparation for an uprising, and insisted that the terroristic acts carried out by Hödel and Nobiling had been expressions of genuine revolutionary spirit. On July 1, 1879, Engels wrote angrily to Becker: "*Freiheit* is prattling on about revolution with fire and sword." [1]

Marx and Engels were quite clear that Most's line was a harmful one, which would demoralise the party, separate it from the masses, and help the Bismarck authorities to organise police provocation. In their numerous letters to workers' leaders, they approved the struggle carried on by the Social-Democratic leaders against this sectarian-anarchist trend and made it quite clear that they had nothing to do with the group led by Most, who was spreading rumours alleging that the two men supported him.

In contrast to these swings to the Right and "Left", Bebel, Liebknecht, Bracke and other party leaders succeeded in finding the correct line. This difficult period brought out Bebel's organisational talent and fighting spirit to the full. As a true proletarian leader, he displayed the ability not only of directing the masses but also of learning from them, of taking up and developing their initiative. Long before the others, he realised that the Executive had been wrong to decide on dissolution, and that it was necessary to work out new forms of party activity designed for underground work. Relying on the leading workers, Bebel exerted much effort to restore the party organisations.

In the autumn of 1878, the Aid Committee in Leipzig, which he headed, assumed the functions of the party's governing body. In the new period of the German working-class movement, Bebel "showed himself to be a real party leader". [2]

While discerning the vital needs of the working-class movement, Bebel did not immediately realise the extent of the danger which opportunism presented to the party in the new situation. Under the in-

---

[1] Marx, Engels, *Werke*, Bd. 34, S. 383.
[2] V. I. Lenin, *Collected Works*, Vol. 19, p. 299.

fluence of the opportunists Liebknecht now and again abandoned his revolutionary tone, as in his speech in the Reichstag on March 17, 1879, when he said that the Social-Democratic Party, as a reform party, would abide by the Anti-Socialist Law.

The conciliatory attitude taken by the party leadership towards Right-wing opportunism made itself felt in the discussion of the composition of the editorial board for a central organ to be published abroad. Hirsch was to be appointed editor, but during the negotiations with him it turned out that apart from the editorial commission in Leipzig, which was to include Bebel and Liebknecht, there was also to be a supervisory or administrative committee in Zurich, where the paper was to be published.

Its members were to be the reformist Karl Höchberg and former followers of Eugen Dühring—Eduard Bernstein and Carl Schramm. This structure of the editorial board and the future paper's financial dependence on Höchberg—whom Marx had described in 1877 as a bourgeois who "had bought his way into the party", while sharply criticising the Berlin *Zukunft* which he was then editing [1]—gave the Zurich group a decisive say on the paper. Unwilling to act as a "straw man" Hirsch refused the invitation to become editor.

Marx and Engels approved of Hirsch's attitude, and withdrew their offer to write for the paper. In a letter to Bebel on August 4, 1879, Engels resolutely declared, on behalf of Marx and himself, that they would have nothing to do with a party organ placed under the control of "social-*philanthropist*" Höchberg.[2]

At first, the Social-Democratic leaders did not understand why Marx and Engels took this attitude and believed that they were being unfair to Höchberg. However, fresh confirmation soon came that the two men had been right. In early September 1879, the first issue of the *Jahrbuch für Sozialwissenschaft und Sozialpolitik*, edited by Höchberg, appeared in Zurich, containing an article enitled "A Retrospective Survey of the Socialist Movement in Germany". In place of the author's name were three asterisks. It soon transpired that the article had been written by Höchberg, Bernstein and Schramm, the three prospective members of the supervisory committee.

This work by the "three-star constellation", as Marx ironically called its authors, was in a sense a manifesto of all Right-wing elements. Marx observed: "Nothing more disgracing for the party has ever been printed." [3] The article condemned the whole of the Social-Democrats' past revolutionary activity, including their support for the Paris Commune. The authors accused the party of having failed to "display moderation", thereby bringing down upon itself the Anti-Socialist Law. The whole article was a philistine call to aban-

---

[1] Marx, Engels, *Werke*, Bd. 34, S. 305.
[2] Ibid., S. 386.
[3] Ibid., S. 413.

don revolutionary aims, to submit slavishly to Bismarck's police regime, and to repent of past revolutionary "sins". It also condemned the party's fight against the bourgeoisie, and suggested the need to attract the bourgeoisie into the party ranks and to fill the leading posts with bourgeois intellectuals, in view of the workers' inadequate education.

Marx and Engels were highly indignant. At the time, Marx was on holiday in Ramsgate, and it was Engels who expressed their attitude to Höchberg, who had just come to London. Marx and Engels decided that there was an urgent need to demand categorically of party leaders that they should review the composition of the editorial board of the central party organ. The two men had usually made known their views to working-class party leaders in the form of advice and recommendations, but on this occasion they felt that the very class basis of the party was being jeopardised. In mid-September 1879, Engels drafted a letter to Bebel, Liebknecht, Bracke and the other Social-Democratic leaders. On September 17, he discussed it with Marx, who had that day returned to London, and having worked out the final text of the circular, as Marx called it, the two men signed and dispatched it. They warned party leaders that if the new party organ became a mouthpiece for Höchberg and his group, "then all we could do — much though we might regret it — would be publicly to declare ourselves opposed to it".[1]

The circular letter was one of the most striking written attacks on opportunism and the conciliatory attitude to it. It was a wrathful condemnation of the policy which the cowardly spokesmen of the petty bourgeoisie sought to impose on the party, thereby jeopardising its proletarian revolutionary character. "Instead of resolute political opposition — general conciliation; instead of a struggle against government and bourgeoisie — an attempt to win them over and talk them round; instead of defiant resistance to maltreatment from above — humble subjection and the admission that the punishment was deserved."[2]

The circular helped Bebel and other German leaders to see the writings of the Zurich group in a truer light. On October 23, 1879, referring to the article in the Zurich paper, Bebel wrote to Engels: "I have read it and I see why you are so indignant."[3] Bracke said the opportunists were trying to "undermine the foundations of the party and to threaten its very *existence*".[4] The party leaders abandoned their plan to involve Höchberg and his friends in the publication of their central organ. Aware of the dissatisfaction in party circles, the representatives of the opportunist trend beat a temporary retreat.

The first sample issue of the weekly *Sozialdemokrat*, whose edito-

---

[1] Marx, Engels, *Collected Works*, Vol. 24, p. 269.
[2] Ibid., p. 267.
[3] A. Bebel, *Aus meinem Leben*, 3. Teil, Berlin, 1953, S. 59.
[4] Karl Marx, Friedrich Engels, *Briefwechsel mit Wilhelm Bracke (1869-1880)*, S. 208.

rial committee included Bebel, Liebknecht and Friedrich Fritzsche, appeared in Zurich on September 28, 1879. However, the choice of Georg Vollmar as chief editor also proved to be unsatisfactory. Under his editorship (from September 1879 to December 1880) the party's central organ frequently made opportunist mistakes. Nevertheless, the newspaper played a major role in organising the party's underground revolutionary activity. Despite police harassment, a large group of party activists organised a regular underground supply of copies from Zurich to Germany.

That the party's leading circles were overcoming their vacillation was seen from its first underground congress held at Wieden Castle in Switzerland, from August 20 to 23, 1880. Its keynote was the struggle against deviations from the revolutionary line. Most and Hasselmann, the leaders of the anarchist-minded elements, were expelled from the party. In spite of resistance from the Right-wingers (Höchberg, Kayser and others) and the moderates, the following amendment was made to the programme: the word "legal" was deleted in the clause which said that the party would work for its goals "by every legal means". This congress decision oriented the party towards the use of both legal and illegal forms of struggle.

The results of the congress were welcomed by Marx and Engels. At the end of September 1880, Liebknecht arrived in London and informed them of the state of affairs. However, the two men were disturbed by Liebknecht's tendency to present the state of the party in a rosy light, and, in particular, to ignore the troubles in the *Sozialdemokrat*, edited by Vollmar.

Soon Bebel also realised the need for a change of editor. He decided to go to London in the first half of December 1880 to discuss this matter with Marx and Engels whom he had never met personally and establish closer contacts with them. He invited Bernstein, one of the Zurich trio, who was then taking a more correct attitude under the impact of criticism, to go to London with him. It subsequently turned out that Bernstein had adopted this stand only under the influence of Engels, for after the latter's death he became the chief ideologist of revisionism.

Bebel and Bernstein arrived in London on December 9, were put up at Engels' house and stayed for about a week. They frequently went to see Marx. Bebel was greatly impressed by the cordiality and hospitality he received from Marx and Engels. In their friendly talks they discussed many questions. Bebel subsequently wrote: "We left London completely satisfied with the results of our visit." [1]

Bernstein was appointed editor of the *Sozialdemokrat*, and Vollmar's removal had a salutary effect on the paper. This was reinforced by Engels' constant contributions to the newspaper and collaboration with the editorial board, beginning from December 1881. Through Engels, Marx also strove to help the newspaper, and in his

---

[1] A. Bebel, *Aus meinem Leben*, S. 150.

letters he advised that more emphasis should be laid on revealing the plight of the workers not only in private but also in government enterprises, in order to expose Bismarck's social demagogy, Bismarck's "state socialism".[1] He frequently criticised Bernstein's mistakes.

Marx was glad to see the German party increasing its influence in the masses despite the reprisals. At the 1881 elections, it managed to win 12 seats in the Reichstag, the same number that it had won in 1877, when it was still a legal party. Marx and Engels had high praise for the steadfastness and courage displayed by the mass of party members, and they valued greatly the activity of the revolutionary leaders of the German proletariat, notably Bebel. When the bourgeois press reported Bebel's death in September 1882, Marx wrote to Engels: "It's frightful—the greatest misfortune for our party! He was a unique phenomenon in the German (one might say in the "European") working class."[2] It was a great relief for Marx and Engels when the report proved to be groundless.

Naturally Marx and Engels were not entirely satisfied with the activity of the German Social-Democratic Party even during this period of its history, which was, taken as a whole, an heroic one. They realised that many members of the party still favoured opportunist tactics. They were also wary of some of the younger members who saw themselves as the party's theorists and publicists. Thus, Marx formed a highly unfavourable impression of Karl Kautsky (the son of the Austrian writer, Minna Kautsky), who visited him in 1881. Ever since joining the socialist movement in 1874 he had been under the influence of diverse ideological trends, from positivism and Malthusianism to Lassalleanism and anarchism, until he began to turn to Marxism in early 1880, when he was working on the *Sozialdemokrat*. On April 11, 1881, Marx wrote to his eldest daughter: "When the charmer ... first came to see me, the first question that rose to my lips was—are you like your mother? Not in the least, he exclaimed, and silently I congratulated his mother. He's mediocrity, narrow in outlook, overwise (only 26 years old), a know-all, hardworking after a fashion, much concerned with statistics out of which, however, he makes little sense, by nature a member of the philistine tribe, for the rest, a decent fellow in his own way."[3] In the first two months of their acquaintanceship, Engels also described Kautsky as a born pedant and hair-splitter, "in whose hands complex questions are not made simple, but simple one complex".[4]

As a result of his association with Engels, Kautsky soon became a prominent propagandist of Marxism and a theorist of the Second International, but the negative traits which Marx discerned in the young Kautsky made themselves felt many years later, and played

---
[1] Marx, Engels, *Werke*, Bd. 35, S. 124.
[2] Ibid., S. 95.
[3] Ibid., S. 178.
[4] Ibid., S. 220.

a definite part in his subsequent political evolution and his switch to opportunism.

Faced with various external and internal problems and not always able to overcome them swiftly or easily, the German working-class movement nevertheless gained steadily in strength, becoming an increasingly powerful factor in German political life and exerting a strong influence on the advance of the proletarian struggle for emancipation in other countries.

CONTRIBUTION TO THE ESTABLISHMENT OF THE FRENCH WORKERS' PARTY

The struggle by the forward-looking members of the French proletariat to establish and strengthen their own, independent revolutionary party was an important element in the socialist movement of the 1870s and 1880s. Marx and Engels closely followed this revolutionary process and strove to promote it in every way possible.

The French police tried to establish control over Marx's connections in France, and the Paris prefecture had a record of intercepted letters which Marx wrote to Hirsch in 1875 and 1876. Marx showed great concern for organising the propaganda of scientific communism among the French workers. He hoped to find forces in France capable of uniting the socialist elements and exerting a decisive influence on the awakening of the class consciousness of the French proletariat.

These forces were in fact there. In the autumn of 1876, Jules Guesde (the pseudonym of Mathieu Jules Basile) returned to France after a period of exile. He was sentenced to five years of imprisonment in his absence for defending the Paris Commune in the press. He fled to Switzerland, and took part in the activity of the International, siding with the Bakuninist wing. During his stay in Switzerland and later in Italy Guesde became disillusioned with anarchism, mainly under the impact of Chernyshevsky's novel, *What Is to Be Done?* and his other works. On his return to France, he met members of the students' socialist circles, Hirsch and other Marxists, and all this helped him to accept Marxism, although he did not immediately abandon his earlier views.

Together with Gabriel Deville, Emile Massard, Chabry and his other associates Guesde inaugurated a new stage in the spread of the ideas of scientific communism in France. In November 1877, he and his friends succeeded in starting publication of the daily newspaper *Egalité*. The editorial board openly supported the "collectivist school which has now been adopted by all the serious thinkers of the proletariat in the Old and the New World". Henceforth "collectivism" in France usually signified Marxism. The newspaper's Marxist line grew even more pronounced when Lafargue became first an active contributor and then one of its editors. On November 5, 1880,

Marx wrote to Sorge: "You have probably noticed that the *Egalité* (thanks principally to *Guesde*'s coming over to us and to the works of my son-in-law Lafargue) has become the first 'French' *workers' paper* in the true sense of this term." [1]

The *Egalité*'s revolutionary influence on the workers and its international ties were a source of alarm to the authorities and brought police reprisals against the editorial board. In the summer of 1878, Guesde and a number of his friends were imprisoned for an attempt to convene an international workers' congress in Paris.

Following Guesde's release, an opportunity occurred for Marx to become personally acquainted with him. The radical organ, *Révolution Francaise*, published a polemic between Guesde and Longuet, who proved unable to overcome his Proudhonist views and take a critical attitude to the social projecteering of the bourgeois radicals. Marx took Guesde's side and wrote him a letter in January 1879. The text of it is not extant, but in a reply sent to London that spring Guesde repeated and quoted some of the ideas it contained. Guesde's reply shows that Marx regarded the establishment of an "independent and militant workers' party" as a pressing task before the French socialists. [2] He believed this could be done by spreading scientific communism among the workers, overcoming the influence of bourgeois radicals and petty-bourgeois socialists, and engaging in extensive agitation activity. Guesde fully accepted these ideas, and informed Marx of his warmest desire to meet him personally.

In the summer of 1879, Guesde and Lafargue (the latter had lived in London until the spring of 1882) began a regular correspondence, and this was the start of their friendship. Lafargue frequently showed Guesde's letters to Marx and Engels and discussed his replies with them. This opened up yet another channel through which Marx and Engels could help the French socialists to set up a proletarian party. The extant letters which Lafargue wrote to Guesde are a reflection of the work done by Marx behind the scenes, and bear the stamp of his thoughtful and tactful influence on prominent members of the working-class movement. These letters urged them to remember the final goals of the movement and at the same time give attention to the day-to-day needs of the working class, to refrain from spreading their negative view of the reformist ideology of the syndicalists and the co-operativists to the trade union and co-operative movement as a whole, and to learn to see and use the rational elements in all aspects of the workers' activity and initiative.

In the friendly discussions between Guesde and Lafargue, Marx and Engels sometimes supported Guesde, whenever his stand reflected his better knowledge of the concrete situation in France, with which Lafargue had long been out of touch. Marx made a point of reading everything published by Guesde and Lafargue. Apart from the items in the *Egalité*, he read Guesde's pamphlet, *Collectivism and*

---

[1] Marx and Engels, *Selected Correspondence*, p. 312.
[2] *Le Combat marxiste*, No. 19, May 1935, p. 20.

Revolution, published in 1879. In the margin he put a question mark where Guesde erroneously stated that in the future society the worker would receive "the full product of his labour".[1] But on the whole, he took a positive view of the pamphlet. Later, Marx made extracts from Guesde's articles on the agrarian question which appeared in November 1880. Among Lafargue's writings, he read his long article entitled "The Movement of Landed Property in France".

The third workers' congress was held at Marseilles from October 20 to 31, 1879. In contrast to the first two congresses—in Paris in October 1876 and in Lyons in January-February 1878—which were dominated by the bourgeois co-operativists, the majority of the Marseilles Congress followed the revolutionary socialists. In spite of reformist and anarchist resistance, it adopted resolutions on the establishment of collective ownership of the means of production as the goal of the working-class movement, and the founding of an independent working-class party. The leaders of the congress asked Guesde (who was ill and did not attend) to draft the party programme. Marx put a high value on this outstanding victory of the French socialists, and wrote that "the first organisation of a genuine workers' party in France dates back to the Marseilles Congress".[2]

Marx and Engels helped the leaders of the French party to work out a coherent platform, to prepare the party for political and electoral action, and to consolidate its ideological stand. In March 1880, the *Egalité* carried two articles by Engels, entitled "Herr Bismarck's Socialism", which showed the illusory nature of the belief among some French socialists that the bourgeois state was capable of carrying out important social reforms. Within two weeks, Marx contributed an item to the *Egalité* on his work *The Poverty of Philosophy,* which preceded the publication of sections from it in the newspaper. He explained the essence of the polemics with Proudhon, stressing the need to combat idealistic and utopian views by expounding the materialist doctrine.

Marx and Engels also contributed to the monthly socialist journal, *La Revue socialiste,* first issued in January 1880. At Lafargue's request, Engels edited three chapters of his *Anti-Dühring,* as a separate essay entitled "Socialism: Utopian and Scientific", which appeared in the March-May 1880 issues of the journal. The same year, it was published as a separate pamphlet, and in May 1880 Marx wrote an introductory biographical note about Engels for the French edition, calling him "one of the foremost representatives of contemporary socialism".[3]

Earlier on, in April 1880, Marx had drawn up a questionnaire for the *Revue socialiste,* which was published in the journal and as a separate supplement. The "Workers' Questionnaire" was widely cir-

---

[1] Central Party Archives of the Institute of Marxism-Leninism.
[2] Marx, Engels, *Werke,* Bd. 35, S. 114.
[3] Marx, Engels, *Collected Works,* Vol. 24, p. 335.

culated, 25,000 copies being printed of the supplement alone. This was a comprehensive programme for a social study of the condition of the working class. Its four sections contained almost 100 questions. But it was more than a questionnaire. It was a fine specimen of skilful socialist agitation, inducing the workers to give thought to the exploiting nature of the capitalist system, and formulating the essential economic demands of the working class: shorter working hours, higher wages, effective insurance under the workers' own control, equal pay for men and women, prohibition of child labour, a shorter working day for juveniles, complete legality for trade union associations, etc. All in all, the document suggested to the workers the need for a fundamental change in the existing social system.

The emerging Workers' Party was in need of a programme above all other things. Guesde found some difficulty in drawing it up and, on Lafargue's advice, turned to Marx. In early May 1880, he came to London, where he met Marx, Engels and Lafargue for the first time.

At Engels' house Marx, Guesde, Lafargue and Engels himself discussed the draft programme of the French Workers' Party. There and then Marx dictated to Guesde the general theoretical preamble, the rest having been drafted beforehand by Guesde, with Lafargue's participation. It contained the minimum programme—a list of political and economic demands to be put through under the bourgeois-democratic system and regarded as a stage in the winning of power by the working class. Marx and Engels gave greater precision to some of its formulations. Marx found the minimum programme highly satisfactory, except for the point on the legislative establishment of minimum wages, because in practice it could be used by the entrepreneurs to limit any wage rise. It contained, as he pointed out, "demands that have, in fact, arisen spontaneously out of the workers' movement itself".[1] It included the demands for a repeal of the laws restricting freedom of assembly, the press and associations, introduction of an eight-hour working day for adults and a six-hour working day for juveniles, equal pay for equal work for men and women, prohibition of any transfer into private hands of state enterprises, banks, railways, mines, etc.

The preamble was the pivot which determined the programme's theoretical level. In highly concise and popular form, without any trace of the high-flown and flowery verbiage which was the hallmark of French socialist documents, Marx stated the communist goals of the proletariat's liberation struggle. He himself wrote about the results of his efforts: "To bring the French workers down to earth out of their verbal-cloud-cuckoo land was a tremendous step forward."[2] It took Marx only a page to formulate the key propositions about the historical mission of the working class, its revolutionary action as the decisive means for overthrowing the capitalist

---

[1] Marx, Engels, *Werke*, Bd. 34, S. 476.
[2] Ibid.

system and establishing social ownership of the means of production, and the proletariat's need for an independent political party. It said that the "emancipation of the producing class is that of all human beings without distinction of sex or race".[1] Engels said that Marx's introduction was "a masterpiece of cogent reasoning calculated to explain things to the masses in a few words".[2]

The first Marxist programme of the French working-class movement was adopted by the Workers' Party Congress at Le Havre on October 14, 1880, marking a major success for Marxism and showing that it had gained strong influence among the leading sections of the French workers. It was also the touchstone for the various trends within French socialism and helped the truly proletarian elements to part ways with the reformists and sectarians.

The struggle over the programme began before the congress at Le Havre. As soon as the draft was published, it was attacked by bourgeois radicals, and some Proudhonist-minded socialists allied with them, including Longuet. The anarchists put up a stiff fight against the programme at the congress at Le Havre, and the Blanquists also took a negative stand. Although in the International they had taken a step towards accepting the materialist outlook and scientific communism, they had yet to overcome their teacher's voluntarist and conspiratorial ideas about tactics, naively believing in the boundless possibilities open to a vigorously active revolutionary minority and its ability to stage instant communist revolution. In 1881, they broke away from the Workers' Party and set up their own Central Revolutionary Committee.

However, it was the opportunist grouping within the Workers' Party itself, headed by former anarchists and active members of the Bakuninist Alliance of Socialist Democracy — Paul Brousse and Benoît Malon, that proved to be the main opponent of the revolutionary Marxist wing. During the Marseilles Congress, both Brousse and Malon had spoken out for collectivism, and had paid lip-service to Marx's doctrine. But Malon himself described his views as "integral socialism" based not only on the Marxist theory, but also on the doctrines of the "true socialist" Karl Grün, Lassalle, and the neo-Kantian Friedrich Lange. Brousse's outlook was also a hodgepodge of reformist and anarchist views. Brousse and Malon expressed the views of the petty-bourgeois elements in the Workers' Party who were discontent with the revolutionary line laid down in its programme.

After the congress at Le Havre, Brousse, Malon and their followers launched a direct attack on the Workers' Party leadership, with the newspaper *Le Prolétaire* as their mouthpiece. They declared the Havre Programme, especially its preamble, to be the cause of all the reverses of the young Workers' Party, particularly its failure in the 1881 election. Brousse's article "Once Again on Socialist Unity"

---

[1] Marx, Engels, *Collected Works*, Vol. 24, p. 340.
[2] Marx, Engels, *Werke*, Bd. 35, S. 232.

(published in November 1881) set out the reformist platform, proposing the abandonment of the "narrow horizon of one doctrine" (meaning Marxism) and broad access to the party for the adherents of various doctrines. Brousse said that the party's orientation towards the ultimate establishment of socialism was tantamount to backing up the "all or nothing" principle. In contrast, he proposed that the party should confine itself to demands which were practicable at that moment, and that it should pursue a "politique des possibilités" (policy of possibilities). The Possibilists, as members of the new opportunist trend became called, discarded the idea of the revolutionary socialist transformation of society in favour of peaceful gradualism, the philistine utopian theory of "municipal socialism", implying the transfer of various industries to local bodies and the establishment on that basis of a "public service" system.

Marx and Engels at once perceived the petty-bourgeois essence of possibilism. Engels said that the Possibilists were corrupting the Workers' Party, and that the spread of their views threatened to reduce it "to the level of the most ordinary trade unions".[1]

Marx and Engels naturally believed that it was the French Marxists who should give a lead in the fight against the Possibilists, and so they were grieved to see Guesde and Lafargue now and again putting trump cards into the hands of their ideological opponents. The leaders of the revolutionary Marxist wing frequently lacked self-control and flexibility, and sometimes took a dogmatic and too straightforward view of some Marxist propositions. There was also the traditional French passion for revolutionary phrases. Engels said that Guesde suffered from the Parisian superstition that "the word revolution is something one must continually bandy about".[2] In attacking the reformist ideology, Guesde and his followers were frequently prepared to deny altogether, in the sectarian spirit, the importance of the struggle for reform. Nor did they pay enough attention in practice to the workers' day-to-day needs. Lafargue, who was theoretically more mature, likewise shared some of Guesde's sectarian mistakes. Complaining of the French Marxists' narrow and dogmatic view of revolutionary theory and tactics, Marx once acidly told Lafargue: "What is clear is that I myself am not a Marxist."[3]

While criticising his French followers for their blunders, Marx fully supported their general line, for he believed that the revolutionary tendencies in the French working-class movement were fully expressed by the Marxist wing of the Workers' Party led by Guesde and Lafargue. Marx believed that the future of the Workers' Party depended on the success of the Guesdists.

Meanwhile, a split within the party was coming to a head. At the Rheims Congress in late October 1881, the Possibilist delegates,

---

[1] Marx, Engels, *Werke*, Bd. 35, S. 118.
[2] Ibid., S. 231.
[3] Ibid.

many from fictitious branches, had a majority, and passed decisions undermining the party's unity in favour of autonomy. Thus, each federation was given the right to have its own programme. The National Committee consisted mainly of Possibilists, and the newspaper *Le Prolétaire* was established as the party's central organ. After the congress, the Possibilists intensified their slander campaign against Guesde and Lafargue.

In this period of tension, Marx and Engels sought to support the French Marxists in every way possible. In response to a request Marx, who was very ill and on his way to Algiers for treatment, stopped over in Paris in February 1882 to meet Guesde, Deville and their Spanish supporter Mesa. In the summer of that year, at Argenteuil on his way back from Algiers, Marx had many conversations with Lafargue, who had by then settled in France. On August 2, he again met Guesde and Deville, together with Lafargue, at Mesa's home in Paris. All this left Marx with the impression that despite the acute situation, "Guesde and his party are gaining the upper hand".[1]

By the autumn, the organisational separation with the opportunists had become imperative. When the St. Etienne Congress of the Workers' Party opened on September 25, 1882, the Marxist delegates, led by Guesde, walked out in protest against the opportunist policy of the Possibilists and convened their own congress at Roanne. The Possibilist congress rejected the Havre Programme, allowing each federation to have its own programme, while the Marxists at their congress reaffirmed their loyalty to the principles set forth in that document. They adopted a special resolution stating that the party's main political goal was the winning of state power by the working class.

Marx and Engels believed that in the circumstances the split in the Workers' Party was inevitable, and they saw what had happened at St. Etienne as being the result of growing objective contradictions within the working-class movement, springing from the existence within it of two different trends: the revolutionary-proletarian, and the petty-bourgeois reformist. In general, they regarded the struggle between these opposite tendencies as a manifestation of the law governing the development of the proletarian parties in a class society. The form of necessary separation from the opportunist elements depended on the concrete conditions. Marx and Engels showed the events in France to have proved that in critical situations, where the maintenance of formal unity threatened the party with reformist degeneration, a split was not a bane but a boon for the working-class movement, for it created the prerequisites for the genuine unity of the proletarian party, unity on a revolutionary basis.

Marx and Engels were not disturbed by the fact that initially the Possibilist branches were stronger numerically. The advantage of

---

[1] Ibid., S. 84.

the Guesdists lay in the fact that they were supported by the proletarian circles, particularly in the large industrial centres, including many industrial workers of Paris, whereas the Possibilists prevailed mainly in the economically backward areas, in the south and the west of France and among the workers of small enterprises in the capital. The French Marxists stood the test of sharp inner-party struggle and safeguarded their programme, their ideological banner. Marx saw this as a guarantee of the future triumph of revolutionary principles in the French working-class movement.

TOWARDS A NEW STAGE IN THE SPREAD OF SOCIALISM IN BRITAIN

Marx and Engels believed that the main reason for the growing reformist tendency in the British working-class movement lay above all in the fact that Britain's capitalist industry dominated the world market, and felt that radical changes would occur only when England lost her monopoly.

Towards the end of the 1870s, there were signs that Britain's industrial monopoly was weakening. American and German industry was clearly growing at a faster rate. While remaining the first colonial power and the chief exporter not only of home-produced goods but of colonial goods also, Britain was gradually losing her industrial leadership. Her economy was in a state of stagnation from 1873, and then, without any upsurge, plunged straight into a sharp crisis in 1878 and 1879.

The condition of sizable sections of the proletariat deteriorated and this had an effect on the mood of the masses. There were signs of disillusionment with the narrow craft unions, which brought together skilled workers only. There was a growing urge among workers and radical intellectuals to be rid of the Liberals' political control. The mounting national and agrarian movement in Ireland was an important element of this ferment. A situation was taking shape in the British Isles in which the seeds of revolutionary socialism sown by the International in the British working-class movement could be expected to produce their first shoots.

All these years, Marx and Engels had been constantly seeking ways and means of activating the British working class and getting its most advanced members to accept socialist theory. They approved the activity of Adam Weiler, the Secretary of the Cabinet-Makers' Union, who had fought in the American Civil War and had been a member of the British Federal Council of the International. Weiler coupled his practical work in the trade unions with an open stand in defence of his socialist views; at the London Trades Union Council and at the annual Trades Union Congresses, to which he was elected as a delegate from 1876 to 1883, he stood up for radical decisions in contrast to the stand taken by the reformist majority. In the autumn of 1880, Marx and Engels started to correspond with Robert Banner, a spokesman for a group of radical-minded trade unionists in Scotland, who were inclined to scientific socialism. On September 17, Banner wrote to Marx from Edinburgh: "It will be no surprise to you, I hope, to hear, that north of the Tweed there are others beside your humble admirer, who have a very high opinion of your past and present work, in the cause of Social-Democracy." [1] We do not have Marx's reply, which he wrote in mid-November, but Banner's letters in December 1880 to Marx and to Engels (whose letter to Banner is not extant either) show that Marx explained the state of affairs in the British working-class movement and the essence of the policy pursued by the Liberals, who had subordinated it to their political influence. He also drew Banner's attention to the economic and social changes in Britain, which were creating the prerequisites for breaking out of the narrow framework of Liberal Labour policy. Banner agreed with this, and wrote: "The silent social revolution you speak about, is taking deep root among us." [2]

Marx was also well known—often from the International period—by members of the radical clubs and societies who had among them former leaders of the British Federation of the International Working Men's Association, and now and again he was invited to lecture on socialism. His works were also known to the leaders of the League campaigning for manhood suffrage which had been set up in London's Soho district in 1879.

Marx and Engels gave every support to the new groups who spread socialist ideas, and helped the most progressive bourgeois intellectuals to side with the working class. However Marx took an implacable stand against those of them who stopped halfway and strove to combine socialist views with anti-revolutionary and vulgar views or to use the socialist movement for personal ends.

This is well illustrated by Marx's relations with the English publicist, Henry Mayers Hyndman, a wealthy lawyer and stockbroker, and a bourgeois radical, who sympathised with the Tories. In 1880, he stood for Parliament as a Tory candidate but lost. Meanwhile, he had won a reputation for exposing some aspects of British colonial rule in India, and also the punitive measures taken by the Liberal Government against the Irish national movement. In June 1880, Hirsch introduced Hyndman to Marx and the two had several conversations. Hyndman's interest in socialism was stimulated by his reading of Volume One of *Capital* in French, but his socialist views were highly superficial and inconsistent.

Marx tried hard to convince Hyndman of the need for adopting the revolutionary doctrine in a coherent form, but Hyndman failed

---

[1] Robert Banner to Karl Marx, September 17, 1880 (Central Party Archives of the Institute of Marxism-Leninism).
[2] Robert Banner to Karl Marx, December 6, 1880 (Central Party Archives of the Institute of Marxism-Leninism).

to understand the revolutionary Marxist conclusions, and gave a distorted interpretation of Marx's proposition that the socialist revolution could develop peacefully in Britain. He tried to substitute for this concept ideas like "social reorganisation" and "social reconstruction", and to combine Marxist views with theories of "state socialism", equating Marx with Rodbertus and Lassalle.

Marx regarded Hyndman as a democrat who sympathised with the working-class movement and so tried to influence the evolution of his ideas, but was by no means inclined to see him as the leader of British socialism, a role Hyndman soon began to claim. In the spring of 1881, he and his friends took steps to unite workers' and democratic radical clubs in one organisation, seeking to bring together in its ranks bourgeois-democratic and socialist elements.

Marx was clearly aware that the organisation Hyndman was setting up—on June 8, 1881, it was officially established as the Democratic Federation—was a semi-bourgeois, semi-proletarian society. Nor did he have any illusions about Hyndman's qualities as a leader. He observed: "All those amiable middle-class writers—if not specialists—have an itching to make money or name or political capital *immediately* out of any new thoughts they may have got at by any favourable windfall."[1]

During the inaugural conference, Hyndman circulated among the delegates his recently published pamphlet, *England for All*, as a commentary on the programme of the Democratic Federation. In two of its chapters ("Labour" and "Capital") he retold and partially reproduced some extracts from Volume One of *Capital*, without mentioning Marx's name and confining himself to an obscure reference in the preface concerning the source of his ideas: "I am indebted to the work of a great thinker and original writer."

When Marx read Hyndman's pamphlet, he found that the author had not only plagiarised him, but had distorted many of the ideas borrowed from *Capital*. Thus, when conveying Marx's theory about the exploiting character of the capitalist system, Hyndman "supplemented" it with praise of bourgeois democracy and Lassallean recipes for solving the social question through state intervention. Marx underlined and put exclamation marks against those sections of the pamphlet where the author, with considerable national arrogance, expounded on the alleged intellectual superiority of the English, who did not allow themselves to be carried away by the "demon of socialism", which pushed other nations into anarchy and destruction. Hyndman also betrayed chauvinism when he claimed a special social mission for Anglo-Saxon democracy with respect to the rest of mankind, suggesting that a union of the English-speaking peoples was the best way for social reconstruction, and stressing England's "selflessness" in her trade relations with other nations.[2]

Marx believed that real propaganda of socialism was incompatible

---

[1] Marx and Engels, *Selected Correspondence*, p. 326.
[2] Central Party Archives of the Institute of Marxism-Leninism.

with this kind of vulgar-democratic and chauvinistic views. In response to Hyndman's attempts to vindicate his unpardonable treatment of *Capital*, Marx replied in a letter of July 2, 1881 that he opposed any hodge-podge of bourgeois-democratic and socialist ideas, adding that he did not share the opinion of Hyndman, and his friends that the English had an organic "horror of socialism", or a mistrust of socialist theories, particularly those of foreign origin. Marx wrote: "I have not found it so during the times of the International and of Chartism." [1] Marx was sure that revolutionary proletarian doctrine would get through to the working class of England.

This was gradually being borne out in practice. There was a growing interest in Marx's theory among English proletarian and democratic circles. In December 1881, the talented journalist, Ernest Belfort Bax, published an article about Marx and his doctrine in the journal *Modern Thought*. Marx sent this article to Lavrov and wrote: "There is a sincerity of speech and a ring of true conviction about him which strike you." [2] The prominent poet, artist and publicist, William Morris, joined in the spreading of socialist ideas. The Marxist doctrine was winning ever greater numbers of supporters among the leading workers as well.

Serious changes were also taking place within the Democratic Federation. In the summer of 1883, it adopted a socialist programme, and in 1884 was transformed into the Social-Democratic Federation, which proclaimed Marxism as its theoretical platform. But the sectarian and opportunist attitudes taken by Hyndman and some other leaders long prevented it from pursuing the correct revolutionary policy.

It took much time and effort to clear the ground for the establishment of a revolutionary proletarian party in Britain. But even in Marx's lifetime steps were taken to bring scientific communism and the working-class movement together in this country, where reformism had struck deep roots.

PROSPECTS BEFORE THE WORKING-CLASS MOVEMENT IN THE U.S.A.

Marx had never been to America, but he knew a great deal about its economic and political affairs and was quick to observe the trends in its development.

In 1882, he and Engels wrote about the "fabulous concentration of capital" in the United States. [3] Marx drew attention to the "monopolising power" "of the great companies swaying industry, commerce, property in land, railroads, finance — at an always acceler-

---

[1] Marx to Hyndman, July 2, 1881 (Central Party Archives of the Institute of Marxism-Leninism).

[2] Marx to P. Lavrov, January 23, 1882 (Central Party Archives of the Institute of Marxism-Leninism).

[3] Marx, Engels, *Collected Works*, Vol. 24, p. 426.

ated rate since the outbreak of the Civil War". [1] He saw agrarian relations in the U.S.A. as an example of the growth of capitalist contradictions on the basis of free enterprise and capitalist development in agriculture, unfettered by any feudal survivals.

The reverse side of American prosperity was large-scale exploitation of the workers through the intensification of labour, extensive social ills, caused by crises, and the unprecedented number of unemployed. "American civilisation" was keeping whole layers of the population, the Negroes above all, in the condition of pariahs; only the upper strata of the U.S. working class enjoyed better conditions, the rest — the bulk — especially the immigrant workers, differed little if at all from their fellows in other countries in terms of lack of rights and social hardship. Marx wrote: "The best Yankee writers are loud in proclaiming the stubborn fact that, if the Anti-Slavery war has broken the chains of the black, it has on the other hand enslaved the white producers." [2] Despite its democratic trappings, the U.S. bourgeois state was acutely hostile to the working class, being an instrument in the hands of big business. Marx described the political regime in the U.S.A. in these words: "Rings and cliques have seized upon the legislature, and politics has been made a trade." [3]

Marx was sure that the American working class would intensify its resistance to the power of capital. He realised that it was developing along specific and intricate lines. Alongside the factors which accelerated its development — the growing numerical strength and concentration of the proletariat, the intensified exploitation and the deepening of class contradictions, the chronic unemployment, etc. — other factors tended to slow down the consolidation of the proletarian forces. In the 1870s, workers, especially native-born workers, were still able to buy tracts of land in the West and to set up as farmers. A formidable obstacle to unity was the mixed national composition of the working class, as more and more immigrants arrived from Ireland, Britain, Germany and Italy, and in the 1870s from the East-European countries, China, and so on. Under the impact of these contradictory tendencies, the U.S. working-class movement swung from one extreme to the other. Ideologically it was also most varied: narrow trade unionist ideology and apolitical attitudes existed side by side with conspiratorial traditions, and Marxism alongside various shades of petty-bourgeois socialism.

A most important result of the International's activity in the U.S.A. was the establishment in the summer of 1876 of the Workingmen's Party of America, which had a Marxist wing, headed by Friedrich Sorge, Otto Weydemeyer and Patrick MacDonnel. The American Marxists were in constant touch with Marx and Engels. MacDonnel, who was appointed editor of the party paper, *The Labor Standard*, invited Marx and Engels to contribute to the paper.

---

[1] Marx, Engels, *Werke*, Bd. 34, S. 359.
[2] Ibid.
[3] *The Chicago Tribune*, January 5, 1879.

He wrote: "A line from you or from Mr. Engels in *The Labor Standard* would be read with general pleasure and would help us very much."[1] In March 1878, the paper published a series of articles by Engels entitled "The Workingmen of Europe in 1877".

The adherents of scientific communism within the Workingmen's Party of America had to carry on a stiff fight against the Lassalleans and other sectarian and reformist elements, mainly from among the German immigrants. In the above-mentioned letter to Marx, MacDonnel said that he, Sorge and the other Marxists were "fighting a great battle here against schemers, fanatics and fools".[2] A congress of the party in 1877, which renamed it the Socialist Labor Party of North America, was dominated by the Lassalleans. Sorge, MacDonnel and their supporters were forced to leave the party, while the Lassallean leadership changed its programme, orienting the party mainly on participation in the electoral struggle. The stand taken by the new leadership, its unwillingness to work among native-born Americans, or even to study the English language, led to the conversion of the party into a narrow sectarian organisation.

The situation improved somewhat when those who inclined to Marxism became more active within the party. The Marxists who were not members of the party likewise constantly sought to exert an influence on it. The party papers *New Yorker Volkszeitung* and *The Socialist*—both founded in 1878—began to spread Marxist ideas. In the early 1880s, the German Social-Democrat Adolf Hepner, who had worked with Marx in the International, worked on the *New Yorker Volkszeitung*, and took steps to arrange for the publication of Marxist pamphlets as the Workers' Library series.

Marx and Engels strove to induce the American socialists to overcome their dogmatic approach to revolutionary theory and tactics, to keep in closer touch with the mass of workers, even if they had not yet matured for socialist ideas, and to carry on the propaganda of socialism not in abstract terms, but in a form comprehensible to the masses, combining it with action in defence of the workers' concrete interests and direct participation in their day-to-day struggle. Lenin stressed that in their recommendations to the socialists of various countries and in criticising their mistakes, the founders of Marxism emphasised this or that line, depending on the specific features of the country's socialist movement and its main shortcomings. While they warned the German Social-Democrats above all of the danger of Right-wing opportunism, they censured the socialists in America and Britain chiefly for their narrow sectarian views, for turning Marxism into a dogma, and for failing to take account of the actual conditions of the struggle. Lenin wrote: "What Marx and Engels criticise most sharply in British and American socialism is its isolation from the working-class movement."[3]

---

[1] MacDonnel to Marx, December 7, 1876 (Central Party Archives of the Institute of Marxism-Leninism).
[2] Ibid.
[3] V. I. Lenin, *Collected Works*, Vol. 12, p. 363.

Marx explained that the setting up of a proletarian party in the U.S.A. was inseparable from the mass struggle of the American proletariat. Only in the thick of that struggle could the socialists hope to lay the foundation for such a party. Marx insisted that the low level of class consciousness and the narrow pragmatism of the proletarian masses were not an insuperable obstacle for this. The participants in the proletarian struggle could first be united on the basis of the concrete practical tasks which were clear to everyone, making use of the spontaneous urge of the masses for unity. This would pave the way for educating the workers in a socialist spirit and helping them to adopt a revolutionary socialist programme.

One of the reasons for the influence exerted by various radical bourgeois theories on the workers was that socialist propaganda was out of touch with the day-to-day struggle of the proletarian masses. Thus, among the highly popular ideas in the U.S.A. were those of the radical publicist and economist Henry George, who held that the nationalisation of landed property was the main instrument for social reconstruction. This was widely accepted by farmers and workers still hoping to go back to farming, who were indignant over the exploitation of land by speculators, railroad companies, etc. George's book *Progress and Poverty*, published in 1880, was considered by many in America, England and Ireland as a socialist work.

Marx read the book — we have his remarks in the margins — and another of George's works published in 1881, entitled *The Irish Land Question*, and his remarks on both these works show the author's mistakes and narrow-mindedness. He stressed that George was wrong in trying to blame all contemporary social ills on private ownership of land, which was only one type, and theoretically not a necessary one at all, of the capitalists' monopoly of the means of production. In the margins of *The Irish Land Question*, Marx wrote that dispossession of the workers "springs not *from landed* property, but from the capitalist *system*".[1] George and other bourgeois economists of his kind failed to understand that abolition of land-rent, or to be more precise, its payment to the state in the form of a land tax, superseding all the other taxes, did not in itself eliminate wage-labour and the appropriation of surplus-value. It would merely help to consolidate capitalism by increasing the other parts of capitalist profit at the expense of rent. Marx said that George's theoretical impotence had prevented him from seeing that it was the cheapness of land and its availability in the United States that had, contrary to George's theory, pushed the capitalist system in the United States "to extremes yet unknown in Europe".[2]

Marx summed up his conclusions in a letter of June 2, 1881 to the American socialist John Swinton, an admirer of George, and on

---

[1] Central Party Archives of the Institute of Marxism-Leninism.
[2] Ibid.

June 20 in a letter to Sorge. He gave George his due as a publicist and did not deny that the demand to abolish land-rent was progressive, recalling that it had been formulated in the *Manifesto of the Communist Party* as one of the proletarian state's transitional measures facilitating the socialist transformation of society. The whole point was that George did not see this radical demand—first advanced by English economists of the Ricardo school—as a transitional measure, but, like the Belgian petty-bourgeois socialist Jean Colins, as a panacea for the social ills. By advertising it in the American way, and himself as its inventor, George spread illusions among the masses, diverting their revolutionary protest along the wrong way, and distracting them from the fight against the pillars of the capitalist system. Marx wrote to Sorge: "So the whole thing is merely an attempt, tricked out with socialism, *to save the capitalist régime* and, indeed, to *re-establish it on an ever broader basis* than at present." [1]

Marx's ideas about the specific features of the development of the American working-class movement, the obstacles and dangers it faced on the way, and the need for American socialists to overcome sectarianism and rebuff the ideology alien to the proletariat gradually exerted an influence on leading workers in the U.S.A.

ANALYSIS OF POST-1861 DEVELOPMENT IN RUSSIA

In the last decade of his life, Marx paid particular attention to Russia, which was then going through a painful period of transition from the backward serf system to capitalism. In 1861 she entered a period marked by exceptionally acute class contradictions and a rapid growth of revolutionary forces.

The causes, substance and consequences of the peasant reform of 1861 were among the main problems studied by Marx. Special interest attaches to his manuscript "Remarks on the 1861 Reform and Russia's Post-Reform Development", which Marx wrote at the end of 1881 or in early 1882 by way of systematising and summing up the material he had accumulated. Marx felt that the reform had been prepared directly under the impact of mounting discontent among the peasantry and the growing peasant movement, an idea he had first suggested in the *New-York Daily Tribune* in 1858. His conclusion was: "A guerrilla war was being fought between the peasants and the landowners." [2]

At a time when not only the official Russian press but the whole European liberal press continued to extol the tsar as an "emancipator" and the reform as a "great act", Marx described it as the robbing of the peasants. He said that being forced to abolish serfdom,

---
[1] Marx, Engels, *Werke*, Bd. 35, S. 200.
[2] Ibid., Bd. 19, S. 414.

the tsar "decided from the outset to give the landowners as much as possible (and the peasants as little as possible)".[1] He perceived the true nature of the reform: "The emancipation merely boils down to the fact that the noble landowner is no longer able to dispose of the *peasant's person*, to sell him, etc. This *personal bondage has been abolished*. The landowners have lost their *personal power over peasant's person.... The peasant* has found himself *economically dependent on his former landowner*."[2] The Regulations of February 19, 1861, Marx stressed, maintained forced labour for the peasants for a long time by introducing a "state of temporary indenture" which preserved semi-serfdom. Marx said that the redemption payments amounted to legislatively formalised robbing of the peasants, and tribute to the landowners for the abolition of serfdom.

Marx said that the predatory nature of the reform caused a fresh explosion of popular wrath and struggle against the landowners. "Following the proclamation of the emancipation *manifesto* of February 19 (March 3), 1861, there were general unrest and disturbances among the peasants; they believed that it was a forged, unauthentic document; military executions; general flogging of serfs during the first three months after the Manifesto."[3]

Marx's numerous notes give a full picture of the condition of the post-reform countryside and of the millions of peasants who lived in dire poverty, had to add chaff and goose-foot to their flour, and starved to death during the increasingly frequent bad harvests. The small farmer was exploited by the big landowners even more intensively than under the serf system. Usurers and kulaks were quick to draw the peasants' tiny holdings into their net. Autocracy, for its part, saddled the "emancipated" peasant with an intolerable burden of duties and levies for the treasury. Marx stressed that the peasants' economic plight was compounded by their lack of political and legal rights.

At the same time, Marx's "Remarks on the 1861 Reform" and other manuscripts show that he saw the reform and its results as marking the rise of the capitalist formation in Russia, and we find him saying again and again that Russia's post-1861 development marked the beginning of a new industrial era. Of course, Marx and Engels dated the origin of the capitalist order in Russia to much earlier periods, and in his manuscripts Marx recorded data showing the development of commodity-capitalist relations long before 1861. But he emphasised 1861 as an important milestone in the history of Russia's economy, and the start of a qualitatively new stage in the country's socio-economic development as a result of the abolition of serfdom.

Marx was very well aware of all the obstacles which stood in the way of Russia's progressive economic development, the main one

---

[1] Marx, Engels, *Werke*, Bd. 19, S. 408.
[2] Ibid., S. 414.
[3] Ibid., S. 407.

being the continued existence of landed estates and the resultant dependence of the peasants on their old masters. Marx saw the extremely intricate pattern of semi-feudal and developing capitalist relations in the Russian countryside after the reform as a specific feature of Russia's economic development, a peculiar characteristic of Russian social life which generated the especially acute class antagonisms in Russia.

Marx saw and correctly assessed many elements of capitalism in Russia's agriculture which were fettered by semi-feudal relations. Thus, he remarked on the switch by some of the landed estates from the corvée to the capitalist system, involving the use of wage-labour and improved implements and farming machinery. The notes Marx made when reading the *Transactions of the Tax Commission* and other sources show that he devoted special attention to landowner enterprises like beet-sugar factories, distilleries and stud farms, and to the emergence of areas of market agriculture and livestock farming on capitalist lines. He took a special interest in facts showing the growing contradictions within the peasantry itself. Dozens of pages in his notebooks contain material on the property stratification of the peasantry, the kulaks' buying up of the landowners' lands, their use of wage-labour, their lease of plots to peasants, and their money-lending operations.

When reading the satirical works of Saltykov-Shchedrin, Marx noted almost all the passages describing the emergence of the "new pillars of society"—the capitalists and the kulaks.

He also made a thorough study of the formation of the social group which confronted the richer sections in the Russian countryside, and his manuscripts contain much information about agricultural labourers, poor landless peasants and other categories of the rural proletariat in Russia. Marx was well aware of the peculiarity of the Russian rural proletariat, namely, that the agricultural labourer and the farmhand usually had an allotment which not only failed to provide its owner with the necessary means of subsistence, but also tied him to the *mir* (village commune), or to be more precise, to the rapacious kulak and the local landowner, that is, made him sell his labour-power on the worst possible terms.

Marx saw that, as in Western Europe in the past, social processes in Russia were leading to an "expropriation of the peasants, that is, broad masses of people",[1] i.e., the Russian form of depriving the small producers of their land and ruining them. Marx was aware that the stratification of the Russian peasantry, the proletarianisation of a large part of it, and the creation of a labour market in Russia likewise went to create the conditions for the establishment of the capitalist mode of production.

He kept a close watch on the growth of Russian industry, the emergence of new factories and plants, the establishment of new in-

---

[1] Ibid., S. 396.

dustries in the areas of St. Petersburg and Moscow, in Vladimir and other gubernias, on the Black and Azov Sea coasts, in Poland and other parts of the Russian Empire. Marx's notes on the *Military Statistical Review* and the *Transactions of the Tax Commission* show that he was also interested in the development of Russian market relations and foreign trade. He collected information on the growth of Russia's seaports and her trade with Central Asia, Persia and China. He also made a special study of railway construction in Russia, and its impact on the further disintegration of patriarchal relations and the development of commodity-capitalist relations.

Proceeding from his analysis of socio-economic relations, Marx revealed the class character and the reactionary role of the Russian autocratic state, and described its domestic and foreign policy. Despite some changes in the political system after 1861 — apart from the peasant reform, the tsarist government had been forced to put through some reforms in the judicial, administrative and military spheres — the country's regime remained an extremely despotic one. Tsarism had taken the first step to transform itself from a feudal monarchy into a bourgeois one, but retained all the basic features of an autocratic power relying on the army and the police.

As the country developed economically, autocracy ran into ever greater contradictions with the requirements of this development. Marx saw the poor state of tsarist finances as a sign that the existing order in Russia was unsound. The efforts to improve them reminded him of those taken in the 18th century to save French absolutism from financial disaster. He remarked ironically that the "alchemists of Russia's finances" were also taking the same way.[1] Having lost its internal stability, the tsarist autocracy could no longer hope to put through its plans of aggrandisement on the international scene as successfully as it had done in the past, and this was evident from its military and diplomatic difficulties during the Balkan crisis in the 1870s, and the Russo-Turkish War of 1877-78. The growing revolutionary movement at home was undermining the whole system of Russian tsarism's aggressive foreign policy. On September 10, 1879, Marx wrote: "The secret of Russian diplomacy's success abroad was the deathly silence of Russia at home, the spell being broken by the movement in that country."[2]

With great satisfaction Marx observed the deepening contradictions between official and revolutionary Russia, and took a warm interest in the assessment of the domestic situation by Russia's leading revolutionaries. Hence his growing interest in Russian social thinking, revolutionary publicistic writings and belles-lettres. Marx compared the latter to a mirror reflecting Russian life and the changing frame of mind among the leading sections of Russian society. Marx, who knew Chernyshevsky's works very well and called

---

[1] Marx to P. Lavrov, October 21, 1876 (Central Party Archives of the Institute of Marxism-Leninism).

[2] Marx, Engels, *Werke*, Bd. 34, S. 108.

Marx in 1882

Marx's grave
in Highgate Cemetery,
London (before the erection
of the monument in 1956)

Page of V. I. Lenin's notebook *Marxism on the State* with extracts from the *Manifesto of the Communist Party*

him "the great Russian scholar and critic",[1] continued with unflagging interest to study his writings, especially those analysing socio-economic relations in Russia during the preparation and implementation of the 1861 Reform. In the early 1870s, Marx read Chernyshevsky's "Letters Without Address", containing a full-scale critique of the reform, which Danielson had sent him in a manuscript copy, and in 1881 he reread this striking publicistic work.

Marx put a high value on Chernyshevsky's programme for a popular revolution against serfdom and the autocracy, and paid tribute to the Russian revolutionary's militant democratism, his faith in the people, and his hatred for tsarism and serfdom.

Marx saw Chernyshevsky and Dobrolyubov not only as profound thinkers and talented writers, but also as leaders of the revolutionary camp, who educated and guided the new generation of Russian revolutionaries. Marx's remarks in the margins of Chernyshevsky's "Critique of Philosophical Preconceptions Against the Communal Ownership of Land" are evidence of his keen interest in the idea put forward by the great revolutionary thinker about Russia's transition to the socialist system, bypassing capitalism. At the time, Chernyshevsky could not see the real social forces which would carry the Russia of that period along a non-capitalist path, and Marx was aware that his idea of using the village commune for Russia's socialist transformation was a utopian one, but he found many rational elements in his statements (on the importance of a "spirit of collectivism and comradely association", on the communal use of farming machinery, scientific achievements, and so on). Marx believed that Chernyshevsky's approach to the question of Russia's socialist prospects was in itself of exceptional importance.

Chernyshevsky's philosophical, historical and publicistic writings and works of fiction were well known in the Marx family. In the above-mentioned review of literary and theatrical life in London, published by the *Frankfurter Zeitung und Handelsblatt* in May 1877, Jenny Marx criticised the lies in the British bourgeois press about Russian revolutionary writings, and called Chernyshevsky "the greatest modern revolutionary writer". She referred to his novel *What Is to Be Done?* and his articles in the journal *Sovremennik*, in which he demanded of the "Russian government the emancipation of the serf peasants (naturally, in a different way to that in which it was actually carried out) and castigated the then pseudo-liberalism of the Petersburg press with such caustic relentlessness that its 'worthy' representatives breathed a sigh of relief when the government exiled him to Siberia".[2]

Marx was aware that the poet Nikolai Nekrasov and the great satirist Mikhail Saltykov-Shchedrin belonged to the trend led by Chernyshevsky and Dobrolyubov. In February 1873, he read Saltykov-Shchedrin's satirical cycles entitled "The Diary of a Provincial

---

[1] Karl Marx, *Capital*, Vol. I, p. 15.
[2] *Beiträge zur Geschichte der deutschen Arbeiterbewegung*, No. 6, 1966, S. 1045.

in St. Petersburg" and "The Gentlemen of Tashkent", sent to him by Danielson. Later, Marx also read his "Abroad" and "The Retreat of Mon Repos". The markings Marx made in 1878 on a pamphlet by M.P. Dragomanov, *The Persecution of Ukrainian Literature by the Russian Government*, show that he had also taken note of the writings of the great Ukrainian poet and revolutionary, Taras Shevchenko.[1]

In general, Marx took a lively interest in Russian literature and culture. Together with Engels he frequently expressed his delight at the flourishing of Russian poetry and belles-lettres in the 19th century. Lafargue recalled the pleasure Marx derived from reading the works of Pushkin, Gogol and Saltykov-Shchedrin. An early edition of *Eugene Onegin* (which Marx quoted in *A Contribution to the Critique of Political Economy* in 1859) was cherished by Marx, and after his death by Engels, as an especially valuable item in their Russian collection. Franziska Kugelmann recorded Marx's views of other Russian writers: "He was of the opinion that Turgenev wonderfully renders the peculiarities of the Russian soul in its veiled Slavonic sensitivity. Lermontov's descriptions of nature, he thought, were hardly to be excelled and seldom equalled."[2] The letters and reminiscences of Marx's close friends tell us that the family often listened to Russian classical music, including popular Russian ballads and pianoforte arrangements of Glinka's operas, which they received from Russia.

For Marx, Russian literature was not only a source of pleasure, but also a reflection of the contemporary socio-historical situation and an aesthetic reproduction of highly interesting and concrete facts from Russian social life.

KEEN EXPECTATION OF REVOLUTION IN RUSSIA

The more Marx studied Russia's socio-economic development and the deeper he penetrated into her social and political processes, the stronger became his conviction that the country was moving towards a great revolutionary upheaval, which would have a decisive influence on the whole of Europe. Lenin stressed: "Marx and Engels naturally possessed the most fervent faith in a Russian revolution and its great world significance."[3]

In the latter half of the 1870s, Marx was firmly convinced that Russia was closer to revolution than any other European country. He hoped that the tsarist government's difficulties over the Russo-Turkish War of 1877-78 would accelerate the revolutionary events. He was highly inspired by the prospect of a Russian revolution, and on September 27, 1877, he wrote to Sorge: "And then there will be

---
[1] Central Party Archives of the Institute of Marxism-Leninism.
[2] *Reminiscences of Marx and Engels*, p. 278.
[3] V.I. Lenin, *Collected Works*, Vol. 12, p. 376.

a fine row. If Mother Nature is not particularly ill-disposed towards us, we shall yet live to see the fun!"[1]

By the time of the second revolutionary situation in Russia at the turn of the 1880s, Marx was quite clear on all the essential issues of the incipient Russian revolution. His conviction that it was inevitable and would be tremendously powerful was based on his profound understanding of its objective prerequisites and his scientific definition of the requirements of the country's progressive development. Marx and Engels believed that the impending revolution in Russia would be a bourgeois-democratic and mainly peasant one, aimed chiefly at abolishing the autocracy, landed estates and semifeudal relations. In contrast to the Narodniks, who had visions of proceeding directly to socialism, Marx clearly saw that the forthcoming revolution in Russia was bound to be a democratic and not a socialist one. The peasantry, with a vital stake in the solution of the land question, was bound to make it highly explosive, and to give it great depth and scope.

Observing the political behaviour of the Russian bourgeoisie, Marx was clearly aware of its indecision and constant inclination to political compromise with autocracy, which had to reckon with the bourgeoisie's economic interests. Marx realised that the Russian bourgeoisie was incapable of putting up any serious resistance to tsarism or of taking action which was in any sense revolutionary.

Marx held that the primary task of a bourgeois-democratic revolution in Russia would be to overthrow autocracy, with the political and agrarian revolutions constituting its two inseparable aspects. A death blow to tsarism would sound the tocsin rousing broad sections of the people for further creative revolutionary action. Marx was sure that the revolutionary movement in Russia would produce great popular leaders, worthy successors of Chernyshevsky and Dobrolyubov.

It was Marx's profound conviction that the overthrow of autocracy would open the floodgates for genuinely progressive development of the Russian and other nationalities in the country. In the event of a victorious proletarian revolution in the West and with its assistance, Russia would be able to advance to socialism, bypassing the capitalist phase of development or substantially shortening it. In allowing for such an eventuality, Marx proceeded from the fact that the overall historical situation had changed markedly not only compared with the period of the French Revolution, to which he frequently likened the coming revolution in Russia as regards scale and progressive development, but also compared with the period of the revolutionary events of 1848. The proletarian movement in the West had risen to a new level, and in the event of a victory could and was bound to influence the course and the historical results of a popular revolution in Russia.

---

[1] Marx and Engels, *Selected Correspondence*, p. 289.

Since the Russian working class had not yet taken shape as an organised force capable of giving a lead in the struggle of the whole people, Marx believed the outcome of a Russian revolution depended on the West-European proletariat, whose assistance to the Russian revolutionaries he held to be almost axiomatic in ensuring the victory of a bourgeois-democratic revolution in Russia and the country's social revival. He also maintained that the joint action of the Russian revolution and the victorious movement of the West-European working class was a guarantee that the revolutionary struggle in Russia would advance beyond the stage of the bourgeois revolution, and ultimately carry the country to socialism.

This idea was reflected in a message which Marx and Engels sent to the Chairman of the Slavonic Meeting held in London in March 1881 to celebrate the 10th anniversary of the Paris Commune. They said that the growing revolutionary movement in Russia, "maybe after long and violent struggles, must ultimately and certainly lead to the establishment of a Russian Commune".[1]

At the same time, Marx and Engels kept emphasising, a Russian democratic revolution as a component part of the European revolutionary process was bound to have an exceptional influence on it. The impending revolution in Russia would be a turning point in world history.

Marx believed that once a popular revolution had occurred in Russia and overthrown tsarism, the whole system of European international relations was bound to change. The ultimate result of the revolution would "put paid to the whole of old Europe's present status quo".[2] Like a "fresh breeze", it would have a beneficial effect on Germany, changing the state of things in that country "at one blow" and bringing about the downfall of the Prussian Junkers and the militarists. He wrote to Liebknecht that a revolution in Russia would "ring Prussia's death-knell".[3] He also believed a Russian revolution would lead to the liberation of Poland, involve other oppressed peoples in Europe in the revolutionary movement, and bring about a revolutionary change in Austria-Hungary and other countries. There would be a fundamental change in the balance of forces in favour of the working class and revolutionary democracy across the European continent. The collapse of the autocracy in Russia would mean "such a change in the whole situation of Europe as must be hailed with joy by the workingmen of every country as a giant step towards their common goal — the universal emancipation of Labor".[4]

Avidly looking forward to a revolution in Russia, and sharing the hopes of the Russian revolutionaries for its early outbreak, Marx and Engels in fact overestimated the prospects. They were wrong

---

[1] Marx, Engels, *Collected Works*, Vol. 24, p. 372.
[2] Marx, Engels, *Werke*, Bd. 34, S. 244.
[3] Ibid., S. 318.
[4] Marx, Engels, *Collected Works*, Vol. 24, p. 229.

about the date, but quite right on the main thing: their analysis of its objective prerequisites and the anticipation of its great depth and scope.

RUSSIAN REVOLUTIONARIES' ADVISER AND FRIEND

In the 1879s, Russia was the scene of an heroic struggle of the Russian revolutionaries against the tsarist autocracy. The clashes were especially acute from 1879 to 1881, when the revolutionary ferment at the grass roots coincided with the start of a "crisis at the top", as government circles vacillated in search of a way out of the unstable situation, and resorted to a policy of "the whip and the carrot". From the establishment of fresh revolutionary circles and groups and the "going among the people" in the first half of the 1870s, the Russian revolutionaries went on to the establishment, in 1876, of an all-Russia centralised and strictly secret organisation, which was somewhat later named Land and Freedom. In August 1879, internal contradictions, mainly over tactics, led to its split into two bodies: the People's Will, which launched a direct attack on tsarism, and the General Redistribution. On March 1, 1881, Tsar Alexander II was killed under a sentence passed by the Executive Committee of the People's Will. After this, the revolutionary movement, which was subjected to especially fierce reprisals and did not receive the necessary support from the people, declined. Revolutionaries had exhausted their strength in fighting the tsar, the unorganised and scattered masses of peasants had not yet realised the need for joint action everywhere, while the working class of Russia was only just taking shape. The liberal sections of the bourgeoisie faintheartedly refused to give any support to the fighters against autocracy. Once again reaction gained ground in Russia. The Narodnik movement itself began to lose its revolutionary traits and gradually developed into a type of liberal opposition.

The revolutionary events of the 1870s had a great impact on social life in Russia and the subsequent development of the emancipation struggle, constituting a definite phase of the bourgeois-democratic period of the Russian revolutionary movement. It was dominated by the commoners, the advanced intellectuals who championed the people's cause. The revolutionary Narodniks of the 1870s expressed the aspirations of broad masses of peasants who were seeking to be rid of the feudal survivals and the despotic, autocratic regime. From their predecessors and teachers, Herzen, Chernyshevsky and Dobrolyubov, they inherited their faith in the power of the people's revolution, preference for revolutionary methods of fighting tsarism, and socialist ideals.

Marx was very well aware that the hopes of the Russian Narodniks for instant socialist revolution were illusory, but he was resolutely opposed to "calling to account", as Engels put it, the people's loyal champions for their misconceptions. Marx and Engels held that their immature ideology corresponded with the contemporary level of Russia's socio-political development, and believed that they would overcome their mistakes as they gained first-hand experience and learned the lessons of the West-European working-class movement, in which many Narodniks displayed a keen interest. Narodism's ideological flaws did not obscure for Marx and Engels its objectively revolutionary bourgeois-democratic character, or the Narodniks' dedicated fight against tsarism.

While regarding various petty-bourgeois socialist trends in the West as an obstacle to the development of the proletariat's class organisation, Marx and Engels took account of the fact that in Russia, where the working-class movement was only taking its first independent steps, and where bourgeois-democratic change was on the order of the day, the petty-bourgeois Narodnik movement had not yet exhausted its revolutionary potentialities. That is why they supported the revolutionary Narodniks, whom they considered allies of the West-European proletariat and the socialist parties. What Marx and Engels valued especially was their fierce hatred of tsarism, their dedication and revolutionary steadfastness, their internationalist tendencies, and their urge to arouse to the struggle the peasantry of Russia, a great reserve of the European proletarian revolution.

Marx read many Narodnik publications, including the journal and newspaper *Vperyod*, which Lavrov published abroad from 1873 to 1876, the underground organs of the Land and Freedom and the People's Will, and their programme documents, Narodnik publicistic writings and similar literature. Apart from his old Russian friends and correspondents—Lavrov, Lopatin and Danielson—there were now Lev Hartmann, Nikolai Morozov, and Vera Zasulich. Marx established close friendly relations with Lavrov, who invariably showed the greatest respect for Marx and Engels, considered their opinions and valued their advice. He was a frequent visitor at Marx's home and carried on an extensive correspondence with him. However, Marx and Engels clearly saw the shortcomings and contradictions in their Russian friend's outlook.

Hartmann and Morozov, both participants in the Narodnik movement, also visited Marx at his home in 1880 and 1881. Through them and Lavrov, he established direct contact with the Executive Committee of the People's Will. Marx provided revolutionary emigrants from Russia with reliable addresses in Germany, and induced his associates in various countries to give their utmost support to the Russian revolutionary movement. He readily responded to various requests from the Russian revolutionaries, notably, the idea proposed by Russian emigrants to publish abroad an English-language weekly *The Nihilist* to win West-European public support for the Russian revolutionary movement. Nothing came of the idea, however.

Marx cherished his contacts with Russian revolutionaries and was proud to show his friends a letter from the Executive Committee of the People's Will of November 6 (October 25, Old Style), 1880, which expressed profound respect for Marx's scientific achievements and his concern for Russian revolutionary activity, and asked him to help Hartmann inform the Western public about the nature of the struggle which had started in Russia. As a mark of sympathy for the Narodniks he had earlier sent two of his autographed photographs to members of the Executive Committee (both soon fell into the hands of the police).

There was also growing respect for Marx among the Russian revolutionaries, in particular, the revolutionary Narodniks, who took a keen interest in his theory and activity. Many of them — especially men of proletarian origin, such as Stepan Khalturin, Pyotr Alexeyev and Andrei Karpenko — avidly read works on scientific communism. *Capital* was widely circulated among young Russian revolutionaries, and many Narodniks quoted it in their talks in study-circles and in their pamphlets (for example, Sergei Kravchinsky's *Fairy-Tale of the Wise Woman Naumovna* and Alexei Bakh's *Hunger the Tsar*). The Executive Committee of the People's Will wrote to Marx that *Capital* had become "a standard work for all intelligent men".[1] Russian revolutionaries were also well acquainted with other writings by Marx and Engels. In March 1881, the police confiscated a copy of the *Manifesto of the Communist Party* when arresting Nikolai Kibalchich, a leader of the People's Will, an outstanding revolutionary, scientist and inventor, who had started to translate it in 1875.

However, the Narodniks were hampered in their understanding of the Marxist doctrine by their idealistic views, for example, that Russia's social development must follow its own unique course, that capitalism meant regress and decline — this was a step back as compared with Chernyshevsky — and their idealistic view of the peasant commune and of the peasantry as a whole as being the most revolutionary class. The Narodniks, petty-bourgeois utopian socialists, believed that Marxist political economy applied only to the capitalist West, but not to Russia. Those were the ideas expressed in a book by the Narodnik publicist Vasily Vorontsov, entitled *The Future of Capitalism in Russia*, which Marx read in 1882. The Narodniks took a superficial view of Marx's theory and now and again tried to combine it mechanically with the ideas of Proudhon, Bakunin, Lassalle and Dühring, and the subjectivist, idealistic views expounded by Lavrov, one of those who insisted on the decisive role the "critically-minded individual" had to play in history, etc.

Marx and Engels sought in every way to help the Russian revolutionaries in their painful quest for the right outlook and tactics, and their attacks on the ideas of Bakunin and Nechayev accelerated the

---

[1] Central Party Archives of the Institute of Marxism-Leninism.

overcoming of the anarchist influence, although some of Bakunin's ideas long continued to influence the Narodniks. Of great importance in exposing the Narodnik ideological mistakes were Engels' articles entitled *Refugee Literature*, which he wrote in 1874 and 1875, with Marx's full backing, against Lavrov and Tkachov, prominent Narodnik ideologists. He showed their outlook to be a haphazard mixture of ideas and insisted that Lavrov would fail in his efforts to reconcile Marxism and anarchism. He exposed Tkachov's erroneous views that the Russian state stood over and above classes, that it would be easy to carry out a revolution in Russia, and that conspiratorial methods were right. These false idealistic views were an essential feature of the Narodniks' outlook, who in general had a very vague idea about the connection between the legal and political institutions and the interests of the various social classes.

On many subsequent occasions, Marx drew the Narodniks' attention to their erroneous views, but as their fight against tsarism advanced he believed that such criticism should be couched in the friendliest and most delicate terms. It was the wrong moment for a public condemnation of the utopian principles of the Narodniks' ideology, for they were fighting in incredibly difficult conditions. At the time, their practical revolutionary action was of much greater importance than the theoretical side of the movement. But Marx never missed an opportunity to express his opinion on the acute problems which agitated the minds of revolutionary intellectuals in Russia, and to show the difference between his own view and that of the Narodniks. He also responded to any attempt to distort his doctrine.

The need for such a critical statement arose at the end of 1877, when, following comments in the Russian press by bourgeois publicists about *Capital* and Marxism, Nikolai Mikhailovsky, an authoritative Narodnik sociologist and a future ideologist of liberal Narodism, published an article in the democratic journal *Otechestvenniye Zapiski*, entitled "Karl Marx on Trial by Mr. Y. Zhukovsky". He wrote it in response to malicious attacks on Marx by Zhukovsky, a vulgar political economist, in the liberal *Vestnik Yevropy*. Mikhailovsky defended Marx the "sanguinian" against his liberal critics from the Narodnik standpoint. He admitted that *Capital* revealed the author's "rare logical power and vast erudition", but added the warning that just because Marx's theory was "something coherent and integral, and therefore alluring", it was not right to "fling open the gateway" before it as a whole.[1] Mikhailovsky denied a priori the existence of capitalism in Russia and so insisted that the conclusions in *Capital* were inapplicable to his country. Like all Narodniks, he was hoping for an exclusive way to socialism—through the peasant commune.

Immediately upon reading Mikhailovsky's article, Marx drafted

---

[1] *Otechestvenniye Zapiski*, No. 10, 1877, pp. 322, 325.

a letter in French to the editors of *Otechestvenniye Zapiski*, protesting against the vulgarisation of his ideas in *Capital* and the attempt to turn dialectical materialism into a universal method for fitting the history of the various nations into a general scheme, instead of studying its actual course. The Marxist method reveals the general regularities governing social development, but does not, contrary to Mikhailovsky's view, proceed from the assumption that social development everywhere necessarily follows a definite pattern, regardless of the peculiar historical conditions of this or that country. Accordingly, Marx resolutely protested against his historical essay on the emergence of capitalism in Western Europe, in the chapter on the primitive accumulation of capital, being changed into "a historico-philosophical theory of general development, imposed by fate on all peoples, whatever the historical circumstances in which they are placed".[1]

Marx said that if the Narodniks wanted to find the right answer to the question of whether Russia could bypass the capitalist stage of development they had to take a strictly realistic view of the economic and social processes going on in their country. He himself took account — and advised the Narodnik ideologists and publicists to do likewise — of the tendency which Russia had manifested "to become a capitalist nation". He added: "If Russia continues along the path it has followed since 1861, it will miss the finest chance that history has ever offered to a nation, only to undergo all the fatal vicissitudes of the capitalist system."[2] Consequently, Marx regarded the capitalist way of Russia's socio-economic development as being a real one as well.

He firmly objected to the Narodnik sociologists' vulgar view of capitalism as an unmitigated evil and stressed that in the context of world history it was large-scale capitalist production that prepared the material prerequisites for socialism.

This letter was discovered by Engels when he was sorting out Marx's papers after his death. He sent a copy to Vera Zasulich and gave another to Lopatin, who took it to Russia, where it was circulated in manuscript form before its publication (abroad in 1886, in Russia in 1888). In a letter to Vera Zasulich, Engels suggested that Marx had failed to post the letter because "his name alone would be sufficient to jeopardise the existence of the journal that would publish his reply".[3] The impression which Marx's letter made on progressive people in Russia can be seen from Gleb Uspensky's article "Bitter Rebuke": "In a few lines written in the same manner as every line in his *Capital*, that is, with impeccable precision and impartiality, Karl Marx shed light on the whole course of our economic life, beginning from 1861."[4]

---

[1] Marx, Engels, *Collected Works*, Vol. 24, p. 200.
[2] Ibid., p. 199.
[3] Marx, Engels, *Werke*, Bd. 36, S. 121.
[4] Gleb Uspensky, *Collected Works*, Vol. 9, Moscow, 1957, p. 166 (in Russian).

Marx's above-mentioned reply to Vera Zasulich in early 1881 likewise testifies to his fundamental differences with the Narodniks over the village commune and the ways of Russia's social development.

Vera Zasulich had written to Marx in connection with the polemics over Vorontsov's article in *Otechestvenniye Zapiski*, in which the author argued that there were no suitable conditions for capitalism in Russia. This article was discussed in Geneva by Vera Zasulich, Kravchinsky, Stefanovich, Deutsch and their Polish friends Dyksztajn and Waryński, who were divided on the issue. Deutsch recalled: "We asked Vera to write to Marx for an answer to the question",[1] and this she did on February 16, 1881. In December 1880, Marx was asked by Morozov, on behalf of the Executive Committee of the People's Will, to write about the Russian commune, and in response to requests from his Russian friends he sent Vera Zasulich a letter on March 8, 1881, which she circulated among many friends, including Deutsch, who sent a copy of it to Plekhanov. In this letter, Marx again protested against his theory of the historical inevitability of capitalist development being turned into a universal scheme. As for the Russian commune, Marx wrote that it could become "the fulcrum of social regeneration in Russia, but in order that it may function, as such, it would first be necessary to eliminate the deleterious influences which are assailing it from all sides, and then ensure for it the normal conditions of spontaneous development".[2]

By emphasising the conditions in which the peasant commune could be used for socialist change, Marx took a resolute stand against its idealisation by the Narodniks. It was not the commune that would on its own become the source of Russia's socialist rejuvenation, but the revolution in Russia and its support by the victorious working class in the developed capitalist countries that were to create the possibility for refurbishing this archaic institution and transforming it on the socialist lines. Marx urged a realistic approach to the actual commune, considering the circumstances which tended to transform it into an instrument of fiscal oppression, and the processes which led to its disintegration. In a draft of his reply he said that drained by "fiscal exactions, the commune became an inert thing, easily exploited by trade, landed property and usury. This oppression from without unleashed in the heart of the commune itself the conflict of interests already present, and rapidly developed the seeds of decay."[3]

Marx rejected the view that the existence of the commune in Russia was evidence that the Russian peasantry had a special socialist mission, and took the truly historical approach by regarding the

---

[1] *Emancipation of Labour Group*, Collection No. 1, Moscow [1924], p. 133 (in Russian).
[2] Marx, Engels, *Collected Works*, Vol. 24, p. 371.
[3] Ibid., pp. 354-55.

commune as a social institution which all nations had at a definite stage of their development.

Marx and Engels expressed their idea about the necessary premises for Russia's non-capitalist development with even greater clarity and precision a little later, on January 21, 1882, in a preface to the second Russian edition of the *Manifesto of the Communist Party*, where they formulated what they believed to be the "only possible" answer at that time to the question of whether the village commune could move directly into the higher, communist form. "If the Russian Revolution becomes the signal for a proletarian revolution in the West, so that the two complement each other, the present Russian common ownership of land may serve as the starting-point for a communist development."[1]

His critique of the Narodnik outlook helped the most advanced members of the Russian revolutionary movement to accept scientific communism.

He noted with satisfaction the progress in the ideological development of the Russian revolutionaries, notably their gradual abandonment of anarchist doctrines and political indifference, and the switch by the People's Will to the fight for political liberties. What he believed to be important was that the Narodniks, first within the Land and Freedom and later the People's Will, set up a centralised underground organisation based on conscious and strict discipline.

Marx and Engels saw the establishment of the People's Will as the emergence in Russia of a revolutionary party with "exceptional devotion and vigour",[2] as Engels put it. Marx told the Narodnik Morozov that the Russian revolutionaries' fight against tsarism was "something fabulous".[3] Marx's notes in the margins of the "Programme of Workers, Members of the People's Will Party" (written mainly by Andrei Zhelyabov), which he received at the end of 1880, showed that he did not share the illusions which made the members of the People's Will akin to the other Narodnik trends, but strongly approved of their revolutionary-democratic demands, such as self-determination for the nationalities within the Russian Empire, a democratic revolution and the winning of political and civil liberties. Marx and Engels took a positive view of the appeal with the demand for political change which the People's Will made on the new tsar after March 1, 1881.[4] In a talk with Lopatin in the autumn of 1883, Engels confirmed Marx's approval of this document, particularly its firm but calm and restrained tone.

The members of the People's Will fought autocracy mainly by terroristic methods, which were largely in response to the tsarist authorities' savage reprisals and arbitrary acts against revolutionaries and those who sympathised with them. While taking a negative view in

---

[1] Ibid., p. 426.
[2] Marx, Engels, *Werke*, Bd. 34, S. 449.
[3] *Reminiscences of Marx and Engels*, p. 303.
[4] On March 1, 1881, Tsar Alexander II was assassinated.

principle of individual acts of terrorism as an instrument of political struggle, Marx and Engels believed that they could be used only in exceptional circumstances. They hoped that the Russian revolutionaries' acts of terrorism would generate a powerful outburst of popular discontent against the autocracy. At the same time, Marx was sure that the Russian revolutionaries themselves regarded terrorism as something to which they were forced to resort temporarily. On April 11, 1881, he wrote to Jenny Longuet that the tactics of the Executive Committee of the People's Will were a far cry from "the bungling way in which Most and other puerile ranters advocate tyrannicide as a 'theory' and 'panacea'". The Russian revolutionaries "on the other hand, are at pains to teach Europe that their *modus operandi* is a specifically Russian and historically inevitable mode of action which no more lends itself to moralising — for or against — than does the earthquake in Chios." [1]

The courageous struggle by a small group of members of the People's Will against the powerful tsarist regime evoked "a most sympathetic echo" in Marx and Engels.[2] It was in this period that Marx read Pyotr Alisov's pamphlet *Alexander II the Emancipator* and Mikhail Dragomanov's *Tyrannicide in Russia*, and followed with deep emotion the trial of those who had organised and taken part in the revolutionary act of March 1. He expressed admiration for the behaviour in court of Zhelyabov, Sophia Perovskaya and Kibalchich, whom he regarded as true heroes and revolutionaries. "That are sterling chaps through and through, *sans pose mélodramatique* [without melodramatic posturing], simple, matter-of-fact, heroic." [3]

Marx took a more critical view of the other Narodnik organisation called the General Redistribution, whose ideas and tactics revealed the influence of anarchist theory, the obsolete Bakuninist dogma of abstention from politics. Marx wrote about their "tedious doctrinairism" and believed that their main mistake was rejection of "political-revolutionary action". In contrast to the People's Will, whose members realised the need for a democratic revolution as a stage leading towards socialist change, the members of the General Redistribution believed that "Russia is to leap head-over-heels into the anarchist-communist-atheist millennium".[4]

At the same time, Marx sought to help the Russian revolutionaries overcome their internal disagreements and unite in the struggle against tsarism, their common enemy. That is why, when in 1880 he received an invitation, conveyed by Morozov, to take part in publishing abroad a Russian Socio-Revolutionary Library series, a joint venture by the People's Will and the General Redistribution, he ag-

---

[1] Marx, Engels, *Werke*, Bd. 35, S. 179.
[2] See V. I. Lenin, *Collected Works*, Vol. 2, p. 27.
[3] Marx, Engels, *Werke*, Bd. 35, S. 179.
[4] Ibid., Bd. 34, S. 477.

reed and offered to put his works at the disposal of the publishers, promising to write a special preface to any they decided to publish.

In 1882, a new Russian translation of the *Manifesto of the Communist Party* was published in this series. Through Lavrov, Marx and Engels sent the translator, Georgi Plekhanov, a leader of the General Redistribution, the preface to the Russian edition which they had written in January of that year. In it they reiterated that a Russian revolution was at hand and would be of great historical importance. With the Russian revolutionaries' heroic acts fresh in their minds, they wrote: "Russia forms the vanguard of revolutionary action in Europe." [1]

Another important fact was that under the influence of this and other scientific communist works, Plekhanov, who had suggested a Russian edition of the *Manifesto*, came to realise that Marx's doctrine alone was the lodestar which would help the Russian revolutionary movement as well to find the right path. In 1883, Plekhanov and his followers founded the first Russian Marxist group, known as the Emancipation of Labour, which paved the way for the establishment of the Russian Social-Democratic Party. Concerning this event, which opened up fresh prospects for the emancipation struggle in Russia, Engels wrote to Vera Zasulich: "... I am proud to know that there is a party among the youth of Russia which frankly and without equivocation accepts the great economic and historical theories of Marx, and has definitely broken with all the anarchist and also the few existing Slavophile traditions of its predecessors. And Marx himself would have been equally proud of this had he lived a little longer." [2]

IRREPARABLE LOSSES. FAILING HEALTH

In the summer of 1880, the health of Jenny Marx, who had been suffering from a liver complaint, deteriorated sharply, and in early October came the terrible news that she had cancer of the liver. On June 6, 1881, Marx wrote to his eldest daughter, Jenny: "You are aware that there is no cure of the illness she suffers from, and she gets indeed weaker." [3]

At the end of June 1881, Marx took his wife to Eastbourne on the coast, where they spent a month. Overcoming his grave apprehensions and yielding to Jenny's great desire to see her grandchildren, he set off with her for France, accompanied by Hélène Demuth.

They arrived at Argenteuil near Paris, where the Longuet family lived, on July 26. In mid-August came the news that Eleanor was gravely ill. Marx left his wife in Hélène's care and set out for London, where he found his youngest daughter in a state of deep

---

[1] Marx, Engels, *Collected Works*, Vol. 24, p. 426.
[2] Marx, Engels, *Werke*, Bd. 36, S. 303-04.
[3] Ibid., Bd. 35, S. 194.

nervous and physical exhaustion. The urgent measures he took had their effect and Eleanor soon began to recover. Jenny and Hélène also returned to London shortly.

From the autumn of 1881, Jenny left her bed less and less often until she was completely bedridden. It was then that Marx himself fell gravely ill: in October he went down with the pleurisy, complicated by bronchitis and pneumonia. His condition was so grave that the doctors feared for his life. His physical suffering was made more acute by the awareness that his wife lay dying in the next room. The crisis passed at the end of October and Marx was able to spend some time at Jenny's bedside. Eleanor recalled: "Never shall I forget the morning he felt himself strong enough to go into Mother's room. When they were together they were young again — she a young girl and he a loving youth, both on life's threshold, not an old disease-ridden man and an old dying woman parting from each other for life."[1]

Jenny Marx died on December 2, 1881.

This was a mortal blow for Marx, and on December 5, the day of Jenny's funeral, he was so weak and so distraught at her death that the doctor insisted on his remaining at home. He was sustained by numerous letters from his party friends, acquaintances and relatives. He was deeply moved by the fact that these expressions of condolence were "animated by a spirit of truth and a depth of feeling rarely found in what are as a rule merely conventional tributes." In a letter to one of his daughters he explained it by the fact that everything about their mother had been "natural and genuine, unforced and without affectation".[2]

As usual in moments of trial, Engels was by his side, and not only handled all the arrangements for the funeral but also felt it his duty to describe in the press Jenny's role in the working-class movement. The *Sozialdemokrat* carried an obituary written by him honouring the memory of this representative of the "old guard of proletarian, revolutionary socialism", and the *Egalité* the text of the speech he made at her graveside, in which he said: "But of one thing I am sure ... will the rest of us have occasion enough to miss her bold and wise advise, bold without ostentation, wise without ever compromising her honour to even the smallest degree."[3]

Marx and Eleanor spent the first three weeks of January 1882 at Ventnor on the Isle of Wight, where they had gone in the hope that the sea air would help Marx get rid of his chronic bronchitis and the painful bouts of coughing which aggravated his insomnia. He did, indeed, feel somewhat better, and was eager to get back to work.

He resumed his scientific studies upon his return to London, but his doctors advised him to go south to escape the changeable London spring weather. Their opinion was that he should go to Algeria.

---

[1] *Reminiscences of Marx and Engels*, p. 127.
[2] Marx, Engels, *Werke*, Bd. 35, S. 250.
[3] Marx, Engels, *Collected Works*, Vol. 24, pp. 423-24.

In the first half of February, Marx went to France, where he spent a week with the Longuet family at Argenteuil. After a two-day stay at Marseilles, he sailed for Algeria where he arrived on February 20. On the way he caught a bad cold, and was disappointed to find rain, strong winds and cold weather, instead of the expected warmth and sunshine. He wrote to his eldest daughter: "Since ten years Algiers had not such a failure of the winter season." [1] Naturally this made his bronchitis worse, and on top of everything he again fell ill with pleurisy.

However, neither the state of his health, nor the long stretch of bad weather, with the odd sunny day, prevented Marx from enjoying the beauties of the land which reminded him of the *Thousand and One Nights*. He spent hours at his window in the Hotel Victoria admiring the picturesque view of the bay and the port, the hilly slope running down to the sea, and the villas with their lush greenery. In the distance lay a majestic range of mountains with snow-capped peaks. He wrote to Engels: "There is nothing more magical than this panorama, ... a wonderful *mélange* of Europe and Africa." [2] When he felt strong enough he went for walks, and visited the famous botanical gardens where he admired the "great longitudinal 'allées' of a wonderful beauty", the palm groves, the plane trees and the magnolias.

But Algeria's natural beauty did not obscure for Marx the deep social and national contradictions of life in that French colony. His frank talks with Judge Fermé, an old republican and a former political exile in Algeria, together with his own observations, left him with a clear picture of the lack of rights of the local people, and the oppressive nature of the colonial regime.

By mid-April, he had completely recovered from pleurisy, but the bronchitis still worried him, and he suffered greatly when the south wind blew in from the desert raising clouds of dust. On the advice of his doctors, Marx left Algiers before the hot season and went to the French Riviera. In early May he arrived in Monte Carlo. But there again he was dogged by bad luck: a local doctor whom he consulted diagnosed a fresh bout of pleurisy. For almost a month, Marx was forced to undergo treatment in the puppet principality of Monaco, "this *repaire* [haunt] of aristocratic idlers or adventurers" [3] who flocked to its gambling tables.

On June 3 Marx left Monte Carlo, after a lung specialist had advised him to continue his treatment in a mountain resort. However, he decided to spend some time with Jenny and his grandchildren at Argenteuil. He felt much better in the family circle, and on that occasion stayed there for some time, from June 8 to August 22, taking a course of sulphur baths and inhalations at neighbouring Enghien. Together with Laura, he then went to Vevey, on Lake Geneva in

---

[1] Marx, Engels, *Werke*, Bd. 35, S. 289.
[2] Ibid., S. 45.
[3] Ibid., S. 68.

Switzerland, where he stayed for a month, until September 25. Before leaving Switzerland, he went to Geneva where he met his old friend Becker. The two men were very glad to see each other again.

Marx returned to Argenteuil on September 28, where the doctors expressed their satisfaction with the results of his stay in Switzerland and allowed him to return to England, but insisted that he should not stay in London for more than two or three weeks at a time. Marx spent almost the whole of October at his home in Maitland Park Road, once again immersed in scientific pursuits, studying the history of primitive society, agrarian relations in Russia and other problems. After this he again went to Ventnor on the Isle of Wight, where he continued his scientific work.

In early January 1883, he learned that Jenny, his eldest daughter, was seriously ill. This news brought on a nervous disorder, and his bouts of coughing developed into dangerous spasms. On January 12, Eleanor brought Marx the terrible news that Jenny had died the day before. He was shattered by the loss of his beloved daughter, who had died at the age of 38, a mother of five children. He returned to London stricken with grief and physically debilitated.

MARCH 14, 1883

The ravages of the disease left no doubt about an imminent tragic outcome. Marx's bronchitis took a turn for the worse, and he developed an inflammation of the larynx, so that for a long time he was unable to take any food, except milk. In February, the doctors diagnosed a lung abscess. Marx was visibly wasting away, and Eleanor, Hélène and Engels fought desperately to save his life. Their heroic efforts appeared to have had some effect, and his condition improved slightly in early March. On March 9, Donkin, Marx's doctor and a friend of the family, made the encouraging announcement that if he could be kept going for another two months, there would be a chance of his pulling through.

However, this was not to be. At 2.30 p.m. on March 14, Engels, who came to see his friend every day, found everyone in tears. That morning Marx had had a haemorrhage and was very weak. When Hélène went up to his room, she found him sitting half asleep in the armchair. She at once ran down and asked Engels to go up. The following day, Engels wrote to Sorge: "When we entered the room he was lying there, asleep, but never to wake again. His pulse and breathing had stopped. In those two minutes he had passed away, peacefully and without pain.

"... Medical skill might have been able to assure him a few more years of vegetative existence, the life of a helpless being, dying—to the triumph of the physicians' art—not suddenly, but inch by inch. Our Marx however would never have borne that. To live, with all the unfinished works before him, tantalised by the desire to complete them and unable to do so, would have been a thousand times more bitter to him than the gentle death that overtook him."[1]

News of the death of the great thinker and revolutionary rapidly spread throughout the world and was reported not only by proletarian but also by bourgeois periodicals in many countries of Europe and America. Friends and enemies alike paid tribute to his intellectual powers. The Russian liberal journal *Yuridichesky Vestnik* said that Marx had been an "outstanding personality,... a scientist of rare calibre". The Austrian bourgeois newspaper *Neues Wiener Tagblatt* stressed on March 17 that "Karl Marx must be *ranked among the most important and the most outstanding contemporaries*".

But even with his death, the bourgeois press did not give any objective assessment of his role, and behind a barrage of talk about his high qualities, sought in every way to minimise his influence, to distort his doctrine and activity, and to pervert his life-story shamelessly. The advocates of the capitalist system, who had always hated and persecuted Marx, intensified their slander after his death, and spread it to his followers.

Marx's death evoked a totally different response in the workers' and socialist circles. Letters from working-class leaders and rank-and-file socialists arrived in London from all over the world with expressions of affection for the teacher and leader of the working class and all oppressed people, expressions of profound grief at the great loss toiling mankind had suffered with his death. These emotions abounded in the obituaries of the working-class press of the various countries, and speeches at memorial meetings and rallies. All voiced firm faith in the immortality of Marx's great ideas and the inevitable triumph of the cause to which he had devoted his life.

Among those who sent messages to Engels were veterans of the proletarian struggle: the old Chartist Harney, who was living in America, Becker, Sorge and Lochner. Lessner wrote to Eleanor Marx: "His name and his teaching will live for ever, so long as man exists on earth. Like the sun his genius will irradiate a wonderful light for all the peoples, and nothing on earth can prevent this."[2]

From Germany came telegrams from August and Julie Bebel, the Erfurt Social-Democratic organisation, and the Social-Democrats of Hanover. The party leadership sent Liebknecht to London to attend the funeral. A telegram was received from the Paris Association of the Workers' Party of France, whose Federation of the Centre held a memorial meeting. Others arrived from José Mesa on behalf of the Spanish Socialist Party, from De Paepe on behalf of the Belgian Socialists, and Nieuwenhuis, on behalf of the Dutch Socialists. From Zurich came a resolution passed by a memorial meeting of the members of Slavia, the Socialist Slavonic Alliance, which pro-

---

[1] Marx, Engels, *Werke*, Bd. 35, S. 460.
[2] Central Party Archives of the Institute of Marxism-Leninism.

posed the establishment of a Marx Fund in aid of victims of the liberation struggle.

In London, a meeting was held by the Democratic Federation to honour the memory of the "great thinker and genius, a friend of the workers of all countries".[1] Memorial meetings were held by the Marylebone branch of the Democratic Federation in London, by the Cabinet-Makers' Society and other organisations. On March 19, a memorial meeting was held by the American Socialists in New York. Cuno, a former member of the International and an active participant in the working-class movement in the U.S.A., informed Engels of the obituary he had written.

Numerous expressions of grief and profound respect were received from revolutionaries in Russia. A message from Russian Socialists, written by Lavrov, said: "The death of Karl Marx is mourned by all who have been able to grasp his thought and appreciate his influence upon our time."[2] A telegram from the Society of Russian Emigrant Socialists, signed by Lopatin, Plekhanov and Sophia Bardina, was received by Engels from Geneva. On March 28, 1883, Lopatin wrote to Eleanor that Marx was a man whom he had "loved as a friend, respected as a teacher and revered as a father".[3] Wreath collections were made and the money sent to Engels in various ways by students of the Peter Agricultural Academy in Moscow, the Technological Institute in St. Petersburg, the colleges of Odessa and by students of women's colleges of Russia. Forward-looking Russians arranged for the publication and extensive circulation of Marx's works. In a letter to Eleanor, Danielson expressed his readiness to make available all the material and letters he had for a future publication of Marx's literary legacy. A message of greetings sent by Plekhanov, Axelrod and Vera Zasulich to the German Social-Democratic Congress in Copenhagen held in late March and early April 1883, expressed the wish to set up a special fund for a "*popular edition* of all the works of Marx".[4]

Progressive intellectuals from various countries sent sincere messages of condolence at the death of the great thinker and revolutionary. The bourgeois radical Edward Spencer Beesly wrote to Eleanor Marx: "He was a very remarkable man and although I did not share his views, I appreciated his motives and had a great respect and regard for him."[5] On March 18, 1883, students of the Agricultural Academy in Berlin wrote to Engels to say that Marx's ideas would be enshrined in the ages, and that "the nineteenth century will be named after him".[6]

---

[1] Central Party Archives of the Institute of Marxism-Leninism.
[2] Marx, Engels, *Collected Works*, Vol. 24, p. 469.
[3] *K. Marx and F. Engels and Revolutionary Russia*, p. 485.
[4] *Literary Legacy of G. V. Plekhanov*, Collection VIII, Part I, Moscow, 1940, p. 26 (in Russian).
[5] Central Party Archives of the Institute of Marxism-Leninism.
[6] Ibid.

Working-class leaders voiced recognition of Marx's tremendous achievements in the great cause of transforming socialism into a science, and of his role as leader of the world proletariat. In a letter to Engels, Deville said that Marx was the man who "did the most for the emancipation of the workers, for the emancipation of mankind".[1] In an obituary published in the Dutch socialist journal *Recht voor Allen* on March 24, 1883, Nieuwenhuis wrote: "He was the man who gave socialism its scientific foundation."[2]

The socialist press and the working-class spokesmen emphasised the internationalist character of Marx's doctrine. His death, they said, was an irreparable loss to the working people of the world, for all those who yearned for progress, and for the whole of world science and culture. This idea was best expressed by Engels when he said: "Mankind is poorer for the loss of this intellect — the most important intellect, indeed, which it could boast today."[3]

In those mournful days working-class leaders were sustained by the thought that the cause of Marx would be carried on by his true associate Engels. Marx's friends and disciples knew that scientific communism was the joint creation of these two brilliant thinkers, "who remarkably complemented each other".[4]

During Marx's illness, Engels had gradually taken over the leadership of the working-class movement, and together with Eleanor he became Marx's literary executor, in accordance with his friend's wish which he expressed verbally before his death.

Marx was buried at Highgate Cemetery on March 17, 1883, in a section normally reserved for persons rejected by official society and the church. The ceremony was a modest one, as Marx himself had wished, for he disliked pompous funeral processions. Among those who attended the ceremony were his relatives, Paul and Laura Lafargue, who also represented the Workers' Party of France, Longuet, and the men who had worked with Marx in the Communist League, Liebknecht, who spoke, Lessner and Lochner. Others present were two prominent scientists, Edwin Ray Lankester, the zoologist, and Carl Schorlemmer, the chemist. Wreaths were laid on behalf of the editorial board of the *Sozialdemokrat* and the London German Workers' Educational Society. The messages were read out by Longuet.

By Marx's graveside, where his wife already lay, Engels spoke impressively and with deep emotion about the importance of Marx's brilliant scientific discoveries, and of his stature as scientist and revolutionary fighter. "Governments, both absolutist and republican, deported him from their territories. Bourgeois, whether conservative or ultra-democratic, vied with one another in heaping slanders upon

---

[1] Ibid.
[2] *Beiträge zur Geschichte der deutschen Arbeiterbewegung*, No. 4, 1966, S. 636.
[3] Marx, Engels, *Werke*, Bd. 35, S. 460.
[4] Becker to Engels, March 18, 1883 (Central Party Archives of the Institute of Marxism-Leninism).

him. All this he brushed aside as though it were cobweb, ignoring it, answering only when extreme necessity compelled him. And he died beloved, revered and mourned by millions of revolutionary fellow-workers—from the mines of Siberia to California, in all parts of Europe and America—and I make bold to say that though he may have had many opponents he had hardly one personal enemy.

"His name will endure through the ages, and so also will his work!" [1]

---

[1] Marx, Engels, *Collected Works*, Vol. 24, p. 469.

CONCLUSION

Marxism is not a dogma, but a guide to action. This maxim by Engels has become a watchword for Communists, expressing the creative and profoundly vital essence of Marxist theory. "This classical statement," Lenin wrote, "stresses with remarkable force and expressiveness that aspect of Marxism which is very often lost sight of. And by losing sight of it, we turn Marxism into something one-sided, distorted and lifeless; we deprive it of its life and blood; we undermine its basic theoretical foundations — dialectics, the doctrine of historical development, all-embracing and full of contradictions; we undermine its connection with the definite practical tasks of the epoch, which may change with every new turn of history."[1]

Marx's teaching is distinguished for its outstanding consistency and the integrity of its conclusions, the indissoluble internal unity of its component parts — philosophy, political economy and scientific communism. Without materialist dialectics and the materialist conception of history it was impossible to develop Marxist political economy; without dialectical and historical materialism, without the economic theory of Marxism, it would have been impossible to transform socialism from a utopia into a science.

Marx's death caused enormous grief among millions of his followers. The international working class had been deprived of its teacher. A great thinker had ceased to think. *Capital*, his life's work, remained unfinished. An outstanding role in continuing Marx's cause was played by his intimate friend and associate Frederick Engels. After Marx's death, he becomes an adviser and leader of socialists in all countries, completes Marx's work on *Capital*, tirelessly

---

[1] V. I. Lenin, *Collected Works*, Vol. 17, p. 39.

champions the purity of Marxist theory and writes his own works which enriched and advanced it.

Engels played a conspicuous part in the establishment of the Second International — an international association of proletarian parties (1889). The Second International helped to spread Marxism among large sections of the proletariat and to develop and consolidate mass working-class organisations such as trade unions, co-operative societies, women's and youth organisations, sports associations and others. But the working-class movement did not develop without a fair share of opportunism and reformism in the Social-Democratic parties. Engels waged a resolute struggle against all distortions of revolutionary theory and tactics, mercilessly exposed opportunist views, opposed a revision of the fundamental principles of Marx's doctrine and at the same time warned against thoughtless dogmatism.

An outstanding role and the historical initiative in defending Marxism from both Right and Left revisionist distortions, in further developing it after Marx and Engels, and in applying the ideas of scientific socialism to the revolutionary transformation of society accord to Lenin and the Bolshevik Party which he created. Lenin's Party was set up on the firm basis of Marxist theory, as the legitimate heir to all that was best in the international workers' and Russian revolutionary-democratic movements.

Back in 1899 Lenin wrote in his article "Our Programme": "We do not regard Marx's theory as something completed and inviolable; on the contrary, we are convinced that it has only laid the foundation stone of the science which socialists *must* develop in all directions if they wish to keep pace with life."[1] These inspiring words were reflected in Lenin's revolutionary activity and scientific works. Opposing all doctrinaire views, he demonstrated in practice his commitment to Marxism, and in new historical conditions defended it from revisionist onslaughts, added new and highly important generalisations and propositions, leading the workers' movement to a triumph about which his great teachers could have only dreamed.

Relying on the firm foundation of Marxist political economy, Lenin studied imperialism, which had emerged at the turn of the 20th century, and showed that it was the highest and last stage in the capitalist formation, being typified by the economic and political rule of monopolies. He made an inestimable contribution to the agrarian theory of Marxism. In his works, Lenin gave dialectical and historical materialism a form according with the level of scientific and social development at the time. He takes credit for a truly magnificent contribution to the theory of socialist revolution, the strategy and tactics of proletarian struggle and the elaboration of a scientific conception of socialism.

It was because the fundamental theoretical principles of Marx

---

[1] V. I. Lenin, *Collected Works*, Vol. 4, pp. 211-12.

and Engels were advanced, given greater precision and enriched that they were able to serve as a mighty theoretical weapon in the hands of the revolutionary forces in the new historical epoch.

The Great October Socialist Revolution of 1917 in Russia — the most outstanding event of the 20th century — ushered in a new era in human history. It was in this revolution that the teaching of Marx, Engels and Lenin proved itself in practice. The working class and all the working people of Russia, led by the Bolshevik Party with Lenin at the helm, set about building a new society based on genuine democracy. Power was established in the hands of the workers and peasants. Private capitalist ownership was replaced by common ownership of the major means of production. A special decree was enacted giving the land for use free of charge to those who worked it. The foundations were laid for the material security of all working people, for genuine equality and fraternity among peoples. The first decrees adopted by the Soviet state and the entire activities of the victorious proletariat provided a solid basis for settling the cardinal problem facing mankind — the safeguarding of peace on earth.

Under the influence of the October Revolution Communist Parties were formed in many countries, which soon joined together to form the Third, or Communist, International. This organisation strengthened the traditions of international proletarian solidarity inherited from Marx and Engels, and produced many militant revolutionary fighters.

The socialist system was exposed to a merciless test of its viability by the Great Patriotic War fought by the Soviet people between 1941 and 1945. In this most arduous and vicious of wars in human history, the advantages of the Soviet socialist political system, the invincible unity of Soviet society, the cohesion and patriotism of the Soviet people manifested themselves as never before. The Soviet Union made the decisive contribution to the rout of the shock-force of world imperialist reaction — German fascism and Japanese militarism. This was yet another triumph for the Marxist-Leninist teaching of the Communists, which lay at the basis of the vast organisational work carried out by the Party both at the front and in the rear.

The Soviet victory in the war tremendously enhanced the prestige of socialism in the eyes of working people throughout the world and created extremely favourable conditions for socialist revolutions in a number of European, Asian and Latin American countries, for the development of the national liberation and democratic movements.

The October Socialist Revolution and the subsequent proletarian class struggles, the construction of socialism, its undoubted historic achievements, as well as difficulties and sometimes serious errors and even tragic episodes in the experience of the pioneers of the social renewal of society, confirmed the truth that not the absolutisation of some or other forms of revolutionary struggle and social models, but a dialectical choice based on concrete historical conditions and concentration on those which most closely accord with the given situation represent the indispensable condition for success. By creatively applying Marxist-Leninist methodology and considering both the general laws of the revolutionary process and the peculiarities of their manifestation in each country, communist and workers' parties are making their contribution to the study of the theoretical and practical problems of the world communist movement. The further development of Marxism-Leninism based on an analysis of the general course of historical development and specific situations is the concern of all fraternal Marxist-Leninist parties.

The world does not stand still. Present-day capitalism differs in many ways from that studied by Marx. And it has undergone numerous profound changes even since Lenin's day. However, it remains a system marked by the exploitation of wage-labour, although the mechanism of exploitation is becoming more sophisticated, taking on increasingly devious and concealed forms. It is still characterised by the contradiction revealed by Marx, namely that between the social nature of production and the private form of appropriation. Neither have overproduction crises become a thing of the past, although desperate attempts are being made to avert or alleviate them through state-monopoly regulation of the economy. Purchasing power constantly lags behind supply. Clear evidence of the serious problems faced by the sphere of material production is provided by state budget deficits, enormous domestic and external debts, the chaotic migration of capital. Cyclical crises are compounded by structural and ecological crises, the idiosyncrasies of exchange rates, wild fluctuations on stock exchanges, protectionism and other manifestations of inter-imperialist conflicts. Enormous wealth is found side by side with destitution, chronic unemployment of unprecedented proportions. Moral and cultural values are becoming increasingly debased. The developing countries tied to the world capitalist market are being suffocated by debts resulting first and foremost from the backward economic structure of the former colonies and non-equivalent exchange with the developed states. Their political liberation from the colonialists has been replaced by the no less arduous neocolonialism. At the close of the 20th century, in the age of incredible achievements in science and technology, the age of nuclear energy and space travel, millions are starving to death.

Objective processes and the heated class struggles in the present-day capitalist world are indubitable proof of the historical tendency of capitalism discovered by Marx: a move towards its negation, towards its disappearance, sooner or later, from the scene of history and its replacement by a higher and more just social system.

A challenge was thrown down to world capitalism in October 1917. Nowadays, even the most die-hard conservatives are forced to admit that this was not just an accidental or temporary historical "zigzag", not the result of poor government on the part of the tsarist autocracy, but a predestined break in the weakest link of the imperialist chain. Attempts by the imperialists to strangle the socialist "experiment" in the cradle by means of "crusades", the civil war and an economic blockade ended in failure. Subsequent onslaughts on socialism also brought a crushing defeat for their organisers. Socialism is alive and well. For all that, however, the ruling parties in the socialist countries are aware of problems and shortcomings in their economic and political systems, they are fearlessly developing honest and courageous criticism and self-criticism in all branches of society and at all levels, mobilising working people for the more efficient use of the advantages and potential of socialism, the achievements of the scientific and technological revolution. They are giving every encouragement to self-government and power vested in the people, to creating conditions in which working people have a more direct impact on the adoption of major political and economic decisions.

For all its contradictions, today's troubled world is an inseparable whole. The various states which compose it may and indeed do have their own interests, but they all share one supreme aim — safeguarding the survival of the human race which is threatened by the Damocles sword of weapons of mass destruction, notably nuclear weapons. Our time calls for swords to be turned into ploughshares. This is the central element of what has come to be known as new political thinking with its orientation on common sense and restraint, with a patient search for exclusively peaceful means of settling existing confrontations and conflicts and any new ones which may emerge. Secure peace on earth is the most important condition for the fulfilment of Marx's dream about human happiness, about the all-round development and liberty of working people.

INDEXES

NAME INDEX

A

Aberdeen, George Hamilton Gordon (1784-1860) — 284
Adam — 231
Aeschylus (525-456 B. C.) — 261
Alembert, Jean Le Rond d' (1717-1783) — 555
Alexander II (1818-1881) — 346, 590, 597, 604
Alexeyev, Pyotr Alexeyevich (1849-1891) — 599
Alisov, Pyotr Fyodorovich (b. 1840) — 604
Allen, Grant — 554
Anneke, Friedrich (1818-1872) — 178, 181, 206
Annenkov, Pavel Vasilyevich (1812-1887) — 104, 109, 111, 117
Aretino, Pietro (1492-1556) — 268
Ariosto, Lodovico (1474-1533) — 268
Auer, Ignaz (1846-1907) — 541
Auerbach, Berthold (1812-1882) — 26
Auerswald, Rudolf von (1795-1866) — 179, 184
Aveling, Edward (1851-1898) — 529
Avenel, Georges (1828-1876) — 560
Axelrod, Pavel Borisovich (1850-1928) — 566, 610
Azeglio, Massimo d' (1798-1866) — 268

B

Babeuf, Gracchus (1760-1797) — 75, 80, 85, 89
Bachofen, Johann Jakob (1815-1887) — 559
Bacon, Francis (1561-1626) — 71
Bakh, Alexei Nikolayevich (1857-1946) — 599
Bakunin, Mikhail Alexandrovich (1814-1876) — 49, 58, 59, 67, 77, 182, 197, 210, 299, 424, 450, 455-64, 466, 467, 498, 502, 512, 516, 593, 599
Balzac, Honoré de (1799-1850) — 261, 315, 335
Bangya, Janos (1817-1868) — 247

Banner, Robert — 583
Bardina, Sophia Illarionovna (1853-1883) — 610
Barry, Maltman (1842-1909) — 509
Bartenev, Victor Ivanovich (pseudonym Netov) (b. 1838) — 466
Bastiat, Frédéric (1801-1850) — 374
Baudelaire, Charles (1821-1867) — 527
Bauer, Bruno (1809-1882) — 25, 26, 32, 33, 49, 69-71, 93-96
Bauer, Edgar (1820-1886) — 25, 33, 39, 54, 70, 71
Bauer, Heinrich — 33, 89, 109, 124, 142, 158, 204, 220, 229, 231, 237
Bax, Ernest Belfort (1854-1926) — 585
Bebel, August (1840-1913) — 436, 452-55, 474, 476, 500, 509, 533, 538-41, 548, 570-74, 609
Bebel, Julie (1843-1910) — 609
Becker, Hermann Heinrich (1820-1885) — 185, 208, 213, 248, 294
Becker, Johann Philipp (1809-1886) — 327, 434, 439, 446, 456, 463, 465, 498, 500, 509, 518, 533, 566, 570, 608, 609
Beckmann, Johann (1739-1811) — 264
Beesly, Edward Spencer (1831-1915) — 479, 610
Belinsky, Vissarion Grigoryevich (1811-1848) — 54, 108
Belyaev, Ivan Dmitriyevich (1810-1873) — 557
Béranger, Pierre Jean (1780-1857) — 527
Bermbach, Adolph (1822-1875) — 250
Bernadotte, Jean Baptiste Jules (1763-1844) — 280
Bernard, Simon François (1817-1862) — 344
Bernays, Karl Ludwig (1815-1879) — 49, 53, 54, 67, 77
Bernier, Francois (1620-1688) — 270
Bernstein, Eduard (1850-1932) — 540
Berthier, Louis Alexandre (1753-1815) — 280
Bessières, Jean Baptiste (1768-1813) — 280

Beust, Friedrich (1817-1899)—188
Bignami, Enrico (1846-1921)—501, 533
Biscamp, Elard—327, 328
Bismarck, Otto von (1815-1898)—333, 338, 364, 429-32, 436, 437, 452, 472-73, 475, 477, 482-84, 537, 538, 566-70, 572, 574, 577
Blagoev, Dimitr (1856-1924)—148
Blanc, Louis (1811-1882)—48, 56, 58, 141, 164, 165, 225, 247, 362
Blanqui, Louis Auguste (1805-1881)—57, 229, 231, 247, 287, 344, 366
Blos, Wilhelm (1849-1927)—524, 533, 548, 549
Blum, Robert (1807-1848)—188, 280
Bobczyński, Konstantin (b. 1817)—439
Bogišić, Valtasar (1834-1908)—557
Boisguillebert, Pierre (1646-1714)—61, 549
Bojardo, Matteo Maria (1441-1494)—268
Bolivar y Ponte, Simon (1783-1830)—280
Bolte, Friedrich—505, 516, 533
Bonald, Louis Gabriel Ambroise (1754-1840)—35
Bonaparte, Louis—see Napoleon III
Bonhorst, Leonhard von (b. 1840)—453
Boon, Martin James—504
Borchardt, Friedrich—187
Borkheim, Sigismund Ludwig (1825-1885)—465
Born, Stephan (Buttermilch, Simon) (1824-1898)—87, 163-66, 204-06, 210,
Börne, Ludwig (1786-1837)—52
Bornstedt, Adalbert von (1808-1851)—67, 132, 159, 356
Börnstein, Heinrich (1805-1892)—67
Borrosch, Alois (1797-1869)—183
Botkin, Vasily Petrovich (1811-1869)—59
Botta, Carlo (1766-1837)—562
Bourbons—108, 331-32
Bourrienne, Louis Antoine Fauvelet de (1769-1834)—280
Bracke, Wilhelm (1842-1880)—453, 454, 475, 533, 540, 541, 548, 568, 570, 572
Brandenburg, Friedrich Wilhelm (1792-1850)—190, 358
Bray, John Francis (1809-1897)—91, 119
Bright, John (1811-1889)—284
Brissot, Jacques Pierre (1754-1793)—115
Brontë, Charlotte (1816-1855)—335, 526
Brontë, Emilie (1818-1848)—526
Brune, Guillaume (1763-1815)—280

Bruno, Giordano (1548-1600)—268
Brunswick, Karl Wilhelm Ferdinand, Duke of (1735-1806)—21
Bücher, Karl (1847-1930)—560
Buchez, Philippe Joseph Benjamin (1796-1865)—56, 362
Büchner, Ludwig (1824-1899)—339, 377
Bulwer-Lytton, Edward George (1803-1873)—526
Buonarroti, Filippo (Philippe) Michele (1761-1837)—80, 85
Bürgers, Heinrich (1820-1878)—58, 67, 77, 85, 127, 132, 136, 167, 169, 185, 248, 252, 273
Burghard, J. E.—148
Burns, Robert (1759-1796)—261
Butashevich-Petrashevsky, Mikhail Vasilyevich (1821-1866)—107

C

Cabet, Etienne (1788-1856)—48, 57, 58, 85
Cade, Jack (d. 1450)—563
Calderón de la Barca, Pedro (1600-1681)—268, 496
Camélinat, Zéphirin (1840-1932)—428
Camphausen, Ludolf (1803-1890)—33, 179
Capponi, Gino (1792-1876)—560
Càrdenas, Francisco (1816-1898)—557
Carey, Henry Charles (1793-1879)—277, 379, 549
Carleton, William (1794-1869)—561
Carlyle, Thomas (1795-1881)—49, 53, 92, 233
Casse, Germain—468
Cavour, Camillo Benso (1810-1861)—329, 331
Cervantes Saavedra, Miguel de (1547-1616)—137, 261, 268, 335
Chabry, Jules (1846-1893)—575
Chamisso, Adelbert von (1781-1838)—261, 527
Charlemagne (Charles the Great) (c. 742-814)—303
Chateaubriand, François René (1768-1848)—46
Chenu, Adolphe (born c. 1817)—234
Chernyshevsky, Nikolai Gavrilovich (1828-1889)—375, 381, 465-66, 516, 552, 575, 593, 595, 597, 599
Chetham, Humphrey—89
Chicherin, Boris Nikolayevich (1828-1904)—557
Clarendon, George William Frederick (1800-1870)—284
Clouth, Wilhelm—180
Cluss, Adolf (c. 1820-d. after

1889) — 162, 251, 252, 274, 276, 322
Cobbett, William (1762-1835) — 562
Cobden, Richard (1804-1865) — 284
Coblenz, Peter Joseph (1808-1854) — 38
Colins, Jean Guillaume (1783-1859) — 589
Collet, Charles Dobson — 300
Combault, Amédée Benjamin (born c. 1838) — 468
Comte, Auguste (1798-1857) — 479
Comyn, Marian — 526
Considérant, Victor (1808-1893) — 39, 85
Cooper, Thomas (1805-1892) — 109
Cornu, Auguste — 12
Cremer, William Randall (1838-1908) — 180, 419, 426
Cuno, Theodor Friedrich (1847-1934) — 501, 509, 514, 533, 610
Czartoryski, Wladyslaw (1828-1894) — 355

D

Dana, Charles Anderson (1819-1897) — 278-80
Daniels, Roland (1819-1855) — 58, 86, 92, 125, 248, 252, 272
Danielson, Nikolai Frantsevich (1844-1918) — 375, 376, 378, 379, 381, 382, 516, 533, 561, 566, 593, 594, 598, 610
Dante, Alighieri (1265-1321) — 242, 261, 268, 321
Darwin, Charles Robert (1809-1882) — 323-25, 527, 558
Daumer, Georg Friedrich (1800-1875) — 234
Delahaye, Pierre Louis (born c. 1820) — 497
Dell, William — 431
Democritus (c. 460-c. 370 B. C.) — 28
Demuth, Hélène (Lenchen) (1820-1890) — 81, 94, 261, 340, 399, 605-06, 608
De Paepe, César (1842-1890) — 380, 382, 428, 434, 446-48, 462, 464, 477, 610
Deprez, Marcel (1843-1918) — 554
Derby, Edward (1799-1869) — 319
Descartes, René (1596-1650) — 555
Desmoulins, Lucie Simplice Camille Benoît (1760-1794) — 60
Destutt de Tracy, Antoine Louis Claude (1754-1836) — 61
Deutsch, Lev Grigoryevich (1855-1941) — 602
Deville, Gabriel (1854-1940) — 533, 575, 581, 611
Dézamy, Théodore (1803-1850) — 57, 85
Dickens, Charles (1812-1870) — 335, 526
Dietzgen, Joseph (1828-1888) — 406, 446, 447, 509, 533, 548

Diksztain, Szymon (1859-1884) — 602
Disraeli, Benjamin (1804-1881) — 284
Dmitriyeva-Tomanovskaya, Yelizaveta Lukinichna (1851-after 1909) — 466, 467, 479, 527
Dmitry Donskoi (1350-1389) — 563
Dobrolyubov, Nikolai Alexandrovich (1836-1861) — 465, 593, 594, 595, 597
Dolcino (d. 1307) — 563
Donkin — 608
Dragomanov, Mikhail Petrovich (1841-1895) — 593, 604
Dronke, Ernst (1822-1891) — 163, 167-69, 180, 185, 187, 203, 211, 214, 229, 273
Du Cange, Charles du Fresne (1610-1688) — 268
Dühring, Eugen (1833-1921) — 374, 547-49, 570, 571, 599
Dumas, Alexandre (1802-1870) — 261
Duncker, Franz (1822-1888) — 319, 320
Dupont, Eugène (c. 1831-1881) — 422, 428, 434, 439, 443, 445, 446, 447, 462, 468, 500, 504, 512, 533

E

Eccarius, Johann Georg (1818-1889) — 204, 220, 222, 237, 239, 272-74, 277, 360, 417, 419, 432, 434, 445-47, 450, 460, 506
Edmonds, Thomas Rowe (1803-1889) — 91
Eichhoff, Frédéric Gustave (1799-1875) — 270
Eichhoff, Wilhelm Karl (1833-1895) — 454, 533
Elsner, Karl Friedrich Moritz (1809-1894) — 281
Engelhardt, Alexander Nikolayevich (1832-1893) — 552, 554
Engels, Frederick (1820-1895) — 19, 25, 33, 41, 47, 49, 51-54, 55, 60, 61, 67, 69-72, 73-77, 79, 81-92, 94-104, 107-09, 111, 116-17, 130-34, 139-43, 149-54, 158-65, 167-70, 172, 175, 177, 180, 181, 185-87, 197-210, 212-14, 219-22, 226-43, 245, 248-51, 253-55, 257, 258, 261-74, 276-82, 285, 289, 293, 295-99, 301, 303, 307, 310, 311, 320, 323-25, 327-29, 333-35, 347-49, 353-56, 359-62, 365, 366, 367, 368, 370-75, 377, 378, 380-85, 399, 402, 406, 417-21, 426, 429-32, 433, 436-38, 436, 446, 449, 452, 454-58, 460, 468-70, 472, 474-76, 478-81, 486, 488, 492, 493, 495-505, 511-19, 522-23, 525, 529, 532-35, 548-51, 554, 555, 558, 559, 562, 563, 565, 566, 570-83,

620

586, 587, 588, 594, 597-99, 601, 603-12
Engels, Friedrich (Senior) (1796-1860) — 51-52
Epicurus (c. 341-c. 270 B.C.) — 27, 28
Erhardt, Johann Ludwig Albert (born c. 1820) — 252
Esser — 48
Esser, Christian Joseph (b. 1809) — 204
D'Ester, Karl Ludwig Johann (1811-1859) — 145, 182, 187-89, 213
Eudes, Émile Desirée François (1843-1888) — 468
Euler, Leonhard (1707-1783) — 555
Ewerbeck, August Hermann (1816-1860) — 58, 67, 109, 112, 205

F

Favre, Jules (1809-1880) — 479, 483, 486, 487, 492
Fermé — 607
Ferré, Théophile Charles (1845-1871) — 468
Feuerbach, Ludwig Andreas (1804-1872) — 25, 30, 31, 45-50, 52, 58, 63, 64, 66, 70, 75, 83, 84, 93, 95, 101, 104, 115, 374, 378
Fichte, Johann Gottlieb (1762-1814) — 23
Fielding, Henry (1707-1754) — 261
Fischer, Friedrich Theodor (1807-1887) — 268
Flerovsky, N. (Bervi, Vasily Vasilyevich) (1829-1918) — 414-15, 465, 466
Fleury, Charles (Krause, Carl Friedrich August) (b. 1824) — 249
Flocon, Ferdinand (1800-1866) — 157
Fontaine, Léon — 428
Fontana, Giuseppe — 419
Fourier, Charles (1772-1837) — 17, 56, 79, 80, 85, 112, 154, 278
Fox, Peter (Peter Fox Andrée) (d. 1869) — 431, 444
Frank, A. — 118
Fränkel — 237
Frankel, Leo (1844-1896) — 148, 468, 483, 484, 507, 509, 533, 535
Frederick William III (1770-1840) — 19
Frederick William IV (1795-1861) — 31, 77, 106, 190, 209
Freiligrath, Ferdinand (1810-1876) — 87, 136, 169, 203, 212, 220, 261, 328, 336, 339
Freytag, Gustav (1816-1895) — 342
Fribourg, Ernest Edouard — 427, 432, 434, 534
Friedländer, Max (1829-1872) — 347, 349

Fritzsche, Friedrich Wilhelm (1825-1905) — 573
Fröbel, Julius (1805-1893) — 48, 71, 136, 182

G

Gabler, Georg Andreas (1786-1853) — 25
Gall, Ludwig (1794-1863) — 18
Ganilh, Charles (1758-1836) — 91
Gans, Eduard (c. 1798-1839) — 22
Garibaldi, Giuseppe (1807-1882) — 331, 332, 356, 449, 527
Gaskell, Elizabeth (1810-1865) — 335
Geib, August (1842-1879) — 523, 533, 541
Genghis Khan (c. 1155-1227) — 303
George, Henry (1839-1897) — 588-89
Gerye, Vladimir Ivanovich (1837-1919) — 557
Gierke, Julius (d. 1855) — 173
Gigot, Philippe Charles (1819-1860) — 88, 108, 127, 158
Gladstone, William Ewart (1809-1898) — 284, 461, 478, 486
Glaser de Willebrord, E. — 533
Glinka, Mikhail Ivanovich (1804-1857) — 594
Gnocchi-Viani, Osvaldo (1837-1917) — 533
Godwin, William (1756-1836) — 85
Goethe, Johann Wolfgang von (1749-1832) — 137, 261, 335, 526
Gogol, Nikolai Vasilyevich (1809-1852) — 594
Golovin, Ivan Gavrilovich (1816-1886) — 299
Gorbunova-Kablukova, Minna Karlovna (1840-1931) — 552
Görtrek, Per (1798-1876) — 148
Göschel, Karl Friedrich (1784-1862) — 25
Gottschalk, Andreas (1815-1849) — 163-65, 179, 181, 188, 198, 205
Gould, Jay (1836-1892) — 552
Gracchus, Tiberius and Gaius (2nd cent. B.C.) — 527
Greeley, Horace (1811-1872) — 278
Green, John Richard (1837-1883) — 557, 562
Greiff — 249
Grimm, Jacob (1785-1863) — 261
Grimm, Wilhelm (1786-1859) — 261
Grote, George (1794-1871) — 559
Grün, Karl (1817-1887) — 96, 104, 112, 116, 114, 579
Guerrazzi, Francesco Domenico (1804-1873) — 268
Guesde, Jules (1845-1922) — 575-78

Guillaume, James (1844-1916) — 580-81
Guizot, François Pierre Guillaume (1787-1874) — 512, 536

H

Hales, John (b. 1839) — 504-07
Haller, Carl Ludwig von (1768-1854) — 35
Hannsen, Georg (1809-1894) — 557
Hansemann, David Justus (1790-1864) — 33, 179, 184
Hapsburgs — 173, 176, 188, 288, 298, 525, 537
Harney, George Julian (1817-1897) — 89, 94, 143, 146, 157, 178, 230, 552, 609
Harney, Mary (d. 1853) — 94
Hartmann, Lev Nikolayevich (1850-1908) — 527, 594
Hartwell, Robert (born c. 1812) — 431
Hasselmann, Wilhelm (b. 1844) — 570, 573
Hatzfeldt, Sophie (1805-1881) — 342-45
Haude — 204
Haxthausen, August von (1792-1866) — 557
Hébert, Jacques René (1757-1794) — 85
Hecker, C. K. — 180
Hegel, Georg Wilhelm Friedrich (1770-1831) — 22-31, 42-47, 48-52, 61, 63, 66, 68, 69, 76, 95, 97, 103, 119, 120, 334, 398, 406, 408-11
Heilberg, Louis (1818-1852) — 109
Heine, Heinrich (1797-1856) — 27, 48, 49, 54, 58, 59, 67, 77, 95, 242, 261
Heinrich der Löwe (1129-1195) — 563
Heinzen, Karl (1809-1880) — 136-38, 249
Helvétius, Claude Adrien (1715-1771) — 71
Hepner, Adolf (1846-1923) — 509, 511, 533-34, 538, 587
Heraclitus of Ephesus (c. 540-c.-480 B.C.) — 334
Herwegh, Georg Friedrich (1817-1875) — 48, 49, 66, 67, 132, 159, 356
Herzen, Alexander Ivanovich (1812-1870) — 54, 59, 107, 299, 380, 462, 464, 604
Hess, Moses (1812-1875) — 27, 33, 49, 85, 94, 143, 205
Hinckeldey, Karl Ludwig Friedrich (1805-1856) — 249
Hinrichs, Hermann Friedrich Wilhelm (1794-1861) — 25
Hins, Eugen (1839-1923) — 459
Hirsch, Karl (1841-1900) — 453, 533, 571, 575, 576, 583
Hirsch, Wilhelm — 249, 251

Hobbes, Thomas (1588-1679) — 71
Höchberg, Karl (1853-1885) — 571-73
Hodde, Lucien de la (1808-1865) — 234
Hödel, Max (1857-1878) — 567, 570
Hoffmann, Ernst Theodor Amadeus (1776-1822) — 261
Hohenzollerns — 173, 176, 287, 358, 359, 472
Holbach, Paul Henri (1723-1789) — 27
Homer — 21, 261, 316, 559
Hospitalier, Edouard — 554
Howell, George (1833-1910) — 534
Hugo, Gustav (1764-1844) — 36
Hugo, Victor (1802-1885) — 242, 449
Hume, David (1711-1776) — 562
Hyndman, Henry Mayers (1842-1921) — 583-85

I

Iglesias, Pablo (1850-1925) — 501, 564
Imandt, Peter (1823-1897) — 272, 327
Imbert, Jacques (1793-1851) — 140
Irving, Henry (1838-1905) — 526
Ivan III (1440-1505) — 303, 563

J

Jacini, Stefano (1827-1891) — 557
Jacobi, Abraham (1830-1919) — 189, 252, 272, 276
Jacoby, Johann (1805-1877) — 31
Jean Paul (Richter, Johann Paul Friedrich) (1763-1825) — 137
Jeanne d'Arc (1412-1431) — 563
Jelačič (Jellachich), Josip Count von Bužim (1801-1859) — 188
Johannard, Jules (1843-1888) — 563
Johnston, James Finlay Weir (1796-1855) — 554
Jones — 90
Jones, Ernest Charles (1819-1869) — 90, 143, 145, 178, 230, 232, 274-76, 293, 344
Jottrand, Lucien Léopold (1804-1877) — 140, 142
Joy, James (1853-1893) — 552
Juárez, Benito Pablo (1806-1872) — 348
Jukes, Joseph Beete (1811-1869) — 554
Jung, Georg (1814-1886) — 81, 434
Jung, Hermann (1830-1901) — 421, 434, 438, 439, 445, 482
Junge, Adolph Friedrich — 88, 127
Juvenal, Decimus Junius Juvenalis (b. in the 60s-d. after 127) — 242

K

Kablukov, Nikolai Alexeyevich (1849-1919) — 552

Kamm, Friedrich (d. 1867)—277, 278
Kant, Immanuel (1724-1804)—23
Karamzin, Nikolai Mikhailovich (1766-1826)—562
Kareyev, Nikolai Ivanovich (1850-1931)—501
Karpenko, Andrei—599
Kaub, Karl—421
Kaufmann, Illarion Ignatyevich (1848-1916)—552
Kautsky, Karl (1854-1938)—574
Kautsky, Minna (1837-1912)—574
Kayser, Max (1853-1888)—570, 573
Kepler, Johannes (1571-1630)—432
Kératry, Emile de (1832-1905)—528
Khalturin, Stepan Nikolayevich (1856-1882)—564-65, 599
Kibalchich, Nikolai Ivanovich (1853-1881)—599, 604
Kinkel, Gottfried (1815-1882)—248
Klein, Johann Jacob (born c. 1818)—252, 342
Klein, Karl Wilhelm—230
Klings, Karl—533
Knille, Otto (1832-1898)—526
Köhler, J. E. M.—221
Komp, Albrecht—277
Köppen, Karl Friedrich (1808-1863)—26, 33, 343
Korff, Hermann—180, 199
Korvin-Krukovskaya (Jaclard), Anna Vasilyevna (1843-1887)—466
Kościelski, Wladislaw (1818-1895)—184
Kościuzko, Tadeusz Andrzej (1746-1817)—360
Koshelev, Alexander Ivanovich (1806-1883)—557
Kossuth, Lajos (Ludwig) (1802-1894)—107, 221
Kostomarov, Nikolai Ivanovich (1817-885)—561
Kovalevsky, Maxim Maximovich (1851-1916)—524, 557, 561
Kravchinsky, Sergei Mikhailovich (Stepnyak) (1851-1895)—527, 599, 602
Kriege, Hermann (1820-1850)—113-14
Kropotkin, Pyotr Alexeyevich (1842-1921)—535
Kugelmann, Franziska (1858- c. 1930)—524, 594
Kugelmann, Gertrud (born c. 1839)—372, 524
Kugelmann, Ludwig (1828-1902)—327, 363, 369, 371, 377, 439, 442, 446, 454, 462, 482, 488, 490, 509, 523, 524, 528
Kuhlmann, Georg (b. 1812)—94, 96
Kühlwetter, Friedrich Christian Hubert von (1809-1882)—180
Kun, Bela (1886-1939)—148

Kyll, Ulrich Franz—187, 199, 202

L

La Châtre, Maurice (1814-1900)—377, 378
Ladendorf, August—446
Lafargue, Paul (1842-1911)—258, 324, 381, 438, 446, 449, 459, 462, 467, 468, 469, 499-504, 509, 511, 517, 527, 553, 556, 565, 575-77, 580, 594, 611
Lagrange, Joseph Louis (1736-1813)—555
Lamennais (La Mennais), Felicité Robert de (1782-1854)—48
Lange, Friedrich Albert (1828-1875)—579
Lankester, Edwin Ray (1847-1929)—611
Lapiński, Teofil (1826-1886)—356
Lassalle, Ferdinand (1825-1864)—192, 215, 232, 281, 319, 331, 324-38, 340, 342, 343, 362-65, 419, 424, 428-32, 436, 437, 539, 565, 579, 584, 599
Lavrov, Pyotr Lavrovich (1823-1900)—482, 527, 533, 535, 552, 598-99, 604, 610
Leclerc, Théophile (b. 1771)—85
Ledru-Rollin, Alexandre Auguste (1807-1874)—141, 214, 247
Lehmann, Albert—237, 238
Leibniz, Gottfried Wilhelm (1646-1716)—18, 21, 555
Lelewel, Joachim (1786-1861)—88, 140, 147, 271
Le Lubez, Victor P. (born c. 1834)—418, 419, 432
Lenin, Vladimir Ilyich (1870-1924)—11, 12, 13, 49, 54, 69, 74, 75, 81, 103, 114, 119, 146, 148, 149, 173, 175, 197, 208, 221, 225, 235, 237, 240, 246, 256, 293, 296, 302, 311, 325, 338, 347, 383, 393, 406, 407, 417, 441, 464, 465, 479, 481, 488, 510, 522, 530, 538, 541, 544, 545, 549, 565, 587, 594
Leo XIII (1810-1903)—568
Leo, Heinrich (1799-1878)—35
Lermontov, Mikhail Yuryevich (1814-1841)—594
Leroux, Pierre (1797-1871)—38, 56
Leroy-Beaulieu, Anatole (1842-1912)—557
Leske, Karl Friedrich Julius (1821-1886)—93
Lessing Gotthold Ephraim (1729-1781)—18, 26
Lessner, Friedrich (1825-1910)—143, 148, 189, 199, 248, 252, 327, 360, 372, 376, 421, 434, 445, 446, 452-54, 456, 500, 504, 609, 611

Levasseur, René (1747-1834) — 60
Levy, Gustav — 273
Liebig, Justus von (1803-1873) — 264, 370
Liebknecht, Ernestine (d. 1867) — 260, 340, 371
Liebknecht, Wilhelm (1826-1900) — 242, 251, 272, 340, 365, 371, 429, 430, 434, 435, 436, 438, 452-55, 460, 474-76, 533, 537-41, 548, 549, 570-73, 596, 609, 611
Limousin, Charles M. — 427, 434
Lincoln, Abraham (1809-1865) — 349, 350-52, 426, 478
Lissagaray, Prosper Olivier (1838-1901) — 534
List, Friedrich (1789-1846) — 82, 549
Lloyd (Overstone, Samuel Jones Lloyd) (1796-1883) — 265
Lochner, Georg (born c. 1824) — 271, 327, 421, 500, 609, 611
Locke, John (1632-1704) — 18, 71
Loers, Vitus (d. 1862) — 20
Longuet, Charles (1839-1903) — 438, 449, 471, 507, 509, 514, 528, 576, 580, 606, 611
Longuet, Edgar (1879-1950) — 529
Longuet, Henri (1878-1883) — 529
Longuet, Jean (1876-1938) — 529
Longuet, Jenny (1882-1952) — 529
Longuet, Marcel (1881-1949) — 529
Lopatin, Hermann Alexandrovich (1845-1918) — 375, 376, 477, 498, 527, 533, 594, 603, 610
Lope de Vega, Felix (1562-1635) — 496
Lorenzo, Anselmo (1841-1914) — 496, 497
Louis XI (1423-1483) — 563
Louis XV (1710-1774) — 432
Louis Philippe (1773-1850) — 156
Lubbock, John (1834-1913) — 559, 590
Lucraft, Benjamin (1809-1897) — 444, 492
Lucretius (Titus Lucretius Carus) (c. 99-55 B.C.) — 28
Lüning, Otto (1818-1868) — 112
Lyubavin, Nikolai Nikolayevich (1845-1918) — 375

M

Mably, Gabriel (1709-1785) — 85
McCulloch, John Ramsay (1798-1864) — 61, 91
MacDonnel, Joseph Patrick (1845-1906) — 533, 586
Macfarlane, Helen — 148
Machiavelli, Niccolò (1469-1527) — 46, 268, 303, 562, 563
Maclaren, James — 320, 555

Maclaurin, Colin (1698-1746) — 555
Maine, Henry James Summer (1822-1888) — 559, 560
Maistre, Joseph de (1753-1821) — 35
Malon, Benoît (1841-1893) — 579, 580
Malthus, Thomas Robert (1766-1834) — 387, 543
Manteuffel, Otto Theodor (1805-1882) — 194, 202, 211, 342
Markheim, Bertha — 369
Markovic, Švetozar (1846-1875) — 466
Marryat, Frederick (1792-1848) — 261
Marx, Edgar (Musch) (1847-1855) — 82, 260, 261
Marx, Eleanor (Aveling) (1855-1898) — 19, 59, 94, 260, 261, 302, 383, 500, 524, 525, 526, 527, 528, 533-34, 561, 606, 607-09, 611
Marx, Emilie (Conrady) (1822-1888) — 19
Marx, Francis Joseph Peter (1816-1876) — 300
Marx, Franziska (1851-1852) — 258
Marx, Heinrich (1782-1838) — 18-22, 49, 187
Marx, Heinrich Guido (1849-1850) — 258
Marx, Henriette (née Pressburg) (1787-1863) — 19, 344
Marx, Jenny (Longuet) (1844-1883) — 53, 261, 376, 434, 461, 500, 526-29, 574, 604-08
Marx, Jenny (née von Westphalen) (1814-1881) — 21-22, 42-43, 49-58, 78, 80, 81, 159, 215-16, 216, 249, 260, 261, 262, 279, 340, 341, 361, 362, 369, 371, 373, 383, 509, 524, 525, 526, 527-28, 593, 605-08
Marx, Laura (Lafargue) (1845-1911) — 84, 94, 261, 324, 380, 435, 468, 469, 501, 509, 526, 527, 528, 607, 608, 611
Marx, Luise (Juta) (1821-1893) — 19
Marx, Sophie (Schmalhausen) (1816-1883) — 22
Massard, Emile — 575
Matthäi, Rudolph — 96
Mäurer, German (1813-c. 1882) — 58
Maurer, Georg Ludwig (1790-1872) — 556
Mayakovsky, Vladimir Vladimirovich (1893-1930) — 11
Mazzini, Giuseppe (1805-1872) — 271, 286, 329, 418, 419, 423, 438, 456
Mehring, Franz (1846-1919) — 13, 258
Meissner, Otto Karl (1819-1902) — 370, 371, 411, 513
Mellinet, François (1768-1852) — 140
Memminger, Anton (1846-c. 1924) — 83
Mesa y Leompart, José (1840-1904) — 148, 501, 533, 564, 581, 609

Metternich, Clemens Wenzel Lothar (1773-1859) — 107, 149, 156
Meyen, Eduard (1812-1870) — 39
Meyer, Julius (1817-1863) — 104
Meyer, Julius Lothar (1830-1895) — 554
Meyer, Rudolph Hermann (1839-1889) — 553
Meyer, Sigfrid (c. 1840-1872) — 379, 380, 463
Mieroslawski, Ludwig (Louis) (1814-1878) — 271
Mignet, François Auguste Marie (1796-1884) — 60
Mikhailovsky, Nikolai Konstantinovich (1842-1904) — 600-01
Mill, James (1773-1836) — 61, 91, 401, 450
Mill, John Stuart (1806-1873) — 91, 381, 446, 450
Milner, George — 504
Miquel, Johannes (1828-1901) — 273
Moleschott, Jakob (1822-1893) — 339
Molière (Poquelin, Jean Baptiste) (1622-1673) — 526
Moll, Joseph (1812-1849) — 89, 109, 124-26, 142, 159, 181, 182, 185-88, 204, 219
Mommsen, Theodor (1817-1903) — 559
Montesquieu, Charles (1689-1755) — 46
Mora, Francisco (1842-1924) — 501
Morelly (18th cent.) — 85
Morgan, Lewis Henry (1818-1881) — 558, 559
Morozov, Nikolai Alexandrovich (1854-1946) — 594, 602, 603, 604
Morris, William (1834-1896) — 585
Möser, Justus (1720-1794) — 46
Most, Johann (1846-1906) — 533, 570, 573, 604
Mülberger, Arthur (1847-1907) — 538
Mulhall, Michael George — 561
Müller, Jacob (b. 1825) — 204
Müller, Eduard (1804-1875) — 268
Murray, Charles — 504

N

Napoleon I Bonaparte (1769-1821) — 15, 16, 197, 244-45
Napoleon III (Louis Napoleon Bonaparte) (1808-1873) — 214, 242-45, 249, 285, 286, 294, 305, 329-33, 337-40, 349, 355, 431, 435, 472, 473, 476, 488, 502, 568
Nechayev, Sergei Gennadyevich (1847-1882) — 498, 599
Nekrasov, Nikolai Alexeyevich (1821-1878) — 593
Newton, Isaac (1642-1727) — 21, 555

Nieuwenhuis, Ferdinand Domela (1846-1919) — 564, 566, 610
Nobiling, Karl Eduard (1848-1878) — 567, 570
Nobre-França, José — 501
Nothjung, Peter (1821-1866) — 204, 248, 252
Nothomb, Jean Baptiste (1805-1881) — 80

O

Obnorsky, Victor Pavlovich (1852-1919) — 564
O'Connor, Feargus (1794-1855) — 110, 231
Odger, George (1813-1877) — 426, 445, 461, 493
Oppenheim, Dagobert (1809-1889) — 41
Oppenheim, Max — 524
Otto, Karl Wunibald (b. 1810) — 252
Owen, Robert (1771-1858) — 17, 53, 85, 91, 154, 424, 441, 549

P

Paine, Thomas (1737-1809) — 18
Palmerston, Henry John Temple (1784-1865) — 284, 295, 302, 355, 462
Perovskaya, Sophia Lvovna (1853-1881) — 604
Perret, Henri — 498, 533
Peter I (1672-1725) — 303
Petty, William (1632-1687) — 399, 549
Peuchet, Jacques (1758-1830) — 85
Pfänder, Karl (1818-1876) — 220, 237, 272, 421
Phears, John (1825-1905) — 557
Philips, Antoinette (Nannette) (c. 1837-1885) — 342, 433
Philips, Lion (1794-1866) — 342, 433
Pieper, Wilhelm (1899-1926) — 271, 272, 274, 277
Pio, Louis (1841-1894) — 533, 534
Plekhanov, Georgi Valentinovich (1856-1918) — 148, 602, 604, 605, 610
Plutarch (c. 46-126) — 28
Poliakoff (Polyakov), Nikolai Petrovich (c. 1841-1905) — 375
Poppe, Johann Heinrich Moritz (1776-1854) — 264
Pottier, Eugène (1816-1887) — 527
Proudhon, Pierre Joseph (1809-1865) — 37, 58, 75, 115-23, 154, 165, 241-43, 323, 378, 380, 423, 427, 429, 430, 435, 439, 442, 449, 578, 599
Pushkin, Alexander Sergeyevich (1799-1837) — 335, 594
Püttmann, Hermann (1811-1894) — 112
Pyat, Félix (1810-1889) — 469

Q

Quesnay, François (1694-1774) — 391-92, 549

R

Racine, Jean Baptiste (1639-1699) — 526
Radetzky, Joseph (1766-1858) — 156, 183, 209
Ranke, Johannes (1836-1916) — 554
Raphael (1483-1520) — 252
Raspail, François (1794-1878) — 287
Razin, Stepan Timofeyevich (d. 1671) — 560
Reiff, Wilhelm Joseph (born c. 1824) — 204, 236
Reinhardt, Richard (1829-1898) — 242
Rembrandt (1606-1669) — 237
Rempel, Rudolph (c.1815- c. 1869) — 103
Ricardo, David (1772-1823) — 61, 66, 91, 92, 117, 119, 121, 264-66, 315, 321, 373, 385, 397-401, 550
Richelieu, Armand Jean du Plessis (1585-1642) — 363
Richter, Johann Paul Friedrich—see Jean Paul
Rings, L. W. — 252
Rrittinghausen, Moritz (1814-1890) — 460
Robespierre, Maximilien (1758-1794) — 60
Robin, Paul (1837-1912) — 462, 479
Rockefeller, John Davison (1839-1937) — 552
Rodbertus-Jagetzow, Johann Karl (1805-1875) — 552, 553, 554
Rogers, James Edwin Thorold (1823-1890) — 371
Romanovs — 359
Roscoe, Henry Enfield (1833-1915) — 554
Röser, Peter Gerhard (1814-1865) — 204, 226, 248, 252
Rousseau, Jean Jacques (1712-1778) — 18, 27, 46
Roux, Jacques (1752-1794) — 85
Roy, Joseph — 378
Rückert, Friedrich (1788-1866) — 261
Ruge, Arnold (1802-1880) — 25, 32, 33, 34, 40-42, 54-56, 58, 67, 68, 94, 136, 248, 299
Rurik — 303
Russell, John (1792-1878) — 284
Rutenberg, Adolf (1808-1869) — 26, 33

S

Saedt, Otto Joseph Arnold (1816-1886) — 252

Saint-Just, Louis Antoine Léon de (1767-1794) — 60
Saint-Paul, Wilhelm (c. 1815-1852) — 40
Saint-Simon, Claude Henri (1760-1825) — 17, 21, 45, 56, 80, 82, 85, 113, 154
Saltykov, Alexei Dmitriyevich (1806-1859) — 270
Saltykov, Mikhail Yevgrafovich (Shchedrin) (1826-1889) — 591, 594
Sand, George (1804-1876) — 123
Savigny, Friedrich Carl von (1779-1861) — 36
Say, Jean Baptiste (1767-1832) — 61, 264
Sazonov, Nikolai Ivanovich (1815-1862) — 59, 299
Schäffle, Albert Eberhard Friedrich (1831-1903) — 553
Schaper von — 34, 38
Schapper, Karl (1812-1870) — 89, 109, 115, 124, 142, 143, 158, 163, 181, 182, 185-88, 193-94, 199, 200, 202, 204, 206, 219, 236-39, 248, 249, 272
Schelling, Friedrich Wilhelm (1775-1854) — 48, 52
Schiller, Johann Christoph Friedrich von (1795-1805) — 335
Schily, Victor (1810-1875) — 182, 427, 446
Schleiden, Matthias Jakob (1804-1881) — 554
Schlöffel, Friedrich Wilhelm (1800-1870) — 189
Schlosser, Friedrich Christoph (1776-1861) — 271, 552
Schmerling, Anton von (1805-1893) — 347
Schmidt, Kaspar (Stirner, Max) (1806-1856) — 39, 93-96
Schneider II, Karl — 182, 193-94, 199, 200, 202, 206, 252, 343
Schönbein, Christian Friedrich (1799-1868) — 370
Schorlemmer, Carl (1834-1892) — 554, 611
Schramm, Carl August — 571
Schramm, Konrad (c. 1822-1858) — 219, 237, 272, 273
Schulze-Delitzsch, Franz Hermann (1808-1883) — 232, 363, 436
Schurz, Karl (1829-1906) — 182
Schwarzer, Ernst (1808-1860) — 183
Schweichel, Robert (1821-1907) — 453
Schweitzer, Johann Baptist (1834-1875) — 429-31, 437-38, 452-54
Scott, Walter (1771-1832) — 261
Ségur, Philippe Paul (1780-1873) — 302, 562
Seiler, Sebastian (c. 1810-c. 1890) — 108
Semmig, Friedrich Hermann (1820-1887) — 96

Semyonov-Tyanshansky, Pyotr Petrovich (1827-1914) — 557
Senior, Nassau William (1790-1864) — 91
Serno-Solovyevich, Alexander Alexandrovich (1838-1869) — 464-66
Serraillier, Auguste (b. 1840) — 477, 482, 500, 512
Shakespeare, William (1564-1616) — 137, 261, 315, 335, 526
Shaw, Robert (d. 1869) — 426
Shelley, Percy Bysshe (1792-1822) — 527
Shevchenko, Taras Grigoryevich (1814-1861) — 594
Siebel, Carl (1836-1868) — 429
Sieber, Nikolai Ivanovich (1844-1888) — 552
Simon, Ludwig (1810-1872) — 189
Simson, Martin Eduard (1810-1899) — 342
Sismondi, Jean Charles Leonard Simonde de (1773-1842) — 92, 374
Skarbek, Fryderyk (Skarbek, Frédéric) (1792-1866) — 61
Smith, Adam (1723-1790) — 61-62, 91, 117, 121, 264, 397-400
Socrates (c. 469-399 B.C.) — 525
Sokolovsky, Pavel Alexandrovich (1842-1906) — 557
Sophocles (c. 497-406 B.C.) — 261
Sorge, Friedrich Adolf (1828-1906) — 277, 382, 446, 505, 507, 509, 511, 514, 516, 518, 523, 533, 536, 539, 547, 552, 576, 587, 588, 589, 595, 608, 609
Spartacus (d. 71 B.C.) — 433
Spencer, Herbert (1820-1903) — 269
Stahl, Friedrich Julius (1802-1861) — 35
Stefanovich, Yakov Vasilyevich (1854-1915) — 602
Stein, Julius (1813-1883) — 184
Steininger, Johann (1794-1874) — 20
Stieber, Wilhelm (1818-1882) — 249, 252
Stirner, Max — see Schmidt, Kaspar
Strauss, David Friedrich (1808-1874) — 25, 30
Struve, Gustav (1805-1870) — 136, 248
Stumpf, Paul (1827-1912) — 446
Swinton, John (1830-1901) — 525, 589

T

Tacitus Publius Cornelius (c. 55-c. 120) — 242
Talleyrand-Périgord, Charles Maurice (1754-1838) — 294
Taylor, Brook (1685-1731) — 555
Tedesco, Victor (1821-1897) — 88
Terence Publius Terentius Afer (c. 185-159 B.C.) — 137

Thackeray, William Makepiece (1811-1863) — 335, 526
Thierry, Augustin (1795-1856) — 60, 269
Thiers, Adolphe (1797-1877) — 480, 483, 487, 492, 527
Thompson, William (1785-1833) — 91, 119
Tirso de Molina (Téllez, Gabriel) (d. 1648) — 496
Tkachov, Pyotr Nikitich (1844-1885) — 600
Tolain, Henri Louis (1828-1897) — 427, 432, 434, 446, 448, 493
Traube, Moritz (1826-1894) — 554
Tridon, Edme Marie Gustave (1841-1871) — 468
Trübner, Nikolaus (1817-1884) — 300
Trusov, Anton Danilovich (1835-1886) — 466
Tschech, Heinrich Ludwig (1789-1844) — 77
Tucker — 300
Turgenev, Ivan Sergeyevich (1818-1883) — 594
Tyler, Wat (Walter) (d. 1381) — 563
Tylor, Edward Burnett (1832-1917) — 559

U

Ure, Andrew (1778-1857) — 264
Urquhart, David (1805-1877) — 300-02
Uspensky, Gleb Ivanovich (1843-1902) — 601
Utiešenovič, Ognieslav M. (b. 1817) — 557
Utin, Nikolai Isaakovich (1841-1883) — 464, 466, 467, 495, 498, 524

V

Vaillant, Edouard (1840-1915) — 498
Vanderbilt, Cornelius (1794-1877) — 552
Varlin, Louis Eugène (1839-1871) — 428, 434, 468, 469, 482
Vasilchikov, Alexander Illarionovich (1818-1881) — 557
Vernouillet, Just — 533
Vésinier, Pierre (1826-1902) — 438
Vidil, Jules — 231
Villeneuve-Bargemont, Jean Paul Albande (1784-1850) — 92
Wilmart, Raimond — 565
Vogler, C.G. — 118
Vogt, August (c. 1830-c. 1883) — 463
Vogt, Karl (1817-1895) — 338-41, 463
Vollmar, Georg (1850-1922) — 573, 574
Voltaire, François Marie (1694-1778) — 18, 26, 526

Vorontsov, Vasily Pavlovich (1847-1918)—599, 602
Vorovsky, Vaclav (1871-1923)—148

W

Wachsmuth, Ernst Wilhelm Gottlieb (1784-1866)—46
Wagner, Adolph (1835-1917)—552, 554
Wallau, Karl (1823-1877)—88, 159, 161, 162, 163
Waryński, Ludwik (1856-1889)—565, 602
Washington, George (1732-1799)—352
Watteau, Louis (pseudonym Devonville) (b. 1824)—343-45
Watts, John (1818-1887)—371
Weerth, Georg (1822-1856)—87, 132, 134, 140, 159, 163, 167, 168, 187, 211, 212, 215, 272
Weiler, Adam (d. 1894)—582
Weill, Alexandre (1811-1899)—67
Weitling, Wilhelm (1808-1871)—58, 67, 108-15, 116, 126, 181
Weston, John—418, 424, 426
Westphalen, Edgar von (1819- c. 1890)—21, 81, 108
Westphalen, Ferdinand von (1799-1876)—21
Westphalen, Caroline von (1779-1856)—21, 42, 81, 258, 259
Westphalen, Ludwig von (1770-1842)—21-22
Weydemeyer, Joseph (1818-1866)—86, 109, 115, 123, 128, 131, 215, 242, 246, 257, 276, 277, 323, 327, 586
Weydemeyer, Luise—340
Weydemeyer, Otto—586

Wigand, Otto (1795-1870)—95, 371
William I (1797-1888)—333, 342, 567
Willich, August (1810-1878)—214, 219, 216, 231, 236-39, 247-50, 253
Wolff, Ferdinand (1812-1895)—87, 108, 109, 125-27, 131, 132, 158, 163, 215
Wolff, Luigi—418, 438
Wolff, Wilhelm (1809-1864)—87, 108, 109, 126-27, 131, 132, 158, 163, 167, 168, 174, 185-87, 202, 204, 206, 222, 250, 271, 328, 360-62, 373, 390-91
Wrangel, Friedrich Heinrich Ernst (1784-1877)—220
Wróblewski, Walery (1836-1908)—486, 507, 509, 512, 533
Wyttenbach, Johann Hugo (1767-1848)—21

Y

York, Theodor (1830-1875)—523

Z

Zaslavsky, Yevgeny Osipovich (1844-1878)—565
Zasulich, Vera Ivanovna (1849-1919)—524, 557, 594, 601, 602, 605, 610
Zedlitz-Neukirch, Konstantin von (b. 1813)—343
Zhelyabov, Andrei Ivanovich (1851-1881)—603, 604
Zhukovsky, Yuli Galaktionovich (1822-1907)—600
Zitz, Franz Heinrich (1803-1877)—189
Zweiffel—180, 193, 194, 199

INDEX OF PERIODICALS

L'Alba (Florence) — 175
Allgemeine Literatur-Zeitung (Charlottenburg) — 70
Allgemeine Zeitung (Augsburg) — 36, 54, 76, 338
Almanacco Repubblicano per l'anno 1874 (Lodi) — 530
Anekdota zur neuesten deutschen Philosophie und Publicistik (Zurich and Winterthur) — 33, 43
L'Atelier Démocratique (Brussels) — 135
Athenäum. Zeitschrift für das gebildete Deutschland (Berlin) — 23
The Bee-Hive Newspaper (London) — 425, 461
The Chicago Tribune — 525-26, 568
The Commonwealth (London) — 446
La Concordia (Turin) — 165
The Contemporary Review (London) — 561
Le Corsaire (Paris) — 514
The Daily News (London) — 250, 476, 492, 514, 568
The Democratic Review of British and Foreign Politics, History and Literature (London) — 231
Demokratisches Wochenblatt (Leipzig) — 446, 454
Deutsche-Brüsseler-Zeitung — 131-36, 141, 145-46, 157, 159
Deutsche Jahrbücher für Wissenschaft und Kunst (Leipzig) — 40
Deutsche Londoner Zeitung — 148, 200
Deutsch-Französische Jahrbücher (Paris) — 49, 51, 53-55, 62, 67
The Economist (London) — 320
L'Egalité (Geneva) — 462-63
L'Egalité (Paris) — 575-76, 606
Die Eisenbahn (Leipzig) — 54
Elberfelder Zeitung — 77
La Emancipacion (Madrid) — 485
Frankfurter Journal — 213
Frankfurter Zeitung und Handelsblatt — 526, 593
La Fraternité de 1845. Organe du communisme (Paris) — 78

The Free Press (London) — 300
Freiheit (London) — 570
Gesellschaftsspiegel (Elberfeld) — 77, 85
Le Globe (Paris) — 77
L'Internationale (Brussels) — 462
The International Herald (London) — 505
Jahrbuch für Sozialwissenschaft und Sozialpolitik (Zurich) — 571
Journal des Débats politiques et littéraires (Paris) — 17
La Justice (Paris) — 528
Kölnische Zeitung — 76, 167, 198
Kommunistische Zeitschrift (London) — 131-33
The Labor Standard (New York) — 587
Leipziger Allgemeine Zeitung — 40
Mannheimer Abendzeitung — 33-34, 54, 76
La Marseillaise (Paris) — 462, 469
Modern Thought (London) — 585
The Morning Advertiser (London) — 299
Narodnoye Dyelo (People's Cause) (Geneva) — 466
National-Zeitung (Berlin) — 198
Neu-England-Zeitung (Boston) — 253
Neue Kölnische Zeitung für Bürger, Bauern und Soldaten — 203
Neue Oder-Zeitung (Breslau) — 280
Neue Rheinische Zeitung. Organ der Demokratie (Cologne) — 128, 162, 165-78, 182-89, 192-94, 199, 202-04, 206, 208-21
Neue Rheinische Zeitung. Politisch-ökonomische Revue (London, Hamburg) — 221-23, 234
Neues Wiener Tagblatt — 609
The New Moral World: and Gazette of the Rational Society (London) — 53
New-York Daily Tribune — 257, 278-81, 292, 304, 309, 311, 341, 345, 348-49, 589
The New York Times — 279
New Yorker Volkszeitung — 587
The Nineteenth Centure (London) — 534

The Northern Star (Leeds, London) — 89, 135, 141, 157-58
Notes to the People (London) — 232
Otechestvenniye Zapiski (Notes of Fatherland) (St. Petersburg) — 600, 602
The Pall Mall Gazette (London) — 479
The People's Paper (London) — 274-75, 293
La Plebe (Lodi) — 501
Le Populaire de 1841 (Paris) — 57
The Portfolio. Diplomatic Review (London) — 270
Die Presse (Vienna) — 348-49
Le Prolétaire (Paris) — 579, 581
Der Radikale (Vienna) — 183
Recht voor Allen (Amsterdam) — 564
The Red Republican (London) — 148, 231
Die Reform (New York) — 277
La Réforme (Paris) — 58, 78, 141-42, 158, 177
Die Revolution (New York) — 242-43
La Révolution Française (Paris) — 576
La Révolution Sociale (Geneva) — 501
Le Revue socialiste (Lyons, Paris) — 577
Rheinischer Beobachter (Cologne) — 76, 133
Rheinische Zeitung (Cologne) — 34-42, 47, 53-54, 58, 70, 136, 162
Rouge et Noire — 528
Schwäbischer Merkur (Stuttgart) — 67
Schweizerischer Republikaner (Zurich) — 53
The Sheffield Free Press — 301

Der Social-Demokrat (Berlin) — 429-30, 453
The Socialist (Chicago) — 587
Der Sozialdemokrat (Zurich) — 572-74, 606, 611
Der Sprudel (Karlsbad) — 525
Der Telegraph für Deutschland (Hamburg) — 52, 67
The Times (London) — 250, 492
Trier'sche Zeitung — 60, 78
Vestnik Yevropy (European Herald) (St. Petersburg) — 600
Das Volk (London) — 327-28, 338
Der Volksfreund (Vienna) — 214
Der Volksstaat (Leipzig) — 462, 474, 514, 538-39, 548-49
Der Volks-Tribun (New York) — 114-15
Der Vorbote (Geneva) — 375
Vorwärts (Leipzig) — 549
Vorwärts! (Paris) — 59, 67-9, 77, 111
Vperyod! Dvukhnedelnoye obozreniye (Forward! A Fortnight Review) (London) — 598
Vperyod! Neperiodicheskoye obozreniye (Forward! An Unperiodical Review) (Zurich, London) — 598
Der weisse Adler (Zurich) — 432
Westdeutsche Zeitung (Cologne) — 213
Das Westphälische Dampfboot (Paderborn) — 104, 115, 124
Wigand's Vierteljahrsschrift (Leipzig) — 93
Yuridichesky Vestnik (The Law Herald) (St. Petersburg) — 609
Die Zukunft (Berlin) — 571

REQUEST TO READERS

Progress Publishers would be glad to have your opinion of this book, its translation and design and any suggestions you may have for future publications.

Please send all your comments to 17, Zubovsky Boulevard, Moscow, USSR.